QUANTITATIVE METHODS
FOR
INVESTMENT ANALYSIS

Richard A. Defusco, CFA
University of Nebraska-Lincoln

Dennis W. McLeavey, CFA
Association for Investment Management and Research

Jerald E. Pinto, CFA
TRM Services

David E. Runkle, CFA
U.S. Bancorp Piper Jaffray

To obtain the AIMR *Publications Catalog,* contact:
AIMR, P.O. Box 3668, Charlottesville, Virginia 22093, U.S.A.
Phone 434-951-5499 or 800-247-8132; Fax 434-951-5262; E-mail Info@aimr.org
or visit AIMR's World Wide Web site at
www.aimr.org
to view the AIMR publications list.

ISBN 0-935015-69-8

Printed in the United States of America
by United Book Press, Inc., Baltimore, MD
August 2001

To Margo, Rachel, and Rebekah.
R.A.D.

To Jan, Christine, and Andy.
D.W.M.

In memory of Irwin Vanderhoof.
J.E.P.

To Patricia, Anne, and Sarah.
D.E.R.

FOREWORD

Quantitative Methods for Investment Analysis represents the second step of an effort by the Association for Investment Management and Research (AIMR) to produce a set of coordinated, comprehensive, and practitioner-oriented textbook readings specifically designed for the three levels of the Chartered Financial Analyst® Program. The first step was the publication in June 2000 of two volumes on fixed income analysis and portfolio management *(Fixed Income Analysis for the Chartered Financial Analyst Program* and *Fixed Income Readings for the Chartered Financial Analyst Program).* Given the favorable reception of these fixed income books and the expected favorable reception of the current book, coordinated textbooks in other topic areas are planned for the future.

In producing this book, AIMR was actively involved in establishing the table of contents, drawing on inputs from CFA charterholder reviewers, quantitative methods specialist consultants, and AIMR professional staff. The chapters were designed to include detailed learning outcome statements at the outset, illustrative in-chapter problems with solutions, and extensive end-of-chapter questions and problems with complete solutions, all prepared with CFA candidate distance learning in mind. This treatment of quantitative methods represents a substantial improvement for CFA candidates over the previous textbook.

Dennis McLeavey, CFA, spearheaded the effort to develop this book. His expertise and tireless attention to detail is quite evident in the finished product. Dennis has a long and distinguished history of involvement with the CFA Program. Before joining AIMR full-time, Dennis served as a member of the Council of Examiners (the group that writes the CFA examinations), an examination reviewer, and an examination grader. Co-authors Richard DeFusco, Jerry Pinto, and David Runkle bring a unique perspective to the application of quantitative analysis to the investment process. All three co-authors are CFA charterholders and have served as CFA examination graders. In addition, Richard has served on the Council of Examiners, Jerry has served as a CFA examination standard setter (the group that provides a recommended minimum passing score for the CFA examinations to the Board of Governors), and David has served on the Candidate Curriculum Committee (the group that selects CFA Program curriculum).

The treatment in this volume, intended to communicate practical quantitative methods knowledge, skills, and abilities for the investment generalist, is a hallmark of the CFA Program. This book provides the evenness of subject matter treatment, consistency of mathematical notation, and continuity of topic coverage so critical to the learning process. Perhaps the greatest improvement over previous materials is that all examples and problems are investment-oriented. In addition, the examples and problems reflect the global investment community. Starting from a U.S.-based program of approximately 2,000 examinees each year during the 1960s and 1970s, the CFA Program has evolved into a pervasive global certification program involving over 83,000 candidates from 143 countries in 2001. Through curriculum improvements such as this book, the CFA Program should continue to appeal to potential new candidates across the globe in future years.

Finally, the strong support of Tom Bowman and the AIMR Board of Governors through their authorization of this book should be acknowledged. Without their encouragement and support, this project, intended to materially enhance the CFA Program, could not have been possible.

Robert R. Johnson, Ph.D., CFA
Senior Vice President
Association for Investment Management and Research

July 2001

PREFACE

This book follows in the tradition of AIMR-produced books dating back to Valentine and Mennis' *Quantitative Techniques for Financial Analysis.* These books seek to fill gaps in the Chartered Financial Analyst (CFA) curriculum where existing materials are not available. Previous AIMR books are Maginn and Tuttle's *Managing Investment Portfolios;* Brown and Kritzman's *Quantitative Methods for Financial Analysis;* and the recent Fabozzi books *Fixed Income Analysis* and *Fixed Income Readings for the CFA Program.*

Specifically designed for CFA candidates, *Quantitative Methods for Investment Analysis* provides a blend of theory and practice to deliver the Candidate Body of Knowledge (CBOK) in the quantitative methods portion of the curriculum. The CBOK is the result of an extensive job analysis conducted every five years, most recently over the last year. Regional job analysis panels of CFA practitioners were formed in ten cities around the world: Boston, Chicago, Hong Kong, London, Los Angeles, New York, Toronto, Seattle, Tokyo, and Zurich. These panels of practitioners specified what the expert needs to know as the Global Body of Knowledge (now in development) and specified what the generalist needs to know as the CBOK. *Quantitative Methods for Investment Analysis* is a book reflecting the work of these expert panels.

Several features of this book are tailored specifically to the CFA candidate. First, learning outcome statements (LOS) specify the objectives of each chapter. Second, examples and problem practice are emphasized so that the candidate can gain confidence in meeting the LOS. Finally, examples and problems seek to present situations faced by the analyst at his or her job.

ACKNOWLEDGEMENTS

We would like to acknowledge the assistance of many individuals who played a role in producing this book.

Robert R. Johnson, CFA, Senior Vice President of Curriculum and Examinations (C&E) at AIMR, saw the need for specialized curriculum materials and initiated this project at AIMR. Gerald W. Buetow, Jr., CFA, currently with BFRC Services, LLC, supervised the project in its early stages and co-authored the first draft of the first three sections of Chapter 11. Jan R. Squires, CFA, Vice President in C&E, contributed an orientation stressing motivation and testability. Philip J. Young, CFA, Vice President in C&E, provided detailed manuscript reviews and a great deal of assistance with learning outcome statements. Mary Erickson, CFA, Vice President in C&E, provided detailed reviews as well as assistance in verifying some important calculations. Donald L. Tuttle, CFA, Vice President in C&E, oversaw the entire job analysis project and provided invaluable guidance on what the generalist needs to know in quantitative methods. Lee Kha Loon, CFA, AIMR Vice President, Global Affairs (Asia) provided valuable manuscript reviews and an international perspective from the Hong Kong office.

We would especially like to thank Ibbotson Associates of Chicago. Ibbotson generously provided the use of their EnCorr Analyzer™ for the generation of much of the data used in this book.

The Executive Advisory Board of the Candidate Curriculum Committee provided invaluable input: Chair, Peter Mackey, CFA, and members James Bronson, CFA, Alan Meder, CFA, and Matt Scanlan, CFA, as well as the Candidate Curriculum Committee Working Body.

Detailed manuscript reviews were provided by Gordon Alexander, Pierre Bouvier, CFA, Michael Broihahn, CFA, Robert Cangemi, CFA, Marilyn Ettinger, CFA, Maura Halbad, Muhammad Iqbal, CFA, Dorothy Kelly, CFA, Robert Lamy, CFA, Chad Martin, Michael McMillan, CFA, Gregory Noronha, CFA, Thomas Robinson, CFA, Sanjiv Sabherwal, CFA, William Sackley, CFA, Gary Sanger, CFA, Sandeep Singh, CFA, Bruce Smith, CFA, David Smith, CFA, John Stowe, CFA, Thomas Struppeck, Zhenyu Wang, and graduate students at the Carlson School of Management at the University of Minnesota. Many of the end-of-chapter problems were written by John Geppert and by John Stowe, CFA, and were reviewed by Zhiyi Song. Extensive contributions came from Lew Randolph, CFA, Lisa Weiss, CFA, and Sanjiv Sabherwal, CFA.

Copy editing was done by Bette Collins, Fiona Russell Cowen, Christine Kemper, and Patricia McKernon Runkle.

Wanda Lauziere, C&E Associate at AIMR, served as the project manager and shepherded the manuscript with great skill and good humor through its many versions.

ABOUT THE AUTHORS

Richard A. DeFusco, CFA, is an Associate Professor of Finance at the University of Nebraska-Lincoln (UNL). He earned his CFA charter in 1999 and started CFA grading in 2000. He is a member of the Omaha-Lincoln Society of Financial Analysts, and serves on committees for the Association for Investment Management and Research. His primary teaching interest is investments and he coordinates the Cornhusker Fund—the student-managed investment fund at UNL. He has published a number of journal articles, primarily in the field of finance. He completed his bachelor's degree in management science at the University of Rhode Island and doctoral degree in finance at the University of Tennessee-Knoxville.

Dennis W. McLeavey, CFA, is Vice President of Curriculum Development at the Association for Investment Management and Research. He obtained his CFA charter in 1990 and began CFA grading in 1995. During the early 1990s, he taught in the Boston University and the Boston Security Analysts' CFA review programs. He subsequently served on the AIMR Council of Examiners and recently received an AIMR Ten-Year Certificate of Achievement for Continuing Education. Active in endowment fund management, he founded a student-managed fund at the University of Rhode Island and co-authored two college texts and several journal articles. He completed a doctorate in production management and industrial engineering at Indiana University in 1972, after studying economics for his bachelor's degree at the University of Western Ontario in 1968.

Jerald E. Pinto, CFA, as principal of TRM Services, consults to corporations, foundations, and partnerships in investment planning, portfolio analysis, and quantitative analysis. Mr. Pinto previously taught finance at the NYU Stern School of Business after working in the banking and investment industries in New York City. He has lectured to business and government executives from the United States and abroad, and participates in the Society of Quantitative Analysts, Inc., and other forums. He holds an MBA from Baruch College and a Ph.D. in finance from the Stern School.

David E. Runkle, CFA, is Vice President and Research Manager at U.S. Bancorp Piper Jaffray. He has been an Adjunct Professor of Finance in the Carlson School of Management at the University of Minnesota since 1989, where he teaches equity security analysis. He has consulted on valuation and financial performance since 1994. Before joining U.S. Bancorp Piper Jaffray, Runkle was a research officer at the Federal Reserve Bank of Minneapolis. He has published more than 20 academic articles and has won a number of awards, including the Wriston Prize for Outstanding Teaching (Brown University), an Elija Watt Sells Award for outstanding performance on the Certified Public Accountant examination, and a four-star rating as an outstanding professor in the Business Week Guide to the Best Business Schools. He is a member of the Minnesota Society of Certified Public Accountants and was a member of the Candidate Curriculum Committee for AIMR. He received a B.A. in economics, summa cum laude, from Carleton College and a Ph.D. in economics from M.I.T.

CONTENTS

C H A P T E R

THE TIME VALUE OF MONEY

1 INTEREST RATES AND DISCOUNT RATES

Would you accept $9,500 in exchange for $10,000? Not likely. But what if the $9,500 were cash today and the $10,000 were cash one year from now? In effect, you would be borrowing $9,500 and paying back $10,000 at the end of the year. Can these amounts be considered equivalent? Yes, if you **discount** the $10,000 by cutting its value in allowance for

1

how far away it is in time. This insight leads directly to the concept of the **time value of money,** which underlies rates of return, interest rates, required rates of return, discount rates, opportunity costs, inflation, and risk.

The time value of money reflects the relationship between time, cash flow, and an interest rate. For investors preferring current to future consumption, the interest rate is the rate of compensation they require to postpone current consumption. The compensation is the return on their investment (in this case, $10,000 − $9,500 = $500). The rate of return is the return divided by the initial investment (in this case, $500/$9,500 = 0.0526, or 5.26 percent). This rate can be thought of as a pure rate of interest that can convert consumers into investors or lenders.

In a **certain world**, the interest rate is called the risk-free rate. Although a certain world is an abstraction, in some instances the cash flows of lending/borrowing arrangements are virtually certain. Many countries have short-term debt that can be considered risk-free. United States Treasury bills (T-bills), for example, are usually considered risk-free because they are backed by the full faith and credit of the U.S. government. We consider the interest rate paid by T-bills to be an example of a risk-free rate of interest.[1]

In an uncertain world, two factors complicate interest rates: inflation and risk.

- *Inflation.* When prices are expected to increase, lenders charge not only an **opportunity cost** of postponing consumption but also an **inflation premium** that takes into account the expected increase in prices. The **nominal cost of money** therefore consists of a pure rate of interest, called the **real rate**, and an inflation premium.[2]
- *Risk.* In contrast to many governments, companies exhibit varying degrees of uncertainty concerning their ability to repay lenders. The interest rate that lenders charge needs to incorporate **default risk**. The return that borrowers pay thus comprises the nominal risk-free rate (the pure rate plus an inflation premium) plus a default risk premium.

Interest rates can be thought of in three ways. First, they can be considered required rates of return—returns required by investors or lenders to induce them to forgo current consumption. Second, interest rates can be considered discount rates. Recalling our original question, the only way we would accept $9,500 as equivalent to $10,000 would be to discount the $10,000 by allowing for the time value of money. Thus, we use the terms *interest rate* and *discount rate* almost interchangeably. Third, interest rates can be considered opportunity costs. An opportunity cost is the value that investors forgo by choosing what they do. In choosing to consume now, would-be investors forgo the opportunity of earning the risk-free rate and consuming one year from now. In choosing to lend money to risky borrowers, investors forgo the opportunity of lending money to more trustworthy borrowers. Thus, investors require an interest rate reflecting the riskiness of the borrowers.

Among the most important factors that affect interest rates are the forces of supply and demand. Investors are suppliers of funds and borrowers are demanders of funds. The price of the funds is the interest rate. This concept brings us full circle to the time value of

---

[1] Other developed countries also issue securities similar to U.S. Treasury securities. In France, the French Treasury issues bonds with maturities of 3 months to 30 years. French T-bills are called BTNs (*bons du Trésor négociables*) and include discount Treasury bills. Japan issues four types of government securities, one of which is the short-term Treasury bill. The German government also issues four types of securities, one of which is Treasury discount paper called *U-schätze*, a discounted money market instrument that can have maturities of up to two years. In the United Kingdom, the British government issues over 100 gilt-edged bonds with nine different names. Short-dated gilts range from zero to seven years in maturity. The Canadian government bond market is closely related to the U.S. market. Canadian Treasury bills have maturities of 3, 6, and 12 months.

[2] Technically, 1 plus the nominal rate equals the product of 1 plus the real rate and 1 plus the inflation rate. As a quick approximation, however, the nominal rate is equal to the real rate and an inflation premium.

money. Clearly, you would exchange $9,500 now for $10,000 at year-end if the interest rate or price were right.

As an analyst, your first job is to understand thoroughly the mathematics behind the time value of money. In this chapter, you will learn formulas to handle the situations you will encounter. All of the formulas are based on the simplifying assumption that a constant discount rate holds for all future points in time. Keep in mind that all of the results depend on this simplifying assumption.

2　THE FUTURE VALUE OF A SINGLE CASH FLOW

In this section, we introduce the simplest form of time value, that associated with a single cash flow or lump-sum investment. We describe the relationship between an initial investment or **present value** (PV) which earns a rate of return (that is, the interest rate per period) denoted as r, and its **future value** (FV) which will be received N years or periods from today.

The following example illustrates this concept. Suppose you invest $100 (PV = $100) in an interest-bearing bank account paying 5 percent annually. At the end of the first year, you will have the $100 plus the interest earned, 5% × $100 = $5, for a total of $105. To formalize this one-period example, we define the following terms:

PV = present value of the investment

FV_N = future value of the investment N periods from today

r = rate of interest per period

With $N = 1$, this example can now be formalized as

$$FV_1 = PV(1 + r) \qquad \text{(1-1)}$$

For this example, we calculate the future value one year from today as $FV_1 = \$100(1.05) = \$105$.

Now suppose you decide to invest the initial $100 for two years with interest earned and credited to your account annually (annual compounding). At the end of the first year (the beginning of the second year) your account will have $105, which you will leave in the bank for another year. Thus, with a beginning amount of $105 (PV = $105), the ending amount at the end of the second year will be $105(1.05) = $110.25. Note that the $5.25 interest earned during the second year is 5 percent of the amount invested at the beginning of Year 2.

Another way to understand this example is to note that the amount invested at the beginning of Year 2 is composed of the original $100 that you invested plus the $5 interest that was earned during the first year. During the second year, the original principal again earns interest, as does the interest that was earned during Year 1. You can see how the original investment grows:

Original investment	$100.00
Interest for the first year (100 × 0.05)	$5.00
Interest for the second year based on original investment ($100 × 0.05)	$5.00
Interest for the second year based on interest earned in the first year	
(0.05 × $5.00 interest on interest)	$0.25
Total	$110.25

The $5 interest that you earned each period on the $100 original investment is known as **simple interest** (that is, the interest rate times the original **principal**). Over the two-year period, you earn $10 of simple interest. The extra $0.25 that you have at the end of Year 2 is the interest you earned on the Year 1 interest of $5 that you reinvested.

The interest earned on interest is our first glimpse of the phenomenon known as **compounding**. Although the interest that is earned on the initial investment is important, for a given interest rate it is fixed in size from period to period. The interest earned on reinvested interest is a far more powerful force because, for a given interest rate, it grows in size each period. The importance of compounding increases with the magnitude of the interest rate. For example, $100 invested in 1900 would be worth about $13,150 after 100 years if compounded annually at 5 percent, but worth more than $20 million if compounded annually over the same time period at a rate of 13 percent.

To verify the $20 million figure, we need a general formula to handle compounding for any number of periods, and we introduce that now. Following the definitions above, we can relate the present value of an initial investment to its future value after N periods with the following general formula:

$$FV_N = PV(1 + r)^N \qquad\qquad (1\text{-}2)$$

where r is the stated interest rate per period and N is the number of compounding periods. In the bank example, $FV_2 = \$100(1 + 0.05)^2 = \$110.25$. In the 13 percent investment example, $FV_{100} = \$100(1.13)^{100} = \$20,316,287.42$.

The most important point about using the future value equation is to remember that the stated interest rate, r, and the number of compounding periods, N, must be compatible. That is, both variables must be defined in the same time units. In the bank example, the annual rate of interest was 5 percent per year and the number of compounding periods was two years; therefore, $r = 5\%$ and $N = 2$. As you can see, 5 percent is the annual interest, and the number of compounding periods is two years. The interest rate here is quoted on an annual basis and the number of compounding periods is measured in years.

A time line helps us to keep track of the compatibility of time units and the interest rate per time period. In the time line, we use the time index t to represent a point in time a stated number of periods from today. Thus the present value is the amount available for investment today, indexed as $t = 0$. We can now refer to a time N periods from today as $t = N$. The time line in Figure 1-1 shows this relationship.

In Figure 1-1, we have positioned the initial investment, PV, at $t = 0$. With Equation 1-2, the present value, PV, is moved forward to $t = N$ by the factor $(1 + r)^N$. This factor is called a future value factor. We denote the future value on the time line as FV and position it at $t = N$. Suppose the future value is to be received exactly 10 periods from today's date ($N = 10$). The present value, PV, and the future value, FV, are separated by time through the factor $(1 + r)^{10}$.

FIGURE 1-1   The Relationship Between an Initial Investment, PV, and Its Future Value, FV

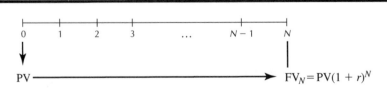

The fact that the present value and the future value are separated by time has important consequences:

- We can only add dollar amounts if they are indexed at the same points in time.
- For a given interest rate, the future value increases with the number of periods.
- For a given number of periods, the future value increases with the interest rate.

To better understand these concepts, consider three examples that illustrate how to apply the future value formula.

EXAMPLE 1-1. **The Future Value of a Lump Sum with Interim Cash Reinvested at the Same Rate.**

You are the lucky winner of your state's lottery of $5 million after taxes. You invest your winnings in a five-year certificate of deposit (CD) at a local financial institution. The CD promises to pay 7 percent per year compounded annually. This institution also lets you reinvest the interest at the same CD rate for the duration of the CD. How much will you have at the end of five years if your money remains invested at 7 percent for five years with no withdrawals of interest?

To solve this problem, compute the future value of the $5 million investment using the following values in Equation 1-2:

$$PV = \$5,000,000$$

$$r = 7\% = 0.07$$

$$N = 5$$

$$\begin{aligned} FV_N = PV(1 + r)^N \\ = \$5,000,000(1.07)^5 \\ = \$5,000,000(1.402552) \\ = \$7,012,758.65 \end{aligned}$$

In most examples in this chapter, note that the factors are reported at six decimal places but the calculations actually carry through at more places. For example, the reported 1.402552 has been rounded up from 1.40255173 (the calculation is actually carried out with greater than eight decimal place precision by the calculator or spreadsheet). Our final result reflects the higher number of decimal places carried by the calculator or spreadsheet.[3]

EXAMPLE 1-2. **The Future Value of a Lump Sum with No Interim Cash.**

A Japanese institution offers you the following terms for a contract: For a premium of JPY2,500,000, the institution promises to pay you a lump sum six years from now at an 8 percent annual interest rate. What future amount can you expect?

---

[3] We could also solve time value of money problems using tables of interest rate factors. Solutions using tabled values of interest rate factors are generally less accurate than solutions properly obtained using calculators or spreadsheets; thus calculators or spreadsheets are preferred in practice.

To solve this problem, use the following data in Equation 1-2 to find the future value:

$$PV = JPY2,500,000$$

$$r = 8\% = 0.08$$

$$N = 6$$

$$\begin{aligned} FV_N &= PV(1 + r)^N \\ &= JPY2,500,000(1.08)^6 \\ &= JPY2,500,000(1.586874) \\ &= JPY3,967,186 \end{aligned}$$

Our third example is a more complicated future value problem that illustrates the importance of keeping track of actual calendar time.

EXAMPLE 1-3.   The More Distant Future Value of a Future Lump Sum.

A pension fund manager estimates that his corporate sponsor will make a $10 million contribution five years from now. The rate of return on plan assets has been estimated at 9 percent per year. The pension fund manager wishes to calculate the future value of this contribution for distribution to the retired work force 15 years from now. What is that future value?

By positioning the initial investment, PV, at $t = 5$, you can calculate the future value of the contribution using the following data in Equation 1-2:

$$PV = \$10 \text{ million}$$

$$r = 9\% = 0.09$$

$$N = 10$$

$$\begin{aligned} FV_N &= PV(1 + r)^N \\ &= \$10,000,000(1.09)^{10} \\ &= \$10,000,000(2.367364) \\ &= \$23,673,636.75 \end{aligned}$$

This problem looks much like the others, but it differs in one important respect: its timing. From the standpoint of today ($t = 0$), the future amount of $23,673,636.75 is 15 years into the future. Although the future value is 10 years from its present value, the present value of $10 million will not be received for another five years.

FIGURE 1-2   The Future Value of a Lump Sum, Initial Investment Not at $t = 0$

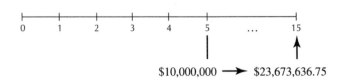

> As Figure 1-2 shows, we have followed the convention of indexing today as $t = 0$ and indexing subsequent times by adding 1 for each period. The additional contribution of $10 million is to be received in five years, so it is indexed as $t = 5$ and appears as such in the figure. The future value of the investment in 10 years is then indexed at $t = 15$; that is, 10 years following the receipt of the $10 million contribution at $t = 5$. Time lines like this one can be extremely useful when dealing with more complicated problems, especially those involving more than one cash flow.

In a later section of this chapter, we will discuss how to calculate today's value of the $10 million to be received five years from now. For the moment, we can use Equation 1-2. Suppose the pension fund manager were to receive $6,499,313.86 today from the corporate sponsor. How much would that sum be worth at the end of five years? How much would it be worth at the end of fifteen years?

$$PV = \$6,499,313.86$$

$$r = 9\% = 0.09$$

$$N = 5$$

$$\begin{aligned} FV_N &= PV(1 + r)^N \\ &= \$6,499,313.86(1.09)^5 \\ &= \$6,499,313.86(1.538624) \\ &= \$10,000,000 \text{ at the 5-year mark} \end{aligned}$$

and

$$PV = \$6,499,313.86$$

$$r = 9\% = 0.09$$

$$N = 15$$

$$\begin{aligned} FV_N &= PV(1 + r)^N \\ &= \$6,499,313.86(1.09)^{15} \\ &= \$6,499,313.86(3.642482) \\ &= \$23,673,636.74 \text{ at the 15-year mark} \end{aligned}$$

Ignoring the one-cent rounding error, these results show that today's present value of around $6.5 million becomes $10 million after five years and $23.67 million after 15 years.

2.1 THE FREQUENCY OF COMPOUNDING

In this section, we examine investments paying interest more than once a year. For instance, many banks offer a monthly interest rate that compounds 12 times a year. In such an arrangement, they pay interest on interest every month. Rather than quote the periodic monthly interest rate, financial institutions often quote an annual interest rate that we refer to as the **stated annual interest rate** or **quoted interest rate**. We denote the stated annual interest rate by r_s. For instance, your bank might state that a particular CD pays 8 percent compounded monthly. The stated annual interest rate is equal to the monthly interest rate times 12. In this example, the monthly interest rate is $0.08/12 = 0.0067$ or 0.67 percent.[4] This rate is strictly a quoting convention because $(1 + 0.0067)^{12} = 1.083$, not 1.08; the

---

[4] To avoid rounding errors when using a financial calculator, divide 8 by 12 and then press the %i key, rather than simply entering 0.67 for %i so we have $(1 + 0.08/12)^{12} = 1.083000$.

term $(1 + r_s)$ is not meant to be a future value factor when compounding is more frequent than annual.

With more than one compounding period per year, the future value formula can be expressed as

$$FV_N = PV\left(1 + \frac{r_s}{m}\right)^{m \times N}$$ (1-3)

where r_s is the stated annual interest rate, m is the number of compounding periods per year, and N now stands for the number of years. Note the compatibility here between the interest rate used, r_s/m, and the number of compounding periods, $m \times N$. The periodic rate, r_s/m, is the stated annual interest rate divided by the number of compounding periods per year. The number of compounding periods, $m \times N$, is the number of compounding periods in one year multiplied by the number of years. The periodic rate, r_s/m, and the number of compounding periods, $m \times N$, must be compatible.

EXAMPLE 1-4.   The Future Value of a Lump Sum with Quarterly Compounding.

Continuing with the CD example, suppose your bank offers you a CD with a two-year maturity, a stated annual interest rate of 8 percent compounded quarterly, and a feature allowing reinvestment of the interest at the same interest rate. You decide to invest $10,000. What will the CD be worth at maturity?

To solve this problem, compute the future value with Equation 1-3 as follows:

$PV = \$10,000$

$r_s = 8\% = 0.08$

$m = 4$

$r_s/m = 0.08/4 = 0.02$

$N = 2$

$m \times N = 4 \times 2 = 8$ interest periods

$$FV = FV_N = PV\left(1 + \frac{r_s}{m}\right)^{m \times N}$$
$$= \$10,000(1.02)^8$$
$$= \$10,000(1.171659)$$
$$= \$11,716.59$$

The future value formula in Equation 1-3 is not different from the one in Equation 1-2. Simply keep in mind that the interest rate to use is the rate per period and the exponent is the number of interest, or compounding, periods.

EXAMPLE 1-5.   The Future Value of a Lump Sum with Monthly Compounding.

An Australian bank offers to pay you 6 percent compounded monthly. You decide to invest AUD1 million for one year. What is the future value of your investment if interest payments are reinvested at 6 percent?

Use Equation 1-3 to find the future value of the one-year investment as follows:

$$PV = AUD1,000,000$$

$$r_s = 6\% = 0.06$$

$$m = 12$$

$$r_s/m = 0.06/12 = 0.0050$$

$$N = 1$$

$$m \times N = 12 \times 1 = 12 \text{ interest periods}$$

$$FV = FV_N = PV\left(1 + \frac{r_s}{m}\right)^{m \times N}$$

$$= AUD1,000,000(1.005)^{12}$$
$$= AUD1,000,000(1.061678)$$
$$= AUD1,061,677.81$$

If you had been paid 6 percent with annual compounding, the future amount would be only AUD1,000,000(1.06) = AUD1,060,000.

2.2 CONTINUOUS COMPOUNDING

The preceding discussion on compounding periods illustrates discrete compounding, which credits interests after a discrete amount of time has elapsed. If the number of compounding periods per year becomes infinite, then interest is compounded continuously. If we want to use the future value formula with continuous compounding, we need to find the limiting value of the future value factor for $m \to \infty$ in Equation 1-2; that is, infinitely many compounding periods per year. The expression for the future value of a sum in N years with <u>continuous compounding</u> is

$$FV_N = PVe^{r_s \times N} \tag{1-4}$$

The term $e^{r_s \times N}$ is the transcendental number $e \approx 2.7182818$ raised to the power $r_s \times N$. Most financial calculators have the function e^x.

EXAMPLE 1-6. The Future Value of a Lump Sum with Continuous Compounding.

Suppose an investment will earn 8 percent compounded continuously for two years. We can compute the future value with Equation 1-4 as follows:

$$PV = \$10,000$$

$$r_s = 8\% = 0.08$$

$$N = 2$$

$$FV = FV_N = PVe^{r_s \times N}$$
$$= \$10,000e^{0.08 \times 2}$$
$$= \$10,000(1.173511)$$
$$= \$11,735.11$$

With the same interest rate but with continuous compounding, the $10,000 investment would grow to $11,735.11 compared to $11,716.59 with quarterly compounding.

TABLE 1-1   The Effect of Compounding Frequency on Future Value

Compounding Frequency	r_s/m	$m \times N$	Future Value of $1
Annual	8%/1 = 8%	1 × 1 = 1	$1.00(1.08) = $1.08
Semiannual	8%/2 = 4%	2 × 1 = 2	$1.00(1.04)^2 = $1.081600
Quarterly	8%/4 = 2%	4 × 1 = 4	$1.00(1.02)^4 = $1.082432
Monthly	8%/12	12 × 1 = 12	$1.00(1.006667)^{12} = $1.083000
Daily	8%/365	365 × 1 = 365	$1.00(1.000219)^{365} = $1.083278
Continuous	8%	1	$1.00(e^{0.08 \times 1}) = $1.083287

Table 1-1 shows how a stated annual interest rate of 8 percent generates different ending dollar amounts with annual, semiannual, quarterly, monthly, daily, and continuous compounding for an initial investment of $1 (carried out to six decimal places).

As Table 1-1 shows, all six cases have the same stated annual interest rate of 8 percent; they have different ending dollar amounts, however, because of differences in the frequency of compounding. With annual compounding, the ending amount is $1.08. More frequent compounding results in larger ending amounts. The ending dollar amount with continuous compounding is the maximum amount that can be earned with a stated annual rate of 8 percent.

Table 1-1 also shows that a $1 investment that earns 8.16 percent compounded annually grows to the same future value at the end of one year as a $1 investment earning 8 percent compounded semiannually. This result leads us to a distinction between the stated annual interest rate and the **effective annual rate** (EAR).[5] For an 8 percent stated annual interest rate with semiannual compounding, the EAR is 8.16 percent.

2.3 STATED AND EFFECTIVE RATES

The stated annual interest rate does not give a future value directly, so we need a formula for the effective annual rate. With an annual interest rate of 8 percent compounded semiannually, we receive a periodic rate of 4 percent. Over the course of a year, an investment of $1 would grow to $1(1.04)^2 = $1.0816, as illustrated in Table 1-1. The interest earned on the $1 investment is $0.0816 and represents an effective annual rate of interest of 8.16 percent. The effective annual rate is

$$(1 + \text{Periodic interest rate})^m - 1 \tag{1-5}$$

The periodic interest rate is the stated annual interest rate divided by m, where m is the number of compounding periods in one year. Using our previous example, we can solve for the effective annual rate as follows: $(1.04)^2 - 1 = 8.16\%$.

---

[5] Among the terms used for the effective annual return on interest-bearing bank deposits are Annual Percentage Yield (APY) in the United States and Equivalent Annual Rate (EAR) in the United Kingdom. By contrast, **Annual Percentage Rate** (APR) is a measure of the cost of borrowing expressed as a yearly rate. In the United States, the APR is calculated as a periodic rate times the number of payment periods per year and, as a result, some writers use APR as a general synonym for the stated annual interest rate. Nevertheless, APR is a term with legal connotations; its calculation follows regulatory standards that vary internationally. Therefore, stated annual interest rate is the preferred general term for an annual interest rate that does not account for compounding within the year.

The concept of effective annual rate extends to continuous compounding. Suppose we have a rate of 8 percent compounded continuously. We can find the effective annual rate in the same way as above by finding the appropriate future value factor. In this case, a \$1 investment would grow to $\$1(e^{0.08 \times 1.0}) = \$1.0833$. The interest earned over one year represents an effective annual rate of 8.33 percent and is larger than the 8.16 percent effective annual rate with semiannual compounding because interest is compounded more frequently. With continuous compounding, we can solve for the effective annual rate as follows:

Effective annual rate $= e^{r_s} - 1$ (1-6)

We can reverse the formulas for effective annual rate with discrete and continuous compounding to find a periodic rate that corresponds to a particular effective annual rate. Suppose we wish to find the appropriate periodic rate for a given effective annual rate of 8.16 percent with semiannual compounding. We can use Equation 1-5 to find the periodic rate

$$0.0816 = (1 + \text{Periodic rate})^2 - 1$$

$$1.0816 = (1 + \text{Periodic rate})^2$$

$$(1.0816)^{1/2} - 1 = \text{Periodic rate}$$

$$1.04 - 1 = \text{Periodic rate}$$

$$4\% = \text{Periodic rate}$$

To calculate the continuously compounded rate (the stated annual interest rate with continuous compounding) corresponding to an effective annual rate of 8.33 percent, we find the interest rate that satisfies Equation 1-6

$$0.0833 = e^{r_s - 1}$$

$$1.0833 = e^{r_s}$$

To solve this equation, we take the natural logarithm of both sides. (Recall that the natural log of $e^{r_s} = \ln e^{r_s} = r_s$.) Therefore, $\ln 1.0833 = r_s$, resulting in $r_s = 8$ percent. We see that a stated annual rate of 8 percent with continuous compounding is equivalent to an EAR of 8.33 percent.

3   THE FUTURE VALUE OF A SERIES OF CASH FLOWS

In this section, we consider series of cash flows, both even and uneven. We begin with a list of terms commonly used when valuing cash flows that are distributed over many time periods.

- *Annuity*: An **annuity** is a finite set of sequential cash flows, all with the same value.
- *Ordinary annuity*: An **ordinary annuity** has a first cash flow that occurs one period from now (indexed at $t = 1$).
- *Annuity due*: An **annuity due** has a first cash flow that is paid immediately (indexed at $t = 0$).
- *Perpetuity*: A **perpetuity** is a perpetual annuity, or a set of never-ending sequential cash flows, with the first cash flow occurring one period from now.

3.1 EQUAL CASH FLOWS — ORDINARY ANNUITY

Consider an ordinary annuity paying 5 percent annually. Suppose we have five separate deposits of $1,000 occurring at equally spaced intervals of one year, with the first payment occurring at $t = 1$. Our goal is to find the future value of this ordinary annuity after the last deposit at $t = 5$. The increment in the time counter is one year, so the last payment occurs five years from now. As the time line in Figure 1-3 shows, we find the future value of each $1,000 deposit at the beginning of Year 5 with Equation 1-2, $FV_N = PV(1 + r)^N$. The arrows in Figure 1-3 extend from the payment date to $t = 5$. For instance, the first $1,000 deposit made at $t = 1$ will compound over four periods. Using Equation 1-2, we find that the future value of the first deposit at $t = 5$ is $1,000(1.05)^4 = \$1,215.51$. We calculate the future value of all other payments in a similar fashion. (Note that we are finding the future value at $t = 5$, so the last payment does not earn any interest.) With all values now at $t = 5$, we can add the future values to arrive at the future value of the annuity. This amount is $5,525.63.

FIGURE 1-3   The Future Value of a Five-Year Annuity

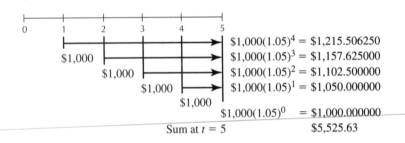

We can arrive at a general annuity formula if we define the annuity amount as A, the number of time periods as N, and the interest rate per period as r. We can then define the future value as

$$FV_N = A[(1 + r)^{N-1} + (1 + r)^{N-2} + (1 + r)^{N-3} + \ldots + (1 + r)^1 + (1 + r)^0]$$

which simplifies to

$$FV = A\left[\frac{(1 + r)^N - 1}{r}\right] \tag{1-7}$$

The term in brackets is the future value annuity factor. This factor gives the future value of an ordinary annuity of $1 per period. Multiplying the future value annuity factor by the annuity amount gives the future value of an ordinary annuity. For the ordinary annuity in Figure 1-3, we find the future value annuity factor from Equation 1-7 as

$$\left[\frac{(1.05)^5 - 1}{0.05}\right] = 5.525631$$

With an annuity amount $A = \$1,000$, the future value of the annuity is $1,000 \times 5.525631 = \$5,525.63$, an amount that agrees with our earlier work.

The next example illustrates how to find the future value of an ordinary annuity using the formula in Equation 1-7.

EXAMPLE 1-7. The Future Value of an Annuity.

Suppose your company's defined contribution retirement plan allows you to invest up to 20,000 euro per year. You plan to invest €20,000 per year in a stock index fund for the next 30 years. Historically, this fund has earned 9 percent per year on average. Assuming that you actually earn 9 percent per year, how much money will you have available for retirement after making the last payment?

To solve this problem, use Equation 1-7 to find the future amount

$$\text{Annuity amount, } A = €20,000$$

$$r = 9\% = 0.09$$

$$N = 30$$

$$\text{Future value annuity factor} = \frac{(1 + r)^N - 1}{r} = \frac{(1.09)^{30} - 1}{0.09} = 136.307539$$

$$\text{Future value of annuity} = €20,000 \times 136.307539$$

$$= €2,726,150.77$$

3.2 UNEQUAL CASH FLOWS

In many cases, the cash flow stream is not level, precluding the simple use of the future value annuity factor. For instance, an individual investor might have a savings plan that involves unequal cash payments depending on the month of the year or lower savings during a planned vacation. You can always find the future value of a series of unequal cash flows by compounding the cash flows one at a time. Suppose you have the five cash flows described in Table 1-2, indexed relative to the present ($t = 0$).

All of the payments shown in Table 1-2 are different. Therefore, the most direct approach to finding the future value at $t = 5$ is to compute the future value of each payment as of $t = 5$ and then sum the individual future values. The future value at Year 5 equals $19,190.76, as shown in the third column. Later in this chapter, you will learn shortcuts to take when the cash flows are close to even; these shortcuts will allow you to combine annuity and single-period calculations.

TABLE 1-2   A Series of Unequal Cash Flows and Their Future Value at 5 Percent

Time	Cash Flow	Future Value at Year 5
$t = 1$	$1,000	$1,000(1.05)^4 =$ $1,215.51
$t = 2$	$2,000	$2,000(1.05)^3 =$ $2,315.25
$t = 3$	$4,000	$4,000(1.05)^2 =$ $4,410.00
$t = 4$	$5,000	$5,000(1.05)^1 =$ $5,250.00
$t = 5$	$6,000	$6,000(1.05)^0 =$ $6,000.00
		Sum $=$ $19,190.76

4   THE PRESENT VALUE OF A SINGLE CASH FLOW

4.1 FINDING THE PRESENT VALUE OF A SINGLE CASH FLOW

Just as the future value factor links today's present value with tomorrow's future value, the present value factor allows us to discount future value to present value. For example, with a 5 percent interest rate generating a future payoff of $105 in one year, what current amount invested at 5 percent for one year will grow to $105? The answer is $100; therefore $100 is the present value of $105 to be received in one year at a discount rate of 5 percent.

Given a future cash flow that is to be received in N periods and an interest rate per period, r, we can use the formula for future value to solve directly for the present value as follows:

$$FV_N = PV(1 + r)^N$$

$$PV = FV_N\left[\frac{1}{(1 + r)^N}\right]$$

$$PV = FV_N(1 + r)^{-N} \tag{1-8}$$

We see from Equation 1-8 that the present value factor, $(1 + r)^{-N}$, is the reciprocal of the future value factor, $(1 + r)^N$.

EXAMPLE 1-8.   The Present Value of a Lump Sum.

An insurance company has issued a Guaranteed Investment Contract (GIC) that promises to pay $100,000 in six years with a promised return of 8 percent. What amount of money must the insurer invest today at 8 percent for six years to make the promised payment?

We can use Equation 1-8 to find the present value using the following data:

$$FV = \$100,000$$

$$r = 8\% = 0.08$$

$$N = 6$$

$$PV = FV_N(1 + r)^{-N}$$

$$= \$100,000 \times \left[\frac{1}{(1.08)^6}\right] = \$100,000 \times (1.08)^{-6}$$

$$= \$100,000(0.6301696)$$

$$= \$63,016.96$$

We can say that $63,016.96 today is equivalent to $100,000 to be received in six years with an interest rate of 8 percent. Discounting the $100,000 makes a future $100,000 equivalent to $63,016.96 when allowance is made for the time value of money. As the time line in Figure 1-4 shows, the $100,000 has been discounted six full periods.

FIGURE 1-4   The Present Value of a Lump Sum to Be Received at Time $t = 6$

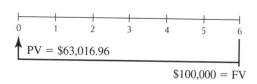

PV = $63,016.96

$100,000 = FV

EXAMPLE 1-9.   The Projected Present Value of a More Distant Future Lump Sum.

Suppose you own a liquid financial asset that will pay you $100,000 ten years from today. Your daughter plans on attending college four years from today and you want to know what the asset's present value will be at that time. Given an 8 percent discount rate, what will the asset be worth four years from today?

The value of the asset is the present value of the asset's promised payment. If you place yourself at $t = 4$, then the cash payment is to be received six years later. With this information, you can solve for the value four years from today using Equation 1-8:

FV = $100,000

$r = 8\% = 0.08$

$N = 6$

$PV = FV_N(1 + r)^{-N}$

$$= \$100,000 \times \left[\frac{1}{(1.08)^6}\right] = \$100,000 \times (1.08)^{-6}$$

$$= \$100,000(0.6301696)$$

$$= \$63,016.96$$

FIGURE 1-5   The Relationship Between Present Value and Future Value

$46,319.35

$63,016.96

$100,000

The time line in Figure 1-5 shows the future payment of $100,000 that is to be received at $t = 10$. The time line also shows the values at $t = 4$ and at $t = 0$. Relative to the payment at $t = 10$, the amount at $t = 4$ is a projected present value, while the amount at $t = 0$ is the present value (as of today).

Present value problems require an evaluation of the present value factor, $(1 + r)^{-N}$. Present values relate to the discount rate and the number of periods in the following ways:

- For a given discount rate, the further in the future the amount to be received, the smaller the amount's present value.
- Holding time constant, the larger the discount rate, the smaller the present value of a future amount.

4.2 THE FREQUENCY OF COMPOUNDING

Recall that interest may be paid semiannually, quarterly, monthly, or even daily. To handle interest payments made more than once a year, we can modify the present value formula (presented as Equation 1-8) as follows. Recall that r_s is the quoted interest rate and is equal to the periodic interest rate times the number of compounding periods per year. In general, with more than one compounding period per year, we can express the formula for present value as

$$PV = FV_N\left(1 + \frac{r_s}{m}\right)^{-m \times N}$$
(1-9)

where

m = number of compounding periods per year

r_s = quoted annual interest rate

N = number of years

The formula in Equation 1-9 is quite similar to that in Equation 1-8. As we have already noted, present value and future value factors are reciprocals. Changing the frequency of compounding does not alter this result. The only difference is the use of the periodic interest rate and the corresponding number of compounding periods.

The following example illustrates Equation 1-9.

EXAMPLE 1-10.   The Present Value of a Lump Sum with Monthly Compounding.

The manager of a Canadian pension fund knows that a lump-sum payment of CAD5 million must be made 10 years from now. She wishes to invest an amount today in a Guaranteed Investment Contract (GIC) so that it will grow to the required amount. She observes an annual interest rate of 6 percent compounded monthly. How much should she invest today in the GIC?

To solve this problem, use Equation 1-9 to find the required present value:

Future value, FV_N = CAD5,000,000

Annual rate, r_s = 6% = 0.06

Compounding periods per year, m = 12

r_s/m = 0.06/12 = 0.005

Number of years = 10

Number of periods, $m \times N$ = 12 $\times$ 10 = 120

$$\text{Present value, PV} = \text{FV}_N\left(1 + \frac{r_s}{m}\right)^{-m \times N}$$

$$= \text{CAD5,000,000}(1.005)^{-120}$$

$$= \text{CAD5,000,000}(0.549633)$$

$$= \text{CAD2,748,163.67}$$

In applying Equation 1-9, we use the periodic rate (in this case, the monthly rate) and the appropriate number of periods with monthly compounding (in this case, 10 years of monthly compounding, or 120 periods).

5 THE PRESENT VALUE OF A SERIES OF CASH FLOWS

Many applications in investment management involve assets that offer a series of cash flows over time. The cash flows may be highly uneven, relatively even, or equal. The cash flows may occur over relatively short periods of time, longer periods of time, or may even stretch on indefinitely. In this section, we discuss how to find the present value of a series of cash flows.

5.1 THE PRESENT VALUE OF A SERIES OF EQUAL CASH FLOWS

We begin with an ordinary annuity. Recall that an ordinary annuity has equal annuity payments, with the first payment starting one period into the future. In total, the annuity makes N payments, with the first payment at $t = 1$ and the last payment at $t = N$. We can express the present value of an ordinary annuity as the sum of the present values of each individual annuity payment, as follows:

$$\text{PV} = \frac{A}{(1 + r)} + \frac{A}{(1 + r)^2} + \frac{A}{(1 + r)^3} + \ldots + \frac{A}{(1 + r)^{N-1}} + \frac{A}{(1 + r)^N} \qquad \text{(1-10)}$$

where

  A = the annuity amount

  r = the interest rate per period corresponding to the frequency of annuity payments (for example, annual, quarterly, or monthly)

  N = the number of annuity payments

Because the annuity payment is a constant in this equation, it can be factored out as a common term. Thus, the sum of the interest factors has a shortcut expression:

$$\text{PV} = A\left[\frac{1 - \dfrac{1}{(1 + r)^N}}{r}\right] \qquad \text{(1-11)}$$

In much the same way that we computed the future value of an ordinary annuity, we find the present value by multiplying the annuity amount by a present value annuity factor (the term above in brackets).

EXAMPLE 1-11.   The Present Value of an Ordinary Annuity.

Suppose you are considering purchasing a financial asset that promises to pay €1,000 per year for five years, with the first payment one year from now. The required rate of return is 12 percent per year. How much should you pay for it?

To find the value of the financial instrument, use the formula for the present value of an ordinary annuity given in Equation 1-11 with the following data:

$$\text{Annuity amount, } A = €1,000$$

$$\text{Interest rate, } r = 12\% = 0.12$$

$$\text{Number of years} = 5$$

$$\text{Present value, PV} = A\left[\dfrac{1 - \dfrac{1}{(1+r)^N}}{r}\right]$$

$$= €1,000 \times \left[\dfrac{1 - \dfrac{1}{(1.12)^5}}{0.12}\right]$$

$$= €1,000(3.604776)$$

$$= €3,604.78$$

The series of cash flows of €1,000 per year for five years is currently worth €3,604.78 when discounted at 12 percent.

Keeping track of the actual calendar time brings us to a specific type of annuity with level payments: the annuity due. An annuity due has its first payment occurring today ($t = 0$). In total, the annuity due will make N payments. We can look at an annuity due that makes four payments of $100 on the time line presented in Figure 1-6.

FIGURE 1-6   An Annuity Due of $100 Per Period

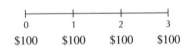

As Figure 1-6 shows, we can view the four-period annuity due as the sum of two parts: a $100 lump sum today and an ordinary annuity of $100 per period for three periods. At a 12 percent discount rate, the four $100 cash flows in this annuity due example will be worth $340.18.[6]

Expressing the value of the future series of cash flows in today's dollars gives us a convenient way of comparing annuities. The next example illustrates this approach.

---

[6] There is an alternative way to calculate the present value of an annuity due. Compared to an ordinary annuity, the payments in an annuity due are each discounted one less period. Thus, we can modify Equation 1-11 to handle annuities due by multiplying the right-hand side of the equation by $(1 + r)$:

$$\text{PV(Annuity due)} = A\{[1 - (1 + r)^{-N}]/r\}(1 + r).$$

EXAMPLE 1-12.   The Present Value of an Immediate Cash Flow Plus an Ordinary Annuity.

You are retiring today and must choose to take your retirement benefits either as a lump sum or as an annuity. Your firm's benefits officer presents you with two alternatives: an immediate lump sum of $2 million or an annuity with 20 payments of $200,000 per year with the first payment starting today. The interest rate at your bank is 7 percent per year compounded annually. Which option do you choose? (Ignore any tax differences between the two options.)

To compare the two options, find the present value of both options at time $t = 0$ and choose the one with the larger value. The first option's present value is $2 million, already expressed in today's dollars. The second option is an annuity due. Because the first payment occurs at $t = 0$, you can separate the annuity benefits into two pieces: an immediate $200,000 to be paid today ($t = 0$) and an ordinary annuity of $200,000 per year for 19 years. To value this option, you need to find the present value of the ordinary annuity using Equation 1-11 and then add $200,000 to it.

$$\text{Annuity amount, } A = \$200,000$$

$$\text{Number of years, } N = 19$$

$$\text{Interest rate, } r = 7\% = 0.07$$

$$\text{Present value, PV} = A \left[\frac{1 - \dfrac{1}{(1 + r)^N}}{r} \right]$$

$$= \$200,000 \times \left[\frac{1 - \dfrac{1}{(1.07)^{19}}}{0.07} \right]$$

$$= \$200,000(10.335595)$$

$$= \$2,067,119.05$$

The 19 payments of $200,000 have a present value of $2,067,119.05. Adding the initial payment of $200,000 to $2,067,119.05, we find that the total value of the annuity option is $2,267,119.05. Because the current value of the annuity is worth more than the lump-sum alternative of $2 million, you should choose the annuity option.

We now look at another example reiterating the equivalence of present and future values.

EXAMPLE 1-13.   The Projected Present Value of an Ordinary Annuity.

A German pension fund manager anticipates that benefits of €1 million per year must be paid to retirees. The pension fund's actuary estimates that retirements will not occur until 10 years from now at time $t = 10$. Once benefits begin to be paid, they will extend until $t = 39$ for a total of 30 payments. What is the present value of the pension liability if the appropriate annual rate of interest for plan liabilities is 5 percent compounded annually?

This problem involves an annuity that starts at $t = 10$. From the perspective of $t = 9$, we have an ordinary annuity with 30 payments. We can compute the present value of this annuity with Equation 1-11 and then look at it on a time line.

Annuity amount, $A = €1,000,000$

Interest rate, $r = 5\% = 0.05$

Number of years, $N = 30$

$$\text{Present value, PV} = A\left[\frac{1 - \dfrac{1}{(1 + r)^N}}{r}\right]$$

$$= €1,000,000 \times \left[\frac{1 - \dfrac{1}{(1.05)^{30}}}{0.05}\right]$$

$$= €1,000,000(15.372451)$$

$$= €15,372,451.03$$

The present value of the pension benefits as of $t = 9$ is €15,372,451.03. The problem now is to find the present value in today's euro (that is, at $t = 0$).

FIGURE 1-7   The Present Value of an Ordinary Annuity Starting at Time $t = 10$ (in millions)

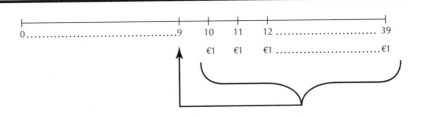

On the time line, we have shown the pension payments of €1 million extending from $t = 10$ to $t = 39$. The bracket and arrow indicate the process of finding the present value of the annuity, discounted back to $t = 9$.

Now we can rely on the equivalence of present value and future value. As Figure 1-7 shows, we can view the amount at $t = 9$ as a future value from the vantage point of $t = 0$. We compute the present value of the amount at $t = 9$ as follows:

Future value, FV $= €15,372,451.03$ (the present value at $t = 9$)

Number of years, $N = 9$

Interest rate, $r = 5\% = 0.05$

$$\text{Present value, PV} = \text{FV}_N(1 + r)^{-N}$$

$$= \text{€}15{,}372{,}451.03\,(1.05)^{-9}$$

$$= \text{€}15{,}372{,}451.03\,(0.644609)$$

$$= \text{€}9{,}909{,}219.00$$

The present value of the pension liability is €9,909,219.00.

Example 1-13 illustrates three procedures emphasized in this chapter:

- finding the present or future value of any cash flow series;
- recognizing the equivalence of present value and appropriately discounted future value; and
- keeping track of the actual calendar time in a problem involving the time value of money.

5.2 THE PRESENT VALUE OF AN INFINITE SERIES OF EQUAL CASH FLOWS— PERPETUITY

Consider the case of an ordinary annuity that extends indefinitely. Such an ordinary annuity is called a perpetuity (that is, a perpetual annuity). To derive a formula for the present value of a perpetuity, we can modify Equation 1-10 to account for an infinite series of cash flows:

$$\text{PV} = A \sum_{t=1}^{\infty} \left[\frac{1}{(1 + r)^t} \right] \tag{1-12}$$

As long as interest rates are positive, the sum of interest factors converges and:

$$\text{PV} = \frac{A}{r} \tag{1-13}$$

To see this, look back at Equation 1-11, the expression for the present value of an ordinary annuity. As N (the number of periods in the annuity) goes to infinity, the term $1/(1 + r)^N$ goes to 0 and Equation 1-11 simplifies to Equation 1-13. This equation will reappear when we value dividends from stocks because stocks have no predefined life span. (A stock paying constant dividends is similar to a perpetuity.) With the first payment a year from now, a perpetuity of $10 per year with a 20 percent required rate of return has a present value of $\frac{\$10}{0.2} = \$50$.

Equation 1-13 is valid only for a perpetuity with level payments. In our development above, the first payment occurred at $t = 1$; therefore, we compute the present value as of $t = 0$.

Other assets also come close to satisfying the assumptions of a perpetuity. Certain government bonds and preferred stocks are typical examples of financial assets that make level payments over an indefinite period of time.

EXAMPLE 1-14.   The Present Value of a Perpetuity.

The British government once issued a type of security called a consol bond, which promised to pay a level cash flow indefinitely. If a consol bond paid GBP100 per year in perpetuity, what would it be worth if the required rate of return were 5 percent?

To answer this question, we can use Equation 1-13 with the following data:

Perpetuity amount, A = GBP100

Interest rate, r = 5% = 0.05

Present value, PV = A/r

= GBP100/0.05

= GBP2,000

5.3   PRESENT VALUES INDEXED AT TIMES OTHER THAN $t = 0$

Especially in our future work with stocks, we will be finding present values indexed at times other than $t = 0$. Subscripting the present value and evaluating a perpetuity beginning with $100 payments in Year 2, we find $PV_1 = \dfrac{\$100}{0.05} = \$2,000$ at a 5 percent discount rate. Further, we can calculate today's PV as $PV_0 = \dfrac{\$2,000}{1.05} = \$1,904.76$.

Consider a similar situation in which cash flows of $6 per year begin at the end of the fourth year and continue at the end of each year thereafter, with the last cash flow at the end of the 10th year. From the perspective of the end of the third year, we are facing a typical seven-year annuity. Therefore, we can find the present value of the annuity from the perspective of the end of the third year and then discount that present value back to the present. At an interest rate of 5 percent, the cash flows of $6 per year starting at the end of the fourth year will be worth $34.72 at the end of the third year ($t = 3$) and $29.99 today ($t = 0$).

The next example illustrates the important concept that an annuity or perpetuity beginning sometime in the future can be expressed in present value terms one period prior to the first payment. That present value can then be discounted back to today's present value.

EXAMPLE 1-15.   The Present Value of a Projected Perpetuity.

Consider a level perpetuity of GBP100 per year with its first payment beginning at $t = 5$. What is its present value today (at $t = 0$), given a 5% discount rate?

First, we find the present value of the perpetuity at $t = 4$ and then discount that amount back to $t = 0$. Recall that a perpetuity or an ordinary annuity has its first payment one period away, explaining the $t = 4$ index for our present value calculation.

  i. Find the present value of the perpetuity at $t = 4$:

Annuity amount, A = GBP100

Interest rate, r = 5% = 0.05

Present value, PV = A/r

= GBP100/0.05

= GBP2,000

ii. Find the present value of the future amount at $t = 4$. From the perspective of $t = 0$, the present value of GBP2,000 can be considered a future value. Now we need to find the present value of a lump sum:

$$\text{Future value, FV} = \text{GBP2,000 (the present value at } t = 4)$$

$$\text{Interest rate, } r = 5\% = 0.05$$

$$\text{Number of years, } N = 4$$

$$\begin{aligned}
\text{Present value, PV} &= \text{FV}(1 + r)^{-N} \\
&= \text{GBP2,000}(1.05)^{-4} \\
&= \text{GBP2,000}(0.822702) \\
&= \text{GBP1,645.40}
\end{aligned}$$

Today's present value of the perpetuity is GBP1,645.40.

As discussed earlier, an annuity is a series of payments of a fixed amount for a specified number of periods. Suppose we own a perpetuity. At the same time, we issue a perpetuity obligating us to make payments; these payments are the same size as those of the perpetuity we own. However, the first payment of the perpetuity we issue is at $t = 5$; payments then continue on forever. The payments on this second perpetuity exactly offset the payments received from the perpetuity we own at $t = 5$ and all subsequent dates. We are left with level non-zero net cash flows at $t = 1, 2, 3,$ and 4. This exactly fits the definition of an annuity with four payments. Thus we can construct an annuity as the difference between two perpetuities with equal, level payments, but differing starting dates. The next example illustrates this result.

EXAMPLE 1-16.   The Present Value of an Ordinary Annuity as the Present Value of a Current Minus Projected Perpetuity.

Given a 5% discount rate, find the present value of a four-year ordinary annuity of GBP100 per year starting in Year 1 as the difference between the following two level perpetuities:

Perpetuity 1	GBP100 per year starting in Year 1 (first payment at $t = 1$)
Perpetuity 2	GBP100 per year starting in Year 5 (first payment at $t = 5$)

If we subtract Perpetuity 2 from Perpetuity 1, we are left with an ordinary annuity of GBP100 per period for four years (payments at $t = 1, 2, 3, 4$). Subtracting the present value of Perpetuity 2 from that of Perpetuity 1, we arrive at the present value of the four-year ordinary annuity:

i. $PV_0(\text{Perpetuity 1}) = \text{GBP100}/0.05 = \text{GBP2,000}$

ii. $PV_4(\text{Perpetuity 2}) = \text{GBP100}/0.05 = \text{GBP2,000}$

iii. $PV_0(\text{Perpetuity 2}) = \text{GBP2,000}/(1.05)^4 = \text{GBP1,645.40}$

iv. $\begin{aligned}[t] PV_0(\text{Annuity}) \ &= PV_0(\text{Perpetuity 1}) - PV_0(\text{Perpetuity 2}) \\ &= \text{GBP2,000} - \text{GBP1,645.40} \\ &= \text{GBP354.60} \end{aligned}$

The four-year ordinary annuity's present value is equal to GBP2,000 − GBP1,645.40 = GBP354.60.

5.4 THE PRESENT VALUE OF A SERIES OF UNEQUAL CASH FLOWS

When we have unequal cash flows, we must first find the present value of each individual cash flow and then sum the respective present values. For a series with many cash flows, we usually use a spreadsheet. Table 1-3 lists a series of cash flows with the time periods in the first column, cash flows in the second column, and each cash flow's present value in the third column. The last row of Table 1-3 shows the sum of the five present values.

TABLE 1-3   A Series of Unequal Cash Flows and Their Present Value at 5 Percent

Time Period	Cash Flow	Present Value at Year 0	
1	$1,000	$1,000(1.05)^{-1}$ =	$952.38
2	$2,000	$2,000(1.05)^{-2}$ =	$1,814.06
3	$4,000	$4,000(1.05)^{-3}$ =	$3,455.35
4	$5,000	$5,000(1.05)^{-4}$ =	$4,113.51
5	$6,000	$6,000(1.05)^{-5}$ =	$4,701.16
		Sum =	$15,036.46

We could calculate the future value of these cash flows by computing them one at a time using the single-payment future value formula. We already know the present value of this series, however, so we can easily apply time-value equivalence. The future value of the series of cash flows, $19,190.76, is equal to the single $15,036.46 amount compounded forward to $t = 5$:

$$\text{Present value, PV} = \$15,036.46$$

$$N = 5$$

$$r = 5\% = 0.05$$

$$\begin{aligned} \text{Future value, FV} &= \text{PV}(1 + r)^N \\ &= \$15,036.46(1.05)^5 \\ &= \$15,036.46(1.276282) \\ &= \$19,190.76 \end{aligned}$$

6 SOLVING FOR RATES, NUMBER OF PERIODS, OR SIZE OF ANNUITY PAYMENTS

In the previous examples, certain pieces of information have been made available. For instance, all problems have given the rate of interest, r, the number of time periods, N, the annuity amount, A, and either the present value, PV, or future value, FV. In real-world applications, however, although the present and future values may be given, you may have to solve for either the interest rate, the number of periods, or the annuity amount. In the subsections that follow, we show these types of problems.

6.1 SOLVING FOR INTEREST RATES AND GROWTH RATES

Suppose a bank deposit of €100 is known to generate a payoff of €111 in one year. With this information, we can infer the interest rate that separates the present value of €100 from the future value of €111 by using Equation 1-2, $FV_N = PV(1 + r)^N$, with $N = 1$. With PV, FV, and N known, we can solve for r directly:

$$1 + r = \frac{FV}{PV}$$

$$1 + r = (€111/€100) = 1.11$$

$$r = 0.11, \text{ or } 11\%$$

The interest rate that equates €100 at $t = 0$ to €111 at $t = 1$ is 11 percent. Thus, we can state that €100 grows to €111 with a growth rate of 11 percent.

As the previous example shows, an interest rate can also be considered a growth rate. The particular application will usually dictate whether we use the term *interest rate* or *growth rate*. Below are two examples that use the concept of a growth rate.

EXAMPLE 1-17. The Compound Growth Rate of Sales Compared to the Compound Interest Rate.

For 1994, IBM recorded net sales of $64,052 million. For 1998, IBM had recorded net sales of $81,667 million. Over the four-year period, what was the rate of growth in IBM's net sales?

To solve this problem, we can use Equation 1-2, $FV_N = PV(1 + r)^N$, this time replacing the interest rate, r, with the growth rate, g. We denote net sales in 1994 as PV and net sales in 1998 as FV. We can then solve for the growth rate as follows:

$$\$81,667 = \$64,052(1 + g)^4$$

$$1.275011 = (1 + g)^4$$

$$(1 + g) = \sqrt[4]{1.275011}$$

$$g = 1.062621 - 1$$

$$= 6.2621\%$$

The growth rate of IBM's sales was 6.26 percent per year over the period 1994 to 1998. Note that we can also use the procedure for finding the growth rate in sales for IBM to find the growth rate in earnings per share.

EXAMPLE 1-18. The Compound Growth Rate of Earnings Compared to the Compound Interest Rate.

In 1996, IBM reported earnings of $2.51 per share. For 2000, analysts estimated that IBM would earn $4.45 per share. What is the growth rate in earnings, assuming that IBM actually earns $4.45 per share in 2000?

Using Equation 1-2, we replace the interest rate, r, with the growth rate, g, as follows: $FV_N = PV(1 + g)^N$. In this case, four years separate year-end 1996 EPS from year-end 2000 EPS.

$$\$4.45 = \$2.51(1 + g)^4$$

$$(1 + g)^4 = 1.772908$$

$$1 + g = \sqrt[4]{1.772908}$$

$$1 + g = 1.153909$$

$$g = 0.153909$$

In general, solving for g gives

$$g = (FV/PV)^{1/N} - 1. \tag{1-14}$$

Here, $g = (4.45/2.51)^{0.25} - 1 = 15.39\%$.

If IBM actually earns $4.45 in 2000, the rate of growth from 1996 will be 15.39 percent per year. Note that we can also refer to 15.39 percent as the compound annual growth rate because it is the single number that compounds 1996 earnings forward to earnings in 2000. Table 1-4 lists the actual reported earnings for IBM from 1996 to 2000 (fiscal year-end December 31).

TABLE 1-4   IBM Earnings Per Share, 1996 to 2000 (Estimated)

Year	Reported Earnings Per Share	$(1 + g)$	t
1996	$2.51		0
1997	$3.01	$3.01/$2.51 = 1.199203	1
1998	$3.29	$3.29/$3.01 = 1.093023	2
1999	$4.12	$4.12/$3.29 = 1.252280	3
2000	$4.45 (estimated)	$4.45/$4.12 = 1.080097	4

Source: Zacks University Analysts Watch

Table 1-4 also shows 1 plus the one-year rate of growth in earnings. We computed the four-year cumulative growth in earnings from 1996 to 2000 with the ratio $4.41/$2.56 as follows:

$$\frac{\$4.45}{\$2.51} = \frac{\$3.01}{\$2.51} \times \frac{\$3.29}{\$3.01} \times \frac{\$4.12}{\$3.29} \times \frac{\$4.45}{\$4.12}$$

$$= (1+g_1) \times (1+g_2) \times (1+g_3) \times (1+g_4)$$

$$1.772908 = 1.199203 \times 1.093023 \times 1.252280 \times 1.080097$$

The right-hand side of the equation is the product of 1 plus the one-year growth rate in EPS for each year. Recall that $4.45/$2.51 = 1.772908 was set equal to $(1 + g)^4$.

In effect, we are solving for the single value of g which, when compounded over four periods, gives the correct product of 1 plus the one-year growth rates.[7]

To solve for g, we take the fourth root and arrive at a solution: $g = 15.39\%$. In our earlier discussion of finding the growth in EPS from 1996 to 2000, we skipped over the intermediate EPS figures and computed a rate of growth.

The compound growth rate, a summary measure that averages a series of different periodic rates, is an excellent measure of past return performance. In our IBM example, the compound growth rate of 15.39 percent is the single growth rate which, when added to 1, compounded over four years, and multiplied by the 1996 EPS, yields the 2000 EPS.

6.2 SOLVING FOR THE NUMBER OF PERIODS

In this section, we demonstrate how to solve for the number of periods given present value, future value, and interest or growth rates.

EXAMPLE 1-19. The Number of Annual Compounding Periods Needed for an Investment to Reach a Value.

You are interested in determining how long it will take an investment of 10,000,000 euro to double in value. The current interest rate is 7 percent compounded annually. How many years will it take €10,000,000 to double to €20,000,000?

Use Equation 1-2, $FV_N = PV(1 + r)^N$, to solve for the number of periods, N, as follows:

$$€20,000,000 = €10,000,000(1.07)^N$$

$$(1.07)^N = 2$$

$$\ln(1.07)^N = \ln 2$$

$$N \times \ln(1.07) = 0.693147$$

$$N \times (0.067659) = 0.693147$$

$$N = 10.24$$

With an interest rate of 7 percent, it will take approximately 10 years for the initial €10,000,000 investment to grow to €20,000,000. Solving for N in the expression $(1.07)^N = 2.0$ requires taking the logarithm of both sides and using the rule that $\ln(x^N) = N \times \ln(x)$. Generally, we find that $N = [\ln(FV/PV)]/\ln(1 + r)$. Here, $N = \ln(20,000,000/10,000,000)/\ln(1.07) = \ln2/\ln1.07 = 10.24$.

To quickly approximate the number of periods, practitioners sometimes use the Rule of 72: Divide 72 by the stated interest rate to get the approximate number of years to double an investment at the interest rate. Here, the approximation gives $72/7 = 10.3$ years.

---

[7] The compound growth rate that we calculate here is an example of a geometric mean, specifically the geometric mean of the EPS growth rates. The geometric mean is defined in the chapter on statistical concepts.

6.3 **SOLVING FOR THE SIZE OF ANNUITY PAYMENTS**

In this section, we discuss how to solve for annuity payments. Mortgages, auto loans, and retirement savings plans are classic examples of applications of annuity formulas.

EXAMPLE 1-20.   The Annuity Payments Needed to Reach a Future Value with Monthly Compounding.

You are planning to purchase a $120,000 house by making a down payment of $20,000 and borrowing the remainder with a 30-year fixed-rate mortgage with monthly payments. The first payment is due at $t = 1$. Current mortgage interest rates are quoted at 8 percent with monthly compounding. What will your monthly mortgage payments be?

The bank will determine the mortgage payments such that, at the stated periodic interest rate, the present value of the payments will be equal to the amount borrowed (in this case, $100,000). With this fact in mind, we can use Equation 1-11,

$$PV = A \left[\frac{1 - \dfrac{1}{(1 + r)^N}}{r} \right],$$ to solve for the annuity amount, A, as the present value

divided by the present value factor:

$$\text{Present value, PV} = \$100,000$$

$$\text{Quoted rate, } r_s = 8\% = 0.08$$

$$\text{Compounding periods per year, } m = 12$$

$$\text{Periodic rate, } r_s/m = 0.08/12 = 0.006667$$

$$\text{Number of years, } N = 30$$

$$\text{Number of periods, } m \times N = 30 \times 12 = 360$$

$$\text{Present value factor} = \left[\frac{1 - \dfrac{1}{\left(1 + \dfrac{r_s}{m}\right)^{m \times N}}}{\dfrac{r_s}{m}} \right] = \left[\frac{1 - \dfrac{1}{(1.006667)^{360}}}{0.006667} \right]$$

$$= 136.283494$$

$$\begin{aligned}
\text{Annuity amount, } A &= \text{PV/Present value factor} \\
&= \$100,000/136.283494 \\
&= \$733.76
\end{aligned}$$

The amount borrowed, $100,000, is equivalent to 360 monthly payments of $733.76 with a stated interest rate of 8 percent. The mortgage problem is a relatively straightforward application of finding a level annuity payment.

Next, we turn to a retirement-planning problem. This problem illustrates the complexity that you might encounter when an individual wants to retire with a specified retirement income. Over the course of a life cycle, the individual may only be able to save a small amount during the early years, but then may have the financial resources to save more during later years. Savings plans often involve uneven cash flows, a topic we will examine in the last part of this chapter. When dealing with uneven cash flows, we take maximum advantage of the principle that dollar amounts indexed at the same point in time are additive—the **additivity principle**.

EXAMPLE 1-21.   The Projected Annuity Amount Needed to Fund a Future Annuity Inflow.

Jill Grant is 22 years old (at $t = 0$) and is planning for her retirement at age 63 (at $t = 41$). She plans to save \$2,000 per year for the next 15 years ($t = 1$ to $t = 15$). She wishes to have retirement income of \$100,000 per year for 20 years, with the first retirement payment starting at $t = 41$. How much must Grant save each year from $t = 16$ to $t = 40$ in order to achieve her retirement goal? Assume Grant plans to invest in a diversified stock-and-bond mutual fund that will earn 8 percent per year on average.

 To help solve this problem, we set up the information on a time line. As Figure 1-8 shows, Grant will save \$2,000 (an outflow) per year for Years 1 to 15. Starting in Year 41, Grant will start to draw retirement income of \$100,000 per year for 20 years. In the time line, the annual savings is recorded in parentheses (\$2) to show that it is an outflow. The problem is to find the savings, recorded as X, from Year 16 to Year 40.

FIGURE 1-8   Solving for Missing Annuity Payments (in thousands)

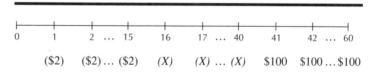

 Solving this problem involves satisfying the following relationship: the present value of savings (outflows) equals the present value of retirement income (inflows). We could bring all the dollar amounts to $t = 40$ or to $t = 15$ and solve for X.

 Let us bring all dollar amounts to $t = 15$. As of $t = 15$, the first payment of X will be one period away (at $t = 16$). Thus we can value the stream of Xs using the formula for the present value of an ordinary annuity. We encourage the reader to repeat the problem by bringing all cash flows to $t = 40$.

 This problem involves three series of level cash flows. The basic idea is that the present value of the retirement income must be equal to the present value of Grant's savings. Our strategy requires the following steps:

 i. Find the future value of the savings of \$2,000 per year and index it at $t = 15$. This value tells us how much Grant will have saved.

 ii. Find the present value of the retirement income at $t = 15$. This value tells us how much Grant needs to meet her retirement goals (as of $t = 15$). Two substeps are necessary. First, calculate the present value of the annuity of \$100,000 per year at $t = 40$. Use the formula for the present value of an annuity. (Note that the present value is indexed at $t = 40$ because the first payment is at $t = 41$.) Next, discount the present value back to $t = 15$ (a total of 25 periods).

iii. Now compute the difference between the amount Grant has saved (Step i) and the amount she needs to meet her retirement goals (Step ii). Her savings from $t = 16$ to $t = 40$ must have a present value equal to the difference between the future value of her savings and the present value of her retirement income.

Our goal is to determine the amount Grant should save in each of the 25 years from $t = 16$ to $t = 40$. We start by bringing the $2,000 savings to $t = 15$, as follows:

Annuity amount, $A = \$2,000$

Interest rate, $r = 8\% = 0.08$

Number of years, $N = 15$

$$\text{Future value, FV} = A\left[\frac{(1 + r)^N - 1}{r}\right]$$

$$= \$2,000\left[\frac{(1.08)^{15} - 1}{0.08}\right]$$

$$= \$2,000(27.152114)$$

$$= \$54,304.23$$

At $t = 15$, Grant's initial savings will have grown to $54,304.23.

Now we need to know the value of Grant's retirement income at $t = 15$. Computing the retirement present value requires two substeps. First, find the present value at $t = 40$ with the formula in Equation 1-11; second, discount this present value back to $t = 15$. Now we can find the retirement income present value at $t = 40$:

Annuity amount, $A = \$100,000$

Interest rate, $r = 8\% = 0.08$

Number of years $= 20$

$$\text{Present value, PV} = A\left[\frac{1 - \dfrac{1}{(1 + r)^N}}{r}\right]$$

$$= \$100,000\left[\frac{1 - \dfrac{1}{(1.08)^{20}}}{0.08}\right]$$

$$= \$100,000(9.8181474)$$

$$= \$981,814.74$$

The present value amount is as of $t = 40$, so we must now discount it back as a lump sum to $t = 15$:

Future value, FV = $981,814.74

Number of years, N = 25

Interest rate, r = 8% = 0.08

Present value, PV = $FV(1 + r)^{-N}$
$$= \$981,814.74(1.08)^{-25}$$
$$= \$981,814.74(0.146018)$$
$$= \$143,362.53$$

Now recall that Grant will have saved $54,304.23 by t = 15. Therefore, in present value terms, the annuity from t = 16 to t = 40 must equal the difference between the amount already saved ($54,304.23) and the amount required for retirement ($143,362.53). This amount is equal to $143,362.53 − $54,304.23 = $89,058.30. Therefore, we must now find the annuity payment, A, from t = 16 to t = 40 that has a present value of $89,058.30. We find the annuity payment as follows:

Present value, PV = $89,058.30

Interest rate, r = 8% = 0.08

Number of years, N = 25

$$\text{Present value factor} = \left[\frac{1 - \dfrac{1}{(1 + r)^N}}{r} \right]$$

$$= \left[\frac{1 - \dfrac{1}{(1.08)^{25}}}{0.08} \right]$$

$$= 10.674776$$

Annuity amount, A = PV/Present value factor
$$= \$89,058.30/10.674776$$
$$= \$8,342.87$$

Grant will need to increase her savings to $8,342.87 per year from t = 16 to t = 40 to meet her retirement goal of having a fund equal to $981,814.74 after making her last payment.

7 ALMOST-EVEN CASH FLOWS

In this final section, we reiterate the equivalence of present value and future value and explore applications of the additivity principle. Both of these concepts facilitate the analysis of cash flows that are even in most periods but cannot be treated as annuities because not all periods are even.

7.1 REVIEW OF PRESENT AND FUTURE VALUE EQUIVALENCE   As we have demonstrated, finding present and future values involves moving currency amounts to different points on a time line. These operations are possible because present value and future value are equivalent measures separated by time. Table 1-5 illustrates this equivalence; it lists the timing of five cash flows, their present values at $t = 0$, and their future values at $t = 5$.

TABLE 1-5   The Equivalence of Present and Future Values

Time	Cash Flow	Present Value at $t = 0$	Future Value at $t = 5$
1	$1,000	$1,000(1.05)^{-1} = \$952.38$	$1,000(1.05)^4 = \$1,215.51$
2	$1,000	$1,000(1.05)^{-2} = \$907.03$	$1,000(1.05)^3 = \$1,157.63$
3	$1,000	$1,000(1.05)^{-3} = \$863.84$	$1,000(1.05)^2 = \$1,102.50$
4	$1,000	$1,000(1.05)^{-4} = \$822.70$	$1,000(1.05)^1 = \$1,050.00$
5	$1,000	$1,000(1.05)^{-5} = \$783.53$	$1,000(1.05)^0 = \$1,000.00$
Sum		$4,329.48	$5,525.64

To interpret Table 1-5, start with the third column, which shows the present values. Note that each $1,000 cash payment is discounted back the appropriate number of periods to find the present value at $t = 0$. The present value of $4,329.48 is exactly equivalent to the series of cash flows. This information illustrates an important point: a lump sum can actually generate an annuity. That is, if we place a lump sum in an account that earns the stated interest rate for all periods, we can generate an annuity that is equivalent to the lump sum. Amortized loans, such as mortgages and car loans, are examples of this principle.

To see how a lump sum can fund an annuity, assume that we place $4,329.48 in the bank today at 5 percent interest. We can calculate the size of the annuity payments by using Equation 1-11. Solving for A, we find

$$A = \frac{PV}{\left[\dfrac{1 - \dfrac{1}{(1 + r)^N}}{r}\right]}$$

$$= \frac{\$4,329.48}{\left[\dfrac{1 - \dfrac{1}{(1.05)^5}}{0.05}\right]}$$

$$= \$1,000$$

Table 1-6 shows how the initial investment of $4,329.48 can actually generate five $1,000 withdrawals over the next five years.

To interpret Table 1-6, start with an initial present value of $4,329.48 at $t = 0$. From $t = 0$ to $t = 1$, the initial investment earns 5 percent interest, generating a future value of $4,329.48(1.05) = \$4,545.95$. We then withdraw $1,000 from our account, leaving $4,545.95 - \$1,000 = \$3,545.95$ (the figure reported in the last column for time period 1). In the next period, we earn one year's worth of interest and then make a $1,000 withdrawal. After the fourth withdrawal, we have $952.38, which earns 5 percent. This amount then grows to $1,000, just enough for us to make the last withdrawal. Thus the initial pres-

TABLE 1-6   How an Initial Present Value Funds an Annuity

Time Period	Amount Available at the Beginning of the Time Period	Ending Amount Before Withdrawal	Withdrawal	Amount Available After Withdrawal
1	$4,329.48	$4,329.48(1.05) = $4,545.95	$1,000	$3,545.95
2	$3,545.95	$3,545.95(1.05) = $3,723.24	$1,000	$2,723.24
3	$2,723.24	$2,723.24(1.05) = $2,859.41	$1,000	$1,859.41
4	$1,859.41	$1,859.41(1.05) = $1,952.38	$1,000	$952.38
5	$952.38	$952.38(1.05) = $1,000	$1,000	$0

ent value, when invested at 5 percent for five years, generates the $1,000 five-year ordinary annuity. The present value of the initial investment is exactly equivalent to the annuity.

Now we can look at how future value relates to annuities. In Table 1-5, we reported that the future value of the annuity was $5,525.64. We arrived at this figure by compounding the first $1,000 payment forward four periods, the second $1,000 forward three periods, and so on. We then added the five future amounts at $t = 5$. The annuity is equivalent to $5,525.64 at $t = 5$ and $4,329.48 at $t = 0$. These two dollar measures are thus equivalent. We can verify the equivalence by finding the present value of $5,525.64, which is $5,525.64 \times (1.05)^{-5} = $4,329.48. We found this result above when we showed that a lump sum can generate an annuity.

To summarize what we have learned so far: A lump sum can be seen as equivalent to an annuity, and an annuity can be seen as equivalent to its future value. Thus present values, future values, and a series of cash flows can all be considered equivalent, as long as they are indexed at the same point in time.

7.2 THE CASH FLOW ADDITIVITY PRINCIPLE

One of the most important concepts in our discussion of the time value of money is that dollar amounts indexed at the same point in time are additive. We can illustrate this relationship with the two series of cash flows shown on the time line in Figure 1-9. The series are denoted A and B. If we assume that the annual interest rate is 2 percent, we can find the future value of each series of cash flows as follows. Series A's future value is $100(1.02) +

FIGURE 1-9   The Additivity of Two Series of Cash Flows

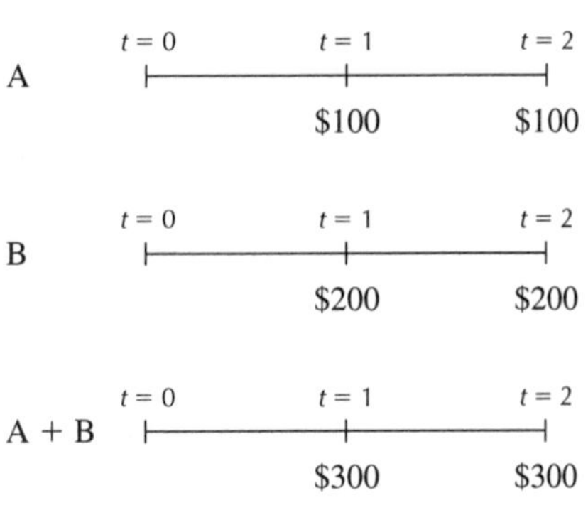

$100 = $202. Series B's future value is $200(1.02) + $200 = $404. The future value of (A + B) is $202 + $404 = $606 by the method we have used up to this point. The alternative way to find the future value is to add the cash flows of each series, A and B (call it A + B), and then find the future value of the combined cash flow, as shown in Figure 1-9.

The third time line in Figure 1-9 shows the combined series of cash flows. Series A has a cash flow of $100 at $t = 1$ and Series B has a cash flow of $200 at $t = 1$. The combined series thus has a cash flow of $300 at $t = 1$. We can easily calculate the cash flow of the combined series at $t = 2$. The future value of the combined series (A + B) is $300(1.02) + $300 = $606; this is the same result we found when we added the future values of each series.

The additivity and equivalence principles are also at work in another commonly encountered situation. Suppose cash flows are $4 at the end of the first year and $24 (actually separate payments of $4 and $20) at the end of the second year. Rather than finding present values of the first year's $4 and the second year's $24, we can treat this situation as a $4 annuity for two years and a second-year $20 lump sum. If the discount rate were 6 percent, the $4 annuity would have a present value of $7.33 and the $20 lump sum a present value of $17.80, for a total of $25.13.

7.3 APPLYING EQUIVALENCE AND ADDITIVITY TO ALMOST-EVEN CASH FLOWS

We can readily solve many uneven cash flow problems if we add dollars indexed at the same point in time. Consider a cash flow series, A, with $1,000 indexed at $t = 1, 2, 3$, and 5, and $0 indexed at $t = 4$. This series is an almost-even cash flow, flawed only by the missing $1,000 at $t = 4$. To value this series, we can use the principles of time-value equivalence and additivity.

How do we find the value of this series at $t = 5$? First, we create two new series: B, an even series with cash flows of $1,000 at $t = 1, 2, 3, 4, 5$; and C (equal to B − A), which isolates the missing cash flow. Series C has a single cash flow of $1,000 at $t = 4$. Next, we subtract the present value of Series C from the present value of Series B to find the present

TABLE 1-7   The Future Value of a Series of Unequal and Equal Cash Flows with Interest Rate 5 Percent

Time	Cash Flow Series A	Cash Flow Series B	Cash Flow Series $C = B - A$ $PV_{B-A} =$ $1,000/(1.05)^4 =$ $\$822.70$	$PV_B = 1000\left[\dfrac{1 - \dfrac{1}{(1 + 0.05)^5}}{0.05}\right]$ $= \$4,329.48$
1	$1,000	$1,000	$0	
2	$1,000	$1,000	$0	
3	$1,000	$1,000	$0	
4	$0	$1,000	$1,000	
5	$1,000	$1,000	$0	
			PV_B	= $4,329.48
			PV_{B-A}	= $ 822.70
			$PV_A = PV_B - PV_{B-A}$	= $4,329.48 − $822.70
				= $3,506.78
			FV_A	= $3,506.78 × (1.05)^5
				= $3,506.79 × 1.27628
				= $4,475.64

value of the almost-even Series A. Finally, we calculate A's future value from its present value by means of the single-payment future value formula.

In Table 1-7, we depict the original series, A, and the two created series, B and C. As discussed, we fill in the missing values and convert A into B. Next, we create the third series, C, equal to B − A. Then, because C = B − A, we can return to A by route of A = B − C = B − (B − A). That is, we subtract the present value of C from the present value of B to get the present value of A.

The future value for Series A, FV_A, is $PV_A \times (1.05)^5 = \$3,506.78 \times 1.276282 = \$4,475.64$.

EXAMPLE 1-22. The Present (or Future) Value of an Annuity with Missing Payments.

Suppose that today is January 1 and you are planning on saving $1,000 at the end of each month for the next 48 months. You recognize that your expenses are higher during December, so you plan to forgo saving in the month of December for the next four years. The bank quotes you a deposit rate of 6 percent compounded monthly, and you expect this rate to stay in effect for the next four years. What is the value of your savings plan on December 31 of the fourth year? (Remember that you will make your last deposit in November of the fourth year.)

This problem uses a series of uneven cash flows as well as a quoted interest rate. Before we begin, we outline the payment stream for your savings plan. For the next 48 months, you will make deposits of $1,000 per month at $t = 1$ to $11, t = 13$ to $23, t = 25$ to 35, and $t = 37$ to 47. You will not make deposits in Months 12, 24, 36, and 48.

To find the future value of your savings plan (call the plan Series A), we can introduce a 48-month ordinary annuity with payments of $1,000 per month and call it Series B. Series B has $1,000 payments for Months 1 to 48. Your savings plan, in contrast, has $1,000 payments in Months 1 to 11, 13 to 23, 25 to 35, and 37 to 47. Series B − A must then have payments of $1,000 in Months 12, 24, 36, and 48 and $0 everywhere else. Now we take the following six steps:

i. Calculate the present value of Series B:

   $N = 48, r = 0.5\%$, and $A = \$1,000$; therefore, PV $= \$42,580.32$.

ii. Calculate the present value of $1,000 for Series B − A, 12 months away:

   $N = 12, r = 0.5\%$, and FV $= \$1,000$; therefore, PV $= \$941.91$.

iii. Note that this $1,000 will be repeated four times, so calculate the equivalent monthly annuity amounts for the $941.91 present value of the first payment in series B − A:

   $N = 12, r = 0.5\%$, and PV $= \$941.91$; therefore, $A = \$81.07$.

iv. Step iii will be replicated three times in Series B − A. Therefore, we calculate the present value of a 48-month annuity as follows:

   $N = 48, r = 0.5\%$, and $A = \$81.07$; therefore, PV $= \$3,451.99$.

v. Calculate the present value of Series A as $PV_A = PV_B - PV_{B-A}$. If $PV_B = \$42,580.32$ from step i and $PV_{B-A} = \$3,451.99$ from Step iv, then

   $PV_A = \$42,580.32 - \$3,451.99 = \$39,128.33$.

vi. Calculate the future value of the payments:

$N = 48$, $r = 0.5\%$, and PV = \$39,128.33; therefore, FV = \$49,712.12.

Step vi alternate: Subtract the Series (B − A) annuity from the Series B annuity and calculate the future value of the result:

$N = 48$, $r = 0.5\%$, and A = \$1,000 − \$81.07 = \$918.93; therefore, FV = \$49,712.12.

8 SUMMARY

In this chapter, we have explored the time value of money. We have compounded and discounted cash flows, and developed and reviewed the following concepts for use in financial applications:

- The interest rate, r, is the required rate of return; r is also called the discount rate or opportunity cost.
- The interest rate, r, makes current and future dollars equivalent based on their time value.
- The future value, FV, is the present value, PV, times the future value factor $(1 + r)^N$.
- The present value, PV, is the future value times the present value factor $(1 + r)^{-N}$.
- In the relation between PV and FV, we can solve for N as $N = [\ln(\text{FV/PV})]/\ln(1 + r)$, where ln stands for the natural log.
- We can also solve for $r = (\text{FV/PV})^{1/N} - 1$.
- The present value of a perpetuity is A/r, where A is the periodic payment to be received forever.
- In the perpetuity formula, we can also solve for $A = \text{PV} \times r$ and for $r = A/\text{PV}$.
- The stated annual interest rate is a quoted interest rate that does not account for compounding within the year.
- The periodic rate is the quoted interest rate per period; it is equal to the stated annual interest rate divided by the number of compounding periods per year.
- The effective annual rate is the amount to which a unit of currency will grow in a year with interest on interest included.
- An annuity is a finite set of sequential cash flows, all with the same value.
- There are two types of annuities, the ordinary annuity and the annuity due. The annuity due has a first cash flow that is paid immediately, while the ordinary annuity has a first cash flow that is paid one period from the present (indexed at $t = 1$).
- We can handle annuities in a similar fashion to single payments if we use annuity factors instead of single-payment factors.
- We can use the cash flow additivity principle to solve problems with uneven cash flows by combining single payments and annuities.
- We can also use the cash flow additivity principle to calculate the present value of an almost-even series of cash flows, A, by creating an annuity, B; isolating an easily evaluated cash flow B − A; and subtracting the present value of B − A from the present value of B.
- On a time line, we can index the present as 0 and then display equally spaced hash marks to represent a number of periods into the future. This representation allows us to index how many periods away each cash flow appears.

PROBLEMS

[handwritten margin notes: 307468.47, 983575.68, 31,863.05, 56049.36, 772,173.49, 819,909.84, 107,185.90, 107229, 107250.80, monthly, 93,295.85, 1000, 233,333.33, .03, 26292.73]

1. A client has a $5 million portfolio and invests 5 percent of it in a money market fund projected to earn 3 percent annually. Estimate the value of this portion of his portfolio after seven years.

2. A client invests $500,000 in a bond fund projected to earn 7 percent annually. Estimate the value of her investment after 10 years.

3. A mother will make her son's first $100,000 college tuition payment 12 years from now. How much will she need to invest today to meet her first tuition goal, if the investment earns 10 percent annually?

4. To cover the first year's total college tuition payments for his two children, a father will make a $75,000 payment five years from now. How much will he need to invest today to meet his first tuition goal, if the investment earns 6 percent annually?

5. A client can choose between receiving 10 annual $100,000 retirement payments, starting one year from today, or receiving a lump sum today. Knowing that he can invest at a rate of 5 percent annually, he has decided to take the lump sum. What lump sum today will be equivalent to the future annual payments?

6. A couple plans to set aside $20,000 per year in a conservative portfolio projected to earn 7 percent per year. If they make their first savings contribution one year from now, how much will they have at the end of 20 years?

7. For liquidity purposes, a client keeps $100,000 in a bank account. The bank quotes a stated annual interest rate of 7 percent. The bank's service representative explains that the stated rate is the rate one would earn if one were to cash out rather than invest the interest payments.
   a. With quarterly compounding, how much will your client have in his account at the end of one year, assuming no additions or withdrawals?
   b. With monthly compounding, how much will he have in his account at the end of one year, assuming no additions or withdrawals?
   c. With continuous compounding, how much will he have in his account at the end of one year, assuming no additions or withdrawals?

8. A bank quotes a rate of 5.89 percent with an effective annual rate of 6.05 percent. Does the bank work with annual, quarterly, or monthly compounding?

9. A client has agreed to invest €100,000 one year from now in a business planning to expand, and she has decided to set aside the funds today in a bank account promising to pay 7 percent compounded quarterly. How much does she need to set aside?

10. A stock position pays quarterly dividends of $1,000 indefinitely (forever). If an investor has an opportunity cost of 12 percent compounded quarterly on this type of investment, how much should he be willing to pay for this dividend stream?

11. Suppose you plan to send a child to college in three years. You expect your child to earn two-thirds of her tuition payment in scholarship money, so you estimate that your payments will be $10,000 per year for four years. To estimate whether you have set aside enough money, you ignore possible inflation in tuition payments and assume that you can earn 8 percent annually on your investments. How much should you set aside now to cover these payments?

12. Two years from now, a client will receive the first of three annual payments of $20,000 from a small business project. If she can earn 9 percent annually on her investments and she plans to retire in six years, how much will the three business project payments be worth at the time of her retirement?

13. A client is confused about two terms on some certificate-of-deposit rates quoted at his bank in the U.S. You explain that the stated annual interest rate is an annual rate that does not take account of compounding within a year. The rate his bank calls APY (Annual Percentage Yield) is the effective annual rate taking account of compounding. The customer service representative mentioned monthly compounding, with $1,000 becoming $1,061.68 at the end of a year. To prepare to explain the terms to your client, calculate the stated annual interest rate that the bank must be quoting.

14. A client seeking liquidity sets aside $35,000 in a bank account today. The account pays 5 percent compounded monthly. Because the client is concerned about the fact that deposit insurance only covers the account for up to $100,000, calculate how many months it will take to reach that amount.

15. A bank pays a stated annual interest rate of 8 percent.
    a. What is the effective annual rate with quarterly compounding?
    b. What is the effective annual rate with monthly compounding?
    c. What is the effective annual rate with continuous compounding?

16. A client plans to send a child to college for four years starting 18 years from now. Having set aside money for tuition, she decides to plan for room and board also. She estimates total costs at $20,000 per year by the time her child goes to college. If she starts next year and makes 17 payments into a savings account paying 5 percent annually, what annual payments must she make?

17. A couple plans to pay their child's college tuition for four years starting 18 years from now. The current annual cost of college is CAD7,000 and they expect this cost to rise at an annual rate of 5 percent. In their planning, they assume that they can earn 6 percent annually. How much must they put aside each year, starting next year, if they plan to make 17 equal payments?

18. At retirement, a client has two payment options: a 20-year annuity at $50,000 per year starting after one year or a lump sum of $500,000 today. If your client's required rate of return on retirement fund investments is 6 percent, which plan has the higher present value and by how much?

19. You are considering investing in two different instruments. If your required rate of return on these investments is 8 percent annually, what should you be willing to pay for each instrument? In evaluating the second instrument, use the formula for a four-year annuity. All payments are made at year end.
    a. The first instrument will pay nothing for three years, but then it will pay $20,000 per year for four years.
    b. The second instrument will pay $20,000 for three years and $30,000 in the fourth year.

20. You are analyzing the last five years of earnings per share for a company. The figures are $4.00, $4.50, $5.00, $6.00, and $7.00. At what annual rate did earnings per share grow over these years?

SOLUTIONS

1. i. Draw a time line.

ii. Identify the problem as the future value of a lump sum.
iii. Use the formula for the future value of a lump sum.

$PV = 0.05 \times \$5,000,000 = \$250,000$

$FV_N = PV(1 + r)^N$ or $\$307,468.47 = \$250,000(1.03)^7$

The future value in seven years of $250,000 received today is $307,468.47 if the interest rate is 3 percent compounded annually.

2. i. Draw a time line.

ii. Identify the problem as the future value of a lump sum.
iii. Use the formula for the future value of a lump sum.

$FV_N = PV(1 + r)^N$ or $\$983,575.68 = \$500,000(1.07)^{10}$

Your client will have $983,575.68 in 10 years if she invests $500,000 today and earns 7 percent annually.

3. i. Draw a time line.

ii. Identify the problem as the present value of a lump sum.
iii. Use the formula for the present value of a lump sum.

$PV = FV_N(1 + r)^{-N}$ or $\$31,863.08 = \$100,000(1 + 0.10)^{-12}$

In summary, the present value of $100,000 received in 12 years is $31,863.08 if the interest rate is 10 percent. She will need to invest $31,863.08 today in order to have $100,000 in 12 years if her investment earns 10 percent annually.

4. **i.** Draw a time line.

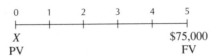

	0	1	2	3	4	5
	X					$75,000
	PV					FV

ii. Identify the problem as the present value of a lump sum.
iii. Use the formula for the present value of a lump sum.

$$PV = FV_N(1 + r)^{-N} \text{ or } \$56,044.36 = \$75,000(1 + 0.06)^{-5}$$

	0	1	2	3	4	5
	$56,044.36					$75,000
	PV					FV

In summary, the father will need to invest $56,044.36 today in order to have $75,000 in five years if his investments earn 6 percent annually.

5. **i.** Draw a time line.

	0	1	2	...	9	10
	X	$100,000	$100,000	...	$100,000	$100,000
	PV					

ii. Identify the problem as the present value of an annuity.
iii. Use the formula for the present value of an annuity.

$$PV = A\left[\frac{1 - \dfrac{1}{(1 + r)^N}}{r}\right] \text{ or } \$772,173.49 = \$100,000\left[\frac{1 - \dfrac{1}{(1 + 0.05)^{10}}}{0.05}\right]$$

	0	1	2	...	9	10
	X	$100,000	$100,000	...	$100,000	$100,000

PV = $772,173.49

iv. As an alternative to Step iii, use a financial calculator. Most of the equations in this chapter can be solved using a financial calculator. Calculators vary in the exact keystrokes required (see your calculator's manual for the appropriate keystrokes), but the table below illustrates the basic variables and algorithms.

Time Value of Money Variable and Notation Used in This Book	Notation Used on Most Calculators	Numerical Value for This Problem
Number of periods or payments = N	N	10
Interest rate per period = r	$\%i$	5
Present value = PV	PV compute	X
Future value = FV	FV	n/a (= 0)
Payment size = A	PMT	$100,000

We have 10 payments of $100,000. The rate is 5 percent and we want to calculate the present value. Enter 10 for N, 5 for $\%i$, and 100,000 for the payment. The future value is not needed, so enter 0. Then let the calculator's built-in function solve for $X = \$772,173.49$. Remember, however, that a financial calculator is only a shortcut way of performing the mechanics and is not a substitute for setting up the problem or knowing which equation is appropriate.

In summary, the present value of 10 payments of $100,000 is $772,173.49 if the first payment is received in one year and the rate is 5 percent compounded annually.

6. **i.** Draw a time line.

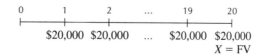

ii. Identify the problem as the future value of an annuity.
iii. Use the formula for the future value of an annuity.

$$FV = A\left[\frac{(1 + r)^N - 1}{r}\right] \text{ or } \$819,909.85 = 20,000\left[\frac{(1 + 0.07)^{20} - 1}{0.07}\right]$$

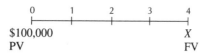

iv. Use a financial calculator.

Notation Used on Most Calculators	Numerical Value for This Problem
N	20
$\%i$	7
PV	n/a (= 0)
FV **compute**	X
PMT	$20,000

Enter 20 for N, the number of periods. Enter 7 for the interest rate and 20,000 for the payment size. The present value is not needed, so enter 0. Calculate the future value. Verify that you get $819,909.85 to make sure you have mastered your calculator's keystrokes.

In summary, if the couple sets aside $20,000 each year (starting next year), they will have $819,909.85 in 20 years if they earn 7 percent annually.

7. **a.** To solve this problem, take the following steps:

i. Draw a time line and recognize that a year consists of four quarterly periods.

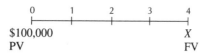

ii. Recognize the problem as the future value of a lump sum with quarterly compounding.

iii. Use the formula for the future value of a lump sum with periodic compounding, where m is the frequency of compounding within a year and N is the number of years.

$$FV_N = PV\left(1 + \frac{r_s}{m}\right)^{m \times N} \text{ or } \$107{,}185.90 = \$100{,}000\left(1 + \frac{0.07}{4}\right)^{4 \times 1}$$

```
0       1       2       3       4
+-------+-------+-------+-------+
$100,000                    $107,185.90
PV                          FV
```

iv. Use a financial calculator.

Notation Used on Most Calculators	Numerical Value for This Problem
N	4
$\%i$	7/4
PV	$100,000
FV **compute**	X
PMT	n/a ($= 0$)

In summary, your client will have $107,185.90 in one year if he deposits $100,000 today in a bank account paying a stated interest rate of 7 percent compounded quarterly.

b.   To solve this problem, take the following steps:

i. Draw a time line and recognize that with monthly compounding, we need to express all values in monthly terms. Therefore, we have 12 periods.

```
0     1     2   ...   12
+-----+-----+---------+
$100,000               X
PV                     FV
```

ii. Recognize the problem as the future value of a lump sum with monthly compounding.

iii. Use the formula for the future value of a lump sum with periodic compounding, where m is the frequency of compounding within a year and N is the number of years.

$$FV_N = PV\left(1 + \frac{r_s}{m}\right)^{m \times N} \text{ or } \$107{,}229.01 = \$100{,}000\left(1 + \frac{0.07}{12}\right)^{12 \times 1}$$

```
0     1     2   ...   12
+-----+-----+---------+
$100,000            $107,229.01
PV                  FV
```

iv. Use a financial calculator.

Notation Used on Most Calculators	Numerical Value for This Problem
N	12
$\%i$	7/12
PV	$100,000
FV **compute**	X
PMT	n/a ($= 0$)

Use your calculator's financial functions to verify that the future value, X, equals $107,229.01.

In summary, your client will have $107,229.01 at the end of one year if he deposits $100,000 today in his bank account paying a stated interest rate of 7 percent compounded monthly.

c.   To solve this problem, take the following steps:

  i. Draw a time line and recognize that with continuous compounding, we need to use the formula for the future value with continuous compounding.

<pre>
0   1
└──────────────────────────┘
$100,000   X
  PV   FV
</pre>

  ii. Use the formula for the future value with continuous compounding (N is the number of years in the expression).

$$FV_N = PV\, e^{r_s \times N} \text{ or } \$107{,}250.82 = \$100{,}000 e^{0.07 \times 1}$$

iii. The notation $e^{0.07 \times 1}$ is the exponential function, where e is a number approximately equal to 2.718282. On most calculators, this function is on the key marked e^x. First calculate the value of X. In this problem, X is $0.07 \times 1 = 0.07$. Key 0.07 into the calculator. Next press the e^x key. You should get 1.072508. If you cannot get this figure, check your calculator's manual.

<pre>
0   1
└──────────────────────────┘
$100,000 $107,250.82
  PV   FV
</pre>

In summary, your client will have $107,250.82 at the end of one year if he deposits $100,000 today in his bank account paying a stated interest rate of 7 percent compounded continuously.

8.   Stated annual interest rate = 5.89 percent.
Effective annual rate on bank deposits = 6.05 percent.

$$1 + EAR = \left(1 + \frac{\text{Stated interest rate}}{m}\right)^m$$

$$1.0605 = \left(1 + \frac{0.0589}{m}\right)^m$$

For annual compounding, with $m = 1$, $1.0605 \neq 1.0589$.
For quarterly compounding, with $m = 4$, $1.0605 \neq 1.060214$.
For monthly compounding, with $m = 12$, $1.0605 \approx 1.060516$.
Hence, the bank uses monthly compounding.

9.   i. Draw a time line and recognize that a year consists of four quarterly periods.

   ii. Recognize the problem as the present value of a lump sum with quarterly compounding.
   iii. Use the formula for the present value of a lump sum with periodic compounding, where m is the frequency of compounding within a year and N is the number of years.

$$PV = FV_N\left(1 + \frac{r}{m}\right)^{-m \times N} \text{ or } €93,295.85 = €100,000\left(1 + \frac{0.07}{4}\right)^{-4 \times 1}$$

   iv. Use a financial calculator.

Notation Used on Most Calculators	Numerical Value for This Problem
N	4
%i	7/4
PV **compute**	X
FV	€100,000
PMT	n/a (= 0)

Use your calculator's financial functions to verify that the present value, X, equals €93,295.85.

In summary, your client will have to deposit €93,295.85 today to have €100,000 in one year if her bank account pays 7 percent compounded quarterly.

10.   i. Draw a time line.

```
      0        1        2      ...
      ├────────┼────────┼──────────
     PV    $1,000  $1,000   ...
```

   ii. Recognize the problem as the present value of a perpetuity.
   iii. Use the formula for the present value of a perpetuity.

$$PV = \left(\frac{A}{r}\right) = \left(\frac{\$1,000}{0.03}\right) = \$33,333.33$$

```
      0        1        2      ...
      ├────────┼────────┼──────────
           $1,000  $1,000   ...

    PV = $33,333.33
```

The investor will have to pay $33,333.33 today to receive $1,000 per quarter for-ever if his required rate of return is 3 percent per quarter (12 percent per year).

11.   i. Draw a time line.

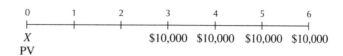

ii. Recognize the problem as a delayed annuity. Delaying the payments requires two calculations.

iii. Use the formula for the present value of an annuity (Equation 1-11),

$$PV = A\left[\frac{1 - \dfrac{1}{(1 + r)^N}}{r}\right],$$ to bring the four payments of $10,000 back to a single

equivalent lump sum of $33,121.27 at $t = 2$. Note that we use $t = 2$ because the first annuity payment is then one period away, giving an ordinary annuity.

Notation Used on Most Calculators	Numerical Value for This Problem
N	4
$\%i$	8
PV **compute**	X
PMT	$10,000

iv. Then use the formula for the present value of a lump sum (Equation 1-8), $PV = FV_N(1 + r)^{-N}$, to bring back the single payment of $33,121.27 to an equivalent single payment of $28,396.15 at $t = 0$.

Notation Used on Most Calculators	Numerical Value for This Problem
N	2
$\%i$	8
PV **compute**	X
FV	$33,121.27
PMT	n/a ($= 0$)

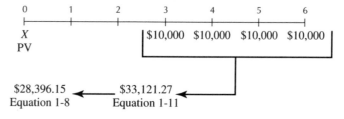

In summary, you should set aside $28,396.15 today to cover four payments of $10,000 starting in three years if your investments earn a rate of 8 percent annually.

12. i. Draw a time line.

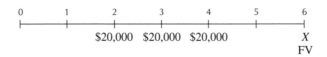

ii. Recognize the problem as the future value of a delayed annuity. Delaying the payments requires two calculations.

iii. Use the formula for the future value of an annuity (Equation 1-7), FV = $A\left[\dfrac{(1 + r)^{N} - 1}{r}\right]$, to bring the three $20,000 payments to an equivalent lump sum of $65,562.00 four years from today.

Notation Used on Most Calculators	Numerical Value for This Problem
N	3
%i	9
PV	n/a (= 0)
FV compute	X
PMT	$20,000

iv. Use the formula for the future value of a lump sum (Equation 1-2), $FV_N = PV\,(1+r)^{N}$, to bring the single lump sum of $65,562.00 to an equivalent lump sum of $77,894.21 six years from today.

Notation Used on Most Calculators	Numerical Value for This Problem
N	2
%i	9
PV	$65,562.00
FV compute	X
PMT	n/a (= 0)

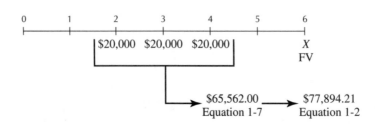

In summary, your client will have \$77,894.21 in six years if she receives three yearly payments of \$20,000 starting in Year 2 and can earn 9 percent annually on her investments.

13. **i.** Draw a time line.

ii. Recognize the problem as the future value of a lump sum with monthly compounding.

iii. Use the formula for the future value of a lump sum with periodic compounding,

$$FV_N = PV\left(1 + \frac{r_s}{m}\right)^{m \times N}$$ and solve for r_s, the stated annual interest rate.

$$\$1,061.68 = \$1,000\left(1 + \frac{r_s}{12}\right)^{12 \times 1} \rightarrow r_s = 0.06$$

iv. Use a financial calculator to solve for r.

Notation Used on Most Calculators	Numerical Value for This Problem
N	12
%i **compute**	X
PV	\$1,000
FV	\$1,061.68
PMT	n/a (= 0)

Use your calculator's financial functions to verify that the stated interest rate of the savings account is 6 percent with monthly compounding.

14. **i.** Draw a time line.

ii. Recognize the problem as the future value of a lump sum with monthly compounding.

iii. Use the formula for the future value of a lump sum, $FV_N = PV\left(1 + \frac{r_s}{m}\right)^{m \times N}$, where m is the frequency of compounding within a year and N is the number of years. Solve for $m \times N$, the number of months.

$$\$100,000 = \$35,000\left(1 + \frac{0.05}{12}\right)^{12 \times N} \rightarrow 12 \times N = 252.48 \text{ months}$$

iv. Use a financial calculator.

Notation Used on Most Calculators	Numerical Value for This Problem
N **compute**	X
$\%i$	5/12
PV	$35,000
FV	$100,000
PMT	n/a ($= 0$)

Use your calculator's financial functions to verify that your client will have to wait 252.48 months to have $100,000 if he deposits $35,000 today in a bank account paying 5 percent compounded monthly.

15. a. Use the formula for the effective annual rate.
Effective annual rate $= (1 + $ Periodic interest rate$)^m - 1$

$$\left(1 + \frac{0.08}{4}\right)^{4\times1} - 1 = 0.0824 \rightarrow 8.24\%$$

b. Effective annual rate $= (1 + $ Periodic interest rate$)^m - 1$

$$\left(1 + \frac{0.08}{12}\right)^{12\times1} - 1 = 0.083 \rightarrow 8.3\%$$

c. Use the formula for the effective annual rate with continuous compounding.
Effective annual rate $= e^{r_s} - 1$.
$e^{0.08} - 1 = 0.0833 \rightarrow 8.33\%$

16. i. Draw a time line.

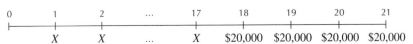

ii. Recognize that you need to equate the values of two annuities.

iii. Equate the value of the four $20,000 payments to a single payment of $70,919 in period 17 using the formula for the present value of an annuity (Equation 1-11), with $r = 0.05$. The present value of the college costs as of $t = 17$ is $70,919.

$$PV = \$20,000 \left[\frac{1 - \dfrac{1}{(1.05)^4}}{0.05} \right] = \$70,919$$

Notation Used on Most Calculators	Numerical Value for This Problem
N	4
$\%i$	5
PV **compute**	X
FV	n/a ($= 0$)
PMT	$20,000

iv. Equate the value of the 17 investments of X to the amount calculated in iii, college costs as of $t = 17$, using the formula for the future value of an annuity (Equation 1-7). Then solve for X.

$$\$70{,}919 = X\left[\frac{(1.05)^{17} - 1}{0.05}\right] = 25.840366X$$

$$X = \$2{,}744.50$$

Notation Used on Most Calculators	Numerical Value for This Problem
N	17
$\%i$	5
PV	n/a ($= 0$)
FV	$70,919
PMT **compute**	X

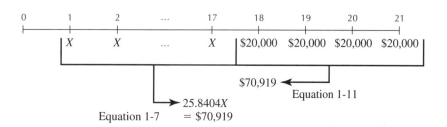

In summary, your client will have to save $2,744.50 each year if she starts next year and makes 17 payments into a savings account paying 5 percent annually.

17. **i.** Draw a time line.

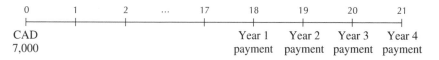

ii. Recognize that the payments in Years 18, 19, 20, and 21 are the future values of a lump sum of CAD7,000 in Year 0.

iii. Use the formula for the future value of a lump sum (Equation 1-2), $FV_N = PV (1 + r)^N$, with $r = 5\%$ four times to find the payments. These future values are shown on the time line below.

iv. Using the formula for the present value of a lump sum ($r = 6\%$), equate the four college payments to single payments as of $t = 17$ and add them together.

$$CAD16{,}846(1.06)^{-1} + CAD17{,}689(1.06)^{-2} + CAD18{,}573(1.06)^{-3} + CAD19{,}502(1.06)^{-4} = CAD62{,}677$$

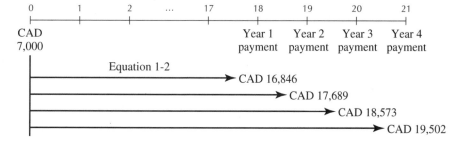

v. Equate the sum of CAD62,677 at $t = 17$ to the 17 payments of X, using the formula for the future value of an annuity (Equation 1-7). Then solve for X.

$$CAD62,677 = X\left[\frac{(1.06)^{17} - 1}{0.06}\right] = 28.21288X,$$

$$X = CAD2,221.58$$

Notation Used on Most Calculators	Numerical Value for This Problem
N	17
$\%i$	6
PV	n/a ($= 0$)
FV	CAD62,677
PMT **compute**	X

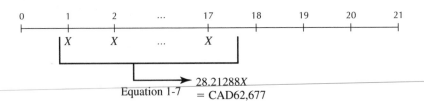

Equation 1-7

In summary, the couple will need to put aside CAD2,221.58 each year if they start next year and make 17 equal payments.

18. **i.** Draw a time line.

```
      0       1       2      ...     20
      |-------|-------|-------|-------|
  $500,000
          $50,000  $50,000   ...  $50,000
```

ii. Recognize that we have to compare a lump sum and an annuity.
iii. Use the formula for the present value of an annuity (Equation 1-11),

$$PV = \$50,000\left[\frac{1 - \dfrac{1}{(1.06)^{20}}}{0.06}\right] = \$573,496.$$

Notation Used on Most Calculators	Numerical Value for This Problem
N	20
$\%i$	6
PV **compute**	X
FV	n/a ($= 0$)
PMT	$50,000

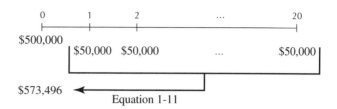

The annuity plan is better by $73,496 in present value terms ($573,496 − $500,000).

19. a. To evaluate the first instrument, take the following steps:

i. Draw a time line.

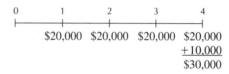

ii. $PV_3 = A\left[\dfrac{1 - \dfrac{1}{(1 + r)^N}}{r}\right] = \$20,000\left[\dfrac{1 - \dfrac{1}{(1 + 0.08)^4}}{0.08}\right] = \$66,242.54$

iii. $PV_0 = \dfrac{PV_3}{(1 + r)^N} = \dfrac{\$66,242.54}{1.08^3} = \$52,585.46$

You should be willing to pay $52,585.46 for this instrument.

b. To evaluate the second instrument, take the following steps:

i. Draw a time line.

The time line shows that this instrument can be analyzed into an ordinary annuity of $20,000 with four payments (valued in step ii below), and a $10,000 payment to be received at $t = 4$ (valued in step iii below).

ii. $PV = A\left[\dfrac{1 - \dfrac{1}{(1 + r)^N}}{r}\right] = \$20,000\left[\dfrac{1 - \dfrac{1}{(1 + 0.08)^4}}{0.08}\right] = \$66,242.54$

iii. $PV = \dfrac{A}{(1 + r)^N} = \dfrac{10,000}{(1 + 0.08)^4} = \$7,350.30$

iv. Total = $66,242.54 + $7,350.30 = $73,592.84

You should be willing to pay $73,592.84 for this instrument.

20. i. Draw a time line.

ii. $\text{FV} = \text{PV}(1 + r)^N$

$7 = 4(1 + r)^4$

$1 + r = (7/4)^{1/4}$

$r = (7/4)^{1/4} - 1$

$= 0.1502 = 15.02\%$

Earnings per share grew at an annual rate of 15.02 percent over the four years.

2

DISCOUNTED CASH FLOW APPLICATIONS

LEARNING OUTCOMES

After completing this chapter, you will be able to do the following:

- Identify the key values for capital budgeting problems.
- Calculate the net present value of a capital investment project.
- Explain the net present value rule for making investment decisions.
- Calculate the internal rate of return of a capital investment project.
- Explain the internal rate of return rule for making investment decisions.
- Describe problems with the internal rate of return method.
- Calculate the bank discount yield for a U.S. Treasury bill.
- Calculate the holding period yield for a U.S. Treasury bill.
- Calculate the effective annual yield for a U.S. Treasury bill.
- Calculate the money market yield for a U.S. Treasury bill.
- Convert between holding period yields, money market yields, and equivalent annual yields.
- Describe the basics of bond valuation.
- Calculate the price of a zero-coupon bond.
- Calculate the yield to maturity of a zero-coupon bond.
- Explain the relationship between zero-coupon bonds and spot interest rates.
- Explain how spot interest rates are used to price complex debt instruments.
- Describe how an ordinary coupon bond can be valued as a portfolio of zero-coupon bonds.
- Calculate the price of an option-free coupon bond, using the arbitrage-free valuation approach.
- Calculate the yield to maturity of a coupon bond.
- Calculate the price of an option-free coupon bond, using the required yield to maturity approach.
- Explain the concept of a growing perpetuity.
- Calculate the price of a stock using the constant growth dividend discount model.
- Explain a case for which the constant growth dividend discount model is appropriate.
- Explain the concept of supernormal growth.

- Calculate the price of a stock using the two-stage dividend discount model.
- Explain a case for which the two-stage dividend discount model is appropriate.
- Calculate the value of a firm using a free cash flow to equity (FCFE) model.
- Describe the basic principles of measuring investment performance.
- Calculate the dollar-weighted rate of return of a portfolio.
- Calculate the time-weighted rate of return of a portfolio.
- Discuss the use of the time-weighted rate of return when the client controls the timing and amount of withdrawals and additions to a portfolio.

1   DISCOUNTED CASH FLOW ANALYSIS

Securities such as stocks and bonds are claims on the future cash flows and assets of a business. Clients ask, How risky is a proposed investment? What is the best time to make the investment? How large an effect will the investment have on our business? What is the appropriate method for evaluating the performance of our investment portfolio? As equity and fixed-income analysts, we must have knowledgeable answers to these questions.

In this chapter, we introduce time value of money applications centered around the discounted cash flow (DCF) model for evaluating the worth of an investment. We also introduce basic tools for measuring portfolio performance. Capital budgeting is a logical starting point for our discussion. Both equity and fixed income analysts need to be able to assess how well managers are investing the assets of their firms. There are three chief areas of financial decision-making in most businesses. **Capital budgeting** is the allocation of funds to relatively long-range projects or investments. From the perspective of capital budgeting, a firm is a portfolio of projects and investments. **Capital structure** is the choice of long-term financing for the investments the firm wants to make. **Working capital management** is the management of the firm's short-term assets (such as inventory) and short-term liabilities (such as money owed to suppliers).

In the next section, we focus on two important concepts in capital budgeting, net present value and internal rate of return. In subsequent sections we will apply these same concepts to valuing financial instruments.

1.1   THE NET PRESENT VALUE RULE

The net present value rule is a method for choosing among investment proposals. The **net present value** (NPV) of an investment is the present value of its cash inflows minus the present value of its cash outflows. The *net* in net present value refers to subtracting the present value of the investment's outflows (costs) from the present value of its inflows (benefits) to arrive at the net benefit.

The steps in computing NPV and applying the NPV rule are as follows:

i. Identify all cash flows associated with the investment. These include all inflows and outflows.[1]

---

[1] In developing cash flow estimates, we observe two principles. First, we include only the **incremental cash flows** resulting from undertaking the project; we do not include sunk costs (costs that have been committed prior to the project). Second, we account for tax effects by using after-tax cash flows. For a full discussion of these and other issues in capital budgeting, see Brealey and Myers (1999).

ii. Determine the appropriate discount rate or opportunity cost, r, for the investment project.[2]

iii. Using that discount rate, find the present value of each cash flow. (Inflows are signed positive and increase NPV; outflows are signed negative and decrease NPV.)

iv. Sum all present values. The sum of the present values of all cash flows (inflows and outflows) is the investment's net present value.

v. Apply the **NPV rule**: If the investment's NPV is positive, we should undertake it; if the NPV is negative, we should not undertake it. If we have two candidates for investment and we have the funds to invest in only one (that is, we have mutually exclusive projects), we should choose the candidate with the higher positive NPV.

What is the meaning of the NPV rule? In calculating the NPV of an investment proposal we use an estimate of the opportunity cost of capital as the discount rate. The opportunity cost of capital is the alternative return that investors forgo in undertaking the investment. When NPV is positive, the investment adds value because it more than covers the opportunity cost of the capital needed to undertake it. So a firm undertaking a positive NPV investment increases shareholders' wealth. An individual investor making a positive NPV investment increases personal wealth. But a negative NPV investment decreases wealth.

When we work problems using the NPV rule it will be helpful to refer to the following formula:

$$NPV = \sum_{t=0}^{N} \frac{CF_t}{(1 + r)^t} \qquad (2\text{-}1)$$

where

CF_t = the expected net cash flow at time t
N = the investment's projected life
r = the discount rate or opportunity cost of capital

As always, we state the inputs on a compatible basis: If cash flows are annual, N is the project's life in years and r is an annual rate. For instance, suppose you are reviewing a proposal that requires an initial outlay of \$2 million ($CF_0 = -\$2$ million). You expect that the proposed investment will generate net positive cash flows of $CF_1 = \$0.50$ million at the end of Year 1, $CF_2 = \$0.75$ million at the end of Year 2, and $CF_3 = \$1.35$ million at the end of Year 3. Using 10 percent as a discount rate, you calculate the NPV as follows:

$$NPV = -\$2 + \$0.50/(1.10) + \$0.75/(1.10)^2 + \$1.35/(1.10)^3$$
$$= -\$2 + \$0.454545 + \$0.619835 + \$1.014275$$
$$= \$0.088655 \text{ million}$$

Because the NPV of \$88,655 is positive, we accept the proposal under the NPV rule.

Consider an example in which a research and development program is evaluated using the NPV rule.

---

[2] The **weighted average cost of capital** (WACC) is often used to discount cash flows. This value is a weighted average of the after-tax required rates of return on the firm's common stock, preferred stock, and long-term debt where the weights are the fraction of each source of financing in the firm's target capital structure. For a full discussion of the issues surrounding the cost of capital, see Brealey and Myers (1999).

EXAMPLE 2-1.   Evaluating a Research and Development Project Using the Net Present Value Rule.

As an analyst covering the RAD Corporation, you are evaluating its research and development (R & D) program for the coming year. Management has announced that it intends to invest $1 million in R & D at the beginning of the next year. Incremental net cash flows are forecasted to be $150,000 per year in perpetuity. If RAD Corporation's opportunity cost of capital is 10 percent, will its R & D program benefit shareholders, as judged by the NPV rule? Do your conclusions change if RAD Corporation's opportunity cost of capital is 15 percent?

The level net cash flows of $150,000, which we can denote by $\overline{CF}$, form a perpetuity. The present value of the annuity is $\overline{CF}/r$, so we calculate the project's NPV as

$$NPV = CF_0 + \overline{CF}/r = -\$1,000,000 + \$150,000/0.10 = \$500,000$$

With an opportunity cost of 10 percent, the present value of the program's cash inflows is $1.5 million. The program's cost is an immediate outflow of $1 million; therefore, its net present value is $500,000. As NPV is positive, you conclude that RAD Corporation's R & D program will benefit shareholders.

With an opportunity cost of capital of 15 percent, you compute the NPV as you did above, but this time you use a 15 percent discount rate:

$$NPV = -\$1,000,000 + \$150,000/0.15 = \$0$$

With a higher opportunity cost of capital, the present value of the inflows is smaller and the program's NPV is smaller: At 15 percent, the NPV exactly equals $0. At NPV = 0, the program generates just enough cash flow to compensate shareholders for the opportunity cost of making the investment. When a firm undertakes a zero-NPV project, the firm becomes larger but shareholders' wealth does not increase.

1.2   THE INTERNAL RATE OF RETURN RULE

Financial managers often wish to have a single number that represents the rate of return generated by an investment. The rate of return computation most often used in investment applications (including capital budgeting) is the internal rate of return, or IRR. The internal rate of return rule is a second method for choosing among investment proposals. The **internal rate of return** (IRR) is that discount rate which makes net present value equal to 0. It equates the present value of the investment's costs (outflows) to the present value of the investment's benefits (inflows). The rate is *internal* because it depends only on the cash flows of the investment; no external data are needed. As a result, we can apply the IRR concept to any investment that can be represented as a series of cash flows. Later in this chapter, we will meet IRR under two other names: yield to maturity for bonds, and dollar-weighted rate of return for portfolios.

Before we continue, however, we should add a note of caution about interpreting IRR: Even if our cash flow projections are correct, we will realize a compound rate of return that is equal to IRR over the life of the investment *only if* we can reinvest all interim cash flows at exactly the IRR rate. Suppose IRR for a project is 15 percent but we consistently reinvest the cash generated by the project at a lower rate. In this case, we will realize a return that is less than 15 percent. (This principle can work in our favor if we can reinvest at rates above 15 percent.)

To return to the definition of IRR, in mathematical terms we said the following:

$$NPV = CF_0 + \frac{CF_1}{(1 + IRR)^1} + \frac{CF_2}{(1 + IRR)^2} + \cdots + \frac{CF_N}{(1 + IRR)^N} = 0 \qquad (2\text{-}2)$$

Again, the IRR in Equation 2-2 must be compatible with the timing of the cash flows. If the cash flows are quarterly, we have a quarterly IRR in Equation 2-2. We can then state the IRR on an annual basis. For some simple projects, the cash flow at $t = 0$, CF_0, captures the single capital outlay or initial investment; cash flows after $t = 0$ are the positive returns to the investment. In such cases, we can say $CF_0 = -$Investment (the negative sign indicates an outflow). Thus, we can rearrange Equation 2-2 in a form that is helpful:

$$Investment = \frac{CF_1}{(1 + IRR)^1} + \frac{CF_2}{(1 + IRR)^2} + \cdots + \frac{CF_N}{(1 + IRR)^N}$$

For most real-life problems, financial analysts use software, spreadsheets, or financial calculators to solve this equation for IRR, so you should familiarize yourself with such tools.[3]

The investment decision rule using IRR, the **IRR rule,** is stated as follows: "Accept projects or investments for which the IRR is greater than the opportunity cost of capital." Note that if the opportunity cost of capital or **hurdle rate** is equal to the IRR, then the NPV is equal to 0. If the project's opportunity cost is less than the IRR, the NPV is greater than 0 (that is, using a discount rate less than the IRR will make the NPV positive). With these comments in mind, we work through two examples that involve the internal rate of return.

EXAMPLE 2-2.   Evaluating a Research and Development Program Using the Internal Rate of Return Rule.

In the previous RAD Corporation example, the initial outlay is $1 million and the program's cash flows are $150,000 in perpetuity. Now you are interested in determining the program's internal rate of return. What is the internal rate of return of this R & D program?

Recall that finding the IRR is equivalent to finding the discount rate that makes the NPV equal to 0. Because the program's cash flows are a perpetuity, you can set up the NPV equation as follows:

$$NPV = -Investment + \overline{CF}/IRR = 0$$

$$NPV = -\$1,000,000 + \$150,000/IRR = 0$$

In Example 2-1, you found that a discount rate of 15 percent made the program's NPV equal to 0. By definition, therefore, the program's IRR is 15 percent. If the opportunity cost of funds is also 15 percent, the R & D program just covers its opportunity costs and neither increases nor decreases shareholder wealth. If it is less than

---

[3] In some real-world capital budgeting problems, the initial investment (which has a minus sign) may be followed by subsequent cash inflows (which have plus signs) and outflows (which have minus signs). In these instances, the project can have more than one IRR. The possibility of multiple solutions is a theoretical limitation of IRR.

15 percent, the IRR rule indicates that management should invest in the program because it more than covers its opportunity cost. If the opportunity cost is greater than 15 percent, the IRR rule tells management to reject the R & D program. For a given opportunity cost, the IRR rule and the NPV rule lead to the same decision in this example.

EXAMPLE 2-3.   The IRR and NPV Rules, Side by Side.

The Japanese company Kageyama Ltd. is considering whether or not to open a new factory to manufacture capacitors used in cell phones. The factory will require an investment of JPY1 billion. The factory is expected to generate level cash flows of JPY0.2948 billion per year in each of the next 5 years. According to information in its financial reports, Kageyama's opportunity cost of capital for this type of project is 11 percent. Using both the IRR and NPV rules, determine whether the project will benefit Kageyama's shareholders.

NPV Rule. The cash flows can be grouped into an initial outflow of JPY1 billion and an ordinary annuity of five inflows of JPY0.2948 billion. The expression for the present value of an annuity is $A[1 - (1 + r)^{-N}]/r$, where A is the level annuity payment. Therefore, with amounts shown in billions of Japanese yen,

$$NPV = -1 + 0.2948[1 - (1.11)^{-5}]/0.11$$
$$= -1 + 1.08955 = 0.08955$$

Because the project's NPV is positive JPY0.08955 billion, it should benefit Kageyama's shareholders.

IRR Rule.   The IRR of the project is the solution to

$$NPV = -1 + 0.2948[1 - (1 + IRR)^{-5}]/IRR = 0$$

This project's positive NPV tells us that the internal rate of return must be greater than 11 percent. Using a financial calculator, we find that IRR is 0.145012 or 14.50 percent. Table 2-1 gives the keystrokes on most calculators.

TABLE 2-1   Computing IRR

Notation Used on Most Calculators	Numerical Value for This Problem
N	5
%*i* **compute**	X
PV	-1
PMT	0.2948
FV	n/a (= 0)

Because the IRR of 14.50 percent is greater than the opportunity cost of the project, Kageyama should build the factory. Whether it uses the IRR rule or the NPV rule, Kageyama makes the same decision: build the factory.

In the previous example, value creation is evident: For a single JPY1 billion payment, Kageyama creates a project worth JPY1.08955 billion, a value increase of JPY0.08955 billion. The project generates an annual operating cash flow of JPY294,800,000. If we subtract a capital charge of JPY270,570,310 (the amount of a five-year annuity having a present value of JPY1 billion at 11 percent), we find JPY294,800,000 − JPY270,570,310 = JPY24,229,690. The present value of a five-year annuity of JPY24,229,690 at an 11 percent cost of capital is exactly what we calculated as the project's NPV: JPY0.08955 billion. Therefore, we can also calculate NPV by converting the initial investment to an annual capital charge against cash flow.

1.3 PROBLEMS WITH THE INTERNAL RATE OF RETURN RULE

The IRR and NPV rules give the same accept or reject decision when projects are independent (that is, when the decision to invest in one project does not affect the decision to undertake another). They can provide conflicting rankings, however, when a firm cannot finance all the projects it would like to undertake (that is, when projects are mutually exclusive). Consider the following one-period investment projects, called A and B, in Table 2-2.

TABLE 2-2   IRR for Mutually Exclusive Projects of Different Size

Project	Investment at $t = 0$	Cash Flow at $t = 1$	IRR	NPV at 8%
A	−10,000	15,000	50%	$3,888.89
B	−30,000	42,000	40%	$8,888.89

Project A requires an immediate investment of $10,000. This project will make a single cash payment of $15,000 at $t = 1$. Because the IRR is the discount rate that equates the present value of the future cash flow with the cost of the investment, the IRR is equal to 50 percent. If we assume that the opportunity cost of capital is 8 percent, then the NPV of Project A is $3,888.89. We compute the IRR and NPV of Project B as 40 percent and $8,888.89, respectively. The IRR and NPV rules indicate that we should undertake both projects.

Suppose, however, that the firm has only $30,000 available to invest.[4] The IRR rule ranks Project A, with the higher IRR, first. The NPV rule ranks Project B, with the higher NPV, first. Because the firm can invest in only one project, the two rules conflict. Choosing Project A because it has the higher IRR would not lead to the largest increase in shareholders' wealth. Investing in Project A effectively leaves $20,000 (B's cost minus A's cost) uninvested. Project A increases wealth by almost $4,000, but Project B increases wealth by almost $9,000. The inconsistency in the ranking between the two rules is caused by the difference in the scale of the two projects.

IRR and NPV can also rank projects of the same scale differently when the timing of cash flows differs. We can illustrate this principle with Projects A and D, presented in Table 2-3.

---

[4] Or suppose the two projects require the same physical or other resources, so that only one can be undertaken.

TABLE 2-3   IRR for Mutually Exclusive Projects with Different Timing of Cash Flows

Project	CF_0	CF_1	CF_2	CF_3	IRR	NPV at 10%
A	$-10,000$	15,000	0	0	50.0%	$3,636.36
D	$-10,000$	0	0	21,220	28.5%	$5,942.90

The terms CF_0, CF_1, CF_2, and CF_3 represent the cash flows at time periods 0, 1, 2, and 3. The IRR for Project A is the same as it was in the previous example. The IRR for Project D is found as follows:

$$-10,000 + \frac{21,220}{(1 + \text{IRR})^3} = 0$$

The IRR for Project D is 28.5 percent as compared to 50 percent for Project A. Because a project's cash flows alone determine the internal rate of return, IRRs and IRR rankings are not affected by any external interest rate or discount rate. By contrast, the calculation of NPV uses an external discount rate, and NPV rankings can depend on the discount rate chosen. Here, Project D has a larger but more distant cash inflow ($21,220 versus $15,000). As a result, Project D has a higher NPV than Project A at lower discount rates.[5]

      The NPV rule incorporates the market-determined opportunity cost of capital as a discount rate. As a consequence, the NPV is the expected addition to shareholder wealth from an investment. Because shareholder wealth is the bottom line, always use the NPV rule when the IRR rule and NPV rule conflict.[6]

2   MONEY MARKET YIELDS

In our discussion of internal rate of return and net present value, we referred to the opportunity cost of capital as a market-determined rate. In this section, we begin a discussion of discounted cash flow analysis in actual markets by considering short-term debt markets. We move on to longer-term debt markets in Section 3 and equity markets in Section 4.

      To understand the various ways returns are presented in debt markets, we must discuss some of the conventions for quoting yields on money-market instruments. The **money market** is the market for low-risk, highly liquid, short-term debt instruments (that is, one-year maturity or less). Some instruments require the issuer to repay the lender the amount borrowed plus interest. Others are **pure discount instruments** that pay interest as the difference between the amount borrowed and the amount paid back.

      In the U.S. money market, the classic example of a pure discount instrument is the U.S. Treasury bill (T-bill) issued by the federal government. In buying a T-bill, investors pay the face amount less the **discount,** and receive the face amount at maturity. Thus, in-

---

[5] There is a crossover discount rate above which Project A has a higher NPV than Project D. This crossover rate is 18.94 percent.

[6] Technically, different reinvestment rate assumptions account for this conflict between the IRR and NPV rules. The IRR rule assumes that the firm can earn the IRR on all reinvested cash flows, but the NPV rule assumes that cash flows are reinvested at the firm's opportunity cost of capital. The NPV assumption is far more realistic. For further details on this and other topics in capital budgeting, see Brealey and Myers (1999).

vestors earn a dollar return equal to the discount if they hold the instrument to maturity. T-bills are by far the most important class of money-market instruments in the United States. Other types of money-market instruments include commercial paper and banker's acceptances, which are discount instruments, and negotiable certificates of deposit, which are interest-bearing instruments. The market for each of these instruments has its own convention for quoting prices or yields. The remainder of this section examines the quoting conventions for T-bills and other money-market instruments. In most instances, the quoted yields must be adjusted for use in other present-value problems.

Pure discount instruments such as Treasury bills are quoted differently from U.S. government bonds. Treasury bills are quoted on a **bank discount basis,** rather than on a price basis. Yield on a bank discount basis is computed as follows:

$$r_{BD} = \frac{D}{F} \times \frac{360}{t}$$

(2-3)

where

r_{BD} = the annualized yield on a bank discount basis

D = the dollar discount, which is equal to the difference between the face value of the bill, F, and its purchase price, P

F = the face value of the T-bill

t = the number of days remaining to maturity

360 = bank convention of the number of days in a year

The bank discount yield (often called simply the discount yield) takes the dollar discount from par, D, and expresses it as a fraction of the **face value** (not the price) of the T-bill. This fraction is then multiplied by the number of periods of length, t, in one year (that is, $360/t$), where the year is assumed to have 360 days. Annualizing in this fashion assumes simple interest (no compounding). Consider the following example.

EXAMPLE 2-4.   The Bank Discount Yield.

Suppose a T-bill with a face value (or par value) of $100,000 and 150 days until maturity is selling for $98,000. What is its bank discount yield?

For this example, the dollar discount, D, is $2,000. The yield on a bank discount basis is 4.8 percent, as computed with Equation 2-3:

$$r_{BD} = \frac{\$2,000}{\$100,000} \times \frac{360}{150} = 4.8\%$$

The bank discount formula takes the T-bill's dollar discount from face or par as a fraction of face value, 2 percent, and then annualizes by the factor $360/150 = 2.4$. The price of discount instruments such as T-bills is quoted using discount yields, so we typically go from discount yield to price.

Suppose we are offered a $100,000 T-bill at a discount yield of 4.8 percent. What is its price? We solve for the dollar discount, D, as follows:

$$D = r_{BD} \times F \times \frac{t}{360}$$

With $r_{BD} = 4.8\%$, the dollar discount is $D = 0.048 \times \$100,000 \times 150/360 = \$2,000$. Once we have computed the dollar discount, the purchase price for the T-bill is its face value minus the dollar discount, $F - D = \$100,000 - \$2,000 = \$98,000$.

Yield on a bank discount basis is not a meaningful measure of the return that is earned by investors, for three reasons. First, the yield is based on the face value of the bond, not on its purchase price. Returns from investments should be evaluated relative to the amount that is invested. Second, the yield is annualized based on a 360-day year rather than a 365-day year. Third, the bank discount yield annualizes with simple interest, which ignores the opportunity to earn interest on interest (that is, compound interest).

We can extend Example 2-4 to discuss three alternative yield measures that are often used. The first measure is the periodic total return over the 150-day period. This periodic return is also called the **holding period yield** (HPY) because it is the return that an investor will earn if the T-bill is held until maturity.[7] For an instrument that makes one cash payment during its life, HPY is

$$\text{HPY} = \frac{P_1 - P_0 + D_1}{P_0} \qquad (2\text{-}4)$$

where

P_0 = the initial purchase price of the instrument
P_1 = the price received for the instrument at its maturity
D_1 = the cash distribution paid by the instrument at its maturity (that is, interest)

When we use this expression to calculate the holding period yield for an interest-bearing instrument (for example, coupon-bearing bonds), we need to observe an important detail: The purchase and sale prices must include any **accrued interest** added to the trade price because the bond was traded between interest payment dates.[8]

Returning to U.S. T-bills, all of the return is derived by redeeming the bill for more than its purchase price. Because the T-bill is a pure discount instrument, it makes no interest payment and therefore $D_1 = 0$. Thus, the holding period yield is the dollar discount divided by the purchase price, $\text{HPY} = D/P_0$, where $D = P_1 - P_0$. The holding period yield is the figure that is annualized in the other measures. For the T-bill in Example 2-4, the investment of \$98,000 will pay \$100,000 in 150 days. The holding period yield on this investment using Equation 2-4 is ($\$100,000 - \$98,000)/\$98,000 = \$2,000/\$98,000 = 2.0408$ percent. For this example, the periodic return of 2.0408 percent is associated with a 150-day period. If we were to use the T-bill rate of return as the opportunity cost of investing, we would use a discount rate of 2.0408 percent for the 150-day T-bill to find the present value of any other cash flow to be received in 150 days. As long as the other cash flow

---

[7] Bond-market participants often use *yield* when referring to total returns (returns incorporating both price change and income). Other examples of this usage in this chapter are *bond equivalent yield* and *yield to maturity*. In other cases, *yield* refers to returns from income alone (as in *current yield,* which is annual interest divided by price). As used in this book and by many writers, *holding period yield* is a bond-market synonym for *holding period return, total return,* and *horizon return.*

[8] The price with accrued interest is called the **full price.** Trade prices are quoted clean (without accrued interest), but accrued interest, if any, is added to the purchase price. For more on accrued interest, see Fabozzi (2000).

has risk characteristics similar to those of the T-bill, this approach is appropriate. If the other cash flow were riskier than the T-bill, then we could use the T-bill's yield as a base rate, to which we would add a risk premium.

The second measure of yield is the **effective annual yield** (EAY). The effective annual yield takes the quantity 1 plus the holding period yield and compounds it forward to one year, then subtracts 1 to recover an annualized return that accounts for the effect of interest-on-interest.[9]

$$EAY = (1 + HPY)^{\frac{365}{t}} - 1$$

In our example, we can solve for the effective annual yield as follows:

$$EAY = (1.020408)^{\frac{365}{150}} - 1 = 1.050388 - 1 = 5.0388\%$$

This example illustrates a general rule: The bank discount yield is less than the effective annual yield.

The third alternative measure of yield is the **money market yield** (also known as the **CD equivalent yield**). This convention makes the quoted yield on a T-bill comparable to yield quotations on interest-bearing money-market instruments that pay interest on a 360-day basis. In general, the money market yield is equal to the annualized holding period yield, assuming a 360-day year, $r_{MM} = HPY \times (360/t)$. Compared to the bank discount yield, the money market yield is computed on the purchase price, so $r_{MM} = r_{BD} \times (F/P_0)$. This equation shows that the money market yield is larger than the bank discount yield. In practice, the following expression is more useful because it does not require knowing the T-bill price:

$$r_{MM} = \frac{360 \times r_{BD}}{360 - t \times r_{BD}} \tag{2-5}$$

For the T-bill example, the money market yield is $r_{MM} = (360 \times 0.048)/(360 - 150 \times 0.048) = 4.898$ percent.

Table 2-4 summarizes the three yield measures we have discussed.

TABLE 2-4   Three Commonly Used Yield Measures

Holding Period Yield (HPY)	Effective Annual Yield (EAY)	Money Market Yield (CD Equivalent Yield)
$HPY = \dfrac{P_1 - P_0 + D_1}{P_0}$	$EAY = (1 + HPY)^{\frac{365}{t}} - 1$	$r_{MM} = \dfrac{360 \times r_{BD}}{360 - t \times r_{BD}}$

The next example will help you consolidate your knowledge of these yield measures.

---

[9] Effective annual yield was called the effective annual rate (Equation 1-5) in the chapter on the time value of money.

EXAMPLE 2-5.   Using the Appropriate Discount Rate.

You need to find the present value of a cash flow of $1,000 that is to be received in 150 days. You decide to look at a T-bill maturing in 150 days to determine the relevant interest rate for calculating the present value. You have found a variety of yields for the 150-day bill. Table 2-5 presents this information.

TABLE 2-5   Short-Term Money Market Yields

Holding period yield	2.0408%
Bank discount yield	4.8%
Money market yield	4.898%
Effective annual yield	5.0388%

Which yield or yields are appropriate for finding the present value of the $1,000 to be received in 150 days?

Holding period yield (2.0408 percent).   This yield is exactly what we want. Because it applies to a 150-day period, we can use it in a straightforward fashion to find the present value of the $1,000 to be received in 150 days. (Recall the principle that discount rates must be compatible with the time period.) The present value is

$$PV = \frac{\$1,000}{1.020408} = \$980.00$$

Now we can see why the other yield measures are inappropriate or not as easily applied.

Bank Discount Yield (4.8 percent).   We should not use this yield measure to determine the present value of the bill. As mentioned earlier, the bank discount yield is based on the face value of the bill and not on its price.

Money Market Yield (4.898 percent).   To use the money market yield we need to convert it to the 150-day holding period yield by dividing it by 360/150. After obtaining the holding period yield 0.04898/(360/150) = 0.020408, we use it to discount the $1,000 as above.

Effective Annual Yield (5.03888 percent).   This yield has also been annualized, so it must be adjusted to be compatible with the timing of the cash flow. We can obtain the holding period yield from the EAY as follows:

$$(1.050388)^{\frac{150}{365}} - 1 = 0.020408$$

Recall that when we found the effective annual yield, the exponent was 365/150, or the number of 150-day periods in a 365-day year. To shrink the effective annual yield to a 150-day yield, we use the reciprocal of the exponent that we used to annualize.

With the concepts of NPV, IRR, and opportunity cost defined, we are now ready to use time value of money tools to cover the basics of bond pricing.

3 BASIC BOND VALUATION

A bond contract specifies the date or dates on which interest and principal must be paid.[10] For some bonds, interest is paid periodically and is called coupon interest—these bonds are called **coupon bonds.** Other bonds may not pay any periodic interest during their lives—these are called **zero-coupon bonds** (also called zeros) or **pure discount bonds.** In bond markets, the internal rate of return on a bond is known as the yield to maturity on the bond. Bond market participants usually don't speak of the NPV of a bond, but the NPV concept applies to all investments. The NPV of a bond is the present value of the bond, discounting the bond's promised payments at the required rate(s) of return, minus the bond's market price. If we take the yield to maturity on comparable bonds as the required rate of return or opportunity cost, the bond's NPV should be 0 as long as it is priced correctly. If the bond is undervalued in the marketplace, its NPV should be positive.

Bonds come in many varieties. They can be issued by corporations, municipalities, and governments. They can differ in maturity, tax status, safety of principal, and other features. To simplify matters in this chapter, we only consider bonds without embedded options (that is, option-free bonds or straight bonds) and we look at only three key features of a bond: term to maturity, coupon, and principal.

Term to maturity is the time difference between today's date and the date on which the issuer will redeem the issue by paying the face or par value. A bond's yield and price depend substantially on its maturity. Bonds with maturities of 1 to 5 years are typically classified as short-term, those with maturities of 5 to 12 years as intermediate-term, and those with maturities greater than 12 years as long-term.

Bonds are also characterized by their coupon and principal. A bond's **coupon** is the periodic interest payment to the owners of the bond; **principal** is the face value to be paid at maturity. We always cite the bond's coupon rate and maturity in the price quotation. The coupon rate is the rate that, when multiplied by the par or face value (the principal), yields the annual dollar interest on the bond. In some European bond markets and on bonds issued in the Eurobond market, the coupon is paid annually. In the United States, corporate bonds have a $1,000 face value and their coupons are typically paid semiannually. U.S. Treasury bonds and notes also make coupon payments twice a year. Thus, the yields for those bonds are based on six-month periods rather than annual periods, as we will discuss later in this section.

3.1 ZERO-COUPON BONDS AND THE ARBITRAGE-FREE VALUATION APPROACH

Zero-coupon bonds do not pay any coupon interest. Zeros are issued at a discount from their face, or par, value, and investors earn interest equal to the difference between the purchase price and the face value. Zero-coupon U.S. Treasury securities are created by dealer firms under the Treasury's Separate Trading of Registered Income and Principal Securities (STRIPS) program. In this chapter, we refer to these bonds as strips. Zeros have also been issued by corporations and municipalities.

The market for zero-coupon bonds provides investors with a wealth of information about yields or interest rates for various maturities. The information contained in the prices of zero-coupon bonds can then be used as a starting point to value all types of bonds.

For a zero-coupon bond, the price is computed as the present value of the single expected cash flow at the required yield or required rate of return. Because the zero has only one cash flow, we can use the formula for lump sums, $PV = FV_N(1 + r)^{-N}$. For zero-coupon bonds, the face value is specified, as well as its maturity date. The bond's face value is FV and its term to maturity is N. The present value equation now has two

---

[10] You can find more details on all the topics covered in this section in Fabozzi (2000).

unknowns, r, the periodic interest rate or yield compatible with N, and PV, the bond's present value. In this context, r is the zero's internal rate of return.

The yield, r, and the present value, PV, are two sides of the same coin. If we know the required rate of return, r, then we can solve for the present value or price. If we know the price, we can compute the yield.

Periodic bond yields for both straight and zero-coupon bonds are conventionally computed based on semiannual periods, as U.S. bonds typically make two coupon payments per year. So, for example, a zero-coupon bond with a maturity of 20 years will mature in 40 six-month periods. The periodic yield for that bond, r, solves the equation Price = Maturity value $\times (1 + r)^{-40}$. This yield r is, of course, an internal rate of return with semiannual compounding. In bond market terminology, it is the semiannual yield to maturity. How do we annualize it? The convention is to double it and call the result the bond's **yield to maturity.** For example, if the semiannual yield to maturity is 4 percent, the bond's yield to maturity is 8 percent. The yield to maturity calculated in this way, which ignores compounding, is a **bond-equivalent yield,** and annualizing a semiannual yield by doubling it is putting the yield on **a bond-equivalent basis.** This yield to maturity (on a bond-equivalent basis) is the actual yield quoted in markets, the one you would use in talking to the bond dealer in the next example.

EXAMPLE 2-6.   Zero-Coupon Bond Calculations.

A bond dealer offers you from inventory a zero-coupon bond that promises to pay $1,000 in five years (10 six-month periods). The yield to maturity on bonds with the same terms and credit risk is 6 percent. The dealer is offering to sell you the bond for $740. Is that a fair price?

To find bond present values using quoted annual yields to maturity, halve the quoted annual YTM to get a semiannual rate and then discount the bond's cash flows using that rate and the number of semiannual periods remaining to final maturity. The method applies to zeros as well as coupon bonds; using it, zeros and coupon bonds are priced consistently.

The general formula for the present value of a future amount, FV_N, to be received in N years, given a stated annual rate, r_s, and m compounding periods per year is $PV = FV_N \left(1 + \dfrac{r_s}{m}\right)^{-m \times N}$. We can use this expression to value zero-coupon bonds as follows, where P stands for price:

$$P = M\left(1 + \frac{\text{YTM}}{2}\right)^{-N}$$

Here, N now stands for the number of semiannual compounding periods to maturity. We calculate P as follows:

Maturity or face value, M = $1,000

Yield to maturity, YTM = 6%

Number of semiannual periods to maturity, $N = 2 \times 5 = 10$

$$
\begin{aligned}
\text{Price, } P &= \$1,000(1 + 0.06/2)^{-10} \\
&= \$1,000(0.744094) \\
&= \$744.09
\end{aligned}
$$

The bond is worth $744.09. The dealer's price, $740, is lower. It appears to be a fair price, or better. At a price of $740 your yield to maturity will be higher than 6 percent (there are several possible explanations for this apparent mispricing; for example, the dealer may need to reduce inventory). Note that with this zero-coupon bond, as with all pure discount instruments, price is less than face value at any positive interest rate.

Suppose the zero's quoted price is $744.09, with face value of $1,000 and five years to maturity as before. Now you can compute the five-year zero's yield to maturity using the above expression solved for yield to maturity:

$$YTM = 2\left[\left(\frac{M}{P}\right)^{\frac{1}{N}} - 1\right]$$

$$= 2[(\$1,000/\$744.09)^{1/10} - 1] = 0.06 \text{ or } 6\%$$

EXAMPLE 2-7. Yield to Maturity for Zero-Coupon Bonds.

Suppose you buy a two-year zero with par value of $1,000 for $923.84. What is the bond's yield to maturity? What is the bond's effective annual yield?

Set up this problem as you did in Example 2-6:

$$\text{Maturity value, } M = \$1,000$$

$$\text{Number of semiannual periods, } N = 2 \times 2 = 4$$

$$\text{Price, } P = \$923.84$$

$$\text{Yield to maturity, YTM} = 2[(\$1,000/\$923.84)^{1/4} - 1]$$
$$= 0.04 \text{ or } 4\%$$

In contrast to yield to maturity, which is a bond-equivalent yield, the effective annual yield takes account of compounding. We calculate EAY by dividing YTM by 2 to get the periodic yield and then computing the annual yield taking account of compounding. We have $EAY = (1.02)^2 - 1 = 4.04$ percent. If you discount the zero's face value at its effective annual yield, you get its price of $923.84 = \$1,000(1.0404)^{-2}$. Is there a reason to be troubled that YTM is different from effective annual yield? Not so long as YTM is applied consistently. Given YTM we can always calculate EAY, and vice versa.

The result in Example 2-7 illustrates an important point about zero-coupon bonds. The realized return on a bond depends on three components: price appreciation to the date the bond is sold or redeemed, the coupons received, and interest earned on reinvested coupons. With zeros, all of the return comes from price appreciation; investors have no uncertainty about the return at which coupons will be reinvested, because they have no coupons. Thus, an investor who holds a default-free zero-coupon bond to maturity will receive a realized return equal to the bond's effective annual yield.

The yields to maturity on zero-coupon bonds have a very important place in fixed income analysis. The YTM on an N-year zero-coupon bond is called the N-year **spot interest rate,** and the graph of spot rates versus term to maturity is called the **spot yield** curve.[11] If you had the right to a cash flow at $N = 5$, for example, you would use the five-year spot rate to find its present value.[12]

We can use spot interest rates to price complex debt instruments, including coupon bonds, by taking each individual cash flow of the instrument and discounting it by the appropriate spot rate of interest. For instance, suppose we have a three-year bond that makes payments of €100 at the end of the first and second years, and a final payment of €1,100 (interest and face value) at the end of the third year. We can treat this bond as a portfolio of three zeros, and then value each cash flow using the corresponding spot rate of interest: the one-year spot rate for the first cash flow, the two-year spot rate for the second cash flow, and the three-year spot rate for the third cash flow. Suppose the present value of these cash flows is €940, but we can buy the bond for €920. We can simultaneously buy the bond for €920 and sell the three component zeros for €940 in total (stripping the bond into three pieces). Ignoring transaction costs, we can pocket a €20 arbitrage profit. The actions of arbitrageurs should bid the bond's price up to €940.

This approach to valuing a fixed-income instrument as a portfolio of zero-coupon bonds is known as an **arbitrage-free valuation approach.** Any cash flow with the same maturity and credit must be discounted back at the same rate. This relation must hold whether the cash flow is part of a package (that is, a coupon bond) or simply a zero.

The following example illustrates these concepts.

EXAMPLE 2-8.   A Coupon Bond as a Portfolio of Zeros.

Suppose we have a $1 million face value Treasury note that matures in 12 months and makes $25,000 semiannual coupon payments at $t = \frac{1}{2}$ and $t = 1$ year.[13] In addition to the note, we can buy a strip (a zero-coupon bond) with face value of $25,000 maturing at $t = \frac{1}{2}$ and a strip with face value of $1,025,000 maturing at $t = 1$. The strip maturing at $t = \frac{1}{2}$ has a current price of $24,390.24 with a yield to maturity of 5 percent, and the strip maturing at $t = 1$ has a price of $966,160.81 and a yield to maturity of 6 percent. We can look at time lines of the two strips (which we label zeros, for short) and the T-note, which will make a payment of $25,000 at $t = \frac{1}{2}$ and a payment of $1,025,000 (interest and principal) at $t = 1$.

When we look at the T-note on the time line in Figure 2-1, we can view it as a portfolio of two discount instruments: one that pays $0.025 million in 6 months and another that pays $1.025 million in 12 months. To see this, add the cash flows on the first two time lines at $t = \frac{1}{2}$ and at $t = 1$ and compare the result to the cash flows on the T-note: holding the two discount instruments replicates the cash flows on the T-note. Two identical assets must sell at the same price, so we are justified in discounting the T-note's first payment at an annual yield to maturity of 5 percent and the T-note's second payment at an annual yield to maturity of 6 percent.

---

[11] In finance, *spot* means "immediately deliverable" or "beginning today." The spot interest rate is a rate on a loan beginning today, in contrast to a forward interest rate, which is the rate on a loan beginning some time in the future.

[12] Here and elsewhere, we assume no difference in the risk of the cash flows we are pricing and the risk of spot rates we are using for pricing. If we find a difference, we can make an appropriate risk adjustment to the spot rate.

[13] U.S. Treasury notes are coupon securities issued in original maturities ranging from 2 to 10 years. Notes are available in denominations ranging from $1,000 to $1,000,000.

FIGURE 2-1   A Coupon Instrument Seen as Two Zeros
              (Amounts in $ Million)

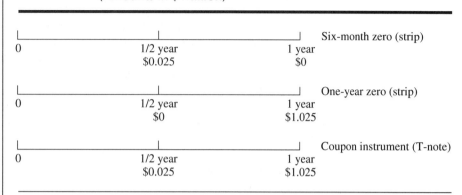

Now we can price the one-year T-note with the yield information from the two discount instruments.

$$
\begin{aligned}
\text{Price} &= \frac{\$25,000}{(1 + 0.05/2)} + \frac{\$1,025,000}{(1 + 0.06/2)^2} \\
&= \$25,000(0.975610) + \$1,025,000(0.942596) \\
&= \$24,390.24 + \$966,160.81 \\
&= \$990,551.05
\end{aligned}
$$

If the T-note is priced less than $990,551.05, it is undervalued and arbitrage involves buying the T-note and selling the T-bills. If the T-note is priced more than $990,551.05, it is overvalued and the arbitrage involves selling the T-note and buying the strips.

This example can be applied to any coupon-bearing bond. If a bond matures in N periods, we can price the bond if we know the zero-coupon rates for bonds maturing in one period, two periods, and so on, up to N periods.

In the previous example, the price of $990,551.05 was based on separate discount rates for each cash flow. Now we turn to the problem of computing the single discount rate (yield) for pricing a one-year coupon bond. As with zero-coupon bonds, this discount rate is the bond's internal rate of return.

3.2 COUPON BONDS AND THE YIELD TO MATURITY VALUATION APPROACH

In contrast to the arbitrage-free valuation approach to valuing coupon bonds, the traditional approach discounts all cash flows at a single interest rate, the yield to maturity. Here again, bond valuation is an application of time value of money principles.

The yield to maturity on a coupon bond is the discount rate that makes the present value of the bond's promised cash flows equal to the bond's market price (plus accrued interest).[14] An implied YTM can be calculated from a bond's market price. In contrast, an implied price or intrinsic value can be calculated from the required YTM on a bond. In

---

[14] Throughout this discussion, we assume that the next coupon is exactly six months in the future (for semiannual coupon bonds) or one year in the future (for annual coupon bonds) so that there is no accrued interest.

pricing a bond using required YTM, investors use information about the YTMs at which comparable bonds are trading to find the discount rate (required YTM) to apply to the bond's cash flows.

Before we can talk about YTM and bond pricing, we need to know the terms of the bond. The bond indenture, or contract creating the bond, specifies the bond's face or principal value, the maturity date at which principal value is paid to bondholders, the bond's coupon rate, and the schedule of the coupon payments.

The coupon rate multiplied by the face value is the amount of annual interest paid on the bond. Coupon or interest payments can be made on any schedule (annual, semiannual, quarterly, monthly, and so on), but most bonds traded in the United States pay coupon interest semiannually. We refer to bonds that pay coupons semiannually as semiannual-pay bonds. For instance, a 10-year U.S. Treasury bond as of the date of issuance will make 20 semiannual coupon payments and at maturity will repay the face or par value. To simplify our presentation, we assume that the next coupon payment is six months from now and that the bond pays a fixed rate of coupon interest. This assumption allows us to view a bond as a package of an ordinary annuity of coupon payments plus the repayment of principal. For instance, suppose we have a 10-year semiannual pay bond with a $1,000 face value and a 6 percent coupon rate. The bond's semiannual coupon payment is determined as follows:

$$\text{Semiannual coupon} = (\text{Coupon rate} \times \text{Par value})/2 = (0.06 \times \$1,000)/2 = \$30$$

The 10-year bond will make 20 coupon payments of $30 (the first of which is six months from now) and repay the par amount of $1,000 in 10 years. Before we begin to discount the cash flow, however, we must be sure that the discount rate, r, and the number of periods, N, are compatible. For the semiannual pay bond, the periodic yield will be a six-month yield and N must be the number of six-month periods during the life of the bond.

When we have a market price for a bond, we can use the price to compute the implied YTM. Given its current price, YTM, then, is the projected compound rate of return on a bond held to maturity. Using YTM in this way requires three assumptions: that the issuer makes all promised cash flows, that the bond is held to maturity, and that all coupons are reinvested at a rate equal to the YTM. Although these assumptions are restrictive, practitioners widely use YTM in investment decision making. The YTM calculation itself is difficult, so analysts typically rely on software, spreadsheets, or financial calculators to calculate YTM quickly and accurately.

Given a required YTM, we can calculate the implied price or intrinsic value of the bond. To find the present value of the coupon and principal payments, we can separate the cash flows into two pieces, the stream of coupon payments and the face value payment at maturity. Because the coupon payments form an ordinary annuity, we can use the formula for the present value of an ordinary annuity, $PV = A[1 - (1 + r)^{-N}]/r$, to find the present value. We can then discount the repayment of principal separately and add it to the present value of the coupon payments to obtain the present value of the bond:

$$P = C\left[\frac{1 - \dfrac{1}{\left(1 + \dfrac{YTM}{2}\right)^N}}{\dfrac{YTM}{2}}\right] + \frac{M}{\left(1 + \dfrac{YTM}{2}\right)^N} \tag{2-6}$$

where

$$P = \text{Price or present value}$$
$$C = \text{Semiannual coupon payment}$$
$$N = \text{Number of semiannual periods to maturity}$$
$$\text{YTM} = \text{Yield to maturity}$$
$$M = \text{Maturity or face value}$$

This calculation reflects a bond-market convention, discussed previously in relation to zero-coupon bonds, that the discount rate, $r = \text{YTM}/2$, is the periodic rate compatible with the semiannual frequency of payments. (The discount rate is the semiannual YTM.) Known as a bond equivalent yield, the annual YTM is computed as twice this periodic rate: $\text{YTM} = 2r$, rather than compounded forward to an effective annual yield using $(1 + r)^2 - 1$.

We now show a standard bond valuation problem using Equation 2-6.

EXAMPLE 2-9.   Price, Coupon Rate, and Yield to Maturity (1).

You are pricing a 10-year, 6 percent coupon bond with a $1,000 face value. Coupon payments are made semiannually and the first payment is due in exactly six months. You have researched other semiannual pay bonds of similar maturity and credit quality and determine that the appropriate yield to maturity is 5 percent. Using this as the required rate of return, compute a fair value for this bond.

Using Equation 2-6, you find the price of the bond as the sum of the present value of the 20 coupon payments and the present value of the maturity value.

$$\text{Semiannual coupon, } C = (0.06 \times \$1,000)/2 = \$30$$

$$\text{Maturity value, } M = \$1,000$$

$$\text{Yield to maturity, YTM} = 5\% = 0.05$$

$$P = \$30\left[\frac{1 - \dfrac{1}{\left(1 + \dfrac{0.05}{2}\right)^{20}}}{\dfrac{0.05}{2}} \right] + \frac{\$1,000}{\left(1 + \dfrac{0.05}{2}\right)^{20}}$$

$$= \$30(15.589162) + \$1,000(0.610271)$$
$$= \$467.67 + \$610.27$$
$$= \$1,077.95$$

The bond should sell for $1,077.95. Note that $1,077.95 is above, or at a premium to, the par value of $1,000 (for that reason, it can be called a **premium bond**). To understand why this is so, consider the following possible relationships:

(a) Coupon rate $>$ YTM   The bond sells at a premium to par.

(b) Coupon rate $=$ YTM   The bonds sells at par.

(c) Coupon rate $<$ YTM   The bond sells at a discount to par.

This bond pays $60 per year in interest. If it sold at par, its yield to maturity would be 6 percent. To yield less than 6 percent, the bond must sell above par, $1,000. Recall that a bond's price is inversely related to the discount rate applied to its cash flows. Also note that when the bond sells above par, its YTM must be less than 6 percent because of the built-in capital loss as the bond's value is pulled down to its maturity value of $1,000. Here, the bond's market-determined yield to maturity is 5 percent. Therefore, case (a) applies and the bond sells above par.

Now we look at the same bond assuming that the market-required yield to maturity is higher.

EXAMPLE 2-10.   Price, Coupon Rate, and Yield to Maturity (2).

Consider the 10-year semiannual pay bond from Example 2-9, but now assume that the required yield to maturity is 7 percent.
    We calculate the bond price as follows:

$$\$30 \left[\frac{1 - \dfrac{1}{\left(1 + \dfrac{0.07}{2}\right)^{20}}}{\dfrac{0.07}{2}} \right] + \frac{\$1,000}{\left(1 + \dfrac{0.07}{2}\right)^{20}}$$

$$= \$30(14.2124) + \$1,000(0.502566)$$
$$= \$426.37 + \$502.57$$
$$= \$928.94$$

The bond now sells for less than its par value. We call this bond a **discount bond** (not to be confused with a pure discount bond or zero). It sells for a discount below the maturity value because its required yield to maturity of 7 percent is greater than the bond's coupon rate of 6 percent. At a price below par, the bond's YTM must be greater than 6 percent because of the built-in capital gain as the bond's price is pulled up to par at maturity.

In this section we have illustrated the pricing of zero-coupon and coupon bonds, the calculation of yield to maturity, and the relationship between yield to maturity, coupon rate, and bond price. Turning to equity valuation, stock represents a residual or ownership stake in a firm. As a result, equity cash flows are generally riskier than bond cash flows. Determining the cash flows to use in valuation is a more complex task for stocks than it is for bonds. However, the underlying principles for discounting cash flows are the same, as we will see as we take up the basics of equity valuation in the next section.

4   BASIC EQUITY VALUATION

Present value concepts can be used to value common stock. As with bonds, we can view the estimated value (intrinsic value) of one share of common stock as equal to the present value of expected future cash flows. We can even relate the net present value concept to equity selection: The NPV of a security is its intrinsic value minus its actual price, a positive (negative) NPV indicating an undervalued (overvalued) security.

In this section, we focus on two discounted cash flow (DCF) models of equity valuation: the dividend discount model (DDM) and the free cash flow to equity (FCFE) model. In all the problems we discuss, we simplify our model by specifying the required rate of return.[15]

An owner of common stock has expected future cash flows that come in two forms: the expected cash dividend and capital gains or losses due to the change in price. Denote the current share price as P_0, the expected price at the end of one year as P_1, and the expected dividend as D_1. If the required rate of return used to discount future cash flows is denoted as r, then we can arrive at the current share price as the present discounted value of the expected future cash flows with the following formula:

$$P_0 = \frac{D_1 + P_1}{(1 + r)} \qquad\qquad (2\text{-}7)$$

Equation 2-7 shows that the current share price is the present value of expected future cash flow. With a holding period of one year, future cash flow comes in two forms: next period's expected dividend, and next period's price (the cash inflow if the share is sold).

We now look at a one-period valuation problem.

EXAMPLE 2-11. Valuing Stock by Discounting its Expected Future Cash Flows.

You have been assigned the task of valuing Basic Industries stock. You forecast that next period's dividend will be $5 per share and next period's stock price will be $225 per share. Your research department indicates that investors are requiring a return of 15 percent on common stocks like Basic. What is your estimate of fair value of Basic stock?

You can use Equation 2-7 to find the fair value (per share) of Basic Industries:

Next period's dividend, $D_1 = \$5$

Next period's stock price, $P_1 = \$225$

Required rate of return, $r = 15\%$

$$\begin{aligned}
\text{Today's price, } P_0 &= (D_1 + P_1)/(1 + r) \\
&= (\$5 + \$225)/(1.15) \\
&= \$200
\end{aligned}$$

Your analysis points to a fair value (per share) of $200.

Now suppose that the price of the stock is equal to its fair value, $200. What rate of return would investors expect to earn if they purchased the stock at $200? With P_0, P_1, and D_1 given, you can solve for r from the single-period model in Equation 2-7:

$$P_0 = (D_1 + P_1)/(1 + r)$$

$$r = (D_1 + P_1 - P_0)/P_0$$

$$r = (\$5 + \$225 - \$200)/\$200 = 0.15$$

---

[15] Note that these simple models provide the basic principles for understanding more complicated DCF models. Block (1999) provides a survey of practice and theory with respect to equity valuation techniques. When we refer to a simple or two-stage dividend discount model in what follows, we could equally well generalize to any cash flows by referring to a simple or two-stage cash flow discount model.

At a current price of $200, investors can expect to earn 15 percent based on their expectations of next period's dividend and price. The numerator of the calculation for return is the $5 dividend plus the $25 capital gain ($225 − $200). We can divide each of these pieces by the current price of $200. The 15 percent rate of return can then be viewed as the sum of two parts: the dividend yield of $5/$200 = 2.5 percent plus the capital gain of $25/$200 = 12.5 percent.

The previous example illustrates how we can use the principles of time value of money to determine the current price of common stock. What, then, determines next period's price? If the single-period model holds today at time period $t = 0$, we can assume that it will hold next period at $t = 1$. We can then determine P_1 as follows:

$$P_1 = \frac{D_2 + P_2}{(1 + r)}$$

We calculate the price at time period $t = 1$ by forecasting the dividends and price expected to hold at time period $t = 2$. Now if we substitute our value for P_1 into Equation 2-7, we get the following expression for P_0:

$$P_0 = \frac{1}{1 + r}(D_1 + P_1) = \frac{1}{1 + r}\left(D_1 + \frac{D_2 + P_2}{(1 + r)}\right) = \frac{D_1}{1 + r} + \frac{D_2 + P_2}{(1 + r)^2}$$

Note that our expression for the current price is expressed as the sum of two components: the present value of next period's dividend and the present value of the dividend and price to be received at time period $t = 2$. Suppose that investors are expecting dividends at time period $t = 2$ of $5.625 per share and a stock price of $253.125 per share. Based on this information, we can calculate the price at time period $t = 1$, P_1, will be

$$P_1 = \frac{D_2 + P_2}{(1 + r)} = \frac{\$5.625 + \$253.125}{1.15} = \$225$$

What determines P_2? We can find the price at time period $t = 2$ with the single-period model as the present value of the dividend and the price expected at time period $t = 3$. This process can be continued to some terminal horizon, H, and we can rewrite Equation 2-7 as

$$P_0 = \frac{D_1}{(1 + r)} + \frac{D_2}{(1 + r)^2} + \frac{D_3}{(1 + r)^3} + \cdots + \frac{D_{H-1}}{(1 + r)^{H-1}} + \frac{D_H + P_H}{(1 + r)^H}, \text{ or}$$

$$P_0 = \sum_{t=1}^{H} \frac{D_t}{(1 + r)^t} + \frac{P_H}{(1 + r)^H} \tag{2-8}$$

This expression for P_0 uses the compact summation notation to express the present value of the dividends from time period $t = 1$ to $t = H$. The price is thus made up of two components: the present value of anticipated dividends out to some horizon date, H, and the price, P_H, at time period H.

Equation 2-8 expresses the price in much the same way Equation 2-7 does: The stock price is the present value of the expected future cash flows. The only difference between Equation 2-7 and Equation 2-8 is how far out we look. In both cases, the current stock price is the present value of future dividends and the future horizon price. When we only look one period ahead, the current price is equal to the present value of the dividend at time period $t = 1$ plus the present value of the price at that time. If we were to look ahead for more than two periods, the price would be computed in the same way. Thus, the current price of a stock is equal to the present value of H future dividends (the dividend stream) plus the present value of the price at time period H (the horizon price).

The version of the stock price in Equation 2-8 can allow the horizon date, H, to extend far into the future. If we allow the horizon date to extend infinitely far into the future, the horizon price, P_H, will approach 0, and the price, P_0, will be the present value of an infinite stream of dividends. We can express the price as

$$P_0 = \sum_{t=1}^{\infty} \frac{D_t}{(1 + r)^t} \tag{2-9}$$

In this model, any dividend stream can be valued because we are discounting dividends directly. For example, this model allows us to value stocks with negative earnings. To do so, we need to establish some future period by which the company may start to earn profits and then project eventual dividend payments.

Although real-world companies deliver ever-changing dividend payment streams, some simplifying assumptions allow us to apply time value of money shortcuts to value dividend-paying companies. For example, Equation 2-9 expresses the price as the present value of a perpetual stream of dividends. If we make the simplifying assumption that the expected dividends are all equal, then Equation 2-9 reduces to finding the present value of a perpetuity. Recall the expression for the present value of a perpetuity. Letting the constant dividend be represented as D_1, the price can be expressed as

$$P_0 = \frac{D_1}{r} \tag{2-10}$$

This simplified valuation method allows us to estimate the price being paid for growth opportunities. Suppose, for example, a firm has no opportunities to invest in projects that earn at least at the opportunity cost of capital; that is, the firm has no projects with positive net present value. Such a no-growth firm should pay out all of its earnings as dividends so that shareholders can redeploy capital to higher-valued investments. In that case, dividends equal earnings period by period, earnings remain constant in perpetuity, and we value the stock as the present value of a perpetuity, $P_0 = E_1/r$, where E_1 is constant level earnings. The quantity E_1/r can be thought of as an estimate of the value of a share of stock under a zero-earnings growth scenario.[16] For example, suppose the market price of a share of stock is $100, but its estimated value under a zero-earnings growth scenario is $60. We can think of investors as valuing the firm's future growth opportunities per share at $40 = $100 − $60.

The level perpetuity example is a special case of a **growing perpetuity,** defined as a stream of cash flows that grow at a constant rate, g, forever. Starting with an initial dividend, D_0, the constant growth assumption implies that dividends grow like this:

$$D_1 = D_0(1 + g)^1$$

$$D_2 = D_1(1 + g)^1 = D_0(1 + g)^2$$

$$D_3 = D_2(1 + g)^1 = D_0(1 + g)^3, \text{ and so on}$$

---

[16] By a similar argument (solving for r), the **earnings yield** $r = E_1/P_0$ has been used as a quick estimate of the required rate of return on a stock under a no-growth scenario.

With the constant growth assumption, Equation 2-9 can be written as

$$P_0 = \sum_{t=1}^{\infty} \frac{D_0(1 + g)^t}{(1 + r)^t} \qquad \text{(2-11)}$$

This infinite sum can be expressed in a simpler form, so long as the growth rate, g, is less than the discount rate ($r > g$):

$$P_0 = \frac{D_1}{r - g} \qquad \text{(2-12)}$$

Note that Equation 2-10 is a special case of Equation 2-12 with $g = 0$. Equation 2-12 is called the **constant growth dividend discount model,** or the **Gordon model,** after Myron J. Gordon. Keep in mind two important points about Equation 2-12. First, the growth rate must be strictly less than the required rate of return. If $g \geq r$, then Equation 2-11 does not converge to the result in Equation 2-12. (To handle cases where $g \geq r$, we will introduce a multistage dividend discount model in Equation 2-13.) Second, the price is the present value of *future* dividends.[17] In Equation 2-12, the dividend in the numerator is D_1, which is next period's dividend; it is equal to $D_0(1 + g)$. The initial dividend, D_0, which was introduced earlier, was a convenient way to start the process for the growing dividend.

If stock prices are generated according to the constant growth model and the price and the growth rate are known, we can solve for the required rate of return, r, as follows:

$$r = \frac{D_1}{P_0} + g$$

Thus, the estimated rate of return has two parts: D_1/P_0 (the dividend yield) and g (the growth rate in dividends). The growth rate in dividends is also the rate at which the stock price will grow.

$$P_0 = \frac{D_1}{r - g}$$

$$P_1 = \frac{D_2}{r - g}$$

$$\frac{P_1 - P_0}{P_0} = \frac{\left(\dfrac{D_2 - D_1}{r - g}\right)}{\dfrac{D_1}{r - g}} = \frac{D_2 - D_1}{D_1}$$

Now we show some examples that illustrate finding the stock price as the present value of either an infinite stream of dividends or a finite stream of dividends plus some horizon price.

---

[17] The required rate of return on equity, r, is also sometimes denoted k or k_e. You may see this notation in other professional readings.

EXAMPLE 2-12.   Using the Constant Growth Dividend Discount Model.

You are working on the valuation of the stock of Unlimited Power, Inc., an electric utility company. The earnings and dividend growth rates of Unlimited Power have been stable and you believe the constant growth dividend discount model is a reasonable choice for valuing the stock. You forecast that Unlimited Power's next dividend is $2 per share. You also estimate that the long-run growth rate in dividends is 5 percent. Comparable firms in Unlimited Power's industry with similar earnings and dividend growth rates have required rates of return of 12 percent. Based on this information, what is your estimate of the price of Unlimited Power's stock?

You can use the constant growth model in Equation 2-12 to arrive at an estimate for Unlimited Power:

$$D_1 = \$2.00 \text{ per share}$$

$$\text{Required return, } r = 12\%$$

$$\text{Estimated growth rate, } g = 5\%$$

$$\begin{aligned} \text{Price, } P_0 &= D_1/(r - g) \\ &= \$2.00/(0.12 - 0.05) \\ &= \$28.57 \text{ per share} \end{aligned}$$

Given your assumptions about dividends, required return, and dividend growth rate, you estimate that Unlimited Power stock should sell at $28.57 per share.

One of the disadvantages of the constant growth model is the necessity of a constant growth figure that is strictly less than the required rate of return. We typically think of the constant growth in perpetuity as the firm's long-term growth rate. In some instances, however, companies experience initial periods of unusually high growth (called **supernormal** growth) that are expected to last for a finite amount of time. In these cases, the high growth may be larger than the required rate of return. We would not use Equation 2-12 in any case, as such companies face two growth rates, not one. The first period of growth might last for a period of time, H. The second period, beginning with the dividend at $t = H + 1$, has dividends reflecting a long-term growth rate strictly less than the required rate of return. The equation that prices this firm's stock is

$$P_0 = \frac{D_1}{(1 + r)} + \frac{D_2}{(1 + r)^2} + \cdots + \frac{D_H}{(1 + r)^H} + \frac{P_H}{(1 + r)^H}$$

where

$$P_H = \frac{D_{H+1}}{(r - g)} \tag{2-13}$$

Equation 2-13 is a restatement of Equation 2-8, $P_0 = \sum_{t=1}^{H} \dfrac{D_t}{(1 + r)^t} + \dfrac{P_H}{(1 + r)^H}$, and is referred to as the **two-stage dividend discount model** (DDM). The only difference between these equations is that Equation 2-13 uses the constant growth model to find the horizon price, P_H. Recall that the formula given by the constant growth model finds the price one period prior to the date of the dividend. In the case of Equation 2-13, putting

D_{H+1} in the numerator of the constant growth model results in the price at time period $t = H$. Suppose your investment horizon extends exactly to the end of this period of super-normal growth. When you reach the end of the holding period, you sell the stock at price P_H. When you sell at price P_H, you are in effect selling off your rights to all future dividends that are assumed to grow at a constant growth rate into the indefinite future.

Now consider an example of a firm with a finite period of supernormal growth.

EXAMPLE 2-13. Using a Two-Stage Dividend Discount Model.

You are now given the task of valuing the stock of DriveMed, Inc., a company that has strong near-term growth prospects. Your research, based on industry and firm projections, shows that DriveMed is likely to grow at a rate of 15 percent per year for the next five years. You forecast that starting in Year 5, the company's long-run sustainable growth rate is likely to stabilize at 5 percent in perpetuity. You decide that a two-stage dividend discount model is appropriate for valuing DriveMed stock. Companies with comparable growth rates and risk in DriveMed's industry have required rates of return of 14 percent.[18] What is your estimate of the price per share of DriveMed?

To value DriveMed stock, you use Equation 2-13 with the data in Table 2-6, which lists the dividends and their present values. Each dividend from $t = 1$ to $t = 5$ has an embedded growth rate of 15 percent, whereas dividends beginning with the dividend at $t = 6$ grow at a rate of 5 percent from the previous level. The last column in the table lists the present value of each individual dividend for the period of supernormal growth. The sum of the present value of the first five dividends is $10.27.

TABLE 2-6 Dividends for DriveMed

Time Period	Dividend at Time t	Present Value of Dividend at Time $t = 0$
1	$2.00(1.15) = $2.30	$2.30(1.14)^{-1} = $2.02
2	$2.30(1.15) = $2.65	$2.65(1.14)^{-2} = $2.04
3	$2.65(1.15) = $3.04	$3.04(1.14)^{-3} = $2.05
4	$3.04(1.15) = $3.50	$3.50(1.14)^{-4} = $2.07
5	$3.50(1.15) = $4.02	$4.02(1.14)^{-5} = $2.09
6	$4.02(1.05) = $4.22	
		Sum = $10.27

The next step is to find the horizon price, P_5, and discount it to time period $t = 0$. The horizon price can be determined with the constant growth model as

$$P_5 = \frac{D_6}{r - g} = \frac{\$4.22}{0.14 - 0.05} = \$46.93$$

---

[18] The model has the flexibility to use a separate discount rate for the supernormal growth and normal growth periods, if the analyst believes that approach is appropriate.

The present value of the horizon price is $46.93(1.14)^{-5} = 24.37. Adding this amount to the present value of the first five dividends yields a price of $34.64 = $24.37 + 10.27. Based on this information, you value DriveMed stock at $34.64 per share. Compare this to the price of $28.57 for Unlimited Power, in Example 2-12. The initial period of supernormal growth for DriveMed results in 21.2 percent higher stock price than for Unlimited Power.

The two-stage dividend discount model is frequently a more realistic way to model stock prices for fast-growing companies that pay dividends. With this model, we must estimate the length of the period of supernormal growth and its rate, as well as a long-term rate of growth. By extension, we can also use a three-stage model to value the stock of high-growth firms that pay dividends. The second stage in three-stage models is typically a transition phase from supernormal to normal growth. In principle, this approach is quite straightforward; in practice, estimating the necessary growth rates or corresponding periods is never easy.

We must also remember that more complex models are not necessarily more accurate or useful. The quality of the analyst's inputs to the model is of paramount importance. At a certain level of complexity, we might just as well project the dividends and horizon price for a long horizon and then discount the dividends directly as $D_t/(1 + r)^t$ for each t and the horizon price as $P_H/(1 + r)^H$.

An alternative to dividend discount formulations is the free cash flow to equity (FCFE) model of equity valuation. To use a FCFE model, the analyst must predict several financial measures for a set investment horizon, say, the next k years (Year 1 to Year k). First, the analyst must predict free cash flow to equity for a firm for each of the next k years.[19] Second, the analyst must predict the multiple of free cash flow that the stock will sell for at the end of k years, M_k.[20] Finally, the analyst must predict the required equity rate of return, r.

Based on these predictions, the estimated value of the firm is

$$P = \frac{FCFE_1}{(1 + r)} + \frac{FCFE_2}{(1 + r)^2} + \cdots + \frac{FCFE_k}{(1 + r)^k} + \frac{M_k \times FCFE_k}{(1 + r)^k}$$

EXAMPLE 2-14.   Free Cash Flow Valuation.

An analyst wants to value Prov-Tel, Inc., a cellular telephone service provider with 10 million shares outstanding. The analyst has decided that the required rate of return on equity for Prov-Tel is 15 percent. Based on his expectations of earnings growth rates for the company and industry prospects, he also predicts that Prov-Tel will sell at a multiple of 30 times predicted free cash flow to equity in five years. Based on fundamental factors for Prov-Tel, the analyst predicts the following free cash flows for each of the next five years.

---

[19] There are many definitions of free cash flow to equity. One common definition is Net income + Depreciation − Capital expenditures − Increase in working capital − Principal repayments + New debt issues.

[20] For alternative methods of finding terminal price see Damodoran (1996). The method presented here is well established in investment practice.

TABLE 2-7   Free Cash Flow for Prov-Tel, Inc.

Year	Free Cash Flow
1	$10,000,000
2	$15,000,000
3	$20,000,000
4	$26,000,000
5	$32,000,000

Table 2-8 shows the present value of the individual free cash flows, the predicted firm value in five years, and the combined present value of the cash flows and predicted firm value. The FCFE model estimates that the value of Prov-Tel is currently $541.25 million. Of that sum, $63.96 million is the value of the discounted free cash flows to equity in the next five years and $477.29 million is the discounted value of the expected firm market value of equity at the end of Year 5. With the 10 million shares outstanding, the estimated price per share is $54.13.

TABLE 2-8   Valuing Prov-Tel with a FCFE Model

Year	Free Cash Flow (millions)	Discount Factor	Present Value of Free Cash Flow
1	$10.00	0.8696	$8.70
2	$15.00	0.7561	$11.34
3	$20.00	0.6575	$13.15
4	$26.00	0.5718	$14.87
5	$32.00	0.4972	$15.91
			Sum = $63.96

FCF multiple
      30

Final free cash flow
      $32.00

Price in Year 5 (final free cash flow × FCF multiple)
      $960.00

Discounted value of price in Year 5 ($960.00 × 0.4972)
      $477.29

Discounted value of price in Year 5 plus discounted value of free cash flow from Year 1 to Year 5 ($477.29 + $63.96)
      $541.25

Note that the overwhelming proportion of firm value is based on the analyst's assumption of the firm's worth in five years (that is, free cash flow in Year 5 times the appropriate multiple). This result is typical for FCFE models. As a consequence, many financial analysts perform sensitivity tests to gauge the effect of changing assumptions about the FCFE model on their valuation. Also, the FCFE multiple estimate implies a long-term growth rate to be examined for plausibility. In this particular case, the firm's worth in five years implies an 11.29 percent long-term growth rate in a simple DCF model. To see this, estimate Prov-Tel's worth in five years with the growing perpetuity formula $FCFE_5(1 + g)/(k - g) = (32 \times 1.11299)/(0.15 - 0.1129) = 960$.

5 PORTFOLIO RETURN MEASUREMENT

Suppose you are an individual or institutional investor and you want to assess the success of your investments. You face two related but distinct tasks. Your first task is **performance measurement,** which involves calculating returns in a logical and consistent manner. Accurate performance measurement provides a basis for your second task, **performance evaluation.**[21] Performance measurement is thus of great importance for all investors and investment managers because it is the foundation for all further analysis.

Particularly when we measure performance over many periods, or when the portfolio is subject to additions and withdrawals, portfolio performance measurement is a challenging task; two of the measurement tools available are the dollar-weighted rate of return measure and the time-weighted rate of return measure. The first measure we discuss, the dollar-weighted rate of return, implements a concept we have already met in the contexts of capital budgeting and bond valuation, internal rate of return.

5.1 DOLLAR-WEIGHTED RATE OF RETURN

The first performance measurement concept that we will discuss is an internal rate of return calculation. In investment management applications, the internal rate of return is called the dollar-weighted rate of return because it accounts for the timing and amount of all dollar flows into and out of the portfolio. To illustrate the dollar-weighted return, we build on a previous example, extending it one more year.

EXAMPLE 2-15. Dollar-Weighted Rate of Return.

At time $t = 0$, an investor buys one share at $200. At time $t = 1$, he purchases an additional share at $225. At the end of Year 2, $t = 2$, he sells both shares for $235 each. During both years, the stock pays a per-share dividend of $5. The $t = 1$ dividend is not reinvested. Table 2-9 shows the total cash inflows and outflows.

TABLE 2-9   Cash Flows

Time	Outlay
0	$200 to purchase the first share
1	$225 to purchase the second share
	Proceeds
1	$5 dividend received from first share (and not reinvested)
2	$10 dividend ($5 per share $\times$ 2 shares) received
2	$470 received from selling two shares at $235 per share

---

[21] In later chapters we will discuss one performance evaluation tool, the Sharpe ratio.

The dollar-weighted return on this portfolio is its internal rate of return over the two-year period. The portfolio's internal rate of return is the rate, r, for which the present value of the cash inflows minus the present value of the cash outflows equals 0, or

$$PV \text{ (outflows)} = PV \text{ (inflows)}$$

$$\$200 + \frac{\$225}{(1 + r)} = \frac{\$5}{(1 + r)} + \frac{\$480}{(1 + r)^2}$$

The left-hand side of this equation details the outflows: $200 at time period $t = 0$ and $225 at time period $t = 1$. The $225 outflow is discounted back one period because it occurs at $t = 1$. The right-hand side of the equation shows the present value of the inflows: $5 at time period $t = 1$ (discounted back one period) and $480 (the $10 dividend plus the $470 sale proceeds) at time period $t = 2$ (discounted back two periods).

To solve for the dollar-weighted return, we use a financial calculator that allows us to enter cash flows or a spreadsheet with an IRR function. The first step is to group net cash flows by time. For this example, we have -200 for the $t = 0$ net cash flow, $-220 = -225 + 5$ for the $t = 1$ net cash flow, and 480 for the $t = 2$ net cash flow. After entering these cash flows, we use the spreadsheet's or calculator's IRR function to find that the dollar-weighted rate of return is 9.39 percent.

Now we take a closer look at what has happened to the portfolio during each of the two years. When talking about equities it is more common to speak of holding period *returns* than holding period *yields*; since this portfolio is invested in stocks, we will use the former term here. In the first year, the portfolio generated a one-period holding period return of ($5 + $225 − $200)/$200 = 15 percent. At the beginning of the second year, the amount invested is $450, calculated as $225 (per share price of stock) × 2 shares, as the $5 dividend was spent rather than reinvested. At the end of the second year, the proceeds from the liquidation of the portfolio are $470 (as detailed in Table 2-9) plus $10 in dividends (as also detailed in Table 2-9). So in the second year the portfolio produced a holding period return of ($10 + $470 − $450)/$450 = 6.67 percent. The dollar-weighted return, which we calculated as 9.39 percent, is pulled downward by the holding period return during the second year, when performance was poor, as more money was invested in the second year than the first.

5.2 TIME-WEIGHTED RATE OF RETURN

An investment measure that is not sensitive to the additions and withdrawals of funds is the time-weighted rate of return. In the investment-management industry, the time-weighted rate of return is the preferred performance measure. The time-weighted return is not affected by cash withdrawals and additions to the portfolio; it measures the compound rate of growth of $1 initially invested in the portfolio over a stated measurement period. The term **time-weighted** refers to the fact that the two returns are averaged over time. To compute an exact time-weighted rate of return on a portfolio, take the following three steps:

i. Price the portfolio immediately prior to any significant addition or withdrawal of funds. Break the overall evaluation period into subperiods based on the dates of cash inflows and outflows.

ii. Calculate the holding period return on the portfolio for each subperiod.

iii. Link or compound holding period returns to obtain an annual rate of return for the year (the time-weighted rate of return for the year). If the investment is for more than one year, take the geometric mean of the annual returns to obtain the time-weighted rate of return over that measurement period.

Let us return to Example 2-15 and calculate the time-weighted rate of return for that investor's portfolio. In that example, we computed the holding period returns on the portfolio, Step ii in the procedure for finding time-weighted rate of return. Given that the portfolio earned returns of 15 percent during the first year and 6.67 percent during the second year, what is the portfolio's time-weighted rate of return over an evaluation period of two years?

We find this time-weighted return by taking the geometric mean of the two holding period returns, Step iii in the procedure above. The calculation of the geometric mean exactly mirrors the calculation of a compound rate of growth. Here, we take the product of 1 plus the holding period return for each period to find the terminal value at $t = 2$ of \$1 invested at $t = 0$. We then take the square root of this product and subtract 1 to get the geometric mean. We interpret the result as the annual compound rate of growth of \$1 invested in the portfolio at $t = 0$. Thus, we have

$$(1 + \text{Time-weighted return})^2 = (1.15)(1.0667)$$

$$\text{Time-weighted return} = \sqrt{(1.15)(1.0667)} - 1 = 10.756\%$$

The time-weighted return on the portfolio was 10.756 percent compared to the dollar-weighted return of 9.39 percent, which gave larger weight to the second year's return. We can see why time-weighted returns are more meaningful for investment managers. If a client gives an investment manager more funds to invest at an unfavorable time, the manager's dollar-weighted rate of return will tend to be depressed. If a client adds funds at a favorable time, the dollar-weighted return will tend to be elevated. The time-weighted rate of return removes these effects.

In defining the steps to calculate an exact time-weighted rate of return, we said that the portfolio should be valued immediately prior to any significant addition or withdrawal of funds. With the amount of cash-flow activity in many portfolios, this task can be costly. We can often obtain a reasonable approximation of the exact time-weighted rate of return by valuing the portfolio less frequently but at regular intervals, particularly if additions and withdrawals are unrelated to market movements. The more frequent the valuation, the more accurate the approximation. (Daily valuation gives more accurate estimates than quarterly valuation, for example.) Suppose that a portfolio is valued monthly over the course of a year. To compute the time-weighted return for the year, we first compute each month's holding period return:

$$r_t = \frac{\text{MVE}_t - \text{MVB}_t}{\text{MVB}_t}$$

where MVB_t equals the market value at the beginning of the month t, and MVE_t equals the market value at the end of month t. We compute twelve such monthly returns, denoted r_1, $r_2, \ldots, r_{12}$. We obtain the annual return for the year by linking the one-month holding period returns in the following way: $(1 + r_1) \times (1 + r_2) \times \cdots \times (1 + r_{12}) - 1$. If withdrawals and additions to the portfolio happen only at month end, this annual return is a precise time-weighted rate of return for the year. Otherwise, it is an approximate time-weighted return for the year.

If we have a number of years of data, we can calculate a time-weighted return for each year individually, as above. If r_i is the time-weighted return for year i, we calculate an annualized time-weighted return as the geometric mean of N annual returns, as follows:

$$r_{TW} = [(1 + r_1) \times (1 + r_2) \times \cdots \times (1 + r_N)]^{1/N} - 1$$

EXAMPLE 2-16.   Time-Weighted Rate of Return.

Strubeck Corporation sponsors a pension plan for its employees. It manages part of the equity portfolio in-house and delegates management of the balance to Super Trust Company. As chief investment officer of Strubeck, you want to review the performance of the in-house and Super Trust portfolios over the last four quarters. You have arranged for outflows and inflows to the portfolio to be made at the very beginning of the quarter. Table 2-10 summarizes the data.

TABLE 2-10   Cash Flows for the In-House Strubeck Account and the Super-Trust Account

	Quarter			
	1	2	3	4
IN-HOUSE ACCOUNT				
Beginning value	$4,000,000	$6,000,000	$5,775,000	$6,720,000
Beginning of period inflow (outflow)	$1,000,000	($500,000)	$225,000	($600,000)
Amount invested	$5,000,000	$5,500,000	$6,000,000	$6,120,000
Ending value	$6,000,000	$5,775,000	$6,720,000	$5,508,000
SUPER TRUST ACCOUNT				
Beginning value	$10,000,000	$13,200,000	$12,240,000	$5,659,200
Beginning of period inflow (outflow)	$2,000,000	($1,200,000)	($7,000,000)	($400,000)
Amount invested	$12,000,000	$12,000,000	$5,240,000	$5,259,200
Ending value	$13,200,000	$12,240,000	$5,659,200	$5,469,568

Table 2-10 provides the valuations of the portfolios needed to compute the time-weighted rate of return for the in-house portfolio and the portfolio managed by Super Trust. The ending value is the portfolio's value just prior to the cash inflow or outflow at the beginning of the quarter. The amount invested is the amount the portfolio manager is responsible for investing. To calculate the time-weighted rate of return, we compute the quarterly holding period returns and link them into an annual return.

In-House Account. The in-house account's time-weighted rate of return is 27 percent, calculated as follows:

Q1 HPR: $r_1 = (\$6,000,000 - \$5,000,000)/\$5,000,000 = 0.20$

Q2 HPR: $r_2 = (\$5,775,000 - \$5,500,000)/\$5,500,000 = 0.05$

Q3 HPR: $r_3 = (\$6,720,000 - \$6,000,000)/\$6,000,000 = 0.12$

Q4 HPR: $r_4 = (\$5,508,000 - \$6,120,000)/\$6,120,000 = -0.10$

$$(1 + r_1) \times (1 + r_2) \times (1 + r_3) \times (1 + r_4) - 1 =$$
$$(1.20) \times (1.05) \times (1.12) \times (0.90) - 1 = 0.27 \text{ or } 27\%$$

Super Trust Account. The account managed by Super Trust has a time-weighted rate of return of 26 percent calculated as follows:

Q1 HPR: $r_1 = (\$13,200,000 - \$12,000,000)/\$12,000,000 = 0.10$

Q2 HPR: $r_2 = (\$12,240,000 - \$12,000,000)/\$12,000,000 = 0.02$

Q3 HPR: $r_3 = (\$5,659,200 - \$5,240,000)/\$5,240,000 = 0.08$

Q4 HPR: $r_4 = (\$5,469,568 - \$5,259,200)/\$5,259,200 = 0.04$

$$(1 + r_1) \times (1 + r_2) \times (1 + r_3) \times (1 + r_4) - 1 =$$
$$(1.10) \times (1.02) \times (1.08) \times (1.04) - 1 = 0.26 \text{ or } 26\%$$

The in-house portfolio's time-weighted rate of return was higher than Super Trust portfolio's by 100 basis points.

Having worked through this exercise, we are ready to look at a more detailed case.

EXAMPLE 2-17. Time-Weighted Rate and Dollar-Weighted Rate of Return Side by Side.

Your task is to compute the investment performance of the Big Red Fund during 2001. On January 1, 2001, the Big Red Fund had a market value of $100 million. On May 1, 2001, the stocks in the fund paid a total dividend of $2 million. Over the year, the stocks in the fund showed a capital gain of $10 million. All dividends were reinvested in additional shares. Because the fund's performance had been exceptional, institutions invested an additional $20 million in Big Red on May 1, 2001, raising assets under management to $132 million ($100 + $10 + $2 + $20). On December 31, 2001, Big Red received total dividends of $2.64 million. The fund's market value on December 31, 2001, not including the dividends, was $140 million. The fund made no other interim cash payments during 2001. Compute the time-weighted and dollar-weighted rates of return.

Time-Weighted Rate of Return. Because interim cash flows were made on May 1, 2001, we must compute two interim total returns and then link them to obtain an annual return. Table 2-11 lists the relevant market values on January 1, May 1, and December 31 as well as the associated interim four-month (January 1 to May 1) and eight-month (May 1 to December 31) holding period returns.

TABLE 2-11   Cash Flows for the Big Red Fund

January 1, 2001	Beginning portfolio value = $100 million
May 1, 2001	Dividends received before additional investment = $2 million
	Ending portfolio value = $110 million

Holding period return $= \dfrac{\$2 + \$10}{\$100} = 12\%$

Dividend received = $2 million
New investment = $20 million
Beginning market value for last 2/3 of year = $132 million

| December 31, 2001 | Dividends received = $2.64 million (2% on $132 million) |
| | Ending portfolio value = $140 million |

Total return $= \dfrac{\$2.64 + \$140 - \$132}{\$132} = 8.06\%$

Now we must geometrically link the four- and eight-month returns to compute an annual return. We compute the time-weighted return as follows:

$$\text{Time-weighted return} = 1.12 \times 1.0806 - 1 = 0.2103$$

In this instance, we compute a time-weighted rate of return of 21.03 percent for one year. The four-month and eight-month intervals combine to equal one year. (Taking the square root of the product 1.12×1.0806 would be appropriate only if 1.12 and 1.0806 each applied to one full year.)

Dollar-Weighted Rate of Return.   To calculate the dollar-weighted return, we find the discount rate that sets the present value of the outflows (purchases) equal to the present value of the inflows (dividends and future payoff). The initial market value of the fund and all additions to it are treated as cash outflows. (Think of them as expenditures.) Withdrawals, receipts, and the ending market value of the fund are counted as inflows. (The ending market value is the amount investors receive on liquidating the fund.) Because interim cash flows have occurred at four-month intervals, we must solve for the four-month internal rate of return. Table 2-11 details the cash flows and their timing.

The present value equation (in millions) is as follows:

$$\text{PV (outflows)} = \text{PV (inflows)}$$

$$\$100 + \frac{\$2}{(1 + r)^1} + \frac{\$20}{(1 + r)^1} = \frac{\$2}{(1 + r)^1} + \frac{\$2.64}{(1 + r)^3} + \frac{\$140}{(1 + r)^3}$$

The left-hand side of the equation shows the investments in the fund or outflows: a $100 million initial investment followed by the $2 million dividend reinvested and an additional $20 million of new investment (both occurring at the end of the first four-month interval, which makes the exponent in the denominator 1). The right-hand side of the equation shows the payoffs or inflows: the $2 million dividend at the first four-month interval followed by the $2.64 million dividend and the terminal market value of $140 million (both occurring at the end of the third four-month interval, which makes the exponent in the denominator 3). The second four-month interval has no cash flow. We can bring all the terms to the right of the equal sign, arranging them in order of time. After simplification, we get

$$0 = -\$100 - \frac{\$20}{(1 + r)^1} + \frac{\$142.64}{(1 + r)^3}$$

Using a spreadsheet or IRR-enabled calculator, we use -100, -20, 0, and \$142.64 for the $t = 0$, $t = 1$, $t = 2$, and $t = 3$ net cash flows, respectively.[22] Using either tool, we get a four-month IRR of 6.28. The quick way to annualize this is to multiply by 3. A more accurate way is $(1.0628)^3 - 1 = 0.20$ or 20 percent.

In this example, the time-weighted return (21.03 percent) is greater than the dollar-weighted return (20 percent). The Big Red Fund's performance was relatively poorer during the eight-month period, when the fund owned more shares. (As we explained earlier, the dollar-weighted return is sensitive to the timing and amount of withdrawals and additions to the portfolio.) Keep in mind that investors controlled the timing and amount of investments into the Big Red Fund. Such inflows and outflows are usually beyond most money managers' control, which is why the use of the time-weighted rate of return is standard practice for money managers.

When we worked through Example 2-16, we stopped short of suggesting that in-house management was superior to Super Trust. Why? As we move from performance measurement to performance evaluation, we need to consider risk. With risk in focus, we can talk of risk-adjusted performance and make comparisons—but only cautiously. In later chapters, we will discuss the Sharpe ratio, an important risk-adjusted performance measure. For now, we have illustrated the major tools for measuring the return on a portfolio.

6 SUMMARY

In this chapter, we applied the concepts of present value, net present value, and internal rate of return to the fundamental problem of valuing investments. We discussed both corporate investment (capital budgeting) and securities (equities and bonds). Finally, we examined the fundamental problem of calculating the return on a portfolio subject to cash inflows and outflows. The following is a summary of key concepts:

- The essential inputs in evaluating capital budgeting projects are the timing and amount of expected cash flows (inflows and outflows) and the opportunity cost of capital.
- The net present value of a project is the present value of the expected cash inflows minus the present value of expected cash outflows, using the required rate of return or opportunity cost of capital as the discount rate.
- The net present value rule for decision making is to accept all projects that have a positive net present value.
- The internal rate of return on an investment is the single discount rate that makes net present value equal to 0. Thus, the internal rate of return is the discount rate that makes the present value of cash outflows equal to the present value of cash inflows.

---

[22] By convention, we denote outflows with a negative sign, and we need 0 as a placeholder for $t = 2$.

- The internal rate of return rule for decision making is to accept all projects with an internal rate of return exceeding the required rate of return, or hurdle rate.

- The internal rate of return decision rule can be affected by problems of scale and of multiple rates.

- We can interpret internal rate of return as an expected compound return only when all interim cash flows can be reinvested at the internal rate of return and the investment is maintained to maturity.

- The bank discount yield for U.S. Treasury bills (and other money-market instruments sold on a discount basis) is given by $r_{BD} = (F - P_0)/F \times 360/t = D/F \times 360/t$, where F is the face amount to be received at maturity, P_0 is the price of the Treasury bill, t is the number of days to maturity, and D is the discount.

- For a stated holding period or horizon, holding period yield (HPY) = (Ending price − Beginning price + Cash distribution(s))/ (Beginning price). For a U.S. Treasury bill, HPY $= D/P_0$.

- The money market yield is given by $r_{MM} = $ HPY $\times 360/t$ where t is the number of days to maturity.

- For a Treasury bill, money market yield can be obtained from the bank discount yield using $r_{MM} = (360 \times r_{BD})/(360 - t \times r_{BD})$.

- The effective annual yield (EAY) is EAY $= (1 + $ HPY$)^{365/t} - 1$.

- We can convert back and forth between holding period yields, money market yields, and equivalent annual yields by using the holding period yield, which is common to all the calculations.

- The price of a zero-coupon bond is the present discounted value of the single future payment at maturity using the required rate of return.

- The price of an option-free coupon bond can be calculated by discounting the interest payments (coupons) and face value at the required yield to maturity.

- The yield to maturity on any bond is the discount rate that equates the promised cash flows on the bond to the bond's price. The yield to maturity is also the bond's internal rate of return.

- In U.S. markets, the calculation of yield to maturity observes a semiannual compounding convention for coupon and zero-coupon bonds.

- The yield to maturity on a zero-coupon bond with N years to maturity is known as the N-year spot interest rate.

- A coupon bond can be evaluated as a collection of zero-coupon bonds. The no-arbitrage approach to bond pricing discounts each promised bond payment at the corresponding spot interest rate.

- Dividend discount models of equity valuation price stock as the present value of expected future dividends, where the discount rate is the required rate of return on the stock. If r is the required rate of return, the value of a share is given by $\sum_{t=1}^{\infty} \dfrac{D_t}{(1 + r)^t}$, where D_t is the expected dividend at time t.

- The constant growth (Gordon) dividend discount model is the expression $P_0 = D_1/(r - g)$, where D_1 is next period's dividend, r is the required rate of return on the stock, and g is the dividend growth rate.

- The chief assumptions of the constant growth model are that dividends grow at a constant rate, g, and that the relation $r > g$ holds.

- When a stock's required rate of return is larger than the dividend growth rate, a multi-stage dividend discount model is used.

- The two-stage dividend discount model calculates the stock price by directly discounting the dividends for the first stage and then discounting the end-of-first-stage price. (The constant growth model price for stage-two dividends is the stock price at the end of the first stage.) Frequently, the first stage is a period of supernormal growth and the second stage is a period of normal growth.

- If the assumptions of the constant growth model are appropriate, we can solve for r to estimate a stock's total return or required rate of return:

  Total return = Dividend yield + Capital gains yield

  $$r = D_1/P_0 + g$$

  where r can be interpreted as either the implied total return or required rate of return.

- The principles of discounted cash flow analysis apply similarly to dividends and free cash flow to equity.

- Dollar-weighted rate of return and time-weighted rate of return are two alternative methods for calculating portfolio returns in a multiperiod setting when the portfolio is subject to additions and withdrawals. Time-weighted rate of return is the standard in the investment-management industry. Dollar-weighted rate of return can be appropriate if the investor exercises control over additions and withdrawals to the portfolio.

- The dollar-weighted rate of return is the internal rate of return on a portfolio, taking account of all cash flows.

- The time-weighted rate of return removes the effects of timing and amount of withdrawals and additions to the portfolio and reflects the compound rate of growth of one unit of currency invested over a stated measurement period.

PROBLEMS

1. A Treasury bill with a face value of $100,000 and 120 days until maturity is selling for $98,500.
   a. What is the T-bill's bank discount yield?
   b. What is the T-bill's money market yield?
   c. What is the T-bill's effective annual yield?

2. Bestfoods, Inc. USA is planning to spend $10 million on advertising. The company expects this expenditure to result in annual incremental cash flows of $1.6 million in perpetuity. The corporate opportunity cost of capital for this type of project is 12.5 percent.
   a. Calculate the NPV for the planned advertising.
   b. Calculate the internal rate of return.
   c. Should the company go forward with the planned advertising? Explain.

3. Waldrup Industries is considering a proposal for a joint venture that will require an investment of $13 million. At the end of the fifth year, Waldrup's joint venture partner will buy out Waldrup's interest for $10 million. Waldrup's chief financial officer has estimated that the appropriate hurdle rate for this proposal is 12 percent. The expected cash flows are given below.

Year	Cash Flow
0	−$13,000,000
1	$3,000,000
2	$3,000,000
3	$3,000,000
4	$3,000,000
5	$10,000,000

   a. Calculate this proposal's NPV.
   b. Make a recommendation to the CFO on whether Waldrup should enter into this joint venture.

4. Trilever is planning to establish a new factory overseas. The project requires an initial investment of $15 million. Management intends to run this factory for six years and then sell it to a local entity. Trilever's finance department has estimated the following yearly cash flows:

Year	Cash Flow
0	−$15,000,000
1	$4,000,000
2	$4,000,000
3	$4,000,000
4	$4,000,000
5	$4,000,000
6	$7,000,000

Trilever's chief financial officer (CFO) decides that the firm's cost of capital of 19 percent is an appropriate hurdle rate for this project.

a. Calculate the internal rate of return (IRR) of this project.

b. Make a recommendation to the CFO on whether to undertake this project.

5. A zero-coupon bond with face value of $10,000 and five years remaining to maturity is selling for $8,000.

a. Calculate this bond's yield to maturity on a bond-equivalent basis.

b. Calculate this bond's effective annual yield.

6. Estimate the price of a six-year zero-coupon bond with par value of $1,000 if the required yield to maturity on comparable bonds is 8 percent. Observe the U.S. convention of semiannual compounding for zero-coupon bonds so that zeros and coupon bonds are priced consistently.

7. Given a required return of 6 percent, how much you would be willing to pay for a semiannual-pay bond with an 8 percent coupon rate, a $1,000 face value, and 15 years remaining to maturity? The next coupon is due six months from now.

8. You are reviewing a printout of bond prices (per $100 of face value):

Bond	Bond Price	Coupon Rate (%)	Yield to Maturity
A	$110	5	4
B	$112	7.5	8
C	$100	6	6
D	$85.50	8	11
E	$90	7.5	6
F	$100	5.5	5.75

You are sure that the prices for some of these bonds have not been correctly reported. Which prices are incorrectly reported?

9. The market price of a 10-year semiannual-pay bond with an 8 percent coupon rate and a face value of $1,000 is $682.20. The first coupon is due in six months. Calculate this bond's yield to maturity. (Use a financial calculator or spreadsheet.)

10. Smith Corporation 7s are semiannual-pay, 7 percent coupon-rate bonds that are being priced to yield 9 percent. These bonds have exactly four years remaining to maturity, and the next coupon payment is in six months.

a. Calculate the bond's price given the 9 percent yield to maturity.

b. Calculate the bond's current yield (CY), defined as annual interest on the bond divided by the bond's price today (from Part a).

c. Suppose that at the end of one-half year the bond will be priced to yield 12 percent (compared to the initial YTM of 9 percent). Recalculate the bond price as of that time given a 12 percent yield to maturity. Using that ending price, calculate the capital gains yield on the bond over the one-half year, defined as change in price divided by beginning price; multiply the figure by 2 to annualize it. The annualized capital gains yield (CGY) added to the current yield is the annualized holding period yield (HPY) on the bond over the half year. Finally, contrast the holding period yield to the bond's initial YTM of 9 percent.

11. Oralee Corporation's dividend in the next year is expected to be $3, and dividends are expected to grow at 10 percent per year forever. The market-required rate of return for Oralee stock is 15 percent. Oralee pays dividends once a year at year end.

a. Using the constant growth dividend discount model, calculate the price for the stock of Oralee Corporation.

b. Assuming annual dividends, calculate the price of Oralee Corporation stock two years from now (at $t = 2$).

12. Presently, the stock of Microsmooth Inc. is selling at $250. Next year's expected dividend is $20. If the required return on Microsmooth stock is 18 percent and the market prices the stock on the basis of the constant growth dividend discount model, forecast Microsmooth's future dividend growth rate.

13. You are planning to buy shares of Sun Corporation. Sun's most recent annual dividend was $5 per share. The next dividend will be paid in exactly one year. Analysts expect dividends to grow at a rate of 10 percent per year for three years (up to and including the $t = 3$ dividend). Thereafter, dividends are expected to grow at a rate of 5 percent per year into the indefinite future. The required rate of return on Sun stock is 12 percent. Calculate the value of Sun stock using the two-stage dividend discount model.

14. John Wilson buys 150 shares of ABM on January 1, 2002 at a price of $156.30 per share. A dividend of $10 per share is paid on January 1, 2003. Assume that this dividend is not reinvested. Also on January 1, 2003, Wilson sells 100 shares at a price of $165 per share. On January 1, 2004, he collects a dividend of $15 per share (on 50 shares) and sells his remaining 50 shares at $170 per share.

a. Write the formula to calculate the dollar-weighted rate of return on Wilson's portfolio.

b. Using any method available to you, compute the dollar-weighted rate of return.

c. Calculate the time-weighted rate of return on Wilson's portfolio.

d. Describe a set of circumstances for which the dollar-weighted rate of return is an appropriate return measure for Wilson's portfolio.

e. Describe a set of circumstances for which the time-weighted rate of return is an appropriate return measure for Wilson's portfolio.

SOLUTIONS

1. In this solution, F stands for face value, P stands for price, and D stands for the discount from face value ($D = F - P$).

   a. Use the discount yield formula (Equation 2-3), $r_{BD} = D/F \times 360/t$:

   $$r_{BD} = (\$1,500/\$100,000) \times (360/120) = 0.0150 \times 3 = 0.045$$

   The T-bill's bank discount yield is 4.5 percent per year.

   b. Use your answer from Part a and the money market yield formula (Equation 2-5), $r_{MM} = (360 \times r_{BD})/(360 - t \times r_{BD})$:

   $$r_{MM} = (360 \times 0.045)/(360 - 120 \times 0.045) = 0.04568$$

   The T-bill's money market yield is 4.57 percent per year.

   c. Calculate the holding period yield (using Equation 2-4), then compound it forward to one year. First, the holding period yield (HPY) is

   $$\text{HPY} = \frac{P_1 - P + D_1}{P_0} = (100,000 - 98,500)/98,500 = 0.015228$$

   Next, compound the 120-day holding period yield, a periodic rate, forward to 1 year:

   $$\text{Effective annual yield} = (1 + \text{HPY})^{365/t} - 1$$

   $$\text{Effective annual yield} = (1.015228)^{365/120} - 1 = 0.047044$$

   The T-bill's effective annual yield is 4.7 percent per year.

2. a. Recall that NPV is the sum of all the cash flows associated with the investment, where inflows are signed positive and outflows are signed negative. This problem has only one outflow, an initial expenditure of $10 million at $t = 0$. The projected cash inflows from this advertising project form a perpetuity. We calculate the present value of a perpetuity as A/r, where A is the level annual cash flow and r is the discount rate. Using the required rate of return of 12.5 percent as the discount rate, we have

   $$\begin{aligned} \text{NPV} &= -\$10,000,000 + 1,600,000/0.125 \\ &= -\$10,000,000 + 12,800,000 \\ &= \$2,800,000 \end{aligned}$$

   b. In this case, the cash inflows are a perpetuity. Therefore, we can solve for the internal rate of return algebraically:

   $$\text{Initial investment} = \text{Annual cash inflow/IRR}$$

   $$10,000,000 = 1,600,000/\text{IRR}$$

   $$\text{IRR} = 16 \text{ percent}$$

   c. Yes, Bestfoods should spend $10 million on advertising. The NPV of $2.8 million is positive. The IRR of 16 percent is also in excess of the required rate of return of 12.5 percent.

3. We can calculate the present value of the cash inflows in several ways. We can discount each cash inflow separately at the required rate of return of 12 percent and then sum the present values. We can also find the present value of a four-year annuity of $3 million, add to it the present value of the $t = 5$ cash flow of $10 million, and subtract the $t = 0$ outflow of $13 million. Or we can compute the present value of a five-year annuity of $3 million, add to it the present value of a cash inflow of $7 million = $10 million − $3 million dated $t = 5$, and subtract the $t = 0$ outflow of $13 million. For this last approach, we illustrate the keystrokes for many financial calculators.

Notation Used on Most Calculators	Numerical Value for This Problem
N	5
%i	12
PV **compute**	X
PMT	3,000,000
FV	7,000,000

We find that the PV of the inflows is $14,786,317.

a. Therefore, NPV = $14,786,317 − $13,000,000 = $1,786,317.

b. Waldrup should undertake this project because it has a positive NPV.

4. Using the IRR function in a spreadsheet or an IRR-enabled financial calculator, we enter the individual cash flows and apply the IRR function. We illustrate how we can solve for IRR in this particular problem using a financial calculator without a dedicated IRR function. The cash flows from $t = 1$ through $t = 6$ can be treated as a six-year, $4 million annuity with $3 million = $7 million − $4 million, entered as a future amount at $t = 6$.

Notation Used on Most Calculators	Numerical Value for This Problem
N	6
%i **compute**	X
PV	−15,000,000
PMT	4,000,000
FV	3,000,000

a. The IRR of the project is 18.25 percent.

b. Because the project's IRR is less than the hurdle rate of 19 percent, the firm should not undertake the project.

5. a. Recall that, following a bond market convention, we use semiannual compounding with zero-coupon bonds. We then convert the semiannual YTM to an annual bond equivalent yield by doubling it. In this example, there are $N = 10$ semiannual periods remaining to maturity. The following is the calculation, where M is maturity or face value and P is price:

$$\text{YTM} = 2\left[\left(\frac{M}{P}\right)^{\frac{1}{N}} - 1\right] \text{YTM} = 2\left[\left(\frac{\$10,000}{\$8,000}\right)^{\frac{1}{10}} - 1\right]$$
$$= 2 \times 0.022565 = 0.04513$$

This bond's YTM on a bond-equivalent basis is 4.513 percent.

b. The effective annual yield is $(1 + \text{Semiannual YTM})^2 - 1 = (1.022565)^2 - 1 = 0.045639$ or 4.56 percent. As expected, this value is higher than the yield to maturity because it accounts for compounding (interest earned on interest).

6. Remembering the convention of semiannual compounding, the equation for the price, P, of a zero with maturity value M and $N = 2 \times 6$ years $= 12$ semiannual periods remaining to maturity is

$$P = M\left(1 + \frac{\text{YTM}}{2}\right)^{-N}$$

$$P = \$1,000\left(1 + \frac{.08}{2}\right)^{-12} = \$624.60$$

If comparable bonds yield 8 percent, this zero should sell for $624.60.

7. Use Equation 2-6 for the price of a semiannual-coupon bond:

$$P = C\left[\frac{1 - \dfrac{1}{\left(1 + \dfrac{\text{YTM}}{2}\right)^N}}{\dfrac{\text{YTM}}{2}}\right] + \frac{M}{\left(1 + \dfrac{\text{YTM}}{2}\right)^N}$$

where

YTM/2, required annual yield to maturity divided by 2 $= 0.06/2 = 0.03$

N, number of semiannual periods to maturity $= 15 \times 2 = 30$

C, semiannual coupon $= \$1,000 \times 0.08/2 = \$40$

M, maturity value $= \$1,000$

Substituting these values gives

$$P = \$40\left[\frac{1 - \dfrac{1}{(1.03)^{30}}}{0.3}\right] + \frac{\$1,000}{(1.03)^{30}}$$
$$= \$784.017654 + \$411.98676 = \$1,196$$

You should be willing to pay $1,196 for this bond.

8. The prices of bonds B, E, and F are incorrectly reported.

- B: The bond's price must be less than $100 because YTM is greater than the coupon rate.

- E: The bond must sell for more than $100 because YTM is less than the coupon rate.
- F: This bond's price cannot be $100 because for a bond selling at par, YTM equals the coupon rate.

9.   The semiannual coupon is $1,000 \times 0.08/2 = \$40$, and the number of payments remaining is $2 \times 10 = 20$. The following keys can be used on many calculators, where N is the number of semiannual periods to maturity.

Notation Used on Most Calculators	Numerical Value for This Problem
N	20
%i **compute**	X
PV	-682.20
PMT	40
FV	1,000

We find that the periodic rate %$i = 0.0699749$ or 7 percent. Doubling this value gives a YTM of 14 percent.

10. a. We calculate the bond's price given a 9 percent YTM, using either the method presented in the solution to problem 7 or an IRR-enabled financial calculator. We have a semiannual coupon of $35, eight semiannual periods to maturity, and a semi-annual YTM of 4.5 percent.

Notation Used on Most Calculators	Numerical Value for This Problem
N	8
%i	4.5
PV **compute**	X
PMT	35
FV	1,000

PV = $934.041139 or $934.04.

b. The current yield (CY) on the bond is the annual interest divided by today's price, $70/934.04 = 0.074943$ or 7.49 percent.

c. With an increase in YTM to 12 percent at the end of the period, the bond drops in price. N is now 7, and the periodic rate is now $6\% = 12\%/2$.

Notation Used on Most Calculators	Numerical Value for This Problem
N	7
%i	6
PV **compute**	X
PMT	35
FV	1,000

The bond's price has fallen to $860.44 from $934.04 calculated in Part a.

The return from capital gains yield on a semiannual basis equals ($860.44 − $934.04)/$934.04 = −0.078797.

Multiplying by 2, the annualized capital gains yield (CGY) is −0.078797 × 2 = −0.157595 or −15.76%. Thus holding period yield (HPY) is

$$HPY = CY + CGY = 7.49\% + (-15.76\%) = -8.27\%$$

The holding period yield is not only less than the initial YTM of 9 percent, it is negative.

11. a. The constant growth dividend discount model is $P_0 = \left(\dfrac{D_1}{r - g}\right)$. We are given these data:

$$D_1 = \$3 \text{ (next year's dividend)}$$
$$r = 0.15 \text{ (the required rate of return on Oralee stock)}$$
$$g = 0.10 \text{ (dividend growth rate)}$$
$$P_0 = 3/(0.15 - 0.10) = \$60$$

Using the constant growth dividend discount model, the price for Oralee stock is $60.

b. Our strategy is to compute Oralee's projected dividend at $t = 3$, one period ahead of the date for valuing Oralee's stock.

$$P_2 = \left(\frac{D_3}{r - g}\right)$$
$$D_3 = D_1(1 + g)^2$$
$$= 3(1 + 0.10)^2$$
$$= 3.63$$
$$r = 0.15$$
$$g = 0.10$$

$$P_2 = \left(\frac{3.63}{0.15 - 0.10}\right)$$

The projected stock price in two years is $72.60.

The constant growth model implies that stock price also grows at a rate of g. Thus, we can directly calculate the stock price as

$$P_2 = D_0(1 + g)^2$$
$$= 60(1 + 0.10)^2$$
$$= \$72.60$$

12. The dividend growth rate forecast for Microsmooth, consistent with the constant growth dividend discount model, is found by solving for g:

$$P_0 = \left(\frac{D_1}{r - g}\right)$$

$$r - g = \frac{D_1}{P_0}$$

$$g = r - \frac{D_1}{P_0}$$
$$= 0.18 - 20/250$$
$$= 0.18 - 0.08$$
$$= 0.10$$

The dividend growth rate forecast is 10 percent.

13. We divide the future stream of Sun dividends into two periods: a 10 percent growth period over $t = 0$ to $t = 3$, and a 5 percent constant growth period thereafter. We value each stream separately and then sum the present values to find stock price. We begin with the 5 percent growth period.

Year	Dividend	Present Value
1	$5(1.10)$ $= \$5.50$	$5.50(1.12)^{-1} = \$4.91$
2	$5(1.10)^2 = \$6.05$	$6.05(1.12)^{-2} = \$4.82$
3	$5(1.10)^3 = \$6.655$	$6.655(1.12)^{-3} = \$4.74$
Sum of PVs:		$14.47

Thus, the present value of the dividends for the 10 percent growth period is $14.47. For the second period with growth at 5 percent, we need to calculate the constant growth rate price as of $t = 3$ and then discount that price back to $t = 0$. To get started, we need to calculate the dividend that will be paid at $t = 4$:

$$D_4 = D_3(1.05) = (\$6.655)\,(1.05) = \$6.99.$$

We are given

$$r = 0.12$$

$$g = 0.05$$

Therefore,

$$P_3 = \left(\frac{D_4}{r - g}\right)$$

$$P_3 = \left(\frac{6.99}{0.12 - 0.05}\right)$$
$$= \$99.86$$

Now we bring this amount back to $t = 0$ at the required rate of return:

$$= \$99.86(1.12)^{-3}$$
$$= \$71.08$$

Summing the two dividends, we value Sun's stock at $\$14.47 + \$71.08 = \$85.55$.

14. a. The dollar-weighted rate of return is the single discount rate that equates the present value of inflows to the present value of outflows.

Outflows:
   At $t = 0$ (January 1, 2002):
   150 shares purchased × $156.30 per share = \$23,445

Inflows:
   At $t = 1$ (January 1, 2003):
   150 shares × $10 dividend per share = \$1,500
   100 shares sold × $165 per share = \$16,500

   At $t = 2$ (January 1, 2004):
   50 shares remaining × $15 dividend per share = \$750
   50 shares sold × $170 per share = \$8,500

$$\text{PV (Outflows)} = \text{PV (Inflows)}$$

$$23,445 = \frac{1,500 + 16,500}{1 + r} + \frac{750 + 8,500}{(1 + r)^2}$$
$$= \frac{18,000}{1 + r} + \frac{9,250}{(1 + r)^2}$$

The last line is the equation for calculating the dollar-weighted rate of return on Wilson's portfolio.

b. We can solve for the dollar-weighted return entering $-23,445$, $18,000$, and $9,250$ in a spreadsheet or calculator with an IRR function. In this case, we can also solve for dollar-weighted rate of return as the real root of the quadratic equation $18,000x + 9,250x^2 - 23,445 = 0$, where $x = 1/(1 + r)$. By any method, the solution is $r = 0.11965$ or approximately 12 percent.

c. The time-weighted rate of return is the solution to $(1 + \text{Time-weighted rate of return})^2 = (1 + r_1)(1 + r_2)$ where r_1 and r_2 are the holding period returns in the first and second years, respectively. The value of the portfolio at $t = 0$ is \$23,445. At $t = 1$, there are inflows of sale proceeds of \$16,500 and \$1,500 in dividends, or \$18,000 in total. The balance of 50 shares is worth $\$8,250 = 50$ shares × $165 per share. So at $t = 1$ the valuation is $\$26,250 = \$18,000 + \$8,250$. Thus

$$r_1 = (\$26,250 - \$23,445)/\$23,445 = 0.119642 \text{ for the first year.}$$

The amount invested at $t = 1$ is $\$8,250 = 50$ shares × $165 per share. At $t = 2$, \$750 in dividends are received, as well as sale proceeds of \$8,500 (50 shares sold × $170 per share). So at $t = 2$ the valuation is $\$9,250 = \$750 + \$8,500$. Thus

$$r_2 = (\$9,250 - \$8,250)/\$8,250 = 0.121212 \text{ for the second year.}$$

Time-weighted rate of return $= \sqrt{(1.119642)(1.121212)} - 1 = 0.120424$ or 12 percent.

d. If Wilson is a private investor who has full discretionary control over the timing and amount of withdrawals and additions to his portfolios, then the dollar-weighted rate of return is an appropriate measure of portfolio returns.

e. If Wilson is an investment manager whose clients exercise discretionary control over the timing and amount of withdrawals and additions to the portfolio, then the time-weighted rate of return is the appropriate measure of portfolio returns. Time-weighted rate of return is standard in the investment management industry.

STATISTICAL CONCEPTS AND MARKET RETURNS

LEARNING OUTCOMES

After completing this chapter, you will be able to do the following:

- Differentiate between a population and a sample.
- Explain the concept of a parameter.
- Explain the differences among the types of measurement scales.
- Define and interpret a frequency distribution.
- Define, calculate, and interpret a total return (holding period return).
- Describe how to construct a frequency distribution.
- Define and explain the use of intervals to summarize data.
- Convert absolute frequencies to relative frequencies.
- Describe the properties of data presented as a histogram or a frequency polygon.
- List the properties of the arithmetic mean and median.
- Define, calculate, and interpret measures of central tendency, including the population mean, sample mean, arithmetic mean, geometric mean, weighted mean, median, and mode.
- Identify whether geometric means are generally larger or smaller than arithmetic means, and give a case where they will be equal.
- Find the location of a given percentile.
- Define, calculate, and interpret a portfolio return as a weighted mean.
- Define, calculate, and interpret a weighted average or mean.
- Define, calculate, and interpret a range and mean absolute deviation.
- Define, calculate, and interpret a sample and a population variance and standard deviation.
- Calculate the proportion of items falling within a certain number of standard deviations of the mean, using Chebyshev's inequality.
- Define, calculate, and interpret the coefficient of variation.
- Define, calculate, and interpret the Sharpe measure of risk-adjusted performance.
- Give the relative location of the mean, median, and mode for a nonsymmetrical distribution.
- Define and interpret skewness.

- Explain why a distribution might be positively or negatively skewed.
- Define and interpret kurtosis.
- Explain why a distribution might have positive excess kurtosis.
- Explain whether an arithmetic mean or a geometric mean is appropriate for making a particular investment statement.
- Explain why a semi-logarithmic scale is often used for return performance graphs.

1 THE NATURE OF STATISTICS

Statistical methods provide a powerful set of tools for analyzing data and drawing conclusions. These tools allow us to forecast sales or earnings, for instance, or to develop inputs for portfolio optimization. As you master a variety of statistical tools and apply them to real-world examples in this chapter, you will gain the perspective you need to make intelligent choices among statistical models.

1.1 WHAT IS STATISTICS?

The term **statistics** can have two broad meanings, one referring to data and the other to method. A company's average earnings per share (EPS) for the last 20 quarters, or its average returns for the past 10 years, are statistics. We may also analyze historical EPS to forecast future EPS, or use the company's past returns to infer its risk. The totality of methods we employ to collect and analyze data is also called statistics.

Statistical methods include descriptive statistics and inferential statistics. **Descriptive statistics** is the study of how data can be summarized effectively to describe the important aspects of large data sets. By consolidating a mass of numerical details, descriptive statistics turns data into information. In this chapter, we discuss descriptive statistics. **Inferential statistics** or **statistical inference**, on the other hand, is concerned with making forecasts, estimates, or judgments about a larger group from the smaller group actually observed. The foundation for statistical inference is probability theory, and both statistical inference and probability theory will be discussed in later chapters.

Our goal in this chapter is to demonstrate the statistical methods that allow analysts to summarize return distributions. We are concerned with the following properties of return distributions: where the data are centered (central tendency), how far the data are dispersed from their center (dispersion), whether the distribution is symmetrically shaped or lopsided (skewness), and whether extreme outcomes are likely (kurtosis). Throughout the chapter, we apply descriptive statistics to historical return data for various U.S. and international markets.

1.2 POPULATIONS AND SAMPLES

A **population** is defined as all members of a specified group. Any descriptive measure of a population characteristic is called a **parameter**. Although a population can have many parameters, investment analysts are usually concerned with only a few, such as the mean value, the range of investment returns, and the variance.

Even if it is possible to observe all the members of a population, it is often too expensive in time or money to attempt this. For example, if the population is all telecommunications customers worldwide and an analyst is interested in their purchasing plans, the analyst will find it too costly to observe the entire population.

Once the population has been defined, we can take a subset or **sample**[1] of the population with a view toward describing the population. Just as a parameter is a descriptive measure of a population characteristic, a statistic is a descriptive measure of a sample characteristic. Much of statistical inference is concerned with the problems involved in using a **sample statistic** to estimate an unknown population parameter.

1.3 MEASUREMENT SCALES

To choose the appropriate statistical methods for summarizing and analyzing data, we need to distinguish between different **measurement scales** or levels of measurement. All data measurements can be classified into one of four major categories:

1. **nominal scale**,
2. **ordinal scale**,
3. **interval scale**, or
4. **ratio scale**.

Nominal scales represent the weakest level of measurement. With integers assigned to mutual funds that have different investment strategies, the number 1 might refer to a small-cap value fund, the number 2 to a large-cap value fund, and so on for each possible style. This nominal scale categorizes the funds according to their style but does not rank them.

Ordinal scales reflect a stronger level of measurement. We have an ordinal scale when all the observations can be placed into separate categories and the categories are ordered with respect to some characteristic. For example, a ranking of 100 balanced mutual funds based on their five-year cumulative return might assign the number 1 to the 10 best-performing funds and 10 to the 10 worst-performing funds. The ordinal scale is stronger than the nominal scale because it reveals that a fund ranked 1 performed better than a fund ranked 2. The scale tells us nothing, however, about the difference in performance between funds ranked 1 and 2 compared with the difference in performance between funds ranked 3 and 4, or 9 and 10.

Interval scales provide not only ranking but also assurance that the differences between scale values are equal. As a result, scale values can be added and subtracted meaningfully. The Celsius and Fahrenheit scales are interval measurement scales. The difference in temperature between 10°C and 11°C is the same as the difference between 40°C and 41°C. We can state accurately that 12°C = 9°C + 3°C, for example. Nevertheless, the zero point of an interval scale does not reflect complete absence of what is being measured; it is not a true zero point or natural zero. Zero degrees Celsius corresponds to the freezing point of water, not the absence of temperature. As a consequence of the absence of a true zero point, we cannot meaningfully form ratios on interval scales. As an example, 50°C, while five times as large a number as 10°C, does not represent five times as much temperature. Also, questionnaire scales are often treated as interval scales. If an investor is asked to rank his risk aversion on a scale from 1 (extremely risk-averse) to 7 (extremely risk-loving), the difference between a response of 1 and a response of 2 is often assumed to represent the same difference in risk aversion as the difference between a response of 6 and a response of 7.

Ratio scales represent the strongest level of measurement. They have all the characteristics of interval measurement scales as well as a true zero point as the origin. With ratio scales we can meaningfully compute ratios, as well as meaningfully add and subtract. As a

---

[1] We discuss sampling in more detail in the chapter on sampling.

result, we can apply the widest range of statistical tools to data measured on a ratio scale. Rates of return are measured on a ratio scale, as is money. If we have twice as much money, then we have twice the purchasing power. Note that the scale has a natural zero—zero means no money.

Now that we have addressed some preliminaries concerning statistics, we can discuss summarizing and describing data. Ibbotson Associates has generously provided much of the data that we use throughout this book.[2] The data cover both U.S. and international markets. To include the general 20th century history of markets around the world, we will also be referring to Dimson, Marsh, and Staunton's *Millennium Book* (2000).

2 FREQUENCY DISTRIBUTIONS

In this section, we discuss one of the simplest ways to summarize data—the frequency distribution. A **frequency distribution** is a tabular display of data summarized into a relatively small number of intervals. Frequency distributions help in the analysis of large amounts of statistical data, and they work with all types of measurement scales.

We can use frequency distributions to summarize rates of return. Rates of return are the fundamental units that analysts and portfolio managers use for making investment decisions. When we analyze rates of return, our starting point is the **total return** (also called the **holding period return**). The total return for time period t, R_t, is defined as follows:

$$R_t = \frac{P_t - P_{t-1} + D_t}{P_{t-1}} \tag{3-1}$$

where

P_t = price per share at the end of time period t

P_{t-1} = price per share at the end of time period $t - 1$, the time period immediately preceding time period t

D_t = cash distributions received during time period t

Thus, the return for time period t is the capital gain (or loss) plus distributions divided by the beginning-period price. (For common stocks, the distribution is the dividend; for bonds, the distribution is the coupon payment.) Equation 3-1 can be used to define the total return on any asset for a day, week, month, or year simply by changing the interpretation of the time interval between successive values of the time index, t.

The total rate of return, as defined in Equation 3-1, has two important characteristics. First, it has an element of time attached to it. For example, if a monthly time interval is used between successive observations for price, then the rate of return is a monthly figure. Second, rate of return has no currency unit attached to it. For instance, suppose that prices are denominated in euro. The numerator and denominator of Equation 3-1 would be expressed in euro, and the resulting ratio would not have any units because the units in the numerator and denominator would cancel one another. This result holds regardless of the currency in which prices are denominated. In many instances, we multiply the result from Equation 3-1 by 100 and express the result as a percentage. Even though both U.S. and German return measures are free of scale, a German investor seeking U.S. returns needs to factor in exchange rate concerns. For a German investor who invests in the United States, the ultimate concern will be the return earned in euro. Because the exchange rate (€/$) is

---

[2] Information about Ibbotson Associates is available at their Web site: www.ibbotson.com.

not likely to remain the same over the time period examined, the return in euro is not necessarily equal to the U.S. return.

With these concerns noted, we now turn to the frequency distribution of the rate of return on the S&P 500.[3] First, we examine annual rates of return; then we look at monthly rates of return. The annual rates of return on the S&P 500 calculated with Equation 3-1 span the period January 1926 to December 1998, for a total of 73 annual observations. Monthly return data cover the period January 1926 to March 1999, for a total of 879 monthly observations.

To begin our discussion of the construction of a frequency distribution, we work with the annual returns on the S&P 500. We begin by looking at the maximum and minimum returns of the series to get a sense of the boundaries of the data. Over the period 1926 to 1998, the return on the S&P 500 had a minimum annual value of −44 percent and a maximum value of +54 percent. To create a frequency distribution, we first set up return intervals between these minimum and maximum values. Then we count the number of observations that fall within certain return intervals.[4] An **interval** is a set of return values within which an observation falls; each observation falls into only one interval, and the total number of intervals covers the entire population. The actual number of observations in a given interval is called the **absolute frequency,** or simply the frequency. The frequency distribution is the list of intervals together with the corresponding measures of frequency.

When we have continuous data such as stock returns, an important consideration is the number of intervals to be used. How much detail should we include? If we use too few intervals, we will summarize too much and lose pertinent characteristics. If we use too many intervals, we may not summarize enough. We need an evenly distributed number of mutually exclusive intervals between the data's minimum and maximum values. We should select lower- and upper-return interval limits such that each return can be placed uniquely into one return interval. If we have continuous data, we must not allow gaps between the intervals.

For the S&P 500 total return series, the range of returns is from −44 percent to +54 percent, or 98 percent. Return intervals of 1 percent width would result in 98 return intervals—in this case, too many. Remember, the general idea of grouping data into a frequency distribution is to summarize the data in a meaningful way. For the annual return data for the S&P 500, we have only 73 annual observations. Grouping 73 observations into 98 intervals would defeat our purpose. Instead, we use return intervals of 2 percent, resulting in 49 return intervals. Return intervals begin with $-44\% \leq R_t < -42\%$ and go up to the last return interval of $52\% \leq R_t \leq 54\%$. Note that we have ensured that the intervals are not overlapping, so each return can be placed uniquely into one return interval. To complete the frequency distribution, we need only count the number of observations that fall into each return interval.

Another useful way to present this information is to divide the absolute frequency of each return interval by the total number of observations. The result is known as the **relative frequency.** We find the **cumulative absolute frequency** and the **cumulative relative frequency** by cumulating the absolute and relative frequencies as we move from the first to the last interval.

The frequency distribution for the annual returns for the S&P 500 is presented in Table 3-1. The first return interval, −44 percent to −42 percent, has one observation; its relative frequency is 1/73 or 1.37 percent. The cumulative frequency for this interval is 1

---

[3] We use the total return series on the S&P 500 from January 1926 to December 1998 provided by Ibbotson Associates.

[4] Return intervals can also be called ranges or bins.

because only one observation is less than −42 percent. The cumulative relative frequency is thus 1/73 or 1.37 percent. The next return interval has zero observations; therefore, its cumulative frequency is 0 plus 1 and its cumulative relative frequency is 1.37 percent (the cumulative relative frequency from the previous interval). We find the other cumulative frequencies by adding the absolute frequency to the previous cumulative frequency. The cumulative frequency, then, tells us the absolute number of observations that are less than the upper limit of each return interval.

As Table 3-1 shows, return intervals have frequencies from 0 to 6 in this sample. Two intervals ($-10\% \leq R_t < -8\%$ and $18\% \leq R_t < 20\%$) have the maximum frequency of 6. These results are shown in bold type in Table 3-1.

You might consider 49 return intervals to be too many. Stock return data, however, are characterized by a few rather large or small outcomes. For instance, from the frequency distribution in Table 3-1, you can see that only five outcomes fall between −44 percent to −14 percent and between 38 percent to 54 percent. We could have collapsed the return intervals in the tails of the frequency distribution, but then we would have lost the information about how extremely poorly or well the stock market had performed. The outcomes in the tails of the distribution may be outliers or they may actually provide important information. How to classify these outcomes is a statistical issue that will be discussed in more detail in the chapters on regression and correlation analysis. For now, we simply note that the issue of outliers is important for risk management.

The frequency distribution gives us a straightforward way to characterize risk. The question remains, however: How many return intervals should we include? A risk manager may need to know the worst possible outcomes and thus may want to have information on the tails. A portfolio manager or analyst, however, may need to know where most of the outcomes lie and thus may require less detailed information on outliers.

In constructing the frequency distribution in Table 3-1, we were careful to use return intervals that were exclusively positive or negative; that is, we chose −2 to 0 and 0 to 2 for the shift from negative to positive. This structure allows us to easily ascertain the number of positive or negative outcomes on the S&P 500. For example, the number of negative returns is 20, as shown in the fourth column, which reports the cumulative frequency. The number of positive returns must then be equal to 73 − 20, or 53. We can express the number of positive and negative outcomes as a percentage of the total to get a sense of the risk inherent in investing in the stock market. During the 73-year period, the S&P 500 had negative annual returns 27.4 percent of the time (that is, 20/73). We can see this result in the fifth column, which reports the cumulative relative frequency.

The frequency distribution gives us a sense of not only where most of the observations lie but also whether the distribution is evenly distributed, lopsided, or peaked. In the case of the S&P 500, we can see that more than half of the outcomes are positive, and many of those annual returns are larger than 10 percent. By describing the data with a frequency distribution, we can summarize the data without destroying its essential elements.

Now we look at the monthly return data for the S&P 500. The monthly return series from January 1926 to March 1999 has 879 observations. Returns range from a minimum of approximately −30 percent to a maximum of approximately +43 percent. With such a large quantity of monthly data we must summarize to get a sense of the distribution, and so we group the data into 38 equally spaced return intervals of 2 percent. The gains from summarizing in this way are substantial. Table 3-2 presents the resulting frequency distribution. The absolute frequencies appear in the second column, followed by the relative frequency. The relative frequencies are rounded to two decimal places. The cumulative absolute and cumulative relative frequencies appear in the fourth and fifth columns, respectively.

TABLE 3-1 Frequency Distribution for the Annual Total Return on the S&P 500: 1926 to 1998

Return ranges are indicated in intervals of 2 percent. The lower class limit is the weak inequality (≤) and the upper class limit is the strong inequality (<). Integer frequency counts appear to the right of each return range.

Return Interval	Frequency	Relative Frequency	Cumulative Frequency	Cumulative Relative Frequency
−44.0% to −42.0%	1	1.37%	1	1.37%
−42.0% to −40.0%	0	0.00%	1	1.37%
−40.0% to −38.0%	0	0.00%	1	1.37%
−38.0% to −36.0%	0	0.00%	1	1.37%
−36.0% to −34.0%	1	1.37%	2	2.74%
−34.0% to −32.0%	0	0.00%	2	2.74%
−32.0% to −30.0%	0	0.00%	2	2.74%
−30.0% to −28.0%	0	0.00%	2	2.74%
−28.0% to −26.0%	1	1.37%	3	4.11%
−26.0% to −24.0%	1	1.37%	4	5.48%
−24.0% to −22.0%	0	0.00%	4	5.48%
−22.0% to −20.0%	0	0.00%	4	5.48%
−20.0% to −18.0%	0	0.00%	4	5.48%
−18.0% to −16.0%	0	0.00%	4	5.48%
−16.0% to −14.0%	1	1.37%	5	6.85%
−14.0% to −12.0%	0	0.00%	5	6.85%
−12.0% to −10.0%	3	4.11%	8	10.96%
−10.0% to −8.0%	**6**	8.22%	14	19.18%
−8.0% to −6.0%	1	1.37%	15	20.55%
−6.0% to −4.0%	1	1.37%	16	21.92%
−4.0% to −2.0%	1	1.37%	17	23.29%
−2.0% to 0.0%	3	4.11%	20	27.40%
0.0% to 2.0%	2	2.74%	22	30.14%
2.0% to 4.0%	0	0.00%	22	30.14%

Return Interval	Frequency	Relative Frequency	Cumulative Frequency	Cumulative Relative Frequency
4.0% to 6.0%	4	5.48%	26	35.62%
6.0% to 8.0%	4	5.48%	30	41.10%
8.0% to 10.0%	1	1.37%	31	42.47%
10.0% to 12.0%	3	4.11%	34	46.58%
12.0% to 14.0%	1	1.37%	35	47.95%
14.0% to 16.0%	1	1.37%	36	49.32%
16.0% to 18.0%	2	2.74%	38	52.05%
18.0% to 20.0%	**6**	8.22%	44	60.27%
20.0% to 22.0%	2	2.74%	46	63.01%
22.0% to 24.0%	5	6.85%	51	69.86%
24.0% to 26.0%	2	2.74%	53	72.60%
26.0% to 28.0%	1	1.37%	54	73.97%
28.0% to 30.0%	1	1.37%	55	75.34%
30.0% to 32.0%	5	6.85%	60	82.19%
32.0% to 34.0%	4	5.48%	64	87.67%
34.0% to 36.0%	0	0.00%	64	87.67%
36.0% to 38.0%	4	5.48%	68	93.15%
38.0% to 40.0%	0	0.00%	68	93.15%
40.0% to 42.0%	0	0.00%	68	93.15%
42.0% to 44.0%	2	2.74%	70	95.89%
44.0% to 46.0%	0	0.00%	70	95.89%
46.0% to 48.0%	1	1.37%	71	97.26%
48.0% to 50.0%	0	0.00%	71	97.26%
50.0% to 52.0%	0	0.00%	71	97.26%
52.0% to 54.0%	2	2.74%	73	100.00%

Source: Frequency distribution generated with Ibbotson Associates EnCorr Analyzer™

TABLE 3-2 Frequency Distribution for the Monthly Total Return on the S&P 500 January 1926 to March 1999

Return ranges are indicated in intervals of 2 percent. The lower class limit is the weak inequality (≤) and the upper class limit is the strong inequality (<). The relative frequency is the absolute frequency or cumulative frequency divided by the total number of observations.

Return Interval	Absolute Frequency	Relative Frequency	Cumulative Absolute Frequency	Cumulative Relative Frequency
−30.0% to −28.0%	1	0.11%	1	0.11%
−28.0% to −26.0%	0	0.00%	1	0.11%
−26.0% to −24.0%	1	0.11%	2	0.23%
−24.0% to −22.0%	1	0.11%	3	0.34%
−22.0% to −20.0%	2	0.23%	5	0.57%
−20.0% to −18.0%	2	0.23%	7	0.80%
−18.0% to −16.0%	2	0.23%	9	1.02%
−16.0% to −14.0%	3	0.34%	12	1.37%
−14.0% to −12.0%	5	0.57%	17	1.93%
−12.0% to −10.0%	5	0.57%	22	2.50%
−10.0% to −8.0%	18	2.05%	40	4.55%
−8.0% to −6.0%	24	2.73%	64	7.28%
−6.0% to −4.0%	51	5.80%	115	13.08%
−4.0% to −2.0%	84	9.56%	199	22.64%
−2.0% to 0.0%	130	14.79%	329	37.43%
0.0% to 2.0%	177	20.14%	506	57.57%
2.0% to 4.0%	148	16.84%	654	74.40%
4.0% to 6.0%	123	13.99%	777	88.40%
6.0% to 8.0%	54	6.14%	831	94.54%
8.0% to 10.0%	19	2.16%	850	96.70%
10.0% to 12.0%	14	1.59%	864	98.29%
12.0% to 14.0%	6	0.68%	870	98.98%
14.0% to 16.0%	2	0.23%	872	99.20%
16.0% to 18.0%	3	0.34%	875	99.54%
18.0% to 20.0%	0	0.00%	875	99.54%
20.0% to 22.0%	0	0.00%	875	99.54%
22.0% to 24.0%	0	0.00%	875	99.54%
24.0% to 26.0%	1	0.11%	876	99.66%
26.0% to 28.0%	0	0.00%	876	99.66%
28.0% to 30.0%	0	0.00%	876	99.66%
30.0% to 32.0%	0	0.00%	876	99.66%
32.0% to 34.0%	0	0.00%	876	99.66%
34.0% to 36.0%	0	0.00%	876	99.66%
36.0% to 38.0%	0	0.00%	876	99.66%
38.0% to 40.0%	2	0.23%	878	99.89%
40.0% to 42.0%	0	0.00%	878	99.89%
42.0% to 44.0%	1	0.11%	879	100.00%

Source: Frequency distribution generated with Ibbotson Associates EnCorr Analyzer™

The advantage of a frequency distribution is evident in Table 3-2, which tells us that the vast majority of observations (578/879 = 66 percent) lie in the four intervals spanning −2 percent to +6 percent. Altogether, we have 329 negative returns and 550 positive returns. Almost 63 percent of the monthly outcomes are positive. If we look at the cumulative relative frequency in the last column, we see that the interval −2 percent to 0 percent shows a cumulative frequency of 37.43 percent, for an upper return limit of 0 percent. This means that 37.43 percent of the observations lie below the level of 0 percent. We can also see that not many observations are greater than +12 percent or less than −12 percent. Note that the frequency distributions of annual and monthly returns are not directly comparable. On average, we should expect the returns measured at shorter intervals (for example, months) to be smaller than returns measured over longer periods (for example, years).

Next, we show an example in which we construct a frequency distribution of monthly price changes on the Dow Jones Industrial Average.

EXAMPLE 3-1.   Constructing a Frequency Distribution

In this example, we compute the monthly price changes of the Dow Jones Industrial Average for June 1995 to June 1999. Table 3-3 shows the frequency distribution. For each period, the percent change in price is $\dfrac{P_t - P_{t-1}}{P_{t-1}}$ the capital gains component of total returns. Note that we ignore the dividend component of total returns in this computation, and we use closing levels of the Dow in constructing the price series.

TABLE 3-3   Closing Prices of the Dow Jones Industrial Average and the Dow's Monthly Percentage Price Change: June 1995 to June 1999

Date	Closing Price	Percent Change in Price	Date	Closing Price	Percent Change in Price
June 1995	4556.1		July 1997	8222.6	7.17%
July 1995	4708.5	3.34%	August 1997	7622.4	−7.30%
August 1995	4610.6	−2.08%	September 1997	7945.3	4.24%
September 1995	4789.1	3.87%	October 1997	7442.1	−6.33%
October 1995	4755.5	−0.70%	November 1997	7823.1	5.12%
November 1995	5074.5	6.71%	December 1997	7908.3	1.09%
December 1995	5117.1	0.84%	January 1998	7906.5	−0.02%
January 1996	5395.3	5.44%	February 1998	8545.7	8.08%
February 1996	5485.6	1.67%	March 1998	8799.8	2.97%
March 1996	5587.1	1.85%	April 1998	9063.4	3.00%
April 1996	5569.1	−0.32%	May 1998	8900.0	−1.80%
May 1996	5643.2	1.33%	June 1998	8952.0	0.58%
June 1996	5654.6	0.20%	July 1998	8883.3	−0.77%
July 1996	5528.9	−2.22%	August 1998	7539.1	−15.13%
August 1996	5616.2	1.58%	September 1998	7842.6	4.03%
September 1996	5882.2	4.74%	October 1998	8592.1	9.56%

Date	Closing Price	Percent Change in Price	Date	Closing Price	Percent Change in Price
October 1996	6029.4	2.50%	November 1998	9116.55	6.10%
November 1996	6521.7	8.16%	December 1998	9181.43	0.71%
December 1996	6448.3	−1.13%	January 1999	9358.83	1.93%
January 1997	6813.1	5.66%	February 1999	9306.58	−0.56%
February 1997	6877.7	0.95%	March 1999	9786.16	5.15%
March 1997	6583.5	−4.28%	April 1999	10789.0	10.25%
April 1997	7009.0	6.46%	May 1999	10559.74	−2.12%
May 1997	7331.0	4.59%	June 1999	10970.8	3.89%
June 1997	7672.8	4.66%			

Source: Closing levels of the Dow were collected from www.yahoo.com.

With 49 price levels, we calculate 48 monthly price changes. (Remember that we cannot compute a return for June 1995 without the closing level of May 1995.) The maximum monthly price change is 10.25 percent and the minimum is −15.13 percent. With 48 returns and a range of returns of 25.38 percent, we arbitrarily set seven return intervals starting at −16 percent, with increments of 4 percent.

As Table 3-4 shows, the Dow can be quite volatile, even from month to month. Most price changes, however, lie within three intervals spanning −4 percent to +8 percent. As is the case for the S&P 500, a few extremely positive and negative percentage changes in price occur. In addition, 29.17 percent of the price changes are negative; that is, less than 0 percent.

TABLE 3-4　Frequency Distribution of the Monthly Price Changes for the Dow: July 1995 to June 1999

Return Interval	Absolute Frequency	Relative Frequency (%)	Cumulative Absolute Frequency	Cumulative Relative Frequency
−16.0% to −12.0%	1	2.08%	1	2.08%
−12.0% to −8.0%	0	0%	1	2.08%
−8.0% to −4.0%	3	6.25%	4	8.33%
−4.0% to 0.0%	10	20.84%	14	29.17%
0.0% to 4.0%	17	35.42%	31	64.59%
4.0% to 8.0%	13	27.08%	44	91.67%
8.0% to 12.0%	4	8.33%	48	100%

Note: Relative frequencies are rounded to add to 100%.

3 GRAPHIC PRESENTATION

A graphical display of data allows us to visualize important characteristics quickly. For example, we may see that the distribution is symmetrically shaped, and this finding may influence which probability distribution we use to describe the data.

In this section, we discuss the histogram, the frequency polygon, and the cumulative frequency distribution as methods for displaying data graphically. We construct all of these graphic presentations with the information contained in the frequency distribution of the S&P 500 shown in either Table 3-1 or Table 3-2.

3.1 THE
HISTOGRAM

A **histogram** is the graphical equivalent of a frequency distribution; it is a bar chart of continuous data that have been grouped into a frequency distribution. The advantage of the visual display is that we can see quickly where most of the observations lie. To see how a histogram is constructed, look at the return interval $18\% \le R_t < 20\%$ in Table 3-1. This interval has an absolute frequency of 6. Therefore, we erect a bar or rectangle with a height of 6 over that return interval on the horizontal axis. Continuing with this process for all other return intervals yields a histogram. Figure 3-1 presents the histogram of the total return series on the S&P 500 from 1926 to 1998.

FIGURE 3-1   Histogram of S&P 500 Annual Total Returns:
December 1926 to December 1998

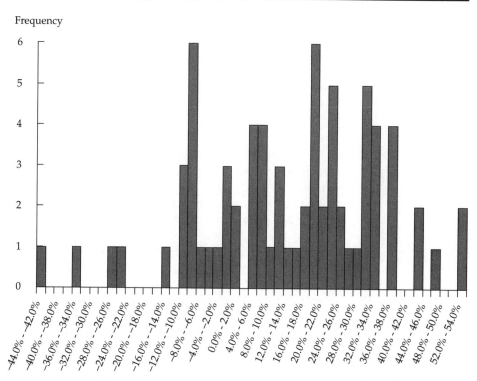

Source: Ibbotson EnCorr Analyzer™

**FIGURE 3-2   Histogram of S&P 500 Monthly Total Returns:
January 1926 to March 1999**

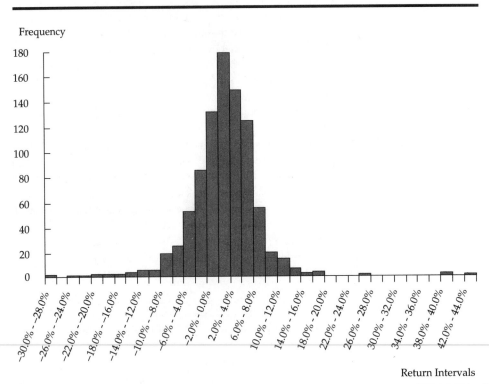

Source: Ibbotson EnCorr Analyzer™

In the histogram in Figure 3-1, the height of each bar represents the absolute frequency for each return interval. Two return intervals ($-10\% \leq R_t < -8\%$ and $18\% \leq R_t < 20\%$) have a frequency of 6 and thus have the tallest bars in the histogram. Because there are no gaps between the interval limits, there are no gaps between the bars of the histogram. Many of the return intervals have zero frequency; therefore, they have no height in the histogram.

The histogram for the distribution of monthly returns on the S&P 500 is presented in Figure 3-2. Slightly more symmetrically shaped than the histogram of annual returns shown in Figure 3-1, the histogram of monthly returns for the S&P 500 appears somewhat more bell-shaped but still highlights the many large negative and positive returns.

**3.2 THE
FREQUENCY
POLYGON AND THE
CUMULATIVE
FREQUENCY
DISTRIBUTION**

Two other graphical tools for displaying data are the frequency polygon and the cumulative frequency distribution. To construct a **frequency polygon,** we plot the midpoint of each interval on the *x*-axis and the absolute frequency for that interval on the *y*-axis; we then connect neighboring points with a straight line. Figure 3-3 shows the frequency polygon for the 879 monthly returns for the S&P 500 from December 1926 to December 1998.

In Figure 3-3, we have replaced the bars in the histogram with points connected with straight lines. For example, the return interval 0 percent to 2 percent has an absolute frequency of 177. In the frequency polygon, we plot the return-interval midpoint of 1 percent

FIGURE 3-3   Frequency Polygon of S&P 500 Monthly Total Returns:
January 1926 to March 1999

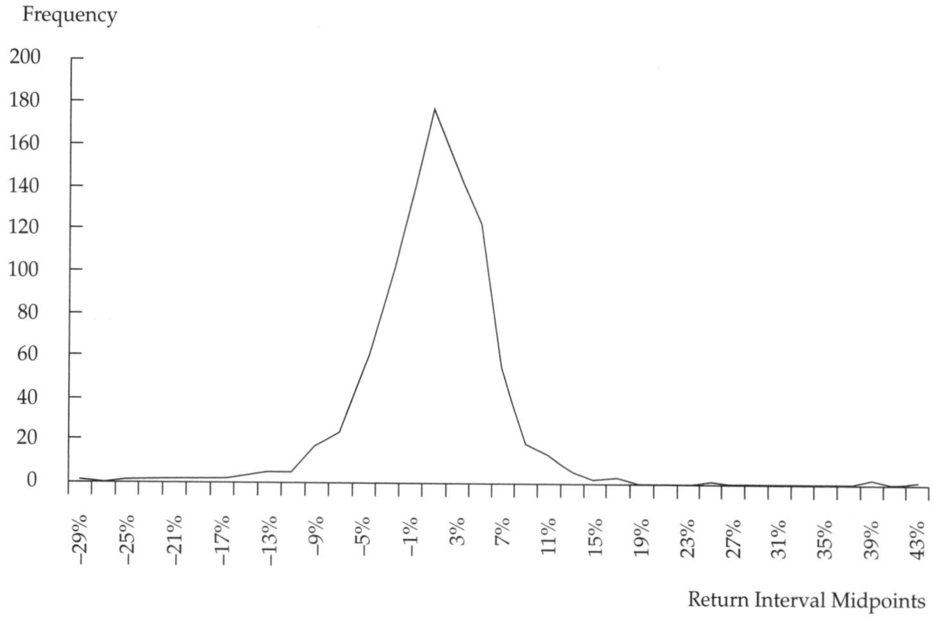

Source: Ibbotson Associates

and a frequency of 177. We plot all other points in a similar way.[5] This form of visual display adds a degree of continuity to the representation of the distribution.

Another form of line graph is the cumulative frequency distribution. Such a graph can plot either the cumulative absolute or cumulative relative frequency against the upper interval limit. The cumulative frequency distribution allows us to see how many or what percent of the observations lie below a certain value. To construct the cumulative frequency distribution, we graph the returns in the fourth or fifth column of Table 3-2 against the upper limit of each return interval. Figure 3-4 presents a graph of the cumulative absolute distribution for the monthly returns on the S&P 500. Notice that the cumulative distribution tends to flatten out when returns are extremely negative or extremely positive. The steep slope in the middle of Figure 3-4 reflects the fact that most of the observations lie in the neighborhood of −2 percent to 10 percent.

We can further examine the relationship between the relative frequency and the cumulative relative frequency by looking at the two return intervals reproduced in Table 3-5. The first return interval (0 percent to 2 percent) has a cumulative relative frequency of 57.57 percent. The next return interval (2 percent to 4 percent) has a cumulative relative frequency of 74.40 percent. The change in the cumulative relative frequency as we move from one interval to the next is the next interval's relative frequency. For instance, as we go from the first return interval (0 percent to 2 percent) to the next return interval (2 percent to 4 percent), the change in the cumulative relative frequency is

---

[5] Even though the upper limit on the interval is not a return falling in the interval, we still average it with the lower limit to determine the midpoint.

FIGURE 3-4   Cumulative Absolute Frequency Distribution of S&P 500 Monthly Total Returns January 1926 to March 1999

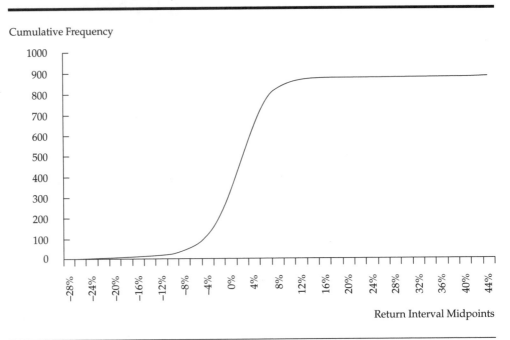

Source: Ibbotson Associates

74.40% −57.57% = 16.83%. (Values in the table have been rounded to two decimal places.) The fact that the slope is steep indicates that these frequencies are large. As you can see in the graph of the cumulative distribution, the slope of the curve changes as we move from the first return interval to the last. A fairly small slope for the cumulative distribution for the first few return intervals tells us that these return intervals do not contain many observations. You can go back to the frequency distribution in Table 3-2 and verify that the cumulative absolute frequency is only 22 observations (the cumulative relative frequency is 2.50 percent) up to the 10th return interval (−12 percent to −10 percent). In essence, the slope of the cumulative absolute distribution at any particular interval is proportional to the number of observations in that interval.

TABLE 3-5   Selected Class Frequencies for the S&P 500

Return Interval	Absolute Frequency	Relative Frequency	Cumulative Absolute Frequency	Cumulative Relative Frequency
0.0% to 2.0%	177	20.14%	506	57.57%
2.0% to 4.0%	148	16.84%	654	74.40%

4 MEASURES OF CENTRAL TENDENCY

So far, we have discussed methods that we can use to group data. Recall that the purpose of grouping data is to provide a logical organization that makes the data more useful and understandable. The frequency distributions of the annual returns on the S&P 500 and the monthly returns on the Dow Jones Industrial Average reveal the nature of the risks that may be encountered by investing in U.S. equities. In particular, the histogram for the annual returns on the S&P 500 clearly shows that large positive and negative annual returns are common.

Although frequency distributions and histograms provide us with a convenient way to summarize a series of observations, these methods are just a first step toward describing the data. We can also summarize data with **measures of central tendency** which specify where the data are centered. Measures of central tendency attempt to find a single number to describe a group of observations. The common measures of central tendency are the mean, median, mode, weighted mean, and geometric mean. Measures of central tendency are probably more widely used than any other statistical measure because they can be computed and applied easily. Measures of location, or location parameters, include not only measures of central tendency but also quartiles, quintiles, deciles, percentiles, and other quantities that provide information on how observations are distributed. After we discuss the various measures of central tendency, we will explain how to use these other location parameters.

4.1 **THE POPULATION MEAN**

Analysts and portfolio managers often want to have one number that describes a representative possible outcome of an investment decision. The population mean return serves that purpose. If a portfolio manager's mandate or assignment is United States large-cap equities, the population from which she must select securities is defined in terms of market capitalization (large-cap) and marketplace (United States). If we can define a population adequately, then we can calculate the population mean as the arithmetic average of all the observations.

We can calculate the **population mean** or average, μ, for a finite population as

$$\mu = \frac{\sum_{i=1}^{N} X_i}{N} \tag{3-2}$$

where upper-case N is the number of observations in the entire population and X_i is the ith observation. The population mean is an example of a parameter. The population mean is unique; that is, a given population has only one mean.

4.2 **THE SAMPLE MEAN**

Many times we cannot observe every member of a set; instead, we observe a subset or sample of the population. The concept of the mean can be applied to the observations in a sample with a slight change in notation. For samples, we define the **sample mean** or average, $\overline{X}$ (read X-bar), as

$$\overline{X} = \frac{\sum_{i=1}^{n} X_i}{n} \tag{3-3}$$

where lower-case n is the number of observations in the sample. The sample mean is also called the arithmetic average.[6] As we discussed earlier, the sample mean is a statistic (that is, a descriptive measure of a sample).

---

[6] Statisticians prefer the term *mean* to *average*. Some writers refer to all measures of central tendency (including the median and mode) as averages. The term *mean* avoids any possibility of confusion.

Means can be computed over individual units or over time. For instance, the sample might be the earnings per share for the 30 companies in the Dow Jones Industrial Average (DJIA) in 1998. In this case, we calculate mean EPS in 1998 as an average across individual units. When we examine the characteristics of some units at a specific point in time (such as EPS for the DJIA), we are examining **cross-sectional data.** The mean of these observations is called a cross-sectional mean. On the other hand, if our sample includes the historical monthly returns on the Nikkei 225 for the past 20 years, then we have **time-series data.** The mean of these observations is called a time-series mean. We will examine specialized statistical methods related to the behavior of time series in the chapter on times-series analysis and forecasting.

Next, we show an example of finding the sample mean return for equities in nine European countries for 1998. In this case, the mean is cross-sectional because we are averaging over individual country returns.

EXAMPLE 3-2.   Calculating a Cross-Sectional Mean.

Suppose we collect a sample of the annual stock market returns of nine European countries followed by Morgan Stanley Capital International (MSCI) for 1998 from Ibbotson Associates. All return series reported by MSCI are in local currency (that is, returns are for investors living in the country). We are interested in finding the sample mean total return for 1998 across these nine countries. This is the mean return in European equity markets in 1998. The calculation is Equation 3-3 applied to the returns in Table 3-6. Because this return is not stated in any single investor's home currency, it is not a return any single investor would earn. Rather, it is an average of returns in nine local currencies.

TABLE 3-6   Total Returns for European Equity Markets

Market	Total Return for 1998 in Local Currency (%)
MSCI Austria	−6.66
MSCI Belgium	56.45
MSCI France	31.91
MSCI Germany	20.32
MSCI Italy	42.88
MSCI Switzerland	16.81
MSCI U.K.	16.50
MSCI Spain	39.99
MSCI Ireland	29.36

Source: Ibbotson EnCorr Analyzer™

We calculate the sample mean by finding the sum of the nine values in the table and dividing by nine. The mean total return for the nine European markets for 1998 is not only (−6.66 + 56.45 + 31.91 + 20.32 + 42.88 + 16.81 + 16.50 + 39.99 + 29.36)/9 = 247.56/9 = 27.51 percent. The mean return for 1998 of 27.51 percent is clearly greater than the annual return for some markets and less than that for others.

In Example 3-2, four markets had returns less than the mean and five had returns that were greater. We should not expect any of the actual observations to be equal to the mean, because sample means provide only a summary of the data being analyzed. As an analyst, you will often need to find a few numbers that describe the characteristics of the distribution. The mean is generally the statistic that you will use as a measure of the typical outcome for a distribution. You can then use the mean to compare the performance of two different markets. For example, you might be interested in comparing the stock market performance of investments in Pacific Rim countries with investments in European countries. The mean returns in these markets are a basis for comparing investment results.

4.3 PROPERTIES OF THE ARITHMETIC MEAN

The arithmetic mean can be compared to the center of gravity of an object. This analogy is expressed graphically in Figure 3-5, which plots nine hypothetical observations on a bar. The nine observations are 2, 4, 4, 6, 10, 10, 12, 12, and 12; the arithmetic mean is $72/9 = 8$. The observations are plotted on the bar with various heights based on their frequency (that is, 2 is one unit high, 4 is two units high, and so on). When the bar is placed on a fulcrum, it balances only when the fulcrum is located at the point on the scale that corresponds to the arithmetic mean.

FIGURE 3-5   Center of Gravity Analogy for the Arithmetic Mean

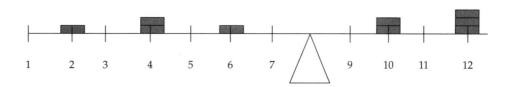

Fulcrum
When the fulcrum is placed at 8, the bar is perfectly balanced.

As analysts, we often use the mean return as a measure of the typical outcome for an asset. As in the example above, however, some outcomes are above the mean and some are below it. We can calculate the distance between the mean and each outcome and call it a deviation. Mathematically, it is always true that the sum of the deviations around the mean is equal to 0. We can see this quite easily by using the definition of the arithmetic mean shown in Equation 3-3, multiplying both sides of the equation by n: $n\overline{X} = \sum_{i=1}^{n} X_i$. Thus, the deviations from the mean can be calculated as follows:

$$\sum_{i=1}^{n}(X_i - \overline{X}) = \sum_{i=1}^{n} X_i - \sum_{i=1}^{n} \overline{X} = \sum_{i=1}^{n} X_i - n\overline{X} = 0$$

Deviations from the arithmetic mean are important information because they are indications of risk. The concept of deviations around the mean is the foundation for the more complex concepts of variance, skewness, and kurtosis, which we will discuss later in this chapter.

4.4 THE MEDIAN

The arithmetic mean can be unduly influenced by extremely large or small values. For example, suppose we compute the arithmetic mean of the following four numbers: 1, 2, 3, and 1,000. The mean is $1,006/4 = 251.50$. This example is extreme, but it highlights the influence of extreme observations on the mean. Because all observations are used to compute the mean, the arithmetic mean can be pulled either upward or downward, depending on the magnitude of the extreme outcomes.

Not influenced by extreme outcomes, the **median** is the middle item of a group that has been sorted into ascending or descending order. In an odd-numbered sample of n items, the median occupies the $(n + 1)/2$ position. In an even-numbered sample, the two middle items occupy the $n/2$ and $(n + 2)/2$ positions, and the median is the mean of these two items. In both cases, an equal number of observations lie above and below the median, and the distribution has only one median.

To demonstrate finding the median, we use the data from Example 3-2, reproduced in Table 3-7 in ascending order of the 1998 total return for European equities. Because this sample has nine observations, the median is the value in the sorted array that occupies the $(9 + 1)/2 =$ fifth position. Ireland's return occupies the fifth position, so the median is 29.36 percent. Note that the median is not influenced by extremely large or small outcomes. Even if Austria's total return had been a much lower value or Belgium's total return a much larger value, the median would still be the return in the fifth position.

TABLE 3-7   Sorted Returns for European Equity Markets

Market	Total Return for 1998 in Local Currency (%)
MSCI Austria	−6.66
MSCI U.K.	16.50
MSCI Switzerland	16.81
MSCI Germany	20.32
MSCI Ireland	29.36
MSCI France	31.91
MSCI Spain	39.99
MSCI Italy	42.88
MSCI Belgium	56.45

Source: Ibbotson Associates.

Suppose the data set above included only eight countries (leaving out Belgium). With $n = 8$, the return in the $n/2 =$ fourth position would be 20.32 percent for Germany, and the return in the $(n + 2)/2 =$ fifth position would be 29.36 percent for Ireland. The median, as the mean of these two returns, would then be $(20.32\% + 29.36\%)/2 = 24.84\%$.

4.5 THE MODE   The **mode** is the most frequently occurring value in a distribution. A distribution can have more than one mode, or even no mode. When a distribution has one most frequently occurring value, the distribution is said to be unimodal. If a distribution has two most frequently occurring values, then the distribution has two modes and we say that it is bimodal. If the distribution has three most frequently occurring values, then it is trimodal. When all the values in a data set are different, the distribution has no mode because no value occurs more frequently than any other value.

Stock return data and other data from continuous distributions may not have a modal outcome. When such data are grouped into intervals, however, we often find an interval (possibly more than one) with the highest frequency. This is the **modal interval** (or intervals). For example, the frequency distribution for the monthly returns on the S&P 500 has a modal interval of 0 percent to 2 percent, as shown in Figure 3-2; this return interval has 177 observations out of a total of 879. The modal interval always has the highest bar in the histogram.

The mode is the only measure of central tendency that can be used with nominal data. When we categorize mutual funds into different styles and assign a number to each style, the mode of these categorized data is the most frequent mutual fund style.

4.6 QUARTILES, QUINTILES, DECILES, AND PERCENTILES

Recall that the median is the value that divides the distribution in half. We can define other dividing lines that split the distribution into smaller sizes. **Quartiles** divide the distribution into quarters, **quintiles** into fifths, **deciles** into tenths, and **percentiles** into hundredths. Because the median divides the distribution in half, we say that the median is the 50th percentile. The first quartile (Q_1) divides the distribution such that 25 percent of the observations lie below it; therefore, the first quartile is also the 25th percentile. The second quartile (Q_2) is the median. The third quartile (Q_3) divides the distribution such that 75 percent of the observations lie below it; the third quartile is also the 75th percentile.

We can express the location of the various percentiles with a formula. Let P_y be the value at or below which y percent of the distribution lies, or the yth percentile. (For example, P_{18} is the point at or below which 18 percent of the observations lie.) The formula for the position of a percentile in an array with n entries sorted in ascending order is

$$L_y = (n + 1)\frac{y}{100}$$

(3-4)

where y is the percentage point at which we are dividing the distribution and L_y is the location (L) of the percentile (P_y) in the array sorted in ascending order.

Suppose we wish to use this formula to find the location of the median. Equation 3-4 indicates that the median is located at the $(n + 1)50/100 = (n + 1)/2$ position in the sorted distribution. This formula, $(n + 1)/2$, is precisely the one that we presented earlier for locating the median when working with an odd number of observations.

In general, the procedure for calculating percentiles is as follows.

- When the location, L_y, is a whole number i (such as $i = 10$), the location corresponds to an actual observation and $P_y = X_i$, where X_i is defined as the value in the ith position of the sorted data. To illustrate, recall the first example we used to demonstrate finding the median in Section 4.4. That example is based on sorted returns for nine European equity markets. The median is P_{50}. With $n = 9$, according to Equation 3-4, the median is located at the $L_{50} =$ fifth position; we need to look up the value standing in the fifth position, X_5. Doing that, we find that $P_{50} = X_5 = 29.36$ percent, or the return on MSCI Ireland.

- When L_y is not a whole number or integer (for example, $i = 10.25$ or $i = 12.57$), we use a linear **interpolation formula** to find P_y. We locate the adjacent X_i and X_j values, where i and j are the whole numbers on either side of L_y. Then $P_y = X_i + (L_y - i)(X_j - X_i)$; that is, we take the smaller of two values, X_i, and add to it a fraction $(L_y - i)$ of the distance between the two values $(X_j - X_i)$. We can check this expression using our second example to demonstrate the calculation of the median. Omitting Belgium from the data in Table 3-7, we use $n = 8$ in Equation 3-4 and find that $L_{50} = 4.5$. Then $i = 4$ and $j = 5$. Noting that $X_4 = 20.32$ and $X_5 = 29.36$, we find that $P_{50} = 20.32 + (4.5 - 4)(29.36 - 20.32)$, or 24.84 percent.

EXAMPLE 3-3.   Calculating Quintiles, Quartiles, and Percentiles.

Using the sorted return data for the Dow in Table 3-8, calculate the 10th percentile, first quartile (25th percentile) and the first four quintiles (20th, 40th, 60th, and 80th percentiles).

TABLE 3-8   Sorted Returns for the Dow Jones Industrial Average in Ascending Order by Column: July 1995 to June 1999

No.	Quintile		No.	Quintile		No.	Quintile		No.	Quintile	
1	Q_1	−15.13%	13	Q_2	−0.32%	25	Q_3	1.93%	37	Q_4	5.12%
2	Q_1	−7.30%	14	Q_2	−0.02%	26	Q_3	2.50%	38	Q_4	5.15%
3	Q_1	−6.33%	15	Q_2	0.20%	27	Q_3	2.97%	39	Q_4	5.44%
4	Q_1	−4.28%	16	Q_2	0.58%	28	Q_3	3.00%	40	Q_5	5.66%
5	Q_1	−2.22%	17	Q_2	0.71%	29	Q_3	3.34%	41	Q_5	6.10%
6	Q_1	−2.12%	18	Q_2	0.84%	30	Q_4	3.87%	42	Q_5	6.46%
7	Q_1	−2.08%	19	Q_2	0.95%	31	Q_4	3.89%	43	Q_5	6.71%
8	Q_1	−1.80%	20	Q_3	1.09%	32	Q_4	4.03%	44	Q_5	7.17%
9	Q_1	−1.13%	21	Q_3	1.33%	33	Q_4	4.24%	45	Q_5	8.08%
10	Q_2	−0.77%	22	Q_3	1.58%	34	Q_4	4.59%	46	Q_5	8.16%
11	Q_2	−0.70%	23	Q_3	1.67%	35	Q_4	4.66%	47	Q_5	9.56%
12	Q_2	−0.56%	24	Q_3	1.85%	36	Q_4	4.74%	48	Q_5	10.25%

Using Equation 3-4, $L_y = (n + 1)\dfrac{y}{100}$, we can identify the position of the various percentiles in the sorted array. In this example, $n = 48$.

$L_{10} = (49)(10/100) = 4.9$	L_{10} is located between the 4th and 5th entries, −4.28% and −2.22%.
$L_{20} = (49)(20/100) = 9.8$	L_{20} is located between the 9th and 10th entries, −1.13% and −0.77%.
$L_{25} = (49)(25/100) = 12.25$	L_{25} is located between the 12th and 13th entries, −0.56% and −0.32%.
$L_{40} = (49)(40/100) = 19.6$	L_{40} is located between the 19th and 20th entries, 0.95% and 1.09%.
$L_{60} = (49)(60/100) = 29.4$	L_{60} is located between the 29th and 30th entries, 3.34% and 3.87%.
$L_{80} = (49)(80/100) = 39.2$	L_{80} is located between the 39th and 40th entries, 5.44% and 5.66%.

To find the value of the 10th percentile, we use the interpolation formula $P_{10} = X_4 + (L_{10} - 4)(X_5 - X_4) = -4.28\% + 0.90[-2.22\% - (-4.28\%)] = -4.28\% + 1.85\% = -2.43\%$. The 10th percentile is located 90 percent of the distance between the fourth and fifth items in the array. The interpolation takes the value of the fourth item and adds to it 90 percent of the difference between the fifth and fourth items.

The first quartile is the 25th percentile; therefore, we can use the interpolation formula to calculate that $P_{25} = -0.56\% + 0.25[-0.32\% - (-0.56\%)] = -0.56\% + 0.06\% = -0.50\%$.

The results for the quintiles are as follows:

First quintile $= -1.13\% + 0.80[-0.77\% - (-1.13\%)] = -1.13\% + 0.29\% = -0.84\%$

Second quintile $= 0.95\% + 0.60(1.09\% - 0.95\%)$ $\qquad = 0.95\% + 0.08\% = 1.03\%$

Third quintile $= 3.34\% + 0.40(3.87\% - 3.34\%)$ $\qquad = 3.34\% + 0.21\% = 3.55\%$

Fourth quintile $= 5.44\% + 0.20(5.66\% - 5.44\%)$ $\qquad = 5.44\% + 0.04\% = 5.48\%$

Notice that the first quintile has 9 observations and the second has 10 observations. Dividing 48 observations into five groups results in some groups having different numbers of observations, as is evident in Table 3-8.

4.7 Using Quantiles for Portfolio Formation

Statisticians use the word **quantile** (or **fractile**) as the most general term for a value at or below which a stated fraction of the data lies. The median, quartiles, quintiles, and percentiles are all types of quantiles. Investment analysts use these statistics every day to rank performance—for example, the performance of mutual funds. Another key use of quantiles is in investment research. Analysts refer to a group defined by a particular quantile as that quantile. For example, analysts often refer to the set of firms with returns falling below the 10th percentile cutoff point as the bottom return decile. Dividing data into quantiles based on some characteristic allows analysts to evaluate the impact of that characteristic on a quantity of interest. For instance, empirical finance studies commonly rank firms based on the market value of their equity and then sort them into deciles. The first decile contains the portfolio of those firms with the smallest market values, and the tenth decile contains those firms with the largest market value. Ranking firms by decile allows analysts to compare the performance of small firms with large ones.

Another way to use this ranking procedure is to categorize stocks as being either growth stocks or value stocks. Typically, value stocks are defined as those for which the market price is relatively low in relation to earnings per share, book value per share, or dividends per share. Growth stocks, on the other hand, have comparatively high prices in relation to those same measures. In a recent study, Bauman, Conover, and Miller (1998) compared the performance of international growth stocks to value stocks. Their classification criteria were measures of value and growth: price to earnings (P/E), price to cash flow (P/CF), price to book value (P/B), and dividend yield (D/P). They assigned one-fourth of the total sample with the lowest P/E on June 30 of each year from 1986 to 1996 (the value group) to Quartile 1, and the one-fourth with the highest P/E of each year (the growth group) to Quartile 4. The stocks with the second-highest P/E formed Quartile 3, and the stocks with the second-lowest P/E, Quartile 2. They repeated this process for each of the four fundamental factors. Treating each quartile group as a portfolio composed of equally weighted stocks, they were able to compare the performance of the various value/growth quartiles. Table 1 from their study is reproduced as Table 3-9.

Table 3-9 reports each valuation factor's median, mean return, and standard deviation for each quartile grouping. Moving from Quartile 1 to Quartile 4, P/E, P/CF, and P/B increase, but D/P decreases. Regardless of the selection criteria, international value stocks outperformed international growth stocks over the sample period.

Bauman, Conover, and Miller also divided firms into one of four quartiles based on market value of equity. Then they examined the returns to the stocks in the quartiles. Table 7 from their article is reproduced as Table 3-10. As the table shows, the small-firm

TABLE 3-9 Mean Annual Returns of Value and Growth Stocks Based on Selected Characteristics: 1986 to 1996

Selection Criteria	Total Observations	Q_1 (Value)	Q_2	Q_3	Q_4 (Growth)	Spread In Return Q_1 to Q_4
Classification by P/E	28,463					
Median P/E		8.7	15.2	24.2	72.5	
Return		15.0%	13.6%	13.5%	10.6%	+4.4%
Standard deviation		46.5	38.3	42.5	50.4	
Classification by P/CF	30,240					
Median P/CF		4.4	8.2	13.3	34.2	
Return		15.5%	13.7%	12.9%	11.2%	+4.3%
Standard deviation		48.7	41.2	41.9	51.4	
Classification by P/B	32,265					
Median P/B		0.80	1.4	2.2	4.3	
Return		18.1%	14.4%	12.6%	12.4%	+5.7%
Standard deviation		69.6	45.9	45.1	57.0	
Classification by D/P	25,394					
Median D/P		5.6%	3.2%	1.9%	0.6%	
Return		14.1%	14.1%	12.5%	9.3%	+4.8%
Standard Deviation		40.5	38.7	38.9	42.0	

Source: Bauman, Conover, and Miller (1998).

portfolio had a median market value of $46.6 million, and the large-firm portfolio had a median value of $2,472.3 million. Large firms were almost 60 times larger than small firms, yet their mean stock returns were less than half those of the small firms (small, 22.0 percent; large, 10.8 percent). Overall, Bauman, Conover, and Miller found two effects. First, international value stocks (as the authors defined them) outperformed international growth stocks. Second, international small stocks outperformed international large stocks.

TABLE 3-10 Mean Annual Returns of International Stocks Grouped by Market Capitalization: 1986 to 1996

Selection Criterion	Total Observations	Q_1 (Small)	Q_2	Q_3	Q_4 (Large)	Spread in Return Q_1 to Q_4
Classification by size	32,555					
Median size (millions)		$46.6	$209.9	$583.7	$2,472.3	
Return		22.0%	13.6%	11.1%	10.8%	+11.2%
Standard deviation		87.8	45.2	39.5	34.0	

Source: Bauman, Conover, and Miller (1998).

The authors' next step was to examine how value and growth stocks performed while controlling for size. This step involved constructing 16 different value/growth and size portfolios ($4 \times 4 = 16$) and investigating the interaction between these two fundamental factors. They found that international value stocks outperformed international growth stocks except when market capitalization was very small. For portfolio managers, these findings suggest that value stocks offered investors relatively more favorable returns than did growth stocks in developed non-U.S. markets over the specific time period studied.

4.8 THE WEIGHTED MEAN

With the concepts of mean, median, and mode established, we must now point out that we gave only a special case of the mean in which the observations were equally weighted by the factor $1/n$. In work with portfolios, we need the more general concept of **weighted mean** to allow different weights on different observations. For example, an investment manager might allocate $75 million to an S&P 500 index fund and $25 million to a long-term corporate bond fund. The total investment of $100 million represents the value of the investment manager's portfolio, with a weight of 0.75 on stocks and 0.25 on bonds.

How do we calculate the return on this portfolio? The portfolio's return clearly involves an averaging of the returns on the stock and bond investments. The mean that we compute, however, needs to reflect the fact that stocks have a 75 percent weight in the portfolio and bonds have a 25 percent weight. The way to reflect this weighting is to multiply the return on the stock investment by 0.75 and the return on the bond investment by 0.25, and then sum the two results. This sum is an example of a weighted mean. By contrast with this calculation, our previous formulas for the arithmetic mean weighted all observations equally. Consider the following example, in which a portfolio manager maintains a portfolio of stocks and bonds for three years.

EXAMPLE 3-4. Portfolio Return as a Weighted Mean.

Determine the rate of return on a hypothetical stock and bond investment for 1996, 1997, and 1998. Use the total returns provided each year by the S&P 500 and long-term corporate bonds. Table 3-11 shows approximate total returns for these years.

TABLE 3-11 Total Returns for S&P 500 and Long-Term Bonds

Year	S&P 500 Total Return	Long-Term Corporate Bonds Total Return
1996	23%	1%
1997	33%	12%
1998	28%	10%

Source: Ibbotson EnCorr Analyzer™.

In January 1996, a portfolio manager decides to allocate $60 million to stocks and $40 million to bonds. During 1996, the portfolio earns the following dollar amounts:

Profit on stocks $= 0.23 \times \$ 60$ million $= \$13.8$ million

Profit on bonds $= 0.01 \times \$ 40$ million $= \underline{\$0.4 \text{ million}}$

Total profit for portfolio in 1996 $\qquad$ $\$14.2$ million

We can then divide the dollar profit by the initial investment of $100 million and arrive at a percentage rate of return of 14.2 percent.

A more direct way to determine the portfolio's rate of return, however, is to use the formula for the weighted mean. The weighted mean, $\bar{X}_w$ (read X-bar sub-w), for a set of observations $X_1, X_2, \ldots, X_n$ with corresponding weights of $w_1, w_2, \ldots, w_n$ is computed as

$$\bar{X}_w = \sum_{i=1}^{n} w_i X_i \qquad\qquad (3\text{-}5)$$

where the sum of the weights equals 1; that is, $\sum_i w_i = 1$. In the context of portfolios, a positive weight represents an asset held long and a negative weight represents an asset held short.

Continuing with our example for 1996, the portfolio return is the weighted average of the return on stocks and bonds. Using Equation 3-5, we find that

$$
\begin{aligned}
\text{Portfolio return for 1996} &= w_{stock}R_{stock} + w_{bonds}R_{bonds} \\
&= 0.60(23\%) + 0.40(1\%) \\
&= 14.2\%
\end{aligned}
$$

This result is the same as our previous calculation. Note that the correct mean to compute in this example is the weighted mean and not the arithmetic mean.[7] If we had computed the arithmetic mean for 1996, we would have calculated a return equal to $\frac{1}{2}(23\%) + \frac{1}{2}(1\%) = (23 + 1)/2 = 12\%$. Given that the portfolio manager invested 60 percent in stocks and 40 percent in bonds, the arithmetic mean would underweight the investment in stocks and overweight the investment in bonds, resulting in a number for portfolio return that is too low by 2.2 percentage points $(14.2\% - 12\%)$.

Now suppose that the portfolio manager maintains constant weights of 60 percent in stocks and 40 percent in bonds for all three years. This method is called a constant-proportions strategy. Because value is price times quantity, price fluctuation causes portfolio weights to change. As a result, the constant-proportion strategy requires rebalancing to restore the weights in stocks and bonds to their target levels. Assuming that the portfolio manager is able to accomplish the necessary rebalancing, we can compute the portfolio returns in 1997 and 1998 with Equation 3-5 as follows:

Portfolio return for 1997 = 0.60(33) + 0.40(12) = 24.60%

Portfolio return for 1998 = 0.60(28) + 0.40(10) = 20.80%

We can now find the time-series mean of the returns for 1996, 1997, and 1998 using Equation 3-2. The time-series mean total return is (14.20 + 24.60 + 20.80)/3 = 59.60/3 = 19.87 percent. We have used the standard arithmetic mean

---

[7] The formula for the weighted mean can be compared to the formula for the arithmetic mean. For a set of observations $X_1, X_2, \ldots, X_n$, let the weights $w_1, w_2, \ldots, w_n$ all equal $1/n$. Under this assumption, the formula for the weighted mean is $(1/n)\sum_{i=1}^{n} X_i$. This is the formula for the arithmetic mean.

Therefore, the arithmetic mean is a special case of the weighted mean where all the weights are equal.

formula here because we have no reason to presume that one year's outcome is more important than any other's.

Instead of calculating the portfolio time-series mean return from portfolio annual returns, we can calculate the mean bond and stock return for the three years and then apply the portfolio weights.

Year	Stock	Bond	Portfolio
1996	23	1	14.2
1997	33	12	24.6
1998	28	10	20.8
Mean	28	7.67	19.87*

*19.87 = (14.2 + 24.6 + 20.8)/3, or
19.87 = 0.6 × 28 + 0.4 × 7.67

The previous example illustrates the general principle that a portfolio return is a weighted sum. Specifically, a portfolio's return is the weighted average of the returns on the assets in the portfolio, where the weight applied to each asset's return is the fraction of the portfolio invested in that asset.

Market indexes are computed as weighted averages. For market-capitalization indexes such as the CAC-40 for France or the S&P 500 for the United States, each included stock receives a weight corresponding to its outstanding market value divided by the total market value of all stocks in the index.

Our illustrations of weighted mean use past data, but they might just as well have used forward-looking data. When we take a weighted average of forward-looking data, the weighted mean is called **expected value**. Suppose we make one forecast for the year-end level of the S&P 500 assuming economic expansion and another forecast for the year-end level of the S&P 500 assuming economic contraction. If we multiply the first forecast by the probability of expansion and the second forecast by the probability of contraction and then add these weighted forecasts, we are calculating the expected value of the S&P 500 at year-end. If we take a weighted average of possible future returns on the S&P 500, we are computing the S&P 500's expected return. Probabilities must sum to 1, satisfying the condition on the weights in the expression for weighted mean (Equation 3-5).

4.9 THE GEOMETRIC MEAN

Although analysts often compute arithmetic means, they also use geometric means—particularly when calculating returns over multiple periods. In the chapter on the time value of money, we worked through an earnings per share growth rate calculation (Example 1-18). That example illustrated one important case in which analysts use the geometric mean. In this section, we define and illustrate the geometric mean. In a later section, we will return to this important topic and offer practical perspectives on using the geometric and arithmetic means.

The standard formula for finding the **geometric mean**, G, of a set of observations X_1, $X_2, \ldots, X_n$ is

$$G = \sqrt[n]{X_1 \times X_2 \times X_3 \times \ldots \times X_n} \qquad (3\text{-}6)$$

Equation 3-6 has a solution only if the product under the radical sign is non-negative; so the geometric mean exists only if all the observations are greater than or equal to zero. We can solve for the geometric mean using Equation 3-6 directly with any calculator that has an exponentiation key (on most calculators, y^x). We can also solve for the geometric mean using natural logarithms. Equation 3-6 can also be stated as

$$\ln G = \frac{1}{n}\ln(X_1 \times X_2 \times X_3 \times \ldots \times X_n)$$

or as

$$\ln G = \frac{\sum_{i=1}^{n} \ln X_i}{n}$$

When we have computed $\ln G$, then $G = e^{\ln G}$ (on most calculators, the key for this step is e^x). Risky assets can have negative returns up to -100 percent (if their price falls to zero), so we must take some care in defining the relevant variables to average in computing a geometric mean. We cannot simply take the product of the returns for the sample and then take the nth root because the returns for any period could be negative. We must redefine the returns to make them positive. We do this by adding 1.0 to the returns. The term $(1 + R_t)$ represents the year-ending value relative to an initial unit of investment at the beginning of the year. As long as we use $(1 + R_t)$, the observations will never be negative because the biggest negative return is -100 percent.

We can now find the geometric mean return, R_G, using a slightly modified version of Equation 3-6:

$$1 + R_G = \sqrt[T]{(1 + R_1)(1 + R_2)\ldots(1 + R_T)} \text{ or}$$

$$1 + R_G = \left[\prod_{t=1}^{T}(1 + R_t)\right]^{\frac{1}{T}}$$

$$R_G = \left[\prod_{t=1}^{T}(1 + R_t)\right]^{\frac{1}{T}} - 1 \tag{3-7}$$

We can use Equation 3-7 to solve for the geometric mean return for any return data series. The next example illustrates the calculations involved in computing the geometric mean.

EXAMPLE 3-5.   A Comparison of the Geometric and Arithmetic Means.

Calculate the geometric and arithmetic mean returns for the S&P 500 for the period 1990 to 1992. The relevant data for the S&P 500 are reproduced below in Table 3-12.

TABLE 3-12   Total Returns for the S&P 500:
1990 to 1992

Year	Return
1990	−3.17%
1991	30.55%
1992	7.67%

Source: Ibbotson Associates.

As noted above, return data can be negative. Adding 1.0 to the three returns in Table 3-12 results in 0.9683, 1.3055, and 1.0767. We can use Equation 3-7 to find the geometric mean of the three rates of return:

$$1 + R_G = \sqrt[3]{0.9683 \times 1.3055 \times 1.0767} = \sqrt[3]{1.3610733} = 1.108223$$
$$R_G = 10.82\%$$

Now we can compare the geometric mean to the arithmetic mean. The arithmetic mean return for the S&P 500 is $(-3.17\% + 30.55\% + 7.67\%)/3 = 11.68\%$. Why are these results different? The geometric mean will always be less than or equal to the arithmetic mean because of a mathematical result known as Jensen's inequality. In general, the difference between the two means increases with the variability in the period-by-period observations. In fact, the only time that the two means will be equal is when there is no variability in the observations; that is, when all the observations in the series are the same. For instance, suppose the return for each of the three years is 10 percent. The arithmetic mean is 10 percent. To find the geometric mean, we first express the returns as $(1 + R_t)$ and then find the geometric mean: $\sqrt[3]{1.10 \times 1.10 \times 1.10} - 1 = 10$ percent.

Arithmetic and geometric means both have a role to play in investment management. Both geometric and arithmetic means are often reported for return series.

Now we look at one more example that illustrates the difference between the two types of means.

EXAMPLE 3-6.   The Compound Rate of Return as a Geometric Mean.

A hypothetical investment in a single stock initially costs €100. One year later, the stock is trading at €200. At the end of the second year, the stock price falls back to the original purchase price of €100. No dividends are paid during the two-year period. Calculate the arithmetic and geometric mean annual returns.

First, we need to find the Year 1 and Year 2 annual returns with Equation 3-1.

Return in Year 1 $= 200/100 - 1 = 100\%$

Return in Year 2 $= 100/200 - 1 = -50\%$

The arithmetic mean of the annual returns is $(100\% - 50\%)/2 = 25\%$.

Before we find the geometric mean, we must convert the percentage rates of return to $(1 + R_t)$. After making this adjustment, the geometric mean from Equation 3-7 is $\sqrt{2.0 \times 0.50} - 1 = 0$ percent.

From this example we should note two points. First, because returns are variable by period, the arithmetic mean is greater than the geometric mean, consistent with our earlier discussion. Second, the geometric mean return of 0 percent accurately reflects that the ending value of the investment in Year 2 equals the starting value in Year 1. The compound rate of return on the investment is 0 percent. In general, when we need to calculate a compound rate of return or growth rate, we use the geometric mean.

In the next example, we compute three different measures of location and the frequency distribution for a small set of monthly returns.

EXAMPLE 3-7.   Descriptive Statistics for a Monthly Return Series.

Compute the arithmetic mean, median, and geometric mean of the monthly returns on the MSCI EAFE Index from April 1998 to March 1999. Also compute the frequency distributions (cumulative and relative) of the 12 returns with return intervals starting at −12 percent with increments of 6 percent. The returns are reported in Table 3-13.

TABLE 3-13   Monthly Returns on the MSCI EAFE Index:
April 1998 to March 1999

Month	Return (%)
April 1998	0.90
May 1998	−0.46
June 1998	0.78
July 1998	1.00
August 1998	−12.00
September 1998	−3.04
October 1998	10.45
November 1998	5.00
December 1998	4.00
January 1999	−0.25
February 1999	−2.00
March 1999	4.50

Source: Ibbotson Associates.

To find the arithmetic mean, we sum the observations and divide by 12. Over this one-year period, the arithmetic mean is 0.74 percent.

To find the geometric mean, we must first convert the returns to $(1 + R_t)$. Because the return data are expressed in percentage form, we must divide by 100 and then add 1. For example, for the April 1998 return of 0.90 percent, we find the value $(1 + R_t)$ as $0.90/100 + 1 = 1.0090$. This value is the first entry under the column "1 + Return" in Table 3-14. To finish calculating the geometric mean, we need to find the product of all the values in the last column. This product is 1.07474. We now find the geometric mean with natural logarithms as follows:

$$\ln G = \ln(1.07474)/12 = 0.072078/12 = 0.0060065$$

To find the geometric mean, G, we raise the constant e to this power and subtract 1:

$$G = \exp(0.0060065) - 1.00 = 1.006024 - 1 = 0.6024 \text{ percent}$$

As expected, the geometric mean is less than the arithmetic mean.

To find the median of the returns, we must first sort the data into either ascending or descending order. The sorted return data are as follows: −12.00, −3.04, −2.00, −0.46, −0.25, 0.78, 0.90, 1.00, 4.00, 4.50, 5.00, 10.45. Because we have an

TABLE 3-14   Calculation of Arithmetic and Geometric Means

Month	Return (%)	1 + Return
April 1998	0.90	1.0090
May 1998	−0.46	0.9954
June 1998	0.78	1.0078
July 1998	1.00	1.0100
August 1998	−12.00	0.8800
September 1998	−3.04	0.9696
October 1998	10.45	1.1045
November 1998	5.00	1.0500
December 1998	4.00	1.0400
January 1999	−0.25	0.9975
February 1999	−2.00	0.9800
March 1999	4.50	1.0450
Sum of Returns (%)	8.88	
Arithmetic Mean (%)	0.74	
Product of (1 + Return)		1.0747
Geometric Mean (%)		0.60

even number of observations, the median is the average of the sixth and seventh observations. The median is therefore equal to $(0.78 + 0.90)/2 = 0.84$ percent.

We construct the frequency distribution of the returns by counting the number of returns that fall in the following intervals: -12 percent $\leq$ return < -6 percent, -6 percent $\leq$ return < 0 percent, 0 percent $\leq$ return < 6 percent, and 6 percent $\leq$ return ≤ 12 percent. Table 3-15 shows the frequency distribution.

TABLE 3-15   Frequency Distribution for the MSCI EAFE Index

Return Interval	Absolute Frequency	Relative Frequency	Cumulative Absolute Frequency	Cumulative Relative Frequency
−12.0% to −6.0%	1	8.33%	1	8.33%
−6.0% to 0.0%	4	33.33%	5	41.67%
0.0% to 6.0%	6	50.00%	11	91.67%
6.0% to 12.0%	1	8.34%*	12	100.00%

*Note: This number has been rounded to 8.34 so that the relative frequencies sum to 100 percent.

The relative frequency (shown in the third column) is calculated by dividing the absolute frequency by the total number of observations. For example, the relative frequency for the second return interval (-6 percent to 0 percent) is $4/12 = 1/3$ or 33.33 percent. To calculate the cumulative frequency, we add the absolute

> frequencies. For the first return interval, the cumulative frequency is 1.0 because
> only the −12 percent return is less than the −6 percent upper return interval limit.
> To find the cumulative frequency for the other return intervals, we add the inter-
> val's absolute frequency to the previous interval's cumulative frequency. The cu-
> mulative relative frequency in the last column results from dividing the cumulative
> frequency by the total number of observations.

5   MEASURES OF DISPERSION AND THEIR APPLICATIONS

As the well-known researcher Fischer Black has written, "[t]he key issue in investments is estimating expected return."[8] Few would disagree with the importance of expected return or mean return in investments: The mean return tells us where returns, and investment results, are centered. To completely understand an investment, however, we also need to know how returns are dispersed around the mean. **Dispersion** is the variability around the central tendency. If mean return addresses reward, dispersion addresses risk.

In this section we examine the most common measures of dispersion: range, mean absolute deviation, variance, and standard deviation. These are all measures of **absolute dispersion**. Absolute dispersion is the amount of variability present without comparison to any reference point or benchmark.

These measures are used throughout investment practice. The variance or standard deviation of return is often used as a measure of risk. As you will see in the chapter on probability, the pioneering work by Nobel laureate Harry Markowitz on modern portfolio theory (MPT) takes account of both variance of return and mean return. Later in this chapter, we will introduce a risk-adjusted measure of performance named after William Sharpe, another winner of the Nobel Prize in economics. That measure makes use of standard deviation of return. Other measures of dispersion, mean absolute deviation and range, are also useful in analyzing data.

5.1   THE RANGE

The simplest of all the measures of dispersion, the **range** can be computed with interval or ratio data. The range is the difference between the maximum and minimum values in a data set:

$$\text{Range} = \text{Maximum value} - \text{Minimum value} \tag{3-8}$$

For example, the largest monthly return for the S&P 500 from January 1926 to March 1999 is 42.56 percent and the smallest is −29.73 percent. The range of returns is therefore 72.29 percent [42.56 percent −(−29.73 percent)]. An alternative definition of the range reports the maximum and minimum values. This alternative definition provides more information than does the range in Equation 3-8.

One advantage of the range is ease of computation. A disadvantage is that the range uses only two pieces of information from the distribution. The range cannot tell us how the data are distributed (that is, the shape of the distribution). Because the range is the difference between the maximum and minimum returns, it can reflect extremely large or small outcomes that may not be representative of the distribution.

---

[8] Black (1993).

5.2 THE MEAN ABSOLUTE DEVIATION

Measures of dispersion can be computed using all the observations in the distribution rather than just the highest and lowest. The question is: How should we measure dispersion? Our previous discussion on properties of the arithmetic mean introduced the notion of distance or deviation from the mean $(X_i - \overline{X})$ as a fundamental piece of information used in statistics. We could compute measures of dispersion as the arithmetic average of the deviations around the mean, but we would encounter a problem: The deviations around the mean always sum to 0. If we computed the mean of the deviations, the result would also equal 0. Therefore, before we compute the average of the deviations around the mean, we must adjust the deviations.

One solution is to examine the absolute deviations around the mean. The mean absolute deviation (MAD) for a sample is defined as follows:

$$\text{MAD} = \frac{\sum_{i=1}^{n} \left| X_i - \overline{X} \right|}{n} \tag{3-9}$$

In calculating MAD, we ignore the signs of the deviations around the mean. The mean absolute deviation uses all of the observations in the sample and is therefore superior to the range as a measure of dispersion.

5.3 POPULATION VARIANCE AND STANDARD DEVIATION

Another way to measure dispersion is to examine the squared deviations around the mean. The variance and standard deviation, which are based on squared deviations, are the two most widely used measures of dispersion. **Variance** is defined as the average of the squared deviations around the mean. The **standard deviation** is the square root of the variance. Later in this section, we will present an important result in statistical theory that provides justification for using the standard deviation as a measure of dispersion.

5.3.1 POPULATION VARIANCE

If we have every member of a population, we can compute the population variance. Denoted by the symbol σ^2, the population variance is the arithmetic average of the squared deviations around the mean. The formula for the population variance is

$$\sigma^2 = \frac{\sum_{i=1}^{N} (X_i - \mu)^2}{N} \tag{3-10}$$

where N is the number of observations in the population.

Although Equation 3-10 is most commonly used to compute the population variance, the following alternative formula is sometimes used because it does not require calculating deviations:

$$\sigma^2 = \frac{\sum_{i=1}^{N} X_i^2}{N} - \left(\frac{\sum_{i=1}^{N} X_i}{N} \right)^2 = \frac{\sum_{i=1}^{N} X_i^2}{N} - \mu^2 \tag{3-11}$$

5.3.2 POPULATION STANDARD DEVIATION

Because the variance is measured in squared units, we must find a way to return to the original units. We can solve this problem by using standard deviation, the square root of the variance. The formula for the population standard deviation is as follows:

$$\sigma = \sqrt{\frac{\sum_{i=1}^{N}(X_i - \mu)^2}{N}} \qquad \text{or} \qquad \sigma = \sqrt{\frac{\sum_{i=1}^{N}X_i^2}{N} - \left(\frac{\sum_{i=1}^{N}X_i}{N}\right)^2} \qquad (3\text{-}12)$$

Both the population variance and standard deviation are examples of parameters of a distribution. In later chapters, we will introduce the notion of variance and standard deviation as risk measures.

5.4 SAMPLE VARIANCE AND STANDARD DEVIATION

5.4.1 SAMPLE VARIANCE

In many instances in investment management, a subset or sample of the population is all that we can observe. When we deal with samples, the summary measures are called statistics. The statistic that measures the dispersion in a sample is called the sample variance. The formula for the sample variance involves a slight change in notation, as follows:

$$s^2 = \frac{\sum_{i=1}^{n}(X_i - \overline{X})^2}{n - 1} \qquad (3\text{-}13)$$

We can express this formula in an alternative way, as we did for the population variance:

$$s^2 = \frac{\sum_{i=1}^{n}X_i^2 - \dfrac{\left(\sum_{i=1}^{n}X_i\right)^2}{n}}{n - 1} \qquad (3\text{-}14)$$

We use s^2 for the sample variance to distinguish it from the population variance, σ^2. The formula for the sample variance is nearly the same as that for population variance except for the use of the sample mean, $\overline{X}$, and the divisor. In the case of the population variance, we divide by the size of the population, N. For the sample variance, however, we divide by the sample size minus 1, or $n - 1$. By using $n - 1$ (rather than n) as the divisor, we improve the statistical properties of the sample variance. In statistical terms, the sample variance defined in Equation 3-13 is an unbiased estimator of the population variance.[9] We also refer to the term $n - 1$ as the degrees of freedom. Once the sample mean is calculated, there are only $n - 1$ independent deviations from it.

5.4.2 SAMPLE STANDARD DEVIATION

Just as we computed a population standard deviation, we can compute a sample standard deviation by taking the positive square root of the sample variance. The sample standard deviation, s, is defined as

$$s = \sqrt{\frac{\sum_{i=1}^{n}(X_i - \overline{X})^2}{n - 1}} \qquad (3\text{-}15)$$

---

[9] This concept is discussed further in the chapter on sampling.

This formula can be restated as

$$s = \sqrt{\frac{\sum_{i=1}^{n} X_i^2 - \frac{\left(\sum_{i=1}^{n} X_i\right)^2}{n}}{n-1}} \qquad (3\text{-}16)$$

We now show an example that uses 12 monthly total returns on the MSCI EAFE index for 1990. This example illustrates how to find the sample variance and the mean absolute deviation.

EXAMPLE 3-8.   Calculating Measures of Dispersion.

Calculate the sample variance with Equations 3-13 and 3-14. Calculate the mean absolute deviation (MAD) with Equation 3-9. Use the data in Table 3-16, which provides monthly total returns for the MSCI EAFE Index during 1990.

Table 3-16   Calculation of Variability Measures for the MSCI EAFE Index: January 1990 to December 1990

Month	Return R_i (%)	Return Deviation $R_i - \bar{R}$	Squared Return Deviation $(R_i - \bar{R})^2$	Squared Return R_i^2	Absolute Return Deviation $|R_i - \bar{R}|$
January 1990	−3.7	−1.9	3.61	13.69	1.9
February 1990	−7.0	−5.2	27.04	49.00	5.2
March 1990	−10.4	−8.6	73.96	108.16	8.6
April 1990	−0.8	1.0	1.00	0.64	1.0
May 1990	11.4	13.2	174.24	129.96	13.2
June 1990	−0.9	0.9	0.81	0.81	0.9
July 1990	2.0	3.8	14.44	4.00	3.8
August 1990	−9.7	−7.9	62.41	94.09	7.9
September 1990	−13.9	−12.1	146.41	193.21	12.1
October 1990	15.6	17.4	302.76	243.36	17.4
November 1990	−5.9	−4.1	16.81	34.81	4.1
December 1990	1.7	3.5	12.25	2.89	3.5
Sum	−21.6	0	835.74	874.62	79.6
Mean (see note)	−1.8		75.98		MAD = 6.63
Standard deviation			8.72		

Source: Ibbotson Associates.

Note: The divisor is 11 for standard deviation, 12 for MAD.

(a) Variance Using Equation 3-13. To compute the sample variance using Equation 3-13, follow these steps: (i) calculate the sample mean, (ii) determine each observation's deviation from the sample mean, (iii) square all the deviations from the sample mean, (iv) sum the squared deviations, and (v) divide the sum by $n - 1$.

(i) We find the sample mean by taking the sum of -21.60 percent and dividing by 12; the result is -1.80 percent. (ii) We now subtract the mean return from each observation. These values are reported in the Return Deviation column. As you can see, some of the values lie above the mean (they have positive deviations) and other observations lie below the mean (they have negative deviations), so the sum of the deviations is 0. (iii) Next, we square each deviation from the mean. These values are reported in the Squared Return Deviation column. (Recall that squaring deviations eliminates the problem of positive and negative deviations canceling. For example, the first deviation is -1.9 percent, and its squared value is 3.61 percent squared.) (iv) Now we sum the squared deviations from the mean. This sum, 835.74, is reported at the bottom of the column. (v) Finally, we divide the sum of squared deviations, 835.74, by $n - 1$ (that is, 11). The sample variance is thus 75.98 percent squared.

(b) Variance Using Equation 3-14. To find the sample variance with Equation 3-14, we find the sum of the squared returns. These values are reported in the Squared Return column of Table 3-16. The sum of the squared returns is 874.62. The sum of the returns, reported at the bottom of the Returns column, is -21.6.

Therefore, the variance is $\dfrac{874.62 - \dfrac{(-21.6)^2}{12}}{11} = 75.98$. This is the same result that we found when using the squared deviations from the mean.

(c) Mean Absolute Deviation Using Equation 3-9. To compute MAD, we follow steps (i) and (ii) for computing the sample variance. Next, we find each deviation's absolute value. Then we compute the mean of the absolute deviations.

(i) As above, we find that the sample mean is -1.80. (ii) We find the deviations from the mean reported in the Return Deviation column. (iii) We convert each deviation to its absolute value, shown in the last column. (iv) We compute the mean of the absolute deviations by dividing the sum of the absolute values, 79.6, by 12. The resulting MAD is 6.63 percent.

Note that the mean absolute deviation is less than the standard deviation. The mean absolute deviation will always be less than or equal to the standard deviation because the standard deviation gives more weight to large deviations than to small ones (remember, the deviations are squared).

5.5 CHEBYSHEV'S INEQUALITY

The Russian mathematician Chebyshev developed an inequality using standard deviation as a measure of dispersion. **Chebyshev's inequality** gives the proportion of elements within k standard deviations of the mean. This inequality holds for samples and populations and for discrete and continuous data regardless of the shape of the distribution.

> *Chebyshev's inequality:* Let k be any positive constant greater than 1. The proportion of the observations within k standard deviations of the mean is at least $1 - 1/k^2$ for all $k > 1$.

Table 3-17 illustrates the proportion of the observations that must lie within a certain number of standard deviations around the sample mean.

Table 3-17   Proportions from Chebyshev's Inequality

k	Interval Around the Sample Mean	Proportion
1.25	$\overline{X} \pm 1.25s$	36%
1.50	$\overline{X} \pm 1.50s$	56%
2	$\overline{X} \pm 2s$	75%
2.50	$\overline{X} \pm 2.50s$	84%
3	$\overline{X} \pm 3s$	89%
4	$\overline{X} \pm 4s$	94%

Note: Standard deviation is denoted as *s*.

When $k = 1.25$, for example, the inequality states that the minimum proportion of the observations that lie within ± 1.25 s is $1 - 1/(1.25)^2 = 1 - 0.64 = 0.36$, or 36 percent. Looking at the last row, we can see that at least 94 percent of the observations must lie within four standard deviations of the sample mean. Thus, if we know the standard deviation, we can use Chebyshev's inequality to measure the minimum amount of dispersion regardless of the shape of the distribution.

The next example illustrates the inequality for the small set of monthly returns on the MSCI EAFE Index for 1990.

EXAMPLE 3-9.   Calculating Chebyshev's Inequality.

Use the 12 monthly returns from the previous example in Table 3-16 and compute the minimum proportion with $k = 2$.

For $k = 2$, Chebyshev's inequality states that at least 75 percent of the observations must lie within two standard deviations of the mean. (That is, $1 - 1/2^2 = 0.75$.) Algebraically, we can say that 75 percent of the observations must lie in the interval $\overline{X} \pm 2s$. Using the data from Table 3-16, we see that the mean return is -1.8 percent and the standard deviation is 8.72 percent. Therefore, the interval for the Chebyshev inequality is $-1.8\% \pm 2 \times 8.72\% = -1.8\% \pm 17.44\%$ or a range of -19.24 percent to 15.64 percent. For a sample size of 12, at least 0.75×12 or nine observations must lie in this interval. Looking back at Table 3-16, you can see that all of the returns lie within this interval, thus satisfying Chebyshev's inequality.

5.6 RELATIVE DISPERSION

If we calculate a measure of dispersion (for example, the standard deviation) for two different distributions, we may encounter problems comparing them. The difference between the dispersion for the monthly returns on T-bills and the dispersion for a portfolio of small stocks is not meaningful because the means of the distributions are far apart. One way to overcome this problem is to standardize the measure of absolute dispersion. **Relative dispersion** is the amount of variability present in comparison to a reference point or benchmark.

A common measure of relative dispersion is the **coefficient of variation,** CV, defined as

$$CV = \frac{s}{\overline{X}} \tag{3-17}$$

The coefficient of variation expresses how much dispersion exists relative to the mean of the distribution, and thus allows for direct comparison of dispersion across different data sets. Because the standard deviation and the mean are measured in the same units, the coefficient of variation is free of scale. For example, the S&P 500 has had a historical mean annual return of about 12 percent with a standard deviation of 20 percent. The historical coefficient of variation is the standard deviation divided by its mean: 20%/12% = 1.67.

The coefficient of variation for various return distributions is shown in the following example using the monthly mean returns and standard deviations for U.S. Treasury bills, the S&P 500, and small U.S. stocks for the period January 1926 to March 1999.[10]

EXAMPLE 3-10.   Calculating the Coefficient of Variation.

Find the coefficient of variation using Equation 3-17. The mean monthly return on T-bills is 0.31 percent with a standard deviation of 0.26 percent. For the S&P 500, the mean is 1.05 percent with a standard deviation of 5.66 percent. The mean monthly return on the portfolio of small U.S. stocks is 1.32 percent with a standard deviation of 8.63 percent.

Although the standard deviations of the three series are measured in the same units, they are not directly comparable. The small-stock portfolio has the larger standard deviation but its returns, on average, are bigger than the returns on T-bills. For this example, we calculate the coefficient of variation for T-bills, small stocks, and the S&P 500 as follows:

$$\text{T-bills: } \frac{0.26}{0.31} = 0.84 \qquad \text{S\&P 500: } \frac{5.66}{1.05} = 5.39 \qquad \text{Small stocks: } \frac{8.63}{1.32} = 6.54$$

The results show that T-bill returns are not only absolutely less variable but also relatively less variable than stock returns. Similarly, the S&P 500 returns are relatively less dispersed than small-stock returns over this period. Note, however, that the coefficients of variation reveal less difference between small-stock and S&P 500 return variability than that suggested by the standard deviations alone.

Before we leave the discussion on dispersion, we show an extended problem using the monthly return data on the MSCI EAFE Index from Example 3-7.

EXAMPLE 3-11.   Absolute and Relative Dispersion of an Index Return Series.

With the monthly return data from Example 3-7 (which are shown in Table 3-18), compute (a) the variance of returns, (b) the coefficient of variation, and (c) the range.

(a) The calculations for the variance appear in Table 3-18. The third column shows the calculations needed to compute the sample variance. The entries in this column are the squared deviations from the mean of 0.74 percent. For example, for April 1998, the squared value is $(0.90 - 0.74)^2 = 0.02560$. The sample variance is equal to the sum of the squared deviations from the mean, 323.82, divided by 11 = 29.44, and the standard deviation is 5.43 percent.

(b) The coefficient of variation is the ratio of the standard deviation to the mean. The coefficient of variation is equal to 5.43%/0.74% = 7.34.

---

[10] Source: Ibbotson Associates.

(c) The range of returns is the maximum return minus the minimum return. The range is $10.45\% - (-12.00\%) = 22.45\%$.

Table 3-18   Calculation of the Variance for the MSCI EAFE Index: April 1998 to March 1999

Month	Return (%)	$(R_i - \bar{R})^2$
April 1998	0.90	0.0256
May 1998	−0.46	1.4400
June 1998	0.78	0.0016
July 1998	1.00	0.0676
August 1998	−12.00	162.3076
September 1998	−3.04	14.2884
October 1998	10.45	94.2841
November 1998	5.00	18.1476
December 1998	4.00	10.6276
January 1999	−0.25	0.9801
February 1999	−2.00	7.5076
March 1999	4.50	14.1376
Sum	8.88	323.82
Mean	0.74	
Variance		29.44

Source: Ibbotson Associates.

5.7 THE SHARPE MEASURE OF RISK-ADJUSTED PERFORMANCE

Although the coefficient of variation was designed as a measure of relative dispersion, its inverse reveals something about return per unit of risk because the standard deviation of returns is commonly used as a measure of investment risk. For example, a portfolio with a mean monthly return of 1.19 percent and a standard deviation of 4.42 percent has an inverse coefficient of variation of $1.19\%/4.42\% = 0.27$. This indicates that each unit of standard deviation provides a 0.27 percent return.

A more precise return-risk measure recognizes the existence of a risk-free return, a return for virtually zero standard deviation. The **Sharpe measure** or ratio for a portfolio, p, is defined as

$$\frac{\bar{r}_p - \bar{r}_f}{\sigma_p} \tag{3-18}$$

where $\bar{r}_f$ is the mean return to a risk-free asset.

The numerator of the Sharpe measure is the portfolio's mean return minus the mean return on the risk-free asset over the sample period. The term $(\bar{r}_p - \bar{r}_f)$ measures the extra reward that investors receive for the added risk taken. We call this difference the **excess return** on portfolio p. Portfolios with large Sharpe ratios are preferred to those with smaller ratios because we assume that investors prefer return and dislike risk.

In the following example, we demonstrate how to calculate the Sharpe ratio for the S&P 500.

EXAMPLE 3-12.   Calculating the Sharpe Ratio.

Over the period January 1972 to March 1999, the mean monthly return on T-bills (the risk-free rate) was 0.55 percent. The S&P 500 mean monthly return over this period was 1.19 percent with a standard deviation of 4.42 percent. We can compute the Sharpe ratio for the S&P 500 with Equation 3-18 as $(1.19 - 0.55)/4.42 = 0.14$. The Sharpe ratio tells us how much extra return (beyond the return on bills) the S&P 500 earned per unit of risk, where risk is measured by standard deviation.

---

6 SYMMETRY AND SKEWNESS IN RETURN DISTRIBUTIONS.

The mean and variance may not adequately describe the distribution of returns. In calculations of the variance, for example, the deviations around the mean are squared, so we do not know whether large deviations are likely to be positive or negative. We need to go beyond measures of central tendency and dispersion to reveal other important characteristics of the distribution. One important characteristic of interest to analysts is the degree of symmetry in return distributions.

If a return distribution is symmetrical about its mean, then each side of the distribution is a mirror image of the other. Thus, equal loss and gain intervals exhibit the same frequencies. Losses from -5 percent to -3 percent, for example, occur with about the same frequency as gains from 3 percent to 5 percent.

One of the most important distributions is the normal distribution, depicted in Figure 3-6. This symmetrical, bell-shaped distribution plays a central role in the mean–variance model of portfolio selection; it is also used extensively in **financial risk management**. The normal distribution has the following characteristics:

- Its mean and median are equal.
- It is completely described by two parameters—its mean and variance.
- Roughly 66 percent of its observations lie between plus and minus one standard deviation from the mean; 95 percent lie between plus and minus two standard deviations; and 99 percent lie between plus and minus three standard deviations.

A distribution that is not symmetrical is called **skewed**. A positively skewed distribution is characterized by many small losses and a few extreme gains. A negatively skewed distribution is characterized by many small gains and a few extreme losses. Figure 3-7 shows positively and negatively skewed distributions. The positively skewed distribution shown has a long tail on its right side; the negatively skewed distribution has a long tail on its left side. For the positively skewed distribution, the mode is less than the median, which is less than the mean. For the negatively skewed distribution, the mean is less than the median, which is less than the mode. Investors should be attracted by positive skewness because the mean return falls above the median. Relative to the mean return, positive skewness amounts to a limited, though frequent, downside compared with a somewhat unlimited, but less frequent, upside.

FIGURE 3-6   Properties of a Normal Distribution (EV = Expected Value)

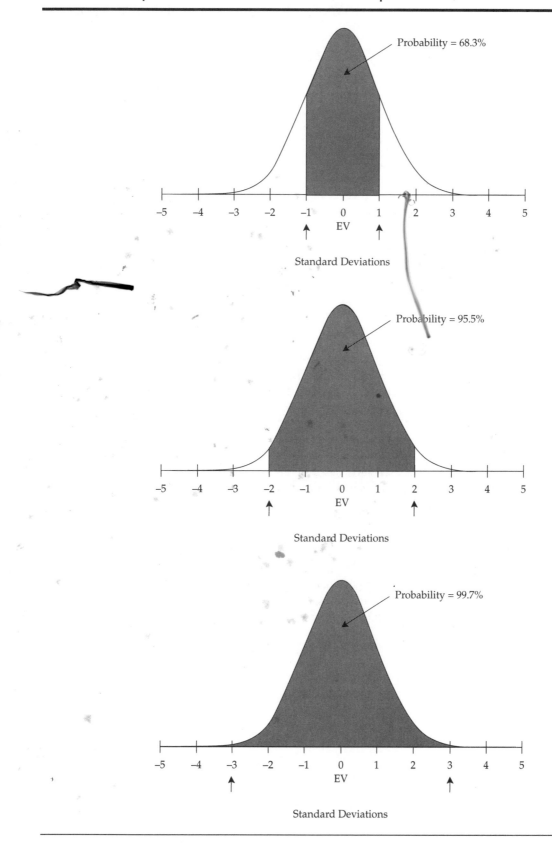

FIGURE 3-7   Properties of a Skewed Distribution

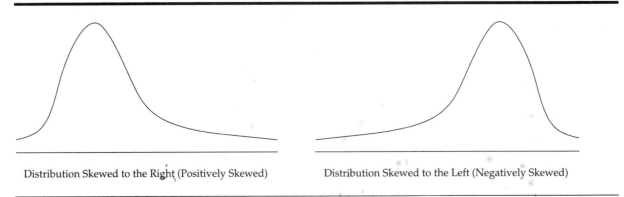

Distribution Skewed to the Right (Positively Skewed)   Distribution Skewed to the Left (Negatively Skewed)

Reprinted with permission from *Fixed Income Readings*
for the Chartered Financial Analyst® *Program.*
Copyright 2000, Frank J. Fabozzi Associates, New Hope, PA.

Skewness is computed in much the same way as variance: by using each observation's deviation from its mean. Absolute skewness is computed as the average cubed deviation from the mean. Cubing, unlike squaring, preserves the sign of the deviation. If a distribution is positively skewed with a mean greater than its median, then more than half of the deviations from the mean are negative and fewer than half are positive. In order for the sum to be positive, the losses must be small and likely, and the gains less likely but more extreme. Thus, if skewness is positive, the average magnitude of positive deviations is larger than the average magnitude of negative deviations.

A simple example with symmetrically distributed data can illustrate how to calculate skewness. Suppose we have the following data: 1, 2, 3, 4, 5, 6, 7, 8, 9. The mean outcome is 5, and the deviations are $-4, -3, -2, -1, 0, 1, 2, 3, 4$. Cubing the deviations yields $-64, -27, -8, -1, 0, 1, 8, 27$, and 64, with a sum of 0. Absolute skewness is thus equal to 0, as we would expect with symmetrically distributed data. Absolute skewness is measured in the units of the original data cubed. Dividing absolute skewness by the standard deviation cubed yields relative skewness, which is free of scale.

The formula for sample relative skewness is

$$S_K = \frac{n}{(n-1)(n-2)} \frac{\sum_{i=1}^{n}(X_i - \overline{X})^3}{s^3} \tag{3-19}$$

where n is the number of observations in the sample and s is the sample standard deviation.[11] We refer to S_K as the skewness coefficient, or skewness, for short. Note that as n gets large, the expression reduces to the mean cubed deviation, $S_K \approx \frac{1}{n} \frac{\sum_{i=1}^{n}(X_i - \overline{X})^3}{s^3}$. As a frame of reference, for a sample size of 100 or larger taken from a normal distribution, a skewness coefficient of ± 0.5 would be considered unusually large.

---

[11] The term $n/(n-1)(n-2)$ in Equation 3-19 corrects for a downward bias in small samples.

EXAMPLE 3-13. Calculating Skewness.

Compute the skewness for the monthly returns on the MSCI EAFE index for 1990 with Equation 3-19. Use Table 3-19, which reproduces the returns, the deviations from the mean return of -1.8 percent, and the cubed value of the deviations.

To calculate skewness, we find the sum of the cubed deviations, divide by the standard deviation cubed, and then multiply by $n/(n - 1)(n - 2)$. The sum of the cubed deviations is 4,550.424. The standard deviation, as we found earlier, is 8.72. Now we find the skewness by substituting the appropriate numbers into Equation 3-19:

$$S_K = \frac{12}{11 \times 10} \times \frac{4550.424}{8.72^3} = 0.749$$

The distribution appears to be positively skewed.

In this example, six deviations are negative and six are positive. Two rather large positive deviations heavily influence the sum of the cubed deviations. For the May 1990 observation (11.4 percent), the deviation is 13.2 with a cube of 2,299.968. For the October 1990 observation (15.6), the deviation is 17.4 with a cube of 5,268.024. Overall, the skewness is positive. The mean return (-1.8 percent) is also greater than the median return (-2.3 percent), revealing that more than half of the observations lie below the mean. If two return distributions are the same except for skewness (for example, if they have the same mean and standard deviation), investors would prefer the distribution with positive skewness because that distribution implies a greater probability of extremely large gains. If we found positive sample skewness to be representative of the overall population, then investors would view this outcome as favorable. Obviously, however, we do not want to draw too many conclusions from only 12 observations. This example simply demonstrates the mechanics and interpretation of skewness.

Table 3-19 Calculating Skewness for the MSCI EAFE Index: January 1990 to December 1990

Month	R_t (%)	$R_t - \overline{R}$	$(R_t - \overline{R})^3$
January 1990	-3.7	-1.9	-6.859
February 1990	-7.0	-5.2	-140.608
March 1990	-10.4	-8.6	-636.056
April 1990	-0.8	1.0	1.000
May 1990	11.4	13.2	2299.968
June 1990	-0.9	0.9	0.729
July 1990	2.0	3.8	54.872
August 1990	-9.7	-7.9	-493.039
September 1990	-13.9	-12.1	-1771.561
October 1990	15.6	17.4	5268.024
November 1990	-5.9	-4.1	-68.921
December 1990	1.7	3.5	42.875
Sum	-21.6	0.0	4,550.424
Standard deviation	8.72		
Skewness	0.749		

Source: Ibbotson Associates.

7 KURTOSIS IN RETURN DISTRIBUTIONS

In the previous section, we discussed how to determine whether a return distribution deviates from a normal distribution because of asymmetry. One other way in which a return distribution might differ from a normal distribution is by having more returns clustered closely around the mean (being more peaked) and more returns with large deviations from the mean (having fatter tails). Relative to a normal distribution, such a distribution has a greater percentage of small deviations from the mean return (more small surprises) and a greater percentage of extremely large deviations from the mean return (more big surprises). Most investors would perceive a greater chance of extremely large deviations from the mean as increasing risk.

Kurtosis is the statistical measure that tells us when a distribution is more or less peaked than a normal distribution. A distribution that is more peaked than normal is called **leptokurtic** (*lepto* from the Greek word for slender), and a distribution that is less peaked than normal is called **platykurtic** (*platy* from the Greek word for broad). A normal distribution is called mesokurtic (*meso* from the Greek word for middle).

Figure 3-8 illustrates a leptokurtic distribution. It is more peaked and has fatter tails than the normal distribution.

The calculation for kurtosis is similar to that for skewness: we find the average deviation from the mean, raise the average deviation to the fourth power, and then divide by the

FIGURE 3-8   Leptokurtic: Fat Tailed

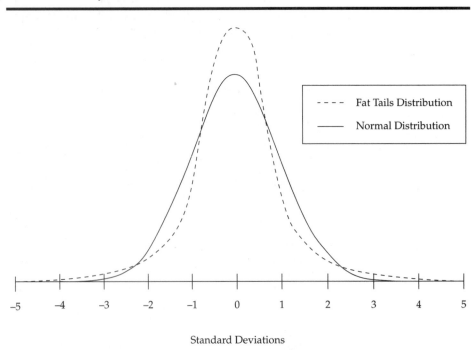

Standard Deviations

standard deviation raised to the fourth power.[12] For all normal distributions, kurtosis is equal to 3. Many statistical packages, however, report **excess kurtosis**, which is kurtosis minus 3. A normal distribution thus has excess kurtosis equal to 0, and a leptokurtic distribution has excess kurtosis greater than 0. (Platykurtic distributions have excess kurtosis less than 0.)

Sample excess kurtosis is computed as follows:

$$\left(\frac{n(n+1)}{(n-1)(n-2)(n-3)} \times \frac{\sum_{i=1}^{n}(X_i - \bar{X})^4}{s^4} \right) - \frac{3(n-1)^2}{(n-2)(n-3)} \tag{3-20}$$

where n is the sample size and s is the sample standard deviation. Note that as n becomes large, Equation 3-20 approximately equals

$$\frac{n^2}{n^3} \times \frac{\sum (X - \bar{X})^4}{s^4} - \frac{3n^2}{n^2} = \frac{1}{n} \frac{\sum (X - \bar{X})^4}{s^4} - 3$$

For a sample of 100 or larger taken from a normal distribution, a sample excess kurtosis of 1.0 or larger would be considered unusually large.

If a return distribution has positive excess kurtosis (leptokurtosis) and we use statistical models that do not account for the fatter tails, we will underestimate the likelihood of very bad or very good outcomes. For example, the return on the S&P 500 for October 19, 1987, was 20 standard deviations away from the mean daily return. Such an outcome is possible with a normal distribution, but its likelihood is almost equal to 0. If daily returns are drawn from a normal distribution, a return four standard deviations or more away from the mean is expected once every 50 years; a return greater than five standard deviations away is expected once every 7,000 years. The return for October 1987 is more likely to have come from a distribution that had fatter tails than a normal distribution.

An important question for anyone managing risk is: Under normal market conditions, what is our maximum likely loss over a particular time horizon? Quantitative analysts have developed a tool called **Value at Risk** (VaR) to provide an answer to this question. One-day VaR, for example, is an estimate of a particular dollar loss that can occur over one day. We expect a dollar loss as large or larger than one-day VaR to occur on a specified small fraction of days (1 out of 100 is a common specification). Analysts often assume a normal distribution of returns when calculating VaR. If returns are not normally distributed, however, then a VaR based on the normal distribution will underestimate the chances of a large loss.

The following example illustrates the calculations for excess kurtosis for the MSCI EAFE's monthly returns from 1990 using Equation 3-20.

EXAMPLE 3-14. Calculating Excess Kurtosis.

Using Equation 3-20, compute the excess kurtosis for the 12 monthly returns for the MSCI EAFE index from 1990 as presented in Table 3-16.

To find the excess kurtosis, we must first find the sum of the deviations raised to the fourth power. The deviations are given in Table 3-20, and their sum

---

[12] This measure is free of scale. It is always positive because the deviations are raised to the fourth power.

is 154,211.2. Next, we find the standard deviation by taking the square root of the sample variance ($\sqrt{75.98} = 8.716$). We can now compute Equation 3-20 as follows:

$$\text{Sample kurtosis} = \left(\frac{12 \times 13}{11 \times 10 \times 9} \times \frac{154,211.2}{8.716^4} \right) - \frac{3(11)^2}{10 \times 9} = 0.176$$

This example indicates positive excess kurtosis. Had this been a sample of size $n = 100$, we would conclude that such a small excess kurtosis statistic might be consistent with a normal distribution. Of course, we do not want to draw too many conclusions from a distribution with only 12 returns. For instance, over the period January 1926 to March 1999, the excess kurtosis for the S&P 500 was 9.89. Excess kurtosis of 0.176 for the MSCI EAFE index during 1990 is thus likely to be considered small.

TABLE 3-20   Calculation of Excess Kurtosis for the MSCI EAFE Index: January 1990 to December 1990

Month	$(R_i - \bar{R})$ (%)	$(R_i - \bar{R})^4$
January 1990	−1.9	13.032
February 1990	−5.2	731.162
March 1990	−8.6	5470.082
April 1990	1.0	1.000
May 1990	13.2	30359.578
June 1990	0.9	0.656
July 1990	3.8	208.514
August 1990	−7.9	3895.008
September 1990	−12.1	21435.888
October 1990	17.4	91663.618
November 1990	−4.1	282.576
December 1990	3.5	150.063
Sum	0.0	154,211.2
Standard deviation	$(75.98)^{1/2}$	8.716
Kurtosis		0.176

8 USING GEOMETRIC AND ARITHMETIC MEANS

With the concepts of descriptive statistics in hand, we will see why the geometric mean is appropriate for making investment statements about past performance. We will also explore why the arithmetic mean is appropriate for making investment statements in a forward-looking context.

For reporting historical returns, the geometric mean has considerable appeal because it is the rate of growth or return we would have had to earn each year to match the actual, cumulative investment performance. In our simplified Example 3-6, for instance, we purchased a stock for €100 and two years later it was worth €100, with an intervening year at €200. The geometric mean of 0 percent is clearly the compound rate of growth over the two years. Specifically, the ending amount is the beginning amount times $(1 + R_G)^2$. The geometric mean is an excellent measure of past performance.

Example 3-6 illustrated how the arithmetic mean can distort our assessment of historical performance. In that example, the total performance over the two-year period was unambiguously 0 percent. With a 100 percent return the first year and -50 percent the second, however, the arithmetic mean was 25 percent. As we noted previously, the arithmetic mean will always be greater than or equal to the geometric mean. If we want to estimate the average return over a one-period horizon, we should use the arithmetic mean because the arithmetic mean is the average of one-period returns. If we want to estimate the average returns over more than one period, however, we should use the geometric mean of returns because the geometric mean captures how the total returns are linked over time.

In reporting historical results, researchers often present real returns in addition to nominal returns. Real returns adjust for the effects of inflation. Using the rate of growth of a consumer price index as a measure of inflation, I, we must have our principal growing at the rate $(1 + I)$ in order to preserve the same purchasing power. To increase our purchasing power, we need a growth rate beyond the inflation rate. This "extra" growth rate is called the real rate, RR_G. Hence $(1 + I) \times (1 + RR_G)$ is the nominal growth factor based on a real growth rate of RR_G. We call this nominal growth factor $(1 + R_G)$ with R_G as the nominal growth rate. Starting with the nominal growth rate and the inflation rate, we can solve for the real growth rate:

$$(1 + RR_G) = \frac{(1 + R_G)}{(1 + I)} \quad \text{and} \quad RR_G = \frac{(1 + R_G)}{(1 + I)} - 1$$

For example, Dimson, Marsh, and Staunton (2000) reported the geometric mean of nominal U.S. returns as 10.3 percent over the 20th century and the geometric mean inflation rate over the same period as 3.2 percent. Thus they report the geometric mean of real returns as 6.9 percent.

As a corollary to using the geometric mean for performance reporting, the use of **semi-logarithmic** rather than arithmetic scales can provide a more realistic picture when graphing past performance.[13] If Dimson et al. had used an arithmetic grid on both horizontal and vertical axes in their 100-year study of stock markets,[14] equal numerical changes in an index would have shown up as equal-sized vertical movements. Thus, a British asset index move from GBP1 to GBP10 over roughly the first 58 years of the century would have been dwarfed by the GBP10 to GBP315 move over the last 42 years. What they actually used, however, was a logarithmic scale on the vertical axis and an arithmetic scale on the horizontal axis, and this mixture is called a semi-logarithmic scale. The vertical axis values are spaced in accordance with the differences between their logarithms. As a result, 1, 10, 100, and 1,000 are equally spaced because the difference in their logarithms is roughly 2.30; that is, $\ln 10 - \ln 1 = \ln 100 - \ln 10 = \ln 1000 - \ln 100 = 2.30$. On a semi-logarithmic scale, equal movements on the vertical axis reflect equal percentage changes. The change from GBP1 to GBP10 is roughly a 4 percent annual return compounded continuously over 58 years. The change from GBP10 to GBP315 is very roughly an 8 percent annual return compounded over the last 42 years. As expected, the Dimson et al. graph shows the vertical difference between the index at GBP315 and the index at GBP10 as approximately twice the distance from the index at GBP1 to the index at GBP10.

---

[13] This explanation is based on Campbell (1974).

[14] Dimson, Marsh, and Staunton (2000).

In addition to reporting historical performance, financial analysts need to calculate expected equity risk premiums in a forward-looking context. For this purpose, the arithmetic mean is appropriate.

We can illustrate the use of the arithmetic mean in a forward-looking context with an example based on an investment's future cash flows. In contrasting the geometric and arithmetic means for discounting future cash flows, the essential issue concerns uncertainty. Suppose an investor with $100,000 faces an equal chance of a 100 percent return or a −50 percent return, represented on the tree diagram as a 50/50 chance of a 100 percent return or a −50 percent return per period. For two periods with both the 100 percent and the −50 percent return occurring, the geometric mean return would be $\sqrt{2 \times 0.5} - 1 = 0$.

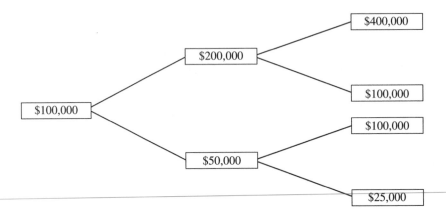

The geometric mean return of 0 percent gives the mode or median of ending wealth after two periods and thus accurately predicts the modal or median ending wealth of $100,000. Nevertheless, the arithmetic mean return better predicts the arithmetic mean ending wealth. With equal chances of 100 percent or −50 percent returns, consider the four equally likely outcomes of $400,000, $100,000, $100,000, and $25,000 as if they actually occurred. The arithmetic mean ending wealth would be $156,250 = ($400,000 + $100,000 + $100,000 + $25,000)/4. The actual returns would be 300 percent, 0 percent, 0 percent, and −75 percent for a two-period arithmetic mean return of (300 + 0 + 0 −75)/4 = 56.25 percent. This arithmetic mean return better predicts the arithmetic mean ending wealth of $100,000 × 1.5625 = $156,250. Noting that 56.25 percent for two periods is 25 percent per period, the expected terminal wealth of $156,250 then needs to be discounted at the 25 percent arithmetic mean rate to reflect the uncertainty in the cash flows.

Uncertainty in cash flows or returns causes the arithmetic mean to be larger than the geometric mean. The more uncertain the returns, the more divergence there is between the arithmetic and geometric means. The geometric mean return approximately equals the arithmetic return minus half the variance of return.[15] Zero variance or uncertainty in returns would leave the geometric and arithmetic return approximately equal, but real world uncertainty presents an arithmetic mean return larger than the geometric. For example, Dimson et al. reported that between 1900 and 2000, U.S. equities had nominal annual returns with an arithmetic mean of 12.2 percent and standard deviation of 20 percent. They reported the geometric mean as 10.3 percent. We can see the geometric mean as approxi-

---

[15] See Bodie, Kane, and Marcus (1999).

mated by the arithmetic mean minus half of the variance of returns: $R_G \approx 0.122 - 1/2 \times 0.2^2 = 0.102$.

9 SUMMARY

In this chapter, we have presented various methods to convert raw data into useful information:

- Frequency distributions in the form of histograms and cumulative distributions, either in tabular or graphical form, allow visual comparisons of actual data to a hypothesized underlying distribution, such as the normal distribution.

- The scale on which data are measured determines the type of analysis that can be performed on the data.

- Sample statistics such as measures of central tendency, measures of dispersion, skewness, and kurtosis help with investment analysis, particularly in making probabilistic statements about returns.

- Measures of central tendency include the mean, median (50th percentile), and mode (most frequently occurring value).

- The median is not influenced by extreme values and is most useful in the case of skewed distributions.

- In investment analysis, the arithmetic mean and the geometric mean are the most frequently used measures for describing average outcomes.

- The geometric mean (which includes compound growth rates) is especially important in reporting investment results (past performance).

- Quantiles such as the median, quartiles, quintiles, deciles, and percentiles are location parameters that divide the distribution into halves, quarters, fifths, tenths, and hundredths, respectively.

- A portfolio's return is a weighted average of the returns on the individual assets, where the weight applied to each asset's return is the fraction of the portfolio invested in that asset.

- Dispersion measures such as the variance, standard deviation, and mean absolute deviation describe the variability of outcomes around the arithmetic mean.

- Range is defined as the maximum value minus the minimum value. Range has the limitation that it uses information from only two observations.

- Variance and standard deviation (the square root of variance) are frequently used as quantitative measures of risk.

- Using standard deviation, we can make probabilistic statements about risk for any distribution with Chebyshev's inequality. When outcomes follow a normal distribution, more precise probabilistic statements are possible using standard deviation.

- Relative variation is measured by scale-free measures of dispersion such as the coefficient of variation (the standard deviation divided by the mean) and the Sharpe ratio (the excess return divided by its standard deviation).

- Skewness describes the degree to which a distribution is not symmetric about its mean. Kurtosis measures the peakedness of a distribution and provides information about the probability of extreme outcomes.

- Skewness and kurtosis are used to assess departures from the normal distribution.

PROBLEMS

The table below contains monthly total returns (in percent) on the S&P 500 from January 1991 to December 1991. Use the information in this table to answer Problems 1 through 7.

January 1991	4.42
February 1991	7.16
March 1991	2.38
April 1991	0.28
May 1991	4.28
June 1991	−4.57
July 1991	4.68
August 1991	2.35
September 1991	−1.64
October 1991	1.34
November 1991	−4.04
December 1991	11.43

1. To describe the data in the table:
   a. Create a frequency distribution with four equally spaced classes.
   b. Construct a histogram.
   c. Interpret the frequency distribution.

2. To describe the central tendency of the data:
   a. Calculate the sample mean return.
   b. Calculate the geometric mean return.

3. To describe the areas where certain returns fall:
   a. Calculate the median.
   b. Calculate the 30th percentile.
   c. Identify the modal interval (or intervals) of the grouped data.

4. To describe the dispersion of the distribution:
   a. Calculate the variance.
   b. Calculate the standard deviation.
   c. Calculate the mean absolute deviation (MAD).

5. To describe the degree to which the distribution departs from normality:
   a. Calculate the skewness.
   b. Calculate the excess kurtosis.

6. To describe the frequency of observations:
   a. Calculate the cumulative frequency distribution.
   b. Calculate the relative, absolute, and cumulative frequencies.

7. To describe the relative dispersion, calculate the coefficient of variation, CV.

8. The table below contains monthly total returns (in percent) on the S&P 500 and small stocks from January 1992 to December 1992.

	S&P 500 Total Return	U.S. Small Stocks Total Return
January 1992	−1.86	11.28
February 1992	1.28	4.52

March 1992	−1.96	−2.49
April 1992	2.91	−4.03
May 1992	0.54	−0.14
June 1992	−1.45	−5.19
July 1992	4.03	3.70
August 1992	−2.02	−2.28
September 1992	1.15	1.31
October 1992	0.36	2.59
November 1992	3.37	8.85
December 1992	1.31	4.41

a. Calculate the arithmetic mean returns on the S&P 500 and small stocks.

b. Calculate the standard deviations of return on the S&P 500 and small stocks.

c. Calculate and interpret the coefficient of variation, CV, for the two series.

d. Calculate the mean return on a portfolio 20 percent invested in the S&P 500 and 80 percent invested in small stocks.

9. The table below contains monthly total returns (in percent) on the S&P 500 and on 30-day T-bills from January 1998 to December 1998.

	S&P 500 Total Return	U.S. 30-Day T-Bills Total Return
January 1998	1.11	0.43
February 1998	7.21	0.39
March 1998	5.12	0.39
April 1998	1.01	0.43
May 1998	−1.72	0.40
June 1998	4.06	0.41
July 1998	−1.06	0.40
August 1998	−14.46	0.43
September 1998	6.41	0.46
October 1998	8.13	0.32
November 1998	6.06	0.31
December 1998	5.76	0.38

Calculate the Sharpe measure of performance for the S&P 500.

10. The table below contains annual total returns (in percent) for two hypothetical stocks, Stock A and Stock B.

Stock A	Stock B
1.1100	1.1100
7.2100	7.2100
5.1200	5.1200
1.0100	1.0100
−1.7200	−1.7200
4.0600	4.0600

Stock A	Stock B
−1.0600	−1.2458
−14.4600	−0.1363
6.4100	2.2100
8.1300	4.9936
6.0600	2.3950
5.7600	2.6236

a. Calculate the mean return and skewness of return for the two stocks.
b. Interpret the differences.

11. The table below contains annual total returns (in percent) for two hypothetical stocks, Stock A and Stock B.

Stock A	Stock B
1.3500	2.0670
2.7500	2.0667
5.2100	2.0667
1.0025	2.0671
−1.7200	2.0675
4.0600	2.0666
−1.0600	2.0675
−14.4600	−17.3783
6.5000	11.1020
2.0000	2.0668
3.0000	2.0667
5.7600	2.0666

a. Calculate the mean return and skewness of return on each stock.
b. Calculate the excess kurtosis of each stock.
c. Interpret the differences between the two stocks.

12. The table below contains monthly total returns (in percent) on the Russell 1000 Index and on 30-day T-bills from January 1990 to December 1990.

	Russell 1000 Total Return	U.S. 30-Day T-Bills Total Return
January 1990	−7.14	0.57
February 1990	1.62	0.57
March 1990	2.48	0.64
April 1990	−2.59	0.69
May 1990	9.37	0.68
June 1990	−0.55	0.63

July 1990	−0.89	0.68
August 1990	−9.19	0.66
September 1990	−5.11	0.60
October 1990	−0.49	0.68
November 1990	6.84	0.57
December 1990	3.04	0.60

Calculate the Sharpe measure of risk-adjusted performance for the Russell 1000.

13. The table below contains monthly total returns on the S&P 500, small stocks, and long-term corporate bonds.

	S&P 500 Total Return	U.S. Small Stocks Total Return	U.S. Long-Term Corporate Bonds Total Return
January 1990	−6.71	−7.64	−1.91
February 1990	1.29	1.87	−0.12
March 1990	2.63	3.68	−0.11
April 1990	−2.47	−2.66	−1.91
May 1990	9.75	5.61	3.85
June 1990	−0.70	1.44	2.16
July 1990	−0.32	−3.82	1.02
August 1990	−9.03	−12.96	−2.92
September 1990	−4.92	−8.29	0.91
October 1990	−0.37	−5.72	1.32
November 1990	6.44	4.50	2.85
December 1990	2.74	1.94	1.67

Calculate the mean return on a portfolio 30 percent invested in the S&P 500, 25 percent invested in small stocks, and 45 percent invested in long-term corporate bonds.

14. The table below contains monthly total returns (in percent) on the Russell 1000 from January 1990 to December 1990.

January 1990	−7.14
February 1990	1.62
March 1990	2.48
April 1990	−2.59
May 1990	9.37
June 1990	−0.55
July 1990	−0.89
August 1990	−9.19
September 1990	−5.11
October 1990	−0.49
November 1990	6.84
December 1990	3.04

a. Create a frequency distribution table with four equally spaced classes.
b. Construct a histogram.
c. Identify the modal interval of the grouped data.

15. Below are 12 annual total returns (in percent) on Stock A and Stock B. Also given are some statistics for these returns.

	Stock A	Stock B
	9.03	12.96
	6.71	8.29
	4.92	7.64
	2.47	5.72
	0.7	3.82
	0.37	2.66
	0.32	−1.44
	−1.29	−1.87
	−2.63	−1.94
	−2.74	−3.68
	−6.44	−4.5
	−9.75	−5.61
Mean	0.1392	1.8375
Median	0.3450	0.6100
Standard deviation	5.3086	5.9047
Skewness	−0.1395	0.4934
Excess kurtosis	−0.0187	−0.8525

Interpret the differences between the statistics for Stock A and Stock B.

16. Below are 12 annual returns on Stock A and Stock B. Also given are some statistics for these returns.

	Stock A	Stock B
	9.03	34.67423
	6.71	3.166395
	4.92	3.165887
	2.47	3.165075
	0.7	3.164588
	0.37	3.164587
	0.32	3.164513
	−1.29	3.164066
	−2.63	3.163722
	−2.74	3.163676
	−6.44	3.163556
	−9.75	−64.6499

Mean	0.1392	0.1392
Median	0.3450	3.1646
Standard deviation	5.3086	22.3237
Skewness	−0.1395	−2.2602
Excess kurtosis	−0.0187	8.0495

Describe the risk and return of the two stocks.

17. At the UXI Foundation, portfolio managers are normally kept on if their annual rate of return meets or exceeds the mean annual return for all portfolio managers of a similar investment style. Recently, the UXI Foundation has also been considering two other evaluation criteria: the median annual return of funds with the same investment style, and two-thirds of the return performance of the top fund with the same investment style.

The table below gives the returns for nine funds with the same investment style as the UXI Foundation.

17.8
21.0
38.0
19.2
2.5
24.3
18.7
16.9
12.6

With the above distribution of fund performance, which of the three evaluation criteria is the most difficult to achieve?

SOLUTIONS

1. a. A frequency distribution is a tabular display of data summarized into a relatively small number of equally sized intervals. In this example, we want four equally sized intervals. To make the frequency distribution table, we take the following five steps.

 i. Rank returns from lowest to highest.

−4.57
−4.04
−1.64
0.28
1.34
2.35
2.38
4.28
4.42
4.68
7.16
11.43

 ii. Calculate the range. Recall that the range formula is

$$\text{Range} = \text{Maximum value} - \text{Minimum value}$$

 In this case, the range is $11.43 - (-4.57) = 16.00$.

 iii. Divide the range by the number of regions:

$$\text{Range/Number of regions} = 16.00/4 = 4.00.$$

 iv. To get the endpoints for each of the four intervals, successively add the width of each interval (4.00 from Step iii) to the lowest value (−4.57) until we reach the maximum value (11.43).

−4.57 + 4.00 = −0.57
−0.57 + 4.00 = 3.43
3.43 + 4.00 = 7.43
7.43 + 4.00 = 11.43

 v. After setting the endpoints for the intervals, count the number of observations in each interval. This count is called the absolute frequency or simply the frequency. The frequency distribution table is shown below.

Range	Absolute Frequency
−4.57 ≤ Interval A < −0.57	3
−0.57 ≤ Interval B < 3.43	4
3.43 ≤ Interval C < 7.43	4
7.43 ≤ Interval D ≤ 11.43	1

b. A histogram is the graphical equivalent of a frequency distribution. Here, it is a bar chart of return data that have been grouped into a frequency distribution.

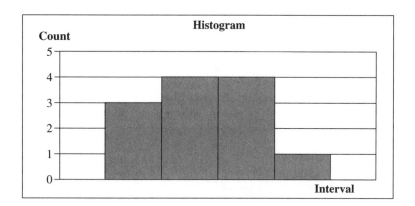

c. In the histogram, we can see a total of 12 observations (3 + 4 + 4 + 1 = 12). The distribution is somewhat bell-shaped, but not symmetric. The maximum return is less than or equal to 11.43, and the minimum return is greater than or equal to −4.57.

2. a. We calculate the sample mean by finding the sum of the 12 values in the table and dividing by 12. The formula (Equation 3-3) for the sample mean, $\overline{X}$, is

$$\overline{X} = \frac{\sum\limits_{i=1}^{n} X_i}{n}$$

In this case,
$\overline{X}$ = (4.42 + 7.16 + 2.38 + 0.28 + 4.28 − 4.57 + 4.68 + 2.35 − 1.64 + 1.34 − 4.04 + 11.43)/12 = 28.07/12 = 2.3392.

b. The geometric mean requires that all the numbers be greater than or equal to 0. To ensure that the returns satisfy this requirement, we add 1 to the S&P 500 returns above. We then use Equation 3-7:

$$R_G = \sqrt[T]{(1 + R_1)(1 + R_2)...(1 + R_T)} - 1$$

$$R_G = \left[\prod_{t=1}^{T}(1 + R_t) \right]^{\frac{1}{T}} - 1$$

To find the geometric mean in this example, we take the following five steps:

i. Divide each figure in the table by 100 to put the returns into decimal representation.

ii. Add 1 to each return to ensure that the figures are positive.

Return	Return in Decimal Form	1 + Return
4.42	0.0442	1.0442
7.16	0.0716	1.0716
2.38	0.0238	1.0238

Return	Return in Decimal Form	1 + Return
0.28	0.0028	1.0028
4.28	0.0428	1.0428
−4.57	−0.0457	0.9543
4.68	0.0468	1.0468
2.35	0.0235	1.0235
−1.64	−0.0164	0.9836
1.34	0.0134	1.0134
−4.04	−0.0404	0.9596
11.43	0.1143	1.1143

iii. Multiply together all the numbers in the third column to get 1.3055.

iv. Take the 12th root of 1.3055 to get $\sqrt[12]{1.3055} = 1.0225$. On most calculators, $\sqrt[12]{1.3055} = 1.0225$ is obtained with the y^x key. Enter 1.3055 with the y^x key. Next, enter 1/12 = 0.0833333. Then press = to get 1.0225.

v. Subtract 1 to get 0.0225, or 2.25 percent per month. The geometric mean return is 2.25 percent. This result means that on average, the compound rate of return for this 12-month period is 2.25 percent. Note that this value is less than the arithmetic mean of 2.3392 percent that we calculated in Solution 2a.

3. a. The median is defined as the value of the middle item of a group that has been sorted into ascending or descending order. In a sample of n items, where n is an odd number, the median is the item in the sorted data set occupying the $(n + 1)/2$ position. When the data set has an even number of observations (as in this example), the median is the mean of the items occupying the $n/2$ and $(n + 2)/2$ positions (the two middle positions). With $n = 12$, these are the sixth and seventh positions.

To find the median, the first step is to rank the data.

Returns	Ranking
11.43	12
7.16	11
4.68	10
4.42	9
4.28	8
2.38	7
2.35	6
1.34	5
0.28	4
−1.64	3
−4.04	2
−4.57	1

The item in the sixth position is 2.35, and the item in the seventh position is 2.38. The median is then $M_d = (2.35 + 2.38)/2 = 2.365$. Note that we can change the values of the extreme large and small values in the sample without affecting the median.

b.   Recall the formula for the location of the percentile (Equation 3-4):

$$L_y = (n + 1)\frac{y}{100}$$

where L_y is the location or position of the yth percentile, P_y, and y is the percentage point at which we want to divide the distribution.

If we apply the percentile location formula to this data, we find $L_{30} = (12 + 1)\frac{30}{100} = 3.9$, which is not a whole number. To find the 30th percentile from the sorted data, we take the value in the third position, -1.64, and add 90 percent of the difference between the items in fourth and third position. The interpolated value is $P_{30} = -1.64 + 0.9[0.28 - (-1.64)] = 0.088$.

Therefore, the 30th percentile is 0.088. By definition, the 30th percentile is that value at or below which 30 percent of the observations lie. In this problem, 25 percent of the observations are below 0.088. The difficulty here is with our small sample size of 12 observations. In general, as the sample size increases, the percentile calculation becomes more accurate.

c.   The distribution of the grouped data in this example is bimodal, meaning that two intervals are tied for the most observations. Interval B and Interval C each have four observations, and they are the two modal intervals.

4. a.   Variance is defined as the mean of the squared deviations around the mean. We find the variance with Equation 3-13:

$$s^2 = \frac{\sum\limits_{i=1}^{n}(X_i - \overline{X})^2}{n - 1}$$

To calculate the variance, we take the following four steps:

i.   Take the original values and calculate their arithmetic mean.
ii. Subtract the arithmetic mean from each value.
iii. Square each deviation from the mean.
iv. Sum the squared deviations and divide by the total number of observations minus 1. The variance, in this case, is 20.8149.

Original Data X_i	Deviation from the Mean $X_i - \overline{X}$	Squared Value of the Deviation from the Mean $(X_i - \overline{X})^2$
4.42	2.0808	4.3297
7.16	4.8208	23.2401
2.38	0.0408	0.0017
0.28	−2.0592	4.2403
4.28	1.9408	3.7667
−4.57	−6.9092	47.7370
4.68	2.3408	5.4793

Original Data X_i	Deviation from the Mean $X_i - \overline{X}$	Squared Value of the Deviation from the Mean $(X_i - \overline{X})^2$
2.35	0.0108	0.0001
−1.64	−3.9792	15.8340
1.34	−0.9992	0.9984
−4.04	−6.3792	40.6942
11.43	9.0908	82.6426

$$\overline{X} = \frac{\sum_i^n X_i}{n} = 2.3392$$

$$\sum_{i=1}^n (X_i - \overline{X})^2 = 228.9641$$

$$s^2 = \frac{\sum_{i=1}^n (X_i - \overline{X})^2}{n-1} = 20.8149$$

Recall that the units of variance are the squared units of the underlying variable, so we have 20.8149 percent squared. To have more intuitive units, we calculate the standard deviation.

b. The standard deviation is the square root of the variance. We calculate the standard deviation with Equation 3-15:

$$s = \sqrt{\frac{\sum_{i=1}^n (X_i - \overline{X})^2}{n-1}}$$

The standard deviation is therefore 4.5623 percent.

c. The mean absolute deviation is defined in Equation 3-9 as

$$MAD = \frac{\sum_{i=1}^n |X_i - \overline{X}|}{n}$$

To find the MAD for this example, we take the following four steps:

i. Take the original values and calculate their arithmetic mean.
ii. Subtract the mean from each value.
iii. Take the absolute value of each deviation from the mean.
iv. Sum the absolute values of the deviations and divide by the total number of observations. The mean absolute deviation in this case is 3.3876.

Original Data X_i	Deviation from the Mean $X_i - \overline{X}$	Absolute Value of the Deviation from the Mean $|X_i - \overline{X}|$
4.42	2.0808	2.0808
7.16	4.8208	4.8208

2.38	0.0408	0.0408
0.28	−2.0592	2.0592
4.28	1.9408	1.9408
−4.57	−6.9092	6.9092
4.68	2.3408	2.3408
2.35	0.0108	0.0108
−1.64	−3.9792	3.9792
1.34	−0.9992	0.9992
−4.04	−6.3792	6.3792
11.43	9.0908	9.0908

$$\overline{X} = \frac{\sum\limits_{i=1}^{n} X_i}{n} = 2.3392 \qquad\qquad \sum_{i=1}^{n} |X_i - \overline{X}| = 40.6516$$

$$\text{MAD} = \frac{\sum\limits_{i=1}^{n} |X_i - \overline{X}|}{n} = 3.3876$$

5. a. The formula for sample skewness is given as Equation 3-19:

$$S_K = \frac{n}{(n-1)(n-2)} \frac{\sum\limits_{i=1}^{n} (X_i - \overline{X})^3}{s^3}$$

The sample size, n, is 12. In 4a, we calculated $s = 4.5623$; therefore, $s^3 = 94.9624$. We previously calculated $\overline{X} = 2.3392$ in 2a. Using this result, we calculate the sum of the cubed deviations from the mean as follows:

$$\sum_{i=1}^{12} (X_i - \overline{X})^3 = \sum_{i=1}^{12} (X_i - 2.3392)^3 = 2.0808^3 + 4.8208^3 + 0.0408^3$$
$$+ (-2.0592)^3 + 1.9408^3 + (-6.9092)^3 + 2.3408^3 + 0.0108^3 + (-3.9792)^3$$
$$+ (-0.9992)^3 + (-6.3792)^3 + 9.0908^3 = 230.3123$$

So finally we have

$$S_K = \frac{12}{(11)(10)} \frac{230.3123}{94.9624} = 0.2646$$

In the sample period, the returns on the S&P 500 were slightly positively skewed.

b. The formula for excess kurtosis is Equation 3-20:

$$\left(\frac{n(n+1)}{(n-1)(n-2)(n-3)} \times \frac{\sum\limits_{i=1}^{n} (X_i - \overline{X})^4}{s^4} \right) - \frac{3(n-1)^2}{(n-2)(n-3)}$$

In Solution 4b, we calculated $s = 4.5623$; therefore, $s^4 = 433.2468$. We previously calculated $\overline{X} = 2.3392$ in Solution 2a. We already have the mean, so we are ready to calculate the sum of the deviations from the mean raised to the fourth power:

$$\sum_{i=1}^{12} (X_i - \overline{X})^4 = \sum_{i=1}^{12} (X_i - 2.3392)^4 = 2.0808^4 + 4.8208^4 + 0.0408^4$$
$$+ (-2.0592)^4 + 1.9408^4 + (-6.9092)^4 + 2.3408^4 + 0.0108^4 + (-3.9792)^4$$
$$+ (-0.9992)^4 + (-6.3792)^4 + 9.0908^4 = 11,637.4037$$

Thus, we have

$$\left(\frac{12(13)}{(11)(10)(9)} \times \frac{11,637.4037}{433.2468} \right) - \frac{3(11)^2}{(10)(9)} = 4.2326 - 4.0333 = 0.1993$$

In the sample period, the returns on the S&P 500 were slightly leptokurtic.

6. a. We find the cumulative frequencies by adding the absolute frequencies as we move from the first interval to the last.

Range	Absolute Frequency	Calculations to Obtain Cumulative Frequency	Cumulative Frequency
$-4.57 \leq$ Interval A < -0.57	3		3
$-0.57 \leq$ Interval B < 3.43	4	4 + 3 =	7
$3.43 \leq$ Interval C < 7.43	4	4 + 7 =	11
$7.43 \leq$ Interval D ≤ 11.43	1	1 + 11 =	12

The cumulative frequency is a running total of the absolute frequency.

b. The relative frequency is the absolute frequency or cumulative frequency divided by the total number of observations.

Range	Absolute Frequency	Relative Frequency	Cumulative Absolute Frequency	Cumulative Relative Frequency
$-4.57 \leq$ Interval A < -0.57	3	3/12 = 25.00%	3	3/12 = 25.00%
$-0.57 \leq$ Interval B < 3.43	4	4/12 = 33.33%	7	7/12 = 58.33%
$3.43 \leq$ Interval C < 7.43	4	4/12 = 33.33%	11	11/12 = 91.67%
$7.43 \leq$ Interval D ≤ 11.43	1	1/12 = 8.33%	12	12/12 = 100.00%
Sum	12			

7. A common measure of relative dispersion is the coefficient of variation, CV, which is the standard deviation divided by the mean:

$$CV = s/\overline{X}$$

(This is Equation 3-17.) The coefficient of variation expresses how much dispersion exists relative to the mean of the distribution. Thus, it allows for direct comparisons of dispersions across different data sets.

From Solution 4b, we know that the standard deviation is 4.5623. From Solution 2a, we know that the mean is equal to 2.3392. The coefficient of variation is thus 4.5623/2.3392 = 1.9504. This result indicates that we have 1.95 units of standard deviation for each unit of mean return.

8. a. Recall that the arithmetic mean, $\overline{X}$, is equal to

$$\overline{X} = \frac{\sum_{i=1}^{n} X_i}{n}$$

Add all the return values and divide by the total number of observations.

	S&P 500 Total Return X_i	U.S. Small Stocks Total Return X_i
January 1992	−1.86	11.28
February 1992	1.28	4.52
March 1992	−1.96	−2.49
April 1992	2.91	−4.03
May 1992	0.54	−0.14
June 1992	−1.45	−5.19
July 1992	4.03	3.70
August 1992	−2.02	−2.28
September 1992	1.15	1.31
October 1992	0.36	2.59
November 1992	3.37	8.85
December 1992	1.31	4.41
$\overline{X} = \dfrac{\sum_{i=1}^{n} X_i}{n}$	0.6383	1.8775

b. Recall that the standard deviation is given as

$$s = \sqrt{\frac{\sum_{i=1}^{n} (X_i - \overline{X})^2}{n-1}}$$

To calculate the standard deviation, we take the following five steps:

i. Take the original values and calculate their arithmetic mean.

ii. Subtract the mean from each value.

iii. Square each deviation from the mean.

iv. Sum the squared deviations and divide by the total number of observations minus 1. This calculation gives the variance.

v. To get the standard deviation, take the square root of the variance. For the S&P 500 data, the standard deviation of return is 2.1269 percent.

Original Data X_i	Deviation from the Mean $X_i - \bar{X}$	Squared Value of the Deviation from the Mean $(X_i - \bar{X})^2$
-1.86	-2.4983	6.2415
1.28	0.6417	0.4118
-1.96	-2.5983	6.7512
2.91	2.2717	5.1606
0.54	-0.0983	0.0097
-1.45	-2.0883	4.3610
4.03	3.3917	11.5036
-2.02	-2.6583	7.0666
1.15	0.5117	0.2618
0.36	-0.2783	0.0775
3.37	2.7317	7.4622
1.31	0.6717	0.4512

$$\bar{X} = \frac{\sum_{i=1}^{n} X_i}{n} = 0.6383$$

$$\sum_{i=1}^{n} (X_i - \bar{X})^2 = 49.7587$$

$$\sqrt{\frac{\sum_{i=1}^{n} (X_i - \bar{X})^2}{n - 1}} = 2.1269$$

For small stocks, the standard deviation of return is 5.0439 percent. Because the standard deviation of return on small stocks is greater than the standard deviation of return on the S&P 500, we can say that small stocks had greater total or stand-alone risk than the S&P 500 stocks had.

Original Data X_i	Deviation from the Mean $X_i - \bar{X}$	Squared Value of the Deviation from the Mean $(X_i - \bar{X})^2$
11.28	9.4025	88.4070
4.52	2.6425	6.9828
-2.49	-4.3675	19.0751
-4.03	-5.9075	34.8986
-0.14	-2.0175	4.0703
-5.19	-7.0675	49.9496
3.70	1.8225	3.3215
-2.28	-4.1575	17.2848
1.31	-0.5675	0.3221
2.59	0.7125	0.5077
8.85	6.9725	48.6158
4.41	2.5325	6.4136

$$\bar{X} = \frac{\sum_{i=1}^{n} X_i}{n} = 1.8775 \qquad\qquad \sum_{i=1}^{n} (X_i - \bar{X})^2 = 279.8489$$

$$s = \sqrt{\frac{\sum_{i=1}^{n} (X_i - \bar{X})^2}{n-1}} = 5.0439$$

c. Recall that the coefficient of variation, CV, is defined as $CV = s / \bar{X}$.
For the S&P 500, $CV_{S\&P500} = 2.1269/0.6383 = 3.3321$.
For small stocks, $CV_{SmallStocks} = 5.0439/1.8775 = 2.6865$.
Thus, small stocks offered more return (reward) for each unit of risk.

d. In this example, the S&P 500 makes up 20 percent of the portfolio and is weighted 0.20, whereas small stocks make up 80 percent of the portfolio and are weighted 0.80. The mean return of this portfolio is thus

$$\bar{X}_w = 0.20(0.6383) + 0.80(1.8775) = 1.6297.$$

9. a. The Sharpe measure or ratio is defined as $\dfrac{\bar{r}_p - \bar{r}_f}{\sigma_p}$ (Equation 3-18.) We calculate the arithmetic mean return of the portfolio (the S&P 500) and the risk-free asset (the T-bill) in the table below.

	S&P 500 Total Return X_i	30-Day T-Bill Total Return X_i	S&P 500 Minus 30-Day T-Bill Total Return
January 1998	1.11	0.43	0.68
February 1998	7.21	0.39	6.82
March 1998	5.12	0.39	4.73
April 1998	1.01	0.43	0.58
May 1998	−1.72	0.40	−2.12
June 1998	4.06	0.41	3.65
July 1998	−1.06	0.40	−1.46
August 1998	−14.46	0.43	−14.89
September 1998	6.41	0.46	5.95
October 1998	8.13	0.32	7.81
November 1998	6.06	0.31	5.75
December 1998	5.76	0.38	5.38
$\bar{X} = \dfrac{\sum_{i=1}^{n} X_i}{n}$	2.3025	0.3958	1.9067

We also need the standard deviation for the portfolio. This statistic is calculated in the following table.

Original Data X_i	Deviation from the Mean $X_i - \overline{X}$	Squared Value of the Deviation from the Mean $(X_i - \overline{x})^2$
1.11	−1.1925	1.4221
7.21	4.9075	24.0836
5.12	2.8175	7.9383
1.01	−1.2925	1.6706
−1.72	−4.0225	16.1805
4.06	1.7575	3.0888
−1.06	−3.3625	11.3064
−14.46	−16.7625	280.9814
6.41	4.1075	16.8716
8.13	5.8275	33.9598
6.06	3.7575	14.1188
5.76	3.4575	11.9543

$$\overline{X} = \frac{\sum_{i=1}^{n} X_i}{n} = 2.3025 \qquad\qquad \sum_{i=1}^{n} (X_i - \overline{X})^2 = 423.5762$$

$$s = \sqrt{\frac{\sum_{i=1}^{n}(X_i - \overline{X})^2}{n-1}} = 6.2054$$

The Sharpe measure for this data is thus $(2.3025 - 0.3958)/6.2054 = 0.3073$. In this text, we are using the above method of calculating the Sharpe measure. An alternative calculation of the Sharpe measure uses in the denominator the standard deviation of the series (S&P 500 return) minus (T-bill return). Using this standard deviation (6.2240), we get a similar number for the Sharpe measure:

$$(2.3025 - 0.3958)/6.2240 = 0.3063$$

10. a.   The mean return for Stock A is $\overline{X} = \dfrac{\sum_{i=1}^{n} X_i}{n} = \dfrac{27.63}{12} = 2.3025$. To calculate skewness, we need the sample size, n; the sum of the cubed deviations of returns, X_i, from the mean return, $\overline{X}$; and the sample standard deviation cubed, s^3. We already know that $n = 12$ and that $\overline{X} = 2.3025$. We can calculate the sum of the cubed deviations from the mean as

$$\sum_{i=1}^{n} (X_i - \overline{X})^3 = \sum_{i=1}^{12} (X_i - 2.3025)^3 = -4{,}309.3411$$

We calculate the sample standard deviation as $s = 6.2054$; therefore, $s^3 = 238.9513$. We then substitute these numbers into the expression for skewness to find that

$$S_{K,Stock\,A} = \frac{n}{(n-1)(n-2)} \sum_{i=1}^{n} \frac{(X_i - \overline{X})^3}{s^3} = \frac{12}{(11)(10)} \frac{-4309.3411}{238.9513} = -1.9674$$

For Stock B, we have $\overline{X} = 2.3025$. We calculate the sum of the cubed deviations from the mean as $\sum_{i=1}^{n} (X_i - \overline{X})^3 = \sum_{i=1}^{12} (X_i - 2.3025)^3 = 37.3841$. Because $s = 2.7016$, $s^3 = 19.7180$. Substituting in, we have

$$S_{K,Stock\ B} = \frac{n}{(n-1)(n-2)} \sum_{i=1}^{n} \frac{(X_i - \overline{X})^3}{s^3} = \frac{12}{(11)(10)} \frac{37.3841}{19.7180} = 0.2068.$$

The table below summarizes what we have learned about Stock A and Stock B.

	Mean Return	Skewness
Stock A	2.3025	−1.9674
Stock B	2.3025	0.2068

b. Stocks A and B have the same mean return, but different skewness. Stock A is negatively skewed; it has a large negative outlier that pulls the mean down.

Now look at the ranked data in the table below.

Stock A	Stock B
8.1300	7.2100
7.2100	5.1200
6.4100	4.9936
6.0600	4.0600
5.7600	2.6236
5.1200	2.3950
4.0600	2.2100
1.1100	1.1100
1.0100	1.0100
−1.0600	−0.1364
−1.7200	−1.2458
−14.4600	−1.7200

Note that Stock A has a larger maximum loss (−14.4600). The mean returns for A and B are the same. However, the returns for B have less variance than the returns for A (a standard deviation of 2.7016 for B versus 6.2054 for A); and skewness for B is positive, whereas skewness for A is negative. Overall, Stock B offers a better risk–return trade-off.

11. a. The mean return for Stock A is $\overline{X} = \dfrac{\sum_{i=1}^{n} X_i}{n} = \dfrac{\sum_{i=1}^{12} X_i}{12} = \dfrac{14.3925}{12} = 1.1994$. We calculate the sum of the cubed deviations from the mean as

$$\sum_{i=1}^{n} (X_i - \overline{X})^3 = \sum_{i=1}^{12} (X_i - 1.1994)^3 = -3,534.5865$$

Using the formula already given, we calculate the sample standard deviation as $s = 5.5461$; therefore, $s^3 = 170.5937$. We substitute these numbers into the expression for skewness to find that

$$S_{K,Stock\,A} = \frac{n}{(n-1)(n-2)} \sum_{i=1}^{n} \frac{(X_i - \overline{X})^3}{s^3} = \frac{12}{(11)(10)} \frac{-3534.5865}{170.5937} = -2.2603$$

The mean return for Stock B is $\overline{X} = 14.3929/12 = 1.1994$. To four decimal places, the mean return for B is the same as the same as the mean return for Stock A. We calculate the sum of the cubed deviations from the mean as

$$\sum_{i=1}^{n} (X_i - \overline{X})^3 = \sum_{i=1}^{12} (X_i - 1.1994)^3 = -5,434.1465$$

We calculate the sample standard deviation as $s = 6.4011$; therefore, $s^3 = 262.2792$. Using the formula for skewness, we find that

$$S_{K,Stock\,B} = \frac{n}{(n-1)(n-2)} \sum_{i=1}^{n} \frac{(X_i - \overline{X})^3}{s^3} = \frac{12}{(11)(10)} \frac{-5434.1465}{262.2792} = -2.2603$$

The mean return and skewness of return are the same for Stocks A and B.

b. To calculate the kurtosis of Stock A, we need the sum of the deviations from the mean raised to the fourth power:

$$\sum_{i=1}^{n} (X_i - \overline{X})^4 = \sum_{i=1}^{12} (X_i - 1.1994)^4 = 61,794.3815$$

Using the sample standard deviation for Stock A from Solution 10a, we have $s^4 = 946.1299$. Substituting all of these values into the formula for kurtosis (Equation 3-20), we have

$$\left(\frac{12(13)}{(11)(10)(9)} \times \frac{61794.3815}{946.1299} \right) - \frac{3(11)^2}{(10)(9)} = 10.2917 - 4.0333 = 6.2584$$

For Stock B, we have $\sum_{i=1}^{n} (X_i - \overline{X})^4 = \sum_{i=1}^{12} (X_i - 1.1994)^4 = 128,737.0830$. Using the sample standard deviation for Stock A from 10a, we have $s^4 = 1,678.8753$.

Then the kurtosis for Stock B is

$$\left(\frac{12(13)}{(11)(10)(9)} \times \frac{128737.0830}{1678.8753} \right) - \frac{3(11)^2}{(10)(9)} = 12.0830 - 4.0333 = 8.0497$$

The table below summarizes what we have learned about Stock A and Stock B.

	Mean Return	Standard Deviation	Skewness	Excess Kurtosis
Stock A	1.1994	5.5461	-2.2603	6.2584
Stock B	1.1994	6.4011	-2.2603	8.0497

c. Both stocks have the same mean return and the same skewness, but the kurtosis for B is larger than the kurtosis for A. We can see this result more clearly if we sort the returns of each stock as shown below.

Stock A	Stock B
−14.4600	−17.3783
−1.7200	2.0666
−1.0600	2.0666
1.0025	2.0667
1.3500	2.0667
2.0000	2.0667
2.7500	2.0668
3.0000	2.0670
4.0600	2.0671
5.2100	2.0675
5.7600	2.0675
6.5000	11.1020

Stock B has larger returns at the extremes, both negative and positive. To summarize, although both stocks have the same mean return and the same skewness, Stock B has the greater standard deviation of return and greater kurtosis. Consequently, Stock A has the better risk–reward profile.

12. The Sharpe measure is defined as follows:

$$\frac{\bar{r}_p - \bar{r}_f}{\sigma_p}$$

The numerator of the Sharpe measure is the portfolio's mean return minus the mean return on the risk-free asset over the sample period. The expression $(\bar{r}_p - \bar{r}_f)$ thus measures the extra reward that investors received for the added risk taken. To implement the Sharpe measure, we need to calculate the mean return on the portfolio (the Russell 1000) and the risk-free asset (the T-bill). These mean returns are calculated below.

	Russell 1000 Total Return X_i	30-Day T-Bill Total Return X_i
January 1990	−7.14	0.57
February 1990	1.62	0.57
March 1990	2.48	0.64
April 1990	−2.59	0.69
May 1990	9.37	0.68
June 1990	−0.55	0.63
July 1990	−0.89	0.68
August 1990	−9.19	0.66

	Russell 1000 Total Return X_i	30-Day T-Bill Total Return X_i
September 1990	−5.11	0.60
October 1990	−0.49	0.68
November 1990	6.84	0.57
December 1990	3.04	0.60
$\overline{X} = \dfrac{\sum\limits_{i=1}^{n} X_i}{n}$	−0.2175	0.6308

We also need the portfolio standard deviation, which is calculated below.

Original Data X_i	Deviation from the Mean $X_i - \overline{X}$	Squared Value of the Deviation from the Mean $(X_i - \overline{X})^2$
−7.14	−6.9225	47.9210
1.62	1.8375	3.3764
2.48	2.6975	7.2765
−2.59	−2.3725	5.6288
9.37	9.5875	91.9202
−0.55	−0.3325	0.1106
−0.89	−0.6725	0.4523
−9.19	−8.9725	80.5058
−5.11	−4.8925	23.9366
−0.49	−0.2725	0.0743
6.84	7.0575	49.8083
3.04	3.2575	10.6113

$$\overline{X} = \frac{\sum\limits_{i=1}^{n} X_i}{n} = -0.2175 \qquad\qquad \sum\limits_{i=1}^{n} (X_i - \overline{X})^2 = 321.6221$$

$$s = \sqrt{\frac{\sum\limits_{i=1}^{n} (X_i - \overline{X})^2}{n-1}} = 5.4073$$

The Sharpe measure for this data is thus $(-0.2175 - 0.6308)/5.4073 = -0.1569$. The negative Sharpe measure indicates particularly bad performance: The asset's return was less than the risk-free rate over the same period.

Be careful when interpreting negative Sharpe ratios. In general, when an asset becomes riskier, its Sharpe measure moves closer to 0. An asset with returns greater than the risk-free rate will show a decreasing Sharpe ratio (for example, from 1 to 0.5) as it becomes riskier. An asset whose returns are less than the risk-free rate will show an increasing Sharpe ratio (for example, from −1 to −0.5) as it becomes riskier. If you are not careful, you may interpret an increasing negative Sharpe ratio (that is, more return per unit of risk) as favorable when, in fact, it indicates increased risk.

13.   Recall that a portfolio's return is a weighted average of the returns on the assets in the portfolio, where the weight applied to each asset's return is the fraction of the portfolio invested in that asset. Similarly, the mean return on a portfolio is a weighted average of the mean returns on the assets in the portfolio. The first step, therefore, is to calculate the mean return on each of the assets in the portfolio.

	S&P 500	U.S. Small Stocks	U.S. Long-Term Corporate Bonds
January 1990	−6.71	−7.64	−1.91
February 1990	1.29	1.87	−0.12
March 1990	2.63	3.68	−0.11
April 1990	−2.47	−2.66	−1.91
May 1990	9.75	5.61	3.85
June 1990	−0.70	1.44	2.16
July 1990	−0.32	−3.82	1.02
August 1990	−9.03	−12.96	−2.92
September 1990	−4.92	−8.29	0.91
October 1990	−0.37	−5.72	1.32
November 1990	6.44	4.50	2.85
December 1990	2.74	1.94	1.67
Mean return $\overline{X} = \dfrac{\sum\limits_{i=1}^{n} X_i}{n}$	−0.1392	−1.8375	0.5675
Weights	0.3	0.25	0.45
Portfolio mean return	−0.2458		

We then use the general formula (Equation 3-5) for the weighted mean for a set of observations $X_1, X_2, \ldots, X_n$ with corresponding weights $w_1, w_2, \ldots, w_n$:

$$\overline{X}_w = \sum_{i=1}^{n} w_i X_i$$

where $\displaystyle\sum_{i=1}^{n} w_i = 1$

and where the observations are the mean returns on the assets. The portfolio's holdings are

- the S&P 500, which makes up 30 percent of the portfolio and so has a weight $w_1 = 0.30$;
- the small-stock index, which makes up 25 percent of the portfolio and has a weight $w_2 = 0.25$; and
- the long-term bond index, which makes up 45 percent of the portfolio and has a weight $w_3 = 0.45$.

Substituting the above numbers into the formula for the weighted mean, we conclude that the mean return on the portfolio is -24.58 percent:

$$0.30(-0.1392) + 0.25(-1.8375) + 0.45(0.5675) = -0.2458$$

14.   To create a frequency distribution table with four equally spaced classes, we take the following four steps:

   i. Rank the returns from smallest to largest.

 ii. Calculate the maximum, minimum, and range of the data.

Maximum	9.37
Minimum	-9.19
Range	18.56

 iii. Divide the range by the number of regions: $18.56/4 = 4.64$.

 iv. Successively add the result above, 4.64, to the lowest value until we reach the maximum value. The four intervals are shown below.

	Lower Boundary	Upper Boundary
Interval A	-9.19	-4.55
Interval B	-4.55	0.09
Interval C	0.09	4.73
Interval D	4.73	9.37

The full frequency table is given below.

	Interval A	Interval B	Interval C	Interval D
Absolute frequency	3	4	3	2
Cumulative absolute frequency	3	7	10	12
Relative frequency	25.00%	33.33%	25.00%	16.67%
Cumulative relative frequency	25.00%	58.33%	83.33%	100.00%

The histogram for this data is shown below.

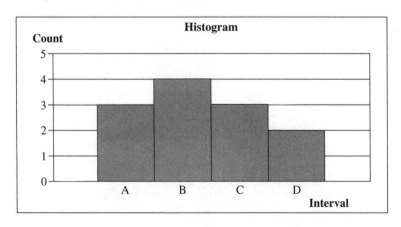

The histogram shows that Interval B has the most members. Interval B is thus the modal interval.

15. *Mean*: The mean return of Stock A is smaller than the mean return of Stock B.

Median: The median takes away the influence of outliers. The median return of Stock B is greater than the median return of Stock A.

Standard Deviation: Standard deviation is a measure of total risk or stand-alone risk. Stock B's stand-alone risk is greater than Stock A's stand-alone risk.

Skewness: Stock A is negatively skewed, and Stock B is positively skewed. We can see that this difference is caused by several large negative returns in Stock A. Stock B's positive skewness is caused by a large positive outlier.

Excess Kurtosis: Neither stock has severe excess kurtosis compared with a normal distribution (in which excess kurtosis = 0). Stock B does have slightly fatter tails than Stock A, however.

Summary: We cannot know which stock is preferred by particular investors without knowing their exact preferences. Stock B has a higher arithmetic mean return and positive skewness, but it also has more risk as measured by the standard deviation of return.

16. Both stocks have the same expected return of 0.1392, as seen by their means. Stock B, however, is riskier by several measures. First, its standard deviation is about four times as great as A's. Second, it has a large negative skewness. Third, it has a larger positive excess kurtosis (fatter tails) than A. From the ranked data, we can see that B has the possibility of very large losses or very large gains relative to A.

17. To determine which evaluation criterion is the most difficult to achieve, we need to (i) calculate the mean return of the nine funds, (ii) calculate the median return of the nine funds, (iii) calculate two-thirds of the return of the highest-performing fund, and (iv) compare the results.

i. Calculate the mean return of the nine funds.

Find the sum of the values in the table and divide by 9.

$\overline{X}$ = (17.8 + 21.0 + 38.0 + 19.2 + 2.5 + 24.3 + 18.7 + 16.9 + 12.6)/9 = 171/9 = 19.0

ii. Calculate the median return of the nine funds. The first step is to sort the returns from largest to smallest.

Return	Ranking
38.0	9
24.3	8
21.0	7
19.2	6
18.7	5
17.8	4
16.9	3
12.6	2
2.5	1

The median is the middle item, which occupies the $(n + 1)/2 =$ fifth position in this odd-numbered sample. We conclude that the median is 18.7.

iii. Calculate two-thirds of the return of the highest-performing fund.

The top return is 38.0; therefore, two-thirds of the top return is $(2/3)38.0 = 25.33$.

iv. The following table summarizes what we have learned about these funds.

Criterion 1	Criterion 2	Criterion 3
19.0	18.7	25.3

Criterion 3, two-thirds of the return on the top fund, is the most difficult to meet.

In analyzing this problem, note that Criterion 3 is very sensitive to the value of the maximum observation. For example, if we were to subtract 10 from the maximum (to make it 28) and add 10 to the minimum (to make it 12.5), the mean and median would be unchanged. Criterion 3 would fall to two-thirds of 28, or 18.67. In this case, the mean, at 19.0, would be the most difficult criterion to achieve.

C H A P T E R

4

PROBABILITY CONCEPTS

- Explain the properties of covariance.
- Explain the relationship among covariance, standard deviation, and correlation.
- Explain the concept of covariance matrices.
- Calculate the expected return on a portfolio.
- Explain the inputs to calculating the variance of return on a portfolio.
- Calculate the variance of return on a portfolio.
- Calculate covariance, given a joint probability function.
- State Bayes' formula.
- Calculate an updated probability, using Bayes' formula.
- Calculate the number of ways a specified number of steps can be done, using the multiplication rule of counting.
- Solve counting problems using the factorial, combination, and permutation notations.
- Distinguish between problems for which different counting methods are appropriate.
- Calculate the number of ways to choose r objects from a total of n objects, where the order in which the r objects is listed does not matter.
- Calculate the number of ways to choose r objects from a total of n objects, where the order in which the r objects is listed does matter.

1 INTRODUCTION

All investment decisions are made in an environment of risk. The tools that allow us to make decisions with consistency and logic in this setting come under the heading of probability. This chapter presents the essential probability tools needed to frame and address many real world problems involving risk. We illustrate how these tools apply to such issues as predicting investment manager performance, forecasting financial variables, and pricing a bond so that it fairly compensates bondholders for default risk. In contrast to most introductions to probability, we de-emphasize mathematics but explore concepts important to investments more fully. One such concept is independence, as independence relates to the predictability of returns and financial variables. Another concept which receives special attention is expectation, as analysts continually look to the future in their analyses and decisions. Analysts and investors must also cope with variability. We present variance, or dispersion around expectation, as a risk concept important in investments. You will acquire specific skills in using portfolio expected return and variance.

The basic tools of probability, including expected value and variance, are set out in Section 2 of this chapter. Section 3 introduces covariance and correlation (measures of relatedness between random quantities) and the principles for calculating portfolio expected return and variance. Two topics end the chapter: Bayes' formula and outcome counting. Bayes' formula is a procedure for updating beliefs based on new information. In several areas, including a widely-used option pricing model, the calculation of probabilities involves defining and counting outcomes. The chapter ends with a discussion of principles and shortcuts for counting.

2 PROBABILITY, EXPECTED VALUE, AND VARIANCE

The probability concepts and tools that an investment analyst needs to know for most of his or her work are relatively few and simple. However, they require thought to apply. This section presents the essential tools for working with probability, expectation, and variance, drawing on examples from equity and fixed income analysis.

An investor's concerns center on returns. The return on a risky asset is an example of a **random variable,** a quantity whose outcomes are uncertain. For example, an investor's expectation in making an investment may be that it will earn a return of 14 percent. How likely is that return? Fourteen percent is a particular value or **outcome** of the random variable. In probability discussions, an outcome is also one type of event. An **event** is any outcome or specified set of outcomes of a random variable. To return to the question: How likely is that return of 14 percent?

The answer to this question is a probability. A probability is a number between 0 and 1 that gives the chance that a stated event occurs. If the probability is 0.10 that a stock earns a return of 14 percent, there is a 10 percent chance of that return happening. If an event is impossible, it has a probability of 0. If an event is certain to happen, it has a probability of 1. If an event is impossible or a sure thing, it is not random at all. So 0 and 1 serve as the two endpoints of probability.

To save words, it is common to use a capital letter in italics, such as A, to represent an event, after it has been defined. P with parentheses stands for "the probability of (the event in parentheses)" as in $P(E)$ for "the probability of event E." Probability as a function of the distinct possible outcomes of a random variable is the probability function of the random variable. There are two properties of probability which together constitute its definition.

- **Definition of Probability.** The two defining properties of a probability are as follows:
    1. $0 \leq P(E) \leq 1$, the probability of any event E is a number between 0 and 1.
    2. The sum of the probabilities of any list of mutually exclusive and exhaustive events equals 1.

In the above definition, the term **mutually exclusive events** means that only one event can occur at a time; **exhaustive** means that the events cover all possible outcomes. The most basic kind of mutually exclusive and exhaustive events is the set of the distinct possible outcomes of the random variable. If we have that set and the assignment of probabilities to those outcomes—the probability distribution of the random variable—we have a complete description of the random variable.

Suppose we have a statement of the possible outcomes of stock returns and we know their probabilities. But we are interested in the probability of a more complex event than a particular outcome: What is the probability that *the stock earns a return above the risk-free rate*? (We use italics to highlight statements that define events, in this chapter.) The probability of any event is the sum of the probabilities of the distinct outcomes—here, stock return outcomes—included in the definition of the event. So if the risk-free rate is 4 percent, we would sum the probabilities of returns above 4 percent. And that raises a question: How do we, in practice, obtain probabilities?

In investments, the probability of an event is very often estimated from data, as a relative frequency of occurrence. This is an **empirical probability.** We will point out empirical probabilities in several places in which they are used in this chapter. Relationships have to be stable through time for empirical probabilities to be accurate. We cannot calculate an empirical probability of an event not in the historical record, or a reliable empirical probability for a very rare event. There are cases, then, in which we may adjust an empirical probability to take account of perceptions of changing relationships. In other cases, we do not have an empirical probability to use at all. We may also make a personal assessment of probability without reference to any particular data. Each of these three probabilities is a **subjective probability,** one drawing on personal or subjective judgment. Subjective probabilities are of great importance in investments. Investors, in making buy and sell decisions that determine asset prices, often draw on subjective probabilities. Subjective probabilities appear in various places in this chapter, notably in our discussion of Bayes' formula. In a more narrow range of well-defined problems, we can sometimes deduce probabilities by reasoning about the problem. The resulting probability is an **a priori probability,** one based on logical analysis rather than on observation or personal judgment. We will use this type of probability in Example 4-6. The counting methods we discuss later are particularly important in calculating an a priori probability. Because a priori and empirical probabilities generally do not vary from person to person, they are often grouped as **objective probabilities.**

In business, we often meet probabilities stated in terms of odds, as "the odds for E," or the "odds against E," for example.[1] These terms can be defined as follows:

- **Probability Stated as Odds.** Given a probability $P(E)$,

    1. Odds for $E = P(E)/[1 - P(E)]$. In words, the odds for E are the probability of E divided by 1 minus the probability of E. Given odds for E of "a to b" (for example, "7 to 2"), the implied probability of E is $a/(a + b)$.
    2. Odds against $E = [1 - P(E)]/P(E)$, the reciprocal of odds for E. Given odds against E of "a to b," the implied probability of E is $b/(a + b)$.

As an example of Statement 1, if $P(E) = 1/3$, the odds for E are $(1/3)/(2/3) = 1/2$, or "1 to 2." For odds of "1 to 2," the implied probability is $1/3 = 1/(1 + 2) = 1/3$, as expected. As an example of Statement 2, in wagering it is common to speak in terms of the odds against something. For odds of "2 to 1" against E (an implied probability of E of 1/3), a \$1 wager on E, if successful, returns \$2 in profits plus the \$1 staked in the wager. The bet's anticipated profit is \$0 because (1/3 probability of winning) $\times$ (\$2 profit if the wager is won) + (2/3 probability of losing) $\times$ (−\$1 loss if the wager is lost) = 0. This is an example of an expected value calculation, which we define later.

EXAMPLE 4-1.   Profiting from Inconsistent Probabilities.

You are examining the common stock of two firms in the same industry in which an important antitrust decision will be announced next week. The first firm, SmithCo Corporation, will benefit by a governmental decision that there is no antitrust obstacle related to a merger in which it is involved. You believe that SmithCo's share price reflects a 0.85 probability of such a decision. A second firm, Selbert Corporation, will equally benefit from a "go ahead" ruling. Surprisingly, you believe Selbert stock

---

reflects only a 0.50 probability of a favorable decision. Assuming your analysis is correct, what investment strategy would profit from this pricing discrepancy?

You start by thinking about the logical possibilities. One possibility is that the probability of 0.50 reflected in Selbert's share price is accurate. In that case, Selbert is fairly valued but SmithCo is overvalued, as its current share price overestimated the probability of a "go ahead" decision. The second possibility is that the probability of 0.85 is accurate. In that case, SmithCo shares are fairly valued, but Selbert shares, which build in a lower probability of a favorable decision, are undervalued. You diagram the situation as shown in Table 4-1.

TABLE 4-1   Worksheet for Investment Problem

	True Probability of a "Go Ahead" Decision	
	0.50	0.85
SmithCo	Shares Overvalued	Shares Fairly Valued
Selbert	Shares Fairly Valued	Shares Undervalued

The 0.50 probability column shows that Selbert shares are a better value than SmithCo shares. Selbert shares are also a better value if a 0.85 probability is accurate. On average, SmithCo shares are overvalued and Selbert shares are undervalued.

Your investment actions depend on your confidence in your analysis and on any investment constraints you face (such as constraints on selling stock short).[2] A conservative strategy would be to buy Selbert shares and reduce or eliminate any current position in SmithCo. The most aggressive strategy is to short SmithCo stock (relatively overvalued) and simultaneously buy the stock of Selbert (relatively undervalued). This is known as a **pairs arbitrage trade**: a trade in two closely related stocks involving the short sale of one and the purchase of the other.

The prices of SmithCo and Selbert shares reflect probabilities that are not consistent. According to the **Dutch Book Theorem,**[3] one of the most important probability results for investments, inconsistent probabilities create profit opportunities. In our example, investors, by their buy and sell decisions to exploit the inconsistent probabilities, should eliminate the profit opportunity and inconsistency.

Probabilities are either unconditional or conditional. The probability in answer to the straightforward question, What is the probability of this event A?, is an **unconditional probability,** denoted $P(A)$. Unconditional probabilities are also frequently referred to as

---

[2] *Selling short or shorting stock* is selling borrowed shares in the hope that you can repurchase them later at a lower price.

[3] The theorem's name comes from the terminology of wagering. Suppose someone places a $100 bet on X at odds of 10 to 1 against X, and later he is able to place a $600 bet against X at odds of 1 to 1 against X. Whatever the outcome of X, that person makes a riskless profit of $500 because the implied probabilities are inconsistent. He is said to have made a *Dutch book* in X. Ramsey (1931) presented the problem of consistent probabilities. See also Lo (1999).

marginal probabilities.[4] Suppose the question is: What is the probability that *the stock earns a return above the risk-free rate*? The answer is an unconditional probability that can be viewed as the ratio of two quantities. In the numerator is the sum of the probabilities of stock returns above the risk-free rate. In the denominator is 1, the sum of the probabilities of all possible returns.

Contrast the question, What is the probability of *A*? with the question, What is the probability of *A*, given that *B* has occurred? The probability in answer to this last question is a **conditional probability,** denoted $P(A \mid B)$ (read: "the probability of *A* given *B*"). For example, suppose we want to know the probability that *the stock earns a return above the risk-free rate*, given that *the stock earns a positive return*. With the words "given that" we are restricting returns to those larger than 0 percent; this is a new element in contrast to the question that brought forth an unconditional probability. The conditional probability is calculated as the ratio of two quantities. The numerator is the sum of the probabilities of stock returns above the risk-free rate; in this particular case, the numerator is the same as it was in the unconditional case. The denominator, however, changes from 1 to the sum of the probabilities for all outcomes (returns) above 0 percent; the denominator is a number less than 1, as negative returns are possible.[5] To review, an unconditional probability is the probability of an event without any restriction; it might even be thought of as a stand-alone probability. A conditional probability, in contrast, is a probability of an event given that another event has occurred.

Investors continually seek an information edge that will help improve their forecasts. In mathematical terms, they are attempting to frame their view of the future using probabilities conditioned on relevant information or events. Investors do not ignore useful information; they adjust their probabilities to reflect it. Thus, the concepts of conditional probability and conditional expectation, which are discussed later, are extremely important in investment analysis and financial markets. To state an exact definition of conditional probability, we need to introduce the concept of joint probability.

Suppose we ask the question: What is the probability of both *A* and *B* happening? The answer to this question is a **joint probability,** denoted $P(AB)$ (read: "the probability of *A* and *B*"). If we think of the probability of *A* and the probability of *B* as sets built of the outcomes of one or more random variables, the joint probability of *A* and *B* is the sum of the probabilities of the outcomes they have in common. For example, consider two events: *the stock earns a return above the risk-free rate* (*A*) and *the stock earns a positive return* (*B*). The outcomes of *A* are contained within (are a subset of) the outcomes of *B*, so $P(AB)$ equals $P(A)$. We can now state a definition of conditional probability that provides a formula for calculating it.

- **Definition of Conditional Probability.** The conditional probability of *A* given that *B* has occurred is equal to the joint probability of *A* and *B* divided by the probability of *B* (assumed not to equal 0).

    $$P(A \mid B) = P(AB)/P(B), P(B) \neq 0 \qquad\qquad (4\text{-}1)$$

---

[4] In analyses of probabilities presented in tables, unconditional probabilities usually appear at the ends or *margins* of the table, thus the term *marginal probability*. Because of possible confusion with the way *marginal* is used in economics (roughly meaning *incremental*), we use the term *unconditional probability* throughout this discussion.

[5] In this example, the conditional probability is larger than the unconditional probability. We cannot generalize from this example, however. For instance, the probability that *the stock earns a return above the risk-free rate* given that *the stock earns a negative return* is 0.

Sometimes we know the conditional probability $P(A \mid B)$ and we want to know the joint probability $P(AB)$. We can obtain the joint probability from the following **multiplication rule for probabilities,** which is Equation 4-1 rearranged.

- **Multiplication Rule for Probabilities.** The joint probability of A and B can be expressed as

$$P(AB) = P(A \mid B)P(B) \tag{4-2}$$

Equation 4-2 states that the joint probability of A and B equals the probability of A given B times the probability of B. As $P(AB) = P(BA)$, the expression $P(AB) = P(BA) = P(B \mid A)P(A)$ is equivalent to Equation 4-2.

EXAMPLE 4-2.   Conditional Probabilities and Predictability of Mutual Fund Performance (1).

Kahn and Rudd (1995) examined whether historical performance predicts future performance for a sample of mutual funds that included 300 actively managed U.S. domestic equity funds. One approach they used involved calculating each fund's exposure to a set of style indexes (the term *style* captures the distinctions of growth/value and large-capitalization/mid-capitalization/small-capitalization). After establishing a style benchmark (a comparison portfolio matched to the fund's style) for each fund, Kahn and Rudd computed the fund's *selection return* for two periods. They defined selection return as fund return minus the fund's style-benchmark return. The first period was October 1990 to March 1992. The top 50 percent of funds by selection return for that period were labeled winners; the bottom 50 percent were labeled losers. Based on selection return in the next period, April 1992 to September 1993, the top 50 percent of funds were tagged as winners and the bottom 50 percent as losers for that period. An excerpt from their results is given in Table 4-2. The winner–winner entry, for example, shows that 79 of the 150 first-period winner funds were winners in the second period (52.6% = 79/150).

**TABLE 4-2   Equity Selection Returns
Period 1: October 1990 to March 1992
Period 2: April 1992 to September 1993
Entries are number of funds (percent of row total in parentheses)**

	Period 2 Winner	Period 2 Loser
Period 1 winner	79 (52.6%)	71 (47.4%)
Period 1 loser	71 (46.9%)	79 (53.1%)

Source: Kahn and Rudd (1995), Table 3.

1. The four entries in parentheses in the table can be viewed as conditional probabilities. State the four events that define the four conditional probabilities.

2. Restate the four entries of the table as conditional probabilities. Use the form $P(this\ event \mid that\ event) = \text{number}$.

---

3. Are the conditional probabilities in Part 2 empirical, a priori, or subjective probabilities?

4. Using information in the table, calculate the probability of the event *a fund is loser in both period 1 and period 2*. (Note that because 50 percent of funds are categorized as losers in each period, the unconditional probability that a fund is labeled a loser in either period is 0.5.)

Solution to 1.   The four events needed to define the conditional probabilities are as follows:

Fund is a period 1 winner
Fund is a period 1 loser
Fund is a period 2 winner
Fund is a period 2 loser

Solution to 2.
From row 1:

P(*fund is a period 2 winner* | *fund is a period 1 winner*) = 0.526
P(*fund is a period 2 loser* | *fund is a period 1 winner*) = 0.474

From row 2:

P(*fund is a period 2 winner* | *fund is a period 1 loser*) = 0.469
P(*fund is a period 2 loser* | *fund is a period 1 loser*) = 0.531

Solution to 3.   These probabilities are calculated from data, so are empirical probabilities.

Solution to 4.   The estimated probability is 0.266. We use Equation 4-2:

P(*fund is a period 2 loser* and *fund is a period 1 loser*) = P(*fund is a period 2 loser* | *fund is a period 1 loser*) $\times$ P(*fund is a period 1 loser*) = 0.531 $\times$ 0.50 = 0.2655, or a probability of 0.266.

When we have two events, A and B, that we are interested in, we often want to know the probability that either A or B occurs. Here by *or* we mean an inclusive-or: that either A or B occurs, or both A and B occur. To put this another way, the probability of A or B is the probability that at least one of the two events occurs. Such probabilities are calculated using the **addition rule for probabilities.**

- **Addition Rule for Probabilities.** Given events A and B, the probability that A or B occurs, or both occur, is equal to the probability that A occurs, plus the probability that B occurs, minus the probability that both A and B occur.

$$P(A \text{ or } B) = P(A) + P(B) - P(AB) \tag{4-3}$$

If we think of the individual probabilities of A and B as sets built of outcomes of one or more random variables as shown in Figure 4-1, the first step in calculating the probability of A or B is to sum the probabilities of the outcomes in A to obtain $P(A)$. If A and B share any outcomes, if we now added $P(B)$ to $P(A)$ we would count twice the probabilities of those shared outcomes. So we add to $P(A)$ the quantity $[P(B) - P(AB)]$, which is the probability of outcomes in B net of the probability of any outcomes already counted when we computed $P(A)$. This is illustrated in Figure 4-1, where we avoid double-counting the outcomes in the intersection of A and B by subtracting $P(AB)$. As an example of the calculation, if $P(A) = 0.50$, $P(B) = 0.40$, and $P(AB) = 0.20$, then $P(A \text{ or } B) = 0.50 + 0.40 - 0.20 = 0.70$. Only if the two events A and B were mutually exclusive, so that $P(AB) = 0$, would it be correct to state that $P(A \text{ or } B) = P(A) + P(B)$.

FIGURE 4-1   **Addition Rule for Probabilities**

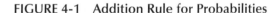

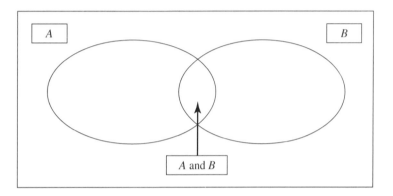

The next example shows how much useful information can be obtained using the few probability rules presented to this point.

EXAMPLE 4-3.   Probability of a Limit Order Executing.

You have two buy limit orders outstanding on the same stock. A limit order to buy stock at a stated price is an order to buy at that price or lower. A number of vendors, including an Internet service that you use, supply the estimated probability that a limit order will be filled within a stated time horizon, given the current stock price and the price limit. One buy order (order 1) was placed at a price limit of $10. The probability that it will execute within one hour is 0.35. The second buy order (order 2), was placed at a price limit of $9.75; it has a 0.25 probability of executing within the same one-hour time frame.

   1. What is the probability that either order 1 or order 2 will execute?
   2. What is the probability that order 2 executes, given that order 1 executes?

     Solution to 1.   The probability is 0.35. The calculation uses the addition rule for probabilities:

     P(order 1 executes or order 2 executes) = P(order 1 executes) + P(order 2 executes) − P(order 1 executes and order 2 executes) = 0.35 + 0.25 − 0.25 = 0.35

Note that *P(order 1 executes and order 2 executes) = P(order 1 executes | order 2 executes)P(order 2 executes)* = 1 × 0.25 = 0.25. *P(order 1 executes | order 2 exe-*

cutes) = 1 because, if order 2 executes, it is certain that order 1 also executes: Price must pass through $10 to reach $9.75.

Note that the outcomes for which order 2 executes are a subset of the outcomes for which order 1 executes. After you count the probability that order 1 executes, you have counted the probability of the outcomes for which order 2 also executes. Therefore, the answer to the question is the probability that order 1 executes, 0.35.

Solution to 2. If the first order executes, the probability that the second order executes (stated as a percent) is 71.4 percent. In the solution to Part 1, you found that *P*(*order 1 executes* and *order 2 executes*) = *P*(*order 1 executes* | *order 2 executes*)*P*(*order 2 executes*) = 1 × 0.25 = 0.25. An equivalent way to state this joint probability is useful here:

P(*order 1 executes* and *order 2 executes*) = 0.25 =
P(*order 2 executes* | *order 1 executes*) × *P*(*order 1 executes*)

Now *P*(*order 1 executes*) = 0.35 was a given, so you have one equation in one unknown:

0.25 = *P*(*order 2 executes* | *order 1 executes*) × 0.35

You conclude that *P*(*order 2 executes* | *order 1 executes*) = 0.25/0.35 = 5/7, or about 0.714.

Of great interest to investment analysts are the concepts of independence and dependence. These concepts bear on such basic investment questions as which financial variables are useful for investment analysis, whether asset returns can be predicted, and whether superior investment managers can be selected on the basis of their past records.

Two events are independent if the occurrence of one event does not affect the probability of occurrence of the other event.

- **Definition of Independent Events.** Two events A and B are **independent** if and only if $P(A| B) = P(A)$ or, equivalently, $P(B | A) = P(B)$.

When two events are not independent, they are **dependent**: the occurrence of one is related to the probability of occurrence of the other. If we are trying to forecast one event, information about a dependent event may be useful, but information about an independent event will not be useful.

When two events are independent, the multiplication rule for probabilities, Equation 4-2, simplifies as follows.

- **Multiplication Rule for Independent Events.** When two events are independent, the joint probability of A and B equals the product of the individual probabilities of A and B.

$$P(AB) = P(A)P(B) \qquad (4\text{-}4)$$

Thus, if we are interested in two independent events with probabilities of 0.75 and 0.50, respectively, the probability that they both occur is 0.375 = 0.75 × 0.50. The multiplication rule for independent events generalizes to more than two events; for example, if A, B, and C are independent events, then $P(ABC) = P(A)P(B)P(C)$.

EXAMPLE 4-4.   BankCorp's Earnings per Share (1).

As part of your work as a banking industry analyst, you build models for forecasting earnings per share (EPS) of the banks you cover. Today you are studying BankCorp. The historical record shows that in 55 percent of recent quarters BankCorp's EPS has increased sequentially, and in 45 percent of quarters EPS has decreased or remained unchanged sequentially.[6] At this point in your analysis, you are assuming that changes in sequential EPS are independent.

　　　Earnings per share for 2Q:2001 (that is, EPS for the second quarter of 2001) was larger than EPS for 1Q:2001.

1. What is the probability that 3Q:2001 EPS will be larger than 2Q:2001 EPS (a positive change in sequential EPS)?

2. What is the probability of two negative changes in sequential EPS (3Q:2001 EPS smaller than 2Q:2001 EPS, and 4Q:2001 EPS smaller than 3Q:2001 EPS)?

　　　Solution to 1.   Under the assumption of independence, the probability that 3Q:2001 EPS will be larger than 2Q:2001 EPS is the unconditional probability of positive change, 0.55. That 2Q:2001 EPS was larger than 1Q:2001 EPS is not useful information, as the next change in EPS is independent of the prior change.

　　　Solution to 2.   The probability of two negative changes in a row is $0.2025 = 0.45 \times 0.45$.

The following example illustrates how hard it is to satisfy a set of independent criteria even when, individually, the criteria may not be stringent.

EXAMPLE 4-5.   Screening Stocks for Investment.

You have developed a stock screen—a set of criteria for selecting stocks. Your investment universe (the set of securities from which you make your choices) is the Russell 1000, an index of 1,000 large-capitalization U.S. equities. Your criteria capture different aspects of the selection problem; you believe that the criteria are independent, to a close approximation.

Criterion	Percent of Russell 1000 Stocks Meeting Criterion
First valuation criterion	50%
Second valuation criterion	50%
Analyst coverage criterion	25%
Profitability criterion for company	55%
Financial strength criterion for company	67%

How many stocks do you expect to pass your screen?

---

[6] *Sequential* comparisons of quarterly EPS are with the immediately prior quarter. A sequential comparison stands in contrast to a comparison with the same quarter one year ago (another frequent type of comparison).

Only 23 stocks out of 1,000 pass through your screen. If you define five events—*the stock passes the first valuation criterion, the stock passes the second valuation criterion, the stock passes the analyst coverage criterion, the company passes the profitability criterion, the company passes the financial strength criterion*, say events *A, B, C, D*, and *E*, respectively—then the probability that a stock will pass all five criteria, under independence, is

$$P(ABCDE) = P(A)P(B)P(C)P(D)P(E) = 0.50 \times$$
$$0.50 \times 0.25 \times 0.55 \times 0.67 = 0.023031$$

Although only one of the five criteria is even moderately strict (the strictest lets 25 percent of stocks through), the probability that a stock can pass all five is only 0.023031, or about 2 percent. The size of the list of candidate investments is $0.023031 \times 1,000 = 23.031$ or 23 stocks.

An area of intense interest to investment managers and their clients is whether past records of performance are useful in identifying repeat winners and losers. The following example shows how this issue relates to the concept of independence.

EXAMPLE 4-6.   Conditional Probabilities and Predictability of Mutual Fund Performance (2).

The purpose of the Kahn and Rudd (1995) study, introduced in Example 4-2, was to address the question of repeat mutual fund winners and losers. If whether a fund is a loser in one period is independent of whether it is winner in the next period, the practical value of performance ranking is questionable. Using the four events defined in Example 4-2 as building blocks, we can define the following events to address the issue of predictability of mutual fund performance:

> *Fund is a period 1 winner* and *fund is a period 2 winner*
>
> *Fund is a period 1 winner* and *fund is period 2 loser*
>
> *Fund is a period 1 loser* and *fund is a period 2 winner*
>
> *Fund is a period 1 loser* and *fund is a period 2 loser*

In Part 4 of Example 4-2, you calculated that

> *P(fund is a period 2 loser* and *fund is a period 1 loser)* = 0.266

If the ranking in one period is independent of the ranking in the next period, what would you expect *P(fund is a period 2 loser* and *fund is a period 1 loser)* to be? Interpret the calculated probability 0.266.

By the multiplication rule for independent events, *P(fund is a period 2 loser* and *fund is a period 1 loser)* = *P(fund is a period 2 loser)* × *P(fund is a period 1 loser)*. Because 50 percent of funds are categorized as losers in each period, the unconditional probability that a fund is labeled a loser either period is 0.50. Thus *P(fund is a period 2 loser)* × *P(fund is a period 1 loser)* = 0.50 × 0.50 = 0.25. If whether a fund is a loser in one period is independent of whether a fund is a loser in the other period, we conclude that *P(fund is a period 2 loser* and *fund is a period 1 loser*) = 0.25. This is an a priori probability because it is obtained from reasoning about the problem. You could also reason that the four events described above define categories, and that if funds were randomly assigned to the four categories, there is a 1/4 probability of *fund is a period 1 loser* and *fund is a period 2 loser*. If the classifications in period 1 and period 2 were dependent, then the assignment of funds to categories would not be random. The calculated probability of 0.266 is only slightly above 0.25. Is this apparent slight amount of predictability the result of chance? A test conducted by Kahn and Rudd indicated a 35.6 percent chance of observing the tabled data if the period 1 and period 2 rankings were independent.

In investments, the question of whether one event (or characteristic) provides information about another event (or characteristic) arises in both time-series settings (across time) and cross-sectional settings (across units at a given point in time). Examples 4-4 and 4-6 illustrated independence in a time-series setting. Example 4-5 illustrated independence in a cross-sectional setting. Independence/dependence relationships are often also explored in both settings using regression analysis, a technique we discuss in a later chapter.

In many practical problems, we logically analyze a problem as follows: We formulate scenarios that we think are important for understanding the likelihood of an event that we are interested in. We then estimate the probability of the event, given the scenario. When the scenarios (conditioning events) are mutually exclusive and exhaustive, no possible outcomes are left out. We can then analyze the event using the **total probability rule.** This rule explains the unconditional probability of the event in terms of probabilities conditional on the scenarios.

The total probability rule is stated below for two cases. Part 1 gives the simplest case, where we have two scenarios. One new notation is introduced. If we have an event or scenario S, the event not-S, called the **complement** of S, is written S^C.[7] Note that $P(S) + P(S^C)$ = 1, as either S or not-S must occur. Part 2 states the rule for the general case of n mutually exclusive and exhaustive events or scenarios.

- **The Total Probability Rule.**

    1. $P(A) = P(A \mid S)P(S) + P(A \mid S^C)P(S^C)$ (4-5)

    2. $P(A) = P(A \mid S_1)P(S_1) + P(A \mid S_2)P(S_2) + \ldots + P(A \mid S_n)P(S_n)$ (4-6)

    where $S_1, S_2, \ldots, S_n$ are mutually exclusive and exhaustive scenarios or events.

Equation 4-6 states the following: The probability of any event [$P(A)$] can be expressed as a weighted average of the probabilities of the event, given scenarios [terms such $P(A \mid S_1)$]; the weights applied to these conditional probabilities are the respective probabilities of the scenarios [terms such as $P(S_1)$ multiplying $P(A \mid S_1)$], and the scenarios must be mutually exclusive and exhaustive. Among other applications, this rule is needed to understand Bayes' formula, which we discuss later in the chapter.

In the next example, we use the total probability rule to develop a consistent set of views about BankCorp's earnings per share.

---

[7] For readers familiar with mathematical treatments of probability, S, a notation usually reserved for a concept called the sample space, is being appropriated to stand for *scenario*.

EXAMPLE 4-7.   BankCorp's Earnings per Share (2).

You are continuing your investigation into whether you can predict the direction of changes in BankCorp's quarterly EPS. You define four events:

Event	Probability
A = *change in sequential EPS is positive next quarter*	0.55
A^C = *change in sequential EPS is 0 or negative next quarter*	0.45
S = *change in sequential EPS is positive the prior quarter*	0.55
S^C = *change in sequential EPS is 0 or negative the prior quarter*	0.45

On inspecting the data, you observe some persistence in EPS changes: increases tend to be followed by increases, and decreases by decreases. The first probability estimate you develop is P(*change in sequential EPS is positive next quarter | change in sequential EPS is 0 or negative the prior quarter*) $= P(A \mid S^C) = 0.40$. The most recent quarter's EPS (2Q:2001) is announced, and the change is a positive sequential change (the event S). You are interested in forecasting EPS for 3Q:2001.

1. Write this statement in probability notation: "The probability that the change in sequential EPS is positive next quarter, given that the change in sequential EPS is positive the prior quarter."

2. Calculate the probability in Part 1. (Calculate the probability that is consistent with your other probabilities or beliefs.)

Solution to 1.   In probability notation, this statement is written $P(A \mid S)$.

Solution to 2.   The probability that the change in sequential EPS is positive for 3Q:2001, given the positive change in sequential EPS for 2Q:2001, is 0.673. The values of the probabilities needed for the $P(A \mid S)$ calculation are already known: $P(A) = 0.55$, $P(S) = 0.55$, $P(S^C) = 0.45$, and $P(A \mid S^C) = 0.40$. According to Equation 4-5,

$$P(A) = P(A \mid S)P(S) + P(A \mid S^C)P(S^C)$$
$$0.55 = P(A \mid S) \times 0.55 + 0.40 \times 0.45$$

Solving for the unknown, $P(A \mid S) = (0.55 - 0.40 \times 0.45)/0.55 = 0.672727$, or 0.673.

You conclude that P(*change in sequential EPS is positive next quarter | change in sequential EPS is positive the prior quarter*) $= 0.673$. Any other probability is not consistent with your other estimated probabilities. Reflecting the persistence in EPS changes, this conditional probability of a positive EPS change, 0.673, is greater than the unconditional probability of an EPS increase, 0.55.

In the chapter on statistical concepts and market returns, we discussed the concept of a weighted average or weighted mean. The example highlighted in that chapter was that portfolio return is a weighted average of the returns on the individual assets in the portfolio, where the weight applied to each asset's return is the fraction of the portfolio invested in that asset. The total probability rule, which is a rule for stating an unconditional probability in terms of conditional probabilities, is also a weighted average. In that formula, probabilities are used as weights. Part of the definition of weighted average is that the weights sum to 1. Probabilities of mutually exclusive and exhaustive events do sum to 1 (that is part of the definition of probability). The next weighted average we discuss, the expected value of a random variable, also uses probabilities as weights.

The expected value of a random variable is an essential quantitative concept in investments. Investors continually make use of expected values: in estimating the rewards of alternative investments, in forecasting EPS and other corporate financial variables and ratios, and in assessing any other factor that may affect their financial position. The expected value of a random variable is defined as follows:

- **Definition of Expected Value.** The **expected value** of a random variable is the probability-weighted average of the possible outcomes of the random variable. For a random variable X, the expected value of X is denoted $E(X)$.

Expected value (for example, expected stock return) looks either to the future, as a forecast, or to the "true" value of the mean (the *population mean*, discussed in the chapter on statistical concepts and market returns). We should distinguish expected value from the concepts of *historical* or *sample mean*. The sample mean also summarizes in a single number a central value. However, the sample mean presents a central value for a particular set of observations as an equally weighted average of those observations. To summarize, the contrast is *forecast* versus *historical*, or *population* versus *sample*.

EXAMPLE 4-8.   BankCorp's Earnings Per Share (3).

You continue with your analysis of BankCorp's EPS. In Table 4-3, you have recorded a probability distribution for BankCorp's EPS for the current fiscal year.

TABLE 4-3   Probability Distribution for BankCorp's EPS

Probability	EPS
0.15	$2.60
0.45	$2.45
0.24	$2.20
0.16	$2.00
Sum = 1.00	

What is the expected value of BankCorp's EPS for the current fiscal year?

Following the definition of expected value, list each outcome, weight it by its probability, and sum the terms.

$$E(\text{EPS}) = (0.15 \times \$2.60) + (0.45 \times \$2.45) + (0.24 \times \$2.20) + (0.16 \times \$2.00) = \$2.3405$$

The expected value of EPS is $2.34.

An equation that summarizes your calculation in Example 4-8 is

$$E(X) = P(x_1) \times x_1 + P(x_2) \times x_2 + \ldots + P(x_n) \times x_n = \sum_{i=1}^{n} P(x_i) \times x_i \qquad (4\text{-}7)$$

where x_i is one of n possible outcomes of the random variable X.[8]

The expected value is our forecast. Because we are discussing random quantities, we cannot count on an individual forecast being realized (although we hope that, on average, forecasts will be accurate). It is important, as a result, to measure the risk we face. Variance and standard deviation measure the dispersion of outcomes around the expected value or forecast.

- **Definition of Variance.** The **variance** of a random variable is the expected value (the probability-weighted average) of squared deviations from the random variable's expected value.

$$\sigma^2(X) = E\{[X - E(X)]^2\} \qquad (4\text{-}8)$$

The two notations for variance are $\sigma^2(X)$ and $\mathrm{Var}(X)$.

Variance is a number greater than or equal to 0 because it is the sum of squared terms. If variance is 0, there is no dispersion or risk. The outcome is certain, and the quantity X is not random at all. Variance greater than 0 indicates dispersion of outcomes. Increasing variance indicates increasing dispersion, all else equal. Variance of X is a quantity in the squared units of X. For example, if the random variable is return in percent, variance of return is in units of percent squared. Standard deviation is easier to interpret than variance, as it is in the same units as the random variable. If the random variable is return in percent, standard deviation of return is also in units of percent.

- **Definition of Standard Deviation. Standard deviation** is the positive square root of variance.

The best way to become familiar with these concepts is to work examples.

EXAMPLE 4-9.   BankCorp's Earnings Per Share (4).

In Example 4-8, you calculated the expected value of BankCorp's EPS as $2.34, which is your forecast. Now you want to measure the dispersion around your forecast. Table 4-4 shows your view of the probability distribution of EPS.

---

[8] For simplicity, we model all random variables in this chapter as *discrete* random variables, which have a countable set of outcomes. For *continuous* random variables, which are discussed along with discrete random variables in the chapter on common probability distributions, the operation corresponding to summation is integration.

TABLE 4-4   Probability Distribution for BankCorp's EPS

Probability	EPS
0.15	$2.60
0.45	$2.45
0.24	$2.20
0.16	$2.00
Sum = 1.00	

What are the variance and standard deviation of BankCorp's EPS for the current fiscal year?

The order of calculation is always expected value, then variance, then standard deviation. Expected value has already been calculated. Following the definition of variance above, calculate the deviation of each outcome from the mean or expected value, square each deviation, weight (multiply) each squared deviation by its probability of occurrence, then sum these terms.

$$
\begin{aligned}
\sigma^2 &= P(\$2.60)[\$2.60 - E(EPS)]^2 + P(\$2.45)[\$2.45 - E(EPS)]^2 \\
&\quad + P(\$2.20)[\$2.20 - E(EPS)]^2 + P(\$2.00)[\$2.00 - E(EPS)]^2 \\
&= [0.15 \times (\$2.60 - \$2.34)^2] + [0.45 \times (\$2.45 - \$2.34)^2] \\
&\quad + [0.24 \times (\$2.20 - \$2.34)^2] + [0.16 \times (\$2.00 - \$2.34)^2] \\
&= 0.01014 + 0.005445 + 0.004704 + 0.018496 \\
&= 0.038785 \text{ dollars squared}
\end{aligned}
$$

Standard deviation is the positive square root of 0.038785 dollars squared.

$$
\sigma(EPS) = (0.038785)^{1/2} = \$0.196939 \text{ or approximately } \$0.20.
$$

An equation that summarizes your calculation of variance in Example 4-9 is

$$
\sigma^2(X) = P(x_1)[x_1 - E(X)]^2 + P(x_2)[x_2 - E(X)]^2 + \\
\dots + P(x_n)[x_n - E(X)]^2 = \sum_{i=1}^{n} P(x_i)[x_i - E(X)]^2 \tag{4-9}
$$

where x_i is one of n possible outcomes of the random variable X.

In investments, we make use of any relevant information available in making our forecasts. When we refine our expectations or forecasts, we are typically making adjustments based on new information or events; in these cases we are using **conditional expected values.** The expected value of a random variable X given an event or scenario S is denoted $E(X \mid S)$. Suppose the random variable X can take on n distinct outcomes x_1, x_2, $\dots$, x_n. The expected value of X conditional on S is the first outcome, x_1, times the probability of the first outcome given S, $P(x_1 \mid S)$, plus the second outcome, x_2, times the probability of the second outcome given S, $P(x_2 \mid S)$, and so forth.

$$
E(X \mid S) = [P(x_1 \mid S) \times x_1] + [P(x_2 \mid S) \times x_2] + \dots + [P(x_n \mid S) \times x_n] \tag{4-10}
$$

We will illustrate this equation shortly.

Parallel to the total probability rule for stating unconditional probabilities in terms of conditional probabilities, there is a principle for stating (unconditional) expected values in terms of conditional expected values. This principle is the **total probability rule for expected value.**

- **The Total Probability Rule for Expected Value.**

1. $E(X) = E(X \mid S)P(S) + E(X \mid S^C)P(S^C)$ (4-11)

2. $E(X) = E(X \mid S_1)P(S_1) + E(X \mid S_2) P(S_2) + \ldots + E(X \mid S_n) P(S_n)$ (4-12)

where $S_1, S_2, \ldots , S_n$ are mutually exclusive and exhaustive scenarios or events.

The general case, Part 2, states that the expected value of X equals the expected value of X given Scenario 1, $E(X \mid S_1)$, times the probability of Scenario 1, $P(S_1)$, plus the expected value of X given Scenario 2, $E(X \mid S_2)$, times the probability of Scenario 2, $P(S_2)$, and so forth.

To use this principle, we formulate mutually exclusive and exhaustive scenarios that are useful for understanding the outcomes of the random variable. This approach was employed in developing the probability distribution of BankCorp's EPS in Examples 4-8 and 4-9.

The earnings of BankCorp are interest rate sensitive, benefiting from a declining interest rate environment. Suppose there is a 0.60 probability that BankCorp will operate in a *declining interest rate environment* in the current fiscal year, and a 0.40 probability that it will operate in a *stable interest rate environment* (assessing the chance of an increasing interest rate environment as negligible). If a *declining interest rate environment* occurs, the probability that EPS will be $2.60 is estimated at 0.25, and the probability that EPS will be $2.45 is estimated at 0.75. Note that 0.60, the probability of *declining interest rate environment*, times 0.25, the probability of $2.60 EPS given a *declining interest rate environment*, equals 0.15, the (unconditional) probability of $2.60 given in the table in Examples 4-8 and 4-9 above. The probabilities are consistent. Also, $0.60 \times 0.75 = 0.45$, the probability of $2.45 EPS given in Table 4-2. The **tree diagram** in Figure 4-2 shows the rest of the analysis.

FIGURE 4-2   BankCorp's Forecasted EPS

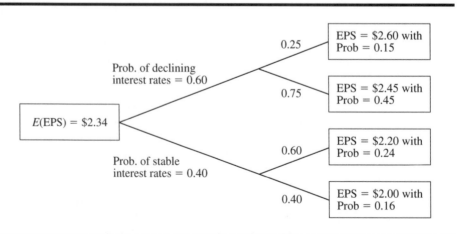

Given a declining interest rate environment, we are at the node of the tree that branches off to outcomes of $2.60 and $2.45. We can find expected EPS given a declining interest rate environment as follows, using Equation 4-10:

$$E(\text{EPS} \mid declining\ interest\ rate\ environment) = (0.25 \times \$2.60)$$
$$+ (0.75 \times \$2.45) = \$2.4875$$

If interest rates are stable

$$E(\text{EPS} \mid stable\ interest\ rate\ environment) = (0.60 \times \$2.20)$$
$$+ (0.40 \times \$2.00) = \$2.12$$

Once we have the new piece of information that interest rates are stable, for example, we revise our original expectation of EPS from $2.34 downward to $2.12. Now using the total probability rule for expected value (Part 1)

$$E(\text{EPS}) = E(\text{EPS} \mid declining\ interest\ rate\ environment)$$
$$\times P(declining\ interest\ rate\ environment)$$
$$+ E(\text{EPS} \mid stable\ interest\ rate\ environment)$$
$$\times P(stable\ interest\ rate\ environment)$$

So $E(\text{EPS}) = (\$2.4875 \times 0.60) + (\$2.12 \times 0.40) = \$2.34$.

This amount is identical to the estimate of the expected value of EPS calculated directly from the probability distribution in Example 4-8. Just as our probabilities must be consistent, so must our expected values, unconditional and conditional; otherwise our investment actions may create profit opportunities for other investors at our expense.

To review, we first developed the factors or scenarios that influence the outcome of the event of interest. After assigning probabilities to these scenarios, we formed expectations conditioned on the different scenarios. Then we worked backward to formulate an expected value as of today. In the problem just worked, EPS was the event of interest, and the interest rate environment was the factor influencing EPS.

We can also calculate the variance of EPS given each scenario:

$$\sigma^2(\text{EPS} \mid declining\ interest\ rate\ environment)$$
$$= P(\$2.60 \mid declining\ interest\ rate\ environment)$$
$$\times [\$2.60 - E(\text{EPS} \mid declining\ interest\ rate\ environment)]^2$$
$$+ P(\$2.45 \mid declining\ interest\ rate\ environment)$$
$$\times [\$2.45 - E(\text{EPS} \mid declining\ interest\ rate\ environment)]^2$$
$$= [0.25 \times (\$2.60 - \$2.4875)^2]$$
$$+ [0.75 \times (\$2.45 - \$2.4875)^2] = 0.004219$$

$$\sigma^2(\text{EPS} \mid stable\ interest\ rate\ environment)$$
$$= P(\$2.20 \mid stable\ interest\ rate\ environment)$$
$$\times [\$2.20 - E(\text{EPS} \mid stable\ interest\ rate\ environment)]^2$$
$$+ P(\$2.00 \mid stable\ interest\ rate\ environment)$$
$$\times [\$2.00 \times E(\text{EPS} \mid stable\ interest\ rate\ environment)]^2$$
$$= [0.60 \times (\$2.20 - \$2.12)^2] + [0.40 \times (\$2.00 - \$2.12)^2] = 0.0096$$

These are **conditional variances,** the variance of EPS given a *declining interest rate environment* and the variance of EPS given a *stable interest rate environment*. The relationship between unconditional variance and conditional variance is a relatively advanced topic.[9] The main points are that variance, like expected value, has a conditional counterpart to the unconditional concept, and that we can use conditional variance to assess risk given a particular scenario.

EXAMPLE 4-10.   BankCorp's Earnings Per Share (5).

Continuing with BankCorp, you focus now on BankCorp's cost structure. One model you are researching for BankCorp's operating costs is

$$\hat{Y} = a + bX$$

where $\hat{Y}$ is a forecast of operating costs in millions of dollars and X is the number of branch offices. (This model was developed using regression analysis, which we will discuss in a later chapter.) You interpret the intercept a as fixed costs and b as variable costs. You estimate the equation as

$$\hat{Y} = 12.5 + 0.65X$$

BankCorp currently has 66 branch offices, and the equation estimates that $12.5 + 0.65 \times 66 = \$55.4$ million. You have two scenarios for growth, pictured in the tree diagram in Figure 4-3.

FIGURE 4-3   BankCorp's Forecasted Operating Costs

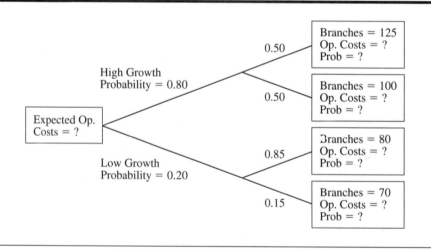

---

[9] The unconditional variance of EPS is the sum of *two* terms: (1) the expected value (probability weighted average) of the conditional variances (parallel to the total probability rules), and (2) the variance of conditional expected values of EPS. The second term arises because the variability in conditional expected value is a source of risk. Term (1) is σ^2(EPS) = P(*declining interest rate environment*) $\times \sigma^2$(EPS | *declining interest rate environment*) + P(*stable interest rate environment*) $\times \sigma^2$(EPS | *stable interest rate environment*) = $(0.60 \times 0.004219) + (0.40 \times 0.0096) = 0.006371$. Term (2) is σ^2[E(EPS | interest rate environment)] = $[0.60 \times (\$2.4875 - \$2.34)^2] + [0.40 \times (\$2.12 - \$2.34)^2] = 0.032414$. Summing the two terms, unconditional variance equals $0.006371 + 0.032414 = 0.038785$.

1. Compute the forecasted operating costs given the different levels of operating costs, using $\hat{Y} = 12.5 + 0.65X$. State the probability of each level of the number of branch offices. These are the answers to the questions in the terminal boxes of the tree diagram.

2. Compute the expected value of operating costs, given the high-growth scenario. Also calculate the expected value of operating costs, given the low-growth scenario.

3. Answer the question in the initial box of the tree: What are BankCorp's expected operating costs?

Solution to 1.   Using $E(X \mid Y) = 12.5 + 0.65Y$, from top to bottom you have

Operating Costs	*Probability*
$\hat{Y} = 12.5 + 0.65 \times 125 = \$93.75$ million	$0.80 \times 0.50 = 0.40$
$\hat{Y} = 12.5 + 0.65 \times 100 = \$77.50$ million	$0.80 \times 0.50 = 0.40$
$\hat{Y} = 12.5 + 0.65 \times 80 = \$64.5$ million	$0.20 \times 0.85 = 0.17$
$\hat{Y} = 12.5 + 0.65 \times 70 = \$58.0$ million	$0.20 \times 0.15 = 0.03$
	Sum $= 1.00$

Solution to 2.   U.S. dollar amounts are in millions.

$E(operating\ costs \mid high\ growth)$
$= (0.50 \times \$93.75) + (0.50 \times \$77.50) = \$85.625$

$E(operating\ costs \mid low\ growth)$
$= (0.85 \times \$64.5) + (0.15 \times \$58.00) = \$63.53$

Solution to 3.   U.S. dollar amounts are in millions.

$E(operating\ costs) = E(operating\ costs \mid high\ growth) \times P(high\ growth)$
$+ E(operating\ costs \mid low\ growth) \times P(low\ growth)$
$= (\$85.625 \times 0.80) + (\$63.53 \times 0.20) = \$81.206$

BankCorp's expected operating costs are $81.206 million.

We will see conditional probabilities again when we discuss Bayes' formula. This section has only introduced some of the problems that can be addressed using probability tools. The following problem draws on these tools, as well as on analytical skills.

EXAMPLE 4-11.   The Default Risk Premium for a One-Period Debt Instrument.

As the co-manager of a short-term bond portfolio, you are reviewing the pricing of a speculative grade, one-year maturity, zero-coupon bond. For this type of bond, the return is the difference between the amount paid and the principal value received at maturity. Your goal is to estimate an appropriate default risk premium for this bond. You define the default risk premium as the extra return above the risk-free return that will compensate investors for default risk. If R is the promised return (yield-to-maturity) on the debt instrument and R_f is the risk-free rate, the default risk premium is $R - R_f$. You assess the probability that the bond defaults as $P(\textit{the bond defaults}) = 0.06$. Looking at current money market yields, you find that one-year Treasury bills (T-bills) are offering a return of 5.8 percent, an estimate of R_f. As a first step, you make the simplifying assumption that bondholders will recover nothing in the event of a default. What is the minimum default risk premium you should require for this instrument?

The challenge in this type of problem is to find a starting point. In many problems, including this one, an effective first step is to divide up the possible outcomes into mutually exclusive and exhaustive events in an economically logical way. Here, from the viewpoint of a bondholder, the two events that affect returns are *the bond defaults* and *the bond does not default*. These two events cover all outcomes. How do these events affect a bondholder's returns? A second step is to compute the value of the bond for the two events. We don't have specifics on bond face value, but we can compute value per $1 or one unit of currency invested. (It is useful to use symbols so that a sensitivity analysis can be done.)

	The Bond Defaults	The Bond Does Not Default
Bond value	$0	$(1 + R)

The third step is to find the expected value of the bond (per $1 invested).

$$E(\text{bond}) = \$0 \times P(\text{the bond defaults}) + \$(1 + R) \times [1 - P(\text{the bond defaults})]$$

So $E(\text{bond}) = \$(1 + R) \times [1 - P(\text{the bond defaults})]$. The expected value of the T-bill per $1 invested is $(1 + R_f)$. In fact, this value is certain because the T-bill is risk-free. The next step requires economic reasoning. You want the default premium to be large enough so that you expect to at least break even. This will happen if the expected value of the bond equals the expected value of the T-bill per $1 invested.

Expected Value of Bond	=	Expected Value of T-Bill
$(1 + R) \times [1 - P(\text{the bond defaults})]$	=	$(1 + R_f)$

Solving for the promised return on the bond, you find $R = \{(1 + R_f)/[1 - P(\text{the bond defaults})]\} - 1$. Substituting in the values in the statement of the problem, $R = [1.058/(1 - 0.06)] - 1 = 1.12553 - 1 = 0.12553$ or about 12.55 percent, and default risk premium is $R - R_f = 12.55\% - 5.8\% = 6.75\%$.

You require a default risk premium of at least 675 basis points. You can state the matter as follows: If the bond is priced to yield 12.55 percent, you will earn a 675 basis-point spread and receive the bond principal with 94 percent probability. If the bond defaults, however, you will lose everything. With a premium of 675 basis points, you expect to just break even relative to an investment in T-bills. Because an investment in the zero-coupon bond has variability, if you are risk averse you might demand a higher risk premium than 675 basis points.

This analysis is a starting point. Bondholders usually recover part of their investment after a default. A next step would be to incorporate a recovery rate. That problem is left for the end-of-chapter problems.

In this section, we have treated random variables such as EPS as stand-alone quantities. We have not explored how descriptors such as expected value and variance of EPS may be functions of other random variables such as sales and costs. To analyze portfolios, we must understand how portfolio expected return and variance of return are a function of characteristics of the individual securities' returns. When we look at the dispersion or variance of portfolio return, we see that how individual security returns move together or covary is important. New concepts, covariance and correlation, are needed. These new concepts are introduced in the next section, which deals with portfolio expected return and variance of return.

3 PORTFOLIO EXPECTED RETURN AND VARIANCE

Modern portfolio theory (MPT) makes frequent use of the idea that investment opportunities can be evaluated using expected return as a measure of reward and variance of return as a measure of risk. Fundamental skills are the calculation and interpretation of portfolio expected return and variance of return. In this section, we will develop an understanding of portfolio expected return and variance of return.[10] Portfolio return is determined by the returns on the individual holdings. As a result, the calculation of portfolio variance, as a function of the individual asset returns, is more complex than the variance calculations illustrated in the previous section.

We work with an example of a portfolio that is 50 percent invested in an S&P 500 index fund, 25 percent invested in a U.S. long-term corporate bond fund, and 25 percent invested in an EAFE index fund. Table 4-5 shows these weights.

TABLE 4-5   Portfolio Weights

Asset Class	Weights
S&P 500	0.50
U.S. long-term corporate bonds	0.25
MSCI EAFE	0.25

The first question is: What is the expected return on the portfolio? In the previous section, we defined the expected value of a random variable as the probability-weighted average of the possible outcomes. Portfolio return, we know, is a weighted average of the returns on the securities in the portfolio. Similarly, the expected return on a portfolio is a weighted average of the expected returns on the securities in the portfolio, using exactly the same weights. When we have estimated the expected returns on the individual securities, we immediately have portfolio expected return. This convenient fact follows from the properties of expected value.

---

[10] Although we outline a number of basic concepts in this section, we do not present mean–variance analysis per se. For extended treatments, consult standard investment textbooks such as Bodie, Kane, and Marcus (1999), Elton and Gruber (1995), Reilly and Brown (2000), and Sharpe, Alexander, and Bailey (1998).

- **Properties of Expected Value.** Let w_i be any constant and R_i be a random variable.

  1. The expected value of a constant times a random variable equals the constant times the expected value of the random variable.

  $E(w_1 R_1) = w_1 E(R_1)$

  2. The expected value of a weighted sum of random variables equals the weighted sum of the expected values, using the same weights.

  $E(w_1 R_1 + w_2 R_2 + \ldots + w_n R_n) = w_1 E(R_1) + w_2 E(R_2)$
  $+ \ldots + w_n E(R_n)$ (4-13)

Suppose we have a random variable with a given expected value. We then multiply each outcome by 2, doubling the value of each outcome. The random variable's expected value doubles as well. That is the meaning of Part 1. The second statement generalizes the principle; it is the rule that directly leads to the expression for portfolio expected return. A portfolio with n securities is defined by its portfolio weights, $w_1, w_2, \ldots, w_n$, which sum to 1. So portfolio return, R_p, is $R_p = w_1 R_1 + w_2 R_2 + \ldots + w_n R_n$. We can state the following principle:

- **Calculation of Portfolio Expected Return.** Given a portfolio with n securities, the expected return on the portfolio is a weighted average of the expected returns on the component securities.

  $E(R_p) = E(w_1 R_1 + w_2 R_2 + \ldots + w_n R_n) = w_1 E(R_1)$
  $+ w_2 E(R_2) + \ldots + w_n E(R_n)$

Suppose we have estimated expected returns on the assets in the portfolio, as given in Table 4-6.

TABLE 4-6   Weights and Expected Returns

Asset Class	Weight	Expected Return (%)
S&P 500	0.50	13
U.S. long-term corporate bonds	0.25	6
MSCI EAFE	0.25	15

We calculate the expected return on the portfolio as 11.75 percent:

$E(R_p) = w_1 E(R_1) + w_2 E(R_2) + w_3 E(R_3) = (0.50 \times 13\%) + (0.25 \times 6\%)$
$+ (0.25 \times 15\%) = 11.75\%$

In the previous section, we studied variance as a measure of dispersion of outcomes around the expected value. Here we are interested in portfolio variance of return as a measure of investment risk. Letting R_P stand for the return on the portfolio, portfolio variance is $\sigma^2(R_P) = E\{[R_P - E(R_P)]^2\}$ according to Equation 4-8. How do we implement this definition? In the chapter on statistical concepts and market returns, we learned how to calculate a historical or sample variance based on a sample of returns. Now we are considering variance in a forward-looking sense. We will use information about the individual assets in the portfolio to obtain portfolio variance of return. To avoid clutter in notation, we write ER_p for $E(R_p)$. We need the concept of covariance.

- **Definition of Covariance.** Given two random variables R_i and R_j, the covariance between R_i and R_j is

$$\text{Cov}(R_i, R_j) = E[(R_i - ER_i)(R_j - ER_j)] \tag{4-14}$$

  Alternative notations are $\sigma(R_i, R_j)$ and σ_{ij}.

Equation 4-14 states that the covariance between two random variables is the probability-weighted average of the cross-product of each random variable's deviation from its own expected value. We will return to discuss covariance after we establish the need for the concept. Working from the definition of variance, we find

$$\sigma^2(R_p) = E[(R_p - ER_p)^2]$$

$$= E\{[w_1R_1 + w_2R_2 + w_3R_3 - E(w_1R_1 + w_2R_2 + w_3R_3)]^2\}$$

$$= E\{[w_1R_1 + w_2R_2 + w_3R_3 - w_1ER_1 - w_2ER_2 - w_3ER_3]^2\}$$
$$\text{(using Equation 4-13)}$$

$$= E\{[w_1(R_1 - ER_1) + w_2(R_2 - ER_2) + w_3(R_3 - ER_3)]^2\} \quad \text{(rearranging)}$$

$$= E\{[w_1(R_1 - ER_1) + w_2(R_2 - ER_2) + w_3(R_3 - ER_3)]$$
$$\times [w_1(R_1 - ER_1) + w_2(R_2 - ER_2) + w_3(R_3 - ER_3)]\}$$
$$\text{(what squaring means)}$$

$$= E[w_1w_1(R_1 - ER_1)(R_1 - ER_1) + w_1w_2(R_1 - ER_1)(R_2 - ER_2)$$
$$+ w_1w_3(R_1 - ER_1)(R_3 - ER_3) + w_2w_1(R_2 - ER_2)(R_1 - ER_1)$$
$$+ w_2w_2(R_2 - ER_2)(R_2 - ER_2) + w_2w_3(R_2 - ER_2)(R_3 - ER_3)$$
$$+ w_3w_1(R_3 - ER_3)(R_1 - ER_1) + w_3w_2(R_3 - ER_3)(R_2 - ER_2)$$
$$+ w_3w_3(R_3 - ER_3)(R_3 - ER_3)] \quad \text{(doing the multiplication)}$$

$$= w_1^2\,E[(R_1 - ER_1)^2] + w_1w_2E[(R_1 - ER_1)(R_2 - ER_2)]$$
$$+ w_1w_3E[(R_1 - ER_1)(R_3 - ER_3)] + w_2w_1E[(R_2 - ER_2)(R_1 - ER_1)]$$
$$+ w_2^2\,E[(R_2 - ER_2)^2] + w_2w_3E[(R_2 - ER_2)(R_3 - ER_3)]$$
$$+ w_3w_1E[(R_3 - ER_3)(R_1 - ER_1)] + w_3w_2E[(R_3 - ER_3)(R_2 - ER_2)]$$
$$+ w_3^2\,E[(R_3 - ER_3)^2] \quad \text{(recalling that the } w_i \text{ terms are constants)}$$

$$= w_1^2\,\sigma^2(R_1) + w_1w_2\text{Cov}(R_1, R_2) + w_1w_3\text{Cov}(R_1, R_3)$$
$$+ w_1w_2\text{Cov}(R_1, R_2) + w_2^2\sigma^2(R_2) + w_2w_3\text{Cov}(R_2, R_3)$$
$$+ w_1w_3\text{Cov}(R_1, R_3) + w_2w_3\text{Cov}(R_2, R_3) + w_3^2\,\sigma^2(R_3) \tag{4-15}$$

The last step follows from the definitions of variance and covariance.[11] For the italicized covariance terms below the diagonal, we used the fact that the order of variables in covari-

---

[11] The calculations leading to Equation 4-15 demonstrate the first of the following useful facts about variance. Let w be any constant, and let R be any random variable: (1) The variance of a constant *times* a random variable equals the constant squared times the variance of the random variable, or $\sigma^2(wR) = w^2\,\sigma^2(R)$; (2) The variance of a constant *plus* a random variable equals the variance of the random variable, or $\sigma^2(w + R) = \sigma^2(R)$.

ance does not matter: $\text{Cov}(R_2, R_1) = \text{Cov}(R_1, R_2)$, for example. As we will show, the diagonal variance terms $\sigma^2(R_1)$, $\sigma^2(R_2)$, and $\sigma^2(R_3)$ can be expressed as $\text{Cov}(R_1, R_1)$, $\text{Cov}(R_2, R_2)$, and $\text{Cov}(R_3, R_3)$, respectively. Using this fact, the most compact way to state Equation 4-15 is $\sigma^2(R_P) = \sum_{i=1}^{3} \sum_{j=1}^{3} w_i w_j \text{Cov}(R_i, R_j)$. The double summation signs say: "Set $i = 1$ then let j run from 1 to 3; then set $i = 2$ and let j run from 1 to 3; next set $i = 3$ and let j run from 1 to 3; finally add the nine terms." This expression generalizes for a portfolio of any size n to

$$\sigma^2(R_P) = \sum_{i=1}^{n} \sum_{j=1}^{n} w_i w_j \text{Cov}(R_i, R_j) \qquad (4\text{-}16)$$

We see from Equation 4-15 that individual variances of return (the bolded diagonal terms) constitute part, but not all, of portfolio variance. The three variances are actually outnumbered by the six covariance terms off the diagonal. For three assets, the ratio is 1 to 2, or 50 percent. If there are 20 assets, there are 20 variance terms and $20 \times 20 - 20 = 380$ off-diagonal covariance terms. The ratio of variance terms to off-diagonal covariance terms is less than 6 to 100, or 6 percent. A first observation, then, is this: As the number of holdings increases, covariance[12] becomes increasingly important, all else equal.

What exactly is the effect of covariance on portfolio variance? The covariance terms capture how the co-movements of returns affect portfolio variance. For example, consider two stocks: one tends to have high returns (relative to its expected return) when the other has low returns (relative to its expected return). The returns on one stock tend to offset the returns on the other stock, lowering the variability or variance of returns on the portfolio. Like variance, the units of covariance are hard to interpret, and we will introduce a more intuitive concept shortly. Meanwhile, from the definition of covariance we can establish two essential observations about covariance.

- **Facts About Covariance.**
   1. We can interpret the sign of covariance as follows:
      Covariance of returns is negative if, when the return on one asset is above its expected value, the return on the other asset is below its expected value (an average inverse relationship between returns). Covariance of returns is 0 if returns on the assets are unrelated.
      Covariance of returns is positive if, when the return on one asset is above its expected value, the return on the other asset is above its expected value (an average positive relationship between returns).
   2. The covariance of a random variable with itself (*own covariance*) is its own variance. $\text{Cov}(R, R) = E\{[R - E(R)][R - E(R)]\} = E\{[R - E(R)]^2\} = \sigma^2(R)$

A complete list of the covariances constitutes all the statistical data needed to compute portfolio variance of return. Covariances are often presented in a square format called a **covariance matrix.** Table 4-7 summarizes the inputs for portfolio expected return and variance of return.

---

[12] Where the meaning of covariance as "off-diagonal covariance" is obvious, as it is here, we omit the qualifying words. Covariance is usually used in this sense.

TABLE 4-7   Inputs to Portfolio Expected Return and Variance

Panel A: Inputs for Portfolio Expected Return

Stock	A	B	C
	$E(R_A)$	$E(R_B)$	$E(R_C)$

Panel B: Covariance Matrix: The Inputs for Portfolio Variance of Return

Stock	A	B	C
A	**$Cov(R_A, R_A)$***	$Cov(R_A, R_B)$	$Cov(R_A, R_C)$
B	$Cov(R_B, R_A)$	**$Cov(R_B, R_B)$****	$Cov(R_B, R_C)$
C	$Cov(R_C, R_A)$	$Cov(R_C, R_B)$	**$Cov(R_C, R_C)$*****

* $Cov(R_A, R_A) = \sigma^2(R_A)$; ** $Cov(R_B, R_B) = \sigma^2(R_B)$; *** $Cov(R_C, R_C) = \sigma^2(R_C)$

With three assets, the covariance matrix has $3^2 = 3 \times 3 = 9$ entries, but it is customary to treat the diagonal terms, the variances, separately from the off-diagonal terms. This is natural, as security variance is a single variable concept. So there are $9 - 3 = 6$ covariances, excluding variances. But $Cov(R_B, R_A) = Cov(R_A, R_B)$, $Cov(R_C, R_A) = Cov(R_A, R_C)$, and $Cov(R_C, R_B) = Cov(R_B, R_C)$. The covariance matrix below the diagonal is the mirror image of the covariance matrix above the diagonal. As a result, there are only $3 = 6/2$ distinct covariance terms to estimate. In general, for n securities there are $n(n - 1)/2$ distinct covariances to estimate, and n variances to estimate.

Suppose we have the covariance matrix shown in Table 4-8:

TABLE 4-8   Covariance Matrix

	S&P 500	U.S. Long-Term Corporate Bonds	MSCI EAFE
S&P 500	400	45	189
U.S. Long-Term Corporate Bonds	45	81	38
MSCI EAFE	189	38	441

Let us take Equation 4-15 and group variance terms together. We have:

$$\sigma^2(R_P) = w_1^2 \sigma^2(R_1) + w_2^2 \sigma^2(R_2) + w_3^2 \sigma^2(R_3) + 2w_1w_2Cov(R_1, R_2)$$
$$+ 2w_1w_3Cov(R_1, R_3) + w_2w_3Cov(R_2, R_3) \tag{4-17}$$

$$= (0.50)^2(400) + (0.25)^2(81) + (0.25)^2(441) + 2(0.50)(0.25)(45)$$
$$+ 2(0.50)(0.25)(189) + 2(0.25)(0.25)(38)$$
$$= 100 + 5.0625 + 27.5625 + 11.25 + 47.25 + 4.75 = 195.875$$

The variance is 195.875. Standard deviation of return is $(195.875)^{1/2} = 14$ percent. To summarize, the portfolio has an expected annual return of 11.75 percent and a standard deviation of return of 14 percent.

Let us look at the first three terms in the calculation above. Their sum, $132.625 = 100 + 5.0625 + 27.5625$, is the contribution of the individual variances to portfolio variance. If the returns on the three assets were independent, according to a fact given above, covariances would be 0 and the standard deviation of portfolio return would be $(132.625)^{1/2} = 11.52$ percent as compared to 14 percent before. The portfolio would have less risk. Suppose the covariance terms were negative. Then a negative number would be added to 132.625, so portfolio variance and risk would be even smaller. At the same time, we have not changed expected return. For the same expected portfolio return, the portfolio has less risk. This risk reduction is a diversification benefit, meaning a risk-reduction benefit from holding a portfolio of assets. The diversification benefit increases with decreasing covariance. This observation is a key insight of modern portfolio theory. It is even more intuitively stated when we can use the concept of correlation. Then we can say that as long as security returns are not perfectly positively correlated, diversification benefits are possible. Furthermore, the smaller the correlation between security returns, the greater the cost of not diversifying (in terms of risk reduction benefits forgone), all else equal.

- **Definition of Correlation.** The correlation between two random variables, R_i and R_j, is defined as $\rho(R_i, R_j) = \text{Cov}(R_i, R_j)/\sigma(R_i)\sigma(R_j)$. Alternative notations are $\text{Corr}(R_i, R_j)$ and ρ_{ij}.

Frequently, covariance is substituted out using the relationship $\text{Cov}(R_i, R_j) = \rho(R_i, R_j)\sigma(R_i)\sigma(R_j)$. The division indicated in the definition makes correlation a pure number (one without a unit of measurement) and places bounds on its largest and smallest possible values. Using the above definition, we can state a correlation matrix from data in the covariance matrix alone. Table 4-9 shows the correlation matrix.

TABLE 4-9   Correlation Matrix of Returns

	S&P 500	U.S. Long-Term Corporate Bonds	MSCI EAFE
S&P 500	1.00	0.25	0.45
U.S. Long-Term Corporate Bonds	0.25	1.00	0.20
MSCI EAFE	0.45	0.20	1.00

For example, the covariance between long-term bonds and EAFE is 38, from Table 4-8. The standard deviation of long-term bond returns is $(81)^{1/2} = 9$ percent, that of EAFE returns is 21 percent, from diagonal terms in Table 4-8. The correlation ρ(Return on long-term bonds, Return on EAFE) is $(38\%^2)/(9\%)(21\%) = 0.201$, rounded to 0.20. The correlation of the S&P 500 with itself equals 1: The calculation is own covariance, which is variance divided by its standard deviation squared, which equals variance.

- **Properties of Correlation.**
  1. Correlation is a number between -1 and $+1$:
     $$-1 \leq \rho(X,Y) \leq +1$$

2. A correlation of 0 (uncorrelated variables) indicates an absence of any linear (straight-line) relationship between the variables.[13] Increasingly positive correlation indicates an increasingly strong positive linear relationship (up to 1, which indicates a perfect linear relationship). Increasingly negative correlation indicates an increasingly strong negative (inverse) linear relationship (down to -1, which indicates a perfect inverse linear relationship).[14]

EXAMPLE 4-12.   Portfolio Expected Return and Variance of Return.

You have a portfolio of two mutual funds, A and B, 75 percent invested in A, as shown in Table 4-10.

TABLE 4-10   Mutual Fund Expected Returns, Return Variances, and Covariances

Fund	A	B
	$E(R_A) = 20\%$	$E(R_B) = 12\%$

	Covariance Matrix	
Fund	A	B
A	625	120
B	120	196

1. Calculate the expected return on the portfolio. 18%
2. Calculate the correlation matrix for this problem. Carry two **decimal places.**
3. Compute portfolio standard deviation of return.

Solution to 1. $E(R_p) = w_A E(R_A) + (1 - w_A E(R_B)) = 0.75 \times 20\% + 0.25 \times 12\% = 18\%$. Portfolio weights must sum to 1: $w_B = 1 - w_A$.

Solution to 2. $\sigma(R_A) = (625)^{1/2} = 25$ percent, $\sigma(R_B) = (196)^{1/2} = 14$ percent. There is one distinct covariance, and thus one distinct correlation:

$$\rho(R_A, R_B) = \text{Cov}(R_A, R_B)/\sigma(R_A)\sigma(R_B) = 120/(25 \times 14) = 0.342857, \text{ or } 0.34.$$

Table 4-11 shows the correlation matrix.

---

[13] If the correlation is 0, $R_1 = a + bR_2 +$ error, with $b = 0$.

[14] If the correlation is positive, $R_1 = a + bR_2, +$ error, with $b > 0$. If the correlation is negative, $b < 0$.

TABLE 4-11   Correlation Matrix

	A	B
A	1.00	0.34
B	0.34	1.00

Diagonal terms are always equal to 1.

Solution to 3.

$$\sigma^2(R_P) = w_A^2\, \sigma^2(R_A) + w_B^2\, \sigma^2(R_B) + 2w_A w_B \text{Cov}(R_A, R_B)$$
$$= (0.75)^2(625) + (0.25)^2\,(196) + 2(0.75)(0.25)(120)$$
$$= 351.5625 + 12.25 + 45 = 408.8125$$
$$\sigma(R_P) = (408.8125)^{1/2} = 20.22 \text{ percent}$$

How do we estimate return covariance and correlation? Frequently, we make forecasts on the basis of historical covariance or other methods based on historical return data, such as a market model regression.[15] We can also calculate covariance using the **joint probability function** of the random variables, if that can be estimated. The joint probability function of two random variables X and Y, denoted $P(X, Y)$, gives the probability of joint occurrences of values of X and Y. For example, $P(3, 2)$, is the probability that X equals 3 and Y equals 2.

Suppose that the joint probability function of the returns on BankCorp stock (R_B) and the returns on NewBank stock (R_N) has the simple structure given in Table 4-12.

TABLE 4-12   Joint Probability Function of BankCorp and NewBank
             Returns (Entries are joint probabilities)

	$R_N = 20\%$	$R_N = 16\%$	$R_N = 10\%$
$R_B = 25\%$	0.20	0	0
$R_B = 12\%$	0	0.50	0
$R_B = 10\%$	0	0	0.30

The expected return on BankCorp stock is $(0.20 \times 25\%) + (0.50 \times 12\%) + (0.30 \times 10\%) = 14\%$. The expected return on NewBank stock is $(0.20 \times 20\%) + (0.50 \times 16\%) + (0.30 \times 10\%) = 15\%$. The joint probability function above might reflect an analysis based on whether banking industry conditions are good, average, or poor. Table 4-13 presents the calculation of covariance.

---

[15] See any of the textbooks mentioned in footnote 10.

TABLE 4-13   Covariance Calculations

Banking Industry Condition	Deviations Bank Corp.	Deviations New Bank	Product of Deviations	Probability of Condition	Probability-Weighted Product
Good	25−14	20−15	55	0.20	11
Average	12−14	16−15	−2	0.50	−1
Poor	10−14	10−15	20	0.30	6
				$\text{Cov}(R_B, R_N) = 16$	

Expected Return: BankCorp 14%, NewBank 15%

The first and second columns of numbers show, respectively, the deviations of BankCorp and NewBank returns from their mean or expected value. The next column shows the product of the deviations. For example, for good industry conditions, $(25 - 14) \times (20 - 15) = 11 \times 5 = 55$. Then 55 is multiplied or weighted by 0.20, the probability that banking industry conditions are good: $55 \times 0.20 = 11$. The calculations for average and poor banking conditions follow the same pattern. Summing up these probability-weighted products, we find that $\text{Cov}(R_B, R_N) = 16$.

A formula for computing the covariance between random variables R_i and R_j is

$$\text{Cov}(R_i, R_j) = \sum_i \sum_j P(R_i, R_j)(R_i - ER_i)(R_j - ER_j) \tag{4-18}$$

The formula tells us to sum all possible cross-products of the two random variables weighted by the appropriate joint probability. In the example we just worked, as you can see from Table 4-13, only three joint probabilities are non-zero. Therefore, in computing the covariance of returns in this case, we need to consider only three cross-products:

$$\begin{aligned}\text{Cov}(R_B, R_N) &= P(25, 20) \times [(25 - 14) \times (20 - 15)] + P(12, 16) \times [(12 - 14) \\ &\quad \times (16 - 15)] + P(10,10) \times [(10 - 14) \times (10 - 15)] \\ &= (0.20 \times 11 \times 5) + [0.50 \times (-2) \times 1] + [0.30 \times (-4) \times (-5)] \\ &= 11 - 1 + 6 = 16\end{aligned}$$

One theme of this chapter has been independence. Two random variables are independent when every possible pair of events—one event corresponding to a value of X and another event corresponding to a value of Y—are independent events. When two random variables are independent, their joint probability function simplifies.

- **Definition of Independence for Random Variables.** Two random variables X and Y are independent if and only if $P(X, Y) = P(X)P(Y)$.

For example, given independence, $P(3, 2) = P(3)P(2)$. We multiply the individual probabilities. *Independence* is a stronger property than *uncorrelatedness* because correlation addresses only linear relationships. The following condition holds for uncorrelated random variables, and therefore also holds for independent random variables.

- **Multiplication Rule for the Expected Value of the Product of Uncorrelated Random Variables.** The expected value of the product of uncorrelated random variables is the product of their expected values.

$E(XY) = E(X)E(Y)$ if X and Y are uncorrelated.

Many financial variables, such as revenue (price times quantity), are the product of random quantities. When applicable, the above rule simplifies calculating expected value of a product of random variables.[16]

4 TOPICS IN PROBABILITY

In the remainder of the chapter we discuss two topics that can be important in solving investment problems. We start with Bayes' formula: what probability theory has to say about learning from experience. Then we move to a discussion of shortcuts and principles for counting.

4.1 BAYES' FORMULA

When we make decisions involving investments, we often start with viewpoints based on our experience and knowledge. These viewpoints may be changed or confirmed by new knowledge and observations. Bayes' formula is a rational method for adjusting our viewpoints as we confront new information.[17] Bayes' formula and related concepts have been applied in many business and investment decision-making contexts, including the evaluation of mutual fund performance.[18]

Bayes' formula makes use of Equation 4-6, the total probability rule. To review, that rule expressed the probability of an event as a weighted average of the probabilities of the event, given a set of scenarios. Bayes' formula works in reverse, or more precisely, reverses the "given that" information. Bayes' formula uses the occurrence of the event to infer the probability of the scenario generating it.[19] In many applications, including the one illustrating its use in this section, an individual is updating his beliefs concerning the causes that may have produced a new observation.

To illustrate Bayes' formula, we work through an investment example that you can adapt to any actual problem. Suppose you are an investor in the stock of DriveMed, Inc. Security analysts make forecasts of earnings per share of the firms they cover, and various services report consensus EPS estimates. Positive earnings surprises relative to consensus EPS estimates often result in positive stock returns, and negative surprises often have the opposite effect. DriveMed will release last quarter's EPS and you are interested in which of these three events happened: *last quarter's earnings exceeded the consensus EPS estimate*, or *last quarter's earnings exactly met the consensus EPS estimate*, or *last quarter's earnings fell short of the consensus EPS estimate*. This list of the alternatives is mutually exclusive and exhaustive. You expect that when the actual earnings become public, you will be benefited or hurt as an investor by the reaction of the stock price to the news.

On the basis of your own research, you jot down the following **prior probabilities** (or **priors,** for short) concerning these three events:

---

[16] Otherwise, the calculation depends on conditional expected value; the calculation can be expressed as $E(XY) = E[X\, E(Y \mid X)]$.

[17] Named after the Reverend Thomas Bayes (1702–1761).

[18] See Baks, Metrick, and Wachter (2001).

[19] For that reason, Bayes' formula is sometimes called an inverse probability.

- $P(EPS\ exceeded\ consensus) = 0.45$
- $P(EPS\ met\ consensus) = 0.30$
- $P(EPS\ fell\ short\ of\ consensus) = 0.25$

These probabilities are *prior* in the sense that they reflect only what you know now, before the arrival of any new information.

The next day, DriveMed announces that it is expanding factory capacity in Singapore and Ireland to meet increased sales demand. You now assess this new information. The decision to expand capacity relates not only to current demand, but probably also to the prior quarter's sales demand. You know that sales demand is positively related to EPS. So now it appears more likely that last quarter's EPS will exceed the consensus.

The question you have is this: In light of the new information, what is my updated probability that the prior quarter's EPS exceeded the consensus estimate?

Bayes' formula provides a rational method for accomplishing this updating. We can abbreviate the new information as *DriveMed expands*. The first step in applying Bayes' formula is to calculate the probability of the new information (here: *DriveMed expands*), given a list of events or scenarios that may have generated it. The list of events should cover all possibilities, as it does here. Formulating these conditional probabilities is the key step in the updating process. Suppose your view is

$P(DriveMed\ expands\ |\ EPS\ exceeded\ consensus) = 0.75$

$P(DriveMed\ expands\ |\ EPS\ met\ consensus) = 0.20$

$P(DriveMed\ expands\ |\ EPS\ fell\ short\ of\ consensus) = 0.05$

Conditional probabilities of an observation (here: *DriveMed expands*) are sometimes referred to as **likelihoods.** Again, likelihoods are required for the updating.

Next, you combine these conditional probabilities or likelihoods with your prior probabilities to get the unconditional probability for DriveMed expanding, P(DriveMed expands), as follows:

$P(DriveMed\ expands) =$
$P(DriveMed\ expands\ |\ EPS\ exceeded\ consensus) \times$
     $P(EPS\ exceeded\ consensus) +$
$P(DriveMed\ expands\ |\ EPS\ met\ consensus) \times$
     $P(EPS\ met\ consensus) +$
$P(DriveMed\ expands\ |\ EPS\ fell\ short\ of\ consensus) \times$
     $P(EPS\ fell\ short\ of\ consensus)$
     $= 0.75 \times 0.45 + 0.20 \times 0.30 + 0.05 \times 0.25 = 0.41$, or 41%

This is Equation 4-6, the total probability rule, in action. Now we can answer the question on your mind. According to Bayes' formula,

$P(EPS\ exceeded\ consensus\ |\ DriveMed\ expands) =$

$$\frac{P(DriveMed\ expands\ |\ EPS\ exceeded\ consensus)}{P(DriveMed\ expands)} \times P(EPS\ exceeded\ consensus)$$

     $= (0.75/0.41) \times 0.45 = 1.829268 \times 0.45 = 0.823171$

Prior to DriveMed's announcement, you thought the probability that DriveMed would beat consensus expectations was 45 percent. On the basis of your interpretation of the announcement, you update that probability to 82.3 percent. This updated probability is called your **posterior probability** because it reflects or comes after the new information.

The Bayes' calculation takes the prior probability, which was 45 percent, and multiplies it by a ratio—the first term on the right-hand side of the equal sign. In the denominator of the ratio is the probability that DriveMed expands, as you view it without considering (conditioning on) anything else. Therefore, this probability is unconditional. The numerator is the probability that DriveMed expands, if last quarter's EPS actually exceeded the consensus estimate. This last probability is larger than unconditional probability in the denominator, so the ratio (1.83 roughly) is greater than 1. As a result, your updated or posterior probability is larger than your prior probability. Thus, the ratio reflects the impact of the new information on your prior beliefs. The following is a general statement of Bayes' formula:

- **Bayes' Formula.** Given a set of prior probabilities for an event of interest, if you receive new information, the rule for updating your probability of the event is

Updated probability of event given the new information =

$$\frac{\text{Probability of the New Information given Event}}{\text{Unconditional Probability of the New Information}} \times \text{Prior probability of event}$$

EXAMPLE 4-13.   Inferring Whether DriveMed's EPS Met Consensus EPS.

You are still an investor in DriveMed stock. To review the givens, your prior probabilities are $P(EPS\ exceeded\ consensus) = 0.45$, $P(EPS\ met\ consensus) = 0.30$, and $P(EPS\ fell\ short\ of\ consensus) = 0.25$. You also have the following conditional probabilities:

$P(DriveMed\ expands\ |\ EPS\ exceeded\ consensus) = 0.75$

$P(DriveMed\ expands\ |\ EPS\ met\ consensus) = 0.20$

$P(DriveMed\ expands\ |\ EPS\ fell\ short\ of\ consensus) = 0.05$

Recall that you updated your probability that last quarter's EPS exceeded the consensus estimate from 45 percent to 82.3 percent after DriveMed announced that it would expand. Now you want to update your other priors.

1. Update your prior probability that DriveMed's EPS met consensus.
2. Update your prior probability that DriveMed's EPS fell short of consensus.
3. Show that the three updated probabilities sum to 1. (Carry each probability to four decimal places.)
4. Suppose, because of lack of prior beliefs about whether DriveMed met consensus, you updated on the basis of prior probabilities that all three possibilities were equally likely: $P(EPS\ exceeded\ consensus) = P(EPS\ met\ consensus) = P(EPS\ fell\ short\ of\ consensus) = 1/3$. What is your estimate of the probability $P(EPS\ exceeded\ consensus\ |\ DriveMed\ expands)$?

Solution to 1.   The probability is P(EPS met consensus | DriveMed expands) =

$$\frac{P(DriveMed\ expands\ |\ EPS\ met\ consensus)}{P(DriveMed\ expands)} \times P(EPS\ met\ consensus)$$

The probability *P(DriveMed expands)* is found by taking each of the three conditional probabilities in the statement of the problem, such as *P(DriveMed expands | EPS exceeded consensus)*; multiplying each one by the prior probability of the conditioning event, such as *P(EPS exceeded consensus)*; then adding the three products. The calculation is unchanged from the problem in the text above: *P(DriveMed expands)* = 0.75 × 0.45 + 0.20 × 0.30 + 0.05 × 0.25 = 0.41, or 41 percent. The other probabilities needed, *P(DriveMed expands | EPS met consensus)* = 0.20 and *P(EPS met consensus)* = 0.30, are givens. So

> *P(EPS met consensus | DriveMed expands)* = [*P(DriveMed expands | EPS met consensus)/P(DriveMed expands)*] × *P(EPS met consensus)*
> = (0.20/0.41) × 0.30 = 0.487805 × 0.30 = 0.146341

After taking account of the announcement on expansion, your updated probability that last quarter's EPS for DriveMed just met consensus is 14.6 percent compared to your prior probability of 30 percent.

Solution to 2. *P(DriveMed expands)* was already calculated as 41 percent. Recall that *P(DriveMed expands | EPS fell short of consensus)* = 0.05 and *P(EPS fell short of consensus)* = 0.25 are givens.

> *P(EPS fell short of consensus | DriveMed expands)*
> = [*P(DriveMed expands | EPS fell short of consensus)/ P(DriveMed expands)*] × *P(EPS fell short of consensus)*
> = (0.05/0.41) × 0.25 = 0.121951 × 0.25 = 0.030488

As a result of the announcement, you have revised your probability that DriveMed's EPS fell short of consensus from 25 percent (your prior probability) to 3 percent.

Solution to 3. The sum of the three updated probabilities is

> *P(EPS exceeded consensus | DriveMed expands)* + *P(EPS met consensus | DriveMed expands)* + *P(EPS fell short of consensus | DriveMed expands)*
> = 0.8232 + 0.1463 + 0.0305 = 1.0000

The three events (*EPS exceeded consensus, EPS met consensus, EPS fell short of consensus*) are mutually exclusive and exhaustive: One of these events or statements must be true, so the conditional probabilities must sum to 1. Whether we are talking about conditional or unconditional probabilities, whenever we have a complete list of the distinct possible events or outcomes, the probabilities must sum to 1. This is a check on your work.

Solution to 4. According to Bayes' formula, *P(EPS exceeded consensus | DriveMed expands)* = [0.75/(1/3)] × (1/3) = 0.75 or 75 percent. This probability is identical to your estimate of *P(DriveMed expands | EPS exceeded consensus)*. This holds true in general: When a decision-maker is uninformed, his beliefs are completely determined by the data or new information. The assumption of equal prior probabilities is called a **diffuse prior.**

4.2 PRINCIPLES OF COUNTING   The first step in addressing a question often involves determining the different logical possibilities. We may also want to know the number of ways each of these possibilities can happen. In back of our mind is often a question about probability. How likely is it that I will observe this particular possibility? Records of success and failure are an example. When we evaluate a market timer's record, one well-known evaluation method uses counting methods presented in this section.[20] An important investment model, the Binomial Option Pricing Model, incorporates the combination formula that you will learn shortly. The methods of this section are also useful for calculating what were called a priori probabilities in Section 2. When we can assume that the possible outcomes of a random variable are equally likely, the probability of an event equals the number of possible outcomes favorable for the event divided by the total number of outcomes.

In counting, enumeration (counting the outcomes one by one) is of course the most basic resource. What we discuss in this section are shortcuts and principles. Without these shortcuts and principles, counting the total number of outcomes can be very difficult and prone to error. The first and basic principle of counting is the multiplication rule.

- **Multiplication Rule of Counting.** If one thing can be done in n_1 ways, and a second thing, given the first, can be done in n_2 ways, and a third thing, given the first two things, can be done in n_3 ways, and so on for k things, then the number of ways the k things can be done is $n_1 \times n_2 \times n_3 \times \ldots \times n_k$.

Suppose we have three steps in an investment decision process. The first step can be done in two ways, the second in four ways, and the third in three ways. Following the multiplication rule, there are $2 \times 4 \times 3 = 24$ ways in which we can carry out the three steps.

Another illustration is the assignment of members of a group to an equal number of positions. For example, suppose you want to assign three security analysts to cover three different industries. In how many ways can the assignments be made? The first analyst may be assigned in three different ways. Then two industries remain. The second analyst can be assigned in two different ways. Then one industry remains. The third and last analyst can be assigned in only one way. The total number of different assignments equals $3 \times 2 \times 1 = 6$. The compact notation for the multiplication we have just performed is 3! (read: 3 factorial). If we had n analysts, the number of ways we could assign them to n tasks would be

$$n! = n \times (n - 1) \times (n - 2) \times (n - 3) \times \ldots \times 1$$

or **n factorial.** (By convention, $0! = 1$.) To review, in this application we repeatedly carry out an operation (here, job assignment) until we use up all members of a group (here, three analysts). With n members in the group, the multiplication formula reduces to n factorial.[21]

The next type of counting problem can be called *labeling problems*.[22] We want to give each object in a group a label, to place it in a category. The following example illustrates this type of problem.

A mutual fund guide ranked 18 bond mutual funds by year 2000 total returns. The guide also assigned each fund one of five risk labels: *high risk* (4 funds), *above average risk* (4 funds), *average risk* (3 funds), *below average risk* (4 funds), and *low risk* (3 funds); as $4 + 4 + 3 + 4 + 3 = 18$, all the funds are accounted for. How many different ways

---

[20] Henriksson and Merton (1981).

[21] The shortest explanation of n factorial is that it is the number of ways we can order n objects in a row. A characteristic of the problems to which we apply this counting method is that we use up all the members of a group (sampling without replacement).

[22] This discussion follows Kemeny, Schleifer, Snell, and Thompson (1972) in terminology and approach.

can we take 18 mutual funds and label 4 of them high risk, 4 above-average risk, 3 average risk, 4 below-average risk, and 3 low risk, so each fund is labeled?

The answer is close to 13 billion. We can label 18 funds *high risk* (the first slot), then 17 funds, then 16 funds, then 15 funds (now we have 4 funds in the *high risk* group); then we can label 14 funds *above average risk*, then 13 funds, and so forth. There are 18! possible sequences. However, order of assignment within a category does not matter. For example, whether a fund occupies the first or third slot of the four funds labeled *high risk*, the fund has the same label (*high risk*). Thus, there are 4! ways to assign a given group of 4 funds to the 4 *high risk* slots. Making the same argument for the other categories, in total there are 4! × 4! × 3! × 4! × 3! equivalent sequences. To eliminate such redundancies from the 18! total, we divide 18! by 4! × 4! × 3! × 4! × 3!. We have 18!/(4! × 4! × 3! × 4! × 3!) = 18!/(24 × 24 × 6 × 24 × 6) = 12,864,852,000. This procedure generalizes as follows.

- **Multinomial Formula (The General Formula for Labeling Problems).** The number of ways that n objects can be labeled with k different labels, with n_1 of the first type, n_2 of the second type, and so on, with $n_1 + n_2 + \ldots + n_k = n$, is given by

$$\frac{n!}{n_1! \times n_2! \times \ldots \times n_k!}$$

The special case of the general rule for when there are just two different labels ($k = 2$) is especially important. The special case is called the combination formula. A **combination** is a listing in which order of listing does not matter. We state the combination formula in a traditional way, but no new concepts are involved. Using the notation in the formula below, the number of objects with the first label is $r = n_1$, and the number with the second label is $n - r = n_2$ (there are just two categories, so $n_1 + n_2 = n$). Here is the formula.

- **Combination Formula (The Binomial Formula).** The number of ways that we can choose r objects from a total of n objects, where the order in which the r objects is listed does not matter, is

$$_nC_r = \binom{n}{r} = \frac{n!}{(n - r)! \times r!}$$

Here $_nC_r$ and $\binom{n}{r}$ are shorthand notations for $n!/[(n - r)!r!]$ (read: n choose r, or n combination r).

If we label the r objects as *belongs to the group* and the remaining objects as *does not belong to the group,* whatever the group of interest, the combination formula tells us how many ways we can select a group of size r. We can illustrate this formula with the binomial option pricing model (BOPM). The BOPM describes the movement of the underlying asset as a series of moves, price up (U) or price down (D). For example, two sequences of five moves containing three up moves, such as UUUDD and UDUUD, result in the same final stock price. At least for an option with a payoff dependent on final stock price, the number but not the order of up moves in a sequence matters. How many sequences of five moves *belong to the group with three up moves?* The answer is 10, calculated using the combination formula ("5 choose 3"):

$$_5C_3 = n!/[(n - r)!r!] = 5!/[(5 - 3)!3!] = (5 \times 4 \times 3 \times 2 \times 1)/$$
$$[(2 \times 1)(3 \times 2 \times 1)] = 120/12 = 10 \text{ ways}$$

A useful fact can be illustrated as follows: $_5C_3 = 5!/(2!3!)$ equals $_5C_2 = 5!/(3!2!)$, as $3 + 2 = 5$; $_5C_4 = 5!/(1!4!)$ equals $_5C_1 = 5!/(4!1!)$, as $4 + 1 = 5$. This symmetrical relationship can save work when we need to calculate many possible combinations.

Suppose jurors want to select three companies out of a group of five to receive the first-, second-, and third-place awards for the best annual report. In how many ways can the jurors make the three awards? Order does matter if we want to distinguish among the three awards (the rank within the group of 3); it is clear that the question considers order important. On the other hand, if the question was "In how many ways can the jurors choose three winners, without regard to place of finish?" we would use the combination formula.

To address the first question above, we need to count ordered listings such as *first place—New Company, second place—Fir Company, third place—Well Company*. An ordered listing is known as a **permutation,** and the formula that counts the number of permutations is known as the permutation formula.[23]

- **Permutation Formula.** The number of ways that we can choose r objects from a total of n objects, where the order in which the r objects is listed does matter, is

$$_nP_r = \frac{n!}{(n - r)!}$$

So the jurors have $_5P_3 = n!/(n - r)! = 5!/(5 - 3)! = (5 \times 4 \times 3 \times 2 \times 1)/(2 \times 1) = 120/2 = 60$ ways in which they can make their awards. To see why this formula works, note that $(5 \times 4 \times 3 \times 2 \times 1)/(2 \times 1)$ reduces to $5 \times 4 \times 3$, after cancellation of terms. This counts the number of ways to fill three slots choosing from a group of five people, according to the multiplication rule of counting. This number is naturally larger than it would be if order did not matter (compare 60 to the value of 10 for "5 choose 3" that we calculated above). For example, *first place—Well Company, second place—Fir Company, third place—New Company* contains the same three companies as *first place—New Company, second place—Fir Company, third place—Well Company*. If we were concerned with *award winners* (without regard to place of finish), the two listings would count as one combination. But when we are concerned with order of finish, the listings count as two permutations.

Answering the following questions may help you apply the counting methods we have presented in this section.

1. Does the thing that I want to count have a finite number of possible outcomes? If the answer is yes, you may be able to use a tool in this section, and you can go to the second question. If the answer is no, the number of outcomes is infinite, and the tools in this section do not apply.

2. Do I want to assign every member of a group of size n to one of n slots (or tasks)? If the answer is yes, use n factorial. If the answer is no, go to the third question.

3. Do I want to count the number of ways to apply one of three or more labels to each member of a group? If the answer is yes, use the multinomial formula. If the answer is no, go to the fourth question.

4. Do I want to count the number of ways that I can choose r objects from a total of n, where the order in which I list the r objects does not matter (can I give the r objects a label)? If the answer to these questions is yes, the combination formula applies. If the answer is no, go to the fifth question.

---

[23] A more formal definition states that a permutation is an ordered subset of n distinct objects.

5. Do I want to count the number of ways I can choose r objects from a total of n, where the order in which I list the r objects is important? If the answer is yes, the permutation formula applies. If the answer is no, go to question 6.

6. Can the multiplication rule of counting be used? If it cannot, you may have to count the possibilities one by one, or use more advanced techniques than those presented here.[24]

5 SUMMARY

In this chapter, we have discussed the essential concepts and tools of probability. We have applied probability, expected value, and variance to a range of investment problems.

- Probability is a number between 0 and 1 that describes the chance that a stated event will occur.

- A random variable is a quantity whose outcome is uncertain.

- An *event* is any outcome or specified set of outcomes of a random variable.

- The probability of an event E is denoted $P(E)$.

- *Mutually exclusive events* can only occur one at a time. *Exhaustive events* cover or contain all possible outcomes.

- The two defining properties of a probability are, first, that $0 \leq$ probability of any event ≤ 1 and second, the sum of the probabilities of any list of mutually exclusive and exhaustive events equals 1.

- A probability estimated from data as a relative frequency of occurrence is an empirical probability. A probability obtained based on logical analysis is an a priori probability. A probability drawing on personal or subjective judgment is a subjective probability.

- A probability of an event E, $P(E)$, can be stated as odds for $E = P(E)/[1 - P(E)]$ or against $E = [1 - P(E)]/P(E)$.

- Probabilities that are not consistent create profit opportunities, according to the Dutch Book Theorem.

- A probability of an event *not* conditioned on another event is an unconditional probability. The unconditional probability of an event A is denoted $P(A)$. Unconditional probabilities are also called marginal probabilities.

- A probability of an event given (conditioned on) another event is a conditional probability. The probability of an event A given an event B is denoted $P(A \mid B)$.

- The probability of both A and B occurring is the joint probability of A and B, denoted $P(AB)$.

- $P(A \mid B) = P(AB)/P(B)$, $P(B) \neq 0$.

- The multiplication rule for probabilities is $P(AB) = P(A \mid B)P(B)$.

- The probability that A or B occurs, or both occur, is denoted by $P(A$ or $B)$.

- The addition rule for probabilities is $P(A$ or $B) = P(A) + P(B) - P(AB)$.

- When events are independent, the occurrence of one event does not affect the probability of occurrence of the other event. Otherwise, the events are dependent.

---

[24] Feller (1957) contains a very full treatment of counting problems and solution methods.

- Two events A and B are independent if and only if $P(A \mid B) = P(A)$ and $P(B \mid A) = P(B)$.

- The multiplication rule for independent events states that if A and B are independent events, $P(AB) = P(A)P(B)$.

- If S_1, S_2, ... , S_n are mutually exclusive and exhaustive scenarios or events, then $P(A) = P(A \mid S_1)P(S_1) + P(A \mid S_2)P(S_2) + ... + P(A \mid S_n)P(S_n)$.

- The expected value of a random variable is a probability-weighted average of the possible outcomes of the random variable. For a random variable X, the expected value of X is denoted $E(X)$.

- The variance of a random variable is the expected value (the probability-weighted average) of squared deviations from its expected value $E(X)$: $\sigma^2(X) = E\{[X - E(X)]^2\}$, where $\sigma^2(X)$ stands for the variance of X. An alternative notation for the variance of X is $\text{Var}(X)$.

- Variance is a measure of dispersion about the mean. Increasing variance indicates increasing dispersion. Variance is measured in squared units of the original variable.

- Standard deviation is the positive square root of variance.

- Standard deviation measures dispersion (as does variance), but it is measured in the same units as the variable.

- If w_1, w_2, ... , w_n are constants and R_1, R_2, ... , R_n are random variables, then $E(w_1R_1 + w_2R_2 + ... + w_nR_n) = w_1E(R_1) + w_2E(R_2) + ... + w_nE(R_n)$.

- The properties of variance include the following, where w and a are constants and R is a random variable: $\sigma^2(wR) = w^2\sigma^2(R)$ and $\sigma^2(a + R) = \sigma^2(R)$.

- Covariance is a measure of the co-movement (linear association) between random variables.

- The covariance between two random variables R_i and R_j is the expected value of the cross-product of the deviations of the two random variables from their respective means: $\text{Cov}(R_i, R_j) = E\{[R_i - E(R_i)][R_j - E(R_j)]\}$.

- The covariance of a random variable with itself is its own variance: $\text{Cov}(R, R) = \sigma^2(R)$.

- Correlation is a number between -1 and $+1$ that measures the co-movement (linear association) between two random variables: $\rho(R_i, R_j) = \text{Cov}(R_i, R_j)/[\sigma(R_i)\,\sigma(R_j)]$.

- When return correlation is less than $+1$, diversification reduces risk.

- To calculate the variance of return on a portfolio of n assets, the inputs needed are the n expected returns on the individual securities, n variances of return on the individual securities, and $n(n - 1)/2$ distinct covariances.

- Portfolio variance of return is $\sigma^2(R_P) = \displaystyle\sum_{i=1}^{n}\sum_{j=1}^{n} w_iw_j\,\text{Cov}(R_i, R_j)$.

- The calculation of covariance in a forward-looking sense requires the specification of a joint probability function, which gives the probability of joint occurrences of values of the two random variables.

- When two random variables are independent, the joint probability function is the product of the individual probability functions of the random variables.

- When two random variables are uncorrelated, the expected value of the product equals the product of the expected values: $E(XY) = E(X)E(Y)$.

- Bayes' formula is a method for updating probabilities based on new information.

- Bayes' formula is expressed as follows: Updated probability of event given the new information = [(Probability of the new information given event)/(Unconditional probability of the new information)] × Prior probability of event.

- The multiplication rule of counting says, for example, that if the first step in a process can be done in 10 ways, the second step, given the first, can be done in 5 ways, and the third step, given the first two, can be done in 7 ways, then the steps can be carried out in $10 \times 5 \times 7 = 350$ ways.

- The number of ways to assign every member of a group of size n to n slots is $n! = n \times (n - 1) \times (n - 2) \times (n - 3) \times \ldots \times 1$. (By convention, $0! = 1$.)

- The number of ways that n objects can be labeled with k different labels, with n_1 of the first type, n_2 of the second type, and so on, with $n_1 + n_2 + \ldots + n_k = n$, is given by $n!/(n_1! \times n_2! \times \ldots \times n_k)$. This expression is the multinomial formula.

- A special case of the multinomial formula is the combination formula. The number of ways that we can choose r objects from a total of n objects, where the order in which the r objects is listed does not matter, is

$$_nC_r = \binom{n}{r} = \frac{n!}{(n - r)! \times r!}$$

- The number of ways that we can choose r objects from a total of n objects, where the order in which the r objects is listed does matter, is

$$_nP_r = \frac{n!}{(n - r)!}$$

This expression is the permutation formula.

PROBLEMS

1. Define the following terms:
   a. Probability
   b. Conditional probability
   c. Event
   d. Independent events
   e. Variance

2. State three mutually exclusive and exhaustive events describing the reaction of a firm's stock price to a corporate earnings announcement on the day of the announcement.

3. Label each of the following as an empirical, a priori, or subjective probability.
   a. The probability that U.S. stock returns exceed long-term corporate bond returns over a 10-year period, based on Ibbotson Associates data.
   b. An updated (posterior) probability of an event arrived at using Bayes' formula and judgment on prior probabilities.
   c. The probability of one particular outcome when there are exactly 12 equally likely possible outcomes.
   d. A historical probability of default for double-B-rated bonds, adjusted to reflect your perceptions of changes in the quality of double-B-rated issuance.

4. You are comparing two firms, BestRest Corporation and Relaxin, Inc. The exports of both firms stand to benefit substantially from the removal of import restrictions on their products in a large export market. The price of BestRest Corporation shares reflects a probability of 0.90 that the restrictions will be removed within the year. The price of Relaxin stock, however, reflects a 0.50 probability that the restrictions will be removed within that time frame. By all other information related to valuation, the two stocks appear comparably valued. How would you characterize the implied probabilities reflected in share prices? Which stock is relatively overvalued, and which stock is relatively undervalued, compared to the other?

5. Suppose you have two limit orders outstanding on two different stocks. The probability that the first limit order executes before the close of trading is 0.45. The probability that the second limit order executes before the close of trading is 0.20. The probability that the two orders both execute before the close of trading is 0.10. What is the probability that at least one of the two limit orders executes before the close of trading?

6. You are using the following three criteria to select a list of 500 companies that may become acquisition targets:

Criterion	Fraction of the 500 Companies Meeting the Criterion
Product lines compatible	0.20
Company will increase combined sales growth rate	0.45
Balance sheet impact manageable	0.78

If the criteria are independent, how many companies will pass the screen?

7. You apply both valuation criteria and financial strength criteria in choosing stocks. The probability that a randomly selected stock (from your investment universe) meets your valuation criteria is 0.25. Given that a stock meets your valuation criteria, the probability that the stock meets your financial strength criteria is 0.40. What is the probability that a stock meets both your valuation and financial strength criteria?

8. Suppose that 5 percent of the stocks meeting your stock selection criteria are in the telecommunications (telecom) industry. Also, dividend-paying telecom stocks are 1 percent of the total number of stocks meeting your selection criteria. What is the probability that a stock is dividend-paying, given that it is a telecom stock that has met your stock selection criteria?

9. The following two facts were cited in a report from Fitch data service.[25]
   - In 2000, the volume of defaulted U.S. high-yield debt was $27.9 billion. The average market size of the high-yield bond market during 2000 was $550 billion.

   - The average recovery rate for defaulted U.S. high-yield bonds in 2000 (defined as average price one month after default) was $0.27 on the dollar.

   Address the following three tasks:
   a. On the basis of the first fact given above, calculate the default rate on U.S. high-yield debt in 2000. Interpret this default rate as a probability.
   b. State the probability computed in Part a as an odds against default.
   c. The quantity 1 minus the recovery rate given in the second fact above is the expected loss per $1 of principal value, given that default has occurred. Suppose you are told that an institution held a diversified high-yield bond portfolio in 2000. Using the information in both facts, what was the institution's expected loss in 2000?

10. You are given the following probability distribution for the annual sales of ElStop Corporation:

**Probability Distribution for
ElStop Annual Sales
(in millions of dollars)**

Probability	Sales
0.20	$275
0.40	$250
0.25	$200
0.10	$190
0.05	$180
Sum = 1.00	

a. Calculate the expected value of ElStop's annual sales.
b. Calculate the variance of ElStop's annual sales.
c. Calculate the standard deviation of ElStop's annual sales.

11. Suppose the prospects for recovery of principal for a defaulted bond issue depends on which of two economic scenarios prevails. Scenario 1 has probability 0.75 and will re-

[25] "High Yield Defaults Soar in 2000," February 12, 2001.

sult in recovery of $0.90 per $1 principal value with probability 0.45, or in recovery of $0.80 per $1 principal value with probability 0.55. Scenario 2 has probability 0.25 and will result in recovery of $0.50 per $1 principal value with probability 0.85, or in recovery of $0.40 per $1 principal value with probability 0.15.

a. Compute the probability of each of the four possible recovery amounts: $0.90, $0.80, $0.50, and $0.40.
b. Compute the expected recovery, given the first scenario.
c. Compute the expected recovery, given the second scenario.
d. Compute the expected recovery.
e. Graph the information in a tree diagram.

12. Suppose we have the expected daily returns (in terms of U.S. dollars), standard deviations, and correlations shown in the table below.

U.S., German, and Italian Bond Returns

U.S. Dollar Daily Returns in Percent			
	U.S. Bonds	German Bonds	Italian Bonds
Expected Return	0.029	0.021	0.073
Standard Deviation	0.409	0.606	0.635

Correlation Matrix			
	A	B	C
U.S. Bonds	1	0.09	0.10
German Bonds		1	0.70
Italian Bonds			1

Source: Kool (2000), Table 1 (excerpted and adapted)

a. Using the data given above, construct a covariance matrix for the daily returns on U.S., German, and Italian bonds.
b. State the expected return and variance of return on a portfolio 70 percent invested in U.S. bonds, 20 percent in German bonds, and 10 percent in Italian bonds.
c. Calculate the standard deviation of return on a portfolio 70 percent invested in U.S. bonds, 20 percent in German bonds, and 10 percent in Italian bonds.

13. The variance of a portfolio of stocks depends on the variances of each individual stock in the portfolio and also the covariances among the stocks in the portfolio. If you have five stocks, how many unique covariances (excluding variances) must you use in order to compute the variance of return on your portfolio? (Recall that the covariance of a stock with itself is the stock's variance.)

14. Calculate the covariance of the returns on Bedolf Corporation (R_B) with the returns on Zedock Corporation (R_Z), using the following data.

Bedolf and Zedock Returns

	$R_Z = 15\%$	$R_Z = 10\%$	$R_Z = 5\%$
$R_B = 30\%$	0.25	0	0
$R_B = 15\%$	0	0.50	0
$R_B = 10\%$	0	0	0.25

Note: Entries are joint probabilities.

15. You have developed a set of criteria for evaluating distressed credits. Firms that do not receive a passing score are classed as likely to go bankrupt within 12 months. You gathered the following information when validating the criteria:

   • Forty percent of the companies to which the test is administered will go bankrupt within 12 months: *P(non-survivor)* = 0.40.

   • Fifty-five percent of the companies to which the test is administered pass it: *P(pass)* = 0.55.

   • The probability that a firm will pass the test (and be classed as a 12-month survivor), given that it will subsequently survive 12 months, is 0.85: *P(pass test | survivor)* = 0.85.

   a. What is *P(pass test | non-survivor)*?
   b. Using Bayes' formula, calculate the probability that a firm is a survivor, given that it passes the test; that is, calculate *P(survivor | pass test)*.
   c. What is the probability that a firm is a *non-survivor*, given that it does not pass the test?
   d. Is the test effective?

16. On a day in March, 3,292 issues traded on the NYSE: 1,303 advanced, 1,764 declined, and 225 were unchanged. In how many ways could this have happened? (Set up the problem but do not solve it.)

17. Your firm intends to select 4 of 10 vice presidents for the investment committee. How many different groups of 4 are possible?

18. As in Example 4-11, you are reviewing the pricing of a speculative grade, one-year maturity, zero-coupon bond. Your goal is to estimate an appropriate default risk premium for this bond. The default risk premium is defined as the extra return above the risk-free return that will compensate investors for default risk. If R is the promised return (yield-to-maturity) on the debt instrument and R_f is the risk-free rate, the default risk premium is $R - R_f$. You assess that the probability that the bond defaults is 0.06: *P(the bond defaults)* = 0.06. One-year T-bills are offering a return of 5.8 percent, an estimate of R_f. In contrast to your approach in Example 4-11, you now do not make the simplifying assumption that bondholders will recover nothing in the event of a default. Rather, you now assume that recovery will be $0.35 on the dollar, given default.

   a. Denote the fraction of principal recovered in default as θ. Following the model of Example 4-11, develop a general expression for the promised return R on this bond.
   b. Given your expression for R and the estimate of R_f, state the minimum default risk premium you should require for this instrument.

SOLUTIONS

1. **a.** *Probability* is defined by the following two properties: (1) the probability of any event is a number between 0 and 1, and (2) the sum of the probabilities of any list of mutually exclusive and exhaustive events equals 1.

   b. *Conditional probability* is the probability of a stated event, given that another event has occurred. For example $P(A \mid B)$ is the probability of A, given that B has occurred.

   c. An *event* is any specified outcome or set of outcomes of a random variable.

   d. Two events are independent if the occurrence of one event does not affect the probability of occurrence of the other event. In symbols, two events A and B are independent if and only if $P(A \mid B) = P(A)$ or, equivalently, $P(B \mid A) = P(B)$.

   e. The variance of a random variable is the expected value (the probability-weighted average) of squared deviations from the random variable's expected value. In symbols, $\sigma^2(X) = E\{[X - E(X)]^2\}$.

2. One logical set of three mutually exclusive and exhaustive events for the reaction of a firm's stock price on the day of a corporate earnings announcement are as follows (wording may vary):

   • Stock price increases on the day of the announcement.

   • Stock price does not change on the day of the announcement.

   • Stock price decreases on the day of the announcement.

   In fact, there are an unlimited number of ways to split up the possible outcomes into three mutually exclusive and exhaustive events. For example, the following list also answers this question satisfactorily:

   • Stock price increases by more than 4 percent on the day of the announcement.

   • Stock price increases by 0 percent to 4 percent on the day of the announcement.

   • Stock price decreases on the day of the announcement.

3. The probability in Part a is an empirical probability. The probability in Part b is a subjective probability. The probability in Part c is an a priori probability. The probability in Part d is a subjective probability.

4. The implied probabilities of 0.90 and 0.50 are *inconsistent* in that they create a potential profit opportunity. The shares of BestRest are relatively overvalued compared to Relaxin, as their price incorporates a much higher probability of the favorable event (lifting of the trade restriction) than the shares of Relaxin, which are relatively undervalued compared to BestRest.

5. The probability that at least one of the two orders executes is given by the addition rule for probabilities. Letting A stand for the event that *the first limit order executes before the close of trading* and letting B stand for the event that *the second limit order executes before the close of trading*, $P(A \text{ or } B) = P(A) + P(B) - P(AB) = 0.45 + 0.20 - 0.10 = 0.55$. The probability that at least one of the two orders executes before the close of trading is 0.55.

6. According to the multiplication rule for independent events, the probability of a company passing all three criteria is the product of the three probabilities. Labeling the event that a company passes the first, second, and third criteria, A, B, and C, respec-

tively $P(ABC) = P(A)P(B)P(C) = 0.20 \times 0.45 \times 0.78 = 0.0702$. As a consequence, $0.0702 \times 500 = 35.10$ or 35 companies pass the screen.

7. Use Equation 4-2, the multiplication rule for probabilities $P(AB) = P(A \mid B)P(B)$, defining *A* as the event that *a stock meets the financial criteria* and defining *B* as the event that *a stock meets the valuation criteria*. Then $P(AB) = 0.40 \times 0.25 = 0.10$. The probability that a stock meets both the financial and valuation criteria, stated as a percent, is 10 percent.

8. Use Equation 4-1 to find this conditional probability: *P(stock is dividend-paying | telecom stock that meets criteria)* = *P(stock is dividend-paying* and *telecom stock that meets criteria)/P(telecom stock that meets criteria)* = 0.01/0.05 = 0.20

9. **a.** The default rate was ($27.9 billion)/($550 billion) = 0.050727 or 5.1 percent. This can be interpreted as the probability that $1 invested in a market-value weighted portfolio of U.S. high-yield bonds was subject to default in 2000.

   b. The odds against an event are denoted $E = [1 - P(E)]/P(E)$. In this case, the odds against default are $(1 - 0.051)/0.051 = 18.607$, or "18.6 to 1."

   c. First, note that *E(loss | bond defaults)* $= 1 - \$0.27 = \$0.73$. According to the total probability rule for expected value, *E(loss)* = *E(loss | bond defaults)P(bond defaults)* + *E(loss | bond does not default)P(bond does not default)* $= \$0.73 \times 0.051 + \$0.0 \times 0.949 = 0.03723$, or $0.03723. Thus, the institution's expected loss was approximately 4 cents per dollar of principal value invested.

10. **a.** Using Equation 4-6 for the expected value of a random variable (where dollar amounts are in millions)

$$E(\text{Sales}) = (0.20 \times \$275) + (0.40 \times \$250) + (0.25 \times \$200)$$
$$+ (0.10 \times \$190) + (0.05 \times \$180) = \$233 \text{ million}$$

   b. Using Equation 4-8 for variance,

$$\sigma^2(\text{Sales}) = P(\$275)[\$275 - E(\text{Sales})]^2 + P(\$250)[\$250 - E(\text{Sales})]^2$$
$$+ P(\$200)[\$200 - E(\text{Sales})]^2 + P(\$190)[\$190 - E(\text{Sales})]^2$$
$$+ P(\$180)[\$180 - E(\text{Sales})]^2$$
$$= [0.20 \times (\$275 - \$233)^2] + [0.40 \times (\$250 - \$233)^2] + [0.25 \times$$
$$(\$200 - \$233)^2] + [0.10 \times (\$190 - \$233)^2] + [0.05 \times (\$180$$
$$- \$233)^2]$$
$$= 352.80 + 115.60 + 272.25 + 184.90 + 140.45$$
$$= (1,066 \text{ million dollars})^2$$

   c. The standard deviation of annual sales is $[(1,066 \text{ million dollars})^2]^{1/2} = \$32.649655$ million, or $32.65 million.

11. **a.** *Outcomes associated with Scenario 1*: The probability of recovering $0.90 is $0.3375 = 0.45$ (the probability of $0.90 recovery per $1 principal value, given Scenario 1) $\times 0.75$ (the probability of Scenario 1). The probability of recovering $0.80 is $0.4125 = 0.55 \times 0.75$.

   Outcomes associated with Scenario 2: The probability of recovering $0.50 is $0.2125 = 0.85$ (the probability of $0.50 recovery per $1 principal value, given Scenario 2) $\times 0.25$ (the probability of Scenario 2). The probability of recovering $0.40 is $0.0375 = 0.15 \times 0.25$.

b. $E(recovery \mid \text{Scenario 1}) = (0.45 \times \$0.90) + (0.55 \times \$0.80) = \$0.845$

c. $E(recovery \mid \text{Scenario 2}) = (0.85 \times \$0.50) + (0.15 \times \$0.40) = \$0.485$

d. $E(recovery) = (\$0.845 \times 0.75) + (\$0.485 \times 0.25) = \$0.755$

e.

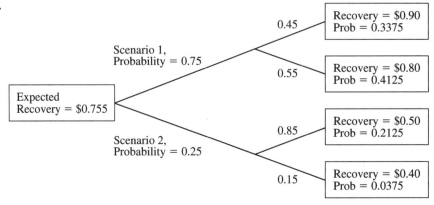

12. a. The diagonal entries in the covariance matrix are the variances, found by squaring the standard deviations.

Var(U.S. bond returns) $= 0.409^2 = 0.167281$
Var(German bond returns) $= 0.606^2 = 0.367236$
Var(Italian bond returns) $= 0.635^2 = 0.403225$

The covariances are found using the relationship $\text{Cov}(R_i, R_j) = \rho(R_i, R_j)\sigma(R_i)\sigma(R_j)$. There are three distinct covariances:

- Cov(U.S. bond returns, German bond returns) = ρ(U.S. bond returns, German bond returns)σ(U.S. bond returns)σ(German bond returns) $= 0.09 \times 0.409 \times 0.606 = 0.022307$

- Cov(U.S. bond returns, Italian bond returns) = ρ(U.S. bond returns, Italian bond returns)σ(U.S. bond returns)σ(Italian bond returns) $= 0.10 \times 0.409 \times 0.635 = 0.025972$

- Cov(German bond returns, Italian bond returns) = ρ(German bond returns, Italian bond returns)σ(German bond returns)σ(Italian bond returns) $= 0.70 \times 0.409 \times 0.635 = 0.181801$

Covariance Matrix of Returns, 1996 to 1998

	U.S. Bonds	German Bonds	Italian Bonds
U.S. Bonds	0.167281	0.022307	0.025972
German Bonds	0.022307	0.367236	0.181801
Italian Bonds	0.025972	0.181801	0.403225

b. Using Equation 4-16, we find

$$\sigma^2(R_P) = w_1^2 \sigma^2(R_1) + w_2^2 \sigma^2(R_2) + w_3^2 \sigma^2(R_3) + 2w_1 w_2 Cov(R_1, R_2)$$
$$+ 2w_1 w_3 Cov(R_1, R_3) + w_2 w_3 Cov(R_2, R_3)$$
$$= (0.70)^2(0.167281) + (0.20)^2(0.367236) + (0.10)^2(0.403225)$$
$$+ 2(0.70)(0.20)(0.022307) + 2(0.70)(0.10)(0.025972)$$
$$+ 2(0.20)(0.10)(0.181801)$$
$$= 0.081968 + 0.014689 + 0.004032 + 0.006246 + 0.003636$$
$$+ 0.007272$$
$$= 0.117843$$

c. The standard deviation of this portfolio is $\sigma^2(R_P) = (0.117843)^{1/2} = 0.343283$, or 34.3 percent.

13. A covariance matrix for five assets has $5 \times 5 = 25$ entries. Subtracting the five diagonal variance terms, we have $25 - 5 = 20$ off-diagonal entries. Because the covariance matrix is symmetric, only 10 entries are unique ($10 = 20/2$). Hence, you must use 10 unique covariances in your five stock portfolio variance calculation.

14. The covariance is 25, computed as follows. First, we calculate expected values:

$$E(R_B) = (0.25 \times 30\%) + (0.50 \times 15\%) + (0.25 \times 10\%) = 17.5\%$$
$$E(R_Z) = (0.25 \times 15\%) + (0.50 \times 10\%) + (0.25 \times 5\%) = 10\%$$

Then we find the covariance as follows:

$$Cov(R_B, R_Z) = P(30, 15) \times [(30 - 17.5) \times (15 - 10)] + P(15, 10)$$
$$\times [(15 - 17.5) \times (10 - 10)] + P(10, 5) \times [(10 - 17.5)$$
$$\times (5 - 10)]$$
$$= (0.25 \times 12.5 \times 5) + [0.50 \times (-2.5) \times 0] + [0.25 \times (-7.5)$$
$$\times (-5)]$$
$$= 15.625 + 0 + 9.375 = 25$$

15. a. We can set up the equation using the total probability rule:

$$P(pass\ test) = P(pass\ test \mid survivor)P(survivor)$$
$$+ P(pass\ test \mid non\text{-}survivor)P(non\text{-}survivor)$$
$$0.55 = 0.85 \times 0.60 + P(pass\ test \mid non\text{-}survivor)$$
$$\times 0.40, \text{ as } P(survivor) = 1 - P(non\text{-}survivor)$$
$$= 1 - 0.40 = 0.60$$

Thus $P(pass\ test \mid non\text{-}survivor) = (0.55 - 0.85 \times 0.60)/0.40 = 0.10$

b. $P(survivor \mid pass\ test) = [P(pass\ test \mid survivor)/P(pass\ test)] \times P(survivor)$
$$= (0.85/0.55) \times 0.60 = 0.927273$$

The information that a firm passes the test causes you to update your probability that the firm is a survivor from 0.60 to approximately 0.927.

c. According to Bayes' formula, $P(non\text{-}survivor \mid not\ pass\ test) = [P(not\ pass\ test \mid non\text{-}survivor)/P(not\ pass\ test)] \times P(non\text{-}survivor) = [P(not\ pass\ test \mid non\text{-}survivor)/0.45] \times 0.40.$

We can set up the following equation to obtain $P(\text{not pass test} \mid \text{non-survivor})$:

$$P(\text{not pass test}) = P(\text{not pass test} \mid \text{non-survivor})P(\text{non-survivor})$$
$$+ P(\text{not pass test} \mid \text{survivor})P(\text{survivor})$$
$$0.45 = P(\text{not pass test} \mid \text{non-survivor}) \times 0.40 + 0.15 \times 0.60$$

where $P(\text{not pass test}|\text{survivor}) = 1 - P(\text{pass test}|\text{survivor}) = 1 - 0.85 = 0.15$. So $P(\text{not pass test}|\text{non-survivor}) = (0.45 - 0.15 \times 0.60)/0.40 = 0.90$. Using this result with the formula above, we find $P(\text{non-survivor}|\text{not pass test}) = [0.90/0.45] \times 0.40 = 0.80$. Seeing that a firm does not pass the test causes us to update the probability that it is a non-survivor from 0.40 to 0.80.

d. Passing the test greatly increases our confidence that the firm is a survivor. Failing the test doubles the probability that the firm is a non-survivor. Therefore, the test appears to be useful.

16. This is a labeling problem where we assign each NYSE issue a label: advanced, declined, or unchanged. The expression to count the number of ways 3,292 issues can be assigned to these three categories such that 1,303 advanced, 1,764 declined, and 225 were unchanged is $3,292!/(1,303! \times 1,764! \times 225!)$.

17. We find the answer using the combination formula $\binom{n}{r} = n!/[(n - r)!r!]$ Here, $n = 10$ and $r = 4$, so the answer is $10!/[(10 - 4)!4!] = 3,628,800/(720 \times 24) = 210$.

18. a. The two events that affect a bondholder's returns are *the bond defaults* and *the bond does not default*. First, compute the value of the bond for the two events per $1 invested.

	The Bond Defaults	*The Bond Does Not Default*
Bond value	$\theta \times \$(1 + R)$	$\$(1 + R)$

Second, find the expected value of the bond (per $1 invested):

$$E(\text{bond}) = \theta \times \$(1 + R) \times P(\text{the bond defaults}) + \$(1 + R)$$
$$\times [1 - P(\text{the bond defaults})]$$

On the other hand, the expected value of the T-bill is the certain value $(1 + R_f)$. Setting the expected value of the bond to the expected value of the T-bill permits us to find the promised return on the bond such that bondholders expect to break even.

$$\theta \times \$(1 + R) \times P(\text{the bond defaults}) + \$(1 + R)$$
$$\times [1 - P(\text{the bond defaults})] = \$(1 + R_f)$$

Rearranging the left-hand side,

$$(1 + R) \times \{\theta \times P(\text{the bond defaults}) + [1 - P(\text{the bond defaults})]\}$$
$$= (1 + R_f)$$
$$R = (1 + R_f)/\{\theta \times P(\text{the bond defaults})$$
$$+ [1 - P(\text{the bond defaults})]\} - 1$$

b. For this problem, $R_f = 0.058$, $P(the\ bond\ defaults) = 0.06$, $1 - P(the\ bond\ defaults) = 0.94$, and $\theta = 0.35$.

$R = [1.058/(0.35 \times 0.06 + 0.94)] - 1 = 0.100937$, or 10.1 percent

With a recovery rate of 35 cents on the dollar, a minimum default risk premium of about 430 basis points is required, calculated as $4.3\% = 10.1\% - 5.8\%$.

COMMON PROBABILITY DISTRIBUTIONS

LEARNING OUTCOMES

After completing this chapter, you will be able to do the following:

- Define the concept of probability distribution.
- Give examples of discrete and continuous random variables.
- Describe the range of possible outcomes of a specified random variable.
- Define a probability function.
- State whether a given function satisfies the conditions for a probability function.
- State the two key properties of a probability function.
- Define a cumulative distribution function.
- Calculate probabilities for a random variable given the random variable's cumulative distribution function.
- Define a discrete uniform random variable.
- Calculate probabilities using a specified discrete uniform probability distribution.
- Define a binomial random variable.
- Describe the types of problems for which the binomial distribution is used.
- Calculate probabilities using a specified binomial probability distribution.
- Calculate the expected value and variance of a binomial random variable.
- Construct a binomial tree to describe asset price movement.
- Calculate the expected terminal stock price with a binomial distribution.
- Describe the continuous uniform distribution.
- Calculate probabilities using a specified continuous uniform probability distribution.
- Describe the key properties of the normal distribution.
- Construct confidence intervals for a normally distributed random variable.
- Describe how to standardize a random variable.
- Define the standard normal distribution.
- Calculate probabilities using the standard normal random probability distribution.
- Explain the distinction between a univariate and a multivariate distribution.
- Explain the role of correlation in the multivariate normal distribution.

- Discuss how the normal distribution is used in modeling asset returns.
- Explain the relationship of the normal distribution to mean–variance analysis.
- Explain the concept of shortfall risk.
- State Roy's safety-first criterion.
- Select an optimal portfolio using Roy's safety-first criterion.
- Explain the relationship between the lognormal and normal distributions.
- Describe the use of the lognormal distribution in modeling asset prices.
- Distinguish between discretely and continuously compounded rates of return.
- Calculate the continuously compounded return associated with a given holding period return.
- Calculate volatility from a historical series of returns for use as an input into an option pricing model.
- Explain the technique of Monte Carlo simulation.
- Describe the major applications of Monte Carlo simulation.
- Describe the relationship of Monte Carlo simulation to analytical methods of valuation.
- Explain the technique of historical simulation.
- Describe the limitations of historical simulation.

1 INTRODUCTION TO COMMON PROBABILITY DISTRIBUTIONS

In nearly all investment decisions we work with random variables. The return on a stock and its earnings per share are familiar examples of random variables which investment analysts work with daily. To make probability statements about a random variable, we need to understand its probability distribution. A **probability distribution** specifies the probabilities of the possible outcomes of a random variable.

In this chapter, we present important facts about four probability distributions and their investment uses. These four distributions—the uniform, binomial, normal, and the lognormal—are used extensively in investment analysis. They are used in such basic valuation models as the Black-Scholes Option Pricing Model, the Binomial Option Pricing Model, and the Capital Asset Pricing Model. Hypothesis testing, regression analysis, and time-series analysis are other quantitative tools that you will be better prepared to study and use when you have the working knowledge of probability distributions that this chapter will provide.

After discussing probability distributions, we end the chapter with an introduction to Monte Carlo simulation, a tool for obtaining information on complex problems using a computer. For example, an investment analyst may want to experiment with an investment idea without actually implementing it. Or she may need to price a complex option for which no simple pricing formula exists. In these cases and many others, Monte Carlo simulation is an important resource. To conduct a Monte Carlo simulation, the analyst must identify the risk factors associated with the problem, and specify probability distributions for them. Monte Carlo simulation is, therefore, a tool that requires an understanding of probability distributions.

Before we discuss specific probability distributions, we define basic concepts and terms. We then illustrate the operation of these concepts through the simplest distribution, the uniform distribution. That done, we address probability distributions that have greater currency in investment work, but also greater complexity.

2 DISCRETE RANDOM VARIABLES

A **random variable** is a quantity whose future outcomes are uncertain. The two basic types of random variables are discrete random variables and continuous random variables. A **discrete random variable** can take on at most a countable number of possible values. For example, suppose we have a random variable, X, that can take on outcomes $x_1, x_2, \ldots$ (without limit) or another random variable Y that can take on outcomes $y_1, y_2, \ldots, y_n$ (n possible outcomes). Because we can count the possible outcomes of each random variable (even if we go on forever), these are both discrete random variables. By contrast, we cannot count the outcomes of a **continuous random variable.** We cannot describe the possible outcomes of a continuous random variable Z with a list $z_1, z_2, \ldots$ because the outcome $(z_1 + z_2)/2$, not in the list, would always be possible. Rate of return is an example of a continuous random variable.

In working with a random variable, we need to understand its possible outcomes. For example, stocks traded on the New York Stock Exchange and Nasdaq are quoted in ticks of $0.01. Quoted stock price is thus a discrete random variable with possible values $0, $0.01, $0.02, \ldots However, we can also model stock price as a continuous random variable (as a lognormal random variable, to look ahead). In many applications, we have a choice between using a discrete or a continuous distribution. We are usually guided by which distribution is most efficient for the task we face. This opportunity for choice is not surprising, as many discrete distributions can be approximated with a continuous distribution, and vice versa. In most practical cases, in fact, a probability distribution is only a mathematical idealization, or approximate model, of the relative frequencies of a random variable's possible outcomes.

EXAMPLE 5-1.   The Distribution of Bond Price.

You are researching a probability model for bond price, and you begin by thinking about the characteristics of bonds that affect price. What are the lowest and the highest possible values for bond price? Why? What are some other characteristics of bonds that may affect the distribution of bond price?

The lowest possible value of bond price is 0, when the bond is worthless. Identifying the highest possible value for bond price is more challenging. The promised payments on a coupon bond are the coupons (interest payments) plus the face amount (principal). The price of a bond is the present discounted value of these promised payments. Because investors require a return on their investments, 0 percent is the lower limit on the discount rate that investors would use to discount a bond's promised payments. At a discount rate of 0 percent, the price of a bond is the sum of the face value and the remaining coupons without any discounting. The discount rate thus places the upper limit on bond price. Suppose, for example, that face value is $1,000 and two $40 coupons remain; the interval $0 to $1,080 captures all possible values of the bond's price. The upper limit, in fact, decreases through time as the number of remaining payments decreases.

Other characteristics of a bond also affect its price distribution. Pull to par value is one such characteristic: As the maturity date approaches, the standard deviation of bond price tends to grow smaller as bond price converges to par value. Embedded options also affect bond price. For example, with bonds that are currently callable, the issuer may retire the bonds at a prespecified premium above par; that option of the issuer cuts off part of the bond's upside. Modeling bond price distribution is a challenging problem.

Every random variable is associated with a probability distribution that describes the variable completely. There are two ways to view a probability distribution. The basic view is the **probability function.** The probability function specifies the probability that the random variable takes on a specific value: $P(X = x)$ is the probability that a random variable X takes on the value x. For a discrete random variable, the shorthand notation for the probability function is $p(x) = P(X = x)$. For continuous random variables, the probability function is denoted $f(x)$ and called the **probability density function** (pdf), or just the density.[1]

A probability function has two key properties.

- $0 \leq p(x) \leq 1$, because probability is a number between 0 and 1.
- The sum of the probabilities $p(x)$ over all values of X equals 1. If we have an exhaustive list of the distinct possible outcomes of a random variable and add up the probabilities of each, the probabilities must sum to 1.

We are often interested in finding the probability of a range of outcomes rather than a specific outcome. In these cases, we take the second view of a probability distribution, the cumulative distribution function (cdf). The **cumulative distribution function,** or *distribution function* for short, gives the probability that a random variable X is less than or equal to a particular value x, $P(X \leq x)$. For both discrete and continuous random variables, the shorthand notation is $F(x) = P(X \leq x)$. How does the cumulative distribution function relate to the probability function? The word *cumulative* tells the story. To find $F(x)$, we sum up, or cumulate, values of the probability function for all outcomes less than or equal to x. The function of the cdf is parallel to that of cumulative relative frequency, which we discussed in the chapter on statistical concepts and market returns.

Next, we illustrate these concepts with examples and show how we use discrete and continuous distributions. We start with the simplest distribution, the discrete uniform.

2.1 THE DISCRETE UNIFORM DISTRIBUTION

The simplest of all probability distributions is the discrete uniform distribution. Suppose that the possible outcomes are the integers (whole numbers) 1 to 8, inclusive, and the probability that the random variable takes on any of these possible values is the same for all outcomes (that is, it is uniform). With eight outcomes, $p(x) = 1/8$, or 0.125, for all x ($X = 1, 2, 3, 4, 5, 6, 7, 8$); the preceding statement is a complete description of this discrete uniform random variable. The distribution has a finite number of specified outcomes, and each outcome is equally likely. Table 5-1 summarizes the two views of this random variable, the probability function and the cumulative distribution function

---

[1] The technical term for the probability function of a discrete random variable, probability mass function (pmf), is less frequently used.

TABLE 5-1   Probability Function and Cumulative Distribution
Function for This Discrete Uniform Random Variable

X = x	Probability Function $p(x) = P(X = x)$	Cumulative Distribution Function $F(x) = P(X \leq x)$
1	0.125	0.125
2	0.125	0.250
3	0.125	0.375
4	0.125	0.500
5	0.125	0.625
6	0.125	0.750
7	0.125	0.875
8	0.125	1.000

We can use Table 5-1 to find three probabilities: $P(X \leq 7)$, $P(4 \leq X \leq 6)$, and $P(4 < X \leq 6)$. The following examples illustrate how to use the cdf to find the probability that a random variable will fall in any interval (for any random variable, not only the uniform).

- The probability that X is less than or equal to 7, $P(X \leq 7)$, is the next-to-last entry in the second column, 0.875 or 87.5 percent.
- To find $P(4 \leq X \leq 6)$, we need to find the sum of three probabilities: $p(4)$, $p(5)$, and $p(6)$. We can find this sum in two ways. We can add $p(4)$, $p(5)$, and $p(6)$ from the first column. Or we can calculate the probability as the difference between two values of the cumulative distribution function:

$$F(6) = P(X \leq 6) = p(6) + p(5) + p(4) + p(3) + p(2) + p(1)$$

$$F(3) = P(X \leq 3) = p(3) + p(2) + p(1)$$

so

$$P(4 \leq X \leq 6) = F(6) - F(3) = p(6) + p(5) + p(4) = 3/8$$

So we calculate the second probability as $F(6) - F(3) = 3/8$.

- Now for the third probability, $P(4 < X \leq 6)$, the probability that X is less than or equal to 6 but greater than 4. This probability is $p(5) + p(6)$. We compute it as follows, using the cdf:

$$P(4 < X \leq 6) = P(X \leq 6) - P(X \leq 4) = F(6) - F(4) = p(6) + p(5) = 2/8$$

So we calculate the third probability as $F(6) - F(4) = 2/8$.

Suppose we want to check that the discrete uniform probability function satisfies the general properties of a probability function given earlier. The first property is $0 \leq p(x) \leq 1$. We see that $p(x) = 1/8$ for all x in the first column of the table. (Note that $p(x)$ equals 0 for numbers such as -14 or 12.215 that are not in that column.) The first property is satisfied. The second property is that the probabilities sum to 1. The entries in the first column of Table 5-1 do sum to 1.

The cdf has two other characteristic properties:

- The cumulative distribution function lies between 0 and 1 for any x.

$$0 \le F(x) \le 1$$

- As we increase x, the cdf either increases or remains constant.

Check these statements by looking at the second column in Table 5-1.

We now have some experience working with probability functions and cdfs for discrete random variables. Later in this chapter, we will discuss Monte Carlo simulation, a methodology driven by random numbers. As we will see, the uniform distribution has an important technical use: It is the basis for generating random numbers, which in turn produce random observations for all other probability distributions.[2]

2.2 THE BINOMIAL DISTRIBUTION

In many investment contexts, we view a result as either a success or a failure, or as binary in some other way. When we make probability statements about a record of successes and failures, or about anything with binary outcomes, we often use the binomial distribution. What is a good model for how stock price moves through time? Different models are appropriate for different uses. Cox, Ross, and Rubinstein (1979) developed an option pricing model based on binary moves, price up or price down, for the asset underlying the option. Their Binomial Option Pricing Model (BOPM) was the first of a class of related option pricing models that have played an important role in the development of the derivatives industry. That fact alone would be sufficient reason for studying the binomial distribution, but the binomial can also be useful in decision-making.

The building block of the binomial distribution is the **Bernoulli random variable,** named after the Swiss probabilist James Bernoulli (1654–1704). Suppose we have a trial (an event that may repeat) that produces one of two outcomes. Such a trial is a **Bernoulli trial.** If we let Y equal 1 when the outcome is success and Y equal 0 when the outcome is failure, then the probability function of the Bernoulli random variable Y is

$$p(1) = P(Y = 1) = p$$
$$p(0) = P(Y = 0) = 1 - p$$

where p is the probability that the trial is a success. Our next example is the very first step on the road to understanding the Binomial Option Pricing Model.

EXAMPLE 5-2.   One-Period Stock Price Movement as a Bernoulli Random Variable.

Suppose we describe stock price movement in the following way. Stock price today is S. Next period stock price can move up or down. The probability of an up move is p and the probability of a down move is $1 - p$. Thus stock price is a Bernoulli random

---

[2] See Hillier and Lieberman (2000). Random numbers initially generated by computers are usually random positive integer numbers that are converted to approximate continuous uniform random numbers between 0 and 1. Then the continuous uniform random numbers are used to produce random observations on other distributions, such as the normal, using various techniques. We will discuss random observation generation further in the section on Monte Carlo simulation.

variable with probability of success (an up move) equal to p. When the stock moves up, ending price is uS, with u equal to 1 plus the rate of return if the stock moves up. For example, if the stock earns 0.01 or 1 percent on an up move, $u = 1.01$. When the stock moves down, ending price is dS, with d equal to 1 plus the rate of return if the stock moves down. For example, if the stock earns -0.01 or -1 percent on a down move, $d = 0.99$. Figure 5-1 shows a diagram of this model of stock price dynamics.

FIGURE 5-1   One-Period Stock Price as a Bernoulli Random Variable

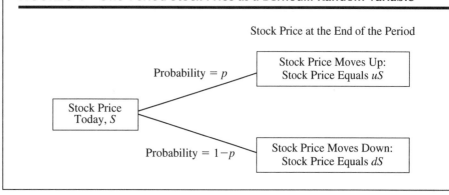

We will continue with the above example later. But sometimes *success* and *failure* have the ordinary financial meaning.

EXAMPLE 5-3.   A Trading Desk Evaluates Block Brokers (1).

You work in equities trading at an institutional money manager that regularly trades with a number of block brokers. Orders to sell or buy that are too large for the liquidity ordinarily available in dealer networks or stock exchanges are blocks. Your firm has known interests in certain kinds of stock. Block brokers call your trading desk when they want to sell blocks of stocks that they think your firm may be interested in buying. You know that these transactions have definite risks. For example, if the broker's client (the seller of the shares) has unfavorable information on the stock, or if the total amount he is selling through all channels is not truthfully communicated to you, you may see an immediate loss on the trade. From time to time, your firm audits the performance of block brokers. Your firm calculates the post-trade, market-risk-adjusted dollar returns on stocks purchased from block brokers. On that basis, you classify each trade as unprofitable or profitable. You have summarized the performance of the brokers in a spreadsheet, excerpted in Table 5-2 for October 2001. (The broker names are coded BB001, BB002.)

TABLE 5-2   Block Trading Gains and Losses

	October 2001	
	Profitable Trades	Losing Trades
BB001	3	9
BB002	5	3

> View each trade as a Bernoulli trial. Calculate the percentage of profitable trades with the two block brokers, for October 2001. These are estimates of p, the probability of a successful (profitable) trade with each broker.
>
> Your firm has logged $3 + 9 = 12$ trades (the row total) with block broker BB001. Because 3 of the 12 trades were profitable, the percentage of profitable trades was 3/12 or 25 percent. With broker BB002, the percentage of profitable trades was 5/8 or 62.5 percent. A trade is a Bernoulli trial, and the above calculations provide estimates of the underlying probability of a profitable trade (success) with the two brokers. For broker BB001, your estimate is $\hat{p} = 0.25$; for broker BB002, your estimate is $\hat{p} = 0.625$.

In n Bernoulli trials, we can have 0 to n successes. If the outcome of an individual trial is random, the total number of successes in n trials is also random. A **binomial random variable** X is defined as the number of successes in n Bernoulli trials. A binomial random variable is the sum of Bernoulli random variables Y_i, $i = 1, 2, \ldots n$:

$$X = Y_1 + Y_2 + \ldots + Y_n$$

where Y_i is the outcome on the ith trial (1 if a success, 0 if a failure). We know that a Bernoulli random variable is defined by the parameter p. The number of trials, n, is the second parameter of a binomial random variable. The binomial distribution makes these assumptions:

- The probability, p, of success is constant for all trials.
- The trials are independent.

The second assumption has great simplifying force. If individual trials were correlated, the calculation for the probability of a given number of successes in n trials would be much more complicated.

Under the above two assumptions, a binomial random variable is completely described by two parameters, n and p. We write

$$X \sim B(n, p)$$

which we read as "X has a binomial distribution with parameters n and p." You can see that a Bernoulli random variable is a binomial random variable with $n = 1$: $Y \sim B(1, p)$.

Now we can find the general expression for the probability that a binomial random variable shows x successes in n trials. We can think in terms of the model of stock price dynamics in Example 5-1. Each period is a Bernoulli trial: with probability p, the stock moves up; with probability $1 - p$, the stock moves down. A success is an up move, and x is the number of up moves or successes in n periods (trials). With each period's moves independent and p constant, the number of up moves in n periods is a binomial random variable. We now develop an expression for $P(X = x)$, the probability function for a binomial random variable.

Any sequence of n periods that shows exactly x up moves must show $n - x$ down moves. We have many different ways to order the up moves and down moves to get a total of x up moves, but each sequence must have the following probability:

$$\underbrace{(p \times p \times p \times p \times \ldots \times p)}_{x \text{ up moves}} \times \underbrace{(q \times q \times q \times \ldots \times q)}_{n - x \text{ down moves}} = p^x q^{n-x}$$

where $q = 1 - p$ is the probability of a down move. (In writing the probability above, we used the assumption of independent trials.) Summarizing, the probability that any one sequence that has x up moves is $p^x q^{n-x}$.

Now we need to multiply this probability by the number of different ways we can get a sequence with x up moves. Using a basic result in counting from the chapter on probability concepts, there are

$$\frac{n!}{(n - x)! \times x!}$$

different sequences in n trials that result in x up moves (or successes) and $n - x$ down moves (or failures). Recall from the chapter on probability concepts that n factorial ($n!$) is defined as $n \times (n - 1) \times (n - 2) \times \dots \times 1$ (and $0! = 1$ by convention). For example, $5! = 5 \times 4 \times 3 \times 2 \times 1 = 120$. The combination formula $n!/[(n - x)! \times x!]$ is denoted by

$$\binom{n}{x}$$

(read: "n combination x" or "n choose x"). For example, over three periods, exactly three different sequences have two up moves: UUD, UDU, and DUU. We confirm this by

$$\binom{3}{2} = \frac{3!}{(3 - 2)! \times 2!} = \frac{3 \times 2 \times 1}{1 \times 2 \times 1} = 3$$

If, hypothetically, each sequence with two up moves had a probability of 0.15, then the total probability of two up moves in three periods would be $0.45 = 3 \times 0.15$. This example should persuade you that for X distributed $B(n, p)$, the probability of x successes in n trials is given by

$$p(x) = P(X = x) = \binom{n}{x} p^x (1 - p)^{n-x} = \frac{n!}{(n - x)! \times x!} p^x (1 - p)^{n-x} \qquad (5\text{-}1)$$

There are distributions that are always symmetric, such as the normal, and distributions that are always asymmetric or skewed, such as the lognormal. The binomial distribution is symmetric when the probability of success on a trial is 0.50, but it is asymmetric or skewed otherwise.

We illustrate Equation 5-1 (the probability function) and the cdf through the symmetrical case. Consider a random variable distributed $B(n = 5, p = 0.50)$. Table 5-3 contains a complete description of this random variable. The fourth column of Table 5-3 is the second column, n combination x, times the third column, $p^x(1 - p)^{n-x}$; column 4 gives the probability for each value of the number of up moves, in the first column. The fifth column, cumulating the entries in the fourth column, is the cumulative distribution function.

What would happen if we kept $n = 5$ but sharply lowered the probability of success on a trial to 10 percent? "Probability for Each Way" for $X = 0$ (no up moves) would then be about 59 percent: $0.10^0(1 - 0.10)^5 = 0.59049$. Because zero successes could still happen one way (column 2), $p(0) = 59$ percent. You may want to check that given $p = 0.10$, $P(X \leq 2) = 99.14$ percent: the probability of two or fewer up moves would be more than 99 percent. The random variable's probability would be massed on 0, 1, and 2 up moves, and a minute amount of probability would attach to larger outcomes. The outcomes of 3 and larger would be the long right tail, and the distribution would be right-skewed. On the

Table 5-3   Binomial Probabilities, $p = 0.50$ and $n = 5$

Number of Up Moves, x (1)	Number of Possible Ways to Reach x Up Moves (2)	Probability for Each Way (3)	Probability for x, $p(x)$ (4) = (2) × (3)	$F(x) = P(X \leq x)$ (5)
0	1	$0.50^0(1 - 0.50)^5 = 0.03125$	0.03125	0.03125
1	5	$0.50^1(1 - 0.50)^4 = 0.03125$	0.15625	0.18750
2	10	$0.50^2(1 - 0.50)^3 = 0.03125$	0.3125	0.50000
3	10	$0.50^3(1 - 0.50)^2 = 0.03125$	0.3125	0.81250
4	5	$0.50^4(1 - 0.50)^1 = 0.03125$	0.15625	0.96875
5	1	$0.50^5(1 - 0.50)^0 = 0.03125$	0.03125	1.00000

other hand, if we set $p = 0.90$, we would have the mirror image of the distribution with $p = 0.10$. The distribution would be left-skewed.

With the binomial probability function in hand, we can continue with our example of block brokers.

EXAMPLE 5-4.   A Trading Desk Evaluates Block Brokers (2).

You now want to evaluate the performance of the block brokers in Example 5-3. You begin with two questions:

1. If you are paying a fair price on average in your trades with a broker, what should be the probability of a profitable trade?
2. Did each broker meet or miss that expectation on probability?

You also realize that the brokers' performance has to be evaluated in light of the sample's size, and for that you need to use the binomial probability function (Equation 5-1). You ask a third question:

3. Under the assumption that the prices of trades were fair, calculate the probability of 3 or fewer profitable trades with broker BB001, and the probability of 5 or more profitable trades with broker BB002. (In answering this question, refer to the data in Example 5-3.)

   Solutions to 1 and 2.   If the price you trade at is fair or fundamental value, 50 percent of the trades you do with a broker should be profitable.[3] The rate of profitable trades with broker BB001 was 25 percent. Therefore, broker BB001 missed your performance expectation. Broker BB002, at 62.5 percent profitable trades, exceeded your expectation.

---

[3] Of course, you need to adjust for the direction in the overall market after the trade (any broker's record will be helped by a bull market) and perhaps make other risk adjustments. Assume that these adjustments have been made.

Solution to 3. For broker BB001, the number of trades (the trials) was $n = 12$, and 3 were profitable. You are asked to calculate the probability of 3 or fewer profitable trades, $F(3) = p(3) + p(2) + p(1) + p(0)$.

Suppose the underlying probability of a profitable trade with BB001 is $p = 0.50$. With $n = 12$ and $p = 0.50$, according to Equation 5-1 the probability of 3 profitable trades is

$$p(3) = \binom{n}{x} p^x (1 - p)^{n-x} = \binom{12}{3} 0.50^3 \times 0.50^9$$

$$= \frac{12!}{(12 - 3)! \times 3!} 0.000061 = 220 \times 0.000244 = 0.053711$$

The probability of exactly 3 profitable trades out of 12 is 5.4 percent if Broker BB001 was giving you fair prices. Now you need to calculate the other probabilities:

$$p(2) = \{12!/[(12 - 2)! \times 2!]\} \times 0.50^2 \times 0.50^{10} = 66 \times 0.000244 = 0.016113$$

$$p(1) = \{12!/[(12 - 1)! \times 1!]\} \times 0.50^1 \times 0.50^{11} = 12 \times 0.000244 = 0.000293$$

$$p(0) = \{12!/[(12 - 0)! \times 0!]\} \times 0.50^0 \times 0.50^{12} = 1 \times 0.000244 = 0.000244$$

Adding all the probabilities, $F(3) = 0.053711 + 0.016113 + 0.000293 + 0.000244 = 0.072998$ or 7.3 percent. The probability of doing 3 or fewer profitable trades out of 12 is 7.3 percent if your trading desk was getting fair prices from broker BB001.

For broker BB002, you are assessing the probability that the underlying probability of a profitable trade with this broker was 50 percent, despite the good results. The question was framed as the probability of doing 5 or more profitable trades if the underlying probability is 50 percent: $1 - F(4) = p(5) + p(6) + p(7) + p(8)$. You could calculate $F(4)$ and subtract it from 1, but you can also calculate $p(5) + p(6) + p(7) + p(8)$ directly. You do that.

You begin by calculating the probability that exactly 5 out of 8 trades were profitable if BB002 was giving you fair prices:

$$p(5) = \binom{8}{5} 0.50^5 \times 0.50^3 = 56 \times 0.003906 = 0.21875$$

The probability is about 21.9 percent. The other probabilities are

$$p(6) = 28 \times 0.003906 = 0.109375$$

$$p(7) = 8 \times 0.003906 = 0.03125$$

$$p(8) = 1 \times 0.003906 = 0.003906$$

So $p(5) + p(6) + p(7) + p(8) = 0.21875 + 0.109375 + 0.03125 + 0.003906 = 0.363281$ or 36.3 percent.[4] This probability of 36.3 percent is quite high. If one of the trades with BB002 had been reclassified from profitable to unprofitable, you would

---

[4] In this example all calculations were worked through by hand; but binomial probability and cdf functions are also available within spreadsheets.

have broken even with 4 out 8 profitable trades. In summary, your trading desk is getting at least fair prices from BB002; you will probably want to accumulate additional evidence before concluding that you are trading at better-than-fair prices.

The magnitude of the profits and losses in these trades is another important consideration. If all profitable trades had small profits but all unprofitable trades had large losses, for example, you might lose money on your trades even if the majority of them were profitable.

The binomial distribution helps in evaluating the performance of an investment manager in the next example.

EXAMPLE 5-5.   Meeting a Tracking Error Objective.

You work for a pension fund sponsor. You have given a new money manager a mandate to manage a $30 million portfolio indexed on MSCI EAFE-Europe. After research, you believe it is reasonable to expect that the manager will keep tracking error within a band of 75 basis points (bps) of the benchmark's return, on a quarterly basis. **Tracking error** is the total return on the portfolio (gross of fees) minus the total return on MSCI EAFE-Europe.[5] To quantify this expectation further, you will be satisfied if tracking error is within the 75 bps band 90 percent of the time. The manager meets the objective in six out of eight quarters. Of course, six out of eight quarters is a 75 percent success rate. But how does the manager's record precisely relate to your expectation of a 90 percent success rate and the sample size, 8 observations? To answer this question, you must find the probability that, given an assumed true or underlying success rate of 90 percent, performance could be as bad or worse than that delivered. Calculate the probability (by hand or with a spreadsheet).

Specifically, you want to find the probability that tracking error is within the 75 bps band in six or fewer quarters out of the eight in the sample. With $n = 8$ and $p = 0.90$, this probability is $F(6) = p(6) + p(5) + p(4) + p(3) + p(2) + p(1) + p(0)$. Start with

$$p(6) = [8!/(6! \times 2!)] \times 0.90^6 \times 0.10^2 = 28 \times 0.005314 = 0.148803$$

and work through the other probabilities

$$p(5) = [8!/(5! \times 3!)] \times 0.90^5 \times 0.10^3 = 56 \times 0.00059 = 0.033067$$

$$p(4) = [8!/(4! \times 4!)] \times 0.90^4 \times 0.10^4 = 70 \times 0.000066 = 0.004593$$

$$p(3) = [8!/(3! \times 5!)] \times 0.90^3 \times 0.10^5 = 56 \times 0.000007 = 0.000408$$

$$p(2) = [8!/(2! \times 6!)] \times 0.90^2 \times 0.10^6 = 28 \times 0.000001 = 0.000023$$

$$p(1) = [8!/(1! \times 7!)] \times 0.90^1 \times 0.10^7 = 8 \times 0.00000009 = 0.00000072$$

$$p(0) = [8!/(0! \times 8!)] \times 0.90^0 \times 0.10^8 = 1 \times 0.00000001 = 0.00000001$$

---

[5] Some practitioners use *tracking error* to describe what we later call *tracking risk*, the standard deviation of the differences between the portfolio's and benchmark's returns.

Summing all these probabilities, you conclude that $F(6) = 0.148803 + 0.033067 + 0.004593 + 0.000408 + 0.000023 + 0.00000072 + 0.00000001 = 0.186895$ or 18.7%. There is a moderate 18.7 percent probability that the manager would show the record he did if he had the skill to meet your expectations 90 percent of the time.

There are other evaluation concepts such as tracking risk, defined as the standard deviation of tracking error, that you can use to assess the manager's performance. The calculation just above would be only one input into any decision you make. But to answer problems involving success rates, you need to be skilled in using the binomial distribution.

Two descriptors of a distribution that are often used in investments are the mean and the variance (or the standard deviation, the positive square root of variance). Table 5-4 gives the expressions for the mean and variance of binomial random variables.

TABLE 5-4   Mean and Variance of Binomial Random Variables

	Mean	Variance
Bernoulli, $B(1, p)$	p	$p(1-p)$
Binomial, $B(n, p)$	np	$np(1-p)$

Because a single Bernoulli random variable, $Y \sim B(1, p)$, takes on the value 1 with probability p and the value 0 with probability $1- p$, its mean or weighted average outcome is p. A general binomial random variable, $B(n, p)$, is the sum of n Bernoulli random variables, and so the mean of a $B(n, p)$ random variable is np. Given that a $B(1, p)$ variable has variance $p(1- p)$, the variance of a $B(n, p)$ random variable is n times that value, or $np(1- p)$, using the independence assumption.[6] We can illustrate the calculation for two binomial random variables with differing probabilities as follows:

Random Variable	Mean	Variance
$B(n = 5, p = 0.50)$	$2.50 = 5(0.50)$	$1.25 = 5(0.50)(0.50)$
$B(n = 5, p = 0.10)$	$0.50 = 5(0.10)$	$0.45 = 5(0.10)(0.90)$

For a $B(n = 5, p = 0.50)$ random variable, the expected number of successes is 2.5 with a standard deviation of $1.118 = (1.25)^{1/2}$; for a $B(n = 5, p = 0.10)$ random variable, the expected number of successes is 0.50 with a standard deviation of $0.67 = (0.45)^{1/2}$.

Earlier, we looked at a simple one-period model for stock price movement. Now we extend the model to describe stock price movement on three consecutive days. Each day is an independent trial. The stock moves up with constant probability p (the **up transition probability**); if it moves up, u is 1 plus the rate of return for an up move. The stock moves down with constant probability $1 - p$ (the **down transition probability**); if it moves down, d is 1 plus the rate of return for a down move. We graph stock price movement in Figure 5-2, where we now associate each of the $n = 3$ stock price moves with time indexed

---

[6] This is the calculation of the variance of a Bernoulli random variable (which can only take on one of two values, 1 or 0): $\sigma^2(Y) = E[(Y - EY)^2] = E[(Y - p)^2] = (1 - p)^2 p + (0 - p)^2(1 - p) = (1 - p)[(1 - p)p + p^2] = p(1 - p)$.

by t. The shape of the graph suggests why it is a called a **binomial tree.** Each boxed value from which successive moves or outcomes branch in the tree is called a **node;** in this example, a node is potential value for the stock price at a specified time.

FIGURE 5-2   Binomial Model of Stock Price Movement

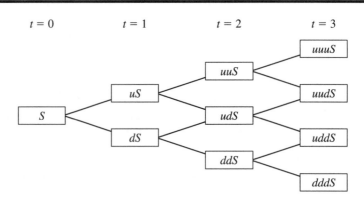

We see from the tree that stock price at $t = 3$ has four possible values: *uuuS*, *uudS*, *uddS*, and *dddS*. The probability that stock price equals any one of these four values is given by the binomial distribution. For example, three sequences of moves result in a final stock price of *uudS*: these are *uud*, *udu*, and *duu*. These sequences have two up moves out of three moves in total; the combination formula confirms that the number of ways to get two up moves (successes) in three periods (trials) is $3!/[(3 - 2)! \times 2!] = 3$. Next note that each of these sequences, *uud*, *udu*, and *duu*, has probability $p^2(1- p)$. So $P(S_3 = uudS) = 3 \times p^2(1 - p)$.

The binomial random variable in this application is the number of up-moves. Final stock price distribution is a function of the initial stock price, the *number* of up moves, and the *size* of the up moves and down moves. We cannot say that stock price itself is a binomial random variable; rather, it is a function of a binomial random variable, as well as of u and d, and initial price. This richness is actually one key to why this way of modeling stock price is useful: It allows us to choose values of these parameters to approximate various distributions for stock price (using a large number of time periods).[7] One distribution that can be approximated is the lognormal, an important continuous distribution model for stock price that we will discuss later. The flexibility extends further. In the tree shown above, the transition probabilities are the same at each node: p for an up move and $1 - p$ for a down move. That is the standard formula you should be familiar with. It describes a process in which stock return volatility is constant through time. Option experts, however, sometimes model changing volatility through time using a binomial tree in which the probabilities for up and down moves are different at different nodes.

The binomial tree also supplies the possibility of testing a condition or contingency at any node. This flexibility is useful in investment applications such as option pricing. Consider an American call option on a dividend-paying stock (an American option can be exercised at any time before expiration, at any node on the tree). It may be optimal to exercise an American call option on stock just before an ex-dividend date, to buy the stock and receive the dividend. If we model stock price with a binomial tree, we can test, at each

---

[7] For example, we can split 20 days into 100 subperiods, taking care to use compatible values for u and d.

node, whether exercising the option is optimal. Also, if we know the value of the call at the four terminal nodes at $t = 3$ and we have a model for discounting values one period, we can step backward one period to $t = 2$ to find the call's value at the three nodes there. Continuing on recursively, we can find the call's value today. This type of recursive operation is convenient for programming a computer. As a result, binomial trees are useful for valuing options even more complex than American calls on stock.

We have said that stock price is a function of a binomial random variable, rather than a binomial variable itself. Nevertheless, it is correct to calculate the expected value and variance of stock price using the underlying binomial probability function to weight the possible stock price outcomes.[8]

EXAMPLE 5-6.   Expected Return and Standard Deviation of Return on a Stock Following a Binomial Process.

You are exploring a simple model for the price dynamics of a stock with a price today of €100. In your model, the stock either moves up by 1 percent ($u = 1.01$) or down by 1 percent ($d = 0.99$) each day over the next three days. The probability of an up move is $p = 0.60$, and the probability of a down move is 0.40. Table 5-5 summarizes the model.

TABLE 5-5   Terminal Stock Price: $n = 3$, $p = 0.60$

Terminal Price	Path: Number of ways	Probability
€103.0301 = €100$(1.01)^3$	UUU: 1 way	$p(103.0301) = 1(0.60^3)$ = 0.216
€100.9899 = €100$(1.01)^2(0.99)$	UUD: 3 ways	$p(100.9899) = (3)(0.60)^2(0.40) = 0.432$
€98.9901 = €100$(1.01)(0.99)^2$	UDD: 3 ways	$p(98.9901) = (3)(0.60)(0.40)^2 = 0.288$
€97.0299 = €100$(0.99)^3$	DDD: 1 way	$p(97.0299) = 1(0.40)^3$ = 0.064
		Sum = 1.0

What is the expected terminal stock price? What is the standard deviation of the expected terminal stock price?

The expected terminal price is equal to the probability-weighted average of the possible ending stock prices. An ending price of €103.0301 (in the first column) results from three up moves. The weight to apply to €103.03101 is the probability of three up moves, 0.216 (in the third column), and so forth for the other terminal stock prices. You calculate

$$E(\text{Stock price}) = 0.216(\text{€}103.0301) + 0.432(\text{€}100.9899) + 0.288(\text{€}98.9901) \\ + 0.064(\text{€}97.0299) = \text{€}100.60$$

The expected terminal stock price is €100.60.

---

[8] The proposition that we can correctly calculate the expected value (and variance) of a *function* of a random variable X using the probability function of X (rather than that of the function itself) is proved in Ross (1997) and other probability textbooks.

> To calculate standard deviation, first calculate variance, the weighted average of the squared deviations from the mean. (Amounts are in euro.)
>
> $$\sigma^2(\text{Stock price}) = 0.216(103.0301 - 100.60)^2 + 0.432(100.9899 - 100.60)^2$$
> $$+ 0.288(98.9901 - 100.60)^2 + 0.064(97.0299 - 100.60)^2$$
> $$= 2.903388$$
>
> The standard deviation of terminal price is the square root of variance, $(2.903388)^{1/2} = 1.703833$ or about €1.70.
>
> To summarize, we calculate the expected stock price and variance of stock price using as weights the associated probabilities for the number of up moves to reach each terminal node.

3   CONTINUOUS RANDOM VARIABLES

In the previous section, we considered discrete random variables (that is, random variables whose set of possible outcomes is countable). In contrast, the possible outcomes of continuous random variables are never countable. If 1.250 is one possible value of a continuous random variable, for example, we cannot name the next higher or lower possible value. Technically, the range of possible outcomes of a continuous random variable is the real line (all real numbers between $-\infty$ and $+\infty$) or some subset of the real line.

In this section, we focus on the two most important continuous distributions in investment work, the normal and lognormal. As we did with discrete distributions, we introduce the topic through the uniform distribution.

3.1 CONTINUOUS UNIFORM DISTRIBUTION

The continuous uniform distribution is the simplest continuous probability distribution. The uniform distribution has two main uses. As the basis of techniques for generating random numbers, the uniform distribution plays a role in Monte Carlo simulation. As the probability distribution that describes equally likely outcomes, the uniform distribution is an appropriate probability model to represent a particular kind of uncertainty in beliefs in which all outcomes appear equally likely.

The probability density function for a uniform random variable is

$$f(x) = \begin{cases} \dfrac{1}{b-a} & \text{for } a \leq x \leq b \\ 0 & \text{otherwise} \end{cases}$$

For example, with $a = 0$ and $b = 8$, $f(x) = 1/8$ or 0.125. We graph this density in Figure 5-3. The graph of the density function plots as a horizontal line with a value of 0.125.

What is the probability that a uniform random variable with limits $a = 0$ and $b = 8$ is less than or equal to 3, or $F(3) = P(X \leq 3)$? When we were working with the discrete uniform random variable with possible outcomes 0, 1, 2, ... 8, we summed individual probabilities: $p(1) + p(2) + p(3) = 0.375$. In contrast, the probability that a continuous uniform random variable, or any continuous random variable, assumes any given fixed value is 0. For example, even the narrow interval 2.510 to 2.511 holds an infinity of possible values. If each individual value had a positive probability, the sum of the probabilities in that interval alone would be infinite. To find the probability $F(3)$, we find the area under the curve graphing the probability density function, between 0 to 3 on the x-axis. In calcu-

FIGURE 5-3   Continuous Uniform Distribution

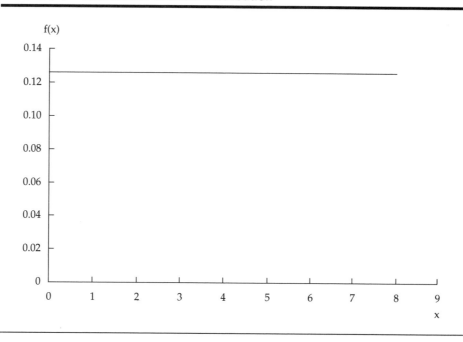

lus, this operation is called integrating the probability function $f(x)$ from 0 to 3. This area under the curve is a rectangle with base $3 - 0 = 3$ and height 1/8. The area of this rectangle equals base times height: $3 \times 1/8 = 3/8$ or 0.375. So $F(3) = 3/8$ or 0.375.

The interval from 0 to 3 is three-eighths of the total length between the limits of 0 and 8, and $F(3)$ is three-eighths of the total probability of 1. The middle line of the expression for the cdf captures this relationship.

$$F(x) = \begin{cases} 0 \text{ for } x \leq a \\ \dfrac{x - a}{b - a} \text{ for } a < x < b \\ 1 \text{ for } x \geq b \end{cases}$$

For our problem, $F(x) = 0$ for $x \leq 0$, $F(x) = x/8$ for $0 < x < 8$, and $F(x) = 1$ for $x > 8$. We graph this cdf in Figure 5-4.

The mathematical operation that corresponds to finding the area under the curve of a probability density function $f(x)$ from a to b is the integral of $f(x)$ from a to b:

$$P(a \leq x \leq b) = \int_{a}^{b} f(x)dx \tag{5-2}$$

where the limits of integration (a and b) can be any real numbers or $-\infty$ and $+\infty$. All probabilities of continuous random variables can be computed using Equation 5-2. For example, $F(7)$ is Equation 5-2 with lower limit $a = -\infty$ and upper limit $b = 7$. For the uniform distribution, the integral corresponding to the cdf reduces to the three-line expression given above. For nearly all other continuous distributions, including the normal and lognormal,

FIGURE 5-4   Continuous Uniform Cumulative Distribution

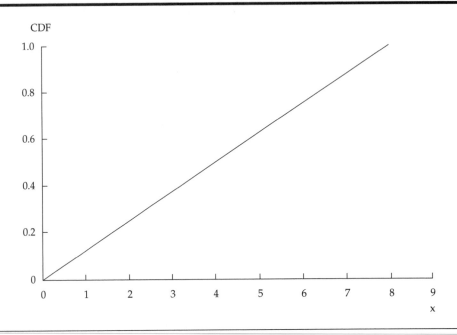

we rely on spreadsheet functions, computer programs, or tables of values to calculate probabilities. Those tools use various numerical methods to evaluate the integral in Equation 5-2.

Recall that the probability of a continuous random variable equaling any fixed point is 0. This fact has an important consequence for working with the cumulative distribution function of a continuous random variable: For any continuous random variable X, $P(a \leq X \leq b) = P(a < X \leq b) = P(a \leq X < b) = P(a < X < b)$ because the probabilities at the endpoints a and b are 0. For discrete random variables these relations of equality are not true, because probability accumulates at points.

EXAMPLE 5-7.   Probability That a Lending Facility Covenant Is Breached.

You are evaluating the bonds of a below-investment-grade credit at a low point in its business cycle. You have many factors to consider, including the terms of the company's bank lending facilities. The contract creating a bank lending facility such as an unsecured line of credit typically has clauses known as covenants. These covenants place restrictions on what the borrower can do, or set minimum levels for financial performance. The firm will be in breach of a covenant in the lending facility if the interest coverage ratio, EBITDA/interest, calculated on EBITDA over the four trailing quarters, falls below 2.0. EBITDA is earnings before interest, taxes, depreciation, and amortization.[9] Compliance with the covenants will be checked at the end of the current quarter. If the covenant is breached, the bank can demand immediate repayment of all borrowings on the facility. That action would probably trigger

---

[9] For a detailed discussion on the use and misuse of EBITDA, see Moody's Investors Service Global Credit Research, *Putting EBITDA in Perspective* (June 2000).

a liquidity crisis for the firm. With a high degree of confidence, you forecast interest charges of $25 million. Your estimate of EBITDA runs from $40 million on the low end to $60 million on the high end.

Address two questions (treating projected interest charges as a constant):

1. If the outcomes for EBITDA are equally likely, what is the probability that EBITDA/interest will fall below 2.0, breaching the covenant?

2. Estimate the mean and standard deviation of EBITDA/interest. For a continuous uniform random variable, the mean is given by $\mu = (a + b)/2$ and the variance is given by $\sigma^2 = (b - a)^2/12$.

Solution to 1. EBITDA/interest is a continuous uniform random variable because all outcomes are equally likely. The ratio can take on values between $1.6 = (\$40 \text{ million})/(\$25 \text{ million})$ on the low end, and $2.4 = (\$60 \text{ million}/\$25 \text{ million})$ on the high end. The range of possible values is $0.8 = 2.4 - 1.6$. What fraction of the possible values falls below 2.0, the level that triggers default? The distance between 2.0 and 1.6 is 0.40; the value 0.40 is one-half the total length of 0.8, or $0.50 = 0.4/0.8$. So the probability that the covenant will be breached is 50 percent.

Solution to 2. In Solution 1, we found that the lower limit of EBITDA/interest is 1.6. This lower limit is *a*. We found that the upper limit is 2.4. This upper limit is *b*. Using the formula given above,

$$\mu = (a + b)/2 = (1.6 + 2.4)/2 = 2.0$$

The variance of the coverage ratio is

$$\sigma^2 = (b - a)^2/12 = (2.4 - 1.6)^2/12 = 0.053333$$

The standard deviation is the positive square root of the variance, $0.230940 = (0.053333)^{1/2}$. The standard deviation is not particularly useful as a risk measure for a uniform distribution, however. The probability that lies within various standard deviation bands around the mean is sensitive to different specifications of the upper and lower limits (although Chebyshev's inequality is always satisfied). Here, a one standard deviation interval around the mean of 2.0 runs from 1.769 to 2.231 and captures $0.462/0.80 = 0.5775$ or 57.8 percent of the probability. A two standard deviation interval runs from 1.54 to 2.46, which extends past both the lower and upper limits of the random variable.

3.2 THE NORMAL DISTRIBUTION

The normal distribution may be the most extensively used probability distribution in quantitative work. It plays key roles in Modern Portfolio Theory and in a number of risk management technologies. Because it has so many uses, the normal distribution must be thoroughly understood by investment professionals.

The role of the normal distribution in statistical inference and regression analysis is vastly extended by a crucial result known as the central limit theorem. The central limit theorem states that the sum (and mean) of a large number of independent random variables is approximately normally distributed.[10]

---

[10] The central limit theorem is discussed further in the chapter on sampling.

The French mathematician Abraham de Moivre (1667–1754) introduced the normal distribution in 1733 in developing a version of the central limit theorem. As Figure 5-5 shows, the normal distribution is symmetrical and bell-shaped.

FIGURE 5-5   Two Normal Distributions

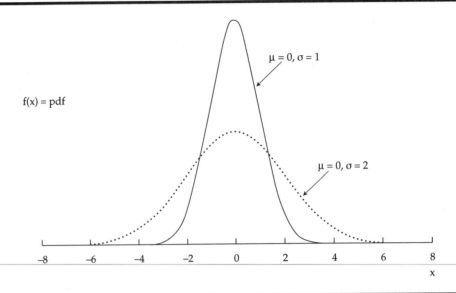

In contrast to the other distributions we discuss in this chapter, the range of possible outcomes of the normal distribution is the entire real line: all real numbers lying between $-\infty$ and $+\infty$. The tails of the bell curve extend without limit to the left and to the right.

The defining characteristics of a normal distribution are as follows:

- The normal distribution is completely described by two parameters—its mean, μ, and variance, σ^2. We indicate this as follows

$$X \sim N(\mu, \sigma^2)$$

  (read: X is distributed normally with mean μ, and variance, σ^2). We can also define a normal distribution in terms of the mean and the standard deviation, σ (this is often convenient because σ is measured in the same units as X and μ). As a consequence, we can answer any probability question about a normal random variable if we know its mean and variance (or standard deviation).

- The normal distribution has a skewness of 0 (that is, it is symmetric). The normal distribution has a kurtosis (measure of peakedness) of 3; its excess kurtosis (kurtosis − 3.0) equals 0.[11] As a consequence of symmetry, the mean, median, and the mode are all equal for a normal random variable.

- A linear combination of two or more normal random variables is also normally distributed.

---

[11] If we have a sample of size n from a normal distribution, we may want to know the possible variation in sample skewness and kurtosis. For a normal random variable, the standard deviation of sample skewness is $6/n$ and the standard deviation of sample kurtosis is $24/n$.

These bullet points concern a single variable or univariate normal distribution: the distribution of one normal random variable. **A univariate distribution** describes a single random variable. **A multivariate distribution** specifies the probabilities for a group of related random variables. You will encounter the **multivariate normal** distribution in investment work and reading and should know the following things about it.

When we have a group of assets, we can model the distribution of returns on each asset individually, or the distribution of returns on the assets as a group. "As a group" is meant that we take account of all the statistical interrelationships between the return series. One model that has often been used for security returns is the multivariate normal distribution. A multivariate normal distribution for the returns on n stocks is completely defined by three lists of parameters:

- the list of the mean returns on the individual securities (n means in total);
- the list of the securities' variances of return (n variances in total);
- the list of all the distinct pairwise return correlations ($n(n-1)/2$ distinct correlations in total).[12]

The need to specify correlations is a distinguishing feature of the multivariate normal distribution in contrast to the univariate normal distribution.

When we read or hear "assume returns are normally distributed," this statement is actually shorthand for joint normally distributed. If we have a portfolio of 30 securities, for example, portfolio return is a weighted average of the returns on the 30 securities. A weighted average is a linear combination. Thus, portfolio return is normally distributed if the individual security returns are (joint) normally distributed. To review, in order to specify the normal distribution for portfolio return, we need the means, variances, and the distinct pairwise correlations of the component securities.

With these concepts in mind, we can return to the normal distribution for one random variable. The curves graphed in Figure 5-5 are the normal density function:

$$f(x) = \frac{1}{\sigma\sqrt{2\pi}} \exp\left(\frac{-(x-\mu)^2}{2\sigma^2}\right) \text{ for } -\infty < x < +\infty \qquad (5\text{-}3)$$

The two densities graphed in Figure 5-5 correspond to a mean of $\mu = 0$ and standard deviations of $\sigma = 1$ and $\sigma = 2$. The normal density with $\mu = 0$ and $\sigma = 1$ is called the **standard normal distribution** (or **unit normal distribution**). Plotting two normal distributions with the same mean and different standard deviations helps us appreciate why standard deviation is a good measure of dispersion. Observations are much more concentrated around the mean for the normal distribution with $\sigma = 1$ than for the normal distribution with $\sigma = 2$.

A normal random variable has no lower limit. This characteristic has several implications for investment applications. An asset price can drop only to 0, when the asset becomes worthless. As a result, practitioners generally do not use the normal distribution to model the distribution of asset prices. Moving from any level of asset price to 0 translates into a return of -100 percent. Because the normal distribution extends below 0 without limit, it cannot be literally accurate as a model for asset returns.

---

[12] For example, a distribution with 2 stocks (a bivariate normal distribution) has 2 means, 2 variances, and 1 correlation [= 2(2 − 1)/2]; a distribution with 30 stocks has 30 means, 30 variances, and 435 distinct correlations [= 30(30 − 1)/2]. The return correlation of Dow Chemical with American Express stock is the same as the correlation of American Express with Dow Chemical stock, so these are counted as one distinct correlation.

However, the normal distribution can be considered an approximate model for returns. Nearly all the probability of a normal random variable is contained within three standard deviations of the mean. For realistic values of mean return and return standard deviation for many assets, the normal probability of outcomes below -100 percent is very small. Whether the approximation is useful in a given application is an empirical question. For example, the normal distribution is a closer fit for quarterly and yearly holding period returns on a diversified equity portfolio than it is for daily or weekly returns.[13] A persistent departure from normality in most equity return series is kurtosis greater than 3, the fat-tails problem. So when we approximate equity return distributions with the normal distribution, we should be aware that the normal distribution tends to underestimate the probability of extreme returns.[14] Option returns are skewed. Because the normal is a symmetrical distribution, we should be cautious in using the normal distribution to model the returns on portfolios containing significant positions in options.

Using the standard deviation, we can make useful probability statements about the dispersion of outcomes of any normal distribution. The last three are illustrated in Figure 5-6.

- Approximately 50 percent of all observations fall in the interval $\mu \pm (2/3)\sigma$.
- Approximately 68 percent of all observations fall in the interval $\mu \pm \sigma$.
- Approximately 95 percent of all observations fall in the interval $\mu \pm 2\sigma$.
- Approximately 99 percent of all observations fall in the interval $\mu \pm 3\sigma$.

FIGURE 5-6   Units of Standard Deviation

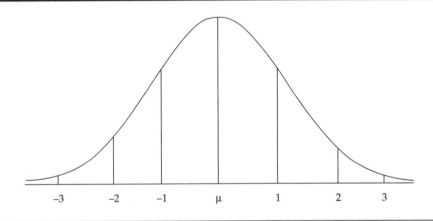

We estimate the population mean, μ, using the sample mean, $\bar{x}$ (sometimes reported as $\hat{\mu}$), and estimate the population standard deviation, σ, using the sample standard deviation, s (sometimes reported as $\hat{\sigma}$). The quantities $\bar{x}$ and s are **point estimates.** Probability statements about a random variable are often framed using **confidence intervals** built around point estimates. In investment work, confidence intervals for a normal random vari-

---

[13] See Fama (1976) and Campbell, Lo, and MacKinlay (1997).

[14] Fat tails can be modeled by a mixture of normal random variables or by a Student-t distribution with a relatively small number of degrees of freedom. See Kon (1984) and Campbell, Lo, and MacKinlay (1997). We discuss the Student-t distribution in the chapter on sampling and estimation.

able in relation to its estimated mean are often used. Some important confidence intervals are given below.

> Exact Confidence Intervals for a Normal Random Variable, X
>
> $P(X$ will be within $\bar{x} \pm 1.645$ standard deviations, s$) = 0.90$ or 90%.
>
> > We say: The 90 percent confidence interval for X is $\bar{x} - 1.645s$ to $\bar{x} + 1.645s$.
>
> $P(X$ will be within $\bar{x} \pm 1.96$ standard deviations, s$) = 0.95$ or 95%.
>
> > We say: The 95 percent confidence interval for X is $\bar{x} - 1.96s$ to $\bar{x} + 1.96s$.
>
> $P(X$ will be within $\bar{x} \pm 2.58$ standard deviations, s$) = 0.99$ or 99%.
>
> > We say: The 99 percent confidence interval for X is $\bar{x} - 2.58s$ to $\bar{x} + 2.58s$.

The practical meaning of the 95 percent confidence interval, for example, is that, in a very large number of observations, we expect the random variable to fall outside the interval only 5 percent of the time. In that sense, we have 95 percent confidence in the interval.

EXAMPLE 5-8. Probabilities for a Common Stock Portfolio (1).

You manage a U.S. core equity portfolio that is sector-neutral to the S&P 500 (its industry sector weights approximately match the S&P 500's). Taking a weighted average of the projected mean returns on the holdings, you forecast a portfolio return of 12 percent. You estimate a standard deviation of annual return of 22 percent, close to the long-run figure for the S&P 500. For the year-ahead return on the portfolio, you are asked to do the following:

1. Calculate and interpret a one standard deviation confidence interval for portfolio return.

2. Calculate and interpret a 90 percent confidence interval, with a normality assumption for returns.

3. Calculate and interpret a 95 percent confidence interval, with a normality assumption for returns.

Solution to 1. A one standard deviation confidence interval is $\bar{x} \pm s$. With $\bar{x} = 12$ percent and $s = 22$ percent, the lower end of a one standard deviation interval is $-10\% = 12\% - 22\%$ and the upper end is $34\% = 12\% + 22\%$. The interval thus runs from -10 percent to 34 percent, and you expect approximately 68 percent of portfolio returns to lie within it, under normality. A compact notation for this one standard deviation confidence interval is $[-10\%, 34\%]$.

Solution to 2. A 90 percent confidence interval, with a normality assumption for returns, runs from $\bar{x} - 1.645s$ to $\bar{x} + 1.645s$. So the lower limit is $-24.19\% = 12\% - 1.645 \times 22\%$, and the upper limit is $48.19\% = 12\% + 1.645 \times 22\%$. Compactly, this interval is $[-24.19\%, 48.19\%]$.

Solution to 3. A 95 percent confidence interval, with a normality assumption for returns, goes from $\bar{x} - 1.96s$ to $\bar{x} + 1.96s$. So the lower limit is $-31.12\% = 12\% - 1.96 \times 22\%$, and the upper limit is $55.12\% = 12\% + 1.96 \times 22\%$. Compactly, this interval is $[-31.12\%, 55.12\%]$.

The 95 percent and 99 percent confidence intervals are probably the two most frequently used in practice. An approximate 95 percent confidence interval using 2 rather than 1.96 standard deviations as the multiplier gives a quick answer, and is frequently used.

The calculation of the lower limit of −31.12 percent in Solution 3 illustrates an earlier point: For many realistic values of mean and standard deviation, the fact that the normal distribution extends to −∞ on the left may not be critical. For a normal distribution, only 2.5 percent of the total probability lies to the left of the mean minus 1.96 standard deviations (and 2.5 percent lies to the right of the mean plus 1.96 standard deviations). Figure 5-7 illustrates these probabilities.

FIGURE 5-7   Tail Probabilities for a 95 Percent Confidence Interval

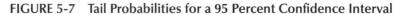

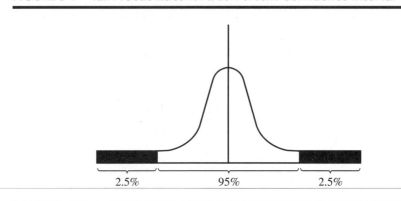

In working with confidence intervals, we specify the desired level of confidence and find the endpoints. We have given the formulas for important conventional intervals, but we may also have questions on other intervals, such as, "How wide do I have to make the confidence interval to capture 75 percent of the returns on this portfolio?" We may also be interested in other probabilities. For example, we may ask, "What is the probability that the annual return on this equity index will be less than the one-year T-bill return?"

There are as many different normal distributions as there choices for mean (μ) and variance (σ^2). We can answer all of the above questions in terms of the normal distribution we are dealing with. Spreadsheets, for example, have functions for the normal cdf for any specification of mean and variance. For the sake of efficiency, however, we would like to refer all probability statements to one set of normal probability values. The standard normal distribution (the normal distribution with $\mu = 0$ and $\sigma = 1$) fills that role.

There are two steps in **standardizing** a random variable X: subtract the mean of X from X, then divide that result by the standard deviation of X. If we have a list of observations on a normal random variable, X, we subtract the mean from each observation to get a list of deviations from the mean, then divide each deviation by the standard deviation. The result is the standard normal random variable, Z. (Z is the conventional symbol for a standard normal random variable.) If we have $X \sim N(\mu, \sigma^2)$, we standardize it using the formula

$$Z = (X - \mu)/\sigma \qquad\qquad\qquad\qquad\qquad (5\text{-}4)$$

Suppose we have a normal random variable, X, with $\mu = 5$ and $\sigma = 1.5$. We standardize X with $Z = (X - 5)/1.5$. For example, a value $X = 9.5$ corresponds to a standardized value of 3, calculated as $Z = (9.5 - 5)/1.5 = 3$. The probability that we will observe a value as small or smaller than 9.5 for $X \sim N(5, 1.5)$ is exactly the same as the probability that we will observe a value as small or smaller than 3 for $Z \sim N(0, 1)$. We can answer all probability questions about X using standardized values and probability tables for Z. We generally do not know the population mean and standard deviation, so we often use the sample mean $\bar{x}$ for μ and the sample standard deviation s for σ in Equation 5-3.

Standard normal probabilities can also be computed with spreadsheets, statistical and econometric software, and programming languages. Tables of the cumulative distribution function for the standard normal random variable are in the back of this book. Table 5-6 shows an excerpt from those tables. $N(x)$ is a conventional notation for the cdf of a standard normal variable.[15]

TABLE 5-6 $P(Z \le x) = N(x)$ for $x \ge 0$ or $P(Z \le z) = N(z)$ for $z \ge 0$

x or z	0	0.01	0.02	0.03	0.04	0.05	0.06	0.07	0.08	0.09
0.00	0.5000	0.5040	0.5080	0.5120	0.5160	0.5199	0.5239	0.5279	0.5319	0.5359
0.10	0.5398	0.5438	0.5478	0.5517	0.5557	0.5596	0.5636	0.5675	0.5714	0.5753
0.20	0.5793	0.5832	0.5871	0.5910	0.5948	0.5987	0.6026	0.6064	0.6103	0.6141
0.30	0.6179	0.6217	0.6255	0.6293	0.6331	0.6368	0.6406	0.6443	0.6480	0.6517
0.40	0.6554	0.6591	0.6628	0.6664	0.6700	0.6736	0.6772	0.6808	0.6844	0.6879
0.50	0.6915	0.6950	0.6985	0.7019	0.7054	0.7088	0.7123	0.7157	0.7190	0.7224

To find the probability that a standard normal variable is less than or equal to 0.24, for example, we go to the row with 0.20, move over to the 0.04 column and find the entry 0.5948. Thus $P(Z \le 0.24) = 0.5948$ or 59.48 percent.

These are some of the most referred to values in the standard normal table:

- 1.282 is the 90th percentile point: $P(Z \le 1.282) = N(1.282) = 0.90$ or 90 percent, and 10 percent of values remain in the right tail.

- 1.645 is the 95th percentile point: $P(Z \le 1.645) = N(1.645) = 0.95$ or 95 percent, and 5 percent of values remain in the right tail. (We used 1.645 standard deviations for the 90 percent confidence interval: 5 percent of values lie outside that interval on both sides.)

- 2.327 is the 99th percentile point: $P(Z \le 2.327) = N(2.327) = 0.99$ or 99 percent, and 1 percent of values remain in the right tail.

The tables that we give for the normal cdf include probabilities for $x \le 0$. Many sources, however, give tables only for $x \ge 0$. Because of the symmetry of the normal distribution we can find all probabilities using tables of the cdf of the standard normal random variable, $P(Z \le x) = N(x)$, for $x \ge 0$. The relations below are helpful for using tables for $x \ge 0$, and in other uses as well:

- For a nonnegative number x, use $N(x)$ from the table. Note that for the probability to the right of x, we have $P(Z \ge x) = 1.0 - N(x)$.

- For a negative number $-x$, $N(-x) = 1.0 - N(x)$: Find $N(x)$ and subtract it from 1. All the area under the normal curve to the left of x is $N(x)$. The balance, $1.0 - N(x)$,

---

[15] Another often-seen notation for the cdf of a standard normal variable is $\Phi(x)$.

is the area and probability to the right of x. By the symmetry of the normal distribution around its mean, the area and the probability to the right of x is equal to the area and the probability to the left of $-x$, $N(-x)$.

For the probability to the right of $-x$, $P(Z \geq -x) = N(x)$.

EXAMPLE 5-9.   Probabilities for a Common Stock Portfolio (2).

Recall that in Example 5-8, the portfolio mean return was forecasted at 12 percent and your estimate of standard deviation of return was 22 percent per year.

You want to estimate the following probabilities, assuming that a normal distribution describes returns. (You can use the above excerpt from the table of normal probabilities to answer these questions.)

1. What is the probability that portfolio return will exceed 20 percent?
2. What is the probability that portfolio return will be between 12 percent and 20 percent? That is, what is $P(12\% \leq$ portfolio return $\leq 20\%)$?
3. You can buy a one-year T-bill that yields 5.5 percent. This yield is effectively a one-year risk-free interest rate. What is the probability that your portfolio's return will be equal to or less than the risk-free rate?

If X is portfolio return, standardized portfolio return is $Z = (X - \bar{x})/s = (X - 12\%)/20\%$. We use this expression throughout the solutions.

Solution to 1.   For $X = 20\%$, $Z = (20\% - 12\%)/20\% = 0.40$. You want to find $P(Z > 0.40)$. First note that $P(Z > x) = P(Z \geq x)$ since the normal is a continuous distribution. Recall that $P(Z \geq x) = 1.0 - P(Z \leq x)$ or $1 - N(x)$. According to the table, $N(0.40) = 0.6554$. Thus, $1 - 0.6554 = 0.3446$. The probability that portfolio return will exceed 20 percent is about 34.5 percent if your normality assumption is accurate.

Solution to 2. $P(12\% \leq$ portfolio return $\leq 20\%) = N(Z$ corresponding to $20\%) - N(Z$ corresponding to $12\%)$. For the first term, $Z = (20\% - 12\%)/20\% = 0.40$ and $N(0.40) = 0.6554$ (as in Solution 1).To get the second term immediately, note that 12 percent is the mean, and for the normal distribution 50 percent of the probability lies on either side of the mean. Therefore, $N(Z$ corresponding to $12\%)$ must equal 50 percent (verify this). So $P(12\% \leq$ portfolio return $\leq 20\%) = 0.6554 - 0.50 = 0.1554$ or 15.5 percent.

Solution to 3.   If X is portfolio return, then we want to find $P($portfolio return $\leq 5.5\%)$. This question is more challenging than 1 or 2, but when you have studied the solution below you will have a useful pattern for calculating other shortfall probabilities.

There are three steps hinging on standardizing the portfolio return and the T-bill return: First, subtract the portfolio mean return from each side of the inequality: $P($portfolio return $- 12\% \leq 5.5\% - 12\%)$. Second, divide each side of the inequality by the standard deviation of portfolio return: $P[($portfolio return $- 12\%)/22\% \leq (5.5\% - 12\%)/22\%] = P(Z \leq -0.295455) = N(-0.295455)$. Third, recognize that on the left-hand side we have a standard normal variable, denoted by Z. As we pointed out above, $N(-x) = 1 - N(x)$. Rounding -0.29545 to -0.30 for use with the excerpted table, we have $N(-0.30) = 1 - N(0.30) = 1 - 0.6179 = 0.3821$, roughly 38 percent. The probability that your portfolio will underperform the one-year risk-free rate is about 38 percent.

We can get the answer above quickly by standardizing 5.5 percent using the mean and standard deviation of portfolio return and evaluating the result (-0.295455) with the standard normal cdf.

3.3 APPLICATIONS OF THE NORMAL DISTRIBUTION

Modern portfolio theory (MPT) makes wide use of the idea that the value of investment opportunities can be meaningfully measured in terms of mean return and variance of return. In economic theory, **mean–variance analysis** holds exactly when investors are risk-averse; when they choose investments so as to maximize expected utility, or satisfaction; and when either (1) returns are normally distributed, or (2) investors have quadratic utility functions.[16] Mean–variance analysis can still be useful, however—that is, it can hold approximately—when either assumption (1) or (2) is violated. Because practitioners prefer to work with observables such as returns, the proposition that returns are at least approximately normally distributed has played a key role in much of MPT.

Without attempting to cover the vast field of MPT, we can usefully illustrate several key ideas relating to the use of mean and variance in investments.

EXAMPLE 5-10.   Mean–Variance Analysis of Commodity Funds (1).

The 1980s saw the fast growth in the United States of a new type of managed investment vehicle called commodity funds. Commodity funds are professionally managed limited partnerships that buy and sell futures contracts. Elton, Gruber, and Rentzler (1990) analyzed the early performance of this category of investment. They gathered monthly returns on all publicly offered commodity funds listed in a major reporting service for the period January 1980 to December 1988, inclusive. Table 5-7 shows the average performance of commodity funds, the S&P 500, and U.S. T-bills over the study period.

TABLE 5-7   Commodity Funds: Returns and Risks, 1980 to 1988

	Mean Annual Return (%)	Standard Deviation of Monthly Return (%)
Commodity funds	2.2565	10.4
S&P 500	14.88	4.91
T-bills	8.64	0.25

Source: Elton, Gruber, and Rentzler (1990), Tables I and II.

Using this information, answer the following questions:

1. How desirable were commodity funds as a stand-alone investment? (We qualify *investment* with *stand-alone* because we are not yet considering the impact of return correlations on the attractiveness of commodity funds as

---

[16] Utility functions are mathematical representations of attitudes toward risk and return.

investments.) Justify your answer in terms of mean return as a measure of reward and standard deviation of return as a measure of risk.

2. What distributional assumption is being made in evaluating investments in these terms?

Solution to 1. Based on the criteria of mean and standard deviation, commodity funds were inferior as stand-alone investments over the study period. Commodity funds had the lowest mean annual return of the three categories of investments; at 2.2565 percent, the mean return was less than 27 percent of the return on T-bills. At the same time, commodity funds had by far the highest risk as measured by standard deviation of return. Any investor who made investment choices on the basis of mean and standard deviation would have preferred to hold either stocks or T-bills over the average commodity fund, during this period.

Solution to 2. The distributional assumption being made is that returns on these assets are described by the normal distribution. If that assumption is correct, we can evaluate these investments in terms of mean return and variance of return alone. We can state the decision rule precisely for a mean–variance investor facing the choice of putting all her money in asset A or all her money in asset B. This investor prefers A to B if either

(1) the mean return on A is equal to or larger than that on B, but A has a smaller standard deviation of return than B; or

(2) the mean return on A is strictly larger than that on B, but A and B have the same standard deviation of return.

This decision rule has been called the **Markowitz decision rule.** Using (1) above, stocks and T-bills, A, are preferred to commodity funds, B. Closely related to condition (2) is the concept of **efficient frontier,** the graph of the set of portfolios that maximize mean return for a given level of standard deviation of return. Commodity funds did not plot on the efficient frontier for the study period.

As we continue with this example, we discuss additional considerations for the investor who holds a portfolio of many assets.

EXAMPLE 5-11. Mean–Variance Analysis of Commodity Funds (2).

Attractiveness as a stand-alone investment is one view of an asset. Investors in practice hold many assets. Modern portfolio theory recommends taking account of how an asset affects the risk and expected return of the total portfolio. To judge that, we need to consider return correlations. Suppose you hold an optimal portfolio P with expected or mean return $E(R_P)$ and standard deviation of return σ_P. Then you are offered the opportunity to invest in a new asset. Will you improve the mean–variance profile of your portfolio by investing in the new asset? (Will you increase mean return for a given level of risk if you add the new asset, or reduce risk without reducing mean return?) To answer this question, you need three inputs: the Sharpe ratio of the new asset, the Sharpe ratio of the portfolio, and the correlation between the new asset's return and portfolio P's return, $\text{corr}(R_{new}, R_P)$. Adding the new asset to your portfolio is optimal if the following condition is met:[17]

$$\frac{E(R_{new}) - R_f}{\sigma_{new}} > \left(\frac{E(R_P) - R_f}{\sigma_P}\right) \text{Corr}(R_{new}, R_P)$$

This expression says that in order to gain by adding the new asset to your holdings, the Sharpe ratio of the new asset needs to be larger than (Sharpe ratio of P) $\times$ (Correlation of new asset with P).

Elton et al. (1990) found that the correlation between commodity fund returns and S&P 500 returns was 0.08 over the period 1980 to 1988. Suppose you held an all-equity portfolio indexed on the S&P 500 during this period. As usual, the return on T-bills can represent the risk-free return.

1. Would you have improved the mean–variance profile of your portfolio if you had added commodity funds to your portfolio over that period?

2. What assumption do you think the above expression makes about the joint distribution of returns on the new asset and the portfolio?

Solution to 1. The Sharpe ratio of the S&P 500 over the study period was $1.271 = (14.88 - 8.64)/4.91$. Multiplied by the correlation, the hurdle that the Sharpe ratio of commodity funds had to meet to benefit your portfolio was $0.102 = 1.271 \times 0.08$. In fact, however, the Sharpe ratio achieved by the average commodity fund was negative, $-0.614 = (2.2565 - 8.64)/10.4$. You conclude that you would not have improved the mean–variance profile of your portfolio over the study period if you had held the average commodity fund.

Solution to 2. The expression assumes multivariate (in particular, bivariate) normality: that the returns on the new asset and the portfolio are each distributed normally, and the relationship between the two can be fully described in terms of correlation.

The simple criterion used to make the decision demonstrates many of the concepts underlying MPT.

In Examples 5-10 and 5-11, we evaluated investment choices considering the whole distribution of returns as summarized by mean and variance. An alternative approach evaluates only downside risk. **Safety-first rules** focus on **shortfall risk,** the risk that portfolio value will fall below some minimum acceptable level over some time horizon. The risk that the assets in a defined benefit plan will fall below plan liabilities is an example of a shortfall risk.

Suppose an investor views any return below a level of R_L as unacceptable. Roy's safety-first criterion states that the optimal portfolio minimizes the probability that portfolio return, R_P, falls below the threshold level, R_L.[18] In symbols, the investor's objective is to choose a portfolio that minimizes $P(R_P < R_L)$. When portfolio returns are normally distributed, we can calculate $P(R_P < R_L)$ using the number of standard deviations R_L lies

---

[17] See Blume (1984) and Elton, Gruber, and Rentzler (1987).

[18] A. D. Roy (1952) introduced this criterion.

below the expected portfolio return, $E(R_P)$. The portfolio for which $E(R_P) - R_L$ is largest in terms of units of standard deviations minimizes $P(R_P < R_L)$. Thus, if returns are normally distributed, the safety-first optimal portfolio *maximizes* the safety-first ratio (SFRatio):

$$\text{SFRatio} = [E(R_P) - R_L]/\sigma_P$$

The quantity $E(R_P) - R_L$ is the distance from the mean return to the shortfall level. Dividing this distance by σ_P gives the distance in units of standard deviation. There are three steps in choosing among portfolios using Roy's criterion (assuming normality):

1. Calculate the portfolio's SFRatio.
2. Evaluate the standard normal cdf at the value calculated for the SFRatio; the probability that return will be less than R_L is $N(-\text{SFRatio})$.
3. Choose the portfolio with the lowest probability.

You may have noticed the similarity of SFRatio to the Sharpe ratio. If we substitute the risk-free rate R_f for the critical level R_L, the SFRatio becomes the Sharpe ratio. The safety-first approach provides a new perspective on the Sharpe ratio: When we evaluate portfolios using the Sharpe ratio, the portfolio with the highest Sharpe ratio is the one that minimizes the probability that portfolio return will be less than the risk-free rate (given a normality assumption).

EXAMPLE 5-12.   The Safety-First Optimal Portfolio for a Client.

You are researching asset allocations for a client with an $800,000 portfolio. Although her investment objective is long-term growth, at the end of a year she may want to liquidate $30,000 of the portfolio to fund educational expenses. If that need arises, she would like to be able to take out the $30,000 without invading the initial capital of $800,000. Table 5-8 shows three alternative allocations.

TABLE 5-8   Mean and Standard Deviation for Three Allocations (in percents)

	A	B	C
Expected annual return	25	11	14
Standard deviation of return	27	8	20
	.7̄4̄7̄	.9063	.5125

Address these questions (assume normality for Parts 2 and 3):

1. Given the client's desire not to invade the $800,000 principal, what is the shortfall level, R_L? Use this shortfall level to answer Part 2.
2. According to the safety-first criterion, which of the three allocations is the best?
3. What is the probability that the return on the safety-first optimal portfolio will be less than the shortfall level, R_L?

Solution to 1. As \$30,000/\$800,000 is 3.75 percent, for any return less than 3.75 percent the client will need to invade principal if she takes out \$30,000. So R_L = 3.75 percent.

Solution to 2. To decide which of the three allocations is safety-first optimal, select the alternative with the highest ratio $[E(R_P) - R_L]/\sigma_P$:

Allocation A: $0.787037 = (25 - 3.75)/27$

Allocation B: $0.90625 = (11 - 3.75)/8$

Allocation C: $0.5125 = (14 - 3.75)/20$

Allocation B, with the largest ratio (0.90625), is the best alternative according to the safety-first criterion.

Solution to 3. To answer this question, note that $P(R_A < 3.75) = N(-0.90625)$. We can round 0.90625 to 0.91 for use with tables of the standard normal cdf. First, we calculate $N(-0.91) = 1 - N(0.91) = 1 - 0.8186 = 0.1814$ or 18.14 percent. Using a spreadsheet function for the standard normal cdf on -0.90625 without rounding, we get 18.24 percent. The safety-first optimal portfolio has a roughly 18 percent chance of not meeting a 3.75 percent return threshold.

Several points are worth noting. First, if the inputs were even slightly different, we would get a different ranking. For example, if the mean return on B were 10 rather than 11 percent, A would be superior to B. Second, if meeting the 3.75 percent return threshold were a necessity rather than a wish, \$830,000 in one year could be modeled as a liability. Fixed-income strategies such as cash flow matching could be used to offset or immunize the \$830,000 quasi-liability.

Roy's safety-first rule was the earliest approach to addressing shortfall risk. The standard mean–variance portfolio selection process can also accommodate a shortfall risk constraint.[19]

Over the past decade, one of the fastest-growing areas in which quantitative tools have been applied is financial risk management. Financial institutions such as investment banks, security dealers, and commercial banks have formal systems to measure and control **financial risk** at various levels, from trading positions to the overall risk for the firm.[20] Two mainstays in managing financial risk are Value at Risk (VaR) and stress testing/ scenario analysis. **Stress testing/scenario analysis,** a complement to VaR, refers to a set of techniques for estimating losses in extremely unfavorable combinations of events or scenarios. Value at Risk addresses the question: "Under normal market conditions, what is the worst loss that can happen over a given time horizon, at a specified confidence level such as 95 percent?" The loss in question may refer to an individual portfolio or position, or at the highest level, to the firm's shareholders' equity.

The 95 percent *t*-day Value at Risk for a portfolio, for example, is the dollar loss over a *t*-day horizon, that is equaled or exceeded (by a larger loss) only 5 percent of the time. Conventionally, VaR is calculated relative to the expected value of a flow variable such as earnings or change in portfolio value, depending on the risk manager's focus. There are

---

[19] See Leibowitz and Henriksson (1989), for example.

[20] *Financial risk* is risk relating to asset prices and other financial variables. The contrast is with other, nonfinancial risks (for example, relating to operations and technology) which require different tools to manage.

several methods for estimating VaR, including Monte Carlo simulation and an approach based on the assumption that returns are normally distributed. Normal VaR is the earliest and simplest methodology for estimating VaR.[21] Using a normal VaR methodology, the 95 percent t-day normal Value at Risk is calculated as

$$\text{VaR} = -[(\text{Expected change in portfolio value over a } t\text{-day horizon}) - 1.645 \times (\text{Standard deviation of change in portfolio value over a } t\text{-day horizon})]$$

We can explain this expression using an example. Suppose the expected change in portfolio value over a seven-day horizon is $10 million. This is the first term within the square brackets. For a normal distribution, if one moves 1.645 standard deviations to the left of the mean or expected value, 5 percent of the probability remains in the left tail. This explains the meaning of the second term in square brackets in relation to *95 percent* in 95 percent VaR. Suppose that the standard deviation of changes in portfolio value over a seven-day horizon is $18.237 million. Then $1.645 \times \$18.237$ million $= \$30$ million. So VaR $= -[\$10$ million $- \$30$ million$] = \$20$ million. We expect a $20 million loss to be equaled or exceeded (by a larger loss) 5 percent of the time.

EXAMPLE 5-13.   Value at Risk for a Common Stock Portfolio.

We continue with our example of the U.S. core equity portfolio with a forecasted annual mean return of 12 percent and a standard deviation of annual return of 22 percent. The current value of the portfolio is $500 million. Suppose the expected change in portfolio value at a one-day horizon is 0.000453 times the starting portfolio value (the daily expected return is close to 0).[22] The standard deviation of one-day changes in portfolio value is $6.128 million.

1. Calculate and interpret the 95 percent one-day Value at Risk for the portfolio under the assumption that portfolio return is normally distributed.
2. What cautions might you have about this daily VaR number?

Solution to 1.   We calculate expected change in portfolio value over a one-day horizon as (Initial portfolio value) $\times 0.000453 = \$500$ million $\times 0.000453 = \$0.2265$ million. Therefore, the specified VaR is $- (\$0.2265$ million $- 1.645 \times \$6.128$ million) $= \$9.854$ million, approximately. This value is 95 percent VaR, so on 5 percent of days we expect it to be exceeded. With approximately 250 trading days in a year, we expect the portfolio to experience a loss larger than $9.854 million on $0.05 \times 250 = 12.5$ or 13 days, under the assumption of normality.

Solution to 2.   For many equity return series, the normal distribution does not describe daily returns adequately, as we mentioned earlier. The multiplier 1.645 may be too small for the specified 95 percent confidence level if the distribution of changes in portfolio value has fat tails.

---

[21] See Linsmeier and Pearson (2000) for a survey. The expression for portfolio VaR presented here is called the delta-normal approach in that paper.

[22] The daily expected change was calculated as the daily return which, compounded forward over 250 days (the number of trading days in a year), gives an annual return of 0.12. This is, however, only one of several possible methods for calculating the daily expected change.

3.4 THE LOGNORMAL DISTRIBUTION

Closely related to the normal distribution, the lognormal distribution is widely used for modeling the probability distribution of stock and other asset prices. One of the lognormal's most important appearances is in the Black-Scholes Option Pricing Model (BSOPM). The BSOPM assumes that the price of the asset underlying the option is lognormally distributed.

A random variable Y follows a lognormal distribution if its natural logarithm, $\ln Y$, is normally distributed. The reverse is also true: If the natural logarithm of random variable Y, $\ln Y$, is normally distributed, then Y follows a lognormal distribution. If you think of the term *lognormal* as "the log is normal," you will have no trouble remembering this relationship.

The two most noteworthy observations about the lognormal distribution are that it is bounded below by 0 and it is skewed to the right (it has a long right tail). Note these two properties in the graphs of the probability density functions of two lognormal distributions in Figure 5-8. Asset prices are bounded from below by 0. In practice, the lognormal distribution has been found to be a usefully accurate description of the distribution of prices for many financial assets.

FIGURE 5-8   Two Lognormal Distributions

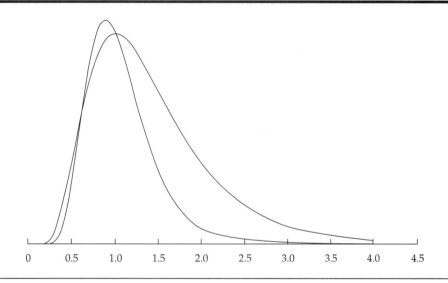

0	0.5	1.0	1.5	2.0	2.5	3.0	3.5	4.0	4.5

Like the normal distribution, the lognormal distribution is completely described by two parameters. Unlike the other distributions we have considered, a lognormal distribution is defined in terms of the parameters of a *different* distribution. The two parameters of a lognormal distribution *are the mean and standard deviation (or variance) of its associated normal distribution*: the mean and variance of $\ln Y$, given that Y is lognormal. Remember, we must keep track of two sets of means and standard deviations (or variances): the mean and standard deviation (or variance) of the associated normal distribution (these are the parameters), and the mean and standard deviation (or variance) of the lognormal variable itself.

The expressions for the mean and variance of the lognormal variable itself are challenging. Suppose a normal random variable X has expected value μ and variance σ^2. Define $Y = \exp(X)$. Remember that the operation indicated by $\exp(X)$ or e^X is the opposite operation from taking logs. Because $\ln Y = \ln [\exp(X)] = X$ is normal (we assumed X is normal), Y is lognormal. What is the expected value of $Y = \exp(X)$? A guess might be that the expected value of Y is $\exp(\mu)$. The expected value is actually $\exp(\mu + 0.50\sigma^2)$, which is larger than $\exp(\mu)$ by a factor of $\exp(0.50\sigma^2) > 1$. To get some insight into this, think of what happens if we increase σ^2. The distribution spreads out; it can spread upward, but it cannot spread downward past 0. As a result the center of its distribution is pushed to the right: its mean increases.[23]

The expressions for the mean and variance of a lognormal variable are summarized below, where μ and σ^2 are the mean and variance of the associated normal distribution (refer to these expressions as needed, rather than memorizing them):

- Mean (μ_L) of a lognormal random variable $= \exp(\mu + 0.5\sigma^2)$
- Variance (σ_L^2) of a lognormal random variable $= \exp(2\mu + \sigma^2) \times [\exp(\sigma^2) - 1]$

We now explore the relationship between the distribution of stock return and stock price. We also introduce some basic concepts such as continuous compounding and the additivity of continuously compounded returns.

If a stock's continuously compounded return is normally distributed, then future stock price is necessarily lognormally distributed. Equally important, stock price can be well described by the lognormal distribution even when continuously compounded returns do not follow a normal distribution, owing to the force of the central limit theorem.

Suppose we have a series of equally spaced observations on stock price: S_0, S_1, S_2, ... , S_T. Current stock price, S_0, is a known quantity and so is non-random. The future prices (such as S_1) however, are random variables. The **price relative**, S_1/S_0, is an ending price, S_1, over a beginning price, S_0; it is equal to 1 plus the holding period return on the stock from $t = 0$ to $t = 1$:

$$S_1/S_0 = 1 + R_{0,1}$$

For example, if $S_0 = \$30$ and $S_1 = \$34.50$, then $S_1/S_0 = \$34.50/\$30 = 1.15$, Therefore, $R_{0,1} = 0.15$ or 15 percent. In general, price relatives have the form

$$S_{t+1}/S_t = 1 + R_{t,t+1}$$

where $R_{t,t+1}$ is the rate of return from t to $t+1$. An important concept is the continuously compounded return associated with a holding period return such as $R_{0,1}$. The **continuously compounded return** associated with a holding period is the natural logarithm of 1 plus that holding period return, or, equivalently, the natural logarithm of the ending price over the beginning price (the price relative).[24] The continuously compounded return from t to $t+1$ is

$$r_{t,t+1} = \ln S_{t+1}/S_t = \ln (1 + R_{t,t+1}) \tag{5-5}$$

For our example, $r_{0,1} = \ln S_1/S_0 = \ln (1 + R_{0,1}) = \ln(34.50/\$30) = \ln(1.15) = 0.139762$. Thus, 13.98 percent is the continuously compounded return from $t = 0$ to $t = 1$. The continuously compounded return is smaller than the associated holding period return. If our investment horizon extends from $t = 0$ to $t = T$, then the continuously compounded return to T is

---

[23] Luenberger (1998) is the source of this explanation.

[24] In this chapter, we use lower-case r for continuously compounded return.

$$r_{0,T} = \ln S_T/S_0$$

Taking the function exp of both sides of the equation, we have $\exp(r_{0,T}) = \exp(\ln S_T/S_0) = S_T/S_0$, so

$$S_T = S_0 \times \exp(r_{0,T})$$

We can also express S_T/S_0 as the product of price relatives:

$$S_T/S_0 = S_T/S_{T-1} \times S_{T-1}/S_{T-2} \times \ldots \times S_1/S_0$$

Taking logs of both sides of this equation, we find that continuously compounded return to T is the sum of the one-period continuously compounded returns:

$$r_{0,T} = r_{T-1,T} + r_{T-2,T-1} + \ldots + r_{0,1} \tag{5-6}$$

Using holding period returns to find the ending value of a $1 investment involves the multiplication of quantities (1 + holding period return). Using continuously compounded returns involves addition.

A key assumption in many investment applications is that returns are **IID,** independently and identically distributed. *Independence* captures the proposition that investors cannot predict future returns using past returns (that is, weak-form market efficiency). *Identically distributed* captures the assumption of stationarity, to which we will return in the chapter on time-series analysis.[25]

Assume that the one-period continuously compounded returns (such as $r_{0,1}$) are IID random variables with mean μ and variance σ^2 (but making no normality or other distributional assumption). Then

$$E(r_{0,T}) = E(r_{T-1,T}) + E(r_{T-2,T-1}) + \ldots + E(r_{0,1}) = \mu T \tag{5-7}$$

(we add up μ for a total of T times) and

$$\sigma^2(r_{0,T}) = \sigma^2 T \tag{5-8}$$

(as a consequence of the independence assumption). The variance of the T-holding period continuously compounded return is T times the variance of the one-period continuously compounded return; and also, $\sigma(r_{0,T}) = \sigma\sqrt{T}$. If the one-period continuously compounded returns on the right-hand side of Equation 5-6 are normally distributed, then the T-holding period continuously compounded return, $r_{0,T}$, is also normally distributed with mean μT and variance $\sigma^2 T$. This is so because a linear combination of normal random variables is also normal. But even if the one-period continuously compounded returns are not normal, by the central limit theorem their sum, $r_{0,T}$, is approximately normal. Now compare $S_T = S_0 \times \exp(r_{0,T})$ to $Y = \exp(X)$, where X is normal and so Y is lognormal (as we discussed above). Clearly, we can model future stock price S_T as a lognormal random variable because $r_{0,T}$ should be at least approximately normal.

---

[25] Stationarity implies that the mean and variance of return do not change from period to period.

EXAMPLE 5-14.   Volatility as Used in Option Pricing Models.

An estimate for volatility is crucial for using option pricing models such as the BSOPM. **Volatility** is a measure of the standard deviation of very short-term returns on the underlying asset.[26] By convention, volatility is stated as an annualized measure.

There are various techniques for estimating volatility, but the most basic method is to calculate the standard deviation of continuously compounded daily returns and then annualize that number. Annualizing is often done on the basis of 250 days in a year, the approximate number of days markets are open for trading. That number may give a better estimate of volatility than 365.

As a standard deviation of return, volatility can be used for other purposes besides pricing options. Suppose, for example, you are researching Lucent Technologies (NYSE: LU) and are interested in Lucent's price action in a week in which a number of news items (including earnings announcements) affected technology stocks. Table 5-9 shows closing prices during that week.

TABLE 5-9   Lucent Technologies Daily Closing Prices

Date	Closing Price
Feb. 26, 2001	$12.59
Feb. 27, 2001	$12.11
Feb. 28, 2001	$11.59
March 1, 2001	$12.00
March 2, 2001	$12.03

Estimate volatility based on the above data (annualize on the basis of 250 days in a year).

First, use Equation 5-5 to calculate the continuously compounded daily returns, then find their standard deviation in the usual way. (In the calculation of sample variance to get sample standard deviation, use a divisor of 1 less than the sample size, as usual.)

$$\ln(12.11/12.59) = -0.038871, \ln(11.59/12.11) = -0.043889$$

$$\ln(12.00/11.59) = 0.034764, \ln(12.03/12.00) = 0.002497$$

$$\text{Sum} = -0.045499, \text{Mean} = -0.011375, \text{Variance} = 0.001378,$$
$$\text{Standard Deviation} = 0.037123$$

The standard deviation of continuously compounded daily returns is 0.037123. Equation 5-8 states that $\hat{\sigma}(r_{0,T}) = \hat{\sigma}\sqrt{T}$. In this example, $\hat{\sigma}$ is the sample standard deviation of one-period continuously compounded returns. Thus, $\hat{\sigma}$ refers to 0.037123. We want to annualize, so the horizon T corresponds to one year. As $\hat{\sigma}$ is in days, we set T equal to the number of trading days in a year (250).

---

[26] Volatility is also called the instantaneous standard deviation, and as such is denoted σ.

We find that annualized volatility for Lucent Technologies stock that week was a very high 58.7 percent, calculated as $0.037123\sqrt{250} = 0.586972$.

Note that the sample mean, -0.011375, is a possible estimate of the mean, μ, of the continuously compounded one-period or daily returns. The sample mean can be translated into an estimate of the expected continuously compounded annual return using Equation 5-7: $\hat{\mu} T = -0.011375 \times 250$ (to be consistent). But four observations are far too few to estimate expected returns. The variability in the daily returns overwhelms any information about expected return in a series this short.

Earlier in this section, we gave bullet-point expressions for the mean and variance of a lognormal random variable. What are those quantities for S_T distributed lognormally? In the bullet-point expressions, the $\hat{\mu}$ and $\hat{\sigma}^2$ would refer, in the context of this discussion, to the mean and variance of the T-horizon (not the one-period) continuously compounded returns, compatible with the horizon of S_T.[27] Because the lognormal distribution is not symmetric, confidence intervals are more complicated than for the normal distribution and will not be discussed in this introductory treatment.[28] Stepping back to Example 5-8, in which a portfolio manager forecasted a 12 percent mean annual return on his portfolio, suppose the portfolio was worth $500 million. If the portfolio manager were asked for a one-year forecast of portfolio year-end value (assuming no withdrawals or additions), he would very likely respond with $560 million, which is $500 million $\times$ 1.12, using the expected holding period return. Over multiple holding periods, however, there can be a meaningful divergence between the ending value from linking expected holding-period returns, and the ending value from converting holding-period expected returns into expected continuously compounded returns and then projecting an ending value based on the lognormal distribution.[29]

4 MONTE CARLO SIMULATION

"What is the last thing you do before you climb on a ladder? You shake it," said Stanford University researcher Sam Savage. "And that is Monte Carlo simulation," he continued.[30]

When a system is too complex to be analyzed using ordinary methods, investment analysts frequently use Monte Carlo simulation. **Monte Carlo simulation** in finance involves the use of a computer to represent the operation of a complex financial system. In some important applications, Monte Carlo simulation is used to find an approximate solution to a complex financial problem. An integral part of Monte Carlo simulation is the generation of a large number of random samples from a probability distribution or distributions; the colorful suggestion of the casinos of Monte Carlo in the name probably comes from this aspect of the method. Monte Carlo simulation has several quite distinct uses in industry.

Just as shaking a ladder helps us assess the risks in climbing it, Monte Carlo simulation allows us to experiment with a proposed policy before actually implementing it. For

---

[27] The expression for the mean is $E(S_T) = S_0 \exp[E(r_{0,T}) + 0.5\sigma^2(r_{0,T})]$, for example.

[28] See Hull (1999) for lognormal confidence intervals.

[29] As analysts, we typically think in terms of holding period returns rather than continuously compounded returns. When we need to move back and forth between means and standard deviations for holding period and continuously compounded returns, we can use expressions found in Ferguson (1993).

[30] *Business Week*, January 22, 2001.

example, investment performance can be evaluated with reference to a benchmark or a liability. Defined benefit pension plans often invest assets with reference to plan liabilities. Pension liabilities are a complex random process. In a Monte Carlo asset-liability financial planning study, the functioning of pension assets and liabilities is simulated over time, given assumptions about how assets are invested, the work force, and other variables. A key specification in this and all Monte Carlo simulations is the probability distributions of the various sources of risk (including interest rates and security market returns, in this case). The implications of different investment policy decisions on the plan's funded status can be assessed through simulated time. The experiment can be repeated for another set of assumptions. We can view Example 5-15 below as coming under this heading. In that example, market return series are not long enough to address researchers' questions on stock market timing, so the researchers simulate market returns to find answers to their questions.

Monte Carlo simulation is also widely used to develop estimates of Value at Risk. This methodology simulates many times the profit and loss performance of the portfolio over a specified horizon. Repeated trials within the simulation (each trial involving a draw of random observations from a probability distribution) produce a frequency distribution for changes in portfolio value. The point that defines the cutoff for the least favorable 5 percent of simulated changes is an estimate of 95 percent Value at Risk.

In an extremely important use, Monte Carlo analysis is a tool for valuing complex securities, particularly European-style options for which no analytic pricing formula is available. For other securities, such as mortgage-backed securities with complex embedded options, Monte Carlo analysis is also an important modeling resource.

Researchers use Monte Carlo simulation to test their models and tools. How critical is a particular assumption to the performance of a model? Because we control the assumptions when we do a simulation, we can run the model through a Monte Carlo simulation to see how sensitive the model is to an assumption.

A simple Monte Carlo simulation generally proceeds along these lines. Steps i through iii describe specifying the simulation; steps iv through vii describe running the simulation.[31]

   i. Specify the quantities of interest (option value, for example, or the funded status of a pension plan) in terms of underlying variables. The underlying variable or variables could be stock price for an equity option, the market value of pension assets, or other variables relating to the pension benefit obligation for a pension plan. Specify the starting values of the underlying variables.

   For example, suppose the quantity of interest is an **Asian call option** on stock. This option is European-style, so it is exercisable only at maturity, T. The value C_{iT} of this option at maturity is (Stock price at maturity − Average stock price during life of option) or $0, whichever is greater. For short, we write $C_{iT} = \max(S_T - S_{ave}, 0)$. For instance, if final stock price is $34 with an average value of $31 over the life of the option, the value of the call at maturity is $C_{iT} = \max(\$34 - \$31, 0) = \$3$.

   ii. Specify a time grid. Take the horizon in terms of calendar time and split it into a number of subperiods, say K in total. Calendar time divided by the number of subperiods, K, is the time increment, Δt.

   iii. Specify distributional assumptions for the risk factors that drive the underlying variables. For example, stock price is the underlying variable for the Asian call, so

---

[31] Although we call these *steps*, the list is an overview rather than a detailed recipe for implementing a Monte Carlo simulation in its many varied applications.

we need a model for stock price movement. Say we choose the following model for changes in stock price, where Z_k stands for the standard normal random variable:

$$\Delta \text{ (Stock Price)} = [\mu \times \text{(Prior Stock Price)} \times \Delta t] + [\sigma \times \text{(Prior Stock Price)} \times Z_k]$$

As we are using the term, we would say that Z_k is a risk factor in the simulation. Through our choice of μ and σ, we control the distribution of stock price. Although this example has one risk factor, a given simulation may have multiple risk factors.

iv. Using a computer program or spreadsheet function, draw K random values of each risk factor. In our example, the spreadsheet function would produce a draw of K values of the standard normal variable Z_k: $Z_1, Z_2, Z_3, \ldots, Z_K$.

v. Calculate the underlying variables using the random observations generated in Step iv. Using the above model of stock price dynamics, the result is K observations on changes in stock price. An additional calculation is needed to convert those changes into K stock prices (using initial stock price, which is given). Another calculation produces the average stock price during the life of the option (the sum of K stock prices divided by K).

vi. Compute the quantities of interest. In our example, the first calculation is the value of an Asian call at maturity, $C_{iT} = \max(S_T - S_{ave}, 0)$. A second calculation discounts this terminal value back to the present to get the call value as of today, C_{i0}. Steps i through vi complete one **simulation trial**. The i subscript in C_{iT} and C_{i0} stands for the ith simulation trial. In a Monte Carlo simulation, a running tabulation is kept of statistics relating to the distribution of the quantities of interest, including their mean value and standard deviation, over the simulation trials to that point.

vii. Iteratively go back to Step iv until a specified number of trials, I, is completed. Finally, produce statistics for the simulation. The key value for our example is the mean value of C_{i0} over the total number of simulation trials. This mean value is the Monte Carlo estimate of the value of the Asian call.

How many simulation trials should be specified? In general, we need to increase the number of simulation trials by a factor of 100 to get each extra digit of accuracy. Depending on the problem, tens of thousands of simulation trials may be needed to obtain accuracy to two decimal places (which is needed for option value, for example). A large number of trials is not necessarily a problem, given today's computing power. The number of trials needed can be reduced using variance reduction procedures, a topic outside the scope of this book.[32]

In Step iv of our example, a computer function produced a set of random observations on a standard normal random variable. Recall that for a uniform distribution, all possible numbers are equally likely. The term **random number generator** refers to an algorithm that produces uniformly distributed random numbers between 0 and 1. In the context of computer simulations, the term **random number** refers to an observation drawn from a uniform distribution.[33] For other distributions, the term *random observation* is used in this context.

---

[32] For details on this and other technical aspects of Monte Carlo simulation, see Hillier and Lieberman (2000).

[33] The numbers that random numbers generators produce depend on a seed or initial value. If the same seed is fed to the same generator, it will produce the same sequence. All sequences eventually repeat as well. Because of this predictability, the technically correct name for the numbers produced by random number generators is **pseudo-random numbers.** Pseudo-random numbers have sufficient qualities of randomness for most practical purposes.

It is a remarkable fact that random observations from any distribution can be produced using the uniform random variable with endpoints 0 and 1. To see why this is so, consider the inverse transformation method of producing random observations. Suppose we are interested in obtaining random observations for a random variable, X, with cumulative distribution function $F(x)$. Recall that $F(x)$ evaluated at x is a number between 0 and 1. Suppose a random outcome of this random variable is 3.21, and that $F(3.21) = 0.25$ or 25 percent. Define an inverse of F, call it F^{-1}, that can do the following: substitute the probability 0.25 into F^{-1} and it returns the random outcome 3.21. That is, $F^{-1}(0.25) = 3.21$. To generate random observations on X, the steps are: (1) Generate a uniform random number, r, between 0 and 1 using the random number generator, and (2) Evaluate $F^{-1}(r)$ to obtain a random observation on X. Random observation generation is a field of study in itself, and we have briefly discussed the inverse transformation method here just to illustrate a point. As a generalist, you do not need to address the technical details of converting random numbers into random observations.

EXAMPLE 5-15.   Potential Gains From Market Timing: A Monte Carlo Simulation.

All active investors want to achieve superior performance. One possible source of superior performance is market timing ability. How accurate does an investor need to be as a bull- and bear-market forecaster for market timing to be profitable? What size gains compared to a buy-and-hold strategy accrue to a given level of accuracy? Because of the variability in asset returns, a huge amount of return data is needed to get statistically reliable answers to these questions. Chua, Woodward, and To (1987) therefore selected Monte Carlo simulation to address the potential gains from market timing. They were interested in the perspective of a Canadian investor.

To understand their study, suppose that at the beginning of a year, an investor predicts that the next year will see either a bull market or bear market. If the prediction is *bull market*, the investor puts all her money in stocks and earns the market return for that year. On the other hand, if the prediction is *bear market*, the investor holds T-bills and earns the T-bill return. A market is categorized as *bull market* if the stock market return, R_{Mt}, minus T-bill return, R_{ft}, is positive for the year; otherwise, the market is classed as *bear market*. The investment results of a market timer can be compared to those of a buy-and-hold investor. A buy-and-hold investor earns the market return every year. For Chua et al., one quantity of interest was the gain from market timing. They defined this quantity as the market timer's average return minus the average return to a buy-and-hold investor.

To simulate market returns, Chua et al. generated 10,000 random standard normal observations, Z_t. At the time of the study, Canadian stocks had a historical mean annual return of 12.95 percent with a standard deviation of 18.30 percent. To reflect these parameters, the simulated market returns are $R_{Mt} = 0.1830Z_t + 0.1295$, $t = 1$, 2, ..., 10,000. Using a second set of 10,000 random standard normal observations, historical return parameters for Canadian T-bills, as well as the historical correlation of T-bill and stock returns, 10,000 T-bill returns were generated.

An investor can have different skills in forecasting bull and bear markets. Chua et al. characterized market timers by accuracy in forecasting bull markets and accuracy in forecasting bear markets. For example, bull market forecasting accuracy of 50 percent means that when the timer forecasts *bull market* for the next year, she is right just half the time, indicating no skill. Suppose an investor has 60 percent accuracy in forecasting *bull market* and 80 percent accuracy in forecasting *bear market* (a

60–80 timer). Once the first observation on $R_{Mt} - R_{ft}$ is generated, it is known whether that observation is a bull or bear market. If the observation is *bull market*, then 0.60 (forecast accuracy for bull markets) is compared to a random number (between 0 and 1). If the random number is less than 0.60 then the market timer is assumed to have correctly predicted *bull market* and her return for that first observation is the market return. If the random number is greater than 0.60 then the market timer is assumed to have made an error and predicted *bear market*; her return for that observation is the risk-free rate. In a similar fashion, if that first observation is *bear market*, the timer has an 80 percent chance of being right in forecasting *bear market* based on a random number draw. In either case, her return is compared to the market return to record her gain versus a buy-and-hold strategy. That is one simulation trial.

The results over 10,000 trials were averaged. Chua et al. specified bull and bear market prediction skill levels of 50, 60, 70, 80, 90, and 100 percent. Table 5-10 presents a very small excerpt from their simulation results for the no transaction costs case (transaction costs were also examined). Reading across the row, the timer with 60 percent bull market and 80 percent bear market forecasting accuracy had a mean annual gain from market timing of -1.12 percent per year. On average, the buy-and-hold investor out-earned this skillful timer by 1.12 percentage points. There was substantial variability in gains across the simulation trials, however: The standard deviation of the gain was 14.77 percent, so in many trials (but not on average) the gain was positive. Row 3 (win/loss) is the ratio of profitable switches between stocks and T-bills to unprofitable switches. This ratio was a favorable 1.2070 for the 60-80 timer. (When transaction costs were considered, however, fewer switches are profitable: the win-loss ratio was 0.5832 for the 60-80 timer.)

TABLE 5-10   Gains from Stock Market Timing (No Transaction Costs)

Bull Market Accuracy (%)		Bear Market Accuracy (%)					
		50	60	70	80	90	100
60	Mean (%)	-2.50	-1.99	-1.57	-1.12	-0.68	-0.22
	S.D. (%)	13.65	14.11	14.45	14.77	15.08	15.42
	Win/Loss	0.7418	0.9062	1.0503	1.2070	1.3496	1.4986

Source: Chua, Woodward, and To (1987), Table II (excerpt)

The authors concluded that the cost of not being invested in the market in bull market years is high. Because a buy-and-hold investor never misses a bull market year, she has 100 percent forecast accuracy for bull markets (at the cost of 0 percent accuracy for bear markets). Given their definitions and assumptions, the authors also concluded that successful market timing requires a minimum accuracy of 80 percent in forecasting both bull and bear markets. Market timing is a continuing area of interest and study, and other perspectives exist. However, this example illustrates how Monte Carlo simulation is used to address important investment issues.

The analyst chooses the probability distributions in Monte Carlo simulation. By contrast, **historic simulation** samples from a historical record of returns (or other underlying variables) to simulate a process. The concept underlying historic simulation (also called back simulation) is that the historical record provides the most direct evidence on distributions (and that the past applies to the future). For example, refer back to Step iv in the outline of Monte Carlo simulation above and suppose the time increment is one day. Further, suppose we base the simulation on the record of daily stock returns over the last five years. In one type of historic simulation, we randomly draw K returns from that record to generate one simulation trial. We put back the observations into the sample, and in the next trial we again randomly sample with replacement. Frequencies in the data are directly reflected in the simulation results. A drawback of this approach is that any risk not represented in the time period selected (for example, a stock market crash) will not be reflected in the simulations. Compared to Monte Carlo simulation, historic simulation does not lend itself to "what-if" analyses. Nevertheless, historic simulation is an established alternative simulation methodology.

Monte Carlo simulation is a complement to analytical methods. It provides only statistical estimates, not exact results. Analytical methods, where available, provide more insight into cause-and-effect relationships. For example, the Black-Scholes Option Pricing Model for the value of a European call option is an analytical method, expressed as a formula. It is a much more efficient method for valuing such a call than Monte Carlo simulation. As an analytical expression, the Black-Scholes model permits the analyst to quickly gauge the sensitivity of call value to changes in current stock price and the other variables that determine call value. In contrast, Monte Carlo simulations do not directly provide such precise insights. However, only some types of options can be priced with analytical expressions. As financial product innovations proceed, the field of applications for Monte Carlo simulation continues to grow.

5   SUMMARY

In this chapter, we have presented the most frequently used probability distributions in investment analysis and Monte Carlo simulation.

- Associated with any random variable is a probability distribution that specifies the probabilities of the possible outcomes of the random variable.
- There are two basic types of random variables: discrete random variables and continuous random variables.
- Discrete random variables take on at most a countable number of possible outcomes that we can list $x_1, x_2, \ldots$. In contrast, we cannot describe the possible outcomes of a continuous random variable Z with a list $z_1, z_2, \ldots$ because the outcome $(z_1 + z_2)/2$, not in the list, would always be possible.
- The two ways in which a probability distribution can be presented are the probability function and the cumulative distribution function.
- The probability function specifies the probability that the random variable will take on a specific value. The probability function is denoted $p(x)$ for a discrete random variable and $f(x)$ for a continuous random variable.
- The cumulative distribution function, denoted $F(x)$ for both continuous and discrete random variables, gives the probability that the random variable is less than or equal to x. All probability questions for both types of random variables can be answered in terms of the cumulative distribution function.
- The discrete uniform and the continuous uniform distribution are the distributions of equally likely outcomes. The uniform distribution plays an essential role in random number generation, an element of Monte Carlo simulation.

- A Bernoulli trial is an experiment with two outcomes, which can represent success or failure, up move or down move, or another binary outcome.

- The binomial distribution is a discrete probability distribution that is used to make probability statements about a record of successes and failures, or about other quantities with binary outcomes.

- The binomial random variable is defined as the number of successes in n Bernoulli trials, where the probability of success, p, is constant for all trials and the trials are independent.

- A binomial random variable has an expected value or mean equal to np and variance equal to $np(1 - p)$.

- A binomial tree is the graphical representation of a model of asset price dynamics in which, at each period, the asset moves up with probability p or down with probability $(1 - p)$. The binomial tree is a flexible method for modeling asset price movement and is widely used in pricing options.

- The normal distribution is a continuous symmetric probability distribution that is completely described by two parameters: its mean, μ, and its variance, σ^2.

- For a normal random variable, approximately 68 percent of all possible outcomes are within a one standard deviation interval about the mean, approximately 95 percent are within a two standard deviation interval about the mean, and approximately 99 percent are within a three standard deviation interval about the mean.

- A linear combination of two or more normal random variables is also normally distributed. As a result, portfolio return is normally distributed if the component securities are normally distributed.

- A univariate distribution specifies the probabilities for a single random variable. A multivariate distribution specifies the probabilities for a group of related random variables.

- To specify a normal distribution for a portfolio when its component securities are normally distributed, we need the means, standard deviations, and distinct pairwise correlations of the securities. When we have those statistics, we have specified a multivariate normal distribution for the securities.

- The standard normal random variable, denoted Z, has mean equal to 0 and variance equal to 1.

- All questions about any normal random variable can be answered by referring to the cumulative distribution function of a standard normal random variable, denoted $N(x)$ or $N(z)$.

- A random variable, X, is standardized using the expression $Z = (X - \mu)/\sigma$, where μ and σ are the mean and standard deviation of X. Generally, we use the sample mean $\bar{x}$ for μ and the sample standard deviation s for σ in this expression.

- If returns are normally distributed, risk-averse investors make portfolio decisions in terms of means and variances. Because the normal distribution is completely defined by its mean and variance, a normal or approximate normal distribution of security returns is the basis for the mean–variance analysis, a branch of modern portfolio theory (MPT).

- Roy's safety-first criterion asserts that the optimal portfolio is the one that minimizes the probability that portfolio return falls below a threshold level.

- According to Roy's safety-first criterion, if returns are normally distributed, the safety-first optimal portfolio P is the one that maximizes the quantity $[E(R_P) - R_L]/\sigma_P$, where R_L is the minimum acceptable level of return.

- Roy's safety-first criterion is one example of models addressing shortfall risk in portfolio selection.

- A random variable follows a lognormal distribution if the natural logarithm of the random variable is normally distributed.

- The lognormal distribution is defined in terms of the mean and variance of its associated normal distribution. The lognormal distribution is bounded below by 0 and skewed to the right (it has a long right tail).

- The lognormal distribution is frequently used to model the probability distribution of asset prices. It plays an important role in option pricing models.

- The continuously compounded return associated with a holding period is the natural log of 1 plus the holding period return, or equivalently, the natural log of ending price over beginning price (the price relative).

- If continuously compounded returns are normally distributed, asset prices are lognormally distributed. This relationship is used to move back and forth between the distributions for return and price. Because of the central limit theorem, continuously compounded returns need not be normally distributed for asset prices to be reasonably well described by a lognormal distribution.

- Standard deviation of continuously compounded daily returns provides an estimate of volatility for use in option pricing models.

- Monte Carlo simulation involves the use of a computer to find approximate solutions to complex problems.

- Monte Carlo simulation involves identifying the risk factors associated with a problem and specifying probability distributions for them. Repeated random sampling from a probability distribution or distributions is used to simulate the risk factors.

- Monte Carlo simulation is used to experiment with a proposed policy without actually implementing it. It is also used to value complex securities, including European options.

- Monte Carlo simulation is a complement to analytical methods.

- Historical simulation is an established alternative to Monte Carlo simulation that involves repeated sampling from a historical data series.

- Historical simulation can only reflect risks represented in the sample. Compared to Monte Carlo simulation, historical simulation does not lend itself to "what-if" analyses.

PROBLEMS

1. A European put option on stock conveys the right but not the obligation to sell the stock at a prespecified price, called the striking price, at the maturity date of the option. The value of this put at maturity is (Striking price − Stock price) or $0, whichever is greater. Suppose the striking price is $100 and the underlying stock trades in ticks of $0.01. As of any time before maturity, the terminal value of the put is a random variable.
   a. Describe the distinct possible outcomes for terminal put value. (Think of the put's maximum and minimum values and its minimum price increments.)
   b. Is terminal put value, viewed as a random variable, a discrete or continuous random variable?
   c. Letting Y stand for terminal put value, express in standard notation the probability that terminal put value is less than or equal to $24. No calculations are necessary.

2. Suppose X, Y, and Z are discrete random variables with these sets of possible outcomes: $X = \{2, 2.5, 3\}$, $Y = \{0, 1, 2, 3\}$, and $Z = \{10, 12, 13\}$. For each of the functions $f(X)$, $g(Y)$, and $h(Z)$, state whether the function satisfies the conditions for a probability function.
   a. $f(2) = -0.01$ $f(2.5) = 0.50$ $f(3) = 0.51$
   b. $g(0) = 0.25$ $g(1) = 0.50$ $g(2) = 0.125$ $g(3) = 0.125$
   c. $h(10) = 0.35$ $h(11) = 0.15$ $h(12) = 0.52$

3. Define *binomial random variable*. Describe the types of problems for which the binomial distribution is used.

4. Over the last 10 years, a company's annual earnings increased from the previous year seven times and decreased from the previous year three times. You decide to model the number of earnings increases over the next decade as a binomial random variable.
   a. What is your estimate of the probability of success, defined as an increase in annual earnings?
   For parts b, c, and d of this problem, take the estimated probability as the actual probability for the next decade.
   b. What is the probability that earnings will increase in exactly 5 of the next 10 years?
   c. Calculate the expected number of yearly earnings increases over the next 10 years.
   d. Calculate the variance and standard deviation of the number of yearly earnings increases over the next 10 years.
   e. The expression for the probability function of a binomial random variable depends on two major assumptions. In the context of this problem, what must you assume about annual earnings increases to apply the binomial distribution in Part b? What cautions might you have about the validity of these assumptions?

5. You have chosen a binomial tree to model the price dynamics of a stock. The probability of an up move is 0.75. If the stock moves up, it earns a 1 percent return. If the stock moves down, it earns a −1 percent return. Current stock price is €100.
   a. What are the possible outcomes for stock price after two periods?
   b. What is the expected value of stock price at the end of two periods?

6. By definition, a down and out call option on stock becomes worthless and terminates if the price of the underlying stock moves down and touches a prespecified point during the life of the call. If the prespecified level is $75, for example, the call expires worthless when and if stock price falls to $75. What feature or features of a binomial tree are useful in valuing a down and out call option?

7. You are forecasting sales for a company in the fourth quarter of its fiscal year. Your low-end estimate of sales is €14 million and your high end estimate is €15 million. You

decide to treat all outcomes for sales between these two values as equally likely, using a continuous uniform distribution.

   a. What is the expected value of sales for the fourth quarter?
   b. What is the probability that fourth-quarter sales will be less than or equal to €14,125,000?

8. State the approximate probability that a normal random variable will fall within the following intervals:

   a. Mean plus or minus one standard deviation
   b. Plus or minus two standard deviations
   c. Plus or minus three standard deviations

9. You are evaluating a diversified equity portfolio. The portfolio's mean monthly return is 0.56 percent, and its standard deviation of monthly returns is 8.86 percent.

   a. Calculate a one standard deviation confidence interval for the return on this portfolio. Interpret this interval.
   b. Calculate an exact 95 percent confidence interval for portfolio return, assuming portfolio returns are described by a normal distribution.
   c. Calculate an exact 99 percent confidence interval for portfolio return, assuming portfolio returns are described by a normal distribution.

10. Find the area under the normal curve up to $z = 0.36$; i.e., find $P(Z \leq 0.36)$. Interpret this value.

11. Profits or losses on futures contracts are settled at the end of each trading day. This procedure is called mark-to-market or daily resettlement. By preventing a trader's losses from accumulating over many days, mark-to-market reduces the risk that traders will default on their obligations. Futures markets participants need a liquidity pool to meet daily mark-to-market. If liquidity is exhausted, a trader may be forced to unwind his position at an unfavorable time.

   Suppose you are using financial futures to hedge a risk in your portfolio. You have a liquidity pool (cash and cash-equivalents) of λ dollars per contract and a time horizon of T trading days. The standard deviation of daily price changes is σ for the contract you are using for hedging. For a given size liquidity pool λ, Kolb, Gay, and Hunter (1985) gave the following expression for the probability that a trader will exhaust his or her liquidity pool within a T-day horizon as a result of daily mark-to-market:

   $$\text{Probability of exhausting liquidity pool} = 2[1 - N(x)]$$

   where $x = \lambda/(\sigma_x \sqrt{T})$ (the liquidity pool size divided by the standard deviation of price changes over the time horizon). $N(x)$ is the standard normal cumulative distribution function.

   a. Your hedging horizon is 5 days and your liquidity pool is $2,000 per contract. You estimate that the standard deviation of daily price changes for the contract is $450. What is the probability that you will exhaust your liquidity pool in the 5-day period?
   b. Suppose your hedging horizon is 20 days, but all the other facts given in Part a are unchanged. What is the probability that you will exhaust your liquidity pool in the 20-day period?

Use the table below to answer questions 12 through 14.

As reported by Liang (1999), U.S. equity funds in three style categories had the following mean monthly returns, standard deviations of return, and Sharpe ratios over the period January 1994 to December 1996.

| | January 1994 to December 1996 | | |
Strategy	Mean Return	Standard Deviation	Sharpe Ratio
Large-cap growth	1.15%	2.89%	0.26
Large-cap value	1.08%	2.20%	0.31
Large-cap blend	1.07%	2.38%	0.28

Source: Liang (1999), Table 5 (excerpt)

12. Basing your estimate of monthly return parameters for a future period on the sample mean and standard deviation for the period January 1994 to December 1996, construct a 90 percent confidence interval for the monthly return on a large-cap blend fund. Assume fund returns are normally distributed.

13. Basing your estimate of monthly return parameters for a future period on the sample mean and standard deviation for the period January 1994 to December 1996, calculate the probability that a large-cap growth fund will earn a monthly return of 0 percent or less. Assume fund returns are normally distributed.

14. Assuming fund returns are normally distributed, which fund category minimized the probability of earning less than the risk-free rate for the period January 1994 to December 1996?

15. **a.** Describe two important characteristics of the lognormal distribution.
    b. Compared to the normal distribution, why is the lognormal distribution a more reasonable model for the distribution of asset prices?
    c. What are the two parameters of a lognormal distribution?

16. The basic calculation for volatility (denoted σ) as used in option pricing is the annualized standard deviation of continuously compounded daily returns. Calculate volatility for Dollar General Corporation (NYSE: DG) based on its closing prices for two weeks, given in the table below. (Annualize on the basis of 250 days in a year.)

Dollar General Corporation Daily Closing Prices

Date	Closing Price
Jan. 29, 2001	$18.37
Jan. 30, 2001	$18.53
Jan. 31, 2001	$19.48
Feb. 1, 2001	$19.50
Feb. 2, 2001	$19.47
Feb. 5, 2001	$19.68
Feb. 6, 2001	$19.50
Feb. 7, 2001	$20.13
Feb. 8, 2001	$19.49
Feb. 9, 2001	$19.28

17. **a.** Define Monte Carlo simulation.
    b. What are the strengths and weaknesses of Monte Carlo simulation for use in valuing securities, compared to analytical methods?

18. By definition, a **lookback call option** on stock has a value at maturity equal to (Value of the stock at maturity − Minimum value of stock during the life of the option) or $0, whichever is greater. If the minimum value reached was $27.11 and the value of the stock at maturity is $23, for example, the call is worthless because $23 is less than $27.11.

Briefly discuss how you might use Monte Carlo simulation in valuing a lookback call option.

SOLUTIONS

1. a. The put's minimum value is $0. The put's value is $0 when the stock price is at or above $100 at the maturity date of the option. The put's maximum value is $100 = $100 (striking price) − $0 (lowest possible stock price). The put's value is $100 when the stock is worthless at the option's maturity date. The put's minimum price increments are $0.01. Thus, the possible outcomes of terminal put value are $0.00, $0.01, $0.02, ..., $100.

b. The price of the underlying has minimum price fluctuations of $0.01: These are the minimum price fluctuations for terminal put value. For example, if the stock finishes at $98.20, the payoff on the put is $1.80 = $100 − $98.20. We can specify that the nearest values to $1.80 are $1.79 and $1.81. With a continuous random variable, we cannot specify the nearest values. So we can characterize terminal put value as a discrete random variable.

c. The probability that terminal put value is less than or equal to $24 is $P(Y \leq 24)$ or $F(24)$, in standard notation, where F is the cumulative distribution function for terminal put value.

2. a. Because $f(2) = -0.01$ is negative, $f(X)$ cannot be a probability function. Probabilities are numbers between 0 and 1.

b. The function $g(Y)$ does satisfy the conditions of a probability function; all the values of $g(Y)$ are between 0 and 1, and the values of $g(Y)$ sum to 1.

c. The function $h(Z)$ cannot be a probability function: the values of $h(Y)$ sum to 1.02, which is more than 1.

3. A binomial random variable is defined as the number of successes in n Bernoulli trials (a trial that produces one of two outcomes). The binomial distribution is used to make probability statements about a record of successes and failures, or about anything with binary (twofold) outcomes.

4. a. The probability of an earnings increase (success) in a year is estimated as 7/10 = 0.70 or 70 percent, based on the record of the past 10 years.

b. The probability that earnings will increase in 5 out of the next 10 years is about 10.3 percent. Define a binomial random variable X counting the number of earnings increases over the next 10 years. From Part a, the probability of an earnings increase in a given year is $p = 0.70$, and the number of trials (years) is $n = 10$. Equation 5-1 gives the probability that a binomial random variable has x successes in n trials, with the probability of success on a trial equal to p.

$$P(X = x) = \binom{n}{x} p^x (1 - p)^{n-x} = \frac{n!}{(n - x)!x!} p^x (1 - p)^{n-x}$$

For this example,

$$\binom{10}{5} 0.7^5 0.3^{10-5} = \frac{10!}{(10 - 5)!5!} 0.7^5 0.3^{10-5}$$

$$= 252 \times 0.16807 \times 0.00243 = 0.102919$$

We conclude that the probability that earnings will increase in exactly 5 of the next 10 years is 0.1029 or approximately 10.3 percent.

c. The expected number of increases is $E(X) = np = 10 \times 0.70 = 7$ or 7 yearly increases.

d. The variance of the number of yearly increases over the next 10 years is $\sigma^2 = np(1 - p) = 10 \times 0.70 \times 0.30 = 2.1$ The standard deviation is 1.449 (the square root of 2.1).

e. You must assume (1) that the probability of an earnings increase (success) is constant from year to year, and (2) that earnings increases are independent trials. If current and past earnings help forecast next year's earnings, assumption (2) is violated. If the firm's business is subject to economic or industry cycles, both assumptions (1) and (2) will probably not hold.

5. a. The possible outcomes for stock price after two periods are €102.01, €99.99, and €98.01. The first column of the table below shows the calculations.

Terminal Stock Price: $n = 2$, $p = 0.750$

Ending Price	Path: Number of Ways to Reach Ending Price	Probability
€102.01 = €100$(1.01)^2$	UU: 1 way	$p(102.01) = (1)(0.75^2) = 0.5625$
€99.99 = €100(1.01)(0.99)	UD: 2 ways	$p(99.99) = (2)(0.75)(0.25) = 0.375$
€98.01 = €100$(0.99)^2$	DD: 1 ways	$p(98.01) = (1)(0.25^2) = 0.0625$
		Sum = 1.0

b. At the end of two periods, expected stock price is approximately €101. This value is a weighted average of terminal stock prices, as given in column 1, weighted by the probabilities in column 3. The calculation is

$$E(\text{Stock Price}) = 0.5625(€102.01) + 0.375(€99.99) + 0.0625(€98.01)$$
$$= €101.0025.$$

6. At each node we can test the condition that stock price is at or below the prespecified level.

Just as in Figure 5-2, we calculate stock price at all nodes of the tree. We calculate the value of the call at the terminal nodes as a function of the terminal price of the stock. Using a model for discounting values one period, we calculate call value one period earlier, and so forth, to reach $t = 0$. But at any node where stock price is at or below the prespecified level, we automatically set call value to $0.

7. a. The expected value of fourth-quarter sales is €14,500,000 calculated as (€14,000,00 + €15,000,000)/2. With a continuous uniform random variable, the mean or expected value is the midpoint between the smallest and largest values. (See Example 5-7.)

b. The probability that fourth-quarter sales will be less than €14,125,000 is 0.125 or 12.5 percent, calculated as (€14,125,000 − €14,000,000)/(€15,000,000 − €14,000,000).

8. a. Approximately 68 percent of all outcomes of a normal random variable fall within the interval mean plus or minus one standard deviation.

b. Approximately 95 percent of all outcomes of a normal random variable fall within the interval mean plus or minus two standard deviations.

c. Approximately 99 percent of all outcomes of a normal random variable fall within the interval mean plus or minus three standard deviations.

9. **a.** The lower limit of a one standard deviation confidence interval is the sample mean return (0.56 percent) minus the sample standard deviation (8.86 percent) or $-8.30\% = 0.56\% - 8.86\%$. The upper limit is the sample mean return (0.56 percent) plus the sample standard deviation (8.86 percent) or $9.42\% = 0.56\% + 8.86\%$. Summarizing, the one standard deviation confidence interval runs from -8.30 percent to 9.42 percent, which we can also write as $[-8.30\%, 9.42\%]$. If the portfolio return is normally distributed, approximately 68 percent (precisely 68.27 percent) of monthly returns should fall in this interval.

   b. The lower limit of a 95 percent confidence interval is the sample mean return minus 1.96 standard deviations or $-16.81\% = 0.56\% - 1.96 \times 8.86\%$. The upper limit is the sample mean return plus 1.96 standard deviations or $17.93\% = 0.56\% + 1.96 \times 8.86\%$. Summarizing, an exact 95 percent confidence interval runs from -16.81 percent to 17.93 percent, which we can also write as $[-16.81\%, 17.93\%]$. Only 5 percent of a large number of returns should fall outside of this interval, under the normality assumption. In that sense, we have 95 percent confidence in this interval.

   c. The lower limit of a 99 percent confidence interval is the sample mean return minus 2.58 standard deviations or $-22.30\% = 0.56\% - 2.58 \times 8.86\%$. The upper limit is the sample mean return plus 2.58 standard deviations or $23.42\% = 0.56\% + 2.58 \times 8.86\%$. Summarizing, an exact 99 percent confidence interval runs from -22.30 percent to 23.42 percent, which we can also write as $[-22.30\%, 23.42\%]$. Only 1 percent of a large number of returns should fall outside of this interval, under the normality assumption. In that sense, we have 99 percent confidence in this interval.

10. The area under the normal curve for $z = 0.36$ is 0.6406 or 64.06 percent. The table below presents excerpts from the tables of the standard normal cumulative distribution function in the back of this book. To locate $z = 0.36$, go down to the fourth row of numbers to 0.30, then move over to the column under 0.06 (the second decimal place of 0.36). The entry is 0.6406 or 64.06 percent.

$P(Z \le x) = N(x)$ for $x \ge 0$ or $P(Z \le z) = N(z)$ for $z \ge 0$

x or z	0	0.01	0.02	0.03	0.04	0.05	0.06	0.07	0.08	0.09
0.00	0.5000	0.5040	0.5080	0.5120	0.5160	0.5199	0.5239	0.5279	0.5319	0.5359
0.10	0.5398	0.5438	0.5478	0.5517	0.5557	0.5596	0.5636	0.5675	0.5714	0.5753
0.20	0.5793	0.5832	0.5871	0.5910	0.5948	0.5987	0.6026	0.6064	0.6103	0.6141
0.30	0.6179	0.6217	0.6255	0.6293	0.6331	0.6368	**0.6406**	0.6443	0.6480	0.6517
0.40	0.6554	0.6591	0.6628	0.6664	0.6700	0.6736	0.6772	0.6808	0.6844	0.6879
0.50	0.6915	0.6950	0.6985	0.7019	0.7054	0.7088	0.7123	0.7157	0.7190	0.7224

The interpretation of 64.06 percent for $z = 0.36$ is that 64.06 percent of observations on a standard normal random variable are smaller than or equal to the value 0.36. (So $100\% - 64.06\% = 35.94\%$ of the values are greater than 0.36.)

11. **a.** The probability of exhausting the liquidity pool is 4.7 percent. First calculate $x = \lambda/(\sigma\sqrt{T}) = \$2,000/(\$450\sqrt{5}) = 1.987616$. We can round this value to 1.99 to use the standard normal tables in the back of this book. Using those tables, we find that $N(1.99) = 0.9767$. Thus, the probability of exhausting the liquidity pool is $2[1 - N(1.99)] = 2[1 - 0.9767] = 0.0466$ or about 4.7 percent.

b. The probability of exhausting the liquidity pool is now 32.2 percent. The calculation follows the same steps as those in Part a. We calculate $x = \lambda/(\sigma\sqrt{T}) = \$2{,}000/(\$450\sqrt{20}) = 0.993808$. We can round this value to 0.99 to use the standard normal tables in the back of this book. Using those tables, we find that $N(0.99) = 0.8389$. Thus, the probability of exhausting the liquidity pool is $2[1 - N(0.99)] = 2[1 - 0.8389] = 0.3222$ or about 32.2 percent. This is a substantial probability that you will run out of funds to meet mark-to-market.

In their paper, Kolb et al. call the probability of exhausting the liquidity pool the *probability of a ruin*, a traditional name for this type of calculation. The expression assumes that the expected change in futures price is 0 and that futures price changes are normally distributed.

12. A 90 percent confidence interval for returns on large-cap blend funds is the interval [2.8451%, 4.9851%]. An exact 90 percent confidence interval is equal to the mean plus and minus 1.645 standard deviations. The lower limit is $-2.8451\% = 1.07\% - 1.645 \times 2.38\%$. The upper limit is $4.9851\% = 1.07\% + 1.645 \times 2.38\%$.

13. Under a normality assumption, the probability that the average large-cap growth fund would earn a negative monthly return is 34.5 percent. We calculate $-0.397924 = (0\% - 1.15\%)/2.89\%$. Rounding this value to -0.40 to use the standard normal tables in the back of the book, we find that $N(-0.40) = 0.3446$. If you use a spreadsheet function on -0.397924, you should get $N(-0.397924) = 0.345343$.

14. The large-cap value fund category minimized the probability of earning a return less than the risk-free rate of return for the period. Large-cap value funds achieved the highest Sharpe ratio during the period. Recall from our discussion of Roy's safety-first criterion that the Sharpe ratio is equivalent to using the risk-free rate as the shortfall level in SFRatio, and that the alternative with the largest SFRatio minimizes the probability of earning a return less than the shortfall level (under a normality assumption). Thus, to answer the question, we select the alternative with the highest Sharpe ratio, the large-cap value fund.

15. a. Two important features of the lognormal distribution are that it is bounded below by 0 and right-skewed.

b. Normal random variables can be negative (the bell curve extends to the left without limit). In contrast, lognormal random variables cannot be negative. Asset prices also cannot be negative. So the lognormal distribution is superior to the normal as a probability model for asset prices.

c. The two parameters of a lognormal distribution are the mean and variance (or standard deviation) of the associated normal distribution. If Y is lognormal and $Y = \ln X$, the two parameters of the distribution of Y are the mean and variance (or standard deviation) of X.

16. To compute volatility for Dollar General Corporation, we begin by calculating the continuously compounded daily returns using Equation 5-5:

$$r_{t,t+1} = \ln S_{t+1}/S_t = \ln (1 + R_{t,t+1})$$

Then we find the variance of those continuously compounded returns, the sum of the squared deviations from the mean divided by 8 (the sample size of 9 continuously compounded returns minus 1). We take the square root of the variance to find the standard deviation. Finally, we multiply the standard deviation by $\sqrt{250}$ to annualize it.

The continuously compounded daily returns are (reading across the line, then down):

$\ln(18.53/18.37) = 0.008672$, $\ln(19.48/18.53) = 0.049997$, $\ln(19.50/19.48) = 0.001026$,

$\ln(19.47/19.50) = -0.001540$, $\ln(19.68/19.47) = 0.010728$, $\ln(19.50/19.68) = -0.009188$,

$\ln(20.13/19.50) = 0.031797$, $\ln(19.49/20.13) = -0.032310$, $\ln(19.28/19.49) = -0.010833$,

Sum = 0.048349, Mean = 0.005372, Variance = 0.000586, Standard deviation = 0.024214

The standard deviation of continuously compounded daily returns is 0.024214. Then $\sigma\sqrt{T} = 0.024214\sqrt{250} = 0.382857$ or 38.3 percent.

17. **a.** Elements that should appear in a definition of Monte Carlo are that it provides a representation and, in some applications, an approximate solution; that it makes use of computer; and that it involves the generation of a large number of random samples from a specified probability distribution. The exact wording can vary, but one definition follows.

Monte Carlo simulation in finance involves the use of a computer to represent the operation of a complex financial system. In some important applications, Monte Carlo simulation is used to find an approximate solution to a complex financial problem. An integral part of Monte Carlo simulation is the generation of a large number of random samples from a probability distribution

b. *Strengths*. Monte Carlo simulation can be used to price complex securities for which no analytic expression is available, particularly European-style options.

Weaknesses. Monte Carlo estimation provides only statistical estimates, not exact results. Analytic methods, where available, provide more insight into cause-and-effect relationships.

18. In the text, we described how we could use Monte Carlo simulation to value an Asian option, a complex European-style option. Just as we can calculate the average value of the stock over a simulation trial to value an Asian option, we can also calculate the minimum value of the stock over a simulation trial. Then, for a given simulation trial, we can calculate the terminal value of the call, given the minimum value of the stock for the simulation trial. We can then discount back this terminal value to the present to get the value of the call today ($t = 0$). The average of these $t = 0$ values over all simulation trials is the Monte Carlo simulated value of the lookback call option.

C H A P T E R

6

SAMPLING AND ESTIMATION

1 INTRODUCTION

Each day, we observe the high, low, and close of stock market indexes from around the world. Indexes such as the S&P 500 and the Nikkei-Dow Jones Average are samples of stocks. Although the S&P 500 and the Nikkei do not represent the populations of U.S. or Japanese stocks, we view them as valid indicators of the behavior of the whole population. As analysts, we are accustomed to using this sample information to assess how various markets from around the world are performing. Any statistics that we compute with sample information, however, are only estimates of the underlying population parameters. A sample, then, is a subset of the population—a subset studied to infer conclusions about the population itself.

How we sample and use sample information to estimate population parameters are the subject of this chapter. In the next section, we discuss **sampling**—the process of obtaining a sample. In investments, we continually make use of the mean as a measure of central tendency of random variables, such as return and earnings per share. Even when the probability distribution of the random variable is unknown, we can make probability statements about the population mean using the central limit theorem. In Section 3, we discuss and illustrate this key result. Following that discussion, we turn to statistical estimation. Estimation seeks precise answers to the question: What is this parameter's value?

The central limit theorem and estimation are the core of the body of methods presented in this chapter. In investments, we apply these and other statistical techniques to financial data; we often interpret the results for the purpose of deciding what works and what does not work in investments. We end this chapter with a discussion of the interpretation of statistical results based on financial data and the possible pitfalls in this process.

2 SAMPLING

In this section, we present the various methods for obtaining information on a population (all members of a specified group) through samples (part of the population). The information for the population that we try to obtain usually concerns the value of a **parameter.** A parameter is a descriptive measure computed from or used to describe a population of data. When we use a sample to estimate a parameter, we make use of sample statistics (statistics, for short). A statistic is a descriptive measure computed from or used to describe a sample of data.

We take samples for one of two reasons. In some cases, we cannot possibly examine every member of the population. In other cases, although we could examine every member of the population, doing so would not be economically efficient. Thus, savings of time and money are two primary factors that cause an analyst to use sampling to answer a question about a population. In this section, we discuss two methods of random sampling: simple random sampling and stratified random sampling. We then define and illustrate the two types of data an analyst uses: cross-sectional data and time-series data.

2.1 SIMPLE RANDOM SAMPLING

Suppose a telecommunications equipment analyst wants to know how much major customers will spend on average for equipment during the coming year. One strategy is to survey the population of telecom equipment customers and inquire what their purchasing plans are. In statistical terms, the characteristics of the population of customers' planned expenditures would then usually be expressed by descriptive measures such as the mean and variance. Surveying all companies would be very costly, however, in terms of time and money.

The alternative strategy for the analyst is to collect a representative sample of companies and survey them about upcoming telecom equipment expenditures. In this case, the analyst will compute the sample mean expenditure, $\bar{x}$, a statistic. This strategy has a substantial advantage over polling the whole population because it can be accomplished more quickly and at lower cost.

Sampling, however, introduces error. The error arises because not all the companies in the population are surveyed. The analyst who decides to sample is trading time and money for sampling error.

When an analyst chooses to sample, he must formulate a sampling plan. A **sampling plan** is the set of rules used to select a sample. The basic type of sample on the basis of which we can draw statistically sound conclusions about a population is the **simple random sample** (random sample, for short).

- **Definition of Simple Random Sample.** A simple random sample is a sample obtained in such a way that each element of the population has an equal probability of being selected.

The procedure of drawing a sample to satisfy the definition of a simple random sample is called **simple random sampling.** How is simple random sampling carried out? We need a method that ensures randomness—the lack of any pattern—in the selection of the sample. For a finite (limited) population, the most common method for obtaining a random sample involves the use of random numbers (numbers with assured properties of randomness). First, we number the members of the population in sequence. For example, if the population contains 500 members, we number the members in sequence with three digits, starting with 001 and ending with 500. Suppose we want a simple random sample of size 50. In that case, using a computer random-number generator or a table of random numbers, we generate a series of three-digit random numbers. We then match these random numbers with the number codes of the members of the population until a sample of size 50 has been selected.

Sometimes we cannot code (or even identify) all the members of a population. We often use **systematic sampling** in such cases. With systematic sampling, we select every kth member until we have a sample of the desired size. The sample that results from this procedure should be approximately random. Real sampling situations may require that we take an approximately random sample.

Suppose the telecommunications equipment analyst polls a random sample of telecom equipment customers to determine the average equipment expenditure. The sample mean will provide the analyst with an estimate of the population mean expenditure. Any difference between the sample mean and the population mean is called **sampling error.**

- **Definition of Sampling Error.** Sampling error is the difference between the observed value of a statistic and the quantity it is intended to estimate.

A random sample reflects the properties of the population in an unbiased way, and sample statistics, such as the sample mean, computed on the basis of a random sample are valid estimates of the underlying population parameters.

A sample statistic is a random variable. In other words, not only do the original data from the population have a distribution, but so does the sample statistic. This distribution is the statistic's sampling distribution.

- **Definition of Sampling Distribution.** The sampling distribution of a statistic is the distribution of all the distinct possible values that the statistic can assume when computed from samples of the same size randomly drawn from the same population.

In the case of the sample mean, for example, we refer to the *sampling distribution of the sample mean* or the distribution of the sample mean. We will have more to say about sampling distributions later in this chapter. Next, however, we look at another sampling method that is useful in investment analysis.

2.2   STRATIFIED RANDOM SAMPLING

The simple random sampling method just discussed may not be the best approach in all situations. One frequently used alternative is stratified random sampling.

- **Definition of Stratified Random Sampling.** In stratified random sampling, the population is subdivided into subpopulations (strata) based on one or more classification criteria. Simple random samples are then drawn from each stratum in sizes proportional to the relative size of each stratum in the population. These samples are then pooled.

Stratified random sampling guarantees that population subdivisions of interest are represented in the sample. Another advantage is that estimates of parameters produced from stratified sampling have greater precision—that is, smaller variance or dispersion—than estimates obtained from simple random sampling.

Bond indexing is one area in which stratified sampling is frequently applied. In pure bond indexing, also called the *full-replication approach*, the investor attempts to fully replicate an index by owning all the bonds in the index in proportion to their market value weights.[1] Many bond indexes consist of thousands of issues, however, so pure bond indexing is difficult to implement. In addition, transaction costs would be high because many bonds do not have liquid markets. Although a simple random sample could be a solution to the cost problem, the sample would probably not match the index's major risk factors—interest rate sensitivity, for example. Because the major risk factors of fixed-income portfolios are well-known and quantifiable, a more effective approach is stratified sampling. In this approach, we divide the population of index bonds into groups of similar duration (interest rate sensitivity), cash flow distribution, sector, credit quality, and call exposure and call each group a stratum or *cell* (a term frequently used in this context).[2] Then, we choose a sample from each stratum proportional to the relative market weighting of the stratum in the index to be replicated.

EXAMPLE 6-1.   Bond Indexes and Stratified Sampling.

Suppose you are the manager of a mutual fund indexed to the Lehman Brothers Government Index. You are exploring several approaches to replicating that bond index, including a stratified sampling approach. You first distinguish agency bonds from Treasury bonds. For each of these two groups, you define 10 maturity intervals—1–2 years, 2–3 years, 3–4 years, 4–6 years, 6–8 years, 8–10 years, 10–12 years, 15–20 years, and 20–30 years—and also separate the bonds in issues with coupons (annual interest rates) of 6 percent or less from the bonds in issues with coupons of more than 6 percent.

---

[1] See Fabozzi (1999). Fabozzi also discusses optimization techniques that can be used with stratified sampling.

[2] See Fabozzi (2000b).

1. How many cells or strata does this sampling plan entail?

2. If you use this sampling plan, what is the minimum number of issues the indexed portfolio can have?

3. Suppose that, in selecting among the securities that qualify for selection within each cell, you apply a criterion concerning the liquidity of the security's market. Is the sample obtained random? Explain your answer.

Solution to 1.   We have 2 issuer classifications, 10 maturity classifications, and 2 coupon classifications. So, in total, this plan entails $2 \times 10 \times 2 = 40$ different strata or cells. (This answer is an application of the multiplication rule of counting discussed in the chapter on probability concepts.)

Solution to 2.   You cannot have fewer than one issue for each cell, so the portfolio must include at least 40 issues.

Solution to 3.   If you apply any additional criteria to the selection of securities for the cells, not every security that might be included has an equal probability of being selected. As a result, the sampling is not random. In practice, indexing using stratified sampling is frequently not strictly random because the selection of issues within cells is subject to various additional criteria. Because the purpose of sampling in this application is not to make an inference about a population parameter but rather to index a portfolio, lack of randomness is not in itself a problem in this application of stratified sampling.

In the next section, we discuss the kinds of data used by financial analysts in sampling and practical issues that arise in selecting samples.

2.3 TIME-SERIES AND CROSS-SECTIONAL DATA

Investment analysts commonly work with both time-series and cross-sectional data. A *time series* is a sequence of returns collected at discrete and equally spaced intervals of time (such as a historical series of monthly stock returns). *Cross-sectional data* are data on some characteristic of individuals, groups, geographical regions, or companies at a single point in time. The 1999 year-end book value per share for all New York Stock Exchange companies is an example of cross-sectional data.

Economic or financial theory offers no basis for determining whether a long or short time period should be selected to collect a sample. As analysts, we might have to look for subtle clues. For example, combining data from a period when exchange rates were fixed with data from a period when exchange rates were floating would be inappropriate. The variance of exchange rates when exchange rates were fixed would certainly be less than when exchange rates were allowed to float. As a consequence, we would not be sampling from a population described by a single set of parameters.[3] Tight versus loose monetary policy also influences the distribution of returns to stocks; thus, combining data from tight-money and loose-money periods would be inappropriate. Calculation of the Sharpe ratio provides a simple illustration of the problem of nonidentical distributions.

---

[3] When the mean or variance of a time series is not constant through time, the time series is not stationary. We discuss stationarity in more detail in the chapter on time-series analysis.

EXAMPLE 6-2.   Calculating Sharpe Ratios: One or Two Years of Quarterly
                Data?

Suppose an analyst wants to evaluate the performance of a managed fund using the
Sharpe ratio. The Sharpe ratio is the average return in excess of the risk-free rate divided by the standard deviation of returns. The Sharpe ratio measures the excess return earned per unit of standard deviation of return.

To compute the Sharpe ratio, the analyst collects eight quarterly excess returns
(i.e., total return in excess of the risk-free rate). During the first year, the investment
manager of the fund followed a low-risk strategy, and during the second year, the
manager followed a high-risk strategy. For each of these years, the analyst also
tracks the quarterly excess returns of some benchmark against which the manager
will be evaluated. For each of the two years, the Sharpe ratio for the benchmark is
0.21. The calculations for the Sharpe ratio of the portfolio are in Table 6-1.

TABLE 6-1   Calculation of Sharpe Ratios: Low-Risk and High-Risk
              Strategies

Quarter/Measure	Year 1 Excess Returns	Year 2 Excess Returns
Quarter 1	−3%	−12%
Quarter 2	5	20
Quarter 3	−3	−12
Quarter 4	5	20
Quarterly average	1%	4%
Quarterly standard deviation	4.62%	18.48%
Sharpe ratio	0.22	0.22

For the first year, during which the manager followed a low-risk strategy, the
average quarterly return in excess of the risk-free rate was 1 percent with a standard
deviation of 4.62 percent. The Sharpe ratio is thus $1/4.62 = 0.22$. The second year's
results mirror the first year except for the higher average return and volatility. The
Sharpe ratio for the second year is $4/18.48 = 0.22$. The Sharpe ratio for the benchmark is 0.21 during the first and second years, so because larger Sharpe ratios are
better (more return per unit of risk), the manager appears to have outperformed the
benchmark.

Now, suppose the analyst believes a larger sample to be superior to a small
one. She thus decides to pool the two years together and calculate a Sharpe ratio
based on eight quarterly observations. The average quarterly excess return for the
two years is the average of each year's average excess return. For the two-year period, the average excess return is $(1 + 4)/2 = 2.5$ percent per quarter. The standard
deviation for all eight quarters measured from the sample mean of 2.5 percent is
12.57 percent. The portfolio's Sharpe ratio for the two-year period is now
$2.5/12.57 = 0.198$; the Sharpe ratio for the benchmark remains 0.21. Thus, when
pooling is used for the two-year period, the manager appears to have provided less

return per unit of risk than the benchmark and less when compared with the separate yearly results.

The problem with using eight quarters of return data is that the analyst has violated the assumption that the returns come from the same population. When she combined return data that came from a distribution with a changing mean, the volatility appeared to have increased relative to the mean—even though asset returns in general were identically distributed through time, as indicated by the constant Sharpe ratio for the benchmark. In our hypothetical example, the underlying strategy used by the manager changed. Clearly, during Year 1, returns were generated by an underlying population with lower mean and variance than the population of the second year. Combining the results for the first and second years yielded a sample that was representative of no population. Although the analyst may have applied sound statistical techniques to the data, because the sample did not satisfy model assumptions, any conclusions she reached are incorrect. For this example, the analyst was better off using a smaller sample than a larger sample because the smaller sample represented a more homogeneous distribution of returns.

The other type of data that an analyst uses is cross-sectional data. The observations in the sample represent a characteristic of individuals, groups, geographical regions, or companies at a single point in time. The telecommunications analyst discussed previously is essentially collecting a cross-section of planned capital expenditures for the coming year.

Whenever we sample cross-sectionally, certain assumptions must be met if we wish to summarize the data in a meaningful way. Again, a useful approach is to think of the observation of interest as a random variable that comes from some underlying population with a given mean and variance. As we collect our sample and begin to summarize the data, we must be sure that all the data do, in fact, come from the same underlying population. For example, an analyst might be interested in how efficiently companies use their inventory assets. Some companies, however, turn their inventory over more quickly than others because of differences in their operating environments (e.g., grocery stores turn over inventory more quickly than automobile manufacturers, in general). So, the distribution of inventory turnover rates may not be characterized by a single distribution with a given mean and variance. Therefore, summarizing inventory turnover across all companies might be inappropriate. If random variables are generated by different underlying distributions, the sample statistics computed from combined samples are not related to one underlying population parameter. The size of the sampling error in such cases is unknown.

In instances such as these, analysts often summarize company-level data by industry. Attempting to summarize by industry partially addresses the problem of differing underlying distributions, but large corporations are likely to be in more than one industrial sector, so analysts should be sure they understand how companies are assigned to the industry groups.

Whether we deal with time-series data or cross-sectional data, we must be sure we have a random sample that is representative of the population we wish to study.

With the objective of inferring information from representative samples, we now turn to the second part of this chapter, which focuses on the central limit theorem and point and interval estimates of the population mean.

3 DISTRIBUTION OF THE SAMPLE MEAN

In the first section, we presented a telecommunications equipment analyst who decided to sample in order to estimate mean planned capital expenditures by his customers. Supposing that the sample is representative of the underlying population, how can the analyst assess the sampling error in estimating the population mean? The sample mean is a random variable and has a probability distribution (its sampling distribution). To estimate how closely the sample mean can be expected to match the underlying population mean, the analyst needs to understand the sampling distribution of the mean. Fortunately, we have a result, the central limit theorem, that helps us understand the sampling distribution of the mean for many of the estimation problems we face.

3.1 THE CENTRAL LIMIT THEOREM

The central limit theorem is one of the most practically useful theorems in probability theory and has important implications for how we construct confidence intervals and test hypotheses. Formally, it is stated as follows:

- **The Central Limit Theorem.** Given a population described by any probability distribution having mean μ and finite variance σ^2, the sampling distribution of sample mean $\bar{x}$ computed from samples of size n from this population will be approximately normal with mean μ (the population mean) and variance σ^2/n (the population variance divided by n) when the sample size n is large.

The central limit theorem allows us to make quite precise probability statements about the population mean by using the sample mean, *whatever the distribution of the population*, because the sample mean follows an approximate normal distribution for large size samples. The obvious question is: When is a sample's size large enough that we can assume the sample mean is normally distributed? In general, when sample size n is greater than or equal to 30, we can assume that the sample mean is approximately normally distributed.[4]

The central limit theorem states that the variance of the distribution of the sample mean is σ^2/n. The positive square root of variance is standard deviation. The standard deviation of a sample statistic is known as the *standard error* of the statistic. The standard error of the sample mean is an important quantity in applying the central limit theorem in practice.

- **Definition of the Standard Error of the Sample Mean.** For sample mean $\bar{x}$ calculated from a sample generated by a population with standard deviation σ, the standard error of the sample mean is given by one of two expressions:

$$\sigma_{\bar{x}} = \frac{\sigma}{\sqrt{n}} \tag{6-1}$$

when we know σ, the population standard deviation, or by

$$s_{\bar{x}} = \frac{s}{\sqrt{n}} \tag{6-2}$$

---

[4] When the underlying population is very nonnormal, a sample size well in excess of 30 may be required for the normal distribution to be a good description of the sampling distribution of the mean.

when we do not know the population standard deviation and need to use the sample standard deviation, s, to estimate it.[5]

In practice, we almost always need to use Equation 6-2. The estimate of s is given by the square root of the sample variance, s^2, calculated as follows:

$$s^2 = \frac{\sum_{i=1}^{n} (x_i - \bar{x})^2}{n - 1}$$

(6-3)

We will soon see how we can use the sample mean and its standard error to make probability statements about the population mean by using the technique of confidence intervals. First, however, we provide a vivid illustration of the force of the central limit theorem.

EXAMPLE 6-3. The Central Limit Theorem.

It is quite remarkable that the sample mean for large sample sizes will be distributed normally regardless of the distribution of the underlying population. To illustrate the central limit theorem in action, we specify in this example a distinctly nonnormal distribution and use it to generate a large number of random samples of size 100. We then calculate the sample mean for each sample. The frequency distribution of the calculated sample means is an approximation of the sampling distribution of the sample mean for that sample size. Does that sampling distribution look like a normal distribution?

Previously, we discussed a telecommunications expert studying the capital expenditure plans of telecom businesses. Suppose that capital expenditures for communications equipment form a continuous uniform random variable with a lower bound equal to $0 and an upper bound equal to $100 [for short, call this a uniform (0, 100) random variable]. The probability function of this continuous uniform random variable has a rather simple shape that is anything but normal. It is a horizontal line with a vertical intercept equal to 1/100. Unlike a normal random variable, for which outcomes close to the mean are most likely, for a uniform random variable, all possible outcomes are equally likely.

To illustrate the power of the central limit theorem, we conduct a Monte Carlo simulation to study the capital expenditure plans of telecom businesses.[6] In this simulation, we collect 200 random samples of the capital expenditures of 100 companies (200 random draws, each consisting of the capital expenditures of 100 companies with $n = 100$). In each simulation trial, 100 values for capital expenditure are

---

[5] We need to note a technical point: When we take a sample of size n from a *finite* population of size N, we apply a shrinkage factor to the estimate of the standard error of the sample mean that is called the *finite population correction factor* (fpc). The fpc is equal to $[(N - n)/(N - 1)]^{1/2}$. Thus, if $N = 100$ and $n = 20$, $[(100 - 20)/(100 - 1)]^{1/2} = 0.808081$. If we have estimated a standard error of, say, 20, according to Equation 6-1 or Equation 6-2, the new estimate is $20 \times 0.808081 = 16.161616$. The fpc applies only when we sample from a finite population without replacement; most practitioners also do not apply the fpc if sample size n is very small relative to N (say, less than 5 percent of N). For more information on the finite population correction factor, see Daniel and Terrell (1995).

[6] Monte Carlo simulation involves the use of a computer to represent the operation of a system subject to risk. An integral part of Monte Carlo simulation is the generation of a large number of random samples from a specified probability distribution or distributions.

generated from the uniform (0, 100) distribution. For each random sample, we then compute the sample mean. We conduct 200 simulation trials in total. Because we have specified the distribution generating the samples, we know that the population mean capital expenditure is equal to ($0 + $100)/2 = $50; the population variance of capital expenditures is equal to $(100 - 0)^2/12 = 833.33$; thus, the standard deviation is $28.87 and the standard error is 2.887.[7]

The results of this Monte Carlo experiment are tabulated in Table 6-2 in the form of a frequency distribution. This distribution is the estimated sampling distribution of the sample mean.

TABLE 6-2   Frequency Distribution: 200 Random Samples of a Uniform (0, 100) Random Variable

Range of Sample Means ($)	Absolute Frequency
42.5 to 44	1
44 to 45.5	6
45.5 to 47	22
47 to 48.5	39
48.5 to 50	41
50 to 51.5	39
51.5 to 53	23
53 to 54.5	12
54.5 to 56	12
56 to 57.5	5

The overall impression is of a bell-shaped distribution centered close to the population mean of 50. The most frequent, or modal, range, with 41 observations, is 48.5 to 50. The overall average of the sample means is $49.92, with a standard error equal to $2.80. The calculated standard error is close to the value of $28.87/\sqrt{100} = 2.887$ given by the central limit theorem. The discrepancy between calculated and expected values of the mean and standard deviation under the central limit theorem is a result of random chance (sampling error).

In summary, although the distribution of the underlying population is very nonnormal, the simulation has shown that the estimated sampling distribution of the sample mean is well described by a normal distribution, with mean and standard error consistent with the values predicted by the central limit theorem.

To summarize, according to the central limit theorem, when we sample from any distribution, the distribution of the sample mean will have the following properties as long as our sample size is large:

---

[7] If a is the lower limit of a uniform random variable and b is the upper limit, then the random variable's mean is given by $(a + b)/2$ and its variance is given by $(b - a)^2/12$. The chapter on common probability distributions fully describes continuous uniform random variables.

- The distribution of sample mean $\bar{x}$ will be approximately normal.
- The mean of the distribution of $\bar{x}$ will be equal to the mean of the population from which the samples are drawn.
- The variance of the distribution of $\bar{x}$ will be equal to the variance of the population divided by the sample size.

With the central limit theorem in hand, we next discuss the concepts and tools related to estimating the population parameters, with a special focus on the population mean. We focus on the mean because in investment analysis, the mean return of a distribution is probably the most important piece of information to analysts and portfolio managers. The means of expected returns on asset classes, for example, are major inputs in asset allocation decisions.

4 POINT AND INTERVAL ESTIMATES OF THE POPULATION MEAN

Whether we are concerned with the mean or another parameter, we may ask two (related) types of questions. One type of question relates to a topic in statistical inference known as *hypothesis testing*. Hypothesis testing addresses the question: Is the value of this parameter (say, a population mean) equal to some specific value (0, for example)? In this process, we have a hunch or a hypothesis concerning the value of a parameter, and we seek to determine whether the evidence from a sample supports or does not support that hypothesis. We discuss hypothesis testing in detail in the chapter on hypothesis testing.

The second type of question comes under the branch of statistical inference known as *estimation*. Estimation seeks an answer to the question: What is this parameter's (for example, the population mean's) value? In contrast to hypothesis testing, in estimating, we do not start with a hypothesis about the value of the parameter and seek to test it. Rather, we try to make the best use of the information in a sample to form one of several types of estimates of the parameter's value. With estimation, we are interested in arriving at a rule for best calculating a single number to estimate the unknown population parameter (a *point estimate*). Together with calculating a point estimate, we may also be interested in calculating a range of values that brackets the unknown population parameter with some specified level of probability (a *confidence interval*). The balance of the discussion in this section concerns estimation. In the next sections, we turn to point estimates of parameters and, then, the formulation of confidence intervals for the population mean.

4.1 POINT ESTIMATORS

An important concept introduced in this chapter is that sample statistics are random variables. The one sample statistic that arises frequently in investment analysis and that we have stressed thus far is the sample mean. The formula for the sample mean tells us to add all the observations in the sample and then divide by the size of the sample. The formulas that we use to compute the sample mean and all the other sample statistics are examples of estimation formulas or **estimators.** The particular value that we calculate from sample observations using an estimator is called an **estimate.** This distinction is subtle but important. The single estimate of the population parameter calculated as a sample mean is called a **point estimate** of the mean. As Example 6-3 illustrated, the formula for the sample mean can and will yield different results in repeated samples as different samples are drawn from the population.

In many applications, we have a choice among a number of possible estimators for estimating a given parameter. How do we make our choice? We often select estimators because they have one or more desirable statistical properties. Following is a brief description of three desirable properties of estimators: unbiasedness (lack of bias), efficiency, and consistency.[8]

- **Definition of Unbiasedness.** An unbiased estimator is an estimator whose expected value (the mean of its sampling distribution) equals the parameter it is intended to estimate.

For example, the expected value of the sample mean, $\bar{x}$, equals μ, the population mean, so we say that the sample mean is an unbiased estimator (of the population mean). The sample variance, s^2, which is calculated using a divisor of $n - 1$ (Equation 6-3), is an unbiased estimator of the population variance, σ^2. If we were to calculate the sample variance using a divisor of n, the estimator would be biased: Its expected value would be smaller than the population variance. We would say that sample variance calculated with a divisor of n is a biased estimator of the population variance.

Whenever one unbiased estimator of a parameter can be found, we can usually find a large number of other unbiased estimators. How do we choose among alternative unbiased estimators? The criterion of efficiency provides a way to make a selection from among unbiased estimators of a parameter.

- **Definition of Efficiency.** An unbiased estimator is efficient if no other unbiased estimator of the same parameter has a sampling distribution with smaller variance.

In repeated samples, we expect the estimates from an efficient estimator to be more tightly grouped around the mean than estimates from other unbiased estimators. Efficiency is an important property of an estimator.[9] Sample mean $\bar{x}$ is an efficient estimator of the population mean; sample variance s^2 is an efficient estimator of σ^2.

Recall that a statistic's sampling distribution is defined for a given sample size. Different sample sizes define different sampling distributions. For example, the variance of sampling distribution of the sample mean is smaller for larger sample sizes. The properties of unbiasedness and efficiency are properties of an estimator's sampling distribution that hold for any size sample. An unbiased estimator is unbiased equally in a sample of size 10 and in a sample of size 1,000. In some problems, however, we cannot find estimators that have such desirable properties as unbiasedness in small samples.[10] In this case, statisticians may justify the choice of an estimator based on the properties of the estimator's sampling distribution in extremely large samples, the estimator's so-called asymptotic properties. Among such properties, the most important is consistency.

- **Definition of Consistency.** A consistent estimator is an estimator for which the probability of accurate estimates (estimates close to the value of the population parameter) increases as sample size increases.

Somewhat more technically, we can define a consistent estimator as an estimator whose sampling distribution becomes concentrated on the value of the parameter it is intended to estimate as the sample size approaches infinity. The sample mean, in addition to being an efficient estimator, is also a consistent estimator of the population mean: As sample size n

---

[8] See Daniel and Terrell (1995) or Greene (1999) for a thorough treatment of the properties of estimators.

[9] An efficient estimator is sometimes referred to as the *best unbiased estimator.*

[10] Such problems frequently arise in regression and time-series analyses, which we discuss in later chapters.

goes to infinity, its standard error, $\sigma/\sqrt{n}$, goes to 0 and its sampling distribution becomes concentrated right over the value of population mean μ. To summarize, we can think of a consistent estimator as one that tends to produce more and more accurate estimates as we increase sample size.

4.2 CONFIDENCE INTERVALS FOR THE POPULATION MEAN

When we need a single number as an estimate of a population parameter, we make use of a point estimate. However, because of sampling error, the point estimate is not likely to be equal to the population parameter in any given sample. Often, a more useful approach than finding a point estimate is to find a range of values that we expect to bracket the parameter with a specified level of probability—an interval estimate of the parameter. A confidence interval fulfills this role.

- **Definition of Confidence Interval.** A confidence interval is an interval for which one can assert with a given probability $1 - \alpha$, called the **degree of confidence,** that it will contain the parameter it is intended to estimate. This interval is often referred to as the $(1 - \alpha)\%$ confidence interval for the parameter.

The end points of a confidence limit are referred to as the lower and upper *confidence limits*. In this chapter, we are concerned only with two-sided confidence intervals—confidence intervals for which we calculate both lower and upper limits.[11]
Confidence intervals are frequently given either a *probabilistic interpretation* or a *practical interpretation*. In the probabilistic interpretation, we interpret a 95 percent confidence interval for the population mean as follows. In repeated sampling, 95 percent of such confidence intervals will, in the long run, include or bracket the population mean. For example, suppose we sample from the population 1,000 times, and based on each sample, we construct a 95 percent confidence interval for each mean. Because of random chance, these confidence intervals will vary from each other, but we expect 95 percent, or 950, of these confidence intervals to include the unknown value of the population mean. In practice, we generally do not carry out such repeated sampling. Thus, in the practical interpretation, we assert that we are 95 percent confident that a single 95 percent confidence interval contains the population mean. We are justified in making this statement because we know that 95 percent of all possible confidence intervals constructed in the same manner will contain the population mean. The confidence intervals that we discuss in this chapter have structures similar to the following basic structure.

- **Construction of Confidence Intervals.** A $(1 - \alpha)\%$ confidence interval for a parameter has the following structure:

$$\text{Point estimate} \pm \text{Reliability factor} \times \text{Standard error}$$

where

Point estimate = a point estimate of the parameter (a value of a sample statistic)

Reliability factor = a number based on the assumed distribution of the point estimate and the degree of confidence $(1 - \alpha)$ for the confidence interval

---

[11] It is also possible to define one-sided confidence intervals, where one limit of the confidence interval is a constant or infinite.

Standard error = the standard error of the sample statistic providing the point estimate[12]

The most basic confidence interval for the population mean arises when we are sampling from a normal distribution with known variance. The reliability factor in this case is based on the standard normal distribution, a normal distribution with a mean of 0 and a variance of 1. A standard normal random variable is conventionally denoted by Z. The notation z_α denotes the point of the standard normal distribution such that α of the probability remains in the right tail. For example, for $z_{0.05} = 1.645$, exactly 0.05 or 5 percent of the possible values of a standard normal random variable are larger than 1.645.

For example, suppose we want to construct a 95 percent confidence interval for the population mean and, for this purpose, we have taken a sample of size 100 from a normally distributed population with known variance of $\sigma^2 = 400$ (so, $\sigma = 20$). We calculate a sample mean of $\bar{x} = 25$. Our point estimate of the population mean is, therefore, 25. If we move 1.96 standard deviations above the mean of a normal distribution, 0.025 or 2.5 percent of the probability remains in the right tail; by symmetry of the normal distribution, if we move 1.96 standard deviations below the mean, 0.025 or 2.5 percent of the probability remains in the left tail. In total, 0.05 or 5 percent of the probability is in the two tails and 0.95 or 95 percent is in-between. So, $z_{0.025} = 1.96$ is the reliability factor for this 95 percent confidence interval. Note the relationship $(1 - \alpha)\%$ for the confidence interval and the $z_{\alpha/2}$ for the reliability factor. The standard error of the sample mean, given by Equation 6-1, is $\sigma_{\bar{x}} = 20/\sqrt{100} = 2$. The confidence interval, therefore, has a lower limit of $\bar{x} - 1.96 \times \sigma_{\bar{x}} = 25 - 1.96 \times 2 = 25 - 3.92 = 21.08$. The upper limit of the confidence interval is $\bar{x} + 1.96 \times \sigma_{\bar{x}} = 25 + 1.96 \times 2 = 25 + 3.92 = 28.92$. The 95 percent confidence interval for the population mean spans 21.08 to 28.92.

- **Confidence Intervals for the Population Mean (Normally Distributed Population with Known Variance).** A $(1 - \alpha)\%$ confidence interval for population mean μ when we are sampling from a normal distribution with known variance σ^2 is given by

$$\bar{x} \pm z_{\alpha/2} \frac{\sigma}{\sqrt{n}} \tag{6-4}$$

The reliability factors for the most frequently used confidence intervals are as follows.

- **Reliability Factors for Confidence Intervals Based on the Standard Normal Distribution.** We use the following reliability factors when we construct confidence intervals based on the standard normal distribution:
  - 90 percent confidence intervals: Use $z_{0.05} = 1.645$.
  - 95 percent confidence intervals: Use $z_{0.025} = 1.96$.
  - 99 percent confidence intervals: Use $z_{0.005} = 2.575$.

These reliability factors highlight an important fact about all confidence intervals. As we increase the degree of confidence, the confidence interval becomes wider and gives us less

---

[12] The quantity (Reliability factor) × (Standard error) is sometimes called the *precision of the estimator;* larger values of the product imply lower precision. This term arises particularly in discussions about selecting the sample size; the larger the sample size, the greater the precision with which we can estimate the population parameter.

precise information about the quantity we want to estimate. "The surer we want to be, the less we have to be sure of."[13]

In practice, assuming that the sampling distribution of the sample mean is at least approximately normal is frequently reasonable, either because the underlying distribution is approximately normal or because we have a large sample and the central limit theorem applies. However, rarely do we know the population variance in practice. When the population variance is unknown—but the sample mean is at least approximately normally distributed—we have two acceptable ways to calculate the confidence interval for the population mean. We will shortly discuss the more conservative approach, which is based on Student's *t*-distribution (the *t*-distribution, for short).[14] In the investments literature, it is the most frequently used approach in both estimation and hypothesis tests concerning the mean when the population variance is not known, whether sample size is small or large.

A second approach to confidence intervals for the population mean, based on the standard normal distribution, is the *z*-alternative. It can be used only when sample size is large. (In general, a sample size of 30 or larger may be considered large.) In contrast to the confidence interval given in Equation 6-4, this confidence interval uses the sample standard deviation, *s*, in computing the standard error of the sample mean (Equation 6-2).

- **Confidence Intervals for the Population Mean—The *z*-Alternative (Large Sample, Population Variance Unknown).** A $(1 - \alpha)\%$ confidence interval for population mean μ when sampling from any distribution with unknown variance and when sample size is large is given by

$$\bar{x} \pm z_{\alpha/2} \frac{s}{\sqrt{n}} \tag{6-5}$$

Because this type of confidence interval is encountered quite often, we illustrate its calculation in Example 6-4.

EXAMPLE 6-4.   Confidence Interval for the Population Mean of Sharpe Ratios—*z*-Statistic.

Suppose an investment advisor takes a random sample of stock mutual funds and calculates the average Sharpe ratio (excess return/standard deviation). The sample size is 100, and the average Sharpe ratio 0.45. The sample has a standard deviation of 0.30.

Calculate and interpret the 90 percent confidence interval for the population mean by using a reliability factor based on the standard normal distribution.

The reliability factor for a 90 percent confidence interval, as given earlier, is $z_{0.05} = 1.645$. The confidence interval will be

$$\bar{x} \pm z_{0.025} \frac{s}{\sqrt{n}} = 0.45 \pm 1.645 \frac{0.30}{\sqrt{100}} = 0.45 \pm 1.645 \times 0.03 = 0.45 \pm 0.05$$

---

[13] Freund and Williams (1977), p. 266.

[14] The distribution of the statistic *t* is called Student's *t*-distribution after the pen name "Student" used by W. S. Gosset, who published his work in 1908.

The confidence interval spans 0.4 to 0.5. The analyst can be confident at the 90 percent level that the interval includes the population mean.

In this example, the analyst makes no specific assumption about the probability distribution describing the population. Rather, the analyst relies on the central limit theorem to produce an approximate normal distribution for the sample mean.

As Example 6-4 shows, even if we are unsure of the underlying population distribution, we can still construct confidence intervals for the population mean as long as the sample size is large because we can apply the central limit theorem.

We now turn to the conservative alternative, using the t-distribution, for constructing confidence intervals for the population mean when the population variance is not known. For confidence intervals based on samples from normally distributed populations with unknown variance, the theoretically correct reliability factor is based on the t-distribution. When sample size is small and population variance is not known (and the population is at least approximately normally distributed), the use of a reliability factor based on the t-distribution is essential. The use of a t reliability factor is also appropriate, however, when the population variance is unknown but we have a large sample and can rely on the central limit theorem to ensure approximate normality of the distribution of the sample mean. In this large sample case, the t-distribution provides more conservative (wider) confidence intervals. In Example 6-4, for instance, the reliability factor was 1.645; using the t-distribution, the reliability factor would be about 1.66, resulting in a slightly wider interval.

The t-distribution is a symmetrical probability distribution defined by a single parameter known as **degrees of freedom** (df). Each value for the number of degrees of freedom defines one distribution in this family of distributions. We will shortly compare t-distributions with the standard normal distribution, but first we need to understand the concept of degrees of freedom. We can do so by examining the calculation of the sample variance.

Equation 6-3 gives the unbiased estimator of the sample variance that we use. The term in the denominator, $n - 1$, which is the sample size minus 1, is the number of degrees of freedom in estimating the population variance when using Equation 6-3. We also use $n - 1$ as the number of degrees of freedom for determining reliability factors based on the t-distribution. The term *degrees of freedom* is used because in a random sample, we assume that observations are selected independently of each other. The numerator of the sample variance, however, uses the sample mean, which is itself calculated from the same sample. How does this added calculation affect the number of observations that are collected independently for the sample variance formula? For example, with a sample of size 10 and a mean of 10 percent, you can freely select only 9 observations. Regardless of the 9 observations selected, you can always find the value for the 10th observation that gives you a mean equal to 10 percent. From the standpoint of the sample variance formula, then, there are 9 degrees of freedom. In other words, given that you must first compute the sample mean from the total of n independent observations, only $n - 1$ observations can be chosen independently for the calculation of the sample variance. The concept of degrees of freedom comes up frequently in statistics, and you will see it often in later chapters.

Suppose we sample from a normal distribution. The ratio $z = (\bar{x} - \mu)/\sigma/\sqrt{n}$ is distributed normally with a mean of 0 and standard deviation of 1; however, the ratio $t = (\bar{x} - \mu)/s/\sqrt{n}$ follows the t-distribution with a mean of 0 and $n - 1$ degrees of freedom. The ratio represented by t is not normal because t is the ratio of two random variables, the sample mean and standard deviation. The definition of the standard normal random variable involves only one random variable, $\bar{x}$. However, as degrees of freedom increase, the *t*-distribution approaches the standard normal distribution. Figure 6-1 shows the standard normal distribution and two *t*-distributions, one with df = 2 and one with df = 8.

FIGURE 6-1   Student's *t*-Distribution Versus the Standard Normal

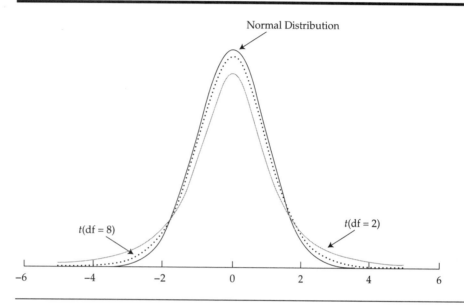

Of the three distributions, the standard normal distribution is clearly the most peaked; it has tails that approach zero faster than the tails of the two *t*-distributions. The *t*-distribution is also symmetrically distributed around its mean value of zero, just like the normal distribution. The *t*-distribution with df = 2 is the least peaked of the three distributions, and its tails lie above the tails for the normal and *t* with df = 8. The *t*-distribution with df = 8 has an intermediate degree of peakedness, and its tails lie above the tails for the normal but below those for *t* with df = 2. As the degrees of freedom increase, the *t*-distribution approaches the standard normal. The *t*-distribution with df = 8 is closer to the standard normal than the *t*-distribution with df = 2.

The standard normal distribution appears to approach 0 at $\sigma = \pm 4$ but both *t*-distributions continue to show some area under each curve at those points. The *t*-distributions have fatter tails, but the tails of the *t*-distribution with df = 8 more closely resemble the normal's tails. As the degrees of freedom increase, the tails of the *t*-distribution become less fat.

Frequently referred to values for the *t*-distribution are presented in tables at the end of the book. For each degree of freedom, five values are given: $t_{0.10}$, $t_{0.05}$, $t_{0.025}$, $t_{0.01}$, and $t_{0.005}$. The values for $t_{0.10}$, $t_{0.05}$, $t_{0.025}$, $t_{0.01}$, and $t_{0.005}$ are such that, respectively, 0.10, 0.05, 0.025, 0.01, and 0.005 of the probability remains in the right tail, for the specified number of degrees of freedom.[15] For example, for df = 30, $t_{0.10} = 1.310$, $t_{0.05} = 1.697$, $t_{0.025} = 2.042$, $t_{0.01} = 2.457$, and $t_{0.005} = 2.750$.

We now give the form of confidence intervals for the population mean using the *t*-distribution.

---

[15] The values $t_{0.10}$, $t_{0.05}$, $t_{0.025}$, $t_{0.01}$, and $t_{0.005}$ are also referred to as *one-sided critical values of t* at the 0.10, 0.05, 0.025, 0.01, and 0.005 significance levels, for the specified number of degrees of freedom.

- **Confidence Intervals for the Population Mean (Population Variance Unknown)—*t*-Distribution.** If we are sampling from a population with unknown variance and either of the conditions below holds
  - the sample is large or
  - the sample is small but the population is normally distributed, or approximately normally distributed,

  then a $(1 - \alpha)\%$ confidence interval for the population mean μ is given by

$$\bar{x} \pm t_{\alpha/2} \frac{s}{\sqrt{n}} \tag{6-6}$$

  where the number of degrees of freedom for $t_{\alpha/2}$ is $n - 1$ and n is the sample size.

EXAMPLE 6-5.   An Investment Manager Estimates Net Client Inflows.

A money manager wants to obtain a 95 percent confidence interval for fund inflows and outflows over the next six months for his existing clients. The money manager begins by calling a random sample of 10 clients and enquiring about their planned additions to and withdrawals from the fund. The manager computes the change in cash flow for each client sampled as a percentage change in total funds placed with the manager. A positive percentage change indicates a net cash inflow to the client's account, and a negative percentage change indicates a net cash outflow from the client's account. The manager weights each response by the relative size of the account within the sample and then computes a weighted average.

As a result of this process, the money manager computes a weighted average of 5.5 percent. Thus, a point estimate is that the total amount of funds under management will increase by 5.5 percent in the next six months. The standard deviation of the observations in the sample is 10 percent. A histogram of past data looks fairly close to normal, so the manager assumes the population is normal.

Calculate a 95 percent confidence interval for the population mean and interpret your findings.

Because the population is unknown and the sample size is small, the manager must use the *t*-statistic in Equation 6-6 to calculate the confidence interval. Based on the sample size of 10, df $= n - 1 = 10 - 1 = 9$. For a 95 percent confidence interval, he needs to use the value of $t_{0.025}$ for df $= 9$. According to the tables in the back of the book, this value is 2.262. Thus, a 95 percent confidence interval for the population mean is

$$\bar{x} \pm t_{0.025} \frac{s}{\sqrt{n}} = 5.5\% \pm 2.262 \frac{10\%}{\sqrt{10}}$$
$$= 5.5\% \pm 2.262 \times 3.16$$
$$= 5.5\% \pm 7.15\%$$

The confidence interval for the population mean spans -1.65 percent to $+12.65$ percent.[16] The manager can be confident at the 95 percent level that this range includes the population mean.

---

[16] We assumed in this example that sample size is sufficiently small compared with the size of the client base that we can disregard the finite population correction factor (mentioned in an earlier footnote).

The manager is frustrated by the lack of precision in his survey results. He decides to see what the confidence interval would look like if he had used a sample size of 20 or 30 and found the same average and standard deviation. He can then decide whether to change the sample size the next time he does the survey.

1. Using the sample mean of 5.5 percent and standard deviation of 10 percent, compute the confidence interval for sample sizes of 20 and 30. For the sample size of 30, use Equation 6-6.
2. Interpret your results.

The calculations for the three sample sizes are presented in Table 6-3. The width of the confidence interval decreases as we increase the sample size. This decrease is a function of the standard error becoming smaller as n increases. The reliability factor also becomes smaller as the df increases. The last column of Table 6-3 shows the relative size of the range of confidence intervals based on $n = 10$ to be 100 percent. Using a sample size of 20 reduces the confidence interval's width to 65.4 percent of the interval width for a sample size of 10. Using a sample size of 30 cuts the width of the interval almost in half.

TABLE 6-3   The 95 Percent Confidence Interval for Three Sample Sizes

Distribution	95% Confidence Interval	Lower Bound	Upper Bound	Range Size
$t(n = 10)$	$5.5\% \pm 2.262 \times 3.16$	−1.65%	12.65%	100.0%
$t(n = 20)$	$5.5\% \pm 2.093 \times 2.23$	0.82	10.18	65.4
$t(n = 30)$	$5.5\% \pm 2.045 \times 1.83$	1.77	9.23	52.2

The money manager decides to use a sample of 30 for the next survey in order to obtain more precise results.[17]

In Table 6-4, we summarize the various reliability factors that we have used.

The quality of inferences depends on the quality of the data and the quality of the sampling plan used. For financial analysts, the challenge in making inferences is increased because financial data pose special problems. These issues are the subject of the final section of this chapter.

---

[17] A formula exists for determining the sample size needed to obtain a desired width for a confidence interval. Define E = (Reliability factor) $\times$ (Standard error). The smaller E is, the smaller the width of the confidence interval needed, because $E \times 2$ is the confidence interval's width. Sample size n to obtain a desired value of E for a given degree of confidence $(1 - \alpha)$ is given by $n = [t_{\alpha/2} \times s/E]^2$.

TABLE 6-4   Basis of Computing Reliability Factors

Sampling from:	Statistic for Small Sample Size	Statistic for Large Sample Size
Normal distribution with known variance	z	z
Normal distribution with unknown variance	t	t^*
Nonnormal distribution with known variance	not available	z
Nonnormal distribution with unknown variance	not available	t^*

*Use of z also acceptable.

5   MORE ON SAMPLING

To provide more perspective on sampling in investments, we next discuss five issues related to the use of financial data: data-snooping/data-mining bias, sample selection bias, look-ahead bias, time-period bias, and the selection of the length of the sample period. All of these issues are important for point and interval estimation and hypothesis testing. As we will see, if the sample is biased in any way, then point and interval estimates and any other conclusions that we draw from the sample will be in error.

5.1   DATA-SNOOPING/DATA-MINING BIAS

New research into the behavior of financial asset prices is often conditioned on past research. For instance, you might read about how a growth or value investment strategy produces superior investment results, or you might read about how high-yielding Dow Jones Industrial Average (DJIA) stocks have performed. You then decide to conduct a study of growth versus value investing or high-yielding DJIA stocks based on prior research findings. You might even use the same or related historical data used in previous research. This strategy is subject to data-snooping bias.

Data-snooping bias is the bias in the inference you draw as a result of prying into the empirical results of others to guide your own analysis. The result of the prying is that what may be chance patterns in the data can appear to be very significant. Data snooping can be a collusive activity of chasing patterns that may be illusory as several analysts study the same pattern in the same data. The antidote is to examine new data. Unfortunately, the data-snooping bias is difficult to avoid because investment analysis relies on historical or hypothesized data rather than experiments, and some finance research has shown that the magnitude of the bias can be significant.[18] All we can do in this chapter is to warn you about this type of bias and caution against interpreting findings and drawing conclusions too strongly that are based solely on previous research.

Data snooping can easily lead investment analysts to a related problem: data mining. **Data mining** is the practice of finding forecasting models by extensive searching through databases for patterns or trading rules (that is, repeatedly "drilling" in the same data until you find something). For example, based on past research about high-yielding DJIA stocks (data snooping), you might test hundreds of variations of the DJIA dividend strategy. After trying a number of different variations, you find, not surprisingly, some trading rule that performs extremely well historically. If the only result that you report is the successful one,

---

[18] Campbell, Lo, and MacKinlay (1990) investigated the magnitude of the bias on tests of the capital asset pricing model.

it is subject to data-mining bias. Data-mining problems arise when a researcher does not report how many different models were tested before finally reporting the successful one. McQueen and Thorley (1999) nicely illustrated this type of data-mining problem.

McQueen and Thorley investigated the popular *Motley Fool's* "Foolish Four" portfolio, which is a slightly revised version of the Dow Dividend Strategy.[19] From 1973 to 1993, the Foolish Four portfolio had an average annual return of 25 percent. The important question is whether these results can persist in the future. McQueen and Thorley took the Foolish Four portfolio one step further: They mined the data to create a "Fractured Four" portfolio. All of the Foolish Four stocks did well in even years but not odd years, so the strategy of the Fractured Four portfolio was to hold the Foolish Four stocks with equal weights in even years and hold only the second-to-lowest-priced stock in odd years. The Fractured Four portfolio earned an average annual return of almost 35 percent from 1973 to 1996 and beat the Foolish Four by almost 8 percentage points. The Fractured Four portfolio, however, is obviously the product of data mining.

McQueen and Thorley discussed several signs that can warn analysts about the potential existence of data mining:

- *Too Much Digging/Too Little Confidence.* The best warning sign to look for is the number of variables used by the researcher. The number of variables actually used might not always be reported, but we should always look closely for hints that the researcher searched over many variables. The use of terms such as "we noted" or "we noticed" should raise suspicions that the researchers were searching through many unreported variables.

- *No Story/No Future.* Research based on slight changes to a trading rule that has worked in the past is another sign warning of possible data mining. Profitable trading strategies should have a plausible theory about why they work. For instance, a value style investing strategy might be based on the theory that certain stocks fall out of favor because of overreaction to bad news. The Fractured Four portfolio model, in contrast, had no coherent explanation for doing one thing in even years and another in odd years.

McQueen and Thorley aptly recommended an antidote to data mining: test the trading rule on out-of-sample data. Using the rule on a set of data other than the set used to create the trading rule should reveal whether the findings are valid out-of-sample or simply the result of data mining. Of course, some published trading strategies might not easily lend themselves to out-of-sample testing because of limited data.

Investment analysts must be vigilant about data snooping and data mining.

5.2 SAMPLE SELECTION BIAS

When researchers look into questions of interest to analysts or portfolio managers, they may exclude certain stocks, bonds, portfolios, or time periods from the analysis for various reasons—perhaps because of data availability. When data availability leads to certain assets being excluded from the analysis, we call the resulting problem **sample selection bias.** For example, you might sample from a database that tracks only companies that are currently in existence. Many mutual fund databases, for instance, provide historical information about only those funds that are currently in existence. Databases that report histor-

---

[19] At the time of McQueen and Thorley's research, the Foolish Four strategy was as follows: At the beginning of each year, the Foolish Four portfolio purchases a 4-stock portfolio from the 5 lowest-priced stocks of the 10 highest-yielding DJIA stocks. The lowest-priced stock of the 5 is excluded, and 40 percent is invested in the second-to-lowest-priced stock, with 20 percent weights in the remaining 3.

ical balance sheet and income statement information suffer from the same sort of bias as the mutual fund databases; funds or companies that are no longer in business do not appear in these databases. So, a study that uses these types of databases suffers from a type of sample selection bias known as **survivorship bias.**

Dimson, Marsh, and Staunton (2000) raised the issue of survivorship bias in international indexes:

> An issue that has achieved prominence is the impact of market survival on estimated long-run returns. Assume that each asset category offers a fair reward for the full range of risky outcomes that may be experienced. Outcomes include not only disappointing performance, but also total loss of value through nationalisation, confiscation, hyperinflation and market failure. By measuring the performance of markets that survive over long intervals, we draw inferences that are conditioned on survival. Yet, as pointed out by Brown, Goetzmann and Ross (1995) and others, one cannot determine in advance which markets will survive and which will perish. (pp. 9–10)

Survivorship bias is sometimes encountered when we use both stock price and accounting data. For example, many studies in finance have used the ratio of a company's market price to book equity per share (i.e., the price-to-book ratio) and found that the price-to-book ratio is inversely related to a company's returns (see Fama and French 1992, 1993). The price-to-book ratio is also used to create many popular value and growth indexes. If the database that we use to collect accounting data excludes failing companies, however, a survivorship bias might result. Kothari, Shanken, and Sloan (1995) investigated just this question and argued that failing stocks would be expected to have low returns and low price-to-book ratios. If we exclude failing stocks, then those stocks with low price-to-book ratios that are included will have returns that are higher on average than if all stocks with low price-to-book ratios were included. Kothari, Shanken, and Sloan suggested that this bias is responsible for the previous findings of an inverse relationship between average return and price-to-book ratio. The only advice we can offer at this point is to be aware of any biases potentially inherent in a sample. Clearly, sample selection biases can cloud the results of any study.

A sample can also be biased because of the removal (or delisting) of a company's stock from an exchange.[20] For example, the Center for Research in Security Prices (CRSP) at the University of Chicago is a major provider of return data used in academic research. When a delisting occurs, CRSP attempts to collect returns for the delisted company, but many times, they cannot collect these returns because of the difficulty involved; CRSP must simply list them as missing. A recent study in the *Journal of Finance* by Shumay and Warther (1999) documented the bias caused by delisting for CRSP Nasdaq return data. The authors showed that delistings associated with poor company performance (e.g., bankruptcy) are missed more often than delistings associated with good or neutral company performance (e.g., merger or moving to another exchange). In addition, delistings occur more frequently for small companies.

5.3 LOOK-AHEAD BIAS

A test design is subject to **look-ahead bias** if it uses information that was not available on the test date. For example, tests of trading rules that use stock market returns and accounting balance sheet data must account for look-ahead bias. In such tests, the book value per share is commonly used to construct the price-to-book variable. Although the market price of a stock is available for all market participants at the same point in time, fiscal year-end book equity per share might not become publicly available until sometime in the following quarter.

---

[20] Delistings occur for a variety of reasons: merger, bankruptcy, liquidation, or migration to another exchange.

5.4 TIME-PERIOD BIAS

A test design is subject to **time-period bias** if it is based on a time period that may make the results time-period specific. A short time series is likely to give period-specific results that may not reflect a longer period. A long time series may give a more accurate picture of true investment performance; its disadvantage lies in the potential for a structural change occurring during the time frame that would result in two different return distributions. In this situation, the distribution that would reflect conditions before the change will be different from the distribution that would describe conditions after the change.

EXAMPLE 6-6.   Biases in Investment Research.[21]

An analyst is reviewing the empirical evidence on historical U.S. equity returns. She finds that value stocks (i.e., those with low price-to-book ratios) outperformed growth stocks (i.e., those with high price-to-book ratios) in some recent time periods. After reviewing the U.S. market, the analyst wonders whether value stocks might be attractive in the United Kingdom. She investigates the performance of value and growth stocks in the U.K. market from January 1987 to December 2000. To conduct this research, the analyst does the following:

- obtains the current composition of the Financial Times Stock Exchange (FTSE) All Share Index, which is a market-capitalization-weighted index;
- eliminates the few companies that do not have December fiscal year-ends;
- uses year-end book values and market prices to rank the remaining universe of companies by price-to-book ratios (P/Bs) at the end of the year;
- based on these rankings, divides the universe into 10 portfolios, each of which contains an equal number of stocks;
- calculates the equal-weighted return of each portfolio and the return for the FTSE All Share Index for the 12 months following the date each ranking was made; and
- subtracts the FTSE returns from each portfolio's returns to derive excess returns for each portfolio.

Describe and discuss each of the following biases introduced by Brown's research design:

- survivorship bias,
- look-ahead bias, and
- time-period bias.

Survivorship bias.   A test design is subject to survivorship bias if it fails to account for companies that have gone bankrupt, merged, or have otherwise departed the database. In this example, the analyst used the current list of FTSE stocks rather than the actual list of stocks that existed at the start of each year. To the extent that the computation of returns excluded companies removed from the index, the performance of the portfolios with the lowest P/B is subject to survivorship bias and may be overstated. At some time during the testing period, those companies not currently in existence were eliminated from testing, and they would probably have been the ones with low prices (and low P/Bs) and poor returns.

---

[21] This example is adapted from the 1998 CFA® Level III examination.

Look-ahead bias.   A test design is subject to look-ahead bias if it uses information unavailable on the test date. In this example, the analyst conducted the test under the assumption that the necessary accounting information was available at the end of the fiscal year. For example, the analyst assumed that book value per share for fiscal 1987 was available on December 31, 1987. Because this information is not released for several months after the close of a fiscal year, the test may have contained look-ahead bias. This bias would make a strategy based on the information appear successful, but it assumes perfect forecasting ability.

Time-period bias.   A test design is subject to time-period bias if it is based on a time period that may make the results time-period specific. Although the test covered a period extending more than 10 years, that period may be too short for testing an anomaly. Ideally, an analyst should test market anomalies over several business cycles to ensure that results are not period specific. This bias can favor a proposed strategy if the time period chosen was favorable to the strategy.

6   SUMMARY

Investment decisions are often made on the basis of the mean and variance of asset returns. In this chapter, we covered the issues surrounding sampling and estimation of the population mean.

- To draw valid inferences from a sample, the sample should be random.
- Two types of sampling were presented. In simple random sampling, each observation has an equal chance of being selected. In stratified random sampling, the population is subdivided into subpopulations, called strata or cells, based on one or more classification criteria; simple random samples are then drawn from each stratum.
- Stratified random sampling ensures that population subdivisions of interest are represented in the sample. Stratified random sampling also produces more precise parameter estimates than simple random sampling.
- Financial analysts use two types of data: times series and cross-sectional. Time-series data are a collection of observations at equally spaced intervals of time. Cross-sectional data are observations that represent individuals, groups, geographical regions, or companies at a single point in time.
- Random sampling makes the assumption that members of the sample come from the same population. With financial data, we must take care that this assumption holds; otherwise, the conclusions we reach will not be valid.
- The central limit theorem states that for large sample sizes, for any underlying distribution for a random variable, the sampling distribution of the sample mean for that variable will be approximately normal, with mean equal to the population mean for that random variable and variance equal to the population variance of the variable divided by sample size.
- Based on the central limit theorem, when the sample size is large, we can compute confidence intervals for the population mean based on the normal distribution regardless of the underlying population from which we are sampling.
- In general, a sample size of 30 or more can be considered large.
- An estimator is a formula for estimating a parameter. An estimate is a particular value that we calculate from a sample by using an estimator.

- Because an estimator or statistic is a random variable, it is described by some probability distribution. We refer to the distribution of an estimator as its sampling distribution. The standard deviation of the sampling distribution of the sample mean is called the standard error of the sample mean.

- The desirable properties of an estimator are unbiasedness (the expected value of the estimate equals the population parameter), efficiency (the estimator has the smallest variance), and consistency (the estimator gets better as we use more data).

- The two types of estimates of a parameter are point estimates and interval estimates.

- A point estimate is a single number that we use to estimate a parameter.

- An interval estimate is a range of values that brackets the population parameter with some probability. We discussed two-sided confidence intervals.

- A confidence interval is an interval for which we can assert with a given probability $1 - \alpha$, called the degree of confidence, that it will contain the parameter it is intended to estimate. It is often referred to as the $(1 - \alpha)\%$ confidence interval for the parameter.

- A $(1 - \alpha)\%$ confidence interval for a parameter has the following structure: Point estimate $\pm$ Reliability factor $\times$ Standard error, where the reliability factor is a number based on the assumed distribution of the point estimate and the degree of confidence $(1 - \alpha)$ for the confidence interval and where standard error is the standard error of the sample statistic providing the point estimate.

- A $(1 - \alpha)\%$ confidence interval for population mean μ when sampling from a normal distribution with known variance σ^2 is given by $\bar{x} \pm z_{\alpha/2}(\sigma/\sqrt{n})$, where $z_{\alpha/2}$ is the point of the standard normal distribution such that $\alpha/2$ remains in the right tail.

- Student's t-distribution is a family of symmetrical distributions defined by a single parameter, degrees of freedom.

- A random sample of size n is said to have $n - 1$ degrees of freedom for estimating the population variance, in the sense that there are only $n - 1$ independent deviations from the mean on which to base the estimate.

- The degrees of freedom number for use with the t-distribution is also $n - 1$.

- The t-distribution has fatter tails than the standard normal distribution but converges to the standard normal distribution as degrees of freedom go to infinity.

- A $(1 - \alpha)\%$ confidence interval for the population mean μ when sampling from a normal distribution with unknown variance (a t-distribution confidence interval) is given by $\bar{x} \pm t_{\alpha/2}(s/\sqrt{n})$, where $t_{\alpha/2}$ is the point of the standard normal distribution such that $\alpha/2$ remains in the right tail and s is the sample standard deviation. This confidence interval can also be used, because of the central limit theorem, when dealing with a large sample from a population with unknown variance that may not be normal.

- An alternative to the t-distribution confidence interval when using a large sample from a population with unknown variance that may not be normal is the z-distribution: $\bar{x} \pm z_{\alpha/2(s/\sqrt{n})}$. This confidence interval is less conservative (wider) than the corresponding confidence interval based on a t-distribution.

- Table 6-4 summarized the various reliability factors used in the chapter:

Sampling from:	Statistic for Small Sample Size	Statistic for Large Sample Size
Normal distribution with known variance	z	z
Normal distribution with unknown variance	t	t^*
Nonnormal distribution with known variance	not available	z
Nonnormal distribution with unknown variance	not available	t^*

- Sample data in investments can suffer from a variety of problems. Survivorship bias is present if companies are excluded from the analysis because of problems with data availability. Databases may systematically exclude companies or funds not currently in existence, or they may stop tracking them if they have been delisted from the major exchanges. Data-snooping bias occurs when research is based on the possibly spurious empirical results of others. Data-mining bias is the result of finding models by repeatedly searching through databases for patterns. Look-ahead bias exists if the model uses data not available to market participants at the time the market participants act in the model. Finally, time-period bias is present if the time period used makes the results time-period specific or if the time period used includes a point of structural change.

As analysts, we should always use a critical eye when we evaluate results from any study. The quality of the sample is of the utmost importance: If the sample is biased in any way, then none of the results derived by using the techniques in this chapter will hold. No matter how sophisticated the statistical method, a bad sample will always yield unsupportable results.

PROBLEMS

1. Peter Biggs wants to know how growth managers performed last year. Biggs assumes that the population cross-sectional standard deviation of growth manager returns is 6 percent and that the returns are independent across managers.
   a. How large a random sample does Biggs need if he wants the standard deviation of the sample means to be 1 percent?
   b. How large a random sample does Biggs need if he wants the standard deviation of the sample means to be 0.25 percent?

2. Petra Munzi wants to know how value managers did last year. Munzi assumes that the population cross-sectional standard deviation of value manager returns is 4 percent and that the returns are independent across managers.
   a. Munzi wants to build a 95 percent confidence interval for the mean return. How large a random sample does Munzi need if she wants the 95 percent confidence interval to have a total width of 1 percent?
   b. Munzi expects it to cost about $10 to collect each observation. If she has a $1,000 budget, will she be able to construct the confidence interval she wants?

3. Assume that the equity risk premium is normally distributed with a population mean of 6 percent and a population standard deviation of 18 percent. Over the last four years, equity returns (relative to the risk-free rate) have averaged −2.0 percent. You have a large client that is very upset and claims that results this poor should *never* occur. Evaluate your client's concerns.
   a. Construct a 95 percent confidence interval for a sample of four-year returns.
   b. What is the probability of the −2.0 percent returns over a four-year period?

4. Compare the standard normal distribution and Student's t-distribution.

5. Find the reliability factors based on the t-distribution for the following confidence intervals for the population mean (df = degrees of freedom, n = sample size):
   a. A 99 percent confidence interval, df = 20
   b. A 90 percent confidence interval, df = 20
   c. A 95 percent confidence interval, n = 25
   d. A 95 percent confidence interval, n = 16

6. Assume that monthly returns are normally distributed with a mean of 1 percent and a sample standard deviation of 4 percent. The population standard deviation is unknown. Construct a 95 percent confidence interval for the sample mean of monthly returns if the sample size is 24.

7. Ten analysts have given the following fiscal year earnings forecasts for a stock:

Forecast (x_i)	Number of Analysts (n_i)
1.40	1
1.43	1
1.44	3
1.45	2
1.47	1
1.48	1
1.50	1

Because the sample is a small fraction of the number of analysts who follow this stock, assume that we can ignore the finite population correction factor. Assume that the analyst forecasts are normally distributed.

a. What are the mean forecast and standard deviation of forecasts?

b. Provide a 95 percent confidence interval for an individual forecast from the population of forecasters.

c. Provide a 95 percent confidence interval for the population mean of the forecasts.

8. Thirteen analysts have given the following fiscal-year earnings forecasts for a stock:

Forecast (x_i)	Number of Analysts (n_i)
0.70	2
0.72	4
0.74	1
0.75	3
0.76	1
0.77	1
0.82	1

Because the sample is a small fraction of the number of analysts who follow this stock, assume that we can ignore the finite population correction factor.

a. What are the mean forecast and standard deviation of forecasts?

b. What aspect of the data makes us uncomfortable about using t-tables to create confidence intervals for the population mean forecast?

9. Explain the differences between estimating a confidence interval when sampling from a normal population with a known population variance and sampling from a normal population with an unknown variance.

10. An exchange rate has a given expected future value and standard deviation.

a. Assuming that the exchange rate is normally distributed, what are the probabilities that the exchange rate will be at least 1, 2, or 3 standard deviations away from its mean?

b. Assume that you do not know the distribution of exchange rates. Use Chebyshev's inequality (that at least $1 - 1/k^2$ proportion of the observations will be within the standard deviations of the mean for any positive integer greater than 1) to calculate the maximum probabilities that the exchange rate will be at least 1, 2, or 3 standard deviations away from its mean.

11. Although he knows security returns are not independent, a colleague makes the claim that, because of the central limit theorem, if we diversify across a large number of investments, the portfolio standard deviation will eventually approach zero as n becomes large. Is your colleague correct?

12. Why is the central limit theorem important?

13. What is wrong with the following statement of the central limit theorem?

> **Central Limit Theorem.** If the random variables $X_1, X_2, X_3, \dots , X_n$ are a random sample of size n from any given distribution with finite mean μ and variance σ^2, then the distribution of $\bar{x}$ will be approximately normal, with a standard deviation of $\sigma/\sqrt{n}$.

14. Suppose we take a random sample of 30 companies in an industry with 200 companies. We calculate the sample mean of the ratio of cash flow to total debt for the prior year. We find that this ratio is 23 percent. Subsequently, we learn that the population cash flow to total debt ratio (taking account of all 200 companies) is 26 percent. What is the explanation for the discrepancy between the sample mean of 23 percent and the population mean of 26 percent?
    a. Sampling error
    b. Bias
    c. A lack of consistency
    d. A lack of efficiency

15. Godzilla Mutual Funds is placing large advertisements in several financial publications. The advertisements prominently display the returns of 5 of Godzilla's 30 funds for the past 1-, 3-, 5-, and 10-year periods. The results are indeed impressive, with all of the funds beating the major market indexes and a few beating them by a large margin. Is the Godzilla family of funds superior to its competitors?

16. A pension plan executive says, "One hundred percent of our portfolio managers are hired because they have above-average performance records relative to their benchmarks. We do not keep portfolio managers who have below-average records. And yet, each year about half of our managers beat their benchmarks and about half do not. What is going on?" Give a possible statistical explanation.

17. Jacques Quandt has tested several predictive models in order to identify undervalued stocks. Quandt used about 30 company-specific variables and 10 market-related variables to predict returns for about 5,000 North American and European stocks. He found that a final model using eight variables applied to telecommunications and computer stocks yields spectacular results. Quandt wants you to use the model to select investments. Should you? What steps would you take to evaluate the model?

18. Hand Associates manages two portfolios that are meant to closely track the returns of two stock indexes. One index is a value-weighted index of 500 stocks in which the weight for each stock depends on the stock's total market value. The other index is an equal-weighted index of 500 stocks in which the weight for each stock is 1/500. Hand Associates invests in only about 50–100 stocks in each portfolio in order to control transactions costs. Should Hand use simple random sampling or stratified random sampling to choose the stocks in each portfolio?

19. Give an example of each of the following:
    a. Delisting bias.
    b. Look-ahead bias.
    c. Time-period bias.

20. What are some of the desirable statistical properties of an estimator, such as a sample mean?

SOLUTIONS

1. **a.** The standard deviation or standard error of the sample mean is $\sigma_{\bar{x}} = \sigma/\sqrt{n}$. Substituting in the values for $\sigma_{\bar{x}}$ and σ, we have $1\% = 6\%/\sqrt{n}$, or $\sqrt{n} = 6$. Squaring this value, we get a random sample of $n = 36$.

   b. As in Part a, the standard deviation of sample mean is $\sigma_{\bar{x}} = \sigma/\sqrt{n}$. Substituting in the values for $\sigma_{\bar{x}}$ and σ, we have $0.25\% = 6\%/\sqrt{n}$, or $\sqrt{n} = 24$. Squaring this value, we get a random sample of $n = 576$, which is substantially larger than for Part a of this question.

2. **a.** Assume the sample size will be large and thus the 95 percent confidence interval for the mean of a sample of manager returns is $\bar{x} \pm 1.96 s_{\bar{x}}$, where $s_{\bar{x}} = \sigma/\sqrt{n}$. Munzi wants the distance between the upper limit and lower limit in the confidence interval to be 1 percent, which is:

$$(\bar{x} + 1.96 \times s_{\bar{x}}) - (\bar{x} - 1.96 \times s_{\bar{x}}) = 1\%$$

Simplifying this equation, we get $2(1.96 \times s_{\bar{x}}) = 1\%$. Finally, we have $3.92 s_{\bar{x}} = 1\%$, which gives us the standard deviation of the sample mean, $s_{\bar{x}} = 0.255\%$. The distribution of sample means is $s_{\bar{x}} = \sigma/\sqrt{n}$. Substituting in the values for $s_{\bar{x}}$ and σ, we have $0.255\% = 4\%/\sqrt{n}$, or $\sqrt{n} = 15.69$. Squaring this value, we get a random sample of $n = 246$.

   b. With her budget, Munzi can pay for a sample of up to 100 observations, which is far short of the 246 observations needed. Munzi can either proceed with her current budget and settle for a wider confidence interval, or she can raise her budget (to around \$2,460) to get the sample size for a 1 percent width in her confidence interval.

3. **a.** This is a small-sample problem in which the sample comes from a normal population with a known standard deviation; thus, we use the z-distribution in the solution. For a 95 percent confidence interval (and 2.5 percent in each tail), the critical z-value is 1.96. For returns that are normally distributed, a 95 percent confidence interval is of the form

$$\bar{x} \pm 1.96 \frac{\sigma}{\sqrt{n}}$$

The lower limit is $X_l = \bar{x} - 1.96 \dfrac{\sigma}{\sqrt{n}} = 6\% - 1.96 \dfrac{18\%}{\sqrt{4}} = 6\% - 1.96(9\%)$
$= -11.64\%$

The upper limit is $X_u = \bar{x} + 1.96 \dfrac{\sigma}{\sqrt{n}} = 6\% + 1.96 \dfrac{18\%}{\sqrt{4}} = 6\% + 1.96(9\%)$
$= 23.64\%$

There is a 95 percent probability that four-year average returns will be between -11.64 percent and $+23.64$ percent.

   b. The critical z-value associated with the -2.0 percent return is

$$Z = \frac{\bar{x} - \mu}{\sigma/\sqrt{n}} = \frac{-2\% - 6\%}{18\%/\sqrt{4}} = \frac{-8\%}{9\%} = -0.89$$

Using a normal table, the probability of a z-value less than -0.89 is $P(z < -0.89) = 0.1867$. Unfortunately, although your client is unhappy with the investment result, four-year returns of -2.0 percent or lower should occur 18.67 percent of the time.

4. (Refer to Figure 6-1 to help visualize the answer to this question.) Basically, only one standard normal distribution exists, but many t-distributions exist—one for every different number of degrees of freedom. If the degrees of freedom are large, the normal distribution and the t-distribution for the large df are practically the same. The lower the degrees of freedom, the flatter the t-distribution becomes. The t-distribution has less mass (lower probabilities) in the center of the distribution and more mass (higher probabilities) out in both tails. Therefore, the confidence intervals based on t-values will be wider than those based on the normal distribution. Stated differently, the probability of being within a given number of standard deviations (such as within ± 1 standard deviation or ± 2 standard deviations) is lower for the t-distribution than for the normal distribution.

5. a. For a 99 percent confidence interval, the reliability factor we use is $t_{0.005}$; for df $= 20$, this factor is 2.845.

   b. For a 90 percent confidence interval, the reliability factor we use is $t_{0.05}$; for df $= 20$, this factor is 1.725.

   c. Degrees of freedom equals $n - 1$, or in this case $25 - 1 = 24$. For a 95 percent confidence interval, the reliability factor we use is $t_{0.025}$; for df $= 24$, this factor is 2.064.

   d. Degrees of freedom equals $16 - 1 = 15$. For a 95 percent confidence interval, the reliability factor we use is $t_{0.025}$; for df $= 15$, this factor is 2.131.

6. Because this is a small sample from a normal population and we have only the sample standard deviation, we use the following model to solve for the confidence interval of the population mean:

$$\bar{x} \pm t_{\alpha/2} \frac{s}{\sqrt{n}}$$

where we find $t_{0.025}$ (for a 95 percent confidence interval) for df $= n - 1 = 24 - 1 = 23$; this value is 2.069. Our solution is $1\% \pm 2.069 \times 4\%/\sqrt{24} = 1\% \pm 2.069 \times 0.8165 = 1\% \pm 1.69$. The 95 percent confidence interval spans the range from -0.69 percent to $+2.69$ percent.

7. The following table summarizes the calculations used in the answers.

Forecast (x_i)	Number of Analysts (n_i)	$x_i n_i$	$(x_i - \bar{x})$	$(x_i - \bar{x})^2$	$(x_i - \bar{x})^2 n_i$
1.40	1	1.40	-0.05	0.0025	0.0025
1.43	1	1.43	-0.02	0.0004	0.0004
1.44	3	4.32	-0.01	0.0001	0.0003
1.45	2	2.90	0.00	0.0000	0.0000
1.47	1	1.47	0.02	0.0004	0.0004
1.48	1	1.48	0.03	0.0009	0.0009
1.50	1	1.50	0.05	0.0025	0.0025
Sums	10	14.50			0.0070

a. The mean forecast is $\bar{x} = \sum_{i=1}^{10} x_i/n = 14.50/10 = 1.45$. The variance is $s^2 = \sum_{i=1}^{10} (x_i - \bar{x})^2/(n - 1) = 0.0070/9 = 0.0007778$. The sample standard deviation is

$$s = \sqrt{0.0007778} = 0.02789.$$

b. A 95 percent confidence interval for the forecasts is of the form $\bar{x} \pm t_{\alpha/2}(s/\sqrt{n})$. For 9 degrees of freedom, the reliability factor, $t_{0.025}$, is 2.262. Substituting in the appropriate values, the confidence interval is $1.45 \pm 2.262 \times 0.02789$, or 1.387 to 1.513.

c. The confidence interval for the mean can be estimated by using

$$\bar{x} \pm t_{\alpha/2} \frac{s}{\sqrt{n}}$$

For 9 degrees of freedom, the reliability factor, $t_{0.025}$, equals 2.262 and the confidence interval is $1.45 \pm 2.262 \times 0.02789/\sqrt{10} = 1.45 \pm 2.262 \times 0.00882 = 1.45 \pm 0.02$. The confidence interval for the population mean ranges from 1.43 to 1.47.

8. The following table summarizes the calculations used in the answers.

Forecast (x_i)	Number of Analysts (n_i)	$x_i n_i$	$(x_i - \bar{x})$	$(x_i - \bar{x})^2$	$(x_i - \bar{x})^2 n_i$
0.70	2	1.40	−0.04	0.0016	0.0032
0.72	4	2.88	−0.02	0.0004	0.0016
0.74	1	0.74	0.00	0.0000	0.0000
0.75	3	2.25	0.01	0.0001	0.0003
0.76	1	0.76	0.02	0.0004	0.0004
0.77	1	0.77	0.03	0.0009	0.0009
0.82	1	0.82	0.08	0.0064	0.0064
Sums	13	9.62			0.0128

a. The mean forecast is $\bar{x} = \sum_{i=1}^{13} x_i/n = 9.62/13 = 0.74$. The variance is $s^2 = \sum_{i=1}^{13} (x_i - \bar{x})^2/(n - 1) = 0.0128/12 = 0.001067$. The sample standard deviation is

$$s = \sqrt{0.001067} = 0.03266.$$

b. The sample is small, and the distribution appears to be bi-modal. We cannot compute a confidence interval for the population mean because we have probably sampled from a distribution that is not normal.

9. If the population variance is known, the confidence interval is

$$\bar{x} \pm z_{\alpha/2} \frac{\sigma}{\sqrt{n}}$$

The confidence interval for the population mean is centered at the sample mean, $\bar{x}$. The population standard deviation is σ, and the sample size is n. The population standard deviation divided by the square root of n is the standard error of the estimate of the mean. The value of z depends on the desired degree of confidence. For a 95 percent confidence interval, $z_{0.025} = 1.96$ and the confidence interval estimate is

$$\bar{x} \pm 1.96 \frac{\sigma}{\sqrt{n}}$$

If the population variance is not known, we make two changes to the technique used when the population variance is known. First, we must use the sample standard deviation instead of the population standard deviation. Second, we use the t-distribution instead of the normal distribution. The critical t-value will depend on sample size $n - 1$. If the sample size is large, we have the alternative of using the z-distribution with the sample standard deviation.

10. **a.** The probabilities can be taken from a normal table, where the critical z-values are 1.00, 2.00, or 3.00, and we are including the probabilities in both tails. The probabilities of being at least 1, 2, or 3 standard deviations away from the mean are

$$P(|x - \mu| \geq 1\sigma) = 0.3174,$$
$$P(|x - \mu| \geq 2\sigma) = 0.0456, \text{ and}$$
$$P(|x - \mu| \geq 3\sigma) = 0.0026.$$

b. With Chebyshev's inequality, the maximum probability of being at least k standard deviations from the mean is $P(|x - \mu| \geq k\sigma) \leq (1/k)^2$. The maximum probabilities of being at least 1, 2, or 3 standard deviations away from the mean are

$$P(|x - \mu| \geq 1\sigma) \leq (1/1)^2 = 1.0000,$$
$$P(|x - \mu| \geq 2\sigma) \leq (1/2)^2 = 0.2500, \text{ and}$$
$$P(|x - \mu| \geq 3\sigma) \leq (1/3)^2 = 0.1111.$$

The probability of being outside 1, 2, or 3 standard deviations of the mean is much smaller with a known normal distribution than when the distribution is unknown and we are relying on Chebyshev's inequality.

11. No. If security returns were independent of each other, your colleague would be correct. We could diversify across a large number of investments and make the portfolio standard deviation very small, approaching zero. However, the returns of investments are not independent; they are correlated with each other and are correlated with common market factors. Diversifying across many investments reduces *unsystematic* (stock-specific) risk, but it does not rid us of *systematic* (market) risk.

12. In many instances, the distribution that describes the underlying population is not normal or the distribution is not known. The central limit theorem states that, if the sample size is large, regardless of the shape of the underlying population, the distribution of the sample mean is approximately normal. Therefore, even in these instances, we can still construct confidence intervals (and conduct tests of inference) as long as the sample size is large (generally $n \geq 30$).

13. The statement makes the following mistakes:

- Given the conditions in the statement, the distribution of $\bar{x}$ will be approximately normal only for large sample sizes.

- The statement omits the important element of the central limit theorem that the distribution of $\bar{x}$ will have mean μ.

14. The discrepancy arises from sampling error. Sampling error exists whenever you do not observe every element of the population, because a sample statistic can vary from sample to sample. As stated in the text, the sample mean is an unbiased estimator, a consistent estimator, and an efficient estimator of the population mean. Although the sample mean is an unbiased estimator of the population mean—the expected value of the sample mean equals the population mean—because of sampling error, we do not expect the sample mean to exactly equal the population mean in any one sample we may take.

15. Godzilla's advertisement is a ploy. Godzilla is probably guilty of sample selection bias. Godzilla is presenting the investment results from its best performing funds and excluding the results from its funds with poorer results from the presentation.

16. The question raises the issue of whether above-average money management performance is the result of skill or luck. Assembling a group of above-average portfolio managers can be an attempt to exploit survivorship bias. We attempt it by hiring only managers with above-average records and by firing any managers that have below-average records. If past successful performance is a function of skill that can be repeated, then managers with above-average records will perform better than average in the future. An explanation for what is going on in the complaint may be that past superior performance is not a result of skill but a result of luck.

    Say we assume that performance is a matter of luck. Suppose there is a 0.5 chance for a manager to beat his or her benchmark. If we start out with 100 managers and define success as two benchmark-beating years in a row, we will have about 25 successful managers. Their successful track records will not predict future success if performance is random. If performance is random, no matter how we pick our managers, future performance will be above average about half the time and below average about half the time. If we wish to appraise skill, we must discount results that would happen by chance.

17. Jacques Quandt may be guilty of data mining. He has used so many possible combinations of variables on so many stocks, it is not surprising that he found some instances where a model worked. In fact, it would have been more surprising if he had not found something. To decide whether to use his model, you should consider doing two things: First, ask that the model be tested on out-of-sample data—that is, data that were not used in building the model. The model may not be successful with different data. Second, examine his model to make sure that the relationships in the model make economic sense, have a story, and have a future.

18. Hand Associates should use stratified random sampling for its portfolio that tracks the value-weighted index. Using 50–100 stocks to track 500 means that Hand will invest in all or almost all of the largest stocks in the index and few of the smallest. In addition to size, the stocks may be grouped by industry, riskiness, and other traits, and Hand Associates may select stocks to represent each of these groups or strata. For the equal-weighted index, Hand can use simple random sampling, in which each stock is equally likely to be chosen. Even in this case, however, Hand could use stratified random sampling to make sure it is choosing stocks that represent the various factors underlying stock performance.

19. a. An example of delisting bias is the failure to include the returns of delisted stocks in reporting portfolio returns. Because delisted stocks frequently are troubled stocks with poor returns, ignoring their returns will bias upwards the returns of portfolios that do not include them.

b. An example of look-ahead bias is a statistician using data that were not yet available at the time a decision was being made. If you are building portfolios on January 1 of each year, you do not yet have the financial results for fiscal years ending on December 31. So, you do not know this information when you make investment decisions. Suppose a statistician is studying historical portfolio returns and has used annual accounting results to make portfolio selections at the beginning of each year. She is using a statistical model that assumes information is available several weeks before it is actually available. The results of such a model are biased.

c. One kind of time-period bias is an investment manager reporting the results from a short time period that give an inaccurate picture of the investment performance that might be expected over a longer time period. Time-period bias exists when a test is carried out for a time period that may make the results time-period specific. Another type of time-period bias arises with long time series. Long time series may give a more accurate picture of true investment performance than short time series, but they have the potential of including structural changes that would result in two different return distributions within the long period.

20. An estimator should have several desirable properties, including the following.

- Unbiasedness: The expected value of the estimate is equal to the population parameter.
- Efficiency: An efficient estimate is unbiased and has a smaller variance than all other unbiased estimates.
- Consistency: A consistent estimate tends to produce more accurate estimates of the population parameter as sample size increases.

CHAPTER

HYPOTHESIS TESTING

LEARNING OUTCOMES

After completing this chapter, you will be able to do the following:

- Define a hypothesis.
- Describe the steps of hypothesis testing.
- Define and interpret the null hypothesis and alternative hypothesis.
- Discuss the choice of the null and alternative hypotheses.
- Distinguish between one-tailed and two-tailed tests of hypotheses.
- Define and interpret a test statistic.
- Define and interpret a significance level.
- Explain how significance levels are used in hypothesis testing.
- Define and interpret a Type I and a Type II error.
- Define the power of a test.
- Define and interpret a decision rule.
- Explain the relation between confidence intervals and tests of significance.
- Explain the distinction between a statistical decision and an economic decision.
- Discuss the *p*-value approach to hypothesis testing.
- Identify the test statistic for a hypothesis test concerning the population mean of a normally distributed population with unknown variance.
- Identify the test statistic for a hypothesis test concerning the population mean of a normally distributed population with known variance.
- Explain the use of the *z*-test in relation to the central limit theorem.
- Formulate a null and an alternative hypothesis about a population mean and determine whether the null hypothesis is rejected or not rejected at a given level of significance.
- Identify the test statistic for a hypothesis test concerning the equality of two population means of two normally distributed populations, based on independent random samples.
- Formulate a null and an alternative hypothesis about the equality of two population means (normally distributed populations, independent random samples) and determine whether the null hypothesis is rejected or not rejected at a given level of significance.

- Identify the test statistic for a hypothesis test concerning mean difference for two normally distributed populations (paired comparisons test).

- Formulate a null and an alternative hypothesis about the mean difference of two normally distributed populations (paired comparisons test) and determine whether the null hypothesis is rejected or not rejected at a given level of significance.

- Discuss the choice between tests of differences between means and tests of mean differences in relation to the independence of samples.

- Identify the test statistic for a hypothesis test concerning the variance of a normally distributed population.

- Formulate a null and an alternative hypothesis about the variance of a normally distributed population and determine whether the null hypothesis is rejected or not rejected at a given level of significance.

- Identify the test statistic for a hypothesis test concerning the equality of the variance of two normally distributed populations, based on two independent random samples.

- Formulate a null and an alternative hypothesis about the equality of the variances of two normally distributed populations, given the test statistic, and determine whether the null hypothesis is rejected or not rejected at a given level of significance.

- Distinguish between parametric and nonparametric tests.

1 INTRODUCTION

Investors continually confront competing ideas on how financial markets work. Some of these ideas develop through personal research or experience with markets; others come from interactions with colleagues; and many others appear in the professional literature on finance and investments. When we can reduce an idea or assertion to a definite statement about the value of a quantity, such as an underlying or population mean, the idea becomes a statistically testable statement or hypothesis. The analyst may want to explore questions such as: Is the underlying mean return on this mutual fund different from the mean return on its benchmark? Did the volatility of returns on this stock change after the stock was added to a stock market index? The concepts and tools of hypothesis testing provide an objective way to gauge whether the available evidence supports the hypothesis. Hypothesis testing has been a powerful tool in the advancement of investment knowledge and science. As Robert L. Kahn of the Institute for Social Research (Ann Arbor, Michigan) has written, "The mill of science grinds only when hypothesis and data are in continuous and abrasive contact."

The main emphases of this chapter are the framework of hypothesis testing and tests concerning mean and variance, two quantities frequently used in investments. We give an overview of the procedure of hypothesis testing in the next section. We then address testing hypotheses about the mean and hypotheses about the differences between means. In the fourth section of this chapter, we address testing hypotheses about a single variance and hypotheses about the differences between variances. We end the chapter with an overview of some other important issues and techniques in inference.

2 HYPOTHESIS TESTING

Statistical inference is a set of tools for answering questions about a population—all members of a specified group—based on a sample; that is, observations on some members of the group. As long as we can specify our questions precisely, we can use the tools of statistical inference. Traditionally, the field of statistical inference has two subdivisions: **estimation** and **hypothesis testing.** Estimation addresses the question: What is this parameter's (e.g., the population mean's) value? The answer is in the form of a confidence interval built around a point estimate. Take the case of the mean: We build a confidence interval for the population mean around the sample mean as a point estimate. For the sake of specificity, suppose the sample mean is 50 and a 95 percent confidence interval for the population mean is 50 ± 10 (that is, the confidence interval runs from 40 to 60). If this confidence interval has been properly constructed, there is a 95 percent probability that the interval contains the population mean (that the interval from 40 to 60 includes the population mean's value). The construction and interpretation of confidence intervals were discussed in the chapter on sampling. The second branch of statistical inference, hypothesis testing, has a somewhat different focus. A hypothesis testing question is: Is the value of the parameter (say, the population mean) 45 (or some other specific value)? The assertion "the population mean is 45" is a hypothesis. A **hypothesis** is defined as a statement about one or more populations.

The concepts of hypothesis testing are the focus of this section. The need for this set of tools is clear. Suppose we suspect that proportional transaction costs for trades in a particular market are higher currently than they were in the previous year. We want to find out whether the evidence supports this hypothesis about transaction costs. Using a sample of current trades, we can test the hypothesis that transaction costs equal their earlier level. Here, statistical inference is an essential tool, as it is unlikely that we could tabulate the costs of the population of all possible trades. In other cases, we might be able to measure the quantity of interest for the entire population; however, this may be cost inefficient relative to the information that we can obtain using statistical inference.

We organize this introduction to hypothesis testing around the following list of seven steps.

- **Steps in Hypothesis Testing.** The steps in testing a hypothesis are:[1]
  1. Stating the hypotheses.
  2. Identifying the test statistic and its probability distribution.
  3. Specifying the significance level.
  4. Stating the decision rule.
  5. Collecting the data and performing the calculations.
  6. Making the statistical decision.
  7. Making the economic or investment decision.

We will explain each of these steps, using a hypothesis test concerning the sign of the risk premium on U.S. stocks as an illustration. Steps 3 and 4 above constitute a traditional approach to hypothesis testing. We will end the section with a frequently used alternative to those steps, the p-value approach.

---

[1] This list is based on one in Daniel and Terrell (1979).

The first step in hypothesis testing is the statement of the hypotheses. We always state two hypotheses: the null hypothesis (or *null*), designated H_0, and the alternative hypothesis, designated H_a.

- **Definition of Null Hypothesis.** The null hypothesis is the hypothesis to be tested.

The null hypothesis is a proposition that is considered true unless the sample we use to conduct the hypothesis test gives convincing evidence that the null hypothesis is false. When such evidence is present, we are led to the alternative hypothesis.

- **Definition of Alternative Hypothesis.** The alternative hypothesis is the hypothesis accepted when the null hypothesis is rejected.

Suppose our question concerns the value of a population parameter, θ, in relation to one possible value of the parameter, θ_0 (these are read, respectively, "theta" and "theta sub zero").[2] Examples of a population parameter include the population mean, μ, and the population variance, σ^2. We can formulate three different sets of hypotheses, which we label according to the assertion made by the alternative hypothesis.

- **Formulations of Hypotheses.** We can formulate the null and alternative hypotheses in three different ways:
  1. $H_0: \theta = \theta_0$ versus $H_a: \theta \neq \theta_0$ (a "not equal to" alternative hypothesis)
  2. $H_0: \theta \leq \theta_0$ versus $H_a: \theta > \theta_0$ (a "greater than" alternative hypothesis)
  3. $H_0: \theta \geq \theta_0$ versus $H_a: \theta < \theta_0$ (a "less than" alternative hypothesis)

The first formulation is a **two-sided hypothesis test** (or **two-tailed hypothesis test**): The null is rejected in favor of the alternative if the evidence indicates that the population parameter is either smaller or larger than θ_0. In contrast, Formulations 2 and 3 are each a **one-sided hypothesis test** (or **one-tailed hypothesis test**). For Formulation 2 (3) the null is rejected only if the evidence indicates that the population parameter is greater than (smaller than) θ_0. The alternative hypothesis has one side.

Notice that in each case above, we state the null and alternative hypotheses such that they account for all possible values of the parameter. With Formulation 1, for example, the parameter is either equal to the hypothesized value, θ_0 (under the null hypothesis), or not equal to the hypothesized value, θ_0 (under the alternative hypothesis); those two statements logically exhaust all possible values of the parameter.

Despite the different ways to formulate hypotheses, we always conduct a test of the null hypothesis at the point of equality, $\theta = \theta_0$. Whether the null is $H_0: \theta = \theta_0$, $H_0: \theta \leq \theta_0$, or $H_0: \theta \geq \theta_0$, we actually test $\theta = \theta_0$. The reasoning is straightforward. Suppose the hypothesized value of the parameter is 5. Consider $H_0: \theta \leq 5$, with a "greater than" alternative hypothesis, $H_a: \theta > 5$. If we have enough evidence to reject $H_0: \theta = 5$ in favor of $H_a: \theta > 5$, we definitely also have enough evidence to reject that the parameter, θ, is some smaller value, such as 4.5 or 4. To review, the calculation to test the null hypothesis is the same for all three formulations. What is different for the three formulations, we will see shortly, is how the calculation is evaluated to decide whether or not to reject the null.

How do we choose the null and alternative hypotheses? Probably most common are "not equal to" alternative hypotheses. We reject the null because the evidence indicates ei-

---

[2] Greek letters, such as σ, are reserved for population parameters; Roman letters in italics, such as *s*, are used for sample statistics.

ther that the parameter is larger or smaller than θ_0. Sometimes, however, we may have a "suspected" or "hoped for" condition for which we want to find supportive evidence.[3] In that case, we can formulate the alternative hypothesis as the statement that this condition is true; the null hypothesis that we test is the statement that this condition is not true. If the evidence supports rejecting the null and accepting the alternative, we have statistically confirmed what we thought was true. For example, economic theory suggests that investors require a positive risk premium on stocks (the **risk premium** is defined as the expected return on stocks minus the risk-free rate). Following the principle of stating the alternative as the "hoped for" condition, we formulate the following hypotheses:

H_0: The population mean risk premium on stocks is less than or equal to 0.

H_a: The population mean risk premium on stocks is positive.

We will later specialize these hypotheses for the U.S. stock market and use them to illustrate our discussion. Note that "greater than" and "less than" alternative hypotheses reflect the beliefs of the researcher more strongly than a "not equal to" alternative hypothesis. To emphasize an attitude of neutrality, the researcher may sometimes select a "not equal to" alternative hypothesis when a one-sided alternative hypothesis is also reasonable.

The second step in hypothesis testing is identification of the test statistic and its probability distribution.

- **Definition of Test Statistic.** A test statistic is a quantity, calculated on the basis of a sample, whose value is the basis for deciding whether to reject or not reject the null hypothesis.

The value of the test statistic is the focal point of the statistical decision we make. Frequently (in all the cases that we examine in this chapter), the test statistic has the form

$$\text{Test statistic} = \frac{\text{Sample statistic} - \text{Value of the population parameter under } H_0}{\text{Standard error of the sample statistic}} \quad \text{(7-1)}$$

For our risk premium example, the population parameter of interest is the population mean risk premium, μ_{RP}. We label the hypothesized value of the population mean under H_0 as μ_0. Restating the hypotheses using symbols, we test H_0: $\mu_{RP} \leq \mu_0$ versus H_a: $\mu_{RP} > \mu_0$. However, because under the null we are testing $\mu_0 = 0$, we write H_0: $\mu_{RP} \leq 0$ versus H_a: $\mu_{RP} > 0$.

The sample mean provides an estimate of the population mean. Therefore, we can use the sample mean risk premium calculated from historical data, $\bar{x}_{RP}$, as the sample statistic in Equation 7-1. The standard deviation of the sample statistic, known as the "standard error" of the statistic, is the denominator in Equation 7-1. For this example, the sample statistic is a sample mean. For a sample mean, $\bar{x}$, calculated from a sample generated by a population with standard deviation σ, the standard error is given by one of two expressions:

$$\sigma_{\bar{x}} = \frac{\sigma}{\sqrt{n}} \quad \text{(7-2)}$$

---

[3] Part of this discussion of the selection of hypotheses follows Bowerman and O'Connell (1997, p. 386).

when we know σ (the population standard deviation), or

$$s_{\bar{x}} = \frac{s}{\sqrt{n}} \tag{7-3}$$

when we do not know the population standard deviation and need to use the sample standard deviation s to estimate it. For this example, because we do not know the population standard deviation of the process generating return, we use Equation 7-3. The test statistic is, therefore,

$$\frac{\bar{x}_{RP} - \mu_0}{s_{\bar{x}}} = \frac{\bar{x}_{RP} - 0}{s/\sqrt{n}}$$

In making the substitution of 0 for μ_0, we use the fact already highlighted that we test any null hypothesis at the point of equality.

We have identified a test statistic to test the null hypothesis. What probability distribution does it follow? We will meet four distributions for test statistics in this chapter:

- the t-distribution (for a t-test),
- the standard normal or z-distribution (for a z-test),
- the chi-square (χ^2) distribution (for a chi-square test), and
- the F-distribution (for an F-test).

We will discuss the details later, but assume that we can conduct a z-test based on the central limit theorem.[4] To summarize, the test statistic for the hypothesis test concerning the mean risk premium is $\bar{x}_{RP}/s_{\bar{x}}$ and we assume it follows a standard normal distribution so that we can conduct a z-test.

The third step is to specify the significance level. When the test statistic has been calculated, two actions are possible: (1) We reject the null hypothesis or (2) we do not reject the null hypothesis. The action we take is based on comparing the calculated test statistic to a specified possible value or values. The comparison values we choose are based on the level of significance selected. The level of significance reflects how much sample evidence we require to reject the null. Analogous to a court of law, the standard of proof we may demand can change according to the nature of the hypotheses and the seriousness of the consequences of making a mistake. There are four possible outcomes when we test a null hypothesis:

1. We reject a false null hypothesis. This is a correct action.
2. We reject a true null hypothesis. This is a **Type I error.**
3. We do not reject a false null hypothesis. This is a **Type II error.**
4. We do not reject a true null hypothesis. This is a correct action.

We illustrate these outcomes in Table 7-1.

---

[4] The central limit theorem says that the sampling distribution of the sample mean will be approximately normal with mean μ and variance σ^2/n when the sample size is large. The sample we will use for this example has 879 observations.

TABLE 7-1   Type I and Type II Errors in Hypothesis Testing

	True Situation	
Decision	H_0 True	H_0 False
Do not reject H_0	Correct Decision	Type II Error
Reject H_0 (accept H_a)	Type I Error	Correct Decision

When we make a decision in a hypothesis test, we run the risk of making either a Type I or a Type II error. These are mutually exclusive errors: If we reject the null, we can only be possibly making a Type I error; if we fail to reject the null, we can only be possibly making a Type II error.

The probability of a Type I error in testing a hypothesis is denoted by the Greek letter alpha, α. This probability is also known as the **level of significance** of the test. For example, a level of significance of 0.05 for a test means that there is a 5 percent probability of rejecting a true null hypothesis. The probability of a Type II error is denoted by the Greek letter beta, β.

Controlling the probabilities of the two types of errors involves a trade-off. All else equal, if we decrease the probability of a Type I error (by making it very hard to reject the null hypothesis), we increase the probability of making a Type II error (because we reject the null less frequently, including when it is false). The only way to reduce the probabilities of both types of errors simultaneously is to increase the sample size, n.

Quantifying the trade-off between the two types of error in practice is usually not possible because the probability of a Type II error is itself hard to quantify. Consider H_0: $\theta \leq 5$ versus H_a: $\theta > 5$. Because every true value of θ greater than 5 makes the null hypothesis false, each value of θ greater than 5 has a different β (Type II error probability). In contrast, it is sufficient to state a Type I error probability for $\theta = 5$, the point at which we conduct the test of the null hypothesis. Thus, in general, we only specify α, the probability of a Type I error, when we conduct a hypothesis test. If the significance level of a test is the probability of incorrectly rejecting the null, the **power of a test** is the probability of *correctly* rejecting the null. That is, the power of a test is the probability of rejecting the null when it is false.[5] In some cases, more than one test statistic may be available to conduct a hypothesis test. If we have information on the relative power of the test for the competing test statistics—which one is most *powerful*—we can use this information in deciding which test statistic to use.

To summarize, the standard approach to hypothesis testing involves specifying a level of significance (probability of Type I error) only. This significance level is most appropriately specified prior to calculating the test statistic. If we specify it after calculating the test statistic, we may be influenced by the result of the calculation, which detracts from the objectivity of the test.

There are three conventional significance levels at which we conduct hypothesis tests: 0.10, 0.05, and 0.01. Qualitatively, if we can reject a null hypothesis at the 0.10 level of significance, we have *some evidence* that the null hypothesis is false. If we can reject a null hypothesis at the 0.05 level, we have *strong evidence* that the null hypothesis is false. And if we can reject a null hypothesis at the 0.01 level, we have *very strong evidence* that

---

[5] The power of a test is, in fact, 1 minus the probability of a Type II error.

the null hypothesis is false. For the risk premium example, we will specify a 0.05 significance level.

Stating the decision rule is the fourth step in testing a hypothesis. The general principle is simply stated. When we test the null hypothesis, if we find that the calculated value of the test statistic is as extreme or more extreme than a given value or values determined by the specified level of significance, α, we reject the null hypothesis. We say the result is **statistically significant.** Otherwise, we do not reject the null hypothesis and we say the result is **not statistically significant.** The value or values against which the calculated test statistic is compared to make our decision are the rejection points (critical values) for the test.[6]

- **Definition of a Rejection Point (Critical Value) for the Test Statistic.** A rejection point (critical value) for a test statistic is a value against which the computed test statistic is compared to decide whether to reject or not reject the null hypothesis.

For a one-tailed test, we indicate a rejection point using the symbol for the test statistic with a subscript indicating the specified probability of a Type I error, α; for example, z_α. For a two-tailed test, we indicate $z_{\alpha/2}$. To illustrate the use of rejection points, suppose we are using a z-test and have chosen a 0.05 level of significance.

- For a test of H_0: $\theta = \theta_0$ versus H_a: $\theta \neq \theta_0$ two rejection points exist, one negative and one positive. For a two-sided test at the 0.05 level, the total probability of a Type I error must sum to 0.05. Thus, $0.05/2 = 0.025$ of the probability should be in each tail of the distribution of the test statistic under the null. As a consequence, the two rejection points are $z_{0.025} = 1.96$ and $-z_{0.025} = -1.96$. Let z represent the calculated value of the test statistic. We reject the null if we find that $z < -1.96$ or $z > 1.96$.

- For a test of H_0: $\theta \leq \theta_0$ versus H_a: $\theta > \theta_0$ at the 0.05 level of significance, the rejection point is $z_{0.05} = 1.645$. We reject the null hypothesis if $z > 1.645$. The value of the standard normal distribution such that 5 percent of the outcomes lie to the right is $z_{0.05} = 1.645$.

- For a test of H_0: $\theta \geq \theta_0$ versus H_a: $\theta < \theta_0$, the rejection point is $-z_{0.05} = -1.645$. We reject the null hypothesis if $z < -1.645$.

Figure 7-1 illustrates a test H_0: $\mu = \mu_0$ versus H_a: $\mu \neq \mu_0$ at the 0.05 significance level using a z-test. The "acceptance region" is the traditional name for the set of values of the test statistic for which we do not reject the null hypothesis. (The traditional name is, however, not accurate. We should avoid using phrases such as "accept the null hypothesis" because it implies a greater degree of conviction about the null than is warranted when we fail to reject it.)[7] On either side of the acceptance region is a rejection region (or critical region). If the null hypothesis that $\mu = \mu_0$ is true, the test statistic has a 2.5 percent chance of falling in the left rejection region and a 2.5 percent chance of falling in the right rejection region. Any calculated value of the test statistic that falls in either of these two regions causes us to reject the null hypothesis at the 0.05 significance level. The rejection points of

---

[6] *Rejection point* is a descriptive synonym for the more traditional term *critical value*.

[7] The analogy in some courts of law (for example, in the United States) is that if a jury does not return a verdict of guilty (the alternative hypothesis), it is most accurate to say that the jury has failed to reject the null hypothesis, namely, that the defendant is innocent.

1.96 and −1.96 are seen to be the dividing lines between the acceptance and rejection regions.

FIGURE 7-1   Rejection Points (Critical Values), 0.05 Significance Level, Two-Sided Test of the Population Mean Using a z-Test

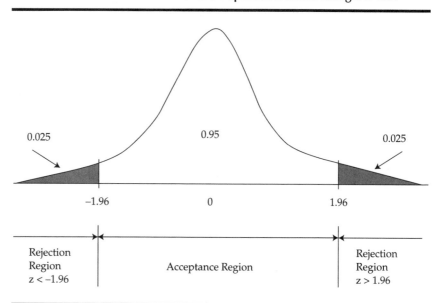

Figure 7-1 affords a good opportunity to highlight the relationship between confidence intervals and hypothesis tests. A 95 percent confidence interval for the population mean, μ, based on sample mean, $\bar{x}$, is given by $\bar{x} - 1.96s_{\bar{x}}$ to $\bar{x} + 1.96s_{\bar{x}}$, where $s_{\bar{x}}$ is the standard error of the sample mean (Equation 7-3).[8]

Now consider one of the conditions for rejecting the null hypothesis:

$$\frac{\bar{x} - \mu_0}{s_{\bar{x}}} > 1.96$$

Here, μ_0 is the hypothesized value of the population mean. The condition states that rejection is warranted if the test statistic exceeds 1.96. Multiplying both sides by $s_{\bar{x}}$, we have $\bar{x} - \mu_0 > 1.96 \, s_{\bar{x}}$, or after rearranging, $\bar{x} - 1.96 \, s_{\bar{x}} > \mu_0$, which we can also write as $\mu_0 < \bar{x} - 1.96 \, s_{\bar{x}}$. This expression says that if the hypothesized population mean, μ_0, is less than the lower limit of the 95 percent confidence interval based on the sample mean, we reject the null hypothesis at the 5 percent level of significance (the test statistic falls in the rejection region to the right). Now, we can take the other condition for rejecting the null hypothesis

$$\frac{\bar{x} - \mu_0}{s_{\bar{x}}} < -1.96$$

---

[8] Just as with the hypothesis test, we can use this confidence interval, based on the standard normal distribution, when we have large samples. An alternative hypothesis test and confidence interval uses the *t*-distribution, which requires concepts that we introduce in the next section.

and, using algebra as before, rewrite this as $\mu_0 > \bar{x} + 1.96\,s_{\bar{x}}$. If the hypothesized population mean is larger than the upper limit of the 95 percent confidence interval, we reject the null hypothesis at the 5 percent level (the test statistic falls in the rejection region to the left). In summary, when the hypothesized value of the population parameter under the null is outside the corresponding confidence interval, the null hypothesis is rejected. We could use confidence intervals to test hypotheses; practitioners, however, usually do not. Computing a test statistic (one number, versus two numbers for the usual confidence interval) is more efficient. Also, a concept of a one-sided confidence interval, to correspond to a one-sided hypothesis test, while possible to define, is rarely encountered. Furthermore, only when we compute a test statistic can we obtain a p-value, a useful quantity relating to the significance of our results (we will discuss p-values shortly).

To return to our risk premium test, we stated hypotheses H_0: $\mu_{RP} \leq 0$ versus H_a: $\mu_{RP} > 0$. We identified the test statistic as $\bar{x}_{RP}/s_{\bar{x}}$, and we stated that it follows a standard normal distribution. We are, therefore, conducting a one-sided z-test. We specified a 0.05 significance level. For this one-sided z-test, the rejection point at the 0.05 level of significance is 1.645. We will reject the null if the calculated z-statistic equals or is larger than 1.645. Figure 7-2 illustrates this test.

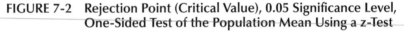

FIGURE 7-2   Rejection Point (Critical Value), 0.05 Significance Level, One-Sided Test of the Population Mean Using a z-Test

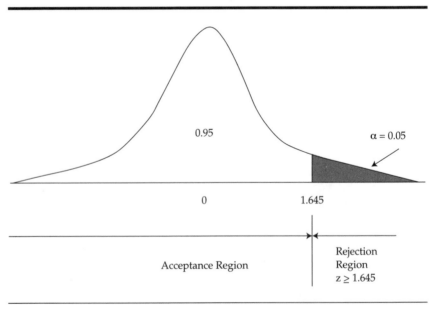

The fifth step in testing a hypothesis involves collecting the data and calculating the test statistic. The quality of our conclusions depends not only on the appropriateness of the statistical model, but also on the quality of the data we use in conducting the test. We need to check for measurement errors in the recorded data, first of all. Other issues to be aware of include, but are not limited to, sample selection bias and time-period bias. Sample selection bias refers to bias introduced by systematically excluding some members of the population according to a particular attribute. One type of sample selection bias is survivorship bias. For example, if we define our sample as U.S. bond mutual funds currently operating and we collect returns for just these funds, we will systematically exclude funds that have not survived to the present. Nonsurviving funds are likely to have underperformed surviving funds, on average; as a result the performance reflected in the sample may be biased upward. Time-period bias refers to the possibility that when using a time-series sample, our statistical conclusion may be sensitive to the starting and ending dates of the sample.[9]

To continue with the risk premium hypothesis, we focus on U.S. equities as captured by the S&P 500. According to Ibbotson Associates, for the period January 1926 to March 1999 (879 monthly observations), the mean excess return on the S&P 500, $\bar{x}_{RP}$, was 0.74 percent per month. The sample standard deviation of monthly returns was 5.66 percent. Using Equation 7-3, the standard error of the sample mean is $s_{\bar{x}} = s/\sqrt{n} = 5.66\%/\sqrt{879} = 0.191\%$. The test statistic is $z = \bar{x}_{RP}/s_{\bar{x}} = 0.74\%/0.191\% = 3.87$.

The sixth step is to make the statistical decision. For our example, because the test statistic $z = 3.87$ is larger than the rejection point of 1.645, we reject the null hypothesis in favor of the alternative hypothesis that the risk premium on U.S. stocks is positive. The first six steps are the statistical steps. The final decision concerns the use we make of the statistical decision.

The final step is to make the economic or investment decision. The economic or investment decision takes into consideration not only the statistical decision, but also all economic issues pertinent to the decision.

As one example, we may be testing an investment strategy and reject a null hypothesis that the mean return to the strategy is zero. We should be aware that slight differences from a hypothesized value may be statistically significant but not economically meaningful. Equation 7-1 shows that the smaller the standard error of the sample statistic (the divisor in the formula), the larger the value of the test statistic and the greater the chance the null will be rejected, all else equal. The standard error decreases as the sample size, n, increases, so that, for very large samples, we can reject the null for small departures from it. We may find that although a strategy provides a mean return that is significantly positive in a statistical sense, the results are not economically significant when we take account of transaction costs, taxes, and risk. Even if we conclude that a strategy's results are economically meaningful, we may explore the logic of why the strategy should work in the future before actually implementing it. Such considerations cannot be incorporated into a hypothesis test.

In reading the investment literature, we frequently find that researchers report the p-value (also called the marginal significance level) associated with tests.

- **Definition of p-Value.** The p-value is the smallest level of significance at which the null hypothesis can be rejected.

For the value of the test statistic of 3.87 in the risk premium hypothesis test, using a spreadsheet function for the standard normal distribution, we calculate a p-value of 0.000054. We can reject the null hypothesis at that level of significance. The smaller the p-value, the stronger the evidence against the null hypothesis and in favor of the alternative hypothesis. The p-value for a two-sided test that a parameter equals zero is frequently generated automatically by statistical and econometric software.

We can use p-values in the hypothesis testing framework presented above as an alternative to using rejection points. If the p-value is less than our specified level of significance, we reject the null hypothesis. Otherwise, we do not reject the null hypothesis. We reach the same conclusion using the p-value in this fashion or using rejection points. For example, because 0.000054 is less than 0.05, we would reject the null hypothesis in the risk premium test. The p-value, however, provides more precise information on the

---

[9] These issue are discussed further in the chapter on sampling.

strength of the evidence than does the rejection points approach. The *p*-value of 0.000054 indicates that the null is rejected at a far smaller level of significance than 0.05.

If one researcher examines a question using a 0.05 significance level and another researcher uses a 0.01 significance level, the reader may have trouble integrating the findings. This concern has given rise to an approach to presenting the results of hypothesis tests that features *p*-values and omits specification of the significance level (Step 3). The interpretation of the statistical results is left to the consumer of the research. This has sometimes been called the *p-value approach* to hypothesis testing.[10]

3   HYPOTHESIS TESTS CONCERNING THE MEAN

Hypothesis tests concerning the mean are among the most common in practice. In this section we discuss conducting such tests for several distinct types of problems. In one type of problem (discussed in Section 3.1), we test whether the population mean of a single population is equal to (or greater or less than) some hypothesized value. Then, we address inference on means based on two samples. Is an observed difference between two sample means due to chance or different underlying (population) means? When we have two random samples that are independent of each other—that is, no relationship exists between the measurements in one sample and the measurements in the other—the techniques of Section 3.2 apply. When the samples are not independent, the methods of Section 3.3 are appropriate.[11]

3.1 TESTS CONCERNING A SINGLE MEAN

An analyst who wants to test a hypothesis concerning the value of an underlying or population mean, will, in the great majority of cases, conduct a *t*-test. A ***t*-test** is a hypothesis test using a statistic (*t*-statistic) that follows a *t*-distribution. The *t*-distribution is a probability distribution defined by a single parameter known as degrees of freedom (df). Each value of degrees of freedom defines one distribution in this family of distributions. The *t*-distribution is closely related to the standard normal distribution. Like the standard normal distribution, a *t*-distribution is a symmetrical distribution with a mean of zero. However, the *t*-distribution is more spread out: It has a standard deviation greater than 1 (compared to 1 for the standard normal)[12] and more probability for outcomes distant from the mean (it has fatter tails than the standard normal distribution). As the number of degrees of freedom, which is based on sample size, increases, the spread decreases and the *t*-distribution approaches the standard normal distribution as a limit.

Why is the *t*-distribution the focus for the hypothesis tests of this section? In practice, investment analysts need to estimate the population standard deviation of the population generating a sample, using the sample standard deviation. That is, the population vari-

---

[10] Davidson and MacKinnon (1993) argued the merits of this approach: "The P value approach does not necessarily force us to make a decision about the null hypothesis. If we obtain a P value of, say, 0.000001, we will almost certainly want to reject the null. But if we obtain a P value of, say, 0.04, or even 0.004, we are not *obliged* to reject it. We may simply file the result away as information that casts some doubt on the null hypothesis, but that is not, by itself, conclusive. We believe that this somewhat agnostic attitude toward test statistics, in which they are merely regarded as pieces of information that we may or may not want to act upon, is usually the most sensible one to take" (p. 80).

[11] When we want to test whether the population means of more than two populations are equal, we use analysis of variance (ANOVA). ANOVA is introduced in its most common application, regression analysis, in the chapter on correlation and regression analysis.

[12] The formula for the variance of a *t*-distribution is df/(df − 2).

ance (or standard deviation) is unknown. For hypothesis tests concerning the population mean of a normally distributed population with unknown variance, the theoretically correct test statistic is the t-statistic. What if a normal distribution does not describe the population? The t-test is **robust** to moderate departures from normality—except for outliers and strong skewness.[13] When we have large samples, departures of the underlying distribution from the normal are of increasingly less concern. With large samples, the sample mean is approximately normally distributed, according to the central limit theorem, whatever the distribution describing the population. In general, a sample size of 30 or more can usually be treated as a large sample and a sample size of 29 or less is treated as a small sample.[14]

- **Test Statistic for Hypothesis Tests of the Population Mean (Practical Case—Population Variance Unknown).** If the population sampled has unknown variance and either of the conditions below holds:
  1. the sample is large, or
  2. the sample is small but the population sampled is normally distributed, or approximately normally distributed,

  then the test statistic for hypothesis tests concerning a single population mean, μ, is

$$t_{n-1} = \frac{\bar{x} - \mu_0}{s/\sqrt{n}} \tag{7-4}$$

  where

$$t_{n-1} = t\text{-statistic with } n - 1 \text{ degrees of freedom (}n\text{ is the sample size)}$$
$$\bar{x} = \text{the sample mean}$$
$$\mu_0 = \text{the hypothesized value of the population mean}$$
$$s = \text{the sample standard deviation}$$

The denominator of the t-statistic is an estimate of the standard error of the sample mean, $s_{\bar{x}} = s/\sqrt{n}$.[15]

In our first example, because the sample size is small, the test would be called a small sample test concerning the population mean.

EXAMPLE 7-1. Risk and Return Characteristics of an Equity Mutual Fund (1).

You are analyzing Sendar Equity Fund, a midcap growth fund that has been in existence for 24 months. Over this period, it has achieved a mean monthly return of 1.50 percent with a sample standard deviation of monthly returns of 3.60 percent. Given

---

[13] See Moore and McCabe (1998). A statistic is robust if the required probability calculations are insensitive to violations of the assumptions.

[14] Although this generalization is useful, the caution should be made that the sample size needed to obtain an approximately normal sampling distribution for the sample mean depends on how nonnormal the original population is. For some populations, *large* may be a sample size well in excess of 30.

[15] A technical note, for reference, is required. When the sample comes from a finite population, estimates of the standard error of the mean, whether from Equation 7-2 or Equation 7-3, overestimate the true standard error. To address this, the computed standard error is multiplied by a shrinkage factor called the finite population correction factor (fpc), equal to $\sqrt{(N - n)/(N - 1)}$, where N is the population size and n is the sample size. When the sample size is small relative to the population size (less than 5 percent of the population size) the fpc is usually ignored. The overestimation problem only arises in the usual situation of sampling without replacement (after an item is selected, it cannot be picked again) as opposed to sampling with replacement.

its level of systematic (market) risk, this mutual fund was expected to have earned a 1.10 percent mean monthly return over that time period. Are the actual results consistent with an underlying or population mean monthly return of 1.10 percent?

1. Formulate null and alternative hypotheses consistent with the verbal description of the goal of the research.
2. Identify the test statistic for conducting a test of the hypotheses in Part 1.
3. Identify the rejection point or points for the hypothesis tested in Part 1 at the 0.10 level of significance.
4. Determine whether the null hypothesis is rejected or not rejected at the 0.10 level of significance. (Use tables in the back of this book.)

Solution to 1.   We have a "not equal to" alternative hypothesis, where μ is the underlying mean return on Sendar Equity Fund—H_0: $\mu = 1.10$ versus H_a: $\mu \neq 1.10$.

Solution to 2.   Because the population variance is not known, we use a t-test with $24 - 1 = 23$ degrees of freedom.

Solution to 3.   Because this is a two-tailed test, we have the rejection point $t_{\alpha/2, n-1} = t_{0.05, 23}$. In the table for the t-distribution, we look across the row for 23 degrees of freedom to the 0.05 column, to find 1.714. There are two rejection points for this two-sided test, 1.714 and -1.714. We will reject the null if we find that $t > 1.714$ or $t < -1.714$.

Solution to 4.

$$t_{23} = \frac{1.5 - 1.10}{3.60/\sqrt{24}} = \frac{0.40}{0.734847} = 0.544331$$

Because 0.544331 does not satisfy either $t > 1.714$ or $t < -1.714$, we do not reject the null hypothesis.

The theoretically correct $100(1 - \alpha)\%$ confidence interval for the population mean of a normal distribution with unknown variance, based on a sample of size n, is

$$\bar{x} - t_{\alpha/2}s_{\bar{x}} \quad \text{to} \quad \bar{x} + t_{\alpha/2}s_{\bar{x}}$$

where $t_{\alpha/2}$ is the value of t such that $\alpha/2$ of the probability remains in the right tail and where $-t_{\alpha/2}$ is the value of t such that $\alpha/2$ of the probability remains in the left tail, for $n - 1$ degrees of freedom. Here, the 90 percent confidence interval runs from $0.240472 = 1.5 - (1.714 \times 0.734847)$ to $2.759528 = 1.5 + (1.714 \times 0.734847)$, compactly [0.240472, 2.759528]. The hypothesized value of mean return, 1.10, is within this confidence interval, and we see from this perspective also that the null hypothesis is not rejected.

EXAMPLE 7-2.   A Slowdown in Payments of Receivables.

FashionDesigns, a supplier of casual clothing to retail chains, is concerned about a possible slowdown in payments by the company's customers. The controller's office measures the rate of payment by the average number of days in receivables.[16] FashionDesigns has generally maintained an average of 45 days in receivables. Because it would be too costly to analyze all of the company's receivables frequently, the controller's office uses sampling to track customers' payment rates. A random sample of 50 accounts shows a mean number of days in receivables of 49 with a standard deviation of 8 days.

1. Formulate null and alternative hypotheses consistent with determining whether the evidence supports the suspected condition that there has been a slowdown in customer payments.

2. Identify the test statistic for conducting a test of the hypotheses in Part 1.

3. Identify the rejection point or points for the hypothesis tested in Part 1 at the 0.05 and 0.01 levels of significance.

4. Determine whether the null hypothesis is rejected or not rejected at the 0.05 and 0.01 levels of significance.

Solution to 1. The suspected condition is that the number of days in receivables has increased relative to the historical rate of 45 days, which suggests a "greater than" alternative hypothesis. With μ as the population mean number of days in receivables, the hypotheses are H_0: $\mu \leq 45$ versus H_a: $\mu > 45$.

Solution to 2. Because the population variance is not known, we use a *t*-test with $50 - 1 = 49$ degrees of freedom.

Solution to 3. The rejection point is found across degrees of freedom of 49. To find the one-tailed rejection point for a 0.05 significance level, we use the 0.05 column: The value is 1.677. To find the one-tailed rejection point for a 0.01 level of significance, we use the 0.01 column: The value is 2.405. To summarize, at a 0.05 significance level, we reject the null if we find that $t > 1.677$; at a 0.01 significance level, we reject the null if we find that $t > 2.405$.

Solution to 4.

$$t_{49} = \frac{49 - 45}{8/\sqrt{50}} = \frac{4}{1.131371} = 3.536$$

Because $3.536 > 1.677$, the null hypothesis is rejected at the 0.05 level. Because $3.536 > 2.405$, the null hypothesis is also rejected at the 0.01 level.

We stated above that when population variance is not known, we use a *t*-test for tests concerning a single population mean. Given at least approximate normality, the *t*-test is always called for when we deal with small samples and do not know the population variance. When we have large samples, the central limit theorem states that the sample mean is approximately normally distributed, whatever the distribution of the population. The *t*-test is still appropriate, but we may also encounter an alternative test when sample size is large.

---

[16] This represents the average length of time that the business must wait after making a sale before receiving payment. The calculation is (accounts receivable)/(average sales per day).

Practitioners sometimes use a z-test in place of a t-test for tests concerning a mean, when sample size is large.[17] The difference between the rejection points for the t-test and z-test becomes quite small when sample size is large. For a two-sided test at the 0.05 level of significance, the rejection points for a z-test are 1.96 and −1.96. For a t-test, the rejection points are 2.045 and −2.045 for df = 29 (about a 4 percent difference between the z and t values) and 2.009 and −2.009 for df = 50 (about a 2.5 percent difference between the z and t values). Because the t-test is readily available as statistical program output and theoretically correct for unknown population variance, we present it as the test of choice.

In a very limited number of cases, we may know the population variance; in this case, the z-test is theoretically correct.[18]

- **The z-Test Alternative.**

  1. If the population sampled is normally distributed with known variance σ^2, then the test statistic for a hypothesis test concerning a single population mean, μ, is

$$z = \frac{\bar{x} - \mu_0}{\sigma/\sqrt{n}} \tag{7-5}$$

  2. If the population sampled has unknown variance and the sample is large, in place of a t-test, an alternative test statistic (relying on the central limit theorem) is

$$z = \frac{\bar{x} - \mu_0}{s/\sqrt{n}} \tag{7-6}$$

In the above,

σ = the known population standard deviation

s = the sample standard deviation

μ_0 = the hypothesized value of the population mean

When we use a z-test, we most frequently refer to a rejection point in the list below.

- **Rejection Points for a z-Test.**

  A. Significance level of $\alpha = 0.10$.

  1. $H_0: \theta = \theta_0$ versus $H_a: \theta \neq \theta_0$. The rejection points are $z_{0.05} = 1.645$ and $-z_{0.05} = -1.645$.
     Reject the null hypothesis if $z > 1.645$ or if $z < -1.645$.

  2. $H_0: \theta \leq \theta_0$ versus $H_a: \theta > \theta_0$. The rejection point is $z_{0.10} = 1.28$.
     Reject the null hypothesis if $z > 1.28$.

  3. $H_0: \theta \geq \theta_0$ versus $H_a: \theta < \theta_0$. The rejection point is $-z_{0.10} = -1.28$.
     Reject the null hypothesis if $z < -1.28$.

---

[17] These practitioners choose between t-tests and z-tests based on sample size. For small samples ($n < 30$), a t-test is used, and for large samples, a z-test is used.

[18] For example, in Monte Carlo simulation, we prespecify the probability distributions for the risk factors. If we use a normal distribution, we know the true values of mean and variance. Monte Carlo simulation involves the use of a computer to represent the operation of a system subject to risk; Monte Carlo simulation is discussed in the chapter on common probability distributions.

B. Significance level of $a = 0.05$.

    1. H_0: $\theta = \theta_0$ versus H_a: $\theta \neq \theta_0$. The rejection points are $z_{0.025} = 1.96$ and $-z_{0.025} = -1.96$.
    Reject the null hypothesis if $z > 1.96$ or if $z < -1.96$.

    2. H_0: $\theta \leq \theta_0$ versus H_a: $\theta > \theta_0$. The rejection point is $z_{0.05} = 1.645$.
    Reject the null hypothesis if $z > 1.645$.

    3. H_0: $\theta \geq \theta_0$ versus H_a: $\theta < \theta_0$. The rejection point is $-z_{0.05} = -1.645$.
    Reject the null hypothesis if $z < -1.645$.

C. Significance level of $a = 0.01$.

    1. H_0: $\theta = \theta_0$ versus H_a: $\theta \neq \theta_0$. The rejection points are $z_{0.005} = 2.575$ and $-z_{0.005} = -2.575$.
    Reject the null hypothesis if $z > 2.575$ or if $z < -2.575$.

    2. H_0: $\theta \leq \theta_0$ versus H_a: $\theta > \theta_0$. The rejection point is $z_{0.01} = 2.33$.
    Reject the null hypothesis if $z > 2.33$.

    3. H_0: $\theta \geq \theta_0$ versus H_a: $\theta < \theta_0$. The rejection point is $-z_{0.01} = -2.33$.
    Reject the null hypothesis if $z < -2.33$.

EXAMPLE 7-3.   The Effect of Commercial Paper Issuance on Stock Prices.

Commercial paper (CP) is unsecured short-term corporate debt that, like U.S. Treasury bills, is characterized by a single payment at maturity. When a company enters the CP market for the first time, how do stock market participants react?

    Nayar and Rozeff (1994) addressed this question using data for the period October 1981 to December 1985. Over this period, 132 CP issues received an initial rating in Standard & Poor's *CreditWeek* or Moody's Investors Service *Bond Survey*. Nayar and Rozeff categorized ratings as superior or inferior. Superior CP ratings were A1+ or A1 from Standard & Poor's and Prime-1 (P1) from Moody's. Inferior CP ratings were A2 or lower from Standard & Poor's and Prime-2 (P2) or lower from Moody's. If CP ratings are informative for stock investors, stock returns should reflect that information when the issue rating is announced. The publication day of the initial ratings was designated $t = 0$. The researchers found, however, that firms themselves often disseminate the rating information prior to publication in *CreditWeek* or the *Bond Survey*. The reaction of stock price the day before publication, $t = -1$, was closer to the actual date of information release.

    If CP ratings provide new information useful for equity valuation, the information should be incorporated in stock prices and returns. Only one component of stock returns is of interest: the return in excess of that predicted given a stock's market risk or beta—called the *abnormal return*. Positive (negative) abnormal returns indicate that investors perceive favorable (unfavorable) corporate news in the ratings announcement. Although Nayar and Rozeff examined abnormal returns for various time horizons or event windows, we report a selection of their findings for the day prior to rating publication ($t = -1$).

All CP Issues ($n = 132$ issues). The null hypothesis was that the average abnormal stock return on day $t = -1$ was 0. The null would be true if stock investors did not find either positive or negative information in the announcement.

Mean abnormal return = 0.39 percent.

Sample standard error of the mean of abnormal returns = 0.1336 percent.[19]

Industrial CP Issues with Superior Ratings ($n = 72$ issues). The null hypothesis was that the average abnormal stock return on day $t = -1$ was 0. The null would be true if stock investors did not find either positive or negative information in the announcement.

Mean abnormal return = 0.79 percent.

Sample standard error of the mean of abnormal returns = 0.197 percent.

Industrial CP Issues with Inferior Ratings ($n = 24$ issues). The null hypothesis was that the average abnormal stock return on day $t = -1$ was 0. The null would be true if stock investors did not find either positive or negative information in the announcement.

Mean abnormal return = -0.57 percent.

Sample standard error of the mean of abnormal returns = 0.38 percent.

The researchers chose to use z-tests.

1. With respect to each of the three cases, suppose that the alternative hypothesis reflects the belief that investors do not, on average, perceive either positive or negative information in initial ratings. State one set of hypotheses (a null hypothesis and an alternative hypothesis) that covers all three cases.

2. Determine whether the null hypothesis formulated in Part 1 is rejected or not rejected at the 0.05 and 0.01 levels of significance for the *All CP Issues* case. Interpret the results.

3. Determine whether the null hypothesis formulated in Part 1 is rejected or not rejected at the 0.05 and 0.01 levels of significance for the *Industrial CP Issues with Superior Ratings* case. Interpret the results.

4. Determine whether the null hypothesis formulated in Part 1 is rejected or not rejected at the 0.05 and 0.01 levels of significance for the *Industrial CP Issues with Inferior Ratings* case. Interpret the results.

Solution to 1. A set of hypotheses consistent with no information in CP credit ratings relevant to stock investors is

H_0: The population mean abnormal return on day $t = -1$ equals 0.
H_a: The population mean abnormal return on day $t = -1$ does not equal 0.

Solution to 2. From the information on rejection points for z-tests we know that we reject the null hypothesis at the 0.05 significance level if $z > 1.96$ or if $z < 1.96$, and at the 0.01 significance level if $z > 2.575$ or if $z < 2.575$. Using the z-test, $z = (0.39\% - 0\%)/0.1336 = 2.92$ is significant at the 0.05 and 0.01 levels. The null is rejected. The fact of CP issuance itself appears to be viewed as favorable news.

Because it is possible that significant results could be due to outliers, the researchers also reported the number of cases of positive and negative abnormal returns. The ratio of cases of positive to negative abnormal returns was 80:52, which tends to support the conclusion of positive abnormal returns from the z-test.

---

[19] This was calculated as a sample standard deviation over the 132 issues (a cross-sectional standard deviation) divided by the square root of 132. Other standard errors were calculated similarly.

Solution to 3. Using the z-test, $z = (0.79\% - 0\%)/0.197\% = 4.01$ is significant at the 0.05 and 0.01 levels. Stocks earned clearly positive abnormal returns in response to the news of a superior initial CP rating. Investors may view rating agencies as certifying through superior ratings that the future prospects of the firms are strong.

The ratio of cases of positive to negative abnormal returns was 48:24, which tends to support the conclusion of positive abnormal returns from the z-test.

Solution to 4. Using the z-test, $z = (-0.57\% - 0\%)/0.38\% = -1.50$ is not significant at the 0.05 and 0.01 levels. In the case of inferior ratings, we cannot conclude that investors found either positive or negative information in the announcements of initial CP ratings.

The ratio of cases of positive to negative abnormal returns was 11:13 and tends to support the conclusion of the z-test, which did not reject the null hypothesis.

Nearly all practical situations involve an unknown population variance. Table 7-2 summarizes our discussion for tests concerning the population mean when the population variance is unknown.

TABLE 7-2 Test Concerning the Population Mean (Population Variance Not Known)

	Large Sample ($n \geq 30$)	Small Sample ($n < 30$)
Population normal	t-Test (z-Test alternative)	t-Test
Population nonnormal	t-Test (z-Test alternative)	Not Available

3.2 TESTS CONCERNING DIFFERENCES BETWEEN MEANS

We often want to know whether a mean value—for example, a mean return—differs between two groups. Is an observed difference due to chance or to different underlying values for the mean? We have two samples, one for each group. When it is reasonable to believe that the samples are from populations at least approximately normally distributed and that the samples are also independent of each other, the techniques of this section apply. We discuss two t-tests for a test concerning differences between the means of two populations. In one case, the population variances, although unknown, can be assumed to be equal. Then, we efficiently combine the observations from both samples to obtain a **pooled** estimate of the common but unknown population variance. In the second case, we do not assume that the unknown population variances are equal and an approximate t-test is then available. Letting μ_1 and μ_2 stand, respectively, for the population means of the first and second populations, we most often want to test whether the population means are equal or whether one is larger than the other. Thus, we usually formulate the following hypotheses:

1. $H_0: \mu_1 - \mu_2 = 0$ versus $H_a: \mu_1 - \mu_2 \neq 0$ (the alternative is that $\mu_1 \neq \mu_2$)
2. $H_0: \mu_1 - \mu_2 \leq 0$ versus $H_a: \mu_1 - \mu_2 > 0$ (the alternative is that $\mu_1 > \mu_2$)
3. $H_0: \mu_1 - \mu_2 \geq 0$ versus $H_a: \mu_1 - \mu_2 < 0$ (the alternative is that $\mu_1 < \mu_2$)

We can, however, formulate other hypotheses, such as $H_0: \mu_1 - \mu_2 = 2$ versus $H_a: \mu_1 - \mu_2 \neq 2$. The procedure is the same.

The definition of the *t*-test follows.

- **Test Statistic for a Test of the Difference between Two Population Means (Normally Distributed Populations, Population Variances Unknown but Assumed Equal).** When we can assume that the two populations are normally distributed and that the unknown population variances are equal, a *t*-test based on independent random samples is given by

$$t = \frac{(\bar{x}_1 - \bar{x}_2) - (\mu_1 - \mu_2)}{\left(\dfrac{s_p^2}{n_1} + \dfrac{s_p^2}{n_2} \right)^{1/2}} \tag{7-7}$$

where $s_p^2 = \dfrac{(n_1 - 1)s_1^2 + (n_2 - 1)s_2^2}{n_1 + n_2 - 2}$ is a pooled estimator of the common variance. The number of degrees of freedom is $n_1 + n_2 - 2$.

EXAMPLE 7-4.   Mean Returns on the S&P 500: A Test of Equality across Decades.

The realized mean monthly return on the S&P 500 in the 1980s appears to have been substantially different than the mean return in the 1970s. Was the difference statistically significant? The data indicate that assuming equal population variances is not unreasonable.

TABLE 7-3

Decade	Number of Months (n)	Mean Monthly Return (%)	Standard Deviation
1970s	120	0.580	4.598
1980s	120	1.470	4.738

1. Formulate null and alternative hypotheses consistent with a two-sided hypothesis test.
2. Identify the test statistic for conducting a test of the hypotheses in Part 1.
3. Identify the rejection point or points for the hypothesis tested in Part 1 at the 0.10, 0.05, and 0.01 levels of significance.
4. Determine whether the null hypothesis is rejected or not rejected at the 0.10, 0.05, and 0.01 levels of significance.

Solution to 1.   Letting μ_1 stand for the population mean return for the 1970s and μ_2 stand for the population mean return for the 1980s, we formulate the following hypotheses:

$$H_0: \mu_1 - \mu_2 = 0 \text{ versus } H_a: \mu_1 - \mu_2 \neq 0.$$

Solution to 2. Because the two samples are drawn from different decades, they are independent samples. The population variances are not known but can be assumed to be equal. Given all these considerations, the *t*-test given in Equation 7-7 has $120 + 120 - 2 = 238$ degrees of freedom.

Solution to 3. In the tables, the closest degrees of freedom to 238 is 200. For a two-sided test, the rejection points are ± 1.653, ± 1.972, and ± 2.601 for, respectively, the 0.10, 0.05, and 0.01 levels for df = 200. To summarize, at the 0.10 level, we will reject the null if $t < -1.653$ or $t > 1.653$; at the 0.05 level, we will reject the null if $t < -1.972$ or $t > 1.972$; and at the 0.01 level, we will reject the null if $t < -2.601$ or $t > 2.601$.

Solution to 4. In calculating the test statistic, the first step is to calculate the pooled estimate of variance:

$$s_p^2 = \frac{(n_1 - 1)s_1^2 + (n_2 - 1)s_2^2}{n_1 + n_2 - 2} = \frac{(120 - 1)(4.598)^2 + (120 - 1)(4.738)^2}{120 + 120 - 2}$$

$$= \frac{5{,}187.239512}{238} = 21.795124$$

$$t = \frac{(\bar{x}_1 - \bar{x}_2) - (\mu_1 - \mu_2)}{\left(\dfrac{s_p^2}{n_1} + \dfrac{s_p^2}{n_2}\right)^{1/2}} = \frac{(0.580 - 1.470) - 0}{\left(\dfrac{21.795124}{119} + \dfrac{21.795124}{119}\right)^{1/2}}$$

$$= \frac{-0.89}{0.605231} = -1.471$$

The *t* value of -1.471 is not significant at the 0.10 level, so it is also not significant at the 0.05 or 0.01 levels.

In many cases of practical interest, we cannot assume that population variances are equal. The following test statistic is often used in the investment literature in such cases:

- **Test Statistic for a Test of the Difference between Two Population Means (Normally Distributed Populations, Unequal and Unknown Population Variances).** When we can assume that the two populations are normally distributed but do not know the population variances and cannot assume that they are equal, an approximate *t*-test based on independent random samples is given by

$$t = \frac{(\bar{x}_1 - \bar{x}_2) - (\mu_1 - \mu_2)}{\left(\dfrac{s_1^2}{n_1} + \dfrac{s_2^2}{n_2}\right)^{1/2}} \tag{7-8}$$

where we use tables of the *t*-distribution using "modified" degrees of freedom computed with the formula

$$df = \frac{\left(\dfrac{s_1^2}{n_1} + \dfrac{s_2^2}{n_2}\right)^2}{\dfrac{(s_1^2/n_1)^2}{n_1} + \dfrac{(s_2^2/n_2)^2}{n_2}} \tag{7-9}$$

A practical tip is to compute the *t*-statistic before computing the degrees of freedom. Whether the *t*-statistic is significant will sometimes be obvious.

EXAMPLE 7-5.   Recovery Rates on Defaulted Bonds: A Hypothesis Test.

How are the required yields on risky corporate bonds determined? Two key factors are the expected probability of default and the expected amount that will be recovered in the event of default, or the recovery rate. Altman and Kishore (1996) documented for the first time the average recovery rates on defaulted bonds stratified by industry and seniority. For their study period, 1971 to 1995, Altman and Kishore discovered that defaulted bonds of public utilities and chemicals, petroleum, and plastics manufacturers experienced much higher recovery rates than did other industrial sectors. Could the differences be explained by a greater preponderance of senior debt in the higher-recovery sectors? They studied this by examining recovery rates stratified by seniority. We discuss their results for senior secured bonds. With μ_1 denoting the population mean recovery rate for the senior secured bonds of utilities and μ_2 denoting the population mean recovery rate for the senior secured bonds of other sectors (non-utilities), the hypotheses are $H_0: \mu_1 - \mu_2 = 0$ versus $H_a: \mu_1 - \mu_2 \neq 0$.

Table 7-4 excerpts from their findings. The group "entire sample" is all senior secured bonds except those of utilities.

TABLE 7-4   Utility Versus Aggregate Recovery Rates by Seniority

Industry Group/ Seniority	Industry Group			Entire Sample		
	Number of Observations	Average Price*	Standard Deviation	Number of Observations	Average Price*	Standard Deviation
Public Utilities Senior Secured	21	$64.42	$14.03	64	$55.75	$25.17

Source: Altman and Kishore (1996), Table 5.

*Average price at default is a measure of recovery rate.

On the basis of the data in the table, answer the following questions. Following the researchers, assume that the populations (recovery rates of utilities, recovery rates of non-utilities) are normally distributed and that the samples are independent.

1. Discuss why Altman and Kishore would choose a test based on Equation 7-8 rather than Equation 7-7.
2. Calculate the test statistic to test the null hypothesis given above.
3. What is the modified degrees of freedom of the test?
4. Determine whether the null is rejected at the 0.10 level.

Solution to 1.   The sample standard deviation for the recovery rate on the senior secured bonds of utilities ($14.03) appears much smaller than the sample standard deviation of the comparable bonds for non-utilities ($25.17). Properly choosing not to assume equal variances, Altman and Kishore employed the approximate t-test given in Equation 7-8.

Solution to 2. The test statistic is

$$t = \frac{\bar{x}_1 - \bar{x}_2}{\left(\dfrac{s_1^2}{n_1} + \dfrac{s_2^2}{n_2}\right)^{1/2}}$$

where

$\bar{x}_1$ = sample mean recovery rate for utilities = 64.42
$\bar{x}_2$ = sample mean recovery rate for non-utility sectors = 55.75
s_1^2 = sample variance for utilities = 14.03^2 = 196.8409
s_2^2 = sample standard deviation for non-utilities = 25.17^2 = 633.5289
n_1 = sample size of the utility sample = 21
n_2 = sample size of the non-utility sample = 64

Thus, $t = (64.42 - 55.75)/[(196.8409/21) + (633.5289/64)]^{1/2} = 8.67/(9.373376 + 9.898889)^{1/2} = 8.67/4.390019 = 1.974$. The calculated t-statistic is thus 1.974.

Solution to 3.

$$df = \frac{\left(\dfrac{s_1^2}{n_1} + \dfrac{s_2^2}{n_2}\right)^2}{\dfrac{(s_1^2/n_1)^2}{n_1} + \dfrac{(s_2^2/n_2)^2}{n_2}} = \frac{\left(\dfrac{196.8409}{21} + \dfrac{633.5289}{64}\right)^2}{\dfrac{(196.8409/21)^2}{21} + \dfrac{(633.5289/64)^2}{64}}$$

$$= \frac{371.420208}{5.714881} = 64.99$$

or 65 degrees of freedom.

Solution to 4. The closest entry to df = 65 in the tables for the t-distribution is df = 60. For α = 0.10, we find $t_{\alpha/2}$ = 1.671. Thus, we reject the null if $t < -1.671$ or $t > 1.671$. Based on the computed value of 1.974, we reject the null at the 0.10 level. Some evidence exists that recovery rates differ between utilities and other industries. Why? Altman and Kishore suggest that the differing nature of the firms' assets and industry competitive structures may explain the different recovery rates.

3.3 TESTS CONCERNING MEAN DIFFERENCES

In the previous section, we presented two t-tests for discerning differences between population means. The basis for the tests was two samples. An assumption for the validity of those tests was that the samples were independent; that is, they were not related. When we want to conduct tests on two means based on samples that we believe are not independent, the methods of this section apply.

The basis of the t-test in this section is data that are arranged in **paired observations,** and the test itself is sometimes called a **paired comparisons test.** For example, we may be concerned with the dividend policy of firms before and after a change in the tax law affecting the taxation of dividends. We then have pairs of before and after observations on the same companies. We may test a hypothesis about the mean of the differences (mean differences) that we observe across firms. In other cases, the paired observations are not in the same units (the firm in the above example). For example, we may be testing whether the mean returns earned by two investment strategies were equal over a study period. Because the returns to both strategies are likely to be related to some common risk factors, such as the market return, the samples are dependent. By calculating a standard error based on differences, the t-test presented below takes account of correlation between the observations.

Suppose we have observations on A and B, and the samples are dependent. We arrange the observations in pairs. Let d_i denote the difference between two paired observations. We can use the notation $d_i = x_{Ai} - x_{Bi}$, where x_{Ai} and x_{Bi} are the ith pair observations, $i = 1, 2, ..., n$. Let μ_d stand for the population mean difference. We can formulate the following hypotheses, where μ_{d0} is a hypothesized value for the population mean difference:

1. $H_0: \mu_d = \mu_{d0}$ versus $H_a: \mu_d \neq \mu_{d0}$
2. $H_0: \mu_d \leq \mu_{d0}$ versus $H_a: \mu_d > \mu_{d0}$
3. $H_0: \mu_d \geq \mu_{d0}$ versus $H_a: \mu_d < \mu_{d0}$

In practice, the most commonly used value for μ_{d0} is 0.

As usual, we are concerned with the case of normally distributed populations with unknown population variances, and we will formulate a t-test. To calculate the t-statistic, we first need to find the sample mean difference:

$$\bar{d} = \frac{1}{n}\sum_{i=1}^{n} d_i \tag{7-10}$$

where n is the number of pairs of observations. The sample variance, denoted by s_d^2, is

$$s_d^2 = \frac{\sum_{i=1}^{n}(d_i - \bar{d})^2}{n-1} \tag{7-11}$$

Taking the square root of this quantity, we have the sample standard deviation, s_d, which then allows us to calculate the standard error of the mean difference as

$$s_{\bar{d}} = \frac{s_d}{\sqrt{n}} \tag{7-12}$$

- **Test Statistic for a Test of Mean Differences (Normally Distributed Populations, Unknown Population Variances).** When we have data consisting of paired observations from samples generated by normally distributed populations with unknown variances, a t-test is based on

$$t = \frac{\bar{d} - \mu_{d0}}{s_{\bar{d}}} \tag{7-13}$$

with $n-1$ degrees of freedom, where n is the number of paired observations, $\bar{d}$ is the sample mean of the differences (as given by Equation 7-10), and $s_{\bar{d}}$ is the standard error of $\bar{d}$ (as given by Equation 7-12).

In some time periods, small-cap stocks outperform large-cap stocks, and in other periods, large-cap stocks have better performance. Suppose we want to test the hypothesis that the mean monthly return on the S&P 500 (dominated by large-cap stocks) equaled the mean monthly return on small-cap stocks over 1997 and 1998. Because they share many common risk factors, returns on small-cap stocks and returns on the S&P 500 over a given time period are not independent, so a paired comparisons test is appropriate. Let μ_d stand for the population mean value of difference between S&P 500 returns and small-cap stock returns over this period. We test H_0: $\mu_d = 0$ versus H_a: $\mu_d \neq 0$ at a 0.05 significance level. Table 7-5 illustrates the mechanics of obtaining the inputs needed to conduct the test.

TABLE 7-5   Returns on the S&P 500 and Small-Cap Stock: 1997 and 1998

Month	S&P 500 Return (%)	Small-Cap Stock Return (%)	Difference (S&P 500 − Small-Cap Stock)
Jan 1997	6.21	4.20	2.01
Feb 1997	0.81	−2.06	2.87
Mar 1997	−4.16	−4.90	0.74
Apr 1997	5.97	−2.76	8.73
May 1997	6.14	10.22	−4.08
Jun 1997	4.46	4.98	−0.52
Jul 1997	7.94	6.05	1.89
Aug 1997	−5.56	5.09	−10.65
Sep 1997	5.48	8.44	−2.96
Oct 1997	−3.34	−3.86	0.52
Nov 1997	4.63	−1.55	6.18
Dec 1997	1.72	−1.71	3.43
Jan 1998	1.11	−0.59	1.70
Feb 1998	7.21	6.49	0.72
Mar 1998	5.12	4.81	0.31
Apr 1998	1.01	1.68	−0.67
May 1998	−1.72	−4.97	3.25
Jun 1998	4.06	−2.06	6.12
Jul 1998	−1.06	−6.71	5.65
Aug 1998	−14.46	−20.10	5.64
Sep 1998	6.41	3.69	2.72
Oct 1998	8.13	3.56	4.57
Nov 1998	6.06	7.58	−1.52
Dec 1998	5.76	2.52	3.24
Mean	2.41	0.75	1.66

Sample standard deviation of differences = 4.02

Source: Ibbotson Associates.

The sample mean difference, $\bar{d}$, between S&P 500 and small-cap stock returns is 1.66 percent per month. The standard error of the sample mean difference is $s_{\bar{d}} =$

$4.02/\sqrt{24} = 0.820579$. The calculated test statistic is $t = (1.66 - 0)/0.820579 = 2.023$ with $n - 1 = 24 - 1 = 23$ degrees of freedom. At the 0.05 significance level, we reject the null if $t > 2.069$ or if $t < -2.069$. As 2.023 does not exceed 2.069, we fail to reject the null. The p-value associated with a t of 2.023 with 23 degrees of freedom is 0.054848. The difference was significant at the 0.10 level, but not at the 0.05 level we had chosen.

The following example illustrates the application of this test to evaluate two competing investment strategies.

EXAMPLE 7-6.   The Dow-10 Investment Strategy.

McQueen, Shields, and Thorley (1997) examined the popular investment strategy of investing in the 10 stocks with the highest yields (rebalancing annually) in the Dow Jones Industrial Average, versus a buy-and-hold strategy in all 30 stocks of the DJIA. Their study period was the 50 years from January 1946 to December 1995.

TABLE 7-6   **Annual Return Summary for Dow-10 and Dow-30 Portfolios: January 1946 to December 1995 ($n = 50$)**

Strategy	Mean Return	Standard Deviation
Dow-10	16.77%	19.10%
Dow-30	13.71	16.64
Difference	3.06	6.62

Source: McQueen, Shields, Thorley (1997, Table 1).

From Table 7-6 we have $\bar{d} = 3.06\%$ and $s_d = 6.62\%$.

1. Formulate null and alternative hypotheses consistent with a two-sided test that the mean difference between the Dow-10 and Dow-30 strategies equals 0.
2. Identify the test statistic for conducting a test of the hypotheses in Part 1.
3. Identify the rejection point or points for the hypothesis tested in Part 1 at the 0.01 level of significance.
4. Determine whether the null hypothesis is rejected or not rejected at the 0.01 level of significance. (Use tables in the back of this book.)
5. Discuss the choice of paired comparisons test.

Solution to 1.   With μ_d as the underlying mean difference between the Dow-10 and Dow-30 strategies, we have H_0: $\mu_d = 0$ versus H_a: $\mu_d \neq 0$.

Solution to 2.   Because the population variance is not known, the test statistic is a t-test with $50 - 1 = 49$ degrees of freedom.

Solution to 3.   In the table for the t-distribution, we look across the row for 49 degrees of freedom to the 0.005 column, to find 2.68. We will reject the null if we find that $t > 2.68$ or $t < -2.68$.

Solution to 4.

$$t_{49} = \frac{3.06}{6.62/\sqrt{50}} = \frac{3.06}{0.936209} = 3.2685$$

Because $3.2685 > 2.68$, we reject the null hypothesis. The authors concluded that the difference in mean returns was clearly statistically significant. However, after adjusting for the Dow-10's higher risk, extra transaction costs, and unfavorable tax treatment, they found that the Dow-10 did not beat the Dow-30 economically.

Solution to 5.   The Dow-30 includes the Dow-10. As a result, they are not independent samples; in general, the correlation of returns on the Dow-10 and Dow-30 should be positive. Because the samples are dependent, a paired comparisons test was appropriate.

4 HYPOTHESIS TESTS CONCERNING VARIANCE

Because variance and standard deviation are widely used quantitative measures of risk in investments, familiarity with hypothesis tests concerning variance is useful. We examine two cases: tests concerning the value of a single population variance and tests concerning the differences between two population variances.

4.1 TESTS CONCERNING A SINGLE VARIANCE

In this section, we discuss testing hypotheses about the value of the variance, σ^2, of a single population. We use σ_0^2 to denote the hypothesized value of σ^2. We can formulate hypotheses as follows:

1. $H_0: \sigma^2 = \sigma_0^2$ versus $H_a: \sigma^2 \neq \sigma_0^2$ (a "not equal to" alternative hypothesis)
2. $H_0: \sigma^2 \leq \sigma_0^2$ versus $H_a: \sigma^2 > \sigma_0^2$ (a "greater than" alternative hypothesis)
3. $H_0: \sigma^2 \geq \sigma_0^2$ versus $H_a: \sigma^2 < \sigma_0^2$ (a "less than" alternative hypothesis)

In tests concerning the variance of a single normally distributed population, we make use of a chi-square test statistic, denoted by χ^2. The chi-square distribution, unlike the normal and t-distributions, is asymmetrical. Like the t-distribution, the chi-square distribution is a family of distributions. A different distribution exists for each possible value of degrees of freedom, $n - 1$ (n is sample size). Unlike the t-distribution, the chi-square distribution is bounded below by 0 (χ^2 does not take on negative values).

- **Test Statistic for Tests Concerning the Value of a Population Variance (Normal Population).** If we have n independent observations from a normally distributed population, the appropriate test statistic is

$$\chi^2 = \frac{(n - 1)s^2}{\sigma_0^2} \qquad\qquad (7\text{-}14)$$

with $n - 1$ degrees of freedom. In the numerator of the expression is the sample variance, calculated as

$$s^2 = \frac{\sum_{i=1}^{n} (x_i - \bar{x})^2}{n - 1} \qquad\qquad (7\text{-}15)$$

In contrast to the t-test, for example, the chi-square test is sensitive to violations of its assumptions. If the sample is not actually random or if it does not come from a normally distributed population, inferences based on a chi-square test are likely to be faulty.

If we choose a level of significance, α, the rejection points for the three kinds of hypotheses are as follows:

- **Rejection Points for Hypothesis Tests on the Population Variance.**

  1. "Not equal to" H_a: Reject the null hypothesis if the test statistic is equal to or greater than the upper $\alpha/2$ point (denoted $\chi^2_{\alpha/2}$) or less than the lower $\alpha/2$ point (denoted $\chi^2_{1-\alpha/2}$) of the chi-square distribution with df $= n - 1$.[20]

  2. "Greater than" H_a: Reject the null hypothesis if the test statistic is greater than or equal to the upper α point of the chi-square distribution with df $= n - 1$.

  3. "Less than" H_a: Reject the null hypothesis if the test statistic is less than or equal to the lower a point of the chi-square distribution with df $= n - 1$.

EXAMPLE 7-7.   Risk and Return Characteristics of an Equity Mutual Fund (2).

You continue with your analysis of Sendar Equity Fund, a midcap growth fund that has been in existence for only 24 months. Recall that over this period, Sendar Equity achieved a sample standard deviation of monthly returns of 3.60 percent. You now want to test a claim that the particular investment disciplines followed by Sendar result in a standard deviation of monthly returns of less than 4 percent.

1. Formulate null and alternative hypotheses consistent with the verbal description of the goal of the research.

2. Identify the test statistic for conducting a test of the hypotheses in Part 1.

3. Identify the rejection point or points for the hypothesis tested in Part 1 at the 0.05 level of significance.

4. Determine whether the null hypothesis is rejected or not rejected at the 0.10 level of significance. (Use tables in the back of this book.)

Solution to 1.   We have a "less than" alternative hypothesis, where σ is the underlying standard deviation of return on Sendar Equity Fund. Being careful to square standard deviation to obtain a test in terms of variance, the hypotheses are H_0: $\sigma^2 \geq 16.0$ versus H_a: $\sigma^2 < 16.0$.

Solution to 2.   The test statistic is chi-square with $24 - 1 = 23$ degrees of freedom.

---

[20] Just as with other hypothesis tests, the chi-square test can be given a confidence interval interpretation. Unlike confidence intervals based on z- or t-statistics, chi-square confidence intervals for variance are asymmetric. A two-sided confidence interval for population variance, based on a sample of size n, has lower limit (L) equal to L $= (n - 1)s^2\chi^2_{\alpha/2}$ and upper limit (U) equal to U $= (n - 1)s^2/\chi^2_{1-\alpha/2}$. Under the null hypothesis, the hypothesized value of the population variance should fall within these two limits.

Solution to 3.   The rejection point is found across degrees of freedom of 23, under the 0.95 column (95 percent probability in the right tail, to give 0.95 probability of getting a test statistic this large or larger). It is 13.091. We will reject the null if we find that chi-square is less than 13.091.

Solution to 4.

$$\chi^2 = \frac{(n-1)s^2}{\sigma_0^2} = \frac{23 \times 3.60^2}{4^2} = \frac{298.08}{16} = 18.63$$

Because 18.63 (the calculated value of the test statistic) is not less than 13.091, we do not reject the null hypothesis. We conclude that Sendar's investment disciplines do result in a standard deviation of monthly returns of less than 4 percent.

4.2 TESTS CONCERNING DIFFERENCES BETWEEN VARIANCES

Suppose we have a hypothesis about the relative values of the variances of two normally distributed populations with means μ_1 and μ_2 and variances σ_1^2 and σ_2^2. Because the labeling of populations as "1" or "2" is arbitrary, we can formulate all hypotheses as one of the choices below:

1. $H_0: \sigma_1^2 = \sigma_2^2$ versus $H_a: \sigma_1^2 \neq \sigma_2^2$
2. $H_0: \sigma_1^2 \leq \sigma_2^2$ versus $H_a: \sigma_1^2 > \sigma_2^2$
3. $H_0: \sigma_1^2 \geq \sigma_2^2$ versus $H_a: \sigma_1^2 < \sigma_2^2$

Note that at the point of equality, the null hypothesis $\sigma_1^2 = \sigma_2^2$ implies that the ratio of population variances equals 1: $\sigma_1^2/\sigma_2^2 = 1$. Given independent random samples from these populations, tests related to these hypotheses are based on an F-test, which is the ratio of sample variances. Suppose we use n_1 observations in calculating the sample variance s_1^2 and n_2 observations in calculating the sample variance s_2^2. Tests concerning the difference between the variances of two populations make use of the F-distribution. Like the chi-square distribution, the F-distribution is a family of asymmetrical distributions that are bounded from below by 0. Each F-distribution is defined by two values of degrees of freedom, called the numerator and denominator degrees of freedom.[21]

- **Test Statistic for Tests Concerning Differences between the Variances of Two Populations (Normally Distributed Populations).** Suppose we have two samples, the first with n_1 observations and sample variance s_1^2, the second with n_2 observations and sample variance s_2^2. The samples are random, independent of each other, and generated by normally distributed populations. A test concerning differences between the variances of the two populations is based on the ratio of sample variances

$$F = \frac{s_1^2}{s_2^2} \tag{7-16}$$

---

[21] The relationship between the chi-square and F-distributions is as follows: If χ_1^2 is one chi-square random variable with m degrees of freedom and χ_2^2 is another chi-square random variable with n degrees of freedom, then $F = (\chi_1^2/m)/(\chi_2^2/n)$ follows an F-distribution with m numerator and n denominator degrees of freedom.

with $df_1 = n_1 - 1$ numerator degrees of freedom and $df_2 = n_2 - 1$ denominator degrees of freedom. Note that df_1 and df_2 are the divisors used in calculating s_1^2 and s_2^2, respectively.

The F-test, like the chi-square test, is not robust to violations of its assumptions.

A convention, or usual practice, is to use the larger of the two ratios s_1^2/s_2^2 or s_2^2/s_1^2 as the actual test statistic. When we follow this convention, the value of the test statistic is always greater than or equal to 1; tables of critical values of F then need only include values greater than or equal to 1. Under this convention, the rejection point for any formulation of hypotheses is a single value in the right-hand side of the relevant F-distribution. Note that the labeling of populations as "1" or "2" is arbitrary in any case.

- **Rejection Points for Hypothesis Tests on the Relative Values of Two Population Variances.** Follow the convention of using the larger of the two ratios s_1^2/s_2^2 and s_2^2/s_1^2 and consider two cases:

  1. A "not equal to" alternative hypothesis: Reject the null hypothesis at the α significance level if the test statistic is greater than the upper $\alpha/2$ point of the F-distribution with the specified numerator and denominator degrees of freedom.
  2. A "greater than" or "less than" alternative hypothesis: Reject the null hypothesis at the α significance level if the test statistic is greater than the upper α point of the F-distribution with the specified number of numerator and denominator degrees of freedom.

Thus, if we conduct a two-sided test at the 0.01 level of significance, we need to find the rejection point in F-tables of $\alpha = 0.01/2 = 0.005$ (Part 1). But a one-sided test at 0.01 uses rejection points in F-tables for $\alpha = 0.01$ (Part 2).

If the convention stated above is not followed and we are given a calculated value of F less than 1, can we still use F-tables? The answer is yes; using a reciprocal property of F-statistics, we can calculate the needed value. The easiest way to present this property is to show a calculation. Suppose our chosen level of significance is 0.05 for a two-tailed test and we have a value of F of 0.11, with 7 numerator degrees of freedom and 9 denominator degrees of freedom. We take the reciprocal, $1/0.11 = 9.09$. Then we look this up in the F-tables for 0.025 (because it is a two-tailed test) with degrees of freedom reversed: F for 9 numerator and 7 denominator degrees of freedom. In other words, $F_{9,7} = 1/F_{7,9}$ and 9.09 exceeds the critical value of 4.82, so $F_{7,9} = 0.11$ is significant at the 0.05 level.

EXAMPLE 7-8.   Volatility and the Crash of 1987.

You are investigating whether the population variance of returns on the S&P 500 changed subsequent to the market crash of October 1987. You gather the data in Table 7-7 for 120 months of returns before October 1987 and 120 months of returns after October 1987. You have specified a 0.05 level of significance (level of Type I error).

TABLE 7-7

	n	Mean Monthly Return (%)	Standard Deviation (%)	Variance
Before October 1987	120	1.498	4.333	18.776
After October 1987	120	1.392	3.619	13.097

1. Formulate null and alternative hypotheses consistent with the verbal description of the goal of the research.
2. Identify the test statistic for conducting a test of the hypotheses in Part 1.
3. Determine whether the null hypothesis is rejected or not at the 0.01 level of significance. (Use F-tables in the back of this book.)

Solution to 1. We have a "not equal to" alternative hypothesis:

$$H_0: \sigma^2_{Before} = \sigma^2_{After} \text{ versus } H_a: \sigma^2_{Before} \neq \sigma^2_{After}.$$

Solution to 2. To test a null hypothesis of the equality of two variances, we use an F-test $F = \dfrac{s_1^2}{s_2^2}$ with $120 - 1 = 119$ numerator and denominator degrees of freedom.

Solution to 3. The "before" sample variance is larger, so following a convention for calculating F-statistics, the "before" sample variance goes in the numerator: $F = 18.776/13.097 = 1.434$. Because this is a two-tailed test, we use F-tables for the 0.005 level ($= 0.01/2$). The closest value to 119 degrees of freedom is 120 degrees of freedom in the tables in the back of the book. At the 0.01 level the rejection point is 1.61. Because 1.434 is less than the critical value 1.61, we reject the null hypothesis. We cannot reject the null hypothesis that the population variance of returns is the same in the pre- and post-crash periods.

5 OTHER ISSUES IN INFERENCE

In this introduction to inference and hypothesis testing, we have restricted our attention to tests concerning means and variances. Investment analysts will encounter other issues and techniques, some of which we briefly mention in this section.

The hypothesis-testing procedures we have discussed in this chapter have two characteristics in common. First, they are concerned with parameters, and second, their validity depends on a definite set of assumptions. Mean and variance, for example, are two parameters, or defining quantities, of a normal distribution. The tests also made specific assumptions—in particular, assumptions about the distribution of the population producing the sample. Any test or procedure with either of the above two characteristics is a **parametric test** or procedure. In some cases, however, we are concerned about quantities other than parameters of distributions or we believe that the assumptions of parametric tests do not hold for the particular data we have. In such cases, a **nonparametric** test or procedure can be useful. A nonparametric test is a test that is not concerned with a parameter, or a test that makes minimal assumptions about the population from which the sample comes.

We primarily use nonparametric procedures in three situations. The first situation occurs when the data available for analysis suggest that the distributional assumption of the parametric test is not appropriate. For example, the null hypothesis may suggest a *t*-test, but if the population is strongly nonnormally distributed, we may seek an alternative, nonparametric test. For example, we presented *t*-tests for testing differences between means that assumed normally distributed populations. When that distributional assumption is not defensible, a nonparametric alternative (a *median test*) is available based on the median as a measure of central tendency.[22] Similarly, a nonparametric alternative (the *sign test*) that tests the median difference is available for the paired comparisons *t*-test.

Nonparametric procedures are also used when the data consist merely of ranks. For example, if the information on investment performance available to us consisted only of rankings (from best to worst), we would use nonparametric statistics to analyze it. Parametric tests generally require a stronger measurement scale than ranks (an ordinal scale).[23]

A third situation in which we use nonparametric procedures is when our question does not concern a parameter. For example, if the question concerns whether a sample is random or not, we use the appropriate nonparametric test (a *runs test*). Another type of question nonparametrics can address is whether a sample came from a population following a particular probability distribution (the *Kolmogorov-Smirnov test*, among others).

Nonparametric statistical procedures extend the reach of inference because they make few assumptions, can be used on ranked data, and may address questions not related to parameters. Quite frequently, nonparametric tests are reported alongside parametric tests. The reader can then assess how sensitive the statistical conclusion is to the assumptions underlying the parametric test. However, if the assumptions of the parametric test are met, the parametric test (where available) is generally preferred to the nonparametric test because the parametric test usually permits us to draw sharper conclusions.[24] For complete coverage of all the nonparametric procedures that may be encountered in the finance and investment literature, it is best to consult a specialist textbook.[25]

One particularly important concept in investments is independence; it relates to such questions as the predictability of financial variables and the persistence of superior performance from time period to time period.[26] Tests of independence are often presented in contingency tables, which are tables into which data are classified according to two criteria or variables. For example, a 2×2 contingency table occurs when both criteria or variables have two values (are dichotomous). One variable might be Period-1 performance (Period-1 winner or Period-1 loser), and the second variable might be Period-2 performance (Period-2 winner or Period-2 loser). The entries would be count data (frequencies). A test of independence of the two variables of classification is based on a chi-square test statistic.[27]

---

[22] The median is the middle item in an array sorted by size from smallest to largest.

[23] Measurement scales were discussed in the chapter on statistical concepts and market returns.

[24] To use a concept introduced in an earlier section, the parametric test is often more powerful.

[25] See, for example, Hettmansperger and McKean (1998) or Siegel (1956).

[26] Two random variables or quantities are independent if they are unrelated in the sense that knowing the value of one variable does not help you predict the value of the other variable.

[27] For more on this test and on the analysis of data in contingency tables in general, see a business statistics textbook, for example Daniel and Terrell (1995).

6 SUMMARY

In this chapter, we have presented the concepts and methods of inference and hypothesis testing.

- A hypothesis is a statement about one or more populations.
- The steps in testing a hypothesis are:
  1. Statement of the hypotheses.
  2. Identification of the test statistic and its probability distribution.
  3. Specification of the significance level.
  4. Statement of the decision rule.
  5. Collecting the data and performing the calculations.
  6. Making the statistical decision.
  7. Making the economic or investment decision.
- We state two hypotheses: The null hypothesis is the hypothesis to be tested; the alternative hypothesis is the hypothesis accepted when the null hypothesis is rejected.
- There are three ways to formulate hypotheses:
  1. $H_0: \theta = \theta_0$ versus $H_a: \theta \neq \theta_0$
  2. $H_0: \theta \leq \theta_0$ versus $H_a: \theta > \theta_0$
  3. $H_0: \theta \geq \theta_0$ versus $H_a: \theta < \theta_0$

  where θ_0 is a hypothesized value of the population parameter and θ is the true value of the population parameter.
- In the above, Formulation 1 is a two-sided test and Formulations 2 and 3 are one-sided tests.
- We always conduct a hypothesis test at the point of equality, $\theta = \theta_0$.
- When we have a "suspected" or "hoped for" condition for which we want to find supportive evidence, we frequently set that condition up as the alternative hypothesis.
- A test statistic is a quantity, calculated on the basis of a sample, whose value is the basis for deciding whether to reject or not to reject the null hypothesis.
- In reaching a statistical decision, we can make two possible errors: We may reject a true null hypothesis (a Type I error) or we may fail to reject a false null hypothesis (a Type II error).
- The level of significance of a test is the probability of a Type I error that we accept in conducting the test.
- The probability of a Type I error is denoted by the Greek letter alpha, α.
- The probability of a Type II error is denoted by the Greek letter beta, β.
- The probability of a Type II error is very hard to determine in practice.
- There is a trade-off between α and β. The only way we can reduce both simultaneously is to increase sample size.
- The power of a test is the probability of correctly rejecting the null (rejecting the null when it is false).
- The standard approach to hypothesis testing involves specifying a level of significance (probability of Type I error) only.

- Three conventional significance levels exist at which we conduct hypothesis tests: 0.10, 0.05, and 0.01.

- A critical value (rejection point) for a test statistic is a value against which the computed value of the test statistic is compared to decide whether to reject, or not to reject, the null hypothesis.

- We indicate a rejection point using the symbol for the test statistic with a subscript related to the specified probability of a Type I error, α; for example, z_α or $z_{\alpha/2}$ for a z-statistic.

- Values of a test statistic fall into the acceptance region (for which the null hypothesis is not rejected) or a rejection (critical) region or regions (for which the null hypothesis is rejected). Rejection points are dividing lines between the acceptance and rejection regions.

- The p-value is the smallest level of significance at which the null hypothesis can be rejected.

- The smaller the p-value, the stronger the evidence against the null hypothesis and in favor of the alternative hypothesis.

- For hypothesis tests concerning the population mean of a normally distributed population with unknown variance, the theoretically correct test statistic is the t-statistic.

- The t-test is robust to moderate departures from the normal distribution.

- For large samples (generally, samples of 30 or more observations), the z-statistic may be used in place of the t-statistic.

- The t-distribution is a symmetrical distribution defined by a single parameter: degrees of freedom. Compared to the standard normal distribution, the t-distribution has fatter tails.

- As the number of degrees increases, the t-distribution converges to the standard normal distributions and the rejection points for hypothesis tests converge.

- When we want to test whether the observed difference between two means is because of chance, we must decide whether the samples are independent or dependent (related). If the samples are independent, we conduct tests concerning differences between means. If the samples are dependent, we often conduct tests of mean differences (paired comparisons tests).

- When we conduct a test of the difference between two population means from normally distributed populations with unknown variances, if we can assume the variances are equal, we use a t-test based on pooling the observations of the two samples to estimate the common (but unknown) variance. This test is based on an assumption of independent samples.

- When we conduct a test of the difference between two population means from normally distributed populations with unknown variances, if we cannot assume that the variances are equal, we use an approximate t-test using modified degrees of freedom given by a formula. This test is based on an assumption of independent samples.

- In tests concerning two means based on samples that are not independent, we often can arrange the data in paired observations and conduct a test of mean differences (a paired comparisons test).

- When we have data consisting of paired observations from samples generated by normally distributed populations with unknown variance, the test statistic is a t-statistic. The denominator of the statistic, the standard error of the mean differences, takes account of correlation between the samples.

- In tests concerning the variance of a single, normally distributed population, the test statistic is chi-square (χ^2) with $n - 1$ degrees of freedom, where n is sample size.
- The chi-square is a family of asymmetrical distributions, each distribution defined by the number of degrees of freedom.
- The chi-square test is sensitive to violations of its assumptions.
- For tests concerning differences between the variances of two normally distributed populations based on two random, independent samples, the appropriate test statistic is based on an F-test (the ratio of the sample variances).
- The F-statistic is defined by the numerator and denominator degrees of freedom. The numerator degrees of freedom is the divisor used in calculating the sample variance in the numerator (number of observations minus 1). The denominator degrees of freedom is the divisor used in calculating the sample variance in the denominator (number of observations minus 1).
- In forming an F-test, a convention is to use the larger of the two ratios, s_1^2/s_2^2 or s_2^2/s_1^2, as the actual test statistic.
- An F-test is sensitive to violations of its assumptions.
- A parametric test is a hypothesis test concerning a parameter or a hypothesis test not based on specific distributional assumptions. In contrast, a nonparametric test either is not concerned with a parameter, or makes minimal assumptions about the population from which the sample comes.

PROBLEMS

1. Define the following terms:
   a. Null hypothesis
   b. Alternative hypothesis
   c. Test statistic
   d. Rejection point (critical value)
   e. Type I error
   f. Type II error
   g. Power of a test

2. Suppose that, on the basis of a sample, we want to test the hypothesis that the mean debt-to-total-assets ratio of firms that become takeover targets is the same as the mean debt-to-total-assets ratio of firms in the same industry that do not become takeover targets. Explain under what conditions we would commit a Type I error and under what conditions we would commit a Type II error.

3. Suppose we are testing a null hypothesis, H_0, versus an alternative hypothesis, H_a, and the p-value for the test statistic is 0.031. At which of the following levels of significance—$\alpha = 0.10$, $\alpha = 0.05$, $\alpha = 0.01$—would we reject the null hypothesis?

4. Identify the appropriate test statistic or statistics for conducting the following hypothesis tests. (Clearly identify the test statistic and, if applicable, the number of degrees of freedom. For example, "We conduct the test using a y-statistic with z degrees of freedom.")
   a. H_0: $\mu = 0$ versus H_a: $\mu \neq 0$, where μ is the mean of a normally distributed population with unknown variance. The test is based on a sample of 15 observations.
   b. H_0: $\mu = 0$ versus H_a: $\mu \neq 0$, where μ is the mean of a normally distributed population with unknown variance. The test is based on a sample of 40 observations.
   c. H_0: $\mu \leq 0$ versus H_a: $\mu > 0$, where μ is the mean of a normally distributed population with known variance σ^2. The sample size is 45.
   d. H_0: $\sigma^2 = 200$ versus H_a: $\sigma^2 \neq 200$, where σ^2 is the variance of a normally distributed population. The sample size is 50.
   e. H_0: $\sigma_1^2 = \sigma_2^2$ versus H_a: $\sigma_1^2 \neq \sigma_2^2$, where σ_1^2 is the variance of one normally distributed population and σ_2^2 is the variance of a second normally distributed population. The test is based on two independent random samples.
   f. H_0: (Population mean 1) − (Population mean 2) = 0 versus H_a: (Population mean 1) − (Population mean 2) ≠ 0, where the samples are drawn from normally distributed populations with unknown variances. The observations in the two samples are correlated.
   g. H_0: (Population mean 1) − (Population mean 2) = 0 versus H_a: (Population mean 1) − (Population mean 2) ≠ 0, where the samples are drawn from normally distributed populations with unknown but assumed equal variances. The observations in the two samples (of size 25 and 30, respectively) are independent.

5. For each of the following hypotheses tests concerning the population mean (μ), state the rejection point condition or conditions for the test statistic (e.g., $t > 1.25$); n denotes sample size.
   a. H_0: $\mu = 10$ versus H_a: $\mu \neq 10$, using a t-test with $n = 26$ and $\alpha = 0.05$.
   b. H_0: $\mu = 10$ versus H_a: $\mu \neq 10$, using a t-test with $n = 40$ and $\alpha = 0.01$.
   c. H_0: $\mu \leq 10$ versus H_a: $\mu > 10$, using a t-test with $n = 40$ and $\alpha = 0.01$.
   d. H_0: $\mu \leq 10$ versus H_a: $\mu > 10$, using a t-test with $n = 21$ and $\alpha = 0.05$.
   e. H_0: $\mu \geq 10$ versus H_a: $\mu < 10$, using a t-test with $n = 19$ and $\alpha = 0.10$.
   f. H_0: $\mu \geq 10$ versus H_a: $\mu < 10$, using a t-test with $n = 50$ and $\alpha = 0.05$.

6. For each of the following hypotheses tests concerning the mean, μ, state the rejection point condition or conditions for the test statistic (e.g., $z > 1.25$).

   a. H_0: $\mu = 10$ versus H_a: $\mu \neq 10$, using a z-test with $n = 50$ and $\alpha = 0.01$.

   b. H_0: $\mu = 10$ versus H_a: $\mu \neq 10$, using a z-test with $n = 50$ and $\alpha = 0.05$.

   c. H_0: $\mu = 10$ versus H_a: $\mu \neq 10$, using a z-test with $n = 50$ and $\alpha = 0.10$.

   d. H_0: $\mu \leq 10$ versus H_a: $\mu > 10$, using a z-test with $n = 50$ and $\alpha = 0.05$.

7. Identify the correct test statistic to use for a hypothesis test concerning the mean of a single population under the following conditions:

   a. The sample comes from a normally distributed population with known variance.

   b. The sample comes from a normally distributed population with unknown variance.

   c. The sample comes from a population following a nonnormal distribution with unknown variance. The sample size is large.

8. Willco is a manufacturer in a mature cyclical industry. Over the most recent industry cycle, its net income averaged $30 million per year with a standard deviation of $10 million ($n = 6$ observations). Management claims that Willco's performance over the most recent cycle results from new approaches, and that we can dismiss profitability expectations based on its average or normalized earnings of $24 million per year in prior cycles.

   a. With μ as the population value of mean annual net income, formulate null and alternative hypotheses consistent with testing Willco management's claim.

   b. Assuming that Willco's net income is at least approximately normally distributed, identify the appropriate test statistic.

   c. Identify the rejection point or points at the 0.05 level of significance for the hypothesis tested in Part a.

   d. Determine whether the null hypothesis is rejected or not rejected at the 0.05 significance level.

Use the following table to answer Questions 9 and 10.

Performance in Forecasting Quarterly Earnings per Share

	Number of Forecasts	Mean Forecast Error (Predicted − Actual)	Standard Deviations of Forecast Errors
Analyst A	101	0.05	0.10
Analyst B	121	0.02	0.09

9. Investment analysts often make use of earnings per share (EPS) forecasts. One test of forecasting quality is the zero-mean test, which states that optimal forecasts should have a mean forecasting error of 0. (Forecasting error = Predicted value of variable − Actual value of variable.)

   You have collected data (shown in the table above) for two analysts who cover two different industries: Analyst A covers the telecom industry; Analyst B covers automotive parts and suppliers.

   a. With μ as the population mean forecasting error, formulate null and alternative hypotheses for a zero-mean test of forecasting quality.

   b. For Analyst A, determine, using both a t-test and a z-test, whether the null is rejected at the 0.05 and 0.01 levels of significance.

c. For Analyst B, determine, using both a *t*-test and a *z*-test, whether the null is rejected at the 0.05 and 0.01 levels of significance.

10. Reviewing the EPS forecasting performance data for Analyst A and B, you want to investigate whether the larger average forecast errors of Analyst A are due to chance or to a higher underlying mean value for Analyst B. Assume that the forecast errors of both analysts are normally distributed and that the samples are independent.

    a. Formulate null and alternative hypotheses consistent with determining whether the population mean value of Analyst A's forecast errors (μ_1) are larger than Analyst B's (μ_2).

    b. Identify the test statistic for conducting a test of the null hypothesis formulated in Part a.

    c. Identify the rejection point or points for the hypothesis tested in Part a.

    d. Determine whether the null hypothesis is rejected or not at the 0.05 level of significance.

11. Altman and Kishore (1996), in the course of a study on the recovery rates on defaulted bonds, investigated the recovery of utility bonds versus other bonds, stratified by seniority. The following table excerpts their findings. The group Entire Sample is all senior unsecured bonds except those of utilities.

Utility versus Aggregate Recovery Rates by Seniority

Industry Group/ Seniority	Industry Group			Entire Sample		
	Number of Observations	Average Price*	Standard Deviation	Number of Observations	Average Price*	Standard Deviation
Public Utilities						
Senior Unsecured	32	$77.74	$18.06	189	$42.56	$24.89

Source: Altman and Kishore (1996, Table 5).

*Average Price at default is a measure of recovery rate.

Assume that the populations (recovery rates of utilities, recovery rates of non-utilities) are normally distributed and that the samples are independent. The population variances are not known; do not assume they are equal. The test hypotheses are H_0: $\mu_1 - \mu_2 = 0$ versus H_a: $\mu_1 - \mu_2 \neq 0$, where μ_1 is the population mean recovery rate for utilities and μ_2 is the population mean recovery rate for non-utilities.

    a. Calculate the test statistic.

    b. Determine whether the null is rejected at the 0.01 significance level without reference to degrees of freedom.

    c. Calculate the degrees of freedom.

12. The table below gives data on the monthly returns on the S&P 500 and small-cap stocks for the period January 1960 through March 1999 and statistics relating to their mean differences.

Measure	S&P 500 Return (%)	Small-Cap Stock Return (%)	Difference (S&P 500 − Small-Cap Stock)
January 1960–March 1999, 471 months			
Mean	1.043	1.260	−0.217
Standard deviation	4.227	5.962	3.726
January 1960–December 1979, 240 months			
Mean	0.635	1.274	−0.639
Standard deviation	4.081	6.583	4.096
January 1980–March 1999, 231 months			
Mean	1.467	1.246	0.221
Standard deviation	4.342	5.253	3.249

Let μ_d stand for the population mean value of difference between S&P 500 returns and small-cap stock returns. Use a significance level of 0.05 and suppose that mean differences are approximately normally distributed.

a. Formulate null and alternative hypotheses consistent with testing whether there is any difference between the mean returns on the S&P 500 and small-cap stocks.

b. Determine whether the null hypothesis is rejected or not rejected at the 0.05 significance level for the January 1960 to March 1999 period.

c. Determine whether the null hypothesis is rejected or not rejected at the 0.05 significance level for the January 1960 to December 1979 subperiod.

d. Determine whether the null hypothesis is rejected or not rejected at the 0.05 significance level for the January 1980 to March 1999 subperiod.

13. Over a 10-year period, the standard deviation of annual returns on a portfolio you are analyzing was 15 percent a year. You want to see whether this record is sufficient evidence to support the conclusion that the portfolio's underlying variance of return was less than 400, the return variance of the portfolio's benchmark.

a. Formulate null and alternative hypotheses consistent with the verbal description of your objective.

b. Identify the test statistic for conducting a test of the hypotheses in Part a.

c. Identify the rejection point or points at the 0.05 significance level for the hypothesis tested in Part a.

d. Determine whether the null hypothesis is rejected or not rejected at the 0.05 level of significance.

14. You are investigating whether the population variance of returns on the S&P 500/BARRA Growth Index changed subsequent to the market crash of October 1987. You gather the following data for 120 months of returns before October 1987 and for 120 months of returns after October 1987. You have specified a 0.05 level of significance (level of Type I error).

Time Period	n	Mean Monthly Return (%)	Standard Deviation (%)	Variance
Before October 1987	120	1.416	4.729	22.367
After October 1987	120	1.436	3.974	15.795

a. Formulate null and alternative hypotheses consistent with the verbal description of the goal of the research.
b. Identify the test statistic for conducting a test of the hypotheses in Part a.
c. Determine whether the null hypothesis is rejected or not rejected at the 0.05 level of significance. (Use F-tables in the back of this book.)

SOLUTIONS
1. a. The null hypothesis is the hypothesis to be tested.

   b. The alternative hypothesis is the hypothesis accepted when the null hypothesis is rejected.

   c. A test statistic is a quantity, calculated on the basis of a sample, whose value is the basis for deciding whether to reject or not reject the null hypothesis.

   d. The rejection point (critical value) is a value against which a computed test statistic is compared to decide whether to reject or not reject the null hypothesis.

   e. A Type I error occurs when we reject a true null hypothesis.

   f. A Type II error occurs when we do not reject a false null hypothesis.

   g. The power of a test is the probability of correctly rejecting the null hypothesis (rejecting the null hypothesis when it is false).

2. If we reject the hypothesis of the equality of the mean debt-to-total-assets ratios of takeover target firms and non-takeover-target firms when, in fact, the means were equal, we would be committing a Type I error.

   On the other hand, if we fail to reject the equality of the mean debt-to-total-assets ratios of takeover target firms and non-takeover-target firms when the means were different, we would be committing a Type II error.

3. By the definition of p-value, 0.031 is the smallest level of significance at which we can reject the null hypothesis. As 0.031 is smaller than 0.10 and 0.05, we can reject the null hypothesis at the 0.10 and 0.05 significance levels. However, because 0.031 is larger than 0.01, we cannot reject the null hypothesis at the 0.01 significance level.

4. a. The appropriate test statistic is a t-statistic with $n - 1 = 15 - 1 = 14$ degrees of freedom. A t-statistic is theoretically correct when the sample comes from a normally distributed population with unknown variance. When the sample size is also small, there is no practical alternative.

   b. The appropriate test statistic is a t-statistic with $40 - 1 = 39$ degrees of freedom. A t-statistic is theoretically correct when the sample comes from a normally distributed population with unknown variance.

   When the sample size is large (generally, 30 or larger is a "large" sample), it is also possible to use a z-statistic, whether the population is normally distributed or not. A test based on a t-statistic is more conservative than a z-statistic test.

   c. The appropriate test statistic is a z-statistic because the sample comes from a normally distributed population with known variance. (The known population standard deviation is used to compute the standard error of the mean using Equation 7-2 in the text.)

   d. The appropriate test statistic is chi-square (χ^2) with $50 - 1 = 49$ degrees of freedom.

   e. The appropriate test statistic is the F-statistic (the ratio of the sample variances).

   f. The appropriate test statistic is a t-statistic for a paired observations test (a paired comparisons test), because the samples are correlated.

   g. The appropriate test statistic is a t-statistic using a pooled estimate of the population variance. The t-statistic has $25 + 30 - 2 = 53$ degrees of freedom. This statistic is appropriate because the populations are normally distributed with unknown variances; because the variances are assumed equal, the observations can be pooled to estimate the common variance. The requirement of independent samples for using this statistic has been met.

5. a. With degrees of freedom (df) $n - 1 = 26 - 1 = 25$, the rejection point conditions for this two-sided test are $t > 2.060$ and $t < -2.060$. Because the significance level is 0.05, $0.05/2 = 0.025$ of the probability is in each tail. The tables give one-sided (one-tailed) probabilities, so we used the 0.025 column. Read across df $= 25$ to the $\alpha = 0.025$ column to find 2.060, the rejection point for the right tail. By symmetry, -2.060 is the rejection point for the left tail.

   b. With df $= 39$, the rejection point conditions for this two-sided test are $t > 2.708$ and $t < -2.708$. This is a two-sided test, so we use the $0.01/2 = 0.005$ column. Read across df $= 39$ to the $\alpha = 0.005$ column to find 2.708, the rejection point for the right tail. By symmetry, -2.708 is the rejection point for the left tail.

   c. With df $= 39$, the rejection point condition for this one-sided test is $t > 2.426$. Read across df $= 39$ to the $\alpha = 0.01$ column to find 2.426, the rejection point for the right tail. Because we have a "greater than" alternative, we are only concerned with the right tail.

   d. With df $= 20$, the rejection point condition for this one-sided test is $t > 1.725$. Read across df $= 20$ to the $\alpha = 0.05$ column to find 1.725, the rejection point for the right tail. Because we have a "greater than" alternative, we are only concerned with the right tail.

   e. With df $= 18$, the rejection point condition for this one-sided test is $t < -1.330$. Read across df $= 18$ to the $\alpha = 0.10$ column to find 1.330, the rejection point for the right tail. By symmetry, the rejection point for the left tail is -1.330.

   f. With df $= 49$, the rejection point condition for this one-sided test is $t < -1.677$. Read across df $= 49$ to the $\alpha = 0.05$ column to find 1.677, the rejection point for the right tail. By symmetry, the rejection point for the left tail is -1.677.

6. Recall that with a z-test (in contrast to the t-test), we do not employ degrees of freedom. The standard normal distribution is a single distribution applicable to all z-tests. You should refer to "Rejection Points for a z-Test" in Section 3.1 to answer these questions.

   a. This is a two-sided test at a significance level of 0.01. In Part c of "Rejection Points for a z-Test," we find that the rejection point conditions are $z > 2.575$ and $z < -2.575$.

   b. This is a two-sided test at a significance level of 0.05. In Part b of "Rejection Points for a z-Test," we find that the rejection point conditions are $z > 1.96$ and $z < -1.96$.

   c. This is a two-sided test at a significance level of 0.10. In Part a of "Rejection Points for a z-Test," we find that the rejection point conditions are $z > 1.645$ and $z < -1.645$.

   d. This is a one-sided test at a significance level of 0.05. In Part b of "Rejection Points for a z-Test," we find that the rejection point condition for a test with a "greater than" alternative hypothesis is $z > 1.645$.

7. a. When sampling from a normally distributed population with known variance, the correct test statistic for hypothesis tests concerning the mean is the z-statistic.

   b. When sampling from a normally distributed population with unknown variance, the theoretically correct test statistic for hypothesis tests concerning the mean is the t-statistic.

c. When the sample size is large, the central limit theorem applies. As a consequence, the sample mean will be approximately normally distributed. When the population variance is not known, a test using the t-statistic is theoretically preferred. A test using the z-statistic is also sufficient when the sample size is large, as in this case.

8. a. As stated in the text, we often set up the "hoped for" or "suspected" condition as the alternative hypothesis. Here, that condition is that the population value of Willco's mean annual net income exceeds \$24 million. Thus, we have H_0: $\mu \leq 24$ versus H_a: $\mu > 24$.

b. Given that net income is normally distributed with unknown variance, the appropriate test statistic is t with $n - 1 = 6 - 1 = 5$ degrees of freedom.

c. In the t-distribution table in the back of the book, in the row for df = 5 under $\alpha = 0.05$, we read the rejection point (critical value) of 2.015. We will reject the null if $t > 2.015$.

d. The t-test is given by Equation 7-4:

$$t_5 = \frac{\bar{x} - \mu_0}{s/\sqrt{n}} = \frac{30 - 24}{10/\sqrt{6}} = \frac{6}{4.082483} = 1.469694$$

or 1.47. Because 1.47 does not exceed 2.015, we do not reject the null hypothesis. The difference between sample mean \$30 million and the hypothesized value of \$24 million under the null is statistically insignificant.

9. a. H_0: $\mu = 0$ versus H_a: $\mu \neq 0$.

b. The t-test is based on $t = \dfrac{\bar{x} - \mu_0}{s/\sqrt{n}}$ with $n - 1 = 101 - 1 = 100$ degrees of freedom. At the 0.05 significance level, we reject the null if $t > 1.984$ or if $t < -1.984$. At the 0.01 significance level, we reject the null if $t > 2.626$ or if $t < -2.626$. For Analyst A, we have $t = (0.05 - 0)/(0.10/\sqrt{101}) = 0.05/0.00995 = 5.024938$ or 5.025. We clearly reject the null hypothesis at both the 0.05 and 0.01 levels.

The calculation of the z-statistic with unknown variance, as in this case, is the same as the calculation of the t-statistic. The rejection point conditions for a two-tailed test are as follows: $z > 1.96$ and $z < -1.96$ at the 0.05 level; and $z > 2.575$ and $z < -2.575$ at the 0.01 level. Note that the z-test is a less conservative test than the t-test, so when the z-test is used, the null is easier to reject. Because $z = 5.02$ is greater than 2.575, we reject the null at the 0.01 level; we also reject the null at the 0.05 level.

In summary, Analyst A's EPS forecasts appear to be biased upwards—that is, they tend to be too high.

c. For Analyst B, the t-test is based on t with $121 - 1 = 120$ degrees of freedom. At the 0.05 significance level, we reject the null if $t > 1.980$ or if $t < -1.980$. At the 0.01 significance level, we reject the null if $t > 2.617$ or if $t < -2.617$. We calculate $t = (0.02 - 0)/(0.09/\sqrt{121}) = 0.02/0.008182 = 2.444444$ or 2.44. Because $2.44 > 1.98$, we reject the null at the 0.05 level. However, 2.44 is not larger than 2.617, so we do not reject the null at the 0.01 level.

For a z-test, the rejection point conditions are the same as given in Part b, and we come to the same conclusions as with the t-test. Because $2.44 > 1.96$, we reject the null at the 0.05 significance level; however, because 2.44 is not greater than 2.575, we do not reject the null at the 0.01 level.

The mean forecast error of Analyst B is only $0.02; but because the test is based on a large number of observations, it is sufficient evidence to reject the null of mean zero forecast errors.

10. a. Stating the suspected condition as the alternative hypothesis, we have

$$H_0: \mu_1 - \mu_2 \le 0 \text{ versus } H_a: \mu_1 - \mu_2 > 0$$

where

$\mu_1 =$ the population mean value of Analyst A's forecast errors
$\mu_2 =$ the population mean value of Analyst B's forecast errors

b. We have two normally distributed populations with unknown variances. Based on the samples, it is reasonable to assume that the population variances are equal. The samples are assumed to be independent; this assumption is reasonable because the analysts cover quite different industries. The appropriate test statistic is t using a pooled estimate of the common variance. The number of degrees of freedom is $n_1 + n_2 - 2 = 101 + 121 - 2 = 222 - 2 = 220$.

c. For df $= 200$ (the closest value to 220), the rejection point for a one-sided test at the 0.05 significance level is 1.653.

d. We first calculate the pooled estimate of variance:

$$s_p^2 = \frac{(n_1 - 1)s_1^2 + (n_2 - 1)s_2^2}{n_1 + n_2 - 2} = \frac{(101 - 1)(0.10)^2 + (121 - 1)(0.09)^2}{101 + 121 - 2}$$

$$= \frac{1.972}{220} = 0.008964$$

Then

$$t = \frac{(\bar{x}_1 - \bar{x}_2) - (\mu_1 - \mu_2)}{\left(\frac{s_p^2}{n_1} + \frac{s_p^2}{n_2}\right)^{1/2}} = \frac{(0.05 - 0.02) - 0}{\left(\frac{0.008964}{101} + \frac{0.008964}{121}\right)^{1/2}}$$

$$= \frac{0.03}{0.01276} = 2.351018$$

or 2.35. Because $2.35 > 1.653$, we reject the null in favor of the alternative hypothesis that the population mean forecast error of Analyst A is greater than that of Analyst B.

11. a. The test statistic is

$$t = \frac{\bar{x}_1 - \bar{x}_2}{\left(\frac{s_1^2}{n_1} + \frac{s_2^2}{n_2}\right)^{1/2}}$$

where

$\bar{x}_1 =$ sample mean recovery rate for utilities $= 77.74$
$\bar{x}_2 =$ sample mean recovery rate for non-utility sectors $= 42.56$
$s_1^2 =$ sample variance for utilities $= 18.06^2 = 326.1636$
$s_2^2 =$ sample standard deviation for non-utilities $= 24.89^2 = 619.5121$

n_1 = sample size of the utility sample = 32

n_2 = sample size of the non-utility sample = 189

Thus, $t = (77.74 + 42.56)/[(326.1636/32) + (619.5121/189)]^{1/2} = 35.18/(10.192613 + 3.277842)^{1/2} = 35.18/3.670212 = 9.585$. The calculated t-statistic is thus 9.585.

b. Usually, we need to know degrees of freedom to determine whether a t-statistic is significant. The magnitude of the t-statistic is so large that, in this case, there is actually no doubt about its significance even at the 0.01 level. For a two-sided test at the 0.01 level of significance, we look under the 0.005 column (0.01/2 = 0.005). For all but the very first two entries, for 1 and 2 degrees of freedom, the calculated test statistic is larger than the indicated rejection point (critical value). Clearly, with samples of size 32 and 189, there are more than 2 degrees of freedom.

c. This question confirms that we can calculate the degrees of freedom for the test, if needed:

$$df = \frac{\left(\dfrac{s_1^2}{n_1} + \dfrac{s_2^2}{n_2}\right)^2}{\dfrac{(s_1^2/n_1)^2}{n_1} + \dfrac{(s_2^2/n_2)^2}{n_2}} = \frac{\left(\dfrac{326.1636}{32} + \dfrac{619.5121}{189}\right)^2}{\dfrac{(326.1636/32)^2}{32} + \dfrac{(619.5121/189)^2}{189}}$$

$$= \frac{181.453139}{3.30339} = 54.93$$

or 55 degrees of freedom.

12. a. We test H_0: $\mu_d = 0$ versus H_a: $\mu_d \neq 0$.

b. This is a paired comparisons t-test with $n - 1 = 471 - 1 = 470$ degrees of freedom. At the 0.05 significance level, we reject the null if either $t > 1.96$ or $t < -1.96$. We use df = ∞ in the t-distribution table under $\alpha = 0.025$ because we have a very large sample and a two-sided test.

$$t = \frac{\bar{d} - \mu_{d0}}{s_{\bar{d}}} = \frac{-0.217 - 0}{3.726/\sqrt{471}} = \frac{-0.217}{0.171685} = -1.263943 \text{ or } -1.26$$

At the 0.05 significance level, because neither rejection point condition is met, we do not reject the null that the mean difference between the returns on the S&P 500 and small-cap stocks over the entire sample period was 0.

c. This t-test now has $n - 1 = 240 - 1 = 239$ degrees of freedom. At the 0.05 significance level, we reject the null if either if $t > 1.972$ or $t < -1.972$, using df = 200 in the t-distribution tables.

$$t = \frac{\bar{d} - \mu_{d0}}{s_{\bar{d}}} = \frac{-0.639 - 0}{4.096/\sqrt{240}} = \frac{-0.639}{0.264396} = -2.416832 \text{ or } -2.42$$

Because $-2.42 < -1.972$, we reject the null hypothesis at the 0.05 significance level. During this subperiod, small-cap stocks significantly outperformed the S&P 500.

d. This t-test now has $n - 1 = 231 - 1 = 230$ degrees of freedom. At the 0.05 significance level, we reject the null if either if $t > 1.972$ or $t < -1.972$, using df = 200 in the t-distribution tables.

$$t = \frac{\bar{d} - \mu_{d0}}{s_{\bar{d}}} = \frac{0.221 - 0}{3.249/\sqrt{231}} = \frac{0.221}{0.213769} = 1.033829 \text{ or } 1.03$$

At the 0.05 significance level, because neither rejection point condition is met, we do not reject the null that for the January 1980–March 1999 period, the mean difference between the returns on the S&P 500 and small-cap stocks was zero.

13. a. We have a "less than" alternative hypothesis where σ^2 is the variance of return on the portfolio. The hypotheses are H_0: $\sigma^2 \geq 400$ versus H_a: $\sigma^2 < 400$, where 400 is the hypothesized value of variance, σ_0^2.

b. The test statistic is chi-square with $10 - 1 = 9$ degrees of freedom.

c. The rejection point is found across degrees of freedom of 9, under the 0.95 column (95 percent of probability above the value). It is 3.325. We will reject the null if we find that chi-square < 3.325.

d. The test statistic is calculated as

$$\chi^2 = \frac{(n - 1)s^2}{\sigma_0^2} = \frac{9 \times 15^2}{400} = \frac{2,025}{400} = 5.0625 \text{ or } 5.06$$

Because 5.06 is not less than 3.325, we do not reject the null hypothesis.

14. a. We have a "not equal to" alternative hypothesis:

$$H_0: \sigma^2_{Before} = \sigma^2_{After} \text{ versus } H_a: \sigma^2_{Before} \neq \sigma^2_{After}$$

b. To test a null hypothesis of the equality of two variances, we use an F-test:

$$F = \frac{s_1^2}{s_2}$$

c. The "Before" sample variance is larger, so following a convention for calculating F-statistics, the Before sample variance goes in the numerator. $F = 22.367/15.795 = 1.416$, with $120 - 1 = 119$ numerator and denominator degrees of freedom. Because this is a two-tailed test, we use F-tables for the 0.025 level (df = 0.05/2). Using the tables in the back of the book, the closest value to 119 is 120 degrees of freedom. At the 0.05 level, the rejection point is 1.43. (Using the insert statistical function on an Excel spreadsheet, we would find FINV(0.025, 119, 119) = 1.434859 as the critical F-value.) Because 1.416 is not greater than 1.43, we do not reject the null hypothesis that the Before and After variances are equal.

CORRELATION AND REGRESSION

LEARNING OUTCOMES

After completing this chapter, you will be able to do the following:

- Define and interpret a scatter plot.
- Define and calculate the covariance between two random variables.
- Define and calculate a correlation coefficient.
- Describe how correlation analysis is used to measure the strength of a relationship between variables.
- Interpret a given correlation coefficient.
- Formulate a test of the hypothesis that the population correlation coefficient equals zero and determine whether the hypothesis is rejected or not rejected at a given level of significance.
- Explain how outliers can affect correlations.
- Explain the nature of a spurious correlation.
- Explain the difference between dependent and independent variables in a linear regression.
- Differentiate between the slope and the intercept terms in a regression equation.
- List the assumptions underlying linear regression.
- Define and calculate the standard error of estimate.
- Calculate the coefficient of determination and explain its meaning.
- Calculate confidence intervals for a regression coefficient.
- Identify the test statistic for a hypothesis test about the population value of a regression coefficient.
- Formulate a null and an alternative hypothesis about a population value of a regression coefficient and determine whether the null hypothesis is rejected or not rejected at a given level of significance.
- Interpret a regression coefficient.
- Use an estimated regression model to predict the dependent variable, given a value of the independent variable.
- Calculate a confidence interval for a prediction made using an estimated regression equation.
- Describe the use of analysis of variance (ANOVA) in regression analysis.

- Identify the test statistic for a hypothesis test that the slope coefficients in a regression are all equal to zero.
- Interpret an *F*-statistic reported in regression output.
- Describe the limitations of regression analysis.
- Interpret the economic meaning of the results of regression and correlation analysis.

1   INTRODUCTION

As a financial analyst, you will often need to examine the relationship between two or more financial variables. You might want to know, for example, whether inflation is associated with a bear market in stocks, or whether returns to different stock market indexes are related. To see what kinds of questions you might ask, look at Table 8-1, which shows the annual returns from 1989 to 1998 for three stock indexes: the S&P 500 (a broad U.S. market index dominated by large cap stocks), the Wilshire 4500 (U.S. small-cap stocks), and the MSCI EAFE (an index of stocks from Europe, Australasia, and the Far East).

TABLE 8-1   Annual Returns to Stock Indexes (in percent)

Year	S&P 500	Wilshire 4500	MSCI EAFE
1989	31.0	23.9	10.4
1990	−3.2	−13.6	−23.6
1991	30.8	43.5	12.2
1992	7.7	11.9	−12.2
1993	10.1	14.6	32.7
1994	1.3	−2.7	7.8
1995	37.4	33.5	11.3
1996	22.8	17.2	6.1
1997	33.2	25.7	1.6
1998	28.4	8.6	20.1
Compound Return	19.1	15.1	5.5

How closely related are the returns to the indexes in this table? What makes them move up and down together? Why do they sometimes move in opposite directions? Is one index less closely related to the others? These questions are important to investment managers because they relate to risk and the benefits from diversification. The principal methods discussed in this chapter, correlation analysis and linear regression, help us examine these issues.

2 CORRELATION ANALYSIS

We have many ways to examine how two sets of data are related. Two of the most useful methods are scatter plots and correlation analysis. We will first look at scatter plots and then introduce correlation analysis.

2.1 SCATTER PLOTS

A **scatter plot** is a graph that shows the relationship between the observations for two data series in two dimensions. Suppose, for example, that we wish to graph the relation between total returns to the S&P 500 and the total returns to U.S. small-cap stocks. Table 8-2 shows the monthly returns to both the S&P 500 and U.S. small-cap stocks from January 1998 to June 1998.[1]

TABLE 8-2   Monthly Total Returns to the S&P 500 and U.S. Small-Cap Stocks:
             January 1998–June 1998

	S&P 500 Total Returns	U.S. Small-Cap Stocks Total Returns
January 1998	1.11%	−0.59%
February 1998	7.21%	6.49%
March 1998	5.12%	4.81%
April 1998	1.01%	1.68%
May 1998	−1.72%	−4.97%
June 1998	4.06%	−2.06%
Average	2.80%	0.89%

Source: Ibbotson Associates

To translate the data in Table 8-2 into a scatter plot, we take the data for each date and mark a point on a graph. For each point, the x-axis coordinate is the return to the S&P 500 and the y-axis coordinate is the return to the small-stock index. Figure 8-1 shows a scatter plot of the data in Table 8-2.

Note that each observation in the scatter plot is represented as a point, and the points are not connected. The scatter plot does not show which observation comes from which period; it shows only the actual observations of both data series plotted as pairs.[2] For example, the upper right point is the February 1998 pair of returns. The data plotted in Figure 8-1 show a fairly strong linear relationship with a positive slope. Next we will examine how to quantify this linear relationship.

---

[1] In this case, small-cap stocks are those stocks in the smallest two deciles according to market value (capitalization) on the NYSE, Amex, and Nasdaq markets combined. The data come from Ibbotson Associates and were constructed by Dimensional Fund Advisors. *Return* as used here and throughout this chapter refers to *total return,* which includes capital appreciation and income (dividends for stocks, interest for bonds).

[2] In this case, the choice of which variable we show on the x-axis and which we show on the y-axis is irrelevant.

FIGURE 8-1   Scatter Plot of Monthly
S&P 500 Returns and
U.S. Small-Cap Returns:
January 1998 Through
June 1998

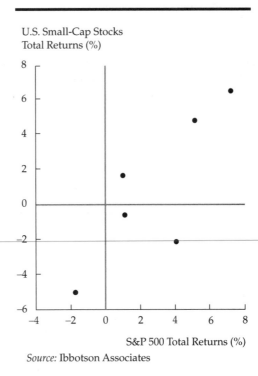

U.S. Small-Cap Stocks
Total Returns (%)

S&P 500 Total Returns (%)

Source: Ibbotson Associates

2.2 CORRELATION ANALYSIS

In contrast to a scatter plot, which graphically depicts the relation between two data series, **correlation analysis** expresses this same relation using a single number. The correlation coefficient is a measure of how closely related two data series are. In particular, the correlation coefficient measures the direction and extent of **linear association** between two variables. A correlation coefficient can have a maximum value of 1 and a minimum value of -1. A correlation coefficient greater than 0 implies a positive linear association between the two variables: When one variable increases (or decreases), the other also tends to increase (or decrease). A correlation coefficient less than 0 implies a negative linear association between the two variables: When one increases (or decreases), the other decreases (or increases). A correlation coefficient of 0 implies no linear relation between the two variables.[3] Figure 8-2 shows the scatter plot of two variables with a correlation of 1.

Note that all the points on the scatter plot in Figure 8-2 lie on a straight line with a positive slope. Whenever variable A increases by one unit, variable B increases by half a unit. Because all of the points in the graph lie on a straight line, an increase of one unit in variable A is associated with exactly the same half-unit increase in variable B, regardless of the level of variable A. Even if the slope of the line in the figure were different (but positive), the correlation between the two variables would be 1 as long as all the points lie on that straight line.

---

[3] Later, we show that variables with a correlation of 0 can have a strong nonlinear relation.

FIGURE 8-2   Variables with a Correlation of 1

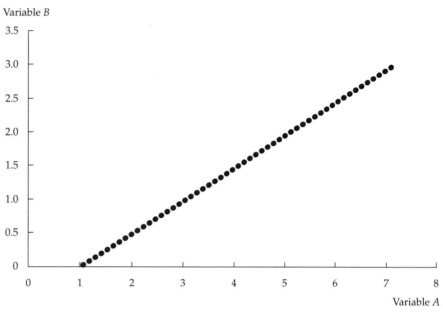

Figure 8-3 shows a scatter plot for two variables with a correlation coefficient of −1. Once again, the plotted observations fall on a straight line. In this graph, however, the line has a negative slope. As variable *A* increases by one unit, variable *B* decreases by half a unit, regardless of the initial value of variable *A*.

FIGURE 8-3   Variables with a Correlation of −1

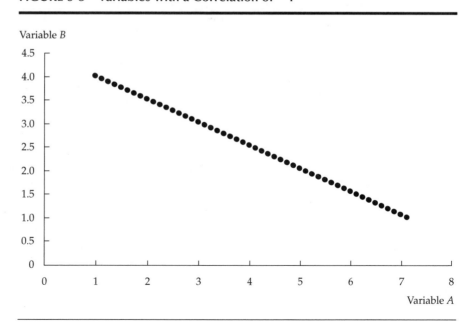

FIGURE 8-4   Variables with a Correlation of 0

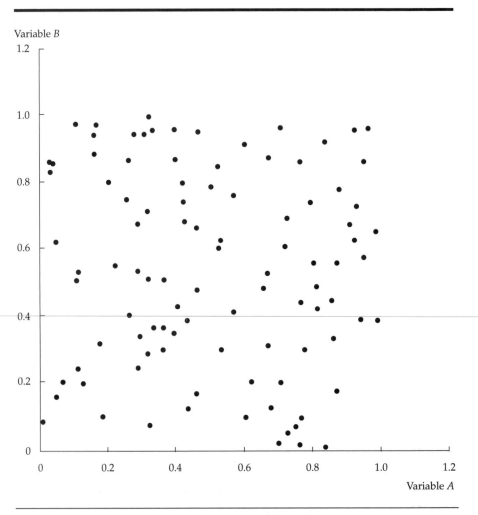

Figure 8-4 shows a scatter plot of two variables with a correlation of 0; they have no linear relation. This graph shows that the value of variable A tells us absolutely nothing about the value of variable B.

2.3 CALCULATING AND INTERPRETING THE CORRELATION COEFFICIENT

To define and calculate the correlation coefficient, we need another measure of linear association: covariance. In the chapter on probability concepts, we defined covariance as the expected value of the product of the deviations of two random variables from their respective means. That was the definition of population covariance, which we would also use in a forward-looking sense. To study historical or sample correlations, we need to use sample covariance. The sample covariance of X and Y, for a sample of size n, is

$$\text{Cov}(X, Y) = \sum_{i=1}^{n} (X_i - \overline{X})(Y_i - \overline{Y})/(n - 1) \tag{8-1}$$

The sample covariance is the average value of the product of the deviations of observations on two random variables from their sample means.[4] If the random variables are returns, the unit of covariance would be returns squared. Far easier to interpret is the sample correlation coefficient.

The formula for computing the sample correlation coefficient is

$$r = \frac{\text{Cov}(X_i, Y_i)}{s_x s_y}$$

(8-2)

The correlation coefficient is the covariance of two variables (X_i and Y_i) divided by the product of their sample standard deviations (s_x and s_y). Like covariance, the correlation coefficient is a measure of linear association. The correlation coefficient, however, has the advantage of being a simple number, with no unit of measurement attached. It has no units because it results from dividing the covariance by the product of the standard deviations. Because we will be using sample variance, standard deviation, and covariance in this chapter, we will repeat the calculations for these statistics. The sample variance of X is

$$s_X^2 = \sum_{i=1}^{n} (X_i - \overline{X})^2/(n - 1)$$

The sample standard deviation is

$$s_X = \sqrt{s_X^2}$$

Table 8-3 shows how to compute the various components of the correlation equation from the data in Table 8-2. The individual observations on S&P 500 total returns are the first variable, X_i, and U.S. small-cap returns are the second variable, Y_i. The remaining columns show the calculations for the inputs to correlation: the sample covariance and the sample standard deviations.

Using the data shown in Table 8-3 on page 368, we can compute the sample correlation coefficient for these two variables as follows:

$$r = \frac{0.001153}{(0.03254)(0.04303)} = \frac{\text{Cov}(X_i, Y_i)}{s_x s_y}$$
$$= 0.8234$$

The correlation coefficient of 0.8234 shows, in this small sample, a strong linear association between returns to the S&P 500 and returns to U.S. small-cap stocks. The correlation coefficient captures this strong association numerically, whereas the scatter plot in Figure 8-1 shows the information graphically.

What assumptions are necessary to compute the correlation coefficient? Correlation coefficients can be validly computed if the means and variances of X_i and Y_i, as well as the covariance of X_i and Y_i, are finite and constant. Later, we will show that when these assumptions are not true, correlations between two different variables can depend greatly on the sample that is used.

---

[4] The use of $n - 1$ in the denominator is a technical point; it ensures that the sample covariance is an unbiased estimate of population covariance.

TABLE 8-3   Sample Covariance and Sample Deviations, S&P 500 and U.S. Small-Cap Stock Monthly Total Returns: January 1998–June 1998

Month	S&P 500 Total Returns X_i	U.S. Small-Cap Stocks Total Returns Y_i	$(X_i - \bar{X})(Y_i - \bar{Y})$ Cross Product	$(X_i - \bar{X})^2$ Squared Deviations	$(Y_i - \bar{Y})^2$ Squared Deviations
January	0.0111	−0.0059	0.000250	0.000285	0.000220
February	0.0721	0.0649	0.002470	0.001948	0.003132
March	0.0512	0.0481	0.000910	0.000539	0.001534
April	0.0101	0.0168	−0.000141	0.000321	0.000062
May	−0.0172	−0.0497	0.002649	0.002041	0.003438
June	0.0406	−0.0206	−0.000373	0.000160	0.000872
Sum	0.1679	0.0536	0.005765	0.005291	0.009258
Average	0.0280	0.0089			
Covariance			0.001153		
Variance				0.001059	0.001852
Std. Dev.				0.03254	0.04303

Source for data: Ibbotson Associates

Notes:

1. Divide the cross-product sum by $n - 1$ (6 − 1) and the result is the covariance of X_i and Y_i.

2. Divide the squared deviations sums by $n - 1$ (6 − 1) and the results are the variances of X_i and Y_i.

2.4   USES AND LIMITATIONS OF CORRELATION ANALYSIS

Correlation is a measure of the linear association between two variables, but it may not always be reliable. Two variables can have a strong **nonlinear relation** and still have a very low correlation. For example, variable A and variable B in Figure 8-5 have a very strong nonlinear association. Below a level of 4 for variable A, variable B decreases with increasing values of A. When variable A is 4 or higher, however, variable B increases whenever variable A increases. Even though the association between these two variables is perfect, the correlation between them is 0.[5]

Correlation may also not be a reliable measure when outliers are present in one or both of the series. **Outliers** are small numbers of observations at either extreme (small or large) of a sample. Figure 8-6 shows a scatter plot of the monthly returns to the S&P 500 and the monthly inflation rate in the United States from January 1990 through March 1999.

In the scatter plot in Figure 8-6, we can see that most of the data lie clustered together with little discernible relation between the two variables. However, in three cases when inflation was greater than 0.8 percent in a particular month (the three circled observations), stock returns were strongly negative. These observations are outliers. If we compute the correlation coefficient for the entire data sample, that correlation is −0.3133. If we eliminate the three outliers, however, the correlation is −0.1321.

The correlation in the previous example is quite sensitive to excluding only three observations. Does it make sense to exclude those observations? Are they noise or news? One possible partial explanation of Figure 8-6 is that during the 1990s, whenever inflation was very high during a month, the market became concerned that the Federal Reserve would raise interest rates, which would cause the value of stocks to decline. This story is a very

---

[5] The two variables are related mathematically by Variable $B = $ (Variable $A - 4)^2$.

FIGURE 8-5   Variables with a Strong Non-Linear Association

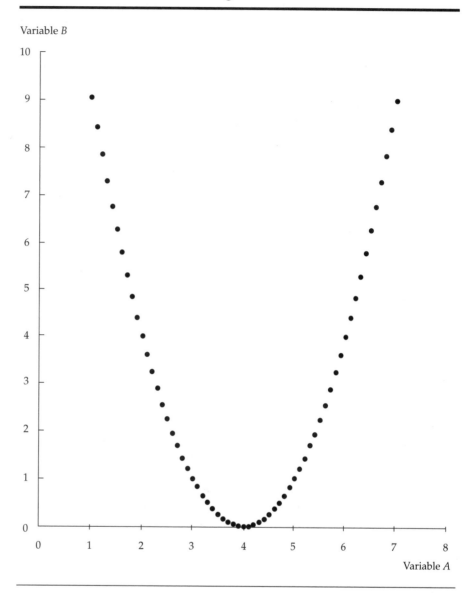

plausible explanation for how investors reacted to large inflation announcements. As a consequence, the outliers may give us important information about how markets actually reacted. Therefore, the correlation that includes the outliers may actually make more sense than the correlation that excludes them.

As a general rule, we must determine whether a computed sample correlation changes greatly by removing a few outliers. But we must also use judgment to determine whether those outliers contain information about the relation between the two variables (and should thus be included in the correlation analysis) or do not contain information (and should thus be excluded).

Also, be aware that correlation does not imply causation. Even if two variables are highly correlated, one does not necessarily cause the other. Spurious correlation can make

FIGURE 8-6   Inflation and Stock Returns in the 1990s

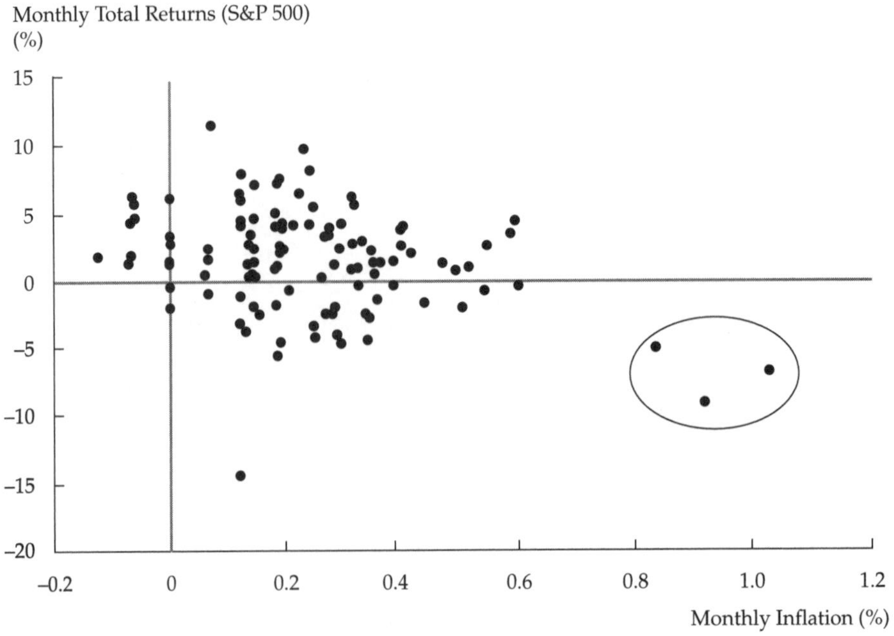

Source: Ibbotson Associates

two series appear closely associated when no causal relation exists. **Spurious correlation** between two variables is based not on any theoretical relationship, but rather on a relation that arises in the data solely because each of those variables is related to some third variable. For example, the number of cars and televisions in Japan both increased greatly after 1950, but certainly the increase in the popularity of cars did not cause people to buy televisions, or vice versa. Instead, economic growth and improved incomes made it possible for people to purchase both cars and televisions. Investment professionals must be particularly cautious when attributing causation to correlated variables. Spurious correlation may suggest investment strategies that appear profitable but actually would not be so, if implemented.

EXAMPLE 8-1.   Evaluating Economic Forecasts.

The strength of overall economic activity greatly affects asset returns. Forecasts of real economic growth are thus very important for many investment decisions. Since the late 1960s, the Survey of Professional Forecasters (SPF) has gathered the predictions of professional forecasters about many economic variables, including economic growth.[6] If these forecasts of economic growth were perfect predictors of actual economic growth, the correlation between forecasts and actual growth would be 1; that is, predicted and actual economic growth would always be the same.

---

[6] The survey was originally developed by Victor Zarnowitz for the American Statistical Association and the National Bureau of Economic Research. Starting in 1990, the survey has been directed by Dean Croushire of the Federal Reserve Bank of Philadelphia.

Figure 8-7 shows a scatter plot of the median forecast of current-quarter, real-output growth on an annualized basis, and actual growth in real output from the third quarter of 1969 through the fourth quarter of 1996.[7] In this scatter plot, the forecast for each quarter is plotted as the *x*-coordinate and the actual real growth rate is plotted as the *y*-coordinate.

As Figure 8-7 shows, a fairly strong linear association exists between the forecast and the actual growth rate. In fact, the correlation between the two series is 0.8164. Therefore, we can say that the forecasts of real-output growth explained a high proportion of the variation in the actual growth rates, suggesting that those forecasts can be used for investment decisions.

EXAMPLE 8-2.   Style-Analysis Correlations.

One important issue in evaluating a portfolio manager's performance is determining an appropriate benchmark for the portfolio manager. In recent years, style analysis has been an important component of benchmark selection.[8] To illustrate, suppose a portfolio manager uses small-cap stocks in an investment portfolio. By applying style analysis, we can try to determine whether the portfolio manager uses a small-cap growth style or a small-cap value style.

In the United States, the Russell 2000 Growth Index and the Russell 2000 Value Index are often used as benchmarks for small-cap growth and small-cap value managers, respectively. Correlation analysis shows, however, that the returns to these two indexes are very closely associated. Between January 1979 and March 1999, the correlation between the monthly returns to the Russell 2000 Growth Index and the Russell 2000 Value Index was 0.9264.

If the correlation between the returns to the two indexes were 1, there would be absolutely no difference in equity-management style between small-cap value and small-cap growth. That is, if we knew the return to one style, we could be certain about the return to the other style. Because the returns to the two indexes are almost perfectly correlated, we can say that very little difference exists between the two returns, and therefore, we may not be able to justify treating small-cap growth and small-cap value as different investment styles.

The previous examples in this chapter have examined the correlation between two variables. Often, however, investment managers need to understand the correlation among many asset returns. For example, investors who have any exposure to movements in exchange rates must understand the correlations of the returns to different foreign currencies and other assets in order to determine their optimal portfolios and hedging strategies.[9] In the following example, we see how a correlation matrix shows correlation between pairs of variables when we have more than two variables. We also see one of the main challenges to investment managers: Investment-return correlations can change substantially over time.

---

[7] In this scatter plot, the actual real growth rate is the initial announcement of real growth made one month after the end of each quarter. These growth rates are subject to many data revisions.

[8] See, for example, Sharpe (1992) and Buetow, Johnson, and Runkle (2000).

[9] See, for example, Clarke and Kritzman (1996).

FIGURE 8-7   Actual Real Growth vs. Real Growth Forecast

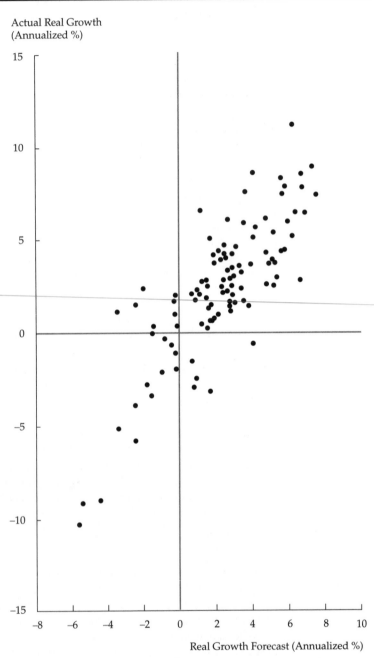

Source: Federal Reserve Bank of Philadelphia and U.S. Department of Commerce

---

EXAMPLE 8-3.   Exchange-Rate Return Correlation.

Exchange rates are usually quoted from the perspective of an investor purchasing foreign currency with the investor's home currency. For example, from the perspective of a U.S. investor, the British pound exchange rate is quoted as USD/GBP: the number of dollars (USD) it takes to buy one pound (GBP). This is known as a direct quote for foreign exchange. If one dollar could buy two-thirds of a pound, the exchange rate would be quoted as $1/(2/3) = 1.5$.

Exchange rates can also be quoted from the perspective of the number of units of foreign currency that can be purchased with one unit of the investor's home currency. The exchange rate between the Japanese yen and the U.S. dollar is usually quoted in this manner. For example, from the perspective of a U.S. investor, the yen (JPY) exchange rate would be quoted as JPY/USD, the number of yen that can be purchased for $1. This is known as an indirect quote for foreign exchange. For example, if $1 buys 100 yen, the exchange rate would be quoted as $100/1 = 100$.

The exchange-rate return measures the periodic domestic currency return to holding foreign currency. Suppose a change in inflation rates in the United Kingdom and the United States results in one dollar being worth 0.8 pounds rather than two-thirds of a pound. The price of a pound would then be $1/(0.8) = \$1.25$ rather than $1/(2/3) = \$1.50$. If this change occurred in one month, the return in that month to holding pounds would be $(1.25 - 1.50)/1.50 = -16.67$ percent, in terms of dollars.

Table 8-4 shows a correlation matrix of monthly returns in U.S. dollars to holding Canadian, Japanese, Swedish, or UK currencies.[10] We can understand how to interpret a correlation matrix by examining the top panel of this table. The first column of numbers of that panel shows the correlations between USD returns to holding the Canadian dollar and USD returns to holding Canadian, Japanese, Swedish, and British currencies. Of course, any variable is perfectly correlated with itself, and so the correlation between USD returns to holding the Canadian dollar and USD returns to holding the Canadian dollar is 1. The second row of this column shows that the correlation between USD returns to holding the Canadian dollar and USD returns to holding the Japanese yen was 0.2593 from 1980 to 1989. The remaining correlations in the panel show how the USD returns to other combinations of currency holdings were correlated in this period.

Note that Table 8-4 omits many of the correlations. For example, column 2 of the panel omits the correlation between USD returns to holding yen and USD returns to holding Canadian dollars. This correlation is omitted because it is identical to the correlation between USD returns to holding Canadian dollars and USD returns to holding yen shown in row 2 of column 1. Other omitted correlations would also have been duplicative. In fact, correlations are always symmetrical: The correlation between X and Y is always the same as the correlation between Y and X.

If you compare the two panels of this table, you will find that many of the currency–return correlations changed dramatically between the 1980s and the 1990s. In the 1980s, for example, the correlation between the return to holding Japanese yen and the return to holding either Swedish kronor (0.6576) or British pounds (0.6068) was almost as high as the correlation between the return to holding kronor and the return to holding pounds (0.6840). In the 1990s, however, the correlation between yen returns and either krona or pound returns dropped by more than half (to 0.2828 and 0.2899, respectively), but the correlation between krona and pound returns hardly changed at all (0.6439). Some of the correlations between returns to the Canadian dollar and returns to other currencies dropped even more dramatically. In the

[10] Data for the 1980s are from January 1980 through December 1989. Data for the 1990s are from January 1990 through March 1999.

1980s, the correlation between Canadian dollar returns and Japanese yen returns was 0.2593. By the 1990s, that correlation actually became negative (−0.0779). The correlation between the Canadian dollar returns and British pound returns dropped from 0.3925 in the 1980s to 0.0529 in the 1990s.

TABLE 8-4   Correlations of Monthly USD Returns to Selected Foreign Currencies

1980–1989	Canada FX Return	Japan FX Return	Sweden FX Return	U.K. FX Return
Canada FX return	1.0000			
Japan FX return	0.2593	1.0000		
Sweden FX return	0.2834	0.6576	1.0000	
U.K. FX return	0.3925	0.6068	0.6840	1.0000

1990–1999	Canada FX Return	Japan FX Return	Sweden FX Return	U.K. FX Return
Canada FX return	1.0000			
Japan FX return	−0.0779	1.0000		
Sweden FX return	0.1920	0.2828	1.0000	
U.K. FX return	0.0529	0.2899	0.6439	1.0000

Source for data: Ibbotson Associates

These changes in correlations are important because optimal asset allocation depends on expectations of future correlations. With less than perfect positive correlation between two assets' returns, there are potential risk-reduction benefits to holding both assets. We discuss these issues in detail in the chapter on portfolio concepts.

EXAMPLE 8-4.   Correlations among Stock-Return Series.

Portfolio managers often concentrate on either large-cap or small-cap stocks. Some investment managers prefer to hold a broadly diversified group of equities of all capitalization values. Examining the correlations among large-cap, small-cap, and broad-market returns can tell us just how different these style categories are. This type of analysis has serious diversification and asset allocation consequences because the strength of the correlations among the assets tells us how successfully the assets can be combined to diversify risk.

Table 8-5 shows the correlation matrix of monthly returns to three U.S. stock indexes using data from January 1971 through March 1999. The large-cap style is represented by the return to the S&P 500 Index, the small-cap style is represented by the return to the Dimensional Fund Advisors U.S. Small-Stock Index, and the broad-market returns are represented by the return to the Wilshire 5000 Index.

TABLE 8-5   Correlations of Monthly Returns to Various U.S. Stock Indexes

1971–1999	S&P 500	U.S. Small-Stock	Wilshire 5000
S&P 500	1.0000		
U.S. Small-Stock	0.7740	1.0000	
Wilshire 5000	0.9896	0.8344	1.0000

1970–1979	S&P 500	U.S. Small-Stock	Wilshire 5000
S&P 500	1.0000		
U.S. Small-Stock	0.7873	1.0000	
Wilshire 5000	0.9906	0.8375	1.0000

1980–1989	S&P 500	U.S. Small-Stock	Wilshire 5000
S&P 500	1.0000		
U.S. Small-Stock	0.8440	1.0000	
Wilshire 5000	0.9914	0.8950	1.0000

1990–1999	S&P 500	U.S. Small-Stock	Wilshire 5000
S&P 500	1.0000		
U.S. Small-Stock	0.7051	1.0000	
Wilshire 5000	0.9864	0.7942	1.0000

Source for data: Ibbotson Associates

The first column of numbers in the top panel of Table 8-5 shows very little difference between returns to the S&P 500 and returns to the Wilshire 5000: The correlation between the two return series is 0.9896. This result should not be surprising, because both the S&P 500 and the Wilshire 5000 are value-weighted indexes, and large-cap stock returns receive most of the weight in both indexes. In fact, the companies in the S&P 500 have about 80 percent of the total market value of all companies in the Wilshire 5000.

Small stocks also have a reasonably high correlation with large stocks. In this sample, the correlation between the S&P 500 returns and the U.S. Small-Stock returns was 0.7740. The correlation between U.S. Small-Stock returns and returns to the Wilshire 5000 is slightly higher (0.8344). This result is also not too surprising because the Wilshire 5000 contains small-cap stocks and the S&P 500 does not. The second, third, and fourth panels of Table 8-5 show that certain correlations among the various stock-market return series have changed substantially from decade to decade. For example, the correlation between returns to the S&P 500 and U.S. small-cap stocks dropped from 0.8440 in the 1980s to 0.7051 in the 1990s.[11]

---

[11] The correlation coefficient for the 1990s was less than that for the 1980s at the 0.01 significance level. A test for this type of hypothesis on the correlation coefficient can be conducted using Fisher's z-transformation. See Daniel and Terrell (1995) for information on this method.

EXAMPLE 8-5.   Correlation of Debt and Equity returns.

Table 8-6 shows the correlation matrix for various U.S. debt returns and S&P 500 returns using monthly data from January 1926 to March 1999.

TABLE 8-6   Correlations among U.S. Stock and Debt Returns: 1926–1999

All	S&P 500	U.S. Long-Term Corp.	U.S. Long-Term Govt.	U.S. 30-Day T-Bill	High-Yield Corp.
S&P 500	1.0000				
U.S. Long-term corp.	0.2368	1.0000			
U.S. Long-term govt.	0.1784	0.8488	1.0000		
U.S. 30-day T-bill	−0.0200	0.1008	0.1159	1.0000	
High-yield corp.	0.6536	0.4282	0.3257	0.0192	1.0000

Source for data: Ibbotson Associates

The first column of numbers, in particular, shows the correlations of S&P 500 returns with various debt returns. Note that S&P 500 returns were almost completely uncorrelated (−0.0200) with 30-day Treasury bill returns. Long-term corporate debt returns were somewhat more correlated (0.2368) with S&P 500 returns. Returns on high-yield corporate bonds have the highest correlation (0.6536) with S&P 500 total returns. This high correlation is understandable; high-yield debt securities behave partially like equities because of their high default risk. If a company defaults, bondholders of high-yield debt typically lose most of their investment.

Long-term government bonds, however, have a low correlation (0.1784) with S&P 500 returns. We expect some correlation between these variables because increases in interest rates reduce the present value of the future cash flows of both bonds and stocks. The relatively low correlation between these two return series, however, shows that other factors affect the returns on stocks besides interest rates. Without these other factors, the correlation between bond and stock returns would be higher.

The second column of numbers in Table 8-6 shows that the correlation between long-term government bond and corporate bond returns was quite high (0.8488). Although this correlation is the highest in the entire matrix, it is not 1. The correlation is lower than 1 because the default premium for long-term corporate bonds changes, whereas government bonds do not incorporate a default premium. As a result, interest rates for government bonds have a correlation less than 1 with interest rates for corporate bonds. For the same reason, return correlations between government bonds and corporate bonds are below 1. Note also that the correlation of high-yield corporate bond total returns with long-term government total returns (0.3257) is only about half of the correlation of high-yield bond returns with S&P 500 returns. This relatively low correlation is another indicator that high-yield-bond returns behave more like equity returns than debt returns.

Note finally that 30-day Treasury bills returns have a very low correlation with all other return series. In fact, the correlations between T-bill returns and other return series are lower than any of the other correlations in this table. These low correlations show that changes in short-term interest rates do not explain much of the variation in returns to either long-term debt securities or the S&P 500.

2.5 TESTING THE SIGNIFICANCE OF THE CORRELATION COEFFICIENT

Significance tests allow us to assess whether apparent relationships between random variables are real or due to chance. If we decide that the relationships are real, we will be inclined to use this information in projections about the future. The data in Table 8-3 showed that the correlation between stock returns for the S&P 500 and stock returns for U.S. Small-Stocks was 0.8234 between January 1998 and June 1998. That estimated correlation seems high, but is it significantly different from 0? Before we can answer this question, we must know something about the distribution of the underlying variables themselves. For purposes of simplicity, let us assume that both of the variables are normally distributed.[12]

We propose two hypotheses: the null hypothesis, H_0, that the correlation in the population is 0 ($\rho = 0$); and the alternative hypothesis, H_a, that the correlation in the population is different from 0 ($\rho \neq 0$).

The alternative hypothesis is a test that the correlation is not equal to 0; therefore, the two-tailed test is the correct test of the null hypothesis.[13] As long as the two variables are distributed normally, we can test to determine whether the null hypothesis should be rejected using the sample correlation, r. The formula for the t-test is

$$t = \frac{r\sqrt{n-2}}{\sqrt{1-r^2}} \tag{8-3}$$

This test statistic has a t distribution with $n - 2$ degrees of freedom if the null hypothesis is true.

The sample size, n, plays a critical role in tests of the significance of the correlation coefficient. Consider the case when $r > 0$.[14] As you can see from Equation 8-3, a larger sample size (n) means a larger value of t. This, in turn, implies that t is more likely to be greater than t_c, the critical value of the test statistic.[15] Furthermore, a larger sample size means more degrees of freedom, and consequently a lower critical-value t_c. This also implies that t is more likely to be greater than t_c. Thus the null hypothesis (H_0: $\rho = 0$) is more likely to be rejected for larger samples, all else equal.

EXAMPLE 8-6. Testing Stock-Return Correlation.

Earlier in this chapter, we showed that the sample correlation between the S&P 500 returns and U.S. small-stock returns from January 1998 to June 1998 is 0.8234. Suppose we want to test the null hypothesis, H_0, that the true correlation in the population is 0 ($\rho = 0$) against the alternative hypothesis, H_a, that the correlation in the population is different from 0 ($\rho \neq 0$). Recalling that this sample has six observations, we can compute the statistic for testing the null hypothesis as follows:

---

[12] Actually, we must assume that the variables come from a bivariate normal distribution. If two variables, X and Y, come from a bivariate normal distribution, then for each value of X the distribution of Y is normal. See, for example, Ross (1997) or Greene (1999).

[13] See the chapter on hypothesis testing for a more in-depth discussion of two-tailed tests.

[14] We could make a similar argument when $r < 0$; in this case the null hypothesis is rejected when $t < -t_c$.

[15] See the chapter on hypothesis testing for a discussion of critical values.

$$t = 2.9020 = \frac{0.8234\sqrt{6-2}}{\sqrt{1-0.8234^2}}$$

The value of the test statistic is 2.9020. As the table of critical values of the t-distribution for a two-tailed test shows, for a t distribution with $n - 2 = 6 - 2 = 4$ degrees of freedom at the 0.05 level of significance, we can reject the null hypothesis (that the population correlation is equal to 0) if the value of the test statistic is greater than 2.776 or less than -2.776. The fact that we can reject the null hypothesis of no correlation when we have only six observations is quite unusual; it further demonstrates the strong relation between the returns to the S&P 500 and returns to small stocks during this period.

EXAMPLE 8-7. Testing the Krona–Yen Return Correlation.

The data in Table 8-4 show that the sample correlation between the USD monthly returns to Swedish kronor and Japanese yen was 0.2828 for the period from January 1990 through March 1999. If we observe this sample correlation, should we believe that the correlation is not equal to 0 in the population?

With 111 months from January 1990 through March 1999, we use the following statistic to test the null hypothesis, H_0, that the true correlation in the population is 0, against the alternative hypothesis, H_a, that the correlation in the population is different from 0:

$$t = 3.0782 = \frac{0.2828\sqrt{111-2}}{\sqrt{1-0.2828^2}}$$

At the 0.05 significance level, the critical level for this test statistic is 1.98 ($n = 111$, degrees of freedom $= 109$). When the test statistic is either larger than 1.98 or smaller than -1.98, we can reject the hypothesis that the correlation in the population is 0. The test statistic is 3.0782, so we can reject the null hypothesis.

Note that the sample correlation coefficient in this case is significantly different from 0 at the 0.05 level, even though the coefficient is much smaller than that in the previous example. The correlation coefficient, though smaller, is still significant because the sample is much larger (111 observations instead of 6 observations).

The above example shows the importance of sample size in tests of the significance of the correlation coefficient. The following example also shows the importance of sample size.

EXAMPLE 8-8. The Correlation between Bond Returns and T-Bill Returns.

When the sample size is large enough, correlations can be significantly different from 0 even if the estimated correlations are rather low. For example, Table 8-6 shows that the sample correlation between monthly returns to U.S. government bonds and monthly returns to 30-day Treasury bills was 0.1159 from January 1926 through March 1999. Suppose we want to test whether the correlation coefficient is statistically significant. From January 1926 to March 1999, there were 891 months. Therefore, to test the null hypothesis, H_0 (that the true correlation in the population is 0), against the alternative hypothesis, H_a (that the correlation in the population is different from 0), we use the following test statistic:

$$t = 3.4791 = \frac{0.1159\sqrt{891-2}}{\sqrt{1-0.1159^2}}$$

At the 0.05 significance level, the critical value for the test statistic is approximately 1.96. At the 0.01 significance level, the critical value for the test statistic is approximately 2.58. The test statistic is 3.4791, so we can reject the null hypothesis of no correlation in the population at both the 0.05 and 0.01 levels. This example shows that, in large samples, even relatively small correlation coefficients can be significantly different from 0. The significance levels of correlations can be important when correlations are used in determining optimal portfolios according to modern portfolio theory, as will be illustrated in the chapter on portfolio concepts.

The scatter plot gives the analyst a visual picture of the relationship between two variables, while the correlation coefficient quantifies the existence of any linear relationship. Large absolute values of the correlation coefficient indicate strong linear relationships. Positive coefficients indicate a positive relationship and negative coefficients a negative relationship between two data sets. In Examples 8-7 and 8-8, we saw that relatively small correlation coefficients (0.2828 and 0.1159) can be statistically significant and thus might provide valuable information about the behavior of economic variables.

Next we will introduce linear regression, another tool useful in examining the relationship between two variables.

3 LINEAR REGRESSION

3.1 LINEAR REGRESSION WITH ONE INDEPENDENT VARIABLE

As a financial analyst, you will often need to use information about one variable to draw a conclusion about another variable. For example, you may want to know the impact of inflation on returns to the S&P 500. If the relationship between those two variables is linear, you can use linear regression to summarize that relation.

Linear regression allows you to use one variable to make predictions about another, test hypotheses about the relation between two variables, and quantify the strength of the relationship between the two variables. The remainder of this chapter focuses on linear regression with a single independent variable. The next chapter will examine regression with more than one independent variable.

Regression analysis begins with the dependent variable (denoted Y), the variable that you are seeking to explain. The independent variable (denoted X) is the variable you are using to explain changes in the dependent variable. For example, you might try to explain small-stock returns (the dependent variable) based on returns to the S&P 500 (the independent variable). Or you might try to explain inflation (the dependent variable) as a function of growth in a country's money supply (the independent variable).

Linear regression assumes a linear relation between the dependent and the independent variables. The following regression equation explains that relation:

$$Y_i = b_0 + b_1 X_i + \epsilon_i, i = 1, \dots, n \tag{8-4}$$

This equation states that the **dependent variable,** Y, is equal to the intercept, b_0, plus a slope coefficient, b_1, times the **independent variable,** X, plus an **error term,** ϵ. The error term represents the portion of the dependent variable that cannot be explained by the independent variable.

Two principal types of data are used in regression analysis: cross-sectional data and time-series data. Cross-sectional data uses many observations on X and Y for the same time period. Those observations could come from different companies, asset classes, investment funds, people, countries, or other entities, depending on the regression model. For example, a cross-sectional model might use data from many companies to test whether predicted earnings-per-share growth explains differences in P/E ratios among companies in a specific time period. If we use cross-sectional observations in a regression, we usually denote the observations $i = 1, 2, \ldots, n$.

Time-series data use many observations from different time periods for the same company, asset class, investment fund, person, country, or other entity, depending on the regression model. For example, a time-series model might use monthly data from many years to test whether U.S. inflation rates determine U.S. short-term interest rates.[16] If we use time-series data in a regression, we usually denote the observations $t = 1, 2, \ldots, T$.[17] Time-series models are discussed in greater detail in the chapter on time-series analysis.

Exactly how does linear regression estimate b_0 and b_1? Linear regression, also known as linear least squares, computes a line that best fits the observations; it chooses values for the slope, b_0, and intercept, b_1, that minimize the sum of the squared vertical distances between the observations and the regression line. That is, linear regression chooses the **estimated** or **fitted parameters** $\hat{b}_0$ and $\hat{b}_1$ in Equation 8-4 to minimize[18]

$$\sum_{i=1}^{n} (Y_i - \hat{b}_0 - \hat{b}_1 X_i)^2 \tag{8-5}$$

In this equation, the term $(Y_i - \hat{b}_0 - \hat{b}_1 X_i)^2$ is (Dependent variable − Predicted value of dependent variable)^2. Using this method to estimate the values of $\hat{b}_0$ and $\hat{b}_1$ we can fit a line through the observations on X and Y that best explains the value that Y takes for any particular value of X.[19]

Note that we never observe the actual parameter values b_0 and b_1 in a regression model. Instead, we observe only the estimated values $\hat{b}_0$ and $\hat{b}_1$. All of our prediction and testing must be based on the estimated values of the parameters rather than their actual values.

Figure 8-8 gives a visual example of how linear regression works. The figure shows the linear regression that results from estimating the regression relation between returns to small-cap stocks (the dependent variable) and returns to the S&P 500 (the independent variable) from January 1998 through June 1998.[20] The equation to be estimated is Monthly small-cap stock returns = $b_0 + b_1$ (Monthly S&P returns) + ϵ.

---

[16] A mix of time-series and cross-sectional data, also known as panel data, is now frequently used in financial analysis. The analysis of panel data is an advanced topic that Greene (1999) discusses in detail.

[17] In this chapter, we primarily use the notation $i = 1, 2, \ldots, n$ even for time series to prevent confusion that would be caused by switching back and forth between different notations.

[18] Hats over the symbols for coefficients indicate estimated values.

[19] For a discussion of the precise statistical sense in which the estimates of b_0 and b_1 are optimal, see Greene (1999).

[20] These data appear in Table 8-2.

FIGURE 8-8   Fitted Regression Line Explaining Small-Cap Returns Using S&P 500 Returns

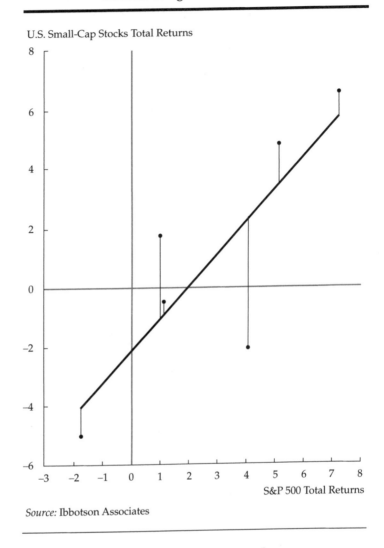

U.S. Small-Cap Stocks Total Returns

S&P 500 Total Returns

Source: Ibbotson Associates

Figure 8-8 shows a vertical line from each of the six data points to the fitted regression line. That distance is the regression residual, which is the difference between the actual value of the dependent variable and the predicted value of the dependent variable made by the regression equation. Linear regression chooses the estimated coefficients $\hat{b}_0$ and $\hat{b}_1$ in Equation 8-4 such that the sum of the squared vertical distances is minimized. The estimated regression equation is Monthly small stock returns $= -0.0216 + 1.0889 \times$ (Monthly S&P 500 returns).[21]

According to this regression equation, if the return to the S&P 500 is 0 in any particular month, the returns to small stocks in that month will be -2.16 percent. For every 1-percentage-point increase in the returns to the S&P 500 during the month, small stock returns are predicted to increase by 1.0889 percentage points. In a regression such as this one,

---

[21] We entered the monthly returns as decimals.

which contains one independent variable, the slope coefficient equals $\text{Cov}(Y_i, X_i)/\text{Var}(X_i)$. We can solve for the slope coefficient using data from Table 8-3, excerpted here:

TABLE 8-3 (EXCERPTED)

Month	S&P 500 Total Returns X_i	U.S. Small-Cap Stocks Total Returns Y_i	$(X_i - \bar{X})(Y_i - \bar{Y})$ Cross Product	$(X_i - \bar{X})^2$ Squared Deviations	$(Y_i - \bar{Y})^2$ Squared Deviations
Sum	0.1679	0.0536	0.005765	0.005291	0.009258
Average	0.0280	0.0089			
Covariance			0.001153		
Variance				0.001059	0.001852
Std. Dev.				0.03254	0.04303

$$\text{Cov}(Y_i, X_i) = 0.001153$$
$$\text{Var}(X_i) = 0.001059$$
$$\text{Cov}(Y_i, X_i)/\text{Var}(X_i) = 0.001153/0.001059$$
$$\hat{b}_1 = 1.0889$$

In a linear regression, the regression line fits through the point corresponding to the means of the dependent and the independent variables. As shown in Table 8-2 (excerpted below), the mean monthly return for the S&P 500 during these six months was 2.80 percent, whereas the mean monthly return to small stocks was 0.89 percent.

TABLE 8-2 (EXCERPTED)

	S&P 500 Total Returns	U.S. Small-Cap Stocks Total Returns
Average	2.80%	0.89%

Because the point (2.80, 0.89) lies on the regression line $\hat{b}_0 = \bar{Y} - \hat{b}_1\bar{X}$, we can solve for the intercept using this point as follows:

$$\hat{b}_0 = 0.0089 - 1.0889 \times 0.0280 = -0.0216$$

We are showing how to solve the linear regression equation by hand so it is clear where the numbers come from. Typically, the analyst will use the data analysis function on a spreadsheet or a statistical package to perform linear regression analysis.

Later, we will discuss how to use regression residuals to quantify the uncertainty in a regression model.

3.2 THE ASSUMPTIONS OF THE LINEAR REGRESSION

We have discussed how to interpret the coefficients in a linear regression model. Now we turn to the statistical assumptions underlying a linear regression model. Suppose that we have n observations on both the dependent variable, Y_i, and the independent variable, X_i, and we wish to estimate the equation

$$Y_i = b_0 + b_1 X_i + \epsilon_i, i = 1, \dots, n \qquad (8\text{-}6)$$

To be able to draw valid conclusions from a linear regression model with a single independent variable, we need to make the following six assumptions, known as the classical normal linear regression model assumptions:

1. A linear relation exists between the dependent variable, Y_i, and the independent variable, X_i. The relation is linear in the parameters b_0 and b_1.
2. The independent variable, X_i, is not random.[22]
3. The expected value of the error term is 0, that is, $E(\epsilon_i) = 0$.
4. The variance of the error term is the same for all observations:
   $E(\epsilon_i^2) = \sigma_\epsilon^2, i = 1, \dots, n$.
5. The error term, ϵ_i, is uncorrelated across observations. Consequently, $E(\epsilon_i \epsilon_j) = 0$ for all i not equal to j.[23]
6. The error term, ϵ_i, is normally distributed.[24]

Now we can take a closer look at each of these assumptions.

Assumption 1 is critical for a valid linear regression. If the independent and dependent variables have a nonlinear relation, as they do in Figure 8-5, then estimating that relation with a linear regression model will be invalid. In fact, using linear regression on the data shown in Figure 8-5 produces an estimated slope coefficient of 0, even though the two variables are strongly related.

Sometimes a nonlinear relation between variables can be transformed easily into a linear relation to satisfy Assumption 1. For example, suppose we postulate the relation $Y_i = e^{(b_0 + b_1 X_i + \epsilon_i)}$. This equation is nonlinear, so Assumption 1 is violated. If we take the natural log of both sides of this equation, however, the resulting equation is $Y_i^* = \ln Y_i = b_0 + b_1 X_i + \epsilon_i$. This equation is log-linear. That is, the log of Y, Y_i^* depends on X in a linear way.[25]

Even if the variables in a regression model are nonlinear, linear regression can be used as long as the variable can be transformed such that the equation is linear in the parameters. So, for example, linear regression can be used to estimate the equation $Y_i = b_0 + b_1(X_i^2) + \epsilon_i$.

---

[22] Although we assume that the independent variable in the regression model is not random, that assumption is clearly often not true. For example, it is unrealistic to assume that the monthly returns to the S&P 500 are not random. If the independent variable is random, then is the regression model incorrect? Fortunately, no. Econometricians have shown that even if the independent variable is random, we can still rely on the results of regression models. The mathematics underlying this result, however, are quite difficult. See, for example, Greene (1999) or Goldberger (1998).

[23] $\mathrm{Var}(\epsilon_i) = E(\epsilon_i - E(\epsilon_i))^2 = E(\epsilon_i - 0)^2 = E(\epsilon_i)^2$.

$\mathrm{Cov}(\epsilon_i, \epsilon_j) = E[(\epsilon_i - E(\epsilon_i))(\epsilon_j - E(\epsilon_j))] = E[(\epsilon_i - 0)(\epsilon_j - 0)] = E(\epsilon_i \epsilon_j) = 0$.

[24] If the regression errors are not normally distributed, can we still use regression analysis? Fortunately, yes. Econometricians who dispense with the normality assumption use chi-square tests of hypotheses, rather than F-tests. But this difference usually does not affect whether a test about a particular null hypothesis is rejected.

[25] The most important difference between these two equations, however, is that the parameters in this new equation affect the dependent variable [$\ln(Y)$] linearly. In the chapter on time-series, we will model sales trends using this log-linear approximation.

Assumptions 2 and 3 are needed to ensure that linear regression produces the correct estimates of b_0 and b_1.[26]

Assumptions 4, 5, and 6 let us use the linear regression model to determine the distribution of the estimated parameters $\hat{b}_0$ and $\hat{b}_1$, and therefore test whether those coefficients have a particular value.

- *Assumption 4*, that the variance of the error term is the same for all observations, is also known as the homoskedasticity assumption. The chapter on regression analysis discusses how to test for and correct for violations of this assumption.
- *Assumption 5*, that the errors are uncorrelated across observations, is also necessary for correctly estimating the variances of the estimated parameters $\hat{b}_0$ and $\hat{b}_1$. The chapter on multiple regression discusses violations of this assumption.
- *Assumption 6*, that the error term is normally distributed, allows us to easily test a particular hypothesis about a linear regression model.[27]

EXAMPLE 8-9.   Evaluating Economic Forecasts.

If economic forecasts were completely accurate, every prediction of real growth in a quarter would exactly match the growth that occurs in that quarter. Of course, when we learn new things about the predicted variable after the forecast has been made, we often discover that forecasts are not accurate. Even though forecasts can be inaccurate, we hope at least that they are unbiased; that is, that the expected value of the forecast error is 0. An unbiased forecast can be expressed as E(Actual growth − Predicted growth) = 0. In fact, most evaluations of forecast accuracy test whether forecasts are unbiased.[28]

Figure 8-9 repeats the scatter plot of predicted current-quarter real growth and actual real growth from the Survey of Professional Forecasters shown in Figure 8-7.[29] This figure also includes the fitted regression line for the equation Actual real growth = $b_0 + b_1$(Predicted real growth) + ϵ. If the forecasts are unbiased, the intercept, b_0, should be 0 and the slope, b_1, should be 1. We should also find E(Actual growth − Predicted growth) = 0. As long as $b_0 =$ and $b_1 = 1$, the error term [Actual growth − $b_0 - b_1$(Predicted growth)] will have an expected value of 0, as required by Assumption 3 of the linear regression model. Any other values of b_0 and b_1 would yield an error term with an expected value different from 0.

If $b_0 = 0$ and $b_1 = 1$, our best guess of actual real growth would be 0 if professional forecasters' predictions of real growth were 0. For every 1-percentage-

---

[26] At this point, do not be concerned about Assumptions 2 and 3. We use them here to avoid the need for more-difficult mathematics. Advanced texts, such as Greene (1999), allow the independent variable, X_i, to be random, and assume that $E(X_i\epsilon_j) = 0$. This alternative assumption does not change how we interpret regression results, however.

[27] We may be able to drop the assumption of normality for large data by appeal to the central limit theorem, which was discussed in the chapter on sampling; see Greene (1999). Asymptotic theory shows that, in many cases, the test statistics produced by standard regression programs are valid even if the error term is not normally distributed. As illustrated in the chapter on statistical concepts and market returns, however, non-normality of some financial time series can be quite severe. With severe non-normality, even with a relatively large number of observations, invoking asymptotic theory to justify using test statistics from linear regression models may be inappropriate.

[28] See, for example, Keane and Runkle (1990).

[29] The predicted growth for the current quarter is compared with the estimate of actual growth that is released about 45 days after the end of the quarter.

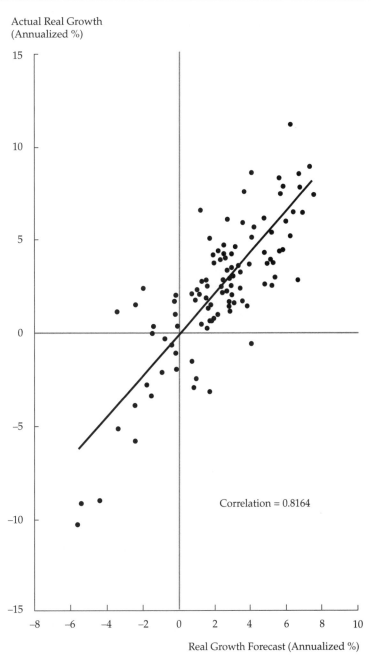

FIGURE 8-9   Actual Real Growth vs. Real Growth Forecast

Actual Real Growth
(Annualized %)

Correlation = 0.8164

Real Growth Forecast (Annualized %)

Source: Federal Reserve Bank of Philadelphia and U.S. Department of Commerce

point increase in the prediction of real growth by the professional forecasters, the regression model would predict a 1-percentage-point increase in actual real growth.

The fitted regression line in Figure 8-9 has the equation Actual real growth = $-0.0017 + 1.0847 \times$ (Predicted real growth). Note that the estimated values of both

b_0 and b_1 are very close to the values they would need to have if the forecast were unbiased. Later in this chapter, we discuss how to test the hypotheses that $b_0 = 0$ and $b_1 = 1$.

3.3   THE STANDARD ERROR OF ESTIMATE

Linear regression models differ greatly in how well the independent variable explains the dependent variable. Sometimes two variables do not have a linear relationship or have only a weak relationship. In these cases, a linear regression using the two variables is not informative. Therefore, in this section and in the next section, we discuss statistics that measure how well regression analysis explains the model's dependent variable.

Figure 8-9, for example, shows a strong relation between predicted real growth and actual real growth. If we knew professional forecasters' predictions for economic growth in a particular quarter, we would be reasonably certain that we could use this regression model to make a relatively accurate forecast of actual real growth. In other cases, however, the relation between the dependent and independent variables is not strong. Figure 8-10 adds a fitted regression line to the data on inflation and stock returns in the 1990s from Figure 8-6. In this figure, the actual observations are much farther from the fitted regression line, in general. Using this regression to predict monthly stock returns assuming a particular level of inflation might result in an inaccurate forecast.

As you can see, the regression relation in Figure 8-10 is less precise than that in Figure 8-9. The standard error of estimate (sometimes called the standard error of the regression) measures this uncertainty. This statistic is very much like the standard deviation for a single variable, except that it measures the standard deviation of $\hat{\epsilon}_i$, the residual term in the regression.

FIGURE 8-10   Inflation and Stock Returns in the 1990s

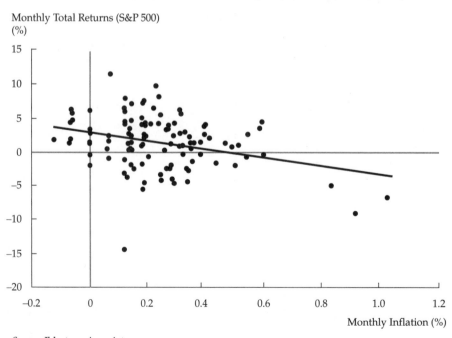

Source: Ibbotson Associates

The formula for the standard error of estimate (SEE) for a linear regression model with one independent variable is

$$\left(\sum_{i=1}^{n} \frac{(Y_i - \hat{b}_0 - \hat{b}_1 X_i)^2}{n-2} \right)^{1/2} = \left(\sum_{i=1}^{n} \frac{(\hat{\epsilon}_i)^2}{n-2} \right)^{1/2} \tag{8-7}$$

In the numerator of this equation, we are computing the difference between the actual value of the dependent variable for each observation and its predicted value $(\hat{b}_0 + \hat{b}_1 X_i)$ for each observation. The difference between the actual and predicted values of the dependent variable is the regression residual, $\hat{\epsilon}_i$.

Equation 8-7 looks very much like the formula for computing a standard deviation, except that $n - 2$ appears in the denominator instead of $n - 1$. We see $n - 2$ because the sample includes n observations and the linear regression model estimates two parameters $(\hat{b}_0$ and $\hat{b}_1)$; the difference between the number of observations and the number of parameters is $n - 2$. This difference is also called the degrees of freedom; it is the denominator needed to ensure that the estimated standard error of estimate is unbiased.

EXAMPLE 8-10. Computing the Standard Error of Estimate.

Recall that the estimated regression equation for the data shown in Figure 8-8 was $Y_i = -0.0216 + 1.0889 X_i$. Table 8-7 uses this estimated equation to compute the data needed for the standard error of estimate for this equation.[30]

TABLE 8-7 Computing the Standard Error of Estimate

	S&P 500 Returns X_i	Small-Stock Returns Y_i	Predicted Small-Stock Returns $\hat{Y}_i$	Regression Residual $Y_i - \hat{Y}_i$	Squared Residual $(Y_i - \hat{Y}_i)^2$
January 1998	1.11%	−0.59%	−0.95%	0.36%	0.000013
February 1998	7.21%	6.49%	5.70%	0.79%	0.000063
March 1998	5.12%	4.81%	3.42%	1.39%	0.000193
April 1998	1.01%	1.68%	−1.06%	2.74%	0.000750
May 1998	−1.72%	−4.97%	−4.03%	−0.94%	0.000089
June 1998	4.06%	−2.06%	2.27%	−4.33%	0.001874
Sum					0.002981

Source for data: Ibbotson Associates

The first and second columns of numbers in Table 8-7 show the returns on the S&P 500, X_i, and small-stock returns, Y_i. The third column of numbers shows the predicted value of the dependent variable from the fitted regression equation for each

---

[30] In this and most examples in this chapter, note that calculation results (intermediate as well as final) are reported at fewer decimal places than actually carried through for calculations. Our final result reflects the higher number of decimal places carried by the calculator or spreadsheet.

observation. In January 1998, for example, the predicted value of $-0.0095 = -0.0216 + (1.0889 \times 0.0111)$ or -0.95%. The next-to-last column contains the regression residual, which is the difference between the actual value of the dependent variable, Y_i, and the predicted value of the dependent variable, $(\hat{Y}_i = \hat{b}_0 + \hat{b}_1 X_i)$. So for January 1998, the residual is equal to $-0.59\% - (-0.95\%) = 0.36\%$. The last column contains the squared regression residual. The sum of the squared residuals is 0.002981. Applying the formula for the standard error of estimate, we obtain

$$\left(\frac{0.002981}{6 - 2}\right)^{1/2} = 0.02730$$

Thus, the standard error of estimate is about 2.73 percent.

Later, we will combine this estimate with estimates of the uncertainty about the parameters in this regression to determine confidence intervals for predicting small-stock returns from returns to the S&P 500. We will see that smaller standard errors result in more-accurate predictions.

3.4   THE COEFFICIENT OF DETERMINATION

Although the standard error of estimate gives some indication of how certain we can be about a particular prediction of Y using the regression equation, it still does not tell us how well the independent variable explains variation in the dependent variable. The coefficient of determination does exactly this: It measures the fraction of the total variance in the dependent variable that is explained by the independent variable.

We can compute the coefficient of determination in two ways. The simpler method, which can be used in a linear regression with one independent variable, is to square the correlation coefficient between the dependent and independent variables. For example, recall that the correlation coefficient for the returns on the S&P 500 and the returns on small stocks between January 1998 and June 1998 was 0.8234. Thus, the coefficient of determination in the regression shown in Figure 8-8 is $(0.8234)^2 = 0.6780$. So, in this regression, the returns to the S&P 500 explain 67.80 percent of the variance in small-stock returns over the period.

The problem with squaring the correlation coefficient in order to measure the coefficient of determination is that this method cannot be used when we have more than one independent variable.[31] Therefore, we need an alternative method of computing the coefficient of determination. Now we present the logic behind that alternative. If we did not know the regression relationship, our best guess of the value of any particular observation of the dependent variable would simply be $\overline{Y}$, the mean of the dependent variable. One measure of accuracy in predicting Y_i based on $\overline{Y}$ is the sample variance of Y_i, $\sum_{i=1}^{n} \frac{(Y_i - \overline{Y})^2}{n - 1}$.

An alternative to using $\overline{Y}$ to predict a particular observation Y_i would be to use the regression relationship to make that prediction. In that case, our predicted value would be $\hat{Y}_i = \hat{b}_0 + \hat{b}_1 X_i$. If the regression relationship works well, the error in predicting Y_i using $\hat{Y}_i$ should be much smaller than the error in predicting Y_i using $\overline{Y}$. If we call $\sum_{i=1}^{n} (Y_i - \overline{Y})^2$ the total variation of Y and $\sum_{i=1}^{n} (Y_i - \hat{Y}_i)^2$ the unexplained variation from the regression, then we can measure the explained variation from the regression using the following equation:

---

[31] We will discuss such models in the chapter on multiple regression.

$$\text{Total variation} = \text{Unexplained variation} + \text{Explained variation} \qquad (8\text{-}8)$$

The coefficient of determination is the fraction of the total variation that is explained by the regression. This gives us the relationship

$$R^2 = \frac{\text{Explained variation}}{\text{Total variation}} = \frac{\text{Total variation} - \text{Unexplained variation}}{\text{Total variation}} \qquad (8\text{-}9)$$

$$= 1 - \frac{\text{Unexplained variation}}{\text{Total variation}}$$

Note that total variation equals explained variation plus unexplained variation, as shown in Equation 8-8. Most regression programs report the coefficient of determination as R^2.[32]

EXAMPLE 8-11.   Small-Stock Returns and Returns to the S&P 500.

Using the data in Table 8-7, we can see that the unexplained variation from the regression, which is the sum of the squared residuals, equals 0.002981. Table 8-8 shows the computation of total variation in the dependent variable, small-stock returns.

TABLE 8-8   Computing Total Variation

	S&P 500 Returns X_i	Small-Stock Returns Y_i	Deviation from Mean $Y_i - \overline{Y}_i$	Squared Deviation $(Y_i - \overline{Y}_i)^2$
January 1998	1.11%	−0.59%	−1.48%	0.000220
February 1998	7.21%	6.49%	5.60%	0.003132
March 1998	5.12%	4.81%	3.92%	0.001534
April 1998	1.01%	1.68%	0.79%	0.000062
May 1998	−1.72%	−4.97%	−5.86%	0.003438
June 1998	4.06%	−2.06%	−2.95%	0.000872
	Average	0.89%	Sum	0.009258

Source: Ibbotson Associates

The average small-stock return for this period is 0.89 percent. The next-to-last column shows the deviation of each period's small-stock return from that average; the last column shows the square of that deviation. The sum of those squared deviations is the total variation in Y_i for the sample (0.009258), shown in Table 8-8.
    The coefficient of determination for the regression is

$$\frac{\text{Total variation} - \text{Unexplained variation}}{\text{Total variation}} = \frac{0.009258 - 0.002981}{0.009258} = 0.6780$$

---

[32] As you will see in the tables of regression output later in this chapter, regression programs also report **multiple R,** which is the correlation between the actual values and the forecast values of Y. The coefficient of determination is the square of multiple R.

Note that this method gives the same result that we obtained earlier. We will use this method again in the chapter on multiple regression—when we have more than one independent variable, this will be the only way to compute the coefficient of determination.

EXAMPLE 8-12.   Inflation and Stock Returns in the 1990s.

Earlier in this chapter, when we discussed the data on inflation and stock returns in the 1990s shown in Figure 8-10, we determined that the correlation coefficient between inflation and monthly stock returns in the 1990s was -0.3133. With this information, we can use both methods to compute the coefficient of determination.

The first method computes the coefficient of determination as $-0.3133^2 = 0.098$. The second method is based on the regression output (shown in Table 8-9 below) for computing the fitted regression line shown in Figure 8-10.

TABLE 8-9   Sources of Variation Explaining Stock Returns in the 1990s with Inflation

Explained Variation	0.0163
Unexplained Variation	0.1502
Total Variation	0.1665

As Table 8-9 shows, the total variation in the dependent variable in the sample is 0.1665 and the unexplained variation from the regression is 0.1502. Therefore, using the second method for computing the coefficient of determination, we see that the coefficient of determination is

$$\frac{\text{Total variation} - \text{Unexplained variation}}{\text{Total variation}} = \frac{0.1665 - 0.1502}{0.1665} = 0.098$$

Therefore, only 9.82 percent of the variation in monthly stock-market returns in the 1990s is explained by variation in the monthly rate of inflation. Contemporaneous inflation explains very little of the variation in monthly stock returns during that period.

3.5 CONFIDENCE INTERVALS AND TESTING HYPOTHESES

Suppose we want to check the valuation of a stock using the capital asset pricing model (CAPM); we may hypothesize that the stock has a market-average beta or level of systematic risk. Or suppose we want to test whether economists' forecasts of the economy's real growth rate are unbiased (not overestimates or underestimates, on average). Questions such as these can be addressed with hypothesis tests within a regression model. Such tests are often t-tests of the value of the intercept or slope coefficient(s). To understand the concepts involved in this test, it is useful to first review a simple, equivalent approach based on confidence intervals.

We can perform a hypothesis test using the confidence interval approach if we know three things:

1. The estimated parameter value, $\hat{b}_0$ or $\hat{b}_1$;
2. The hypothesized value of the parameter, b_0 or b_1; and
3. A confidence interval around the estimated parameter.

A confidence interval is an interval that we believe includes the true parameter value, b_1, with a given degree of confidence. To compute a confidence interval, we must select the significance level for the test and know the standard error of the estimated coefficient.

To illustrate the procedure, suppose we regress a stock's returns on a stock market index's returns and find that beta, the slope coefficient ($\hat{b}_1$), is 1.5 with a standard error ($s_{\hat{b}_1}$) of 0.200. Assume we used 62 monthly observations in our regression analysis. The hypothesized value of the parameter (b_1) is 1.0, the market average beta. Our null hypothesis is that $b_1 = 1.0$ and $\hat{b}_1$ is the estimate for b_1. We will use a 95 percent confidence interval for our test, or we could say that the test has a significance level of 0.05.

Our confidence interval will span the range

$$\hat{b}_1 - t_c s_{\hat{b}_1} \text{ to } \hat{b}_1 + t_c s_{\hat{b}_1}, \text{ or}$$
$$\hat{b}_1 \pm t_c s_{\hat{b}_1} \tag{8-10}$$

where t_c is the critical t value.[33] The critical value for the test depends on the number of degrees of freedom for the t-distribution under the null hypothesis. The number of degrees of freedom equals the number of observations minus the number of parameters estimated. In a regression with one independent variable, there are two estimated parameters, the intercept term and the coefficient on the independent variable. For 62 observations and two parameters estimated in this example, we have 60 degrees of freedom ($62 - 2$). For 60 degrees of freedom, the table of critical values in the back of the book shows that the critical t value at the 0.05 significance level is 2.00. Substituting the values from our example into Equation 8-10 gives us the interval

$$\hat{b}_1 \pm t_c s_{\hat{b}_1} = 1.5 \pm (2.00 \times 0.200)$$
$$= 1.5 \pm 0.400$$
$$= 1.10 \text{ to } 1.90$$

Under the null hypothesis, the probability that the confidence interval includes b_1 is 95 percent. Because we are testing $b_1 = 1.0$ and because our confidence interval does not include 1.0, we can reject the null hypothesis. Therefore, we can be 95 percent confident that the stock's beta of 1.5 is different from 1.0.

As we stated above, in practice, the most common way to test a hypothesis using a regression model is a t-test of significance. To test the hypothesis, we can compute the statistic $\dfrac{\hat{b}_1 - b_1}{s_{\hat{b}_1}} = t$. This test statistic has a t-distribution with $n - 2$ degrees of freedom since there were two parameters estimated in the regression. We would compare the absolute value of the t-statistic to t_c. If the absolute value of t is greater than t_c, then we can reject the null hypothesis. Substituting the values from the above example into this relationship gives the t-statistic associated with the probability that the stock's beta equals 1.0 ($b_1 = 1.0$).

---

[33] We use the t-distribution for this test because we use a sample estimate of the standard error, $s_{\hat{b}}$, rather than its true (population) value. This test statistic has a t-distribution with $n - 2$ degrees of freedom, because there were two parameters estimated in the regression. In the chapter on sampling and estimation, we discussed the concept of degrees of freedom.

$$t = \frac{\hat{b}_1 - b_1}{s_{\hat{b}_1}}$$ (8-11)
$$= (1.5 - 1.0)/0.200$$
$$= 2.50$$

Since $t > t_c$ (2.5 > 2.0), we reject the null hypothesis that $b_1 = 1.0$.

The t-statistic in our example above is 2.50, and at the 0.05 significance level $t_c = 2.00$; thus we reject the null hypothesis because $t > t_c$. This statement is equivalent to saying that a 95 percent confidence interval for the slope coefficient does not contain the value 1.0. If we were performing this test at the 0.01 level, however, t_c would be 2.66 and we would not reject because t would not be greater than t_c at this significance level. A 99 percent confidence interval for the slope coefficient does contain the value 1.0.

The choice of significance level is always a matter of judgment. When we use higher levels of confidence, the t_c increases. This choice leads to wider confidence intervals and to a decreased likelihood of rejecting the null hypothesis. Analysts often choose the 0.05 level of significance, which indicates a 5 percent chance of rejecting the null hypothesis when, in fact, it is true (a Type I error). Of course, decreasing the level of significance from 0.05 to 0.01 decreases the probability of Type I error, but it increases the probability of Type II error—failing to reject the null hypothesis when, in fact, it is false.[34]

Often, financial analysts do not simply report whether a particular hypothesis about a regression parameter is rejected. Instead, they report the p-value or probability value for a particular hypothesis. The p-value is the smallest level of significance at which the null hypothesis can be rejected. The p-value allows the reader to make an interpretation of the results, rather than be told that a certain hypothesis has been rejected or accepted. In most regression packages, the p-values printed for regression coefficients apply to a test of null hypothesis that the true parameter is equal to 0 against the alternative that the parameter is not equal to 0, given the estimated coefficient and the standard error for that coefficient. For example, if the p-value is 0.005, we can reject the hypothesis that the true parameter is equal to 0 at the 0.5 percent significance level.

The standard error of the estimated coefficient is an important input for a hypothesis test concerning the regression coefficient (and for a confidence interval for the estimated coefficient). Stronger regression results lead to smaller standard errors of an estimated parameter and will result in tighter confidence intervals. If the standard error ($s_{\hat{b}_1}$) in the above example was 0.100 instead of 0.200, the confidence interval range would have been half as large and the t-statistic twice as large. With a standard error this small, we would reject the null hypothesis even at the 0.01 significance level since we would have

$$t = \frac{1.5 - 1}{0.1} = 5.00 \text{ and } t_c = 2.66.$$

With this background, we can turn to hypothesis tests using actual regression results. In Example 8-13, we test the beta of Microsoft stock, and in Example 8-14, we examine the forecasting performance of a group of professional economic forecasters.

EXAMPLE 8-13.   Estimating Beta for Microsoft Stock.

You are an investor in Microsoft stock and want an estimate of its beta. As in the text example, you also have a hypothesis that Microsoft has an average level of market

---

[34] For a fuller discussion of Type I and Type II errors, see the chapter on hypothesis testing.

risk, and that its required return above the risk-free rate equals that of the market as a whole. One regression for this is

$$(R - R_f) = \alpha + \beta(R_m - R_f) + \epsilon \tag{8-12}$$

where R_f is the periodic risk-free rate of return (known at the beginning of the period), R_m is the periodic return on the market, R is the periodic return to the stock of the company, and $\beta = Cov(R, R_m)/\sigma_m^2$. Estimating this equation with linear regression provides an estimate of β, $\hat{\beta}$, which tells us the size of the required return premium for the security, given expectations about market returns.[35]

Suppose we want to test the null hypothesis, H_0, that $\beta = 1$ for Microsoft stock to see whether Microsoft stock has the same required return premium as the market as a whole. We need data on returns to Microsoft stock, a risk-free interest rate, and the returns to the market index. For this example, we use data from April 1994 through March 1999 ($n = 60$). The return to Microsoft stock is R. The monthly return to 30-day Treasury bills is R_f. The return to the S&P 500 is R_m.[36] We are estimating two parameters, so the number of degrees of freedom is $n - 2 = 60 - 2 = 58$. Table 8-10 shows the results from the regression $(R - R_f) = \alpha + \beta(R_m - R_f) + \epsilon$.

TABLE 8-10   Estimating Beta for Microsoft Stock

Regression Statistics

Multiple R	0.5411
R-squared	0.2928
Standard error of estimate	0.0835
Observations	60

	Coefficients	Standard Error	t-Statistic
Alpha	0.0267	0.0117	2.2819
Beta	1.3531	0.2761	4.9001

Sources for data: Ibbotson Associates and Bloomberg L.P.

We are testing the null hypothesis, H_0, that β for Microsoft equals 1 ($\beta = 1$) against the alternative hypothesis that $\beta \neq 1$. The estimated $\hat{\beta}$ from the regression equals 1.3531. The estimated standard error for that coefficient in the regression, $s_{\hat{\beta}}$, is 0.2761. The regression equation has 58 degrees of freedom ($60 - 2$), so the crit-

---

[35] β is typically estimated using 60 months of historic data, but the data-sample length sometimes varies. Although monthly data is typically used, some financial analysts estimate β using daily data. For more information on methods to estimate β, see Reilly and Brown (2000). The expected excess return for Microsoft stock above the risk-free rate $(R - R_f)$ is $\beta(R_m - R_f)$, given a particular excess return to the market above the risk-free rate $(R_m - R_f)$. This result holds because we regress $(R - R_f)$ against $(R_m - R_f)$. For example, if a stock's beta is 1.5, its expected excess return is 1.5 times that of the market portfolio.

[36] Data on Microsoft stock returns came from Bloomberg. Data on Treasury-bill returns and S&P 500 returns came from Ibbotson Associates.

ical value for the test statistic is approximately $t_c = 2.00$ at the 0.05 significance level. Therefore, the 95 percent confidence interval for the data for any particular hypothesized value of β is shown by the range

$$\hat{\beta} \pm t_c s_{\hat{\beta}}$$
$$1.3531 \pm 2.00 \times 0.2761$$
$$0.8009 \text{ to } 1.9053$$

In this case, the hypothesized parameter value is $\beta = 1$ and the value 1 falls inside this confidence interval, so we cannot reject the hypothesis at the 0.05 significance level. This means that we cannot reject the hypothesis that Microsoft stock has the same systematic risk as the market as a whole.

Another way of looking at this issue is to compute the t-statistic for the Microsoft beta hypothesized parameter using Equation 8-11:

$$t = \frac{\hat{\beta} - \beta}{s_{\hat{\beta}}}$$
$$= \frac{1.3531 - 1.0}{0.2761}$$
$$= 1.2789$$

This t-statistic is less than the critical t_c value of 2.00. Thus, neither approach allows us to reject the null hypothesis. Note that the t-statistic associated with $\hat{\beta}$ in the regression results in Table 8-10 is 4.9001. Given the significance level we are using, we cannot reject the null hypothesis that $\beta = 1$ but we could reject the hypothesis that $\beta = 0$.[37]

Note also that the R^2 in this regression is only 0.2928. This result suggests that only about 29 percent of the total variance in the excess return to Microsoft stock (that is, the return to Microsoft above the risk-free rate) can be explained by excess return to the market portfolio. The remaining 71 percent of the variance of the excess return to Microsoft's stock is the nonsystematic component, which can be attributed to company-specific risk. This portion is the variance that is diversifiable through holding a portfolio containing many stocks.

EXAMPLE 8-14.   Testing Whether Forecasts of Real Growth Are Unbiased.

Example 8-9 introduced the concept of testing whether forecasts are unbiased. That example showed that if a forecast were unbiased, its expected error would be 0. Of course, we never observe the expected error for an individual forecast. We can, however, examine whether a time-series of forecasts of a particular economic variable is unbiased by comparing the forecast at each date with the actual value of the economic variable that is announced after the forecast. If the forecasts are unbiased, then, by definition, the average realized forecast error should be close to 0. In that case, if we regress the actual values on a constant and the predicted values, the value

---

[37] The t-statistics for a coefficient automatically reported by statistical software programs assume that the null hypothesis states that the coefficient is equal to 0. If you have a different null hypothesis, as we do in this example ($\beta = 1$), then you must either construct the correct test statistic yourself or instruct the program to compute it.

of b_0 (the constant) should be 0 and the value of b_1 (the slope) should be 1, as discussed in Example 8-9.

Refer once again to Figure 8-9, which shows the current-quarter predictions of real growth made by professional economic forecasters and actual real growth from the third quarter of 1969 through the fourth quarter of 1996 ($n = 110$). To test whether the forecasts are unbiased, we must first regress actual growth on a constant and predicted growth. The results of this regression are reported in Table 8-11. The equation to be estimated is

$$\text{Actual growth}_t = b_0 + b_1(\text{Predicted growth}_t) + \epsilon_t$$

This regression estimates two parameters (the constant and the slope); therefore, the regression has $n - 2 = 110 - 2 = 108$ degrees of freedom.

**TABLE 8-11 Testing Whether Forecasts of Real Growth Are Unbiased
Dependent Variable: Real Growth Expressed in Percent**

Regression Statistics

Multiple R	0.8164
R-squared	0.6666
Standard error of estimate	0.0211
Observations	110

	Coefficients	Standard Error	t-Statistic
Intercept	−0.17	0.26	−0.6515
Forecast (slope)	1.0847	0.0738	14.6942

Sources for data: Federal Reserve Bank of Philadelphia and U.S. Bureau of Economic Analysis

We can now test two null hypotheses about the parameters in this regression. Our first null hypothesis, H_0, is that the constant in this regression is 0 ($b_0 = 0$). The alternative hypothesis, H_a, is that the constant is not equal to 0 ($b_0 \neq 0$). Our second null hypothesis, H_0, is that the slope in this regression is 1 ($b_1 = 1$). The alternative hypothesis, H_a, is that the slope is not equal to 1 ($b_1 \neq 1$).

To test the hypotheses about b_0 and b_1, we must first decide on a critical value based on a particular significance level, and then construct the confidence intervals for each parameter. If we choose the 0.05 significance level, with 108 degrees of freedom, the critical value, t_c, is approximately 1.98. The estimated value of the parameter $\hat{b}_0$, is −0.17, and the estimated value of the standard error for $\hat{b}_0 (s_{\hat{b}_0})$ is 0.26. Some people use B_0 as any particular hypothesized value. Therefore, under the null hypothesis that $b_0 = B_0$, a 95 percent confidence interval for b_0 is

$$\hat{b}_0 \pm t_c s_{\hat{b}_0}$$
$$-0.17 \pm 1.98 \times 0.26$$
$$-0.68 \text{ to } 0.34$$

In this case, B_0 is 0. The value of 0 falls within this confidence interval, so we cannot reject the first null hypothesis that $b_0 = 0$. We explain how to interpret this result shortly.

Our second null hypothesis is based on the same sample as our first null hypothesis. Therefore, the critical value for testing that hypothesis is the same as the critical value for testing the first hypothesis ($t_c = 1.98$). The estimated value of the parameter $\hat{b}_1$ is 1.0847, and the estimated value of the standard error for $\hat{b}_1$, $s_{\hat{b}_1}$, is 0.0738. Therefore, the 95 percent confidence interval for any particular hypothesized value of b_1 can be constructed as follows:

$$\hat{b}_1 \pm t_c s_{\hat{b}_1}$$
$$1.0847 \pm 1.98 \times 0.0738$$
$$0.9386 \text{ to } 1.2308$$

In this case, our hypothesized value of b_1 is 1. The value 1 falls within this confidence interval, so we cannot reject the null hypothesis that $b_1 = 1$ at the 0.05 significance level. Because we did not reject either of the null hypotheses ($b_0 = 0$, $b_1 = 1$) about the parameters in this model, we cannot reject the hypothesis that the forecasts of real growth were unbiased.[38]

Many times, you will need forecasts of economic growth to help you make recommendations about asset allocation, expected returns, and other investment decisions. The hypothesis tests just conducted suggest that you cannot reject the hypothesis that the real-growth predictions in the Survey of Professional Forecasters are unbiased. If you need an unbiased forecast of future growth for your asset-allocation decision, you might want to use these forecasts.

3.6 ANALYSIS OF VARIANCE IN A REGRESSION WITH ONE INDEPENDENT VARIABLE

Analysis of variance (ANOVA) is a statistical procedure for analyzing the total variability of a set of data into components which can be attributed to different sources.[39] In regression analysis, we use ANOVA to gain information about the usefulness of the independent variable or variables in explaining variation in the dependent variable. An important statistical test conducted in analysis of variance is the F-test. The F-statistic tests whether all the slope coefficients in a linear regression are equal to 0. In a regression with one independent variable, this is a test of the null hypothesis H_0: $b_1 = 0$ against the alternative hypothesis H_a: $b_1 \neq 0$.

To correctly determine the test statistic for the null hypothesis that the slope coefficient is equal to 0, we need to know four things:

- the total number of observations (n);
- the total number of parameters to be estimated (two: intercept and slope);
- the sum of squared errors or residuals $\left(\sum_{i=1}^{n}(Y_i - \hat{Y}_i)^2, \text{ abbreviated SSE}\right)$. This value is also known as the residual sum of squares; and

[38] Jointly testing the hypothesis $b_0 = 0$ and $b_1 = 1$ would require us to take into account the covariance of $\hat{b}_0$ and $\hat{b}_1$. For information on testing joint hypotheses of this type, see Greene (1999).

[39] In this chapter we focus on regression applications of ANOVA, the most common context in which financial analysts will encounter this tool. We will see that, in this context, ANOVA is used to test whether all the regression slope coefficients are equal to 0. Analysts also use ANOVA to conduct a test of a hypothesis that the means of two or more populations are equal. See Daniel and Terrell (1995) for details.

- the regression sum of squares $\left(\sum_{i=1}^{n} (\hat{Y}_i - \overline{Y})^2, \text{ abbreviated RSS} \right)$. This value is the amount of total variation in Y that is explained in the regression equation.

The F-test for determining whether the slope coefficient is equal to 0 is based on an F-statistic, constructed using these four values. The F-statistic measures how well the regression equation explains the variation in the dependent variable. The F-statistic is the ratio of the average regression sum of squares to the average sum of the squared errors. The average regression sum of squares is computed by dividing the regression sum of squares by the number of slope parameters estimated (in this case, one). The average sum of squared errors is computed by dividing the sum of squared errors by the number of observations, n, minus the total number of parameters estimated (in this case, two: the intercept and the slope). These two divisors are the degrees of freedom for an F-test. If there are n observations, the F-test for the null hypothesis that the slope coefficient is equal to 0 is here denoted $F_{\text{\# slope parameters}, n - \text{\# parameters}} = F_{1, n-2}$, and the test has 1 and $n - 2$ degrees of freedom.

Suppose, for example, that the independent variable in a regression model explains none of the variation in the dependent variable. Then the predicted value for the regression model, $\hat{Y}_i$, is the average value of the dependent variable $\overline{Y}$. In this case, the regression sum of squares $\sum_{i=1}^{n} (\hat{Y}_i - \overline{Y})^2$ is 0. Therefore, the F-statistic is 0. Thus, if the independent variable does not explain the dependent variable, the value of the F-statistic will be very small.

The formula for the F-statistic in a regression with one independent variable is

$$F = \frac{\text{RSS}/1}{\text{SSE}/(n - 2)} = \frac{\text{Mean regression sum of squares}}{\text{Mean squared error}} \tag{8-13}$$

If the regression model does a good job of explaining variation in the dependent variable, then this ratio should be high. That is, the explained regression sum of squares per estimated parameter will be high relative to the unexplained variation for each degree of freedom. A table of critical values for this F-statistic is given in the back of this book.

Even though the F-statistic is commonly computed by regression packages, analysts typically do not use ANOVA and F-tests in regressions with just one independent variable. Why? In such regressions, the F-statistic is the square of the t-statistic for the slope coefficient. Therefore, the F-test is duplicative of the t-test for the significance of the slope coefficient. This relation is not true for regressions with two or more slope coefficients. Nevertheless, the one-slope coefficient case gives a foundation for understanding the multiple-slope coefficient cases.

EXAMPLE 8-15.   Performance Evaluation: The Fidelity Select Technology Fund.

Often, mutual-fund performance is evaluated on whether the fund has significant excess returns beyond the returns that would be expected, given the amount of systematic market risk that the fund takes. The CAPM states that the expected excess return for any asset is based on the beta of the asset's returns. One common way to test whether a fund has an excess return is to estimate the regression

$$(R_i - R_f) = \alpha_i + \beta_i(R_m - R_f) + \epsilon_i \tag{8-14}$$

where R_f is the periodic risk-free rate of return (known at the beginning of the period), R_m is the periodic return on the market, R_i is the periodic return to the mutual fund, and β_i is the fund's beta.

A fund has no risk-adjusted excess return if $\alpha_i = 0$. To determine whether there has been an excess return to a particular fund, we must test the null hypothesis, H_0, that the fund has no risk-adjusted excess return (that is, $\alpha = 0$) against the alternative hypothesis, H_a, that $\alpha \neq 0$.

Table 8-12 presents results evaluating the excess return to the Fidelity Select Technology Fund from April 1994 to March 1999. Note that the estimated beta, $\hat{\beta}_i$, in this regression is 1.5202. That is, the Fidelity Select Technology Fund was estimated to be about 1.5 times riskier than the market as a whole.

TABLE 8-12   Performance Evaluation Dependent Variable: Excess Return to the Fidelity Select Technology Fund, April 1994–March 1999

Regression Statistics

Multiple R	0.7507
R-squared	0.5635
Standard error of estimate	0.0531
Observations	60

ANOVA	Degrees of Freedom (df)	Sum of Squares (SS)	Mean Sum of Squares (MSS)	F
Regression	1	0.2113	0.2113	74.86
Residual	58	0.1637	0.0028	
Total	59	0.3750		

	Coefficients	Standard Error	t-Statistic
Alpha	−0.22	0.74	−0.3001
Beta	1.5202	0.1757	8.6529

Source for data: Ibbotson Associates

Note also that the estimated alpha ($\hat{\alpha}$) in this regression is actually negative (−0.22). The absolute value of the coefficient is only about one-third the size of the standard error for that coefficient (0.74), however, so the t-statistic for the coefficient is only −0.300. Therefore, we cannot reject the null hypothesis ($\alpha = 0$) that the fund did not have a significant excess return beyond the return associated with the market risk of the fund. This means that the returns to the fund were explained by the market risk of the fund, and there was no additional statistical significance to the excess returns to the fund during this period.[40]

---

[40] This example introduces a well-known investment use of regression. Researchers, however, recognize qualifications to the interpretation of alpha from a linear regression. The systematic risk of a managed portfolio is controlled by the portfolio manager. If, as a consequence, portfolio beta is correlated with the return on the market (as could result from market timing), inferences on alpha based on least-squares beta, as here, can be mistaken. This advanced subject is discussed in Dybvig and Ross (1985a) and (1985b).

Since the t-statistic for the slope coefficient in this regression is 8.6529, the p-value for that coefficient is very low: 4.28E $-$ 12, or 4.28×10^{-12}. Therefore, the probability that the true value of this coefficient is actually 0, given the data, is microscopic.

How can we use an F-test to determine whether the slope coefficient in this regression is equal to 0? The ANOVA portion of Table 8-12 provides the data we need. In this case

- The total number of observations (n) is 60.
- The total number of parameters to be estimated is 2 (intercept and slope).
- The sum of squared errors or residuals, SSE, is 0.1637.
- The regression sum of squares, RSS, is 0.2113.

Therefore, the F-statistic to test whether the slope coefficient is equal to 0 is

$$\frac{0.2113/1}{0.1637/(60 - 2)} = 74.86$$

The ANOVA output would show that the p-value for this F-statistic is 4.28E $-$ 12, or 4.28×10^{-12}, exactly the same as the p-value for the t-statistic for the slope coefficient. Therefore, the F-test tells us nothing more than we already knew from the t-test. Note also that the F-statistic (74.86) is the square of the t-statistic (8.65), as discussed in Section 2.6.

3.7 PREDICTION INTERVALS

Financial analysts often want to use regression results to make predictions about a dependent variable. For example, we might ask, "How fast will the sales of XYZ Corporation grow this year if real GDP grows by 4 percent?" But we are not merely interested in making these forecasts; we also want to know how certain we should be about our forecasts. For example, if we predicted that sales for XYZ Corporation would grow by 6 percent this year, our prediction would mean more if we believed that there was a 95 percent chance that sales growth would be between 5 percent and 7 percent than if we thought there was only a 25 percent chance that sales growth would be between 5 percent and 7 percent. Therefore, we need to understand how to compute confidence intervals around regression forecasts.

We must take into account two sources of uncertainty when taking the regression model $Y_i = b_0 + b_1 X_i + \epsilon_i, i = 1, \ldots, n$ and using the estimated parameters, $\hat{b}_0$ and $\hat{b}_1$, to make a prediction. First, the error term itself contains uncertainty. The standard deviation of the error term, σ, can be estimated from the standard error of estimate for the regression equation. A second source of uncertainty in making predictions about Y, however, comes from uncertainty in the estimated parameters, $\hat{b}_0$ and $\hat{b}_1$.

If we knew the true values of the regression parameters, b_0 and b_1, then the variance of our prediction of Y, given any particular predicted (or assumed) value of $\hat{X}$, would simply be s^2, the squared standard error of estimate. The variance would be s^2 because the prediction, $\hat{Y}$, would come from the equation and $\hat{Y} = b_0 + b_1 X$ and $(Y - \hat{Y}) = \epsilon$.

Because we must estimate the regression parameters $\hat{b}_0$ and $\hat{b}_1$ however, our prediction of Y, $\hat{Y}$, given any particular predicted value of X, is actually $\hat{Y} = \hat{b}_0 + \hat{b}_1 X$. The estimated variance of the prediction error, s_f^2, of Y, given X, is

$$s_f^2 = s^2 \left[1 + \frac{1}{n} + \frac{(X - \overline{X})^2}{(n-1)s_x^2} \right] \qquad\qquad (8\text{-}15)$$

This estimated variance depends on

- the squared standard error of estimate, s^2;
- the number of observations, n;
- the value of the independent variable used to predict the dependent variable, X;
- the estimated mean, $\overline{X}$; and
- variance, s_x^2, of the independent variable.[41]

Once we have this estimate of the variance of the prediction error, determining a prediction interval around the prediction is very similar to estimating a confidence interval around an estimated parameter, as shown earlier in this chapter. We need to take the following four steps to determine the prediction interval for the prediction:

1. Make the prediction.
2. Compute the variance of the prediction error using Equation 8-15.
3. Choose a significance level, α, for the forecast. For example, the 0.05 level, given the degrees of freedom in the regression, determines the critical value for the forecast interval, t_c.
4. Compute the $(1 - \alpha)$ percent prediction interval for the prediction, namely $\hat{Y} \pm t_c s_f$.

EXAMPLE 8-16.   Predicting the Returns to Microsoft Stock.

We continue with the example of Microsoft stock. You expect the S&P 500 to have a return 5 percentage points lower than the risk-free rate next month. The mean excess return to the S&P 500 during the sample period was $\overline{X} = 0.0163$ and the variance of the excess return to the S&P 500 during the sample period was $s_x^2 = 0.001550$. Using the estimated regression from Example 8-13 (repeated in the table below), what is the 95 percent confidence interval for the excess return on Microsoft stock for that month?

Using the data provided in Table 8-13, take the following steps:

1. Make the prediction.
   Expected monthly excess return = $0.0267 + 1.3531(-0.05) = -0.0410$
   This regression suggests that, if the excess return to the S&P 500 was -5 percent, the excess return to Microsoft stock would be -4.1 percent.

2. Compute the variance of the prediction error.
   To compute the variance of the forecast error, we must know
   - the standard error of the estimate of the equation, $s = 0.0835$ (as shown in Table 8-13);
   - the mean excess return to the S&P 500 during the sample period, $\overline{X} = 0.0163$ (this computation is not shown in the table); and

---

[41] For a derivation of this equation, see Pindyck and Rubinfeld (1998).

PROBLEMS

1. Variable X takes on the values shown in the following table for five observations. The table also shows the values for five other variables, Y_1 through Y_5. Which of the variables Y_1 through Y_5 have a zero correlation with variable X?

X	Y_1	Y_2	Y_3	Y_4	Y_5
1	7	2	4	4	1
2	7	4	2	1	2
3	7	2	0	0	3
4	7	4	2	1	4
5	7	2	4	4	5

2. Calculate the statistics requested below from the following sample:

$$\sum_{i=1}^{n} X_i = 220 \qquad \sum_{i=1}^{n}(X_i - \bar{X})^2 = 440 \qquad \sum_{i=1}^{n}(X_i - \bar{X})(Y_i - \bar{Y}) = -568$$

$$\sum_{i=1}^{n} Y_i = 385 \qquad \sum_{i=1}^{n}(Y_i - \bar{Y})^2 = 1120 \qquad n = 11$$

a. Calculate the sample mean, variance, and standard deviation for X.
b. Calculate the sample mean, variance, and standard deviation for Y.
c. Calculate the sample covariance between X and Y.
d. Calculate the sample correlation between X and Y.

3. Statistics for three variables are given below. X is the monthly return for a large-stock index, Y is the monthly return on a small-stock index, and Z is the monthly return on a corporate bond index. There are 60 observations.

$$\bar{X} = 0.760 \qquad \sum_{i=1}^{n}(X_i - \bar{X})^2 = 769.081 \qquad \sum_{i=1}^{n}(X_i - \bar{X})(Y_i - \bar{Y}) = 720.535$$

$$\bar{Y} = 1.037 \qquad \sum_{i=1}^{n}(Y_i - \bar{Y})^2 = 1243.309 \qquad \sum_{i=1}^{n}(X_i - \bar{X})(Z_i - \bar{Z}) = 231.007$$

$$\bar{Z} = 0.686 \qquad \sum_{i=1}^{n}(Z_i - \bar{Z})^2 = 183.073 \qquad \sum_{i=1}^{n}(Y_i - \bar{Y})(Z_i - \bar{Z}) = 171.816$$

a. Calculate the sample variance and standard deviation for X, Y, and Z.
b. Calculate the sample covariance between X and Y, X and Z, and Y and Z.
c. Calculate the sample correlation between X and Y, X and Z, and Y and Z.

4. Home sales and interest rates should be negatively related. The following table gives the annual sales for Packard Homes and mortgage rates for four recent years. Calculate the sample correlation between sales and mortgage rates.

Year	Sales (units)	Interest Rate (percent)
2000	50	8.0
2001	70	7.0

Year	Sales (units)	Interest Rate (percent)
2002	80	6.0
2003	60	7.0

5. The following table shows the sample correlations between the monthly returns for four different mutual funds and the S&P 500. The correlations are based on 36 monthly observations. The funds are:

Fund 1	Large-cap fund
Fund 2	Mid-cap fund
Fund 3	Large-cap value fund
Fund 4	Emerging markets fund
S&P 500	U.S. domestic stock index

	Fund 1	Fund 2	Fund 3	Fund 4	S&P 500
Fund 1	1				
Fund 2	0.9231	1			
Fund 3	0.4771	0.4156	1		
Fund 4	0.7111	0.7238	0.3102	1	
S&P 500	0.8277	0.8223	0.5791	0.7515	1

Test the null hypothesis that each of these correlations, individually, is equal to zero against the alternative hypothesis that it is not equal to zero. Use a 5 percent significance level.

6. Juan Martinez, Dieter Osterburg, and Sara Durbin are discussing the correlations between monthly stock returns. Martinez believes that returns are random and that the correlation of stock returns from one month to the next should be zero. Osterburg believes that high or low returns are followed by strong reversals, causing monthly returns to have a negative month-to-month correlation. Durbin believes there is a tendency for positive or negative returns to be followed by returns in the same direction, resulting in positive month-to-month correlation.

They give you a series of 60 monthly returns for the S&P 500 over the 1994–98 time period. You create two variables, where X is the first 59 monthly returns and Y is the last 59 monthly returns. For the first observation, X is the January 1994 return and Y is the February 1994 return; for the second observation, X is the February 1994 return and Y is the March 1994 return, etc. The result is 59 paired, contiguous monthly returns. The calculated sample correlation coefficient between X and Y is -0.0641.
   a. Interpret the meaning of the negative correlation.
   b. Is this correlation significantly different from zero? Use a two-tailed test and a 5 percent significance level.

7. You have monthly returns for four indexes and want to test for serial correlation. You have 29 years of data, or 348 monthly observations. When you compare monthly returns, your sample is reduced to 347 because Month 1 is compared with Month 2,

Month 2 with Month 3, until Month 347 is compared with Month 348. Below are the sample correlations calculated for the indexes:

Index	S&P 500	MSCI Europe	MSCI Pacific	MSCI Far East
Serial correlation	0.0034	0.0335	0.1121	0.1052

For each index, test the hypothesis that its serial correlation is equal to 0. Use a 5 percent significance level.

8. Bouvier Co. is a Canadian company that sells forestry products to several Pacific Rim customers. Bouvier's sales are very sensitive to exchange rates. The following table shows recent annual sales (in millions of Canadian dollars) and the average exchange rate for the year (expressed as the units of foreign currency needed to buy one Canadian dollar).

Year i	X_i = Exchange Rate	Y_i = Sales
1	0.40	20
2	0.36	25
3	0.42	16
4	0.31	30
5	0.33	35
6	0.34	30

a. Calculate the sample mean and standard deviation for X (the exchange rate) and Y (sales).
b. Calculate the sample covariance between the exchange rate and sales.
c. Calculate the sample correlation between the exchange rate and sales.
d. Calculate the intercept and coefficient for an estimated linear regression with the exchange rate as the independent variable and sales as the dependent variable.

9. Julie Moon ran a regression explaining the variation in energy consumption as a function of temperature. The total variation of the dependent variable was 140.58, the explained variation was 60.16, and the unexplained variation was 80.42. There were 60 monthly observations.
a. Compute the coefficient of determination.
b. What was the sample correlation between energy consumption and temperature?
c. Compute the standard error of the estimate of Moon's regression model.
d. Compute the sample standard deviation of monthly energy consumption.

10. You are examining the results of estimating a regression that attempts to explain the unit sales growth of a business you are researching. The analysis of variance output for the regression is given in the table below. The regression was based on five observations ($n = 5$).

ANOVA

	df	SS	MSS	F	Significance F
Regression	1	88	88	36.667	0.00904
Residual	3	7.2	2.4		
Total	4	95.2			

a. How many independent variables are in the regression to which the ANOVA refers?
b. Define Total SS.
c. Calculate the sample variance of the dependent variable using information in the above table.
d. Define Regression MSS and explain how its value of 88 is obtained in terms of other quantities reported in the above table.
e. What hypothesis does the F-statistic test?
f. Explain how the value of the F-statistic of 36.667 is obtained in terms of other quantities reported in the above table.
g. Is the F-test significant at the 5 percent significance level?

11. The first table below contains the regression results for a regression with monthly returns on a large-cap mutual fund as the dependent variable and monthly returns on a market index as the independent variable. The analysis is performed using only 12 monthly observations. The second table provides summary statistics for the dependent and independent variables.
a. What is the predicted return on the large-cap mutual fund for a market index return of 8.00 percent?
b. Find a 95 percent prediction interval for the expected mutual fund return.

Regression Statistics

Multiple R	0.776
R-squared	0.602
Standard Error	4.243
Observations	12

Regression Equation

	Coefficients	Standard Error	t-Statistic	p-Value
Intercept	−0.287	1.314	−0.219	0.831
Slope coefficient	0.802	0.206	3.890	0.003

Statistic	Market Index Return (%)	Large-Cap Fund Return (%)
Mean	2.30	1.56
Standard deviation	6.21	6.41
Variance	38.51	41.13
Count	12	12

12. Industry automobile sales should be related to consumer sentiment. The following table provides a regression analysis in which sales of automobiles and light trucks (in millions of vehicles) are estimated as a function of a consumer sentiment index.

Regression Statistics

Multiple R	0.80113
R-squared	0.64181
Standard Error	0.81325
Observations	120

Regression Equation

	Coefficients	Standard Error	t-Statistic	p-Value
Intercept	6.071	0.58432	10.389	0
Slope coefficient	0.09251	0.00636	14.541	0

For the independent variable and dependent variable, the means, standard deviations, and variances are

	X = Sentiment Index	Y = Automobile Sales (millions of units)
Mean	91.0983	14.4981
Standard deviation	11.7178	1.35312
Variance	137.3071	1.83094

a. Find the expected sales and a 95 percent prediction interval for sales if the sentiment index has a value of 90.
b. Find the expected sales and a 95 percent prediction interval for sales if the sentiment index has a value of 100.

13. Use the following information to create a regression model:

$$\sum_{i=1}^{n} X_i = 81 \qquad \sum_{i=1}^{n} (X_i - \bar{X})^2 = 60 \qquad \sum_{i=1}^{n} (X_i - \bar{X})(Y_i - \bar{Y}) = 84$$

$$\sum_{i=1}^{n} X_i^2 = 789$$

$$\sum_{i=1}^{n} Y_i = 144 \qquad \sum_{i=1}^{n} (Y_i - \bar{Y})^2 = 144 \qquad \sum_{i=1}^{n} (Y_i - \hat{b}_0 - \hat{b}_1 X_i)^2 = 26.4$$

$$n = 9$$

a. Calculate the sample mean, variance, and standard deviation for X and for Y.
b. Calculate the sample covariance and the correlation between X and Y.
c. Calculate $\hat{b}_0$ and $\hat{b}_1$ for a regression of the form $Y_i = \hat{b}_0 + \hat{b}_1 X_i$.
For the remaining three parts of this question, assume that the calculations shown above already incorporate the correct values for $\hat{b}_0$ and $\hat{b}_1$.

d. Find the total variation, explained variation, and unexplained variation.

e. Find the coefficient of determination.

f. Find the standard error of the estimate.

14. Short-term interest rates can be highly correlated with each other. Assume you have 436 monthly rates for 3-month Treasury bills and for 3-month certificates of deposit (CDs). The data run from June 1964 through September 2000. Over this time period, the T-bill rate averaged 6.363% with a standard deviation of 2.526%, and the CD rate averaged 7.166% with a standard deviation of 2.944%. Below are the results of a regression analysis using the T-bill rate as the independent variable and the CD rate as the dependent variable. Several items in the regression output are intentionally left out. Use the information that is reported to find the missing items.

Regression Statistics

Multiple R	X2
R-squared	X1
Standard Error	X3
Observations	436

ANOVA

	df	SS	MSS	F	Significance F
Regression	X5	3676.651	X7	X9	0
Residual	X6	93.567	X8		
Total	X4	3770.219			

Regression Equation

	Coefficients	Standard Error	t-Statistic	p-Value	Lower 95%	Upper 95%
Intercept	−0.15815	0.060332	−2.62138	0.009065	−0.27673	−0.03957
Slope coefficient	1.15105	0.008814	X10	0	X11	X12

15. An economist collected the monthly returns for KDL's portfolio and a diversified stock index. The data collected are shown below:

Month	Portfolio Return (%)	Index Return (%)
1	1.11	−0.59
2	72.1	64.9
3	5.12	4.81
4	1.01	1.68
5	−1.72	−4.97
6	4.06	−2.06

The economist calculated the correlation between the two returns and found it to be 0.996. The regression results with the KDL return as the dependent variable and the index return as the independent variable are given below:

Regression Statistics

Multiple R	0.996
R-Squared	0.992
Standard Error	2.861
Observations	6

ANOVA	df	SS	MSS	F	Significance F
Regression	1	4101.62	4101.62	500.79	0
Residual	4	32.76	8.19		
Total	5	4134.38			

Regression Equation

	Coefficients	Standard Error	t-Statistic	p-Value
Intercept	2.252	1.274	1.768	0.1518
Slope	1.069	0.0477	22.379	0

When reviewing the results, Andrea Fusilier suspected that they were unreliable. She found that the returns for Month 2 should have been 7.21 percent and 6.49 percent, instead of the large values shown in the first table. Correcting these values resulted in a revised correlation of 0.824 and the revised regression results shown below:

Regression Statistics

Multiple R	0.824
R-Squared	0.678
Standard Error	2.062
Observations	6

ANOVA	df	SS	MSS	F	Significance F
Regression	1	35.89	35.89	8.44	0.044
Residual	4	17.01	4.25		
Total	5	52.91			

Regression Equation

	Coefficients	Standard Error	t-Statistic	p-Value
Intercept	2.242	0.863	2.597	0.060
Slope	0.623	0.214	2.905	0.044

Explain how the bad data affected the results.

16. Diet Partners charges its clients a small management fee plus a percentage of gains whenever portfolio returns are positive. Cleo Smith believes that strong incentives for portfolio managers produce superior returns for clients. In order to demonstrate this, Smith runs a regression with the Diet Partners' portfolio return (in percent) as the dependent variable and its management fee (in percent) as the independent variable. The estimated regression for a 60-month period is

$$\text{RETURN} = -3.021 + 7.062(\text{FEE})$$
$$(-7.28)\ (14.95)$$

The calculated t-values are given in parentheses below the intercept and slope coefficients. The coefficient of determination for the regression model is 0.794.
a. What is the predicted RETURN if FEE is 0 percent? If FEE is 1 percent?
b. Using a two-tailed test, is the relationship between RETURN and FEE significant at the 5 percent level?
c. Would Smith be justified in concluding that high fees are good for clients?

17. Kenneth McCoin, CFA, is a fairly tough interviewer. Last year, he handed each job applicant a sheet of paper with the information in the following table, and he then asked several questions about regression analysis. Some of McCoin's questions, along with a sample of the answers he received to each, are given below. McCoin told the applicants that the independent variable is the level of Treasury-bill rates (in percent) and the dependent variable is the monthly return in the S&P 500 (with dividends reinvested, in percent).

Which of the answers given is the best answer to each of McCoin's questions?

Regression Statistics

Multiple R	0.1717
R-Squared	0.0295
Standard Error	4.6813
Observations	120

ANOVA

	df	SS	MSS	F	Significance F
Regression	1	78.553	78.553	3.58	0.0608
Residual	118	2585.868	21.914		
Total	119	2664.422			

Regression Equation

	Coefficients	Standard Error	t-Statistic	p-Value
Intercept	4.010	1.408	2.848	0.0052
Slope	−0.288	0.152	−1.893	0.0608

17-1. What is the value of the coefficient of determination?
  a. −0.288
  b. 0.0295
  c. 0.1717
  d. −1.893

17-2. Suppose that you deleted several of the observations that had small residual values. If you re-estimated the regression equation using this reduced sample, what would likely happen to the standard error of the estimate and the R-squared?

Standard error of the estimate	R-squared
a. Decrease	Decrease
b. Decrease	Increase
c. Increase	Decrease
d. Increase	Increase

17-3. What is the correlation between X and Y?
  a. −0.1717
  b. −0.0295
  c. 0.0295
  d. 0.1717

17-4. Where did the F-value in the ANOVA table come from?
  a. You look up the F-value in a table. The F depends on the numerator and denominator degrees of freedom.
  b. Divide the "Mean Square" for the regression by the "Mean Square" of the residuals.
  c. The F-value is equal to the reciprocal of the t-value for the slope coefficient.
  d. Subtract the standard errors of the intercept and the slope from the standard error of the estimate.

17-5. If the interest rate is 5 percent, what is the predicted monthly return of the stock index?
  a. $1.408 - 0.152(5.0) = 0.648$
  b. $1.408 + 0.152(5.0) = 2.168$
  c. $4.010 - 0.288(5.0) = 2.570$
  d. $4.010 + 0.288(5.0) = 5.450$

17-6. Is the relationship between interest rates and monthly index returns significant at the 5 percent level?
  a. Yes, because the R-squared is less than 0.05.
  b. Yes, because the standard error (4.68) is less than 5.
  c. Yes, because the p-value of the intercept is less than 0.05 (although the p-value of the slope is not).
  d. No, because the p-values for F and t for the slope coefficient are not less than 0.05.

18. Howard Golub, CFA, is preparing to write a research report on Stellar Energy Corp.
common stock. One of the world's largest companies, Stellar is in the business of re-
fining and marketing oil. As part of his analysis, Golub wants to evaluate the sensitivity of the stock's returns to various economic factors. For example, a client recently asked Golub whether the price of Stellar Energy Corporation stock has tended
to rise following increases in retail energy prices. Golub believes the association between the two variables to be negative, but he does not know the strength of the association.

Golub directs his assistant, Jill Batten, to study the relationships between Stellar
monthly common stock returns versus the previous month's percent change in the U.S.
Consumer Price Index for Energy (CPIENG), and Stellar monthly common stock returns versus the previous month's percent change in the U.S. Producer Price Index for
Crude Energy Materials (PPICEM). Golub wants Batten to run both a correlation and
linear regression analysis. In response, Batten compiles the summary statistics shown
in Exhibit 1 for the 248 months between January 1980 and August 2000. All of the
data are in decimal form, where a 1 percent increase is recorded as 0.01. The monthly
mean return for Stellar of 0.0123 means that Stellar's mean return is 1.23 percent. Batten also runs a regression analysis using Stellar monthly returns as the dependent variable and the monthly change in CPIENG as the independent variable. This regression
model is shown in Exhibit 2.

EXHIBIT 1   Descriptive Statistics

	Monthly Return Stellar Common Stock	Lagged Monthly Change (%) CPIENG	PPICEM
Mean	0.0123	0.0023	0.0042
Standard Deviation	0.0717	0.0160	0.0534
Covariance, Stellar vs. CPIENG	−0.00017		
Covariance, Stellar vs. PPICEM	−0.00048		
Covariance, CPIENG vs. PPICEM	0.00044		
Correlation, Stellar vs. CPIENG	−0.1452		

EXHIBIT 2   Regression Analysis with CPIENG

Regression Statistics	
Multiple R	0.1452
R-Squared	0.0211
Standard Error of the Estimate	0.0710
Observations	248

	Coefficients	Standard Error	t-Statistic
Intercept	0.0138	0.0046	3.0275
Slope Coefficient	−0.6486	0.2818	−2.3014

18-1. Batten wants to determine whether the sample correlation between the Stellar and CPIENG variables (−0.1452) is statistically significant. The critical value for the test statistic at the 0.05 level of significance is approximately 1.96. Batten should conclude that the statistical relationship between Stellar and CPIENG is

 a. significant, because the calculated test statistic has a lower absolute value than the critical value for the test statistic.

 b. significant, because the calculated test statistic has a higher absolute value than the critical value for the test statistic.

 c. not significant, because the calculated test statistic has a higher absolute value than the critical value for the test statistic.

 d. not significant, because the calculated test statistic has a lower higher absolute value than the critical value for the test statistic.

18-2. Did Batten's regression analyze cross-sectional or time-series data, and what was the expected value of the error term from that regression?

Data Type	Expected Value of Error Term
a. Time-series	0
b. Time-series	ϵ_I
c. Cross-sectional	0
d. Cross-sectional	ϵ_I

18-3. Based on the regression which used data in decimal form, if the CPIENG *decreases* by 1.0 percent, what is the expected return on Stellar common stock during the next period?

 a. 0.0065 (0.65 percent)

 b. 0.0073 (0.73 percent)

 c. 0.0138 (1.38 percent)

 d. 0.0203 (2.03 percent)

18-4. Based on Batten's regression model, the coefficient of determination indicates that

 a. 2.11 percent of the variability in CPIENG is explained by Stellar's returns.

 b. 14.52 percent of the variability in CPIENG is explained by Stellar's returns.

 c. 2.11 percent of the variability in Stellar's returns is explained by changes in CPIENG.

 d. 14.52 percent of the variability in Stellar's returns is explained by changes in CPIENG.

18-5. For the regression model run by Batten, the standard error of the estimate shows that the standard deviation of

 a. the residuals from the regression is 0.0710.

 b. values estimated from the regression is 0.0710.

       c. Stellar's observed common stock returns is 0.0710.

       d. the intercept estimate from the regression is 0.0710.

18-6. For the analysis run by Batten, which of the following is an *incorrect* conclusion from the regression output?

       a. The estimated intercept coefficient from Batten's regression is statistically significant.

       b. In the month after the CPIENG index declines, Stellar's common stock is expected to exhibit a positive return.

       c. Viewed in combination, the slope and intercept coefficients from Batten's regression are not statistically significant.

       d. In the month after no change occurs in the CPIENG index, Stellar's common stock is expected to exhibit a positive return.

SOLUTIONS

1. The first four variables, Y_1 through Y_4, have a zero correlation with X. Notice that while Y_3 and Y_4 are clearly nonlinearly related to X (decreasing and then increasing as the value of X increases), their overall linear relationship is zero. Variable Y_5 has a correlation of 1.0 with X.

2. a. The sample mean, variance, and standard deviation of X are

$$\bar{X} = \sum_{i=1}^{n} X_i/n = 220/11 = 20$$

$$s_x^2 = \sum_{i=1}^{n} (X_i - \bar{X})^2/(n-1) = 440/10 = 44$$

$$s_X = \sqrt{s_X^2} = \sqrt{44} = 6.633$$

b. The sample mean, variance, and standard deviation of Y are

$$\bar{Y} = \sum_{i=1}^{n} Y_i/n = 385/11 = 35$$

$$s_Y^2 = \sum_{i=1}^{n} (Y_i - \bar{Y})^2/(n-1) = 1120/10 = 112$$

$$s_Y = \sqrt{s_Y^2} = \sqrt{112} = 10.583$$

c. The sample covariance between X and Y is

$$\text{Cov}(X,Y) = \left[\sum_{i=1}^{n} (X_i - \bar{X})(Y_i - \bar{Y}) \right]/(n-1) = -568/10 = -56.8$$

d. The sample correlation between X and Y is

$$r = \frac{\text{Cov}(X,Y)}{s_X s_Y} = \frac{-56.8}{6.633 \times 10.583} = -0.809$$

3. a. The sample variances and standard deviations are

$$s_X^2 = \sum_{i=1}^{n} (X_i - \bar{X})^2/(n-1) = 769.081/59 = 13.035$$

$$s_X = \sqrt{13.035} = 3.610$$

$$s_Y^2 = \sum_{i=1}^{n} (Y_i - \bar{Y})^2/(n-1) = 1243.309/59 = 21.073$$

$$s_Y = \sqrt{21.073} = 4.591$$

$$s_Z^2 = \sum_{i=1}^{n} (Z_i - \bar{Z})^2/(n-1) = 183.073/59 = 3.103$$

$$s_Z = \sqrt{3.103} = 1.762$$

b. The sample covariances are

$$\text{Cov}(X,Y) = \sum_{i=1}^{n} (X_i - \bar{X})(Y_i - \bar{Y})/(n-1) = 720.535/59 = 12.212$$

$$Cov(X,Z) = \sum_{i=1}^{n} (X_i - \bar{X})(Z_i - \bar{Z})/(n-1) = 231.007/59 = 3.915$$

$$Cov(Y,Z) = \sum_{i=1}^{n} (Y_i - \bar{Y})(Z_i - \bar{Z})/(n-1) = 171.816/59 = 2.912$$

c. The sample correlations are

$$r_{XY} = \frac{Cov(X,Y)}{s_X s_Y} = \frac{12.212}{3.610 \times 4.591} = 0.737$$

$$r_{XZ} = \frac{Cov(X,Z)}{s_X s_Z} = \frac{3.915}{3.610 \times 1.762} = 0.615$$

$$r_{YZ} = \frac{Cov(Y,Z)}{s_Y s_Z} = \frac{2.912}{4.591 \times 1.762} = 0.360$$

4. Sample mean sales are $(50 + 70 + 80 + 60)/4 = 260/4 = 65$.

Sample mean interest rate is $(8.0 + 7.0 + 6.0 + 7.0)/4 = 28.0/4 = 7.0$.

Sample variance of sales is $[(50 - 65)^2 + (70 - 65)^2 + (80 - 65)^2 + (60 - 65)^2]/3 = 500/3 = 166.7$.

Sample standard deviation of sales is the square root the variance, or 12.91.

Sample variance of interest rates is $[(8 - 7)^2 + (7 - 7)^2 + (6 - 7)^2 + (7 - 7)^2]/3 = 2/3 = 0.667$.

Sample standard deviation of interest rates is the square root of this result, or 0.8165.

Sample covariance between sales and interest rates is $[(50 - 65)(8 - 7) + (70 - 65)(7 - 7) + (80 - 65)(6 - 7) + (60 - 65)(7 - 7)]/3 = -30/3 = -10$.

Sample correlation is the covariance divided by the product of the standard deviations:

$$r = \frac{Cov(X_i, Y_i)}{s_x s_y} = \frac{-10}{14.14 \times 0.8165} = -0.9487$$

5. The critical t-value for $n - 2 = 34$ df, a 5 percent significance level, and a two-tailed test is 2.032. First, take the smallest correlation in the table, the correlation between Fund 3 and Fund 4, and see if it is significantly different from zero. Its calculated t-value is

$$t = \frac{r\sqrt{n-2}}{\sqrt{1-r^2}} = \frac{0.3102\sqrt{36-2}}{\sqrt{1-0.3102^2}} = 1.903$$

This correlation is not significantly different from zero. If we take the next lowest correlation, between Fund 2 and Fund 3, this correlation of 0.4156 has a calculated t-value of 2.664. So this correlation is significantly different from zero. All of the other correlations in the table (besides the 0.3102) are greater than 0.4156, so they are significantly different from zero.

6. a. The negative correlation, as Osterburg hypothesizes, is consistent with reversals. An above-average return has a tendency to be followed by a below-average return. Similarly, a below-average return has a tendency to be followed by an above-average return.

b. The null hypothesis, H_0, is that the correlation is 0 ($\rho = 0$); and the alternative hypothesis, H_a, is that the correlation is different from $0(\rho \neq 0)$. We can test this hypothesis with a t-test. The calculated value of the t-test is as follows:

$$t = \frac{r\sqrt{n-2}}{\sqrt{1-r^2}} = \frac{-0.0641\sqrt{59-2}}{\sqrt{1-(-0.0641)^2}} = -0.485$$

This test statistic has a t-distribution with $n - 2 = 59 - 2 = 57$ df, so the critical t-value (for a two-tailed test and 5 percent significance) is approximately 2.00. So we cannot reject the hypothesis that $\rho = 0$ with 95 percent confidence. We cannot reject Martinez's opinion that the returns are random.

7. The null hypothesis, H_0, is that the correlation is 0 ($\rho = 0$); and the alternative hypothesis, H_A, is that the correlation is different from 0 ($\rho \neq 0$). The calculated value of the t-test for the S&P 500 is

$$t = \frac{r\sqrt{n-2}}{\sqrt{1-r^2}} = \frac{0.0034\sqrt{347-2}}{\sqrt{1-0.0034^2}} = 0.063$$

The t-values for the other indices are calculated similarly. They are

MSCI Europe: 0.623
MSCI Pacific: 2.095
MSCI Far East: 1.965

The critical t-value for $n - 2 = 347 - 2 = 345$ df is approximately 1.97. At a 5 percent significance level (two-tailed test with 345 df), the S&P 500 and MSCI Europe are not significantly different from zero. The MSCI Pacific apparently is significantly different from zero. The computed t-value for MSCI Far East is slightly below the critical value, so technically we conclude that it is not different from zero at a 5 percent significance level.

8. The following table provides several useful calculations:

Year i	$X_i =$ Exchange Rate	$Y_i =$ Sales	$(X_i - \bar{X})^2$	$(Y_i - \bar{Y})^2$	$(X_i - \bar{X})(Y_i - \bar{Y})$
1	0.4	20	0.0016	36	−0.24
2	0.36	25	0	1	0
3	0.42	16	0.0036	100	−0.6
4	0.31	30	0.0025	16	−0.2
5	0.33	35	0.0009	81	−0.27
6	0.34	30	0.0004	16	−0.08
Sum	2.16	156	0.009	250	−1.39

a. The sample mean and standard deviation of the exchange rate are

$$\bar{X} = \sum_{i=1}^{n} X_i/n = 2.16/6 = 0.36, \text{ and}$$

$$s_x = \sqrt{\sum_{i=1}^{n} (X_i - \bar{X})^2/(n-1)} = \sqrt{0.009/5} = 0.042426$$

The sample mean and standard deviation of sales are

$$\bar{Y} = \sum_{i=1}^{n} Y_i/n = 156/6 = 26, \text{ and}$$

$$s_Y = \sqrt{\sum_{i=1}^{n} (Y_i - \bar{Y})^2/(n-1)} = \sqrt{250/5} = 7.0711$$

b. The sample covariance between the exchange rate and sales is

$$Cov(X_iY_i) = \sum_{i=1}^{n} (X_i - \bar{X})(Y_i - \bar{Y})/(n-1) = -1.39/5 = -0.278$$

c. The sample correlation between the exchange rate and sales is

$$r = \frac{Cov(X_i,Y_i)}{s_X s_Y} = \frac{-0.278}{(0.042426)(7.0711)} = -0.927$$

d. We want to estimate a regression equation of the form $Y_i = b_0 + b_1 X_i + \epsilon_i$. The estimates of the slope coefficient and the intercept are

$$\hat{b}_1 = \frac{\sum_{i=1}^{n} (Y_i - \bar{Y})(X_i - \bar{X})}{\sum_{i=1}^{n} (X_i - \bar{X})^2} = \frac{-1.39}{0.009} = -154.44, \text{ and}$$

$$\hat{b}_0 = \bar{Y} - \hat{b}_1\bar{X} = 26 - (-154.444)(0.36) = 26 + 55.6 = 81.6.$$

So the regression equation is $Y_i = 81.6 - 154.444X_i$.

9. a. The coefficient of determination is

$$\frac{\text{Explained variation}}{\text{Total variation}} = \frac{60.16}{140.58} = 0.4279$$

b. For a linear regression with one independent variable, the absolute value of correlation between the independent variable and the dependent variable is equal to the square root of the coefficient of determination, so the correlation is $\sqrt{0.4279}=$ 0.6542. (The correlation will have the same sign as the slope coefficient.)

c. The standard error of the estimate is

$$\left(\sum_{i=1}^{n} \frac{(Y_i - \hat{b}_0 - \hat{b}_1X_i)^2}{n-2}\right)^{1/2} = \left(\frac{\text{Unexplained variation}}{n-2}\right)^{1/2} = \sqrt{\frac{80.42}{60-2}} = 1.178$$

d. The sample variance of the dependent variable is

$$\sum_{i=1}^{n} \frac{(Y_i - \bar{Y})^2}{n-1} = \frac{\text{Total variation}}{n-1} = \frac{140.58}{60-1} = 2.3827$$

The sample standard deviation is $\sqrt{2.3827} = 1.544$.

10. a. The degrees of freedom (df) for the regression is the number of slope parameters in the regression, which is the same as the number of independent variables in the regression. Because regression df $= 1$, we conclude that there is one independent variable in the regression.

b. Total SS is the sum of the squared deviations of the dependent variable Y about its mean.

c. The sample variance of the dependent variable is the total SS divided by its degrees of freedom ($n - 1 = 5 - 1 = 4$ as given). Thus the sample variance of the dependent variable is $95.2/4 = 23.8$.

d. The Regression SS is the part of total sum of squares explained by the regression. Regression sum of squares equals the sum of the squared differences between predicted values of the Y and the sample mean of Y: $\left(\sum_{i=1}^{n} (\hat{Y}_i - \overline{Y}) \right)^2$. In terms of other values in the table, Regression sum of squares is equal to Total SS minus Residual SS: $95.2 - 7.2 = 88$.

e. The F-statistic tests whether all the slope coefficients in a linear regression are equal to 0.

f. The calculated value of F in the table is equal to the Regression MSS divided by the Residual MSS: $88/2.4 = 36.667$.

g. The significance of 0.00904 given in the table is the p-value of the test (the smallest level at which we can reject the null hypothesis). This value of 0.00904 given is less than the specified significance level of 0.05, so we reject the null hypothesis. The regression equation has significant explanatory power.

11. a. For the large-cap fund, the predicted rate of return, $\hat{Y}$, is

$$\hat{Y} = \hat{b}_0 + \hat{b}_1 X = -.287 + 0.802(8.00) = 6.129$$

b. The estimated variance of the prediction error, s_f^2, of Y, given X, is

$$s_f^2 = s^2 \left[1 + \frac{1}{n} + \frac{(X - \overline{X})^2}{(n - 1)s_x^2} \right] = 4.243^2 \left[1 + \frac{1}{12} + \frac{(8.00 - 2.30)^2}{(12 - 1)(38.51)} \right] = 20.884$$

The standard deviation of the prediction error is the square root of this, or 4.57. For 10 degrees of freedom, the critical t-value is 2.228. A 95 percent prediction interval would be $\hat{Y} \pm t_c s_f$, or $6.129 \pm 2.228(4.57)$, or 6.129 ± 10.182.

Prob $(-4.053 < \hat{Y} < 16.311) = 0.95$

12. a. For a sentiment index of 90, predicted auto sales, $\hat{Y}$, are $\hat{Y} = \hat{b}_0 + \hat{b}_1 X = 6.071 + 0.0925(90) = 14.397$ (about 14.4 million vehicles). The estimated variance of the prediction error, s_f^2, of Y, given X, is

$$s_f^2 = s^2 \left[1 + \frac{1}{n} + \frac{(X - \overline{X})^2}{(n - 1)s_x^2} \right] = 0.81325^2 \left[1 + \frac{1}{120} + \frac{(90 - 91.0983)^2}{(120 - 1)(137.3071)} \right]$$

$$= 0.66689$$

The standard deviation of the prediction error is the square root of this, or 0.8167. For 118 degrees of freedom and a 0.05 level of significance, the critical t-value is approximately 1.98. The 95 percent prediction interval for $X = 90$ is $\hat{Y} \pm t_c s_f$, or $14.397 \pm 1.98(0.8167)$, or 14.397 ± 1.617.

Prob $(12.780 < \hat{Y} < 16.014) = 0.95$

b. For a sentiment index of 100, predicted auto sales, $\hat{Y}$, are

$$\hat{Y} = \hat{b}_0 + \hat{b}_1 X = 6.071 + 0.09251(100) = 15.322$$

The estimated variance of the prediction error, s_f^2, of Y, given X, is

$$s_f^2 = s^2 \left[1 + \frac{1}{n} + \frac{(X - \bar{X})^2}{(n-1)s_x^2} \right] = 0.81325^2 \left[1 + \frac{1}{120} + \frac{(100 - 91.0983)^2}{(120 - 1)(137.3071)} \right]$$
$$= 0.67009$$

The standard deviation of the prediction error is the square root of this, or 0.81859. For 118 degrees of freedom, the critical t-value is approximately 1.98. A 95 percent prediction interval would be $\hat{Y} \pm t_c s_f$, or $15.322 \pm 1.98(0.81859)$ or 15.322 ± 1.621.

Prob$(13.701 < \hat{Y} < 16.943) = 0.95$

13. a. The sample size is $n = 9$.

For X, the sample mean is $\bar{X} = \sum_{i=1}^{N} X_i/n = 81/9 = 9$, the sample variance is

$$s_X^2 = \sum_{i=1}^{N} (X_i - \bar{X})^2/(n-1) = 60/8 = 7.5,$$ and the sample standard deviation is

$$s_X = \sqrt{7.5} = 2.7386$$

For Y, the sample mean is $\bar{Y} = \sum_{i=1}^{N} Y_i/n = 144/9 = 16$, the sample variance is

$$s_Y^2 = \sum_{i=1}^{N} (Y_i - \bar{Y})^2/(n-1) = 144/8 = 18,$$ and the sample standard deviation is

$$s_Y = \sqrt{18} = 4.2426$$

b. The sample covariance is

$$\text{Cov}(X_i, Y_i) = \sum_{i=1}^{n} (X_i - \bar{X})(Y_i - \bar{Y})/(n-1) = 84/8 = 10.5$$

The sample correlation between X and Y is

$$r = \frac{\text{Cov}(X_i, Y_i)}{s_X s_Y} = \frac{10.5}{(2.7386)(4.2426)} = 0.9037$$

c. The coefficients for the regression equation are

$$\hat{b}_1 = \frac{\displaystyle\sum_{i=1}^{n}(Y_i - \overline{Y})(X_i - \overline{X})}{\displaystyle\sum_{i=1}^{n}(X_i - \overline{X})^2} = \frac{84}{60} = 1.4, \text{ and}$$

$$\hat{b}_0 = \overline{Y} - \hat{b}_1\overline{X} = 16 - 1.4(9) = 3.4$$

So the regression equation is $Y_i = 3.4 + 1.4X_i$.

d. The total variation is $\displaystyle\sum_{i=1}^{n}(Y_i - \overline{Y})^2 = 144$ and the unexplained variation is

$\displaystyle\sum_{i=1}^{n}(Y_i - \hat{b}_0 - \hat{b}_1X_i)^2 = 26.4$. So the explained variation is $144 - 26.4 = 117.6$.

e. The coefficient of variation, the R-squared, is

$$\frac{\text{Explained variation}}{\text{Total variation}} = \frac{117.6}{144} = 0.81667$$

f. The standard error of the estimate is

$$SEE = \left(\sum_{i=1}^{n}\frac{(Y_i - \hat{b}_0 - \hat{b}_1X_i)^2}{n - 2}\right)^{1/2} = \left(\frac{26.4}{9 - 2}\right)^{1/2} = 1.942$$

14. The R-squared (**X1**) is the explained variation/total variation = 3676.651/3770.219 = 0.9572. The Multiple R (**X2**) is the correlation between the two variables, which is the square root of the R-squared, or $\sqrt{0.9752} = 0.9875$. The standard error (**X3**) is the square root of unexplained variation divided by $(n - 2)$, which is $\sqrt{93.5674/(436 - 2)} = 0.4643$.

The Total df (degrees of freedom), **X4**, is the sample size minus 1, or $n - 1 = 436 - 1 = 435$. The Regression df (**X5**) is equal to the number of independent variables, which is 1. The Residual df (**X6**) is the difference between the Total df and Regression df, which is also $n - (k + 1)$ where n is the sample size (436) and k is the number of independent variables (1). X6 is $436 - (1 + 1) = 434$. MSS is the "Mean Square," which is the sum of squares divided by the degrees of freedom. For **X7**, the MS Regression is $3676.651/1 = 3676.651$. For **X8**, the MSS Residual is 93.567/434 $= 0.2156$. The F (**X9**) is testing the hypothesis that the regression coefficient is equal to zero, and it is equal to MSS Regression/MSS Residual, or $3676.651/0.2156 = 17{,}053.1$. This F has 1 df in the numerator and 434 df in the denominator. This is an extremely large F, and the probability of an F this large is practically zero.

X10, the calculated t-value for the slope coefficient, is the coefficient divided by its standard error: $t = 1.15105/0.008814 = 130.59$. This is an extremely large t, with a probability of practically zero. (Notice that the square root of the F is equal to the t for a regression with one independent variable.) Finally, **X11** and **X12** are the upper and lower bounds for a 95 percent confidence interval for the slope coefficient. The critical t for a two-tailed test, 5 percent significance, and 434 degrees of freedom is approximately 1.965. The lower bound, **X11**, is $\hat{b}_1 - t_c s_{\hat{b}_1} = 1.15105 - 1.965(.008814) = 1.134$. The upper bound, **X12**, is $\hat{b}_1 + t_c s_{\hat{b}_1} = 1.15105 + 1.965(.008814) = 1.168$.

15. The Month 3 data point is an outlier, lying far away from the other data values. Because this outlier was caused by a data entry error, correcting the outlier improves the validity and reliability of the regression. In this case, the true correlation is reduced from 0.996 to 0.824. The revised R-squared is substantially lower (0.678 versus 0.992). The significance of the regression is also lower, as can be seen in the decline of the F-value from 500.79 to 8.44 and the decline in the t-statistic of the slope coefficient from 22.379 to 2.905.

    The total sum of squares and regression sum of squares were greatly exaggerated in the incorrect analysis. The slope coefficient changes from 1.069 to 0.623. This change is important. When the index moves up or down, the original model indicates that the portfolio return goes up or down by 1.069 times as much, while the revised model indicates that the portfolio return goes up or down by only 0.623 times as much. In this example, the outlier was caused by incorrect data entry. If the outlier was a valid observation, not caused by a data error, then the analyst would have to decide whether the results were more reliable including or excluding the outlier.

16. a. If FEE = 0%, RETURN = $-3.021 + 7.062(0) = -3.021\%$
       If FEE = 1%, RETURN = $-3.021 + 7.062(1) = 4.041\%$

    b. The calculated t-value for the coefficient of FEE is 14.95. The critical t-value for 58 degrees of freedom, a two-tailed test, and significance level of 5 percent is 2.00. Because the calculated t exceeds the critical t, we may conclude that the coefficient of FEE is not equal to zero and the relationship between RETURN and FEE is significant.

    c. Smith's analysis may be inadequate to conclude that high fees are good. Clearly, high returns cause high fees (because of the compensation contract that Diet Partners has with its clients). The regression may be recognizing this relationship. Unfortunately, the reverse may not be true, that fees cause returns. As an analogy, assume that income taxes are a function of income. A regression of income as a function of income taxes would find a strong positive relationship. Does this mean that taxes cause income, or the reverse? The experiment designed by Smith is too simplistic to address the issue of whether a particular compensation contract is good or bad for client returns.

17. 17-1. B is correct. The coefficient of determination is the same as R-squared.

    17-2. C is correct. Deleting observations with small residuals will degrade the strength of the regression resulting in an *increase* in the standard error and a *decrease* in R-squared.

    17-3. A is correct. For a regression with one independent variable, the correlation is the same as the Multiple R with the sign of the slope coefficient. Because the slope coefficient is negative, the correlation is -0.1717.

    17-4. B is correct. This answer describes the calculation of the F-statistic.

    17-5. C is correct. To make a prediction using the regression model, multiply the slope coefficient by the forecast of the independent variable and add the result to the intercept.

    17-6. D is correct. The p-values reflects the strength of the relationship between the two variables. In this case the p-value is greater than 0.05, and thus the regression of S&P 500 monthly returns on the level of T-bill rates is not significant at the 5 percent level.

18. 18-1. B is correct because the calculated test statistic is

$$t = \frac{r\sqrt{n-2}}{\sqrt{1-r^2}} = \frac{-0.1452\sqrt{248-2}}{\sqrt{1-(-0.1452)^2}} = -2.3017$$

Because the absolute value of $t = -2.3017$ is greater than 1.96, the correlation coefficient is statistically significant. For a regression with one independent variable, the t-value (and significance) for the slope coefficient (which is -2.3014) should equal the t-value (and significance) of the correlation coefficient. The slight difference in these t-values is caused by rounding error.

18-2. A is correct because the data are time series, and the expected value of the error term $[E(\epsilon_1)]$ is 0.

18-3. D is correct. From the regression equation, Expected return $= 0.0138 + -0.6486(-0.01) = 0.0138 + 0.006486 = 0.0203$ (or, 2.03 percent).

18-4. C is correct. R-squared is the coefficient of determination. In this case it shows that 2.11 percent of the variability in Stellar's returns is explained by changes in CPIENG.

18-5. A is correct, because the standard error of the estimate is the standard deviation of the regression residuals.

18-6. C is the correct response, because it is a false statement. The slope and intercept are both statistically significant.

MULTIPLE REGRESSION AND ISSUES IN REGRESSION ANALYSIS

LEARNING OUTCOMES

After completing this chapter, you will be able to do the following:

- Describe a multiple regression equation.

- Write a multiple regression equation to describe the relationship between a dependent variable and several independent variables.

- Determine whether each independent variable in a multiple regression is statistically significant in explaining the dependent variable.

- Formulate a null and an alternative hypothesis about the population value of a regression coefficient and determine whether the null hypothesis is true at a given level of significance, using a one-tailed or two-tailed test.

- Formulate the confidence interval for the population value of a regression coefficient in a multiple regression.

- List and explain the assumptions of a multiple regression model.

- Discuss the residual and its relationship to the standard error of estimate.

- Calculate the standard error of estimate given the sum of squared residuals from the regression, the number of observations, and the number of independent variables.

- Predict a dependent variable given estimated coefficients and assumed values of independent variables.

- Discuss the two types of uncertainty involved in regression model predictions.

- Define the F-statistic and show how it can be used to analyze the regression equation.

- Formulate and evaluate a test of the hypothesis that all the independent variable coefficients together are jointly equal to 0.

- Define and interpret the R^2 and adjusted R^2 in a regression.

- Infer how well a regression model explains the dependent variable by analyzing the output of an estimated regression equation and an ANOVA table.

- Modify a multiple regression equation to address qualitative independent variables, using dummy variables.

- Discuss the types of heteroskedasticity and the effect of conditional heteroskedasticity on statistical inference.

- Explain how to test and correct for conditional heteroskedasticity.

> - Discuss the effect of serial correlation on statistical inference in the linear regression model.
> - Explain how to test and correct for serial correlation.
> - Calculate a Durbin-Watson statistic, determine its significance, and interpret the results of this test for serial correlation.
> - Discuss the causes and effects of multicollinearity on statistical inference in the linear regression model.
> - Discuss models for qualitative dependent variables.
> - Interpret the economic meaning of the results of multiple regression analysis.

1   INTRODUCTION

As financial analysts, we often need to use more sophisticated statistical methods than simple correlation or regression analysis, which rely on a single independent variable. For example, we might want to test whether returns to small stocks were unusually high, on average, in any particular month of the year. We might also want to know whether returns to a technology mutual fund behaved more like the returns to growth stocks or the returns to value stocks. We can answer these questions using linear regression with more than one independent variable—with multiple linear regression.

In the first part of the chapter, we introduce and illustrate the basic concepts and models of multiple regression analysis. These models rest on assumptions that, in practice, are sometimes violated. The following sections present remedial steps to take when a model assumption has been violated. Also, in a number of investment applications, we are interested in the probability that one of two outcomes occurs: For example, we may be interested in whether a stock has analyst coverage or not. The chapter ends with an introduction to a class of models, qualitative dependent variable models, that addresses such questions.

2   MULTIPLE LINEAR REGRESSION

In financial analysis, we often need to determine the effect of more than one independent variable on a particular dependent variable. For example, suppose we want to know whether the returns to a particular mutual fund behave more like the returns to a large-cap growth fund or returns to a large-cap value fund. We can address this question with linear regression using the regression model

$$Y_t = b_0 + b_1 X_{1t} + b_2 X_{2t} + \epsilon_t$$

where

Y_t = the return to the mutual fund in period t (the dependent variable)
X_{1t} = the return in period t to a large-cap growth index
X_{2t} = the return in period t to a large-cap value index
ϵ_t = the error term

Of course, linear regression models can use more than two independent variables to explain the dependent variable. The general form of a **multiple linear regression model** is

$$Y_t = b_0 + b_1 X_{1t} + b_2 X_{2t} + \ldots + b_k X_{kt} + \epsilon_t \qquad (9\text{-}1)$$

where

$t = 1, 2, \ldots , T$ observations
$Y_t =$ the t'th observation of the dependent variable
$X_j =$ the independent variables, $j = 1, 2, \ldots , k$
$X_{jt} =$ the t'th observation of the independent variable X_j
$b_0 =$ the intercept of the equation
$b_1, \ldots , b_k =$ the slope coefficients for each of the independent variables
$\epsilon_t =$ the error term

A slope coefficient, b_j, measures how much the dependent variable, Y_t, changes when the independent variable, X_{jt}, changes by one unit, holding all other independent variables constant. For example, if $b_1 = 1$ and all of the other independent variables remain constant, then we predict that if X_{1t} increases by one unit, Y_t will also increase by one unit. If $b_1 = -1$ and all of the other independent variables are held constant, then we predict that if X_{1t} increases by one unit, Y_t will decrease by one unit. Multiple linear regression estimates $b_0, \ldots , b_k$. In this chapter, we will refer to both the intercept, b_0, and the slope coefficients, $b_1, \ldots , b_k$, as *regression coefficients*.

EXAMPLE 9-1.   Explaining Returns to the Fidelity Select Technology Fund.

Suppose you are considering an investment in the Fidelity Select Technology Fund (FSTF), a U.S. mutual fund specializing in technology stocks. You might want to know whether the fund behaves more like a large-cap growth fund or a large-cap value fund. You decide to estimate the regression

$$Y_t = b_0 + b_1 X_{1t} + b_2 X_{2t} + \epsilon_t$$

where

$Y_t =$ the monthly return to the FSTF
$X_{1t} =$ the monthly return to the S&P 500/BARRA Growth Index
$X_{2t} =$ the monthly return to the S&P 500/BARRA Value Index

The S&P 500/BARRA Growth and Value indexes represent predominantly large-cap growth and value stocks, respectively.

Table 9-1 shows the results of this linear regression using monthly data from December 1984 through March 1999. The estimated intercept in the regression is -0.0043. Thus, if both the return to the S&P 500/BARRA Growth Index and the return to the S&P 500/BARRA Value Index equal 0 in a specific month, the regression model predicts that the return to the FSTF will be -0.43 percent. The coefficient on the large-cap growth index is 1.3342. Thus, the model predicts that a 1 percentage point increase in the large-cap growth-return index in a given month is associated with approximately a 1.33 percentage point increase in the return to the FSTF. The coefficient on the large-cap value-index return is -0.0519. Therefore, the model predicts that a 1 percentage point increase in the return to the large-cap value index is associated with approximately a 0.05 percentage point decline in the return to the FSTF.

**TABLE 9-1   Results from Regressing the FSTF Returns
on the S&P 500/BARRA Growth and Value Indexes**

	Coefficients	Standard Error	t-Statistic
Intercept	−0.0043	0.0038	−1.1401
S&P 500/BARRA Growth Index	1.3342	0.1825	7.3105
S&P 500/BARRA Value Index	−0.0519	0.2052	−0.2531

ANOVA	df	SS	MSS	F	Significance F
Regression	2	0.6264	0.3132	143.7483	3.4194E−37
Residual	169	0.3682	0.0022		
Total	171	0.9946			
Residual standard error	0.0467				
Multiple R-squared	0.6298				
n	172				

Source for data: Ibbotson Associates

In addition to interpreting the regression coefficients, we often need to test hypotheses about their population values and assess how well the regression explains the dependent variable overall. The regression output in Table 9-1 helps us address such questions. To review the items in the regression output:

- The Standard Error column gives the standard error (the standard deviation) of the estimated regression coefficients. The test statistic for hypotheses concerning the population value of a regression coefficient has the form (Estimated regression coefficient − Hypothesized population value of the regression coefficient)/(Standard error of the regression coefficient). This is a *t*-test, and to carry it out, we need to determine a quantity called *degrees of freedom* (df). The calculation is Degrees of freedom = (Number of observations, *T*) − (Number of independent variables + 1).[1]

- The *t*-Statistic column reports the results of a *t*-test on the hypothesis that the population value of the regression intercept or slope coefficient, as the case may be, equals 0.

- The ANOVA (analysis of variance) section reports quantities related to the overall explanatory power of the regression. SS stands for sum of squares, and MSS stands for mean sum of squares (SS divided by df); we discussed these quantities in the chapter on correlation and regression. Later in this chapter, we will discuss the *F*-test reported in this section.

- The next section of Table 9-1 presents two measures of how well the estimated regression fits or explains the data. The first, residual standard error, is the standard deviation of the regression residual. This standard deviation is called

---

[1] We add 1 to the number of independent variables to account for the intercept term. The *t*-test and the concept of degrees of freedom are discussed in the chapter on sampling.

the standard error of estimate (SEE). The second measure, known as multiple R^2 or simply R^2 (the square of the correlation between predicted and actual values of the dependent variable) quantifies the degree of linear association between the dependent variable and all of the independent variables jointly.[2] A value of 0 for R^2 indicates no linear association; a value of 1 indicates perfect linear association. The final item in Table 9-1 is the number of observations in the sample (172).

We may want to know whether the coefficient on the returns to the S&P 500/BARRA Value Index is statistically significant in this regression. Our null hypothesis states that the coefficient equals 0 (H_0: $b_2 = 0$); our alternative hypothesis states that the coefficient does not equal 0 (H_a: $b_2 \neq 0$). We use a t-test, rather than a z-test, because we do not know the true or population variance of b_2. We must base our inference on the estimate $s_{\hat{b}_2}$ of the true variance.[3]

Our test of the null hypothesis uses a t-test constructed as follows:

$$\frac{\hat{b}_2 - b_2}{s_{\hat{b}_2}} = \frac{-0.0519 - 0}{0.2052} = -0.2531$$

where

$\hat{b}_2$ = the regression estimate of b_2
b_2 = the hypothesized value[4] of the coefficient (0)
$s_{\hat{b}_2}$ = the estimated standard error of $\hat{b}_2$

This regression has 172 observations and three coefficients (two independent variables and the intercept); therefore, the t-test has $172 - 3 = 169$ degrees of freedom. At the 0.05 significance level, the critical value for the test statistic is about 1.97.[5] The absolute value of the test statistic is 0.2531. Because the test statistic's absolute value is less than the critical value ($0.2531 < 1.97$), we fail to reject the null hypothesis that $b_2 = 0$. (Note that the t-tests reported in Table 9-1, as well as the other regression tables, are tests of the null hypothesis that the population value of a regression coefficient equals zero.)

Similar analysis shows that at the 0.05 significance level, we cannot reject the null hypothesis that the intercept equals 0 (H_0: $b_0 = 0$) against the alternative hypothesis that the intercept does not equal 0 (H_a: $b_0 \neq 0$). Table 9-1 shows that the t-statistic for testing that hypothesis is -1.14, a result smaller in absolute value than the critical value of 1.97. Also at the 0.05 significance level, however, we *can* reject the null hypothesis that the coefficient on the S&P 500/BARRA Growth Index equals 0 (H_0: $b_1 = 0$) against the alternative hypothesis that the coefficient does not equal 0 (H_a: $b_1 \neq 0$). As Table 9-1 shows, the t-statistic for testing that hypothesis is 7.31, a result far above the critical value of 1.97. Thus, multiple regression analysis suggests that returns to the FSTF are very closely associated with the returns to the S&P 500/BARRA Growth Index, but they are not related to S&P 500/BARRA Value Index (the t-statistic of -0.25 is not statistically significant).

[2] Multiple R-squared is also known as the multiple coefficient of determination, or simply the coefficient of determination.

[3] The use of t-tests and z-tests is discussed in the chapter on hypothesis testing.

[4] To economize on notation in stating test statistics, in this context we use b_2 to represent the hypothesized value of the parameter (elsewhere we use it to represent the unknown population parameter).

[5] See Appendix B for t-test values.

2.1 ASSUMPTIONS OF THE MULTIPLE LINEAR REGRESSION MODEL

Before we can conduct correct statistical inference on a multiple linear regression model (ordinary least squares with more than one independent variable), we need to know the assumptions underlying that model. Suppose we have T observations on the dependent variable, Y_t, and the independent variables, $(X_{1t}, X_{2t}, \ldots, X_{kt})$, and we wish to estimate the equation $Y_t = b_0 + b_1 X_{1t} + b_2 X_{2t} + \ldots + b_k X_{kt} + \epsilon_t$.

In order to make a valid inference from a multiple linear regression model, we need to make the following six assumptions, the set of which is known as the classical normal multiple linear regression model:

1. The relationship between the dependent variable, Y_t, and the independent variables, $(X_{1t}, X_{2t}, \ldots, X_{kt})$, is linear as described in Equation 9-1.

2. The independent variables $(X_{1t}, X_{2t}, \ldots, X_{kt})$ are not random.[6] Also, no exact linear relation exists between two or more of the independent variables.[7]

3. The expected value of the error term is 0: $E(\epsilon_t) = 0$.

4. The variance of the error term is the same for all observations:[8] $E(\epsilon_t^2) = \sigma_\epsilon^2$.

5. The error term (ϵ_t) is uncorrelated across observations: $E(\epsilon_t \times \epsilon_s) = 0, s \neq t$.

6. The error term is normally distributed.

Note that these assumptions are almost exactly the same as those for the single-variable linear regression model presented in the chapter on linear regression. Assumption 2 is modified such that no exact linear relation exists between two or more independent variables. If this part of Assumption 2 is violated, then we cannot compute linear regression estimates.[9] Also, even if no exact linear relationship exists between two or more independent variables, linear regression may encounter problems if two or more of the independent variables are highly correlated. Such a high correlation is known as multicollinearity, which we will discuss later in this chapter. We will also discuss the consequences of supposing that Assumptions 4 and 5 are met if, in fact, they are violated.

Although Equation 9-1 may seem to apply only to time series because the notation for the observations is the same ($t = 1, \ldots, T$), all of these results apply to cross-sectional data as well. For example, if we analyze data from one time period for many companies, we would typically use the notation $Y_i, X_{1i}, X_{2i}, \ldots, X_{ki}$, in which the first subscript denotes the variable and the second denotes the ith company.

EXAMPLE 9-2.   Factors Explaining Pension Fund Performance.

Ambachtsheer, Capelle, and Scheibelhut (1998) tested to see which factors affect the performance of pension funds. Specifically, they wanted to know whether the

---

[6] As discussed in the chapter on correlation and regression, even though we assume that independent variables in the regression model are not random, often that assumption is clearly not true. For example, it is absurd to assume that the monthly returns to the S&P 500 are not random. If the independent variable is random, then is the regression model incorrect? Fortunately, no. Even if the independent variable is random, we can still rely on the results of regression models. See, for example, Greene (1999) or Goldberger (1998).

[7] No independent variable can be expressed as a linear combination of any set of the other independent variables. Technically, a constant equal to 1 is included as an independent variable associated with the intercept in this condition.

[8] $\text{Var}(\epsilon_t) = E(\epsilon_t^2)$ and $\text{Cov}(\epsilon_t, \epsilon_s)$ because $E(\epsilon_t) = 0$.

[9] When we encounter this kind of linear relationship (called **perfect collinearity**), we cannot compute the matrix inverse needed to compute the linear regression estimates. See Greene (1999) for a further description of this issue.

risk-adjusted net value added (RANVA) of 80 U.S. and Canadian pension funds depended on the size of the individual fund and the proportion of the fund's assets that were passively managed (indexed). Using data from 80 funds for four years (1993–96), the authors regressed RANVA on the size of the pension fund and the fraction of pension fund assets that were passively managed.[10] They used the equation

$$\text{RANVA}_i = b_0 + b_1\text{Size}_i + b_2\text{Passive}_i + \epsilon_i$$

where

RANVA_i = the average RANVA (in percent) for fund i from 1993–96
Size_i = the log of average assets under management for fund i
Passive_i = the fraction of assets in fund i that were passively managed

Table 9-2 shows the results of their analysis.[11]

TABLE 9-2   Results from Regressing RANVA on Size and Passive Management

	Coefficients	Standard Error	t-Statistic
Intercept	−2.1	0.45	−4.7
Size	0.4	0.14	2.8
Passive management	0.8	0.42	1.9

Source: Ambachtsheer, Capelle, and Scheibelhut (1998)

Suppose we use the results in Table 9-2 to test the null hypothesis that the size of the pension fund had no effect on the fund's RANVA. Our null hypothesis is that the coefficient on the size variable equals 0 (H_0: $b_1 = 0$), and our alternative hypothesis is that the coefficient does not equal 0 (H_a: $b_1 \neq 0$). The t-statistic for testing that hypothesis is

$$\frac{\hat{b}_1 - b_1}{s_{\hat{b}_1}} = \frac{0.4 - 0}{0.14} = 2.8$$

With 80 observations and three coefficients, the t-statistic has $80 - 3 = 77$ degrees of freedom. At the 0.05 significance level, the critical value for t is about 1.99. The resulting t-statistic on the size coefficient is 2.8, which suggests strongly that we can reject the null hypothesis that size is not related to RANVA. Because the estimated coefficient is 0.4, every 10-fold increase in fund size (an increase of 1 in Size_i) is associated with a 0.4 percentage point increase (40 basis points) in RANVA_i. Because

[10] As mentioned in footnote 7, technically a constant equal to 1 is included as an independent variable associated with the intercept term in a regression. As all the regressions reported in this chapter include an intercept term, we will not separately mention a constant as an independent variable in the remainder of this chapter.

[11] Size is the log base 10 of average assets. A log transformation is commonly used for independent variables that can take a wide range of values; company size and fund size are two such variables. One reason to use the log transformation is to improve the statistical properties of the residuals. If the authors had not taken the log of assets and instead used assets as the independent variable, the regression model probably would not have explained RANVA as well.

$Size_i$ is the base 10 log of average assets, an increase of 1 in Size is the same as a 10-fold increase in fund assets.

Of course, a causal relation between size and RANVA is not at all clear: Funds that are more successful may attract more assets. This regression equation is consistent with those results, as well as the result that larger funds perform better. On one hand, we could argue that larger funds are more successful. On the other hand, we could argue that more successful funds attract more assets and become larger.

Now suppose we want to test the null hypothesis that passive management is not related to RANVA; we want to test whether the coefficient on the fraction of assets under passive management equals 0 (H_0: $b_2 = 0$) against the alternative hypothesis that the coefficient on the fraction of assets under passive management does not equal 0 (H_a: $b_2 \neq 0$). The t-statistic to test this hypothesis is

$$\frac{\hat{b}_2 - b_2}{s_{\hat{b}_2}} = \frac{0.8 - 0}{0.42} = 1.9$$

The critical value of the t-test is 1.99 at the 0.05 significance level and about 1.66 at the 0.10 level. Therefore, at the 0.10 significance level, we can reject the null hypothesis that passive management has no effect on fund returns; but we cannot do so at the 0.05 significance level. Although researchers typically use a significance level of 0.05 or smaller, these results and others like them are strong enough that many pension plan sponsors have increased the use of passive management for pension fund assets. We can interpret the coefficient on passive management of 0.8 as implying that an increase of 10 percentage points in the proportion of the passively managed fund was associated with a 0.08 percentage point increase (8 basis points) in RANVA for the fund.

2.2 THE STANDARD ERROR OF ESTIMATE IN MULTIPLE LINEAR REGRESSION

Linear regressions with multiple independent variables can differ greatly in how well the independent variables explain the variation in the dependent variable. We need to quantify the difference so that we can understand how well a set of independent variables explains the variation in a particular dependent variable.

The **standard error of estimate** (SEE) is the standard error of the residual. The formula for SEE in the multiple regression model, however, differs slightly from that with a single independent variable. We demonstrate the calculations with reference to Table 9-1, excerpted here:

TABLE 9-1 (EXCERPT)

ANOVA	df	SS	MSS	F	Significance F
Regression	2	0.6264	0.3132	143.7483	3.4194E−37
Residual	169	0.3682 SSE	0.0022		
Total	171	0.9946			
Residual standard error	0.0467				
Multiple R-squared	0.6298				
n	172				

(SSE is the sum of squared residuals or errors.)

$$SEE = \left(\frac{\sum_{t=1}^{T}(Y_t - \hat{b}_0 - \hat{b}_1 X_{1t} - \hat{b}_2 X_{2t} - \ldots - \hat{b}_k X_{kt})^2}{T - (k+1)} \right)^{1/2} = \left(\frac{\sum_{t=1}^{T} \hat{\epsilon}_t^2}{T - (k+1)} \right)^{1/2}$$

$$= \left(\frac{SS_{residual}}{df_{residual}} \right)^{1/2} = \left(\frac{SSE}{df_{residual}} \right)^{1/2} = \left(\frac{0.3682}{169} \right)^{1/2} = 4.67 \text{ percent} \qquad (9\text{-}2)$$

where SS is the sum of squares in Table 9-1, k is the number of independent variables, and SSE is the sum of squared errors or residuals.

For each observation, we compute the difference between the actual value of the dependent variable and its predicted value. This difference is also known as the regression residual, $\hat{\epsilon}_t$. The numerator in the expression for SEE is the sum of the squared residuals; the denominator is $T - (k+1)$.

The SEE formula looks very much like the formula for computing a standard deviation, except that $T - (k+1)$ appears in the denominator instead of $T - 1$. The multiple linear regression model has T observations in the sample and estimates $k + 1$ parameters (b_0, b_1, b_2, ... , b_k). Therefore, the difference between the number of observations and the number of parameters is $T - (k+1)$. This difference, also called the degrees of freedom, is needed in the denominator to ensure that the standard error of estimate is unbiased.[12]

EXAMPLE 9-3.   Computing the Standard Error of Estimate.

In Example 9-1, we explained the return to the Fidelity Select Technology Fund based on the return to the S&P 500/BARRA Growth Index and the S&P 500/BARRA Value Index. In that regression, the sum of the squared residuals from the estimated regression was 0.3682. With three estimated parameters and 172 observations, there were $172 - 3 = 169$ degrees of freedom. Consequently, we calculate the standard error of estimate as

$$\left(\frac{0.3682}{169} \right)^{1/2} = 0.0467$$

Thus the residual standard error is 4.67 percent a month.

The second measure of how well the estimated regression line explains the data is R^2.

$$\text{Note that } R^2 = 1 - \frac{\text{unexplained variation}}{\text{total variation}}$$

$$= 1 - \frac{SS_{residual}}{SS_{total}}$$

$$= 1 - \frac{0.3682}{0.9946}$$

$$= 0.629801$$

From Table 9-1, R^2 was 0.6298. Therefore, almost 40 percent $(1 - 0.6298)$ of the total variation in the return to the FSTF was unexplained by the regression.

---

[12] See Greene (1999).

2.3 PREDICTING THE DEPENDENT VARIABLE IN A MULTIPLE REGRESSION MODEL

Financial analysts often want to predict the value of the dependent variable in a multiple regression based on assumed values of the independent variables. We have previously discussed how to make such a prediction in the case of only one independent variable. The process for making that prediction with multiple linear regression is very similar.

To predict the value of a dependent variable using a multiple linear regression model, we follow these three steps:

1. Obtain estimates $\hat{b}_0, \hat{b}_1, \hat{b}_2, \ldots, \hat{b}_k$ of the regression parameters $b_0, b_1, b_2, \ldots, b_k$.
2. Determine the assumed values of the independent variables, $\hat{X}_{1t}, \hat{X}_{2t}, \ldots, \hat{X}_{kt}$.
3. Compute the predicted value of the dependent variable, $\hat{Y}_t$, using the equation

$$\hat{Y}_t = \hat{b}_0 + \hat{b}_1\hat{X}_{1t} + \hat{b}_2\hat{X}_{2t} + \ldots + \hat{b}_k\hat{X}_{kt} \tag{9-3}$$

EXAMPLE 9-4. Predicting the Return to the Fidelity Select Technology Fund.

In Example 9-1, we explained the return to the FSTF based on the return to the S&P 500/BARRA Growth Index and the S&P 500/BARRA Value Index using the regression FSTF Return$_t$ = b_0 + b_1Growth Return$_t$ + b_2Value Return$_t$ + ϵ_t. Now we can use the results of the regression reported in Table 9-1 (and excerpted here) to predict the return to the FSTF.

TABLE 9-1 (EXCERPT)

	Coefficients	Standard Error	t-Statistic
Intercept	−0.0043	0.0038	−1.1401
S&P 500/BARRA Growth Index	1.3342	0.1825	7.3105
S&P 500/BARRA Value Index	−0.0519	0.2052	−0.2531

Suppose that in a particular month, the return to the S&P 500/BARRA Growth Index was 1 percent and the return to the S&P 500/BARRA Value Index was 2 percent. In this case, the predicted return to the FSTF for that month, based on the regression, is −0.0043 + (1.3342 × 0.01) + (−0.0519 × 0.02) = 0.0080. Therefore, the regression predicts that the return to the FSTF will be 0.80 percent in a month when the return to the growth index is 1 percent and the return to the value index is 2 percent.

When predicting the dependent variable using a linear regression model, we encounter two types of uncertainty: uncertainty in the regression model itself, as reflected in the standard error of estimate, and uncertainty about the estimates of the regression model's parameters. In the chapter on correlation and regression, we presented procedures for constructing a prediction interval for linear regression with one independent variable. For multiple regression, however, computing a prediction interval to properly incorporate both types of uncertainty requires matrix algebra, which is outside the scope of this book.[13]

---

[13] For more information on using matrix algebra, see Greene (1999).

2.4 TESTING WHETHER ALL POPULATION REGRESSION COEFFICIENTS ARE EQUAL TO ZERO

Earlier, we illustrated how to conduct hypothesis tests on regression coefficients individually. Our focus in this section is on the significance of the regression as a whole. As a group, do the independent variables help explain the dependent variable? To address this question, we test the null hypothesis that all the slope coefficients in a regression are simultaneously equal to 0. In this section, we discuss **analysis of variance (ANOVA),** which provides information on the explanatory power of a regression and the inputs for an F-test of the above null hypothesis.

If none of the independent variables in a regression model helps explain the dependent variable, the slope coefficients should not be significantly different from 0. To test the null hypothesis that all of the slope coefficients in the multiple regression model are jointly equal to 0 (H_0: $b_1 = b_2 = \ldots = b_k = 0$) against the alternative hypothesis that at least one slope coefficient is not equal to 0, we must use an F-test to perform an analysis of variance.

To correctly calculate the test statistic for the null hypothesis, we need four inputs:

- total number of observations (n);
- total number of parameters to be estimated ($k + 1$);
- sum of squared errors or residuals $\sum_{i=1}^{n} (Y_i - \hat{Y}_i)^2$, abbreviated SSE, also known as the residual sum of squares;[14] and
- regression sum of squares $\sum_{i=1}^{n} (\hat{Y}_i - \overline{Y})^2$, abbreviated RSS.[15] This amount is the variation in Y from its mean that the regression equation explains.

The F-test for determining whether the slope coefficients equal 0 is based on an F-statistic calculated using the four values listed above.[16] The F-statistic measures how well the regression equation explains the variation in the dependent variable; it is the ratio of the average regression sum of squares to the average sum of the squared errors.

We compute the average regression sum of squares by dividing the regression sum of squares by the number of slope parameters estimated, k. We compute the average sum of squared errors by dividing the sum of squared errors by the number of observations, n, minus the total number of parameters estimated. The two divisors in these computations are the degrees of freedom for calculating an F-statistic. For n observations and k slope coefficients, the F-test for the null hypothesis that the slope coefficients are all equal to 0 is denoted $F_{k,n-(k+1)}$. The subscript indicates that the test should have k degrees of freedom in the numerator (*numerator degrees of freedom*) and $n - (k + 1)$ degrees of freedom in the denominator (*denominator degrees of freedom*).

The formula for the F-statistic is

$$F = \frac{\dfrac{RSS}{k}}{\dfrac{SSE}{[n - (k + 1)]}} = \frac{\text{Mean regression sum of squares}}{\text{Mean squared error}} = \frac{MSR}{MSE} \qquad (9\text{-}4)$$

where MSR is the mean regression sum of squares and MSE is the mean squared error. If the regression model does a good job of explaining variation in the dependent variable,

---

[14] In a table of regression output, this is the number under the "SS" column, in the row "Residual."

[15] In a table of regression output, this is the number under the "SS" column, in the row "Regression."

[16] F-tests are described in further detail in the chapter on hypothesis testing.

then this ratio will be large. The explained regression sum of squares for each estimated parameter is large relative to the unexplained variation for each degree of freedom.

What does this F-test tell us when the independent variables in a regression model explain none of the variation in the dependent variable? In this case, each predicted value in the regression model, $\hat{Y}_i$, has the average value of the dependent variable, $\overline{Y}$, and the regression sum of squares, $\sum_{i=1}^{n} (\hat{Y}_i - \overline{Y})^2$, is 0. Therefore, the F-statistic for testing the null hypothesis (that all the slope coefficients are equal to 0) has a value of 0 when the independent variables do not explain the dependent variable.

Now we can return to Example 9-1 and test whether returns to the FSTF can be explained by returns to the S&P 500/BARRA Growth Index and returns to the S&P 500/BARRA Value Index. Table 9-1 (excerpted here) presents the results of variance computations for this regression.

TABLE 9-1 (EXCERPT)

ANOVA	df	SS	MSS	F	Significance F
Regression	2	0.6264	0.3132	143.7483	3.4194E−37
Residual	169	0.3682	0.0022		
Total	171	0.9946			

This model has two slope coefficients ($k = 2$), so the number of degrees of freedom in the numerator of this F-test is 2. With 172 observations in the sample, the number of degrees of freedom in the denominator of the F-test is $n - (k + 1) = 172 - 3 = 169$. The sum of the squared errors is 0.3682. The regression sum of squares is 0.6264. Therefore, the F-test for the null hypothesis that the two slope coefficients in this model equal 0 is

$$\frac{\dfrac{0.6264}{2}}{\dfrac{0.3682}{169}} = 143.75$$

This test statistic is distributed as an $F_{2,169}$ random variable under the null hypothesis that the slope coefficients are equal to 0.

Suppose we set the significance level for this test to 0.05 (i.e., a 5 percent probability that we will reject the null hypothesis if it is true). Note that we use a one-tailed F-test.[17] Appendix D provides the critical values for F-statistic significance; we look at the second column, which shows F-distributions with two degrees of freedom in the numerator. Near the bottom of the column, we find that the critical value of the F-test needed to reject the null hypothesis is between 3.00 and 3.07.[18] The actual value of the F-test statistic is 143.75, so we can clearly reject at the 0.05 level the null hypothesis that the growth and value indexes have no relation with the return to the FSTF. In fact, Table 9-1, under

---

[17] A one-tailed test is used because MSR necessarily increases relative to MSE as the explanatory power of the regression increases.

[18] We see a range of values because the denominator has more than 120 degrees of freedom. (Of course, the denominator does not have an infinite number of degrees of freedom.)

"Significance F," reports a p-value of 3.4194×10^{-37}. This p-value means that the smallest level of significance at which the null hypothesis can be rejected is 3.4194×10^{-37}, which is close to zero. The large value for this F-statistic implies a minuscule probability of incorrectly rejecting the null hypothesis (a mistake known as a Type I error).

2.5 Is R^2 Related to Statistical Significance?

We cannot look only at R^2 to determine whether a regression model is well specified (whether it fits well). Unfortunately, R^2 by itself does not tell us whether a regression model is correctly specified. Remember, R^2 is

$$\frac{\text{Total variation} - \text{Unexplained variation}}{\text{Total variation}}$$

Each time we add regression variables to the model, the amount of unexplained variation will decrease if the new independent variable explains any of the unexplained variation in the model. Such a reduction occurs when the new independent variable is even slightly correlated with the dependent variable and is not a linear combination of other independent variables in the regression.[19] Consequently, we can increase R^2 simply by including many additional independent variables that explain even a slight amount of the model's previously unexplained variation, even if they are statistically insignificant.

An alternative measure of equation fit used by some financial analysts is **adjusted R^2,** or $\bar{R}^2$. This measure of fit does not automatically increase when another variable is added to a regression; it is adjusted for degrees of freedom. Adjusted R^2 is typically part of the multiple regression output produced by statistical software packages.

The relation between R^2 and $\bar{R}^2$ is

$$\bar{R}^2 = 1 - \left(\frac{n-1}{n-k}\right)(1 - R^2)$$

where n is the number of observations and k is the number of regression parameters. Note that if $k = 1$ (one independent variable), $R^2 = \bar{R}^2$. If k is greater than one, adjusted R^2 is less than or equal to the unadjusted R^2. When a new independent variable is added, $\bar{R}^2$ can decrease if adding that variable has only a small effect on R^2. In fact, $\bar{R}^2$ can actually be negative if the correlation between the dependent variable and the independent variables is sufficiently low.

3 USING DUMMY VARIABLES IN REGRESSIONS

Often, financial analysts need to use qualitative variables as independent variables in a regression. One type of qualitative variable, called a **dummy variable,** takes on a value of 1 if a particular condition is true and 0 if that condition is false.[20] For example, suppose we want to test whether stock returns were different in January than during the remaining months of the year. We include one independent variable in the regression, X_{1t}, which has a value of 1 for each January and a value of 0 for every other month of the year. We estimate the regression model

---

[19] We say that variable y is a linear combination of variables x and z if $y = ax + bz$ for some constants a and b. A variable can also be a linear combination of more than two variables.

[20] Not all qualitative variables are simple dummy variables. For example, in a trinomial choice model (a model with three choices), a qualitative variable might have the value 0, 1, or 2.

$$Y_t = b_0 + b_1 X_{1t} + \epsilon_t$$

In this equation, the coefficient b_0 is the average value of Y_t in months other than January and b_1 is the difference between the average value of Y_t in January and the average value of Y_t in months other than January.

We need to exercise care in choosing the number of dummy variables in a regression. The rule is that if we want to distinguish between n categories, we need $n - 1$ dummy variables. For example, to distinguish between *during January* and *not during January* above ($n = 2$ categories), we used one dummy variable ($n - 1 = 2 - 1 = 1$). If we want to distinguish between each of the four quarters in a year, as in Example 9-5 below, we would include dummy variables for three of the four quarters in a year. Example 9-5 shows that if we make the mistake of including dummy variables for four rather than three quarters, Assumption 2 of the multiple regression model is violated and we cannot estimate the regression.

EXAMPLE 9-5.   Understanding Dummy Variables.

Table 9-3 shows data for eight quarterly observations of the dependent variable, Y_i; a constant equal to 1, representing the independent variable associated with the intercept in the regression; and the quarterly dummy variables ($X_{1t}, X_{2t}, X_{3t},$ and X_{4t}). The first dummy variable, X_{1t}, has a value of 1 for the first quarterly observation and 0 for the other observations. The second dummy variable, X_{2t}, has a value of 1 for the second quarterly observation and 0 for the other observations. The values for the other dummy variables are determined in the same way.

TABLE 9-3   A Display of Qualitative Independent Variables ($n = 8$)

			Variable			
Observations	Y_t	Constant	X_{1t}	X_{2t}	X_{3t}	X_{4t}
1	1	1	1	0	0	0
2	2	1	0	1	0	0
3	3	1	0	0	1	0
4	4	1	0	0	0	1
5	1	1	1	0	0	0
6	2	1	0	1	0	0
7	3	1	0	0	1	0
8	4	1	0	0	0	1
Mean	2.5					

In this example, we demonstrate three concepts: First, we show the relation between the estimated value for a single dummy variable and the value of the dependent variable during different time periods. Second, we show the relation between the estimated values for multiple dummy variables and the value of the dependent variable during different time periods. Third, we explain the consequences of including too many dummy variables in a regression.

Suppose we estimate the equation $Y_t = b_0 + \epsilon_t$. The estimated value of b_0 is the average value of the dependent variable, 2.5. Now suppose we estimate $Y_t = b_0 + b_1 X_{1t} + \epsilon_t$. The estimated value of b_0, 3.0, is the average value of the dependent variable for all quarters except the first quarter. The estimated value of b_1, -2.0, is the difference between the average value of the dependent variable for the first quarter, 1.0, and the average value of the dependent variable for all quarters except the first quarter (the value of b_0, 3.0). That is, $1.0 - 3.0 = -2.0$ is the estimated value of b_1.

Referring again to Table 9-3, suppose we estimate $Y_t = b_0 + b_1 X_{1t} + b_2 X_{2t} + b_3 X_{3t} + \epsilon_t$. In this case, the estimated value of b_0 is the average value of the dependent variable for all quarters for which a dummy variable is not included. Because the only quarter for which a dummy variable is not included is the fourth quarter, the estimated value of b_0 is 4.0. The estimated value of b_1, -3.0, is the difference between the average value of the dependent variable for the first quarter, 1.0, and the value of b_0, 4.0. The estimated value of b_2, -2.0, is the difference between the average value of the dependent variable for the second quarter, 2.0, and the value of b_0, 4.0. The estimated value of b_3, -1.0, is the difference between the average value of the dependent variable for the third quarter, 3.0, and the value of b_0, 4.0. Thus the regression equation is $y_t = 4 - 3X_1 - 2X_2 - X_3$.

Note that we cannot estimate $Y_t = b_0 + b_1 X_{1t} + b_2 X_{2t} + b_3 X_{3t} + b_{4t} X_{4t} + \epsilon_t$, because $X_{1t} + X_{2t} + X_{3t} + X_{4t} = 1$. Any one of the independent variables can be stated as a linear function of the remaining independent variables, violating Assumption 2 of the multiple linear regression model.

The next example illustrates the use of dummy variables in a regression using monthly data.

EXAMPLE 9-6. Month-of-the-Year Effects on Small Stock Returns.

Financial analysts have been concerned for some time about seasonality in stock returns.[21] In particular, analysts have researched whether returns to small stocks differ during various months of the year. For example, suppose we want to test whether total returns to one small-stock index, the Russell 2000 Index, differ by month. Using data from January 1979 (the first available date for the Russell 2000 data) through the end of 1998, we can estimate a regression including an intercept and 11 dummy variables, one for each of the first 11 months of the year. The equation that we estimate is

$$\text{Returns}_t = b_0 + b_1 \text{Jan}_t + b_2 \text{Feb}_t + \ldots + b_{11} \text{Nov}_t + \epsilon_t$$

where each monthly dummy has a value of 1 when the month occurs (e.g., $\text{Jan}_1 = \text{Jan}_{13} = 1$, as the first observation is a January) and a value of 0 for the other months. Table 9-4 shows the results of this regression.

The intercept, b_0, measures the average return for stocks in December (2.58 percent) because there is no dummy variable for December.[22] Each of the dummy

---

[21] For a discussion of this issue, see Siegel (1998).

[22] When $\text{Jan}_t = \text{Feb}_t = \ldots = \text{Nov}_t = 0$, the month is December and the regression equation simplifies to $\text{Returns}_t = b_0 + \epsilon_t$. Because $E(\text{Returns}_t) = b_0 + E(\epsilon_t) = b_0$, the intercept b_0 represents the mean return for December.

TABLE 9-4   Results from Regressing Russell 2000 Returns on Month Dummies

	Coefficients	Standard Error	t-Statistic
Intercept	0.0258	0.0123	2.1029
January	0.0087	0.0174	0.4986
February	−0.0026	0.0174	−0.1498
March	−0.0141	0.0174	−0.8122
April	−0.0125	0.0174	−0.7175
May	−0.0030	0.0174	−0.1704
June	−0.0196	0.0174	−1.1269
July	−0.0251	0.0174	−1.4473
August	−0.0176	0.0174	−1.0131
September	−0.0230	0.0174	−1.3246
October	−0.0395	0.0174	−2.2718
November	−0.0030	0.0174	−0.1700

ANOVA	df	SS	MSS	F	Significance F
Regression	11	0.0392	0.0036	1.1810	0.3012
Residual	228	0.6876	0.0030		
Total	239	0.7267			
Residual standard error		0.0549			
Multiple R-squared		0.0539			
n		240			

Source for data: Ibbotson Associates

variables shows the estimated difference between returns in that month and returns for December. So, for example, the estimated additional return in January is b_1 which is 0.87 percent higher than December. This gives a January return prediction of 3.45 percent (2.58 December + 0.87 additional).

The low R^2 in this regression (0.0539), however, suggests that a month-of-the-year effect in small-stock returns may not be very important for explaining small-stock returns. We can use the F-test to analyze the null hypothesis that jointly, the monthly dummies all equal 0 (H_0: $b_1 = b_2 = \ldots = b_{11} = 0$). We are testing for significant monthly variation in small-stock returns. Table 9-4 shows the data needed to perform an analysis of variance. The number of degrees of freedom in the numerator of the F-test is 11; the number of degrees of freedom in the denominator is $[240 - (11 + 1)] = 228$. The regression sum of squares equals 0.0392, and the sum of squared errors equals 0.6876. Therefore, the F-statistic to determine whether all of the regression slope coefficients are jointly equal to 0 is

$$\frac{\dfrac{0.0392}{11}}{\dfrac{0.6876}{228}} = 1.18$$

Appendix D shows the critical values for this F-test. If we choose a significance level of 0.05 and look in Column 11 (because the numerator has 11 degrees of freedom), we see that the critical value is 1.87 when the denominator has 120 degrees of freedom. The denominator actually has 228 degrees of freedom, so the critical value of the F-statistic is smaller than 1.87 (for df = 120) but larger than 1.79 (for an infinite number of degrees of freedom). The value of the test statistic is 1.18, so we clearly cannot reject the null hypothesis that all of the coefficients are jointly equal to 0.

The p-value of 0.3012 shown for the F-test in Table 9-4 means that the smallest level of significance at which we can reject the null hypothesis is roughly 0.30, or 30 percent—far above the conventional level of 5 percent. Among the 11 monthly dummy variables, only October has a t-statistic with an absolute value greater than 2. Although the coefficient for the October dummy is statistically significant, we have so many insignificant estimated coefficients that we cannot reject the null hypothesis (that returns are equal across the months). This test suggests that the significance of one or two coefficients in this regression model may be the result of random variation. We may thus want to avoid portfolio strategies calling for differing investment weights for small stocks in different months.

EXAMPLE 9-7. Determinants of Spreads on New High-Yield Bonds.

Fridson and Garman (1998) used data from 1995 and 1996 to examine variables that may explain the initial yield spread between a newly issued high-yield bond and a Treasury bond with similar maturity. They built a model of yield spreads using variables that affect the creditworthiness and interest-rate risk of the bond. Their model included the following factors:

- Rating: Moody's senior-equivalent rating
- Zero-coupon status: Dummy variable (0 = no, 1 = yes)
- BB–B spread: Yield differential (Merrill Lynch Single-B Index minus Double-B Index, in basis points)
- Seniority: Dummy variable (0 = senior, 1 = subordinated)
- Callability: Dummy variable (0 = noncallable, 1 = callable)
- Term: Maturity (years)
- First-time issuer: Dummy variable (0 = no, 1 = yes)
- Underwriter type: Dummy variable (0 = investment bank, 1 = commercial bank)
- Interest rate change

Table 9-5 shows the authors' results.

TABLE 9-5   Multiple Regression Model of New High-Yield Issue Spread: 1995–96

	Coefficient	Standard Error	t-Statistic
Intercept	−213.67	63.03	−3.39
Rating	66.19	4.13	16.02
Zero-coupon status	136.54	32.82	4.16
BB–B spread	95.31	24.82	3.84
Seniority	41.46	11.95	3.47
Callability	51.65	15.42	3.35
Term	−8.51	2.71	−3.14
First-time issuer	25.23	10.97	2.30
Underwriter type	28.13	12.67	2.22
Interest-rate change	40.44	19.08	2.12
R-squared	0.56		
Observations	428		

Source: Fridson and Garman (1998)

We can summarize Fridson and Garman's findings as follows:

- Bond rating has the highest significance level of any coefficient in the regression. This result should not be surprising, because the rating captures rating agencies' estimates of the risk involved with the bond.
- Zero-coupon status increases the yield spread because zero-coupon bonds have more interest-rate risk than coupon bonds of a similar maturity.
- The BB–B spread affects yields because it captures the market's evaluation of how much influence rating differentials have on credit risk.
- Seniority affects yields because subordinated debt has much lower recovery rates in the case of default.
- Callability increases yields because it limits the upside potential on the bond if yields decline.
- Term actually reduces the yield spread. Perhaps term enters with a negative coefficient because the market is willing to buy long-term debt only from high-quality companies; lower-quality companies must issue shorter-term debt.
- First-time issuers must pay a premium because the market does not know much about them.
- Bonds underwritten by commercial banks have a premium over bonds underwritten by investment banks, most likely because the market believes that investment banks have a competitive edge in attracting high-quality corporate clients.
- Interest-rate increases in Treasuries during the previous month cause yield spreads to widen, presumably because the market believes that increasing interest rates will worsen the economic prospects of companies issuing high-yield debt.

Note that all of the coefficients in this regression model are statistically significant at the 0.05 level. The smallest absolute value of a *t*-statistic in this table is 2.12.

4 HETEROSKEDASTICITY

So far, we have made an important assumption that the variance of error in a regression is constant across observations. In statistical terms, we assumed that the errors were homoskedastic. Errors in financial data, however, are often **heteroskedastic;** the variance of the errors differs across observations. In this section, we discuss how heteroskedasticity affects statistical analysis, how to test for heteroskedasticity, and how to correct for it.

We can see the difference between homoskedastic and heteroskedastic errors by comparing two graphs. Figure 9-1 shows the values of the dependent and independent variables and a fitted regression line for a model with homoskedastic errors. There is no systematic relationship between the value of the independent variable and the regression residuals (the vertical distance between one of the plotted points and the fitted regression line). Figure 9-2 shows the values of the dependent and independent variables and a fitted regression line for a model with heteroskedastic errors. Here, a systematic relationship is visually apparent: On average, the regression residuals grow much larger as the size of the independent variable increases.

FIGURE 9-1 Regression with Homoskedasticity

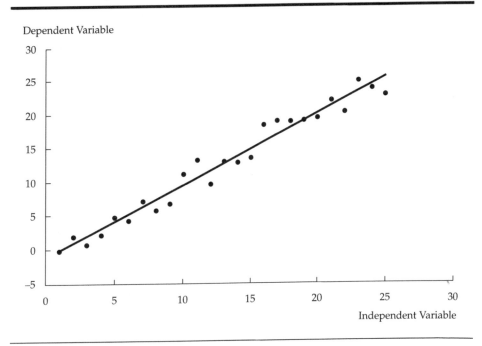

Although heteroskedasticity does not affect the accuracy of the regression parameter estimates, it can have a large effect on both the standard errors for the regression coeffi-

FIGURE 9-2   Regression with Heteroskedasticity

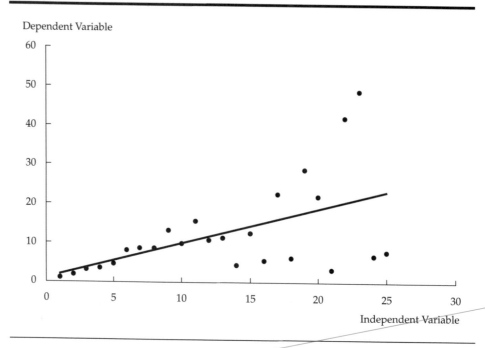

cients and the outcomes of t-tests for hypotheses about a regression equation.[23] If a regression shows significant heteroskedasticity, the standard errors and test statistics computed by regression programs will be incorrect unless they are adjusted for heteroskedasticity.

In regressions with financial data, the most likely result of heteroskedasticity is that the estimated standard errors will be too small and the t-statistics will be too large. When we ignore heteroskedasticity, we tend to find significant relationships where none actually exist.[24] This bias might lead us to adopt a suboptimal investment strategy when a more careful statistical analysis would result in an optimal strategy.

EXAMPLE 9-8.   Tests That Evaluate Heteroskedasticity on Investment Strategies.

MacKinlay and Richardson (1991) examined how heteroskedasticity affects tests of the capital asset pricing model (CAPM).[25] These authors argued that if the CAPM is correct, they should find no significant differences in the risk-adjusted returns for holding small stocks or large stocks. To implement their test, MacKinlay and

---

[23] The use of the term *accuracy* in this sentence is helpful for a general understanding but does not exactly capture the meaning of the technically correct term, *consistency*. Informally, an estimator of a regression parameter is consistent if the probability that regression parameter estimates differ from the true value of the parameter decreases as the number of observations used in the regression increases. The regression parameter estimates from ordinary least squares (OLS) are consistent regardless of whether the errors are heteroskedastic or homoskedastic. See the chapter on sampling and, for a more advanced discussion, see Greene (1999).

[24] Sometimes, however, failure to adjust for heteroskedasticity results in standard errors that are too large (and t-statistics that are too small).

[25] For more on the CAPM, see Bodie, Kane, and Marcus (1999), for example.

Richardson split all stocks on the New York and American exchanges into market-value deciles with annual reassignment. They then tested for systematic differences in risk-adjusted returns across market-capitalization-based stock portfolios. They estimated the following regression:

$$r_{i,t} = \alpha_i + \beta_i r_{m,t} + \epsilon_{i,t}$$

where

$r_{i,t}$ = excess return (return above the risk-free rate) to portfolio i in period t
$r_{m,t}$ = excess return to the market as a whole in period t

The CAPM implies that $\alpha_i = 0$ for every i; no excess return accrues to any portfolio after taking into account its systematic (market) risk.

Using data from January 1926 to December 1988 and a market index based on equal-weighted returns, MacKinlay and Richardson failed to reject the CAPM at the 0.05 level when they assumed that the errors in the regression model are normally distributed and homoskedastic. They found, however, that they could reject the CAPM when they corrected their test statistics to account for heteroskedasticity. They rejected the hypothesis that there are no size-based, risk-adjusted excess returns in historical data.[26]

4.1 TYPES OF HETEROSKEDASTICITY

Although heteroskedasticity can cause problems for statistical inference in the linear regression model, not all types of heteroskedasticity affect statistical inference. **Unconditional heteroskedasticity** occurs when the heteroskedasticity is not correlated with the independent variables in the multiple regression. Although this form of heteroskedasticity violates Assumption 4 of the linear regression model, it creates no major problems for statistical inference.

The type of heteroskedasticity that causes the most problems for statistical inference is **conditional heteroskedasticity**—heteroskedasticity in the error variance that is correlated with (conditional on) the values of the independent variables in the regression. Fortunately, many statistical software packages easily test and correct for conditional heteroskedasticity. The following example illustrates these calculations. In this example, we demonstrate the Breusch–Pagan test for conditional heteroskedasticity.

EXAMPLE 9-9. Testing for Conditional Heteroskedasticity in Commercial-Paper Rates.

Suppose we want to examine the effect of inflation on commercial-paper (CP) interest rates. We use monthly data from January 1972 to June 1999 on CP rates (expressed as annual percentage rates) and inflation (expressed as seasonally adjusted annual rates measured by the CPI). We then regress the CP rate on inflation. The regression equation is

$$\text{CP Rate}_t = b_0 + b_1 \text{Inflation}_t + \epsilon_t$$

---

[26] MacKinlay and Richardson also show that, when using value-weighted returns, the CAPM is rejected whether or not one assumes normally distributed returns and homoskedasticity.

Table 9-6 shows the regression results.

TABLE 9-6   Results from Regressing the CP Rate on Inflation

	Coefficients	Standard Error	t-Statistic
Intercept	5.3628	0.2343	22.8875
Inflation	0.3962	0.0348	11.3898
Residual standard error		2.6328	
Multiple R-squared		0.2834	
n		330	
Durbin-Watson statistic		0.3100	

Source for data: Ibbotson Associates

Suppose we have a colleague who believes that a 100 basis point change in the inflation rate will be reflected in a 50 basis point change in the CP rate. We want to test the null hypothesis that the coefficient on the inflation term is 0.5 ($H_0: b_1 = 0.5$) against the alternative—that the coefficient on the inflation term is not 0.5 ($H_a: b_1 \neq 0.5$). We can easily reject the null hypothesis that the true value of the slope coefficient in this regression is 0.5 by computing the following t-statistic to test the null hypothesis:

$$\frac{\hat{b}_1 - b_1}{s_{\hat{b}_1}} = \frac{0.3962 - 0.5}{0.0348} = -2.983$$

With a t-statistic of -2.983 and $330 - 2 = 328$ degrees of freedom, the critical t-value is about 1.97. We can reject at the 0.05 significance level the hypothesis that the true coefficient in this regression is 0.5. Unfortunately, this result could be erroneous, because the test assumes that any errors in the CP regression were homoskedastic. If those errors prove to be conditionally heteroskedastic, then this test is invalid.

Breusch and Pagan (1979) suggested the following test for conditional heteroskedasticity: Regress the squared residuals from the estimated regression equation on the independent variables in the regression. If no conditional heteroskedasticity exists, the independent variables will not explain much of the variation in the squared residuals. If conditional heteroskedasticity is present in the original regression, however, the independent variables will explain a significant portion of the variation in the squared residuals. The independent variables can explain the variation because the squared residual for each period will be correlated with the independent variables if the independent variables affect the variance of the errors.

Breusch and Pagan showed that, under the null hypothesis of no conditional heteroskedasticity, $n \times R^2$ (from the regression of the squared residuals on the independent variables from the original regression) will be a χ^2 random variable with the number of degrees of freedom equal to the number of independent variables in the regression.[27] Therefore, the null hypothesis states that the regression's squared error

[27] The Breusch–Pagan test is distributed as a χ^2 random variable in large samples. The constant 1 technically associated with the intercept term in a regression is not counted here in computing the number of independent variables. For more on the Breusch–Pagan test, see Greene (1999).

term is uncorrelated with the independent variables. The alternative hypothesis states that the squared error term is correlated with the independent variables.

We can perform the **Breusch–Pagan test** for conditional heteroskedasticity on the squared residuals from the CP rate regression. The test regresses the squared residuals on the inflation rate.[28] The R^2 in the squared residuals regression (not shown here) is 0.0228. The test statistic from this regression, $n \times R^2$, is $330 \times 0.0228 = 7.524$. Under the null hypothesis of no conditional heteroskedasticity, this test statistic is a χ^2 random variable with one degree of freedom (because there is only one independent variable).

We should be concerned about heteroskedasticity only if the value of the test statistic is larger than it would be under the null hypothesis. Therefore, we should use a one-tailed test to determine whether we can reject the null hypothesis. Appendix C shows that the critical value of the test statistic for a variable from a χ^2 distribution with one degree of freedom at the 0.05 significance level is 3.84. The test statistic from the Breusch–Pagan test is 7.524, so we can reject the hypothesis of no conditional heteroskedasticity at the 0.05 level. In fact, we can even reject the hypothesis of no heteroskedasticity at the 0.01 significance level, because the critical value of the test statistic in that case is 6.63. As a result, we can conclude that the commercial-paper regression contains statistically significant conditional heteroskedasticity. We can also conclude that the standard errors computed in the original regression are not correct, because they do not account for heteroskedasticity.[29]

4.2 CORRECTING FOR HETEROSKEDASTICITY

Financial analysts need to know how to correct for heteroskedasticity, because such a correction may reverse the conclusions about a particular hypothesis test—and thus affect a particular investment decision. (In Example 9-8, for instance, MacKinlay and Richardson reversed their investment conclusions after correcting their model's significance tests for heteroskedasticity.)

We can use two different methods to correct the effects of conditional heteroskedasticity in linear regression models. The first method, computing robust standard errors, corrects the standard errors of the linear regression model's estimated parameters to account for the conditional heteroskedasticity. The second method, generalized least squares, modifies the original equation in an attempt to eliminate the heteroskedasticity. The new, modified regression equation is then estimated under the assumption that heteroskedasticity is no longer a problem.[30] The technical details behind these two methods of correcting for conditional heteroskedasticity are outside the scope of this book.[31] Many statistical software packages can easily compute robust standard errors, however, and we recommend using them.[32]

---

[28] The output from the regression of the squared error term on the independent variables is not presented in this text because the estimated coefficients are not needed for the Breusch–Pagan test. As in all regressions mentioned in this chapter, an intercept term is included.

[29] Although the Breusch–Pagan test for heteroskedasticity is one of the simplest to implement, many other tests for conditional heteroskedasticity are frequently used. One of the most widely used tests is White's (1980) test. For more information on White's test and other tests for heteroskedasticity, see Greene (1999).

[30] Generalized least squares requires econometric expertise to implement correctly on financial data. See Greene (1999), Hansen (1982), and Keane and Runkle (1998).

[31] For more details on both methods, see Greene (1999).

[32] This correction is also known as heteroskedastic-consistent standard errors or White-corrected standard errors.

If we correct the standard errors in Table 9-6 for conditional heteroskedasticity, we get the results shown in Table 9-7. In comparing the standard errors between these tables, note that the standard error for the intercept changes very little but the standard error for the coefficient on inflation (the slope coefficient) increases by about 18.4 percent (from 0.0348 to 0.0412). Note also that the regression coefficients are the same in both tables, because the results in Table 9-7 correct only the standard errors in Table 9-6.

TABLE 9-7   Results from Regressing the CP Rate on Inflation
(Standard Errors Corrected for Conditional Heteroskedasticity)

	Coefficients	Standard Error	t-Statistic
Intercept	5.3628	0.2320	23.1186
Inflation	0.3962	0.0412	9.6286
Residual standard error		2.6328	
Multiple R-squared		0.2834	
n		330	

Source for data: Ibbotson Associates

In this case, our test for conditional heteroskedasticity was statistically significant, and correcting for it had an important (although not huge) effect on the estimated standard errors in the equation. Note, for example, that if we were to test whether the slope coefficient could have a true value of 0.5, the test statistic for that hypothesis would now have a value of $(0.3962 - 0.5)/0.0412 = -2.5194$. In absolute value, this number is still much larger than the critical value of 1.97 needed to reject the null hypothesis that the slope equals 0.5.[33] Thus, in this particular example, even though conditional heteroskedasticity was statistically significant, correcting for it had no effect on the result of the test of the hypothesis about the slope of the inflation coefficient. As shown by Example 9-8, however, sometimes conditional heteroskedasticity alone can greatly affect the results of a hypothesis test and the conclusions that a financial analyst should make about the investment implications of a particular regression.

5   SERIAL CORRELATION

A more common—and potentially more serious—problem than violation of the assumption of homoskedasticity is the violation of the assumption that regression errors are independent across observations. Trying to explain a particular financial relation over a number of periods is risky, because errors in financial regression models are often correlated over time.

When regression errors are correlated across observations, we say that they are **serially correlated** (or autocorrelated). In this section, we discuss three aspects of serial correlation: its effect on statistical inference, tests for it, and methods to correct for it.

5.1   THE CONSEQUENCES OF SERIAL CORRELATION

As with heteroskedasticity, the principal problem caused by serial correlation in a linear regression is an incorrect estimate of the regression coefficient standard errors computed by statistical software packages. As long as none of the independent variables is a lagged value of the dependent variable (a value of the dependent variable from a previous period),

---

[33] Remember, this is a two-tailed test.

then the estimated parameters themselves will be accurate (consistent) and need not be adjusted for the effects of serial correlation. If, however, one of the independent variables is a lagged value of the dependent variable—for example, if the CP rate from the previous month was an independent variable in the CP regression—then serial correlation in the error term will cause all the parameter estimates from linear regression to be inaccurate (inconsistent) and they will not be valid estimates of the true parameters. In this chapter, we assume that none of the independent variables is a lagged value of the dependent variable.[34]

Assuming that none of the independent variables is a lagged value of the dependent variable, the effect of serial correlation appears in the regression coefficient standard errors. We will examine it here for the positive serial correlation case, because that case is so common. **Positive serial correlation** is serial correlation in which a positive error for one observation increases the probability of a positive error for the next observation. Positive serial correlation also means that a negative error in one period is likely to be followed by a negative error in the next period.[35] Although the estimated parameters may be accurate, the standard errors for the coefficients are affected by positive serial correlation. Typically, positive serial correlation causes the OLS standard errors for the coefficients to underestimate the true standard errors. As a consequence, if positive serial correlation is present in the regression, standard linear regression analysis will lead us to compute artificially small standard errors for the regression parameters. These small standard errors will cause the estimated t-statistics to be inflated, suggesting significance where perhaps there is none. The inflated t-statistics may, in turn, lead us to incorrectly reject null hypotheses about parameters of the regression model more often than we would if the standard errors were correctly estimated. This Type I error could lead to improper investment recommendations.[36]

5.2 TESTING FOR SERIAL CORRELATION

We can choose from a variety of tests for serial correlation in a regression model,[37] but the most common is based on the Durbin-Watson statistic; in fact, many statistical software packages compute the Durbin-Watson statistic automatically. The equation for the Durbin-Watson test statistic is

$$DW = \frac{\sum_{t=2}^{T} (\hat{\epsilon}_t - \hat{\epsilon}_{t-1})^2}{\sum_{t=1}^{T} \hat{\epsilon}_t^2} \tag{9-5}$$

where $\hat{\epsilon}_t$ is the regression residual for period t.

---

[34] We address this issue in the chapter on time-series analysis.

[35] By contrast, with **negative serial correlation,** a positive error in one period increases the probability of a negative error in the next period, and a negative error in one period increases the probability of a positive error in the next period.

[36] OLS standard errors need not be underestimates of actual standard errors if negative serial correlation is present in the regression. (Negative serial correlation occurs when the error from one observation has a negative correlation with the error from the next observation.) Positive serial correlation is so common in time-series data that we focus on it here.

[37] See Greene (1999) for a detailed discussion of tests of serial correlation.

Because the average value of the residual is 0, we can rewrite this equation as

$$\frac{\frac{1}{T-1}\sum_{t=2}^{T}(\hat{\epsilon}_t^2 - 2\hat{\epsilon}_t\hat{\epsilon}_{t-1} + \hat{\epsilon}_{t-1}^2)}{\frac{1}{T-1}\sum_{t=1}^{T}\hat{\epsilon}_t^2} \approx \frac{\text{Var}(\hat{\epsilon}_t) - 2\,\text{Cov}(\hat{\epsilon}_t, \hat{\epsilon}_{t-1}) + \text{Var}(\hat{\epsilon}_{t-1})}{\text{Var}(\hat{\epsilon}_t)}$$

If the variance of the error is constant over time, then $\text{Var}(\hat{\epsilon}_t) = \hat{\sigma}_\epsilon^2$ for all t. If, in addition, the errors are also not serially correlated, then $\text{Cov}(\hat{\epsilon}_t, \hat{\epsilon}_{t-1}) = 0$. In that case, the Durbin-Watson statistic is approximately equal to

$$\frac{\text{Var}(\hat{\epsilon}_t) - 2\,\text{Cov}(\hat{\epsilon}_t, \hat{\epsilon}_{t-1}) + \text{Var}(\hat{\epsilon}_{t-1})}{\text{Var}(\hat{\epsilon}_t)} = \frac{\hat{\sigma}_\epsilon^2 - 0 + \hat{\sigma}_\epsilon^2}{\hat{\sigma}_\epsilon^2} = 2$$

This equation tells us that if the errors are homoskedastic and not serially correlated, then the Durbin-Watson statistic will be close to 2. Therefore, we can test the null hypothesis that the errors are not serially correlated by testing whether the Durbin-Watson statistic is significantly different from 2.

If the sample is very large, the Durbin-Watson statistic will be approximately equal to $2(1 - r)$, where r is the sample correlation between the regression residuals from one period and those from the previous period. This approximation is very useful because it shows the value of the Durbin-Watson statistic for differing levels of serial correlation.

- If the regression has no serial correlation, then the regression residuals will be un-correlated over time and the value of the Durbin-Watson statistic will be equal to $2 \times (1 - 0) = 2$.
- If the regression residuals are positively serially correlated, then the Durbin-Watson statistic will be less than 2. For example, if the serial correlation of the errors is 1, then the value of the Durbin-Watson statistic will be 0.
- If the regression residuals are negatively serially correlated, then the Durbin-Watson statistic will be greater than 2. For example, if the serial correlation of the errors is -1, then the value of the Durbin-Watson statistic will be 4.

We can now return to Example 9-9, which explains the CP rate based on inflation. As shown in Table 9-6, the Durbin-Watson statistic for the ordinary least squares (OLS) re-gression is 0.31. Therefore,

$$\begin{aligned}
\text{DW} &= 0.31 \\
&\approx 2(1 - r) \\
r &= 1 - \text{DW}/2 \\
&= 1 - 0.3100/2 \\
&= 0.845
\end{aligned}$$

Thus, in the regression that tries to explain CP interest rates based on inflation, the residu-als appear to be positively serially correlated. This correlation may significantly affect sta-tistical inference because the OLS standard errors may be incorrect.

We have just seen that in this case the Durbin-Watson statistic is quite small (0.31). But is it small enough to warrant rejecting the null hypothesis of no positive serial correla-tion? Fortunately, Durbin and Watson (1951) showed exactly how to determine whether that hypothesis should be rejected. They showed that we should reject the null hypothesis, H_0 (that the error in the regression equation is uncorrelated with the error in the previous period) if the Durbin-Watson statistic is below a critical value, d^*. Unfortunately, Durbin and Watson also showed that, for a given sample, we cannot know the true critical value, d^*. Instead, we can determine only that d^* lies either between two values, d_u (an upper value) and d_l (a lower value), or outside those values.[38] Figure 9-3 depicts the upper and lower values of d^* as they relate to the results of the Durbin-Watson statistic.

FIGURE 9-3   Value of the Durbin-Watson Statistic

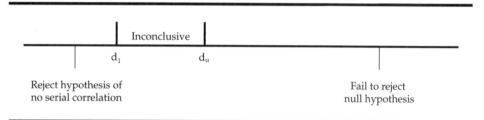

From Figure 9-3, we learn the following:

- When the Durbin-Watson statistic (DW) is less than d_l, we can reject the null hypothesis of no positive serial correlation.
- When DW falls between d_l and d_u, the results of the test are inconclusive.
- When DW is greater than d_u, we fail to reject the null hypothesis of no positive serial correlation.[39]

Returning to our example, the CP rate regression has one independent variable and 330 observations. The Durbin-Watson statistic is 0.31. If we look at Appendix E in the column marked $k = 1$, we see that we can reject the null hypothesis of no correlation at the 0.05 level because the Durbin-Watson statistic is far below d_l for $k = 1$ and $n = 200$ (1.65). The level of d_l would be even higher for a sample of 330 observations. Consequently, we can reject the null hypothesis of no serial correlation in the regression. This finding of significant positive serial correlation suggests that the OLS standard errors in this regression most likely significantly underestimate the true parameter uncertainty in this model.

5.3   CORRECTING FOR SERIAL CORRELATION   As with conditional heteroskedasticity, we have two alternative remedial steps when a regression has significant serial correlation. First, we can adjust the coefficient standard errors for the linear regression parameter estimates to account for the serial correlation. Second, we can modify the regression equation itself to eliminate the serial correlation. We recommend that financial analysts use the first method for dealing with serial correlation; the second method may result in invalid parameter estimates unless implemented with extreme care.

---

[38] Appendix E tabulates the 0.05 significance levels of d_u and d_l for differing numbers of estimated parameters ($k = 1, 2, \ldots, 5$) and time periods between 15 and 200.

[39] Of course, sometimes serial correlation in a regression model is negative rather than positive. For a null hypothesis of no serial correlation, the null hypothesis is rejected if $DW < d_l$ (indicating significant positive serial correlation) or if $DW > 4 - d_l$ (indicating significant negative serial correlation).

The most prevalent method for adjusting standard errors was developed by Hansen (1982) and is a standard feature in many statistical software packages.[40] An additional advantage of Hansen's method is that it simultaneously corrects for conditional heteroskedasticity.[41]

Table 9-8 shows the results of correcting the standard errors from Table 9-6 for serial correlation and heteroskedasticity using Hansen's method. Note that the coefficients for both the intercept and the slope are exactly the same as in the original regression. The robust standard errors are now much larger, however—nearly triple the OLS standard errors. Because of the severe serial correlation in the regression error, OLS greatly underestimates the uncertainty about the estimated parameters in the regression.

Note also that the Durbin-Watson statistic has not changed from Table 9-6. The serial correlation has not been eliminated, but the standard error has been corrected to account for the serial correlation.

TABLE 9-8 Results from Regressing the CP Rate on Inflation
(Standard Errors Corrected for Conditional Heteroskedasticity and Serial Correlation)

	Coefficients	Standard Error	t-Statistic
Intercept	5.3628	0.6469	8.2894
Inflation	0.3962	0.0969	4.0904
Residual standard error		2.6328	
Multiple R-squared		0.2834	
n		330	
Durbin-Watson statistic		0.3100	

Source for data: Ibbotson Associates

Now suppose we want to test our original null hypothesis that the coefficient on the inflation term equals 0.5 (H_0: $b_1 = 0.5$) against the alternative that the coefficient on the inflation term is not equal to 0.5 (H_a: $b_1 \neq 0.5$). With the corrected standard errors, the value of the test statistic for this null hypothesis is

$$\frac{\hat{b}_1 - b_1}{s_{\hat{b}_1}} = \frac{0.3962 - 0.5}{0.0969} = -1.0712$$

The critical values for both the 0.05 and 0.01 significance level are much larger than 1.0712 (absolute value of the t-test statistic), so we cannot reject the null hypothesis.

This conclusion differs from the one we would have made without correcting for serial correlation: Without correcting, we would have falsely rejected the hypothesis that the slope coefficient was equal to 0.5. As a consequence, we would have underestimated the

[40] This correction is known by various names, including serial-correlation consistent standard errors, serial correlation and heteroskedasticity adjusted standard errors, robust standard errors, and Hansen–White standard errors. Analysts may also say that they use the Newey–West method for computing robust standard errors.

[41] We do not always use Hansen's method to correct for serial correlation and heteroskedasticity because sometimes the errors of a regression are not serially correlated.

likely effect of an inflation change on CP rates, to the possible detriment of our portfolio choices.[42]

EXAMPLE 9-10. Predicting Future Spot Rates from Forward Rates.

Managers of international portfolios are often required to anticipate the future value of foreign currencies. We tend to base our projections on the assumption that current forward rates are an unbiased predictor of spot rates in the future, assuming that they are neither too high nor too low, on average. For example, we might assume that the current three-month forward rate for British pounds (denominated in U.S. dollars) is the best predictor of the spot pound–dollar exchange rate three months from now.

We might question, however, whether forward rates give us an accurate forecast. We can test whether the current pound forward rate is, in fact, an unbiased predictor of the future spot rate with data on spot rates and forward rates for the British pound. Specifically, we can use monthly data on three-month forward rates for the British pound (denominated in U.S. dollars) from December 1976 to December 1996. We can then try to determine whether the three-month forward rate is a good predictor of the spot rate three months from now by regressing the spot rate from each period on the three-month forward rate from three months ago.

The regression equation[43] for this analysis is Spot rate$_t$ = b_0 + b_1Forward rate$_{t-3}$ + ϵ_t. Table 9-9 shows the results of this regression. Note that the Durbin-Watson statistic is quite low, suggesting that the residuals in this OLS regression may have significant positive serial correlation.

TABLE 9-9   Results from Regressing British Pound Spot Rates Three Months Ahead on British Pound Three-Month Forward Rates

	Coefficients	Standard Error	t-Statistic
Intercept	0.1516	0.0452	3.3568
Pound forward date	0.9157	0.0263	34.8216
Residual standard error		0.1077	
Multiple R-squared		0.8365	
n		239	
Durbin-Watson statistic		0.5451	

Source for data: Ibbotson Associates

Suppose we want to test the null hypothesis that the errors in this regression are not positively serially correlated against the alternative hypothesis of positive serial correlation. This test will tell us whether we can rely on the estimated standard errors from the linear regression model. (Recall that these standard errors were estimated under the assumption that the errors were not serially correlated.) With one

---

[42] Serial correlation can also affect forecast accuracy. We discuss this issue in the chapter on time series.

[43] Note that the time subscript on the forward rate is $t - 3$ because we are using monthly data and estimating whether the three-month forward rate that occurred three months ago is an unbiased predictor of the current spot rate.

independent variable and 239 observations, the critical value for rejecting the null hypothesis that the errors are serially uncorrelated is at least 1.65 (see Appendix E). The value of the Durbin-Watson statistic is 0.5451, so we reject the hypothesis of no serial correlation at the 0.05 significance level. Therefore, we cannot rely on the estimated coefficient standard errors from linear regression; we must use robust standard errors for proper statistical inference.

Table 9-10 shows the robust standard errors for the coefficients estimated in Table 9-9. Note that the robust standard errors for both regression coefficients are more than 60 percent larger than the OLS estimates of the standard errors. As these results illustrate, relying on OLS standard errors without testing for serial correlation can cause us to underestimate uncertainty about an estimated parameter.[44]

TABLE 9-10   **Results from Regressing British Pound Spot Rates Three Months Ahead on British Pound Three-Month Forward Rates (Corrected for Serial Correlation)**

	Coefficients	Standard Error	t-Statistic
Intercept	0.1516	0.0756	2.0057
Pound forward rate	0.9157	0.0464	19.7183
Residual standard error		0.1077	
Multiple R-squared		0.8365	
n		239	

Source for data: Ibbotson Associates

We can further demonstrate how serial correlation can adversely affect statistical inference by returning to the previous regression and testing the null hypothesis that the slope coefficient in the regression is equal to 1.0 (H_0: $b_1 = 1$) against the alternative hypothesis that the slope coefficient is not equal to 1.0 (H_a: $b_1 \neq 1$). This test tells us whether, for every 1 percentage point increase in the three-month forward rate, the expected spot rate for the British pound three months from now will also increase by 1 percentage point.

When we test this hypothesis using the parameter estimates from OLS as well as the OLS standard errors, the test statistic for testing the null hypothesis, H_0, is

$$\frac{\hat{b}_1 - b_1}{s_{\hat{b}_1}} = \frac{0.9157 - 1}{0.0263} = -3.2053$$

We are testing to see whether the estimated parameter is equal to the hypothesized parameter, 1.0. With 239 observations and two estimated regression coefficients (the intercept and the slope coefficient), the degrees of freedom is 237 and the critical value for this test statistic is about 1.97 at the 0.05 significance level. Because the absolute value of the actual test statistic is greater than the critical value, we reject the null hypothesis at the 0.05 significance level. We conclude that an increase in the forward rate does not lead to a one-for-one increase in the spot rate.

---

[44] The robust standard errors account not only for serial correlation but also for conditional heteroskedasticity.

If we adjust for serial correlation, however, we get a very different answer. Using the robust standard errors in Table 9-10, we calculate the test statistic for the null hypothesis that the slope equals 1 as follows:

$$\frac{\hat{b}_1 - b_1}{s_{\hat{b}_1}} = \frac{0.9157 - 1}{0.0464} = -1.8168$$

The absolute value of the test statistic is only 1.82. Therefore, we cannot reject the null hypothesis that the slope coefficient is equal to 1, because the critical value for rejecting the null hypothesis at the 0.05 significance level is approximately 1.97. We cannot reject the assumption that a 1 percentage point increase in the three-month forward rate for the British pound will be matched by a 1 percentage point increase in the spot rate three months from now.

This example shows that using the incorrect OLS standard errors can result in different conclusions about the null hypothesis than we get relying on the robust standard errors. In this example, using robust standard errors in our analysis could have significant implications for how we manage currency exposure.

6   MULTICOLLINEARITY

One of the greatest difficulties in regression analysis of financial data is that some linear combinations of the independent variables in a regression model may be highly correlated. Data series may be so closely related that the standard errors become quite large, even though the regression equation seems to fit rather well. This problem is known as multicollinearity. Perfect collinearity, a condition obtained when one of the independent variables is an exact linear combination of other independent variables, makes linear regression impossible. We saw a case of perfect collinearity in Example 9-5, where too many dummy variables were included in a regression. More common in practice than perfect collinearity is multicollinearity. **Multicollinearity** occurs when two or more independent variables (or combinations of independent variables) are highly (but not perfectly) correlated with each other. With multicollinearity we can estimate the regression, but the interpretation of the regression output becomes problematic. Consider the following example, which examines how returns to the Fidelity Select Technology Fund depend on the returns to various components of the S&P 500 Index.

EXAMPLE 9-11.   Multicollinearity in Explaining Returns to the Fidelity Select Technology Fund.

Suppose we wish to determine whether returns to the Fidelity Select Technology Fund (FSTF) depend on returns to the S&P 500/BARRA Growth Index or the S&P 500/BARRA Value Index. Table 9-11 shows the results of our regression, which uses data from December 1984 through March 1999. With a standard error of 0.1819, the *t*-statistic on the growth index return is greater than 7.2 and thus is significantly different from 0 at standard significance levels. On the other hand, the *t*-statistic on the value index return is −0.3096 and thus is not statistically significant. This result suggests that the returns to the FSTF are linked to the returns to the growth index and not closely associated with the returns to the value index. The coefficient on the growth index, however, is 1.31. This result indicates that the FSTF is more susceptible to market ups and downs than the growth index. Note also that this regression explains a significant amount of the variation in the returns to the FSTF. Specifically, the R^2 from this regression is 0.6269. Thus, approximately 63 percent of the variation in the returns to the FSTF is explained by returns to the S&P 500/BARRA growth and value indexes.

TABLE 9-11   Results from Regressing the FSTF Returns on the S&P 500/BARRA Growth and Value Indexes

	Coefficients	Standard Error	t-Statistic
Intercept	−0.0043	0.0038	−1.1401
S&P 500/BARRA Growth Index	1.3342	0.1825	7.3105
S&P 500/BARRA Value Index	−0.0519	0.2052	−0.2531

ANOVA	df	SS	MSS	F	Significance F
Regression	2	0.6264	0.3132	143.7483	3.4194E−37
Residual	169	0.3682	0.0022		
Total	171	0.9946			
Residual standard error	0.0467				
Multiple R-squared	0.6298				
n	172				

Source for data: Ibbotson Associates

TABLE 9-12   Results from Regressing FSTF Returns on Returns to the S&P 500/BARRA Growth and Value Indexes and the S&P 500 Index

	Coefficients	Standard Error	t-Statistic
Intercept	−0.0054	0.0039	−1.3885
S&P 500/BARRA Growth Index	−4.2227	4.4185	−0.9557
S&P 500/BARRA Value Index	−5.3677	4.2282	−1.2695
S&P 500 Index	10.8666	8.6331	1.2587

ANOVA	df	SS	MSS	F	Significance F
Regression	3	0.6298	0.2099	96.6917	2.12E−36
Residual	168	0.3648	0.0022		
Total	171	0.9946			
Residual standard error		0.0466			
Multiple R-squared		0.6332			
n		172			

Source for data: Ibbotson Associates

Now suppose we run another linear regression that adds returns to the S&P 500 itself to the returns to the S&P 500/BARRA Growth and Value Indexes. Table 9-12 shows the results of that regression. Note that the R^2 in this regression has changed almost imperceptibly from the R^2 in the previous regression (increasing from 0.6269 to 0.6290), but now the standard errors are much larger. In fact, none of the t-statistics in this regression has an absolute value greater than 1. Adding the return to the S&P 500 to the previous regression does not explain any more of the variance in the returns to the FSTF than the previous regression did, but now none of the coefficients is statistically significant. This odd result is a classic case of multicollinearity, showing a high R^2 (and significant F-statistic) even though the t-statistics on the slope coefficients are insignificant.

Although very high pairwise variable correlations can cause multicollinearity problems, we generally cannot gauge the absence of multicollinearity based on the magnitude of correlations between the independent variables in a regression equation. Pairs of independent variables may not have high correlation, but linear combinations of the variables may still be very highly correlated. If any linear combinations of independent variables are highly correlated, multicollinearity becomes a problem.

The only case in which correlation between variables may be a reasonable indicator of the absence of multicollinearity occurs in a regression with exactly two independent variables. In that case, multicollinearity certainly will not be a problem if the correlation between the two variables is low (say, an absolute value of 0.5 or lower). In that case, the low t-statistics on the two independent variables are not caused by multicollinearity; rather, the independent variables are simply not significant in explaining the variation in the dependent variable.

The most common solution to multicollinearity is excluding one or more of the regression variables. In the example above, we can see that the S&P 500 total returns should not be included if both the S&P 500/BARRA Growth and Value Indexes are included, because the returns to the entire S&P 500 Index are a weighted average of the return to growth stocks and value stocks. In many cases, however, an easy solution to the problem of multicollinearity is not available, and you will need to experiment with including or excluding different independent variables to determine the source of multicollinearity.

7 HETEROSKEDASTICITY, SERIAL CORRELATION, AND MULTICOLLINEARITY: SUMMARIZING THE ISSUES

The previous three sections have discussed some of the problems that heteroskedasticity, serial correlation, and multicollinearity may cause in interpreting regression results. Table 9-13

TABLE 9-13   Problems in Linear Regression and Their Solutions

Problem	Effect	Solution
Heteroskedasticity	Incorrect standard errors	Robust standard errors (corrected for conditional heteroskedasticity)
Serial Correlation	Incorrect standard errors (additional problems if a lagged value of the dependent variable is used as an independent variable)	Robust standard errors (corrected for serial correlation)
Multicollinearity	High R^2 and low t-statistics	Remove one or more independent variables; often no solution based in theory

gives a summary of these problems, the effect they have on the linear regression results (an analyst can see these effects from regression software), and the solutions to these problems.

8 MODELS WITH QUALITATIVE DEPENDENT VARIABLES

Financial analysts often need to be able to explain the outcomes of a qualitative dependent variable. **Qualitative dependent variables** are dummy variables used as dependent variables instead of as independent variables.

For example, to predict whether or not a company will go bankrupt, we need to use a qualitative dependent variable (bankrupt or not) as the dependent variable, and use data on the company's financial performance (e.g., return on equity, debt-to-equity ratio, or debt rating) as independent variables. Unfortunately, linear regression is not the best statistical method to use for estimating such a model. If we use the qualitative dependent variable bankrupt (1) or not bankrupt (0) as the dependent variable in a regression with financial variables as the independent variables, the predicted value of the dependent variable could be much greater than 1 or much lower than 0. Of course, these results would be invalid. The probability of bankruptcy (or of anything, for that matter) cannot be greater than 100 percent or less than 0 percent. Instead of a linear regression model, we should use probit, logit, or discriminant analysis for this kind of estimation.

Probit and **logit models** estimate the probability of a discrete outcome given the values of the independent variables used to explain that outcome. The probit model, which is based on the normal distribution, estimates the probability that $Y = 1$ (a condition is fulfilled) given the value of the independent variable X. The logit model is identical, except that it is based on the logistic distribution rather than the normal distribution.[45] Both models must be estimated using maximum likelihood methods, which are outside the scope of this book.[46]

Another technique to handle qualitative dependent variables is **discriminant analysis**. In his Z-score and Zeta® analysis, Altman (1968 and 1977) reported on the results of discriminant analysis. Altman uses financial ratios to predict the qualitative dependent variable bankruptcy. Discriminant analysis yields a linear function, similar to a regression equation, which can then be used to create an overall score. Based on the score, an observation can be classified into the bankrupt or not bankrupt category.

Qualitative dependent variable models can be useful not only for portfolio management but also for business management. For example, we might want to explain whether a client is likely to continue investing in a company or to withdraw assets from the company. We might also want to explain how particular demographic characteristics might affect the probability that a potential investor would sign on as a new client, or evaluate the effectiveness of a particular direct-mail advertising campaign based on the demographic characteristics of the target audience. These issues can be analyzed with either probit or logit models.

EXAMPLE 9-12. Explaining Analyst Coverage.

In this example, we examine a sample of publicly traded companies using a probit model to determine which factors are statistically significant in explaining whether at least one analyst covers the company. The sample uses 2,047 observations from

---

[45] The logistic distribution $e^{(b_0 + b_1 X)}/[1 + e^{(b_0 + b_1 X)}]$ is easier to compute than the cumulative normal distribution. Consequently, logit models gained popularity when computing power was expensive.

[46] For more on probit and logit models, see Greene (1999).

1999 to estimate a probit model explaining the dependent variable ANALYSTS. All data come from Disclosure, Inc. The analyst coverage data on Disclosure come from I/B/E/S International.

The variables in the probit model are as follows:

ANALYSTS = the discrete dependent variable, which takes on a value of 1 if at least one analyst covers the company and a value of 0 if no analysts cover the company

LNVOLUME = the natural log of trading volume in the most recent week

LNMV = the natural log of market value

ESTABLISHED = a dummy independent variable that takes on a value of 1 if the company's financial data has been audited for at least five years

LNTA = the natural log of total assets (book value)

LNSALES = the natural log of net sales

In this attempt to explain analyst coverage, the market (volume and value) and the book (value and sales) variables might be expected to explain coverage through various dimensions of size and, hence, importance.[47] The audit history variable reflects a possible comfort level that analysts could be expected to have with audited statements. Although some might expect market and book values to be highly correlated, this is not borne out by empirical evidence. Indeed, our probit regression here will show no evidence of multicollinearity. Table 9-14 shows the results of the probit estimation.

TABLE 9-14   Explaining Analyst Coverage Using a Probit Model

Variable	Estimates	Standard Errors	t-Statistics
Constant	−3.0117	0.5912	−5.0946
LNVOLUME	0.0826	0.0204	4.0523
LNMV	0.2504	0.0377	6.6451
ESTABLISHED	−0.1529	0.5469	−0.2796
LNTA	−0.0118	0.0347	−0.3400
LNSALES	0.0080	0.0290	0.2765
Percent correctly predicted		80.95%	

Source: Disclosure, Inc.

As Table 9-14 shows, only two coefficients (besides the constant) have t-statistics with an absolute value greater than 2.0. LNVOLUME has a t-statistic of 4.05. That value is far above the critical value at the 0.05 level for the t-statistic (1.96), so we can reject at the 0.05 level of significance the null hypothesis that the coefficient on LNVOLUME equals 0, in favor of the alternative hypothesis that the coefficient is not equal to 0. The second coefficient with an absolute value greater than 2 is LNMV,

---

[47] The model includes three variables (LNMV, LNTA, and LNSALES) that we may expect to be correlated. On examination, however, the probit results do not show evidence of multicollinearity. For information on tests of multicollinearity, see Greene (1999).

which has a *t*-statistic of 6.65. We can also reject at the 0.05 level of significance the null hypothesis that the coefficient on LNMV is equal to 0, in favor of the alternative hypothesis that the coefficient is not equal to 0. The model does not have multi-collinearity; otherwise, the two independent variables that are highly statistically significant could not have such large *t*-statistics.

Except for the constant, none of the other independent variables is statistically significant at the 0.05 level in this probit analysis. None of the *t*-statistics on the other variables is larger in absolute value than 0.35, so none of them reaches the critical value of 1.96 needed to reject the null hypothesis (that the associated coefficient is significantly different from 0). This result shows that once we take into account a company's market value and trading volume, the other factors—book value of assets, value of sales, and the existence of a five-year audit history—have no power to explain whether at least one analyst will cover the company.

9 SUMMARY

- The general form of a multiple linear regression model is $Y_t = b_0 + b_1 X_{1t} + b_2 X_{2t} + \ldots + b_k X_{kt} + \epsilon_t$ where

  $t = 1, 2, \ldots, T$ observations
  Y_t = the dependent variable
  X_j = the independent variables, $j = 1, 2, \ldots, k$
  X_{jt} = the *t*'th observation on the independent variable X_j
  b_0 = the intercept of the equation
  $b_1, \ldots, b_k$ = the slope coefficients for each of the independent variables
  ϵ_t = the error term

- The assumptions of classical normal multiple linear regression model are as follows:

  1. A linear relation exists between the dependent variable, Y_t, and the independent variables $(X_{1t}, X_{2t}, \ldots, X_{kt})$.
  2. The independent variables $(X_{1t}, X_{2t}, \ldots, X_{kt})$ are not random. Also, no exact linear relation exists between two or more of the independent variables.
  3. The expected value of the error term is 0.
  4. The variance of the error term is the same for all observations.
  5. The error term (ϵ_t) is uncorrelated across observations.
  6. The error term is normally distributed.

- The relation between the regression residual and the standard error of estimate is

$$
\text{SEE} = \left(\sum_{t=1}^{T} \frac{(\hat{\epsilon}_t)^2}{T - (k + 1)} \right)^{1/2}
$$

$$
= \left(\sum_{t=1}^{T} \frac{(Y_t - \hat{b}_0 - \hat{b}_1 X_{1t} - \hat{b}_2 X_{2t} - \ldots - \hat{b}_k X_{kt})^2}{T - (k + 1)} \right)^{1/2}
$$

$$
= \left(\frac{\text{SSE}}{T - (k + 1)} \right)^{1/2}
$$

- To make a prediction using a multiple linear regression model, we take the following three steps:

  1. Obtain estimates $\hat{b}_0, \hat{b}_1, \hat{b}_2, \ldots, \hat{b}_k$ of the regression parameters $b_0, b_1, b_2, \ldots, b_k$.
  2. Determine the assumed values of the independent variables, $\hat{X}_{1t}, \hat{X}_{2t}, \ldots, \hat{X}_{kt}$.
  3. Compute the predicted value of the dependent variable, $\hat{Y}_t$, from the equation $\hat{Y}_t = \hat{b}_0 + \hat{b}_1 \hat{X}_{1t} + \hat{b}_2 \hat{X}_{2t} + \ldots + \hat{b}_k \hat{X}_{kt}$.

- The most important indicators that a regression model explains the dependent variable well are the following:

  1. The coefficients on the independent variables are significantly different from 0. Analysts can test whether at least one coefficient is significantly different from 0 using the F-test shown in an ANOVA table.
  2. The coefficient of determination (R^2) is high. Analysts may want to rely on adjusted R^2, because R^2 automatically increases with the addition of another independent variable.
  3. Analysts must also discover whether there are violations of the assumptions of the multiple regression model (such as heteroskedasticity and serial correlation of the errors). Such violations may invalidate conclusions made about the explanatory power of the model.

- The F-statistic in an ANOVA table tests whether at least one of the slope coefficients on the independent variables is significantly different from 0. If the regression has n observations and k independent variables, the regression sum of squares is denoted RSS, and the sum of squared errors is denoted SSE, then the F-statistic to test whether at least one of the slope coefficients is significantly different from 0 is

$$F = \frac{\dfrac{\text{RSS}}{k}}{\dfrac{\text{SSE}}{[n - (k + 1)]}} = \frac{\text{Mean regression sum of squares}}{\text{Mean squared error}}$$

Under the null hypothesis that none of the slope coefficients is significantly different from 0, this test statistic has a distribution of $F_{k,n-(k+1)}$.

- Dummy variables in a regression model can help analysts determine whether a particular qualitative independent variable explains the model's dependent variable. For example, suppose we want to test whether stock returns are different in January than during the remaining months of the year. We include one independent variable in the regression, the independent variable, X_{1t}, which has the value of 1 for each January and the value of 0 for every other month of the year. Therefore, we estimate the regression model $Y_t = b_0 + b_1 X_{1t} + \epsilon_t$. In this equation, the coefficient b_0 is the average value of Y_t in months other than January and b_1 is the difference between the average value of Y_t in January and the average value of Y_t in months other than January.

- To distinguish between n categories, we use $n - 1$ dummy variables in a regression.

- If a regression shows significant heteroskedasticity, the standard errors and test statistics computed by regression programs will be incorrect unless they are adjusted for heteroskedasticity.

- One simple test for heteroskedasticity is the Breusch–Pagan test. Breusch and Pagan showed that, under the null hypothesis of no conditional heteroskedasticity, $n \times R^2$ (from the regression of the squared residuals on the independent variables from the original regression) will be a χ^2 random variable with the number of degrees of freedom equal to the number of independent variables in the regression.

- The principal effect of serial correlation in a linear regression is that the standard errors and test statistics computed by regression programs will be incorrect unless they are adjusted for serial correlation.

- The most commonly used test for serial correlation is based on the Durbin-Watson statistic. If the value of the Durbin-Watson statistic is sufficiently different from 2, then the regression errors have significant serial correlation.

- Multicollinearity occurs when two or more independent variables (or combinations of independent variables) are highly (but not perfectly) correlated with each other. With multicollinearity, the regression coefficients may not be individually statistically significant even when the overall regression is significant as judged by the F-statistic.

- Probit and logit models estimate the probability of a discrete outcome (the value of a qualitative dependent variable, such as whether a company enters bankruptcy) given the values of the independent variables used to explain that outcome. The probit model, which is based on the cumulative normal distribution, estimates the probability that $Y = 1$ (a condition is fulfilled) given a value of the independent variable. The logit model is virtually identical, except that it is based on the logistic distribution rather than the normal distribution.

PROBLEMS

1. As more companies expand their operations globally, the effect of the U.S. dollar's strength on a U.S. company's returns has become an important investment issue. You would like to determine whether changes in the U.S. dollar's value and the overall U.S. market return affect an asset's returns. You decide to use the S&P 500 as an index reflecting the overall U.S. market.

   a. Write a multiple regression equation to test whether changes in the value of the U.S. dollar and the market return affect an asset's returns. Use the notations below.

   R_{it}: return on the asset in period t

   R_{mt}: return to the S&P 500 Index in period t

   ΔX_t: change in the log of a trade-weighted index of the U.S. dollar's strength in period t. (Note that an *increase* in the index indicates a *weakening* of the dollar.)

   b. The table below shows the results of the linear regression from 1(a) using monthly data for IBM Corporation, the S&P 500, and the trade-weighted exchange value of the U.S. dollar. The data are from July 1994 to March 1999.

   Determine whether changes in the value of the U.S. dollar affect IBM's returns. Use a 5 percent significance level to make your decision.

Results from Regressing IBM's Returns on S&P 500 Index Returns and the Trade-Weighted Exchange Value of the U.S. Dollar: Monthly Data, July 1994–March 1999

	Coefficients	Standard Error	t-Statistic
Intercept	1.6475	1.0345	1.5926
R_{mt}	1.0555	0.2331	4.5281
ΔX_t	−3.6221	1.3580	−2.6672

ANOVA	df	SS	MSS	F	Significance F
Regression	2	2406.5936	1203.2968	18.7673	6.50E-7
Residual	54	3462.3023	64.1167		
Total	56	5868.8959			

Residual Standard Error

R-squared	0.4100
n	57

2. You have been asked to investigate whether you can identify assets with superior return–risk profiles as measured by their Sharpe ratios. You believe that the book-to-market ratio and size (log of market value of equity) may be related to the Sharpe ratio.

   a. Write a multiple regression equation to test whether an asset's book-to-market ratio and size predict its Sharpe ratio. Use the notations below.

   $(B/M)_i$: book-to-market ratio for asset i

   $Sharpe_i$: Sharpe ratio for asset i

   $Size_i$: log of the market value of equity for asset i

b.   The table below shows the results of the linear regression from 2(a) for a cross-section of 38 companies. The size and book-to-market data for each company are for July 1999. The Sharpe ratio for each company is calculated using monthly returns from July 1997 to July 1999.

Results from Regressing the Sharpe Ratio on Book-to-Market Ratio and Size

	Coefficients	Standard Error	t-Statistic
Intercept	0.0244	0.1828	0.1336
$(B/M)_i$	0.1230	0.1603	0.7674
$Size_i$	0.0114	0.0182	0.6257

ANOVA	df	SS	MSS	F	Significance F
Regression	2	0.0269	0.0135	0.3393	0.7146
Residual	35	1.3892	0.0397		
Total	37	1.4161			
Residual Standard Error					
R-squared		0.0190			
n		38			

Determine whether book-to-market ratio and size each help to explain the Sharpe ratio. Use a 5 percent significance level to make your decision.

3.   One of the most important questions in financial economics is what factors determine the cross-sectional variation in an asset's returns. Some have argued that book-to-market ratio and size (market value of equity) play an important role.

a.   Write a multiple regression equation to test whether book-to-market ratio and size explain the cross section of asset returns. Use the notations below.
   $(B/M)_i$:   book-to-market ratio for asset i
   R_i: return ratio for asset i in a particular month
   $Size_i$:   log of the market value of equity for asset i

b.   The table below shows the results of the linear regression from 3(a) for a cross-section of 38 companies. The size, book-to-market, and return data for each company are for July 1999.

Results from Regressing Returns on the Book-to-Market Ratio and Size

	Coefficients	Standard Error	t-Statistic
Intercept	18.2194	10.6576	1.7095
$(B/M)_i$	−11.3383	9.3437	−1.2135
$Size_i$	−0.6930	1.0607	−0.6534

ANOVA	df	SS	MSS	F	Significance F
Regression	2	199.7537	99.8768	0.7406	0.4842
Residual	35	4,720.4082	134.8688		
Total	37	4,920.1619			
Residual Standard Error		11.6133			
R-squared		0.0406			
n		38			

Determine whether the book-to-market ratio and size are each useful for explaining the cross-section of asset returns. Use a 5 percent significance level to make your decision.

4. One possible investment strategy involves exploiting the "neglected-company effect," which states that companies that are followed by fewer analysts will have higher returns on average than companies that are heavily analyzed. To test the neglected-company effect, you have collected data on 38 companies and the number of analysts providing earnings estimates for each company. You have also collected data on the size of each company, to try to distinguish the small company effect from the number of analysts following a company.

The table below shows the results of the linear regression to test the model $R_i = b_0 + b_1 \text{Size}_i + b_2(\text{Number of analysts})_i + \epsilon_i$ for a cross-section of 38 companies. The size, number of analysts, and return data for each company are for July 1999.

Results from Regressing Returns on Size and Number of Analysts

	Coefficients	Standard Error	t-Statistic
Intercept	−2.3429	7.3762	−0.3176
Size_i	0.0727	1.1951	0.0608
$(\text{Number of Analysts})_i$	−0.1608	0.3186	−0.5048

ANOVA	df	SS	MSS	F	Significance F
Regression	2	49.7750	24.8875	0.3266	0.7236
Residual	35	2667.2031	76.2058		
Total	37	2716.9781			
Residual Standard Error		8.7296			
R-squared		0.0183			
n		38			

Determine whether size and the number of analysts are each significantly related to a company's returns. Use a 5 percent significance level to make your decision.

5. Linear regressions with multiple independent variables differ greatly in how well the independent variables explain the variation in the dependent variable. We need to quantify the difference so that we can understand how well a set of independent

variables explains the variation in a particular dependent variable. The standard error of estimate (SEE) for multiple linear regression measures uncertainty just as it does in a linear regression with one independent variable. After each of the following tables, we ask for a calculation of SEE.

Results from Regressing IBM's Returns on the S&P 500 Index's Returns and the Trade-Weighted Exchange Value of the U.S. Dollar. Monthly Data, July 1994–March 1999

	Coefficients		Standard Error		t-Statistic
Intercept	1.6475		1.0345		1.5926
R_{mt}	1.0555		0.2331		4.5281
ΔX_t	-3.6221		1.3580		-2.6672

ANOVA	df	SS	MSS	F	Significance F
Regression	2	2406.5936	1203.2968	18.7673	6.50E-7
Residual	54	3462.3023	64.1167		
Total	56	5868.8959			
Residual Standard Error					
R-squared		0.4100			
n		57			

a. Calculate the standard error of estimate (SEE) for the regression in the table above.

Results from Regressing the Sharpe Ratio on the Book-to-Market Ratio and Size

	Coefficients		Standard Error		t-Statistic
Intercept	0.0244		0.1828		0.1336
$(B/M)_i$	0.1230		0.1603		0.7674
$Size_i$	0.0114		0.0182		0.6257

ANOVA	df	SS	MSS	F	Significance F
Regression	2	0.0269	0.0135	0.3393	0.7146
Residual	35	1.3892	0.0397		
Total	37	1.4161			
Residual Standard Error					
R-squared		0.0190			
n		38			

b. Calculate the SEE for the regression in the table above.

7. The equity risk premium is defined as the return on a risky asset minus the return on a risk-free asset, over the same holding period. Among other things, the equity risk premium may reflect investor sentiment. You decide to test whether the equity risk premium of the S&P 500 reflects changes in investor sentiment. To conduct your test, you have collected the following data:

R_{mt}: monthly return of the S&P 500
R_{ft}: monthly return of a 30-day T-bill
Prem: the equity risk premium $(R_{mt} - R_{ft})$
DS1: change in Market Value Bullish Consensus
DS2: change in American Association of Individual Investors Bearish Consensus
DS3: change in American Association of Individual Investors Bullish Consensus

The table below shows the output from regressing the equity risk premium on the changes in the three investor sentiment measures.

Regression of Equity Risk Premium against Changes in Investor Sentiment: Monthly Data, July 1994–March 1999

	Coefficients	Standard Error	t-Statistic
Intercept	1.0677	0.3178	3.3594
DS1	−0.0883	0.0597	−1.4806
DS2	−0.0778	0.0836	−0.9307
DS3	−0.1334	0.0802	−1.6631

ANOVA	df	SS	MSS
Regression	3	155.91	51.97
Residual	129	1731.4574	13.42
Total	132	1887.3688	
Residual Standard Error	3.6636		
R-squared	0.0826		
n	133		

From the t-statistics, we see that none of the measures is statistically significant at the 5 percent level or better. You wish to test, however, if the three measures *jointly* are statistically related to the equity risk premium. Your null hypothesis is that all three population slope coefficients are 0.

a. What test would you conduct to see whether the three measures *jointly* are statistically related to the equity risk premium at the 5 percent level of significance?

b. What information do you need to conduct the appropriate test?

c. Determine whether the three measures are statistically related to the equity risk premium.

d. Examining the regression results, state the regression assumption that may be violated in this example. Explain your answer.

8. Many developing nations are hesitant to open their equity markets to foreign investment because they fear that rapid inflows and outflows of foreign funds will

increase the volatility of their equity markets. In July 1993, India implemented substantial equity market reforms, one of which allowed foreign institutional investors into the Indian equity markets. You want to test whether the volatility of the Bombay Stock Exchange (BSE) increased after July 1993, when foreign institutional investors were allowed to invest in India. You have collected monthly index data for the BSE from February 1990 to December 1997. You use a measure of return volatility of the BSE and regress it on a dummy variable to indicate "foreign investment allowed." The dummy variable is coded as 1 if foreign investment is allowed, and 0 otherwise.

You believe that market return volatility actually decreases with the opening up of equity markets. The table below shows the results from your regression.

Results from Dummy Regression for Foreign Investment in India with a Volatility Measure as the Dependent Variable

	Coefficients	Standard Error	*t*-Statistic
Intercept	0.0133	0.0020	6.5351
Dummy	−0.0075	0.0027	−2.7604
$n = 95$			

a. State an alternative hypothesis, H_a, for the slope coefficient of the dummy variable that reflects your belief about the effect of opening the equity markets on market return volatility.

b. State a null hypothesis, H_0, that is consistent with the alternative hypothesis in 8(a).

c. Determine whether you can reject the null hypothesis at the 5 percent level of significance (in a one-sided test of significance).

d. According to the estimated regression equation, what is the level of market return volatility before and after the market opening event?

9. Every four years, around the time of U.S. political elections, there is discussion in the popular press as to which of the two leading political parties is better for the stock market. If one party were better for the stock market, this finding would have important asset allocation implications.

a. Write a multiple regression equation to test whether overall market returns, as measured by the annual returns to the S&P 500, are systematically higher when the Republicans or the Democrats control the White House. Use the notations below.

R_{mt}: return to the S&P 500 in period t

Party$_t$: the political party controlling the White House (1 for a Republican president; 0 for a Democratic president)

b. The table below shows the results of the linear regression from 9(a) using annual data for the S&P 500 and a dummy variable for the party that controlled the White House. The data are from 1926 to 1998.

Results from Regressing S&P 500 Returns on a Dummy Variable for the Party That Controlled the White House

	Coefficients		Standard Error		t-Statistic
Intercept	0.1327		0.0304		4.3651
$Party_t$	−0.0435		0.0446		−0.9753

ANOVA	df	SS	MSS	F	Significance F
Regression	1	0.0345	0.0345	0.9567	0.3313
Residual	71	2.5603	0.0361		
Total	72	2.5948			
Residual Standard Error		0.1899			
R-squared		0.0133			
n		73			

Determine at the 0.05 level of significance whether overall market returns are systematically higher when Republicans or Democrats control the White House.

10.   You have heard that companies with low book-to-market ratios have higher returns, on average, than companies with high book-to-market ratios. You estimate the following regression equation to test this hypothesis:

$$R_i = b_0 + b_1 \left(\frac{\text{Book Value}}{\text{Market Value}} \right)_i + \epsilon_i$$

The output from this regression and a graph of the actual and predicted relationship between the book-to-market ratio and return are shown below.

Results from Regressing Returns on the Book-to-Market Ratio

	Coefficients		Standard Error		t-Statistic
Intercept	12.0130		3.5464		3.3874
$\left(\dfrac{\text{Book Value}}{\text{Market Value}} \right)_i$	−9.2209		8.4454		−1.0918

ANOVA	df	SS	MSS	F	Significance F
Regression	1	154.9866	154.9866	1.1921	0.2831
Residual	32	4162.1895	130.0684		
Total	33	4317.1761			
Residual Standard Error		11.4048			
R-squared		0.0359			
n		34			

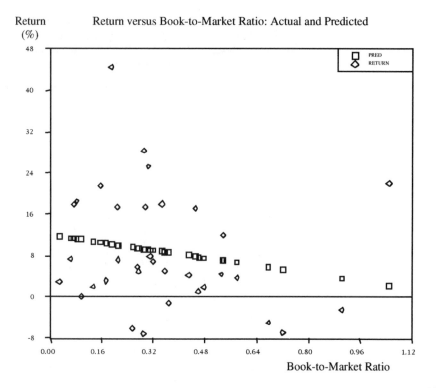

Return versus Book-to-Market Ratio: Actual and Predicted

a. Discuss symptoms of conditional heteroskedasticity in the difference between the actual and predicted relationship.

b. Describe in detail how you could formally test for conditional heteroskedasticity in this regression.

c. Describe a recommended method for correcting for conditional heteroskedasticity.

11. The relative movement of short-term and long-term interest rates is an important issue when hedging fixed-income securities. For example, using a duration immunization strategy to protect a bond fund from interest rate changes generally assumes parallel shifts in the term structure. Parallel shifts imply that a 100 basis point change in the short-term interest rate would be associated with a 100 basis point change in the long-term interest rate.

To test whether a 100 basis point change in the short-term interest rate is associated with a 100 basis point change in the long-term interest rate, you estimate the regression equation:

$$drl_t = b_0 + b_1 drs_t + \epsilon_t$$

where drl_t is the change in the long-term interest rate and drs_t is the change in the short-term interest rate.

The null hypothesis states that $b_1 = 1$. The regression output is given in the table below.

Results from Regressing Changes in Long-Term Interest Rate on Changes in the Short-Term Interest Rate: Monthly Data, January 1983–December 1987

	Coefficients	Standard Error	t-Statistic
Intercept	0.00284	0.03714	0.0764
drs_t	0.63604	0.1156	5.5028
R-squared	0.3430		
n	60		
Durbin-Watson	1.2398		

a. The typical t-statistic output from a regression package is for the null hypothesis that the coefficient is equal to 0. We want to test whether the population slope coefficient on drs_t is equal to 1. Calculate the t-statistic for this null hypothesis.

b. Discuss how the Durbin-Watson statistic of 1.23 affects your interpretation of the t-statistic of -3.1488.

You can use the method of Hansen (1982) to correct the standard error for autocorrelation. The table below shows the regression output with the standard errors corrected for autocorrelation.

Results from Regressing Changes in Long-Term Interest Rate on Changes in the Short-Term Interest Rate: Monthly Data, January 1983–December 1987 (Corrected for Autocorrelation)

	Coefficients	Standard Error	t-Statistic
Intercept	0.0028	0.0369	0.0770
drs_t	0.6360	0.1171	5.4302
R-squared	0.3430		
n	60		
Durbin-Watson	1.2398		

c. Discuss whether the corrected estimation results differ from the original regression estimates, and determine whether the population slope coefficient on drs_t is equal to 1.

12. The book-to-market ratio and the size of a company's equity are two factors that have been asserted to be useful in explaining the cross-sectional variation in asset returns. Based on this assertion, you want to estimate the following regression model:

$$R_i = b_0 + b_1\left(\frac{\text{Book}}{\text{Market}}\right)_i + b_2\text{Size}_i + \epsilon_i$$

where

R_i is the return of asset i

$\left(\dfrac{\text{Book}}{\text{Market}}\right)_i$ is asset i's book-to-market ratio, and

Size_i is the market value of asset i's equity

A colleague suggests that this regression specification may be erroneous, because he believes that the book-to-market ratio may be related to (correlated with) the size of a company.

a.   What is this problem called, and what are its consequences for regression analysis?

b.   How would you determine whether multicollinearity is present in a regression with only two independent variables?

c.   Use the tables below to comment on whether multicollinearity is a likely problem with the regression specification above, and whether that is what is causing the variables to appear insignificant.

Regression of Return on Book-to-Market and Size

	Coefficients	Standard Error	t-Statistic
Intercept	14.1062	4.220	3.3427
$\left(\dfrac{\text{Book}}{\text{Market}}\right)_i$	−12.1413	9.0406	−1.3430
Size_i	0.00005502	0.00005977	−0.92047
R-squared	0.06156		
n	34		

Correlation Matrix

	Book-to-Market Ratio	SIZE
Book-to-Market Ratio	1.0000	
SIZE	−0.3509	1.0000

13.   As a major source of energy and chemicals, oil is one of the most important commodities affecting the overall economy. The health of many industries hinges on the price of oil, although other industries are less affected by it. As a portfolio manager, you are interested in measuring the sensitivity of IBM's returns to changes in the price of oil over and above overall market influences. You have collected the following data:

$R_{IBM,t}$:   monthly returns for IBM, August 1994 to March 1999

$R_{S\&P500,t}$:   monthly returns for the S&P 500, August 1994 to March 1999

ΔP_t: monthly changes in the log of the price of oil, August 1994 to March 1999

a. Using the above notation, write a regression equation to test whether changes in the log of the price of oil affects IBM's returns over and above the influence of the overall market.

The table below shows the output for the regression model $R_{IBM,t} = b_0 + b_1 R_{S\&P500,t} + b_2 \Delta P_t + \epsilon_t$.

Results from Regressing IBM's Returns on S&P 500 Returns and Changes in the Log of the Price of Oil

	Coefficients	Standard Error	t-Statistic
Intercept	0.9857	1.0864	0.9074
$R_{S\&P500,t}$	1.2318	0.2402	5.1292
ΔP_t	1.1929	14.0495	0.0849
R-squared	0.3320		
n	56		

b. Describe how you would test whether IBM's returns are sensitive to changes in the price of oil.

14. Peggy Parsons, CFA, wants to forecast sales of BoneMax, a prescription drug for treating osteoporosis. Osteoporosis is a degenerative disease that primarily affects women over the age of 60.

Parsons has developed the sales regression model, shown in Table 1 below, and supporting data, found in Tables 2 and 3 below, to assist her sales forecast of BoneMax.

TABLE 1 BoneMax Sales Regression Model

SALES = 8.530 + 6.078 (POP) + 5.330 (INC) + 7.380 (ADV)
t-values: (2.48)   (2.23)   (2.10)   (2.75)

Unadjusted R-squared = 0.804
Number of annual observations = 20

Notes:
  SALES = sales of BoneMax (US$ millions)
  POP   = population (millions) of U.S. women over age 60
  INC   = average income (US$ thousands) of U.S. women over age 60
  ADV   = advertising dollars spent on BoneMax (US$ millions)

TABLE 2 Variable Estimates for 1999

POP	34.7
INC	27.4
ADV	8.2

a. i. Calculate a "forecast" for BoneMax for 1999. Show your work.
  ii. Interpret the R^2 statistic.

    b.   Determine whether the regression coefficient of the average income of U.S. women over the age of 60 (INC) is statistically significantly different from 0 at the 5 percent level of significance. Show your calculations.

    c.   Calculate a 95 percent confidence interval for the regression coefficient estimate of the population of U.S. women over the age of 60 (POP). Show your work.

15.   Pat Johnson, CFA, is a stock analyst who follows the toy industry. Johnson has concluded that the two major macroeconomic factors influencing the toy industry's U.S. domestic nominal sales (in US\$ millions, $SALES_t$) are

- the population (in millions) of children 3–14 years old ($CHILD_t$), and
- nominal per capita GDP in the United States (GDP_t).

Using monthly data, Johnson obtains the following regression results (t-values are shown in parentheses):

$$SALES_t = 62.10 + 87.50\ CHILD_t + 0.1974\ GDP_t$$
$$(2.49) \quad (2.02) \qquad\qquad (3.03)$$

Number of observations:	30
Unadjusted R^2:	0.9699
F-statistic:	112.64
Residual standard error:	13.31
Correlation between CHILD and GDP:	0.25 (t-value = 0.75)

    a.   Evaluate the goodness of fit of the regression equation.

    b.   Evaluate and interpret the following hypotheses at the 95 percent significance level.

      i. All estimated coefficients of the independent variables are simultaneously equal to 0.

      ii. Each individual estimated coefficient is equal to 0.

    c. i. Define multicollinearity and determine whether it is likely that multicollinearity exists in Johnson's regression results.

      ii. Discuss the problems in multiple regression analysis when the homoskedasticity assumption is violated.

    d.   Calculate, based on the regression equation, the forecasted "industry nominal sales volume" if nominal per capita GDP (GDP_t) is expected to be \$500 and the population of children 3–14 years old ($CHILD_t$) is expected to be 100 million.

       Johnson's results are evaluated by the company's chief economist, Susan Yost, CFA. Yost suggests that the results can be improved by removing the effects of inflation on $SALES_t$ and GDP_t.

    e.   Justify Yost's suggestion.

SOLUTIONS

1. a. $R_{it} = b_0 + b_1 R_{mt} + b_2 \Delta X_t + \epsilon_{it}$

b. We can test whether the coefficient on the change in the value of the U.S. dollar is statistically significant in this regression. Our null hypothesis is that the coefficient is equal to 0 (H_0: $b_2 = 0$); our alternative hypothesis is that the coefficient is not equal to 0 (H_a: $b_2 \neq 0$). We can test the null hypothesis using a t-test constructed as follows:

$$\frac{\hat{b}_2 - b_2}{s_{\hat{b}_2}} = \frac{-3.6221 - 0}{1.3580} = -2.6672$$

where

$\hat{b}_2$ = the regression estimate of b_2
b_2 = the hypothesized value of the coefficient (here, 0)
$s_{\hat{b}_2}$ = the estimated standard error of $\hat{b}_2$

This regression has 57 observations and 3 coefficients, so the t-test has $57 - 3 = 54$ degrees of freedom. At the 0.05 significance level, the critical value for the test statistic is between 2.01 and 2.0. The absolute value of the test statistic is 2.6672; therefore, we can reject the null hypothesis that $b_2 = 0$.

2. a. $(\text{Sharpe})_i = b_0 + b_1 (\text{B/M})_i + b_2 \text{Size}_i + \epsilon_i$

b. We can test whether the coefficients on the book-to-market ratio and Size are individually statistically significant using t-tests. For the book-to-market ratio, our null hypothesis is that the coefficient is equal to 0 (H_0: $b_1 = 0$); our alternative hypothesis is that the coefficient is not equal to 0 (H_a: $b_1 \neq 0$). We can test the null hypothesis using a t-test constructed as follows:

$$\frac{\hat{b}_1 - b_1}{s_{\hat{b}_1}} = \frac{0.1230 - 0}{0.1603} = 0.7674$$

where

$\hat{b}_1$ = the regression estimate of b_1
b_1 = the hypothesized value of the coefficient (here, 0)
$s_{\hat{b}_1}$ = the estimated standard error of $\hat{b}_1$

This regression has 38 observations and three coefficients, so the t-test has $38 - 3 = 35$ degrees of freedom. At the 0.05 significance level, the critical value for the test statistic is about 2.03. The absolute value of the test statistic is 0.7674; therefore, we cannot reject the null hypothesis that $b_1 = 0$. We can conclude that the book-to-market ratio is not useful in explaining the Sharpe ratio in this sample.

We perform the same analysis to determine whether size (as measured as the log of the market value of equity) can help explain an asset's Sharpe ratio. For size, our null hypothesis is that the coefficient is equal to 0 (H_0: $b_2 = 0$); our alternative hypothesis is that the coefficient is not equal to 0 (H_a: $b_2 \neq 0$). We can test the null hypothesis using a t-test constructed as follows:

$$\frac{\hat{b}_2 - b_2}{s_{\hat{b}_2}} = \frac{0.0114 - 0}{0.0182} = 0.6257$$

where

$$\hat{b}_2 = \text{the regression estimate of } b_2$$
$$b_2 = \text{the hypothesized value of the coefficient (0)}$$
$$s_{\hat{b}_2} = \text{the estimated standard error of } \hat{b}_2$$

Again, because this regression has 38 observations and three coefficients, the t-test has $38 - 3 = 35$ degrees of freedom. At the 0.05 significance level, the critical value for the test statistic is about 2.03. The absolute value of the test statistic is 0.6257; therefore, we cannot reject the null hypothesis that $b_2 = 0$. We can conclude that the size is not useful in explaining the Sharpe ratio in this sample.

3. a. $R_i = b_0 + b_1(B/M)_i + b_2Size_i + \epsilon_i$

b.   We can test whether the coefficients on the book-to-market ratio and size are individually statistically significant using t-tests. For the book-to-market ratio, our null hypothesis is that the coefficient is equal to 0 (H_0: $b_1 = 0$); our alternative hypothesis is that the coefficient is not equal to 0 (H_a: $b_1 \neq 0$). We can test the null hypothesis using a t-test constructed as follows:

$$\frac{\hat{b}_1 - b_1}{s_{\hat{b}_1}} = \frac{-11.3383 - 0}{9.3437} = -1.2135$$

where

$$\hat{b}_1 = \text{the regression estimate of } b_1$$
$$b_1 = \text{the hypothesized value of the coefficient (here, 0)}$$
$$s_{\hat{b}_1} = \text{the estimated standard error of } \hat{b}_1$$

This regression has 38 observations and three coefficients, so the t-test has $38 - 3 = 35$ degrees of freedom. At the 0.05 significance level, the critical value for the test statistic is about 2.03. The absolute value of the test statistic is 1.2135; therefore, we cannot reject the null hypothesis that $b_1 = 0$. We can conclude that the book-to-market ratio is not useful in explaining the cross-sectional variation in returns for this sample.

We perform the same analysis to determine whether size (as measured as the log of the market value of equity) can help explain the cross-sectional variation in asset returns. For size, our null hypothesis is that the coefficient is equal to 0 (H_0: $b_2 = 0$); our alternative hypothesis is that the coefficient is not equal to 0 (H_a: $b_2 \neq 0$). We can test the null hypothesis using a t-test constructed as follows:

$$\frac{\hat{b}_2 - b_2}{s_{\hat{b}_2}} = \frac{-0.6930 - 0}{1.0607} = -0.6534$$

where

$$\hat{b}_2 = \text{the regression estimate of } b_2$$
$$b_2 = \text{the hypothesized value of the coefficient (here, 0)}$$
$$s_{\hat{b}_2} = \text{the estimated standard error of } \hat{b}_2$$

Again, because this regression has 38 observations and three coefficients, the t-test has $38 - 3 = 35$ degrees of freedom. At the 0.05 significance level, the critical value for the test statistic is about 2.03. The absolute value of the test statistic is 0.6534; therefore, we cannot reject the null hypothesis that $b_2 = 0$. We can conclude that asset size is not useful in explaining the cross-sectional variation of asset returns in this sample.

4.   We can test whether the coefficients for size and number of analysts are individually statistically significant using t-tests. For size, our null hypothesis is that the coefficient is equal to 0 (H_0: $b_1 = 0$); our alternative hypothesis is that the coefficient is not equal to 0 (H_a: $b_1 \neq 0$). We can test the null hypothesis using a t-test constructed as follows:

$$\frac{\hat{b}_1 - b_1}{s_{\hat{b}_1}} = \frac{0.0727 - 0}{1.1951} = 0.0608$$

where

$\hat{b}_1$ = the regression estimate of b_1
b_1 = the hypothesized value of the coefficient (here, 0)
$s_{\hat{b}_1}$ = the estimated standard error of $\hat{b}_1$

This regression has 38 observations and three coefficients, so the t-test has $38 - 3 = 35$ degrees of freedom. At the 0.05 significance level, the critical value for the test statistic is about 2.03. The absolute value of the test statistic is 0.0608; therefore, we cannot reject the null hypothesis that $b_1 = 0$. We can conclude that asset size is not useful in explaining the cross-sectional variation in returns for this sample.

We perform the same analysis to determine whether the number of analysts can help explain the cross-sectional variation in asset returns. For the number of analysts variable, our null hypothesis is that the coefficient is equal to 0 (H_0: $b_2 = 0$); our alternative hypothesis is that the coefficient is not equal to 0 (H_a: $b_2 \neq 0$). We can test the null hypothesis using a t-test constructed as follows:

$$\frac{\hat{b}_2 - b_2}{s_{\hat{b}_2}} = \frac{-0.1608 - 0}{0.3186} = -0.5048$$

where

$\hat{b}_2$ = the regression estimate of b_2
b_2 = the hypothesized value of the coefficient (here, 0)
$s_{\hat{b}_2}$ = the estimated standard error of $\hat{b}_2$

Again, because this regression has 38 observations and three coefficients, the t-test has $38 - 3 = 35$ degrees of freedom. At the 0.05 significance level, the critical value for the test statistic is about 2.03. The absolute value of the test statistic is 0.5048; therefore, we cannot reject the null hypothesis that $b_2 = 0$. We can conclude that the number of analysts providing earnings estimates is not useful in explaining the cross-sectional variation of asset returns in this sample. With this data, we do not find evidence supporting the neglected-company effect.

5. a.   The formula for the standard error of the estimate is given by

$$\text{SEE} = \left(\sum_{t=1}^{T} \frac{(Y_t - \hat{b}_0 - \hat{b}_1 X_{1t} - \hat{b}_2 X_{2t} - \ldots - \hat{b}_k X_{kt})^2}{T - (k + 1)} \right)^{1/2}$$

The numerator of the SSE is the sum of the squared residuals from the regression. The denominator of the SSE equation is the number of observations minus the total number of coefficients estimated.

In the regression of IBM's returns on the market return and changes in the exchange rate, the sum of squared errors is 3462.3023. We have 57 observations and three coefficients to estimate, so the number of degrees of freedom is 54. Therefore, the SSE for this estimation is calculated as

$$SEE = \left(\frac{3462.3023}{54}\right)^{1/2} = 8.0073$$

This result tells us that the unexplained variation in the regression equation has a standard error of estimate of 8.0073 percent a month, a fairly high standard error. But this finding merely supports the R^2 of 0.4100 for this regression; 59 percent of the variation of IBM's returns is unexplained by the market return and changes in the value of the U.S. dollar.

b. The sum of the squared residuals for this regression is 1.3892. We have 38 observations and three coefficients to estimate, so the number of degrees of freedom is 35. The standard error of the estimate is thus

$$SEE = \left(\frac{1.3892}{35}\right)^{1/2} = 0.1992$$

or 19.92 percent a month. The standard error is very large for this data set and indicates that the independent variables, book-to-market ratio and size, account for virtually none of the cross-sectional variation in the Sharpe ratio. Again, this finding is confirmed by the very low R^2 for this regression.

7. a. To test the null hypothesis that all of the regression coefficients except for the intercept in the multiple regression model are equal to 0 (H_0: $b_1 = b_2 = \ldots = b_k = 0$) against the alternative hypothesis that at least one slope coefficient is not equal to 0, we must use an F-test to perform an analysis of variance.

b. To conduct the F-test, we need four inputs:

i. total number of observations (n)

ii. total number of parameters to be estimated ($k + 1$)

iii. sum of squared errors or residuals $\sum_{i=1}^{n} (Y_i - \hat{Y}_i)^2$, abbreviated SSE, and

iv. regression sum of squares $\sum_{i=1}^{n} (\hat{Y}_i - \overline{Y})^2$

c. The F-test formula is

$$F = \frac{\dfrac{RSS}{k}}{\dfrac{SSE}{[n - (k + 1)]}} = \frac{\dfrac{155.91}{3}}{\dfrac{1731.457}{[133 - (3 + 1)]}} = 3.8720$$

The F-statistic has degrees of freedom $F\{k, [n - (k + 1)]\} = F(3, 129)$. From the F-test table, the critical value for $F(3, 120) = 2.68$ and $F(3, 129)$ will be less than $F(3, 120)$, so we can reject at the 5 percent level that the slope coefficients are all 0. Changes in the three sentiment measures are jointly statistically related to the equity risk premium.

    d.   The insignificant *t*-statistics and a significant *F*-statistic suggest the possibility of multicollinearity in the independent variables.

8. a. $H_1: b_1 < 0$

    b. $H_0: b_1 \geq 0$

    c.   The critical value for the *t*-statistic with $95 - 2 = 93$ degrees of freedom and a 5 percent one-tailed significance level is about 1.66. The coefficient on the dummy variable is negative and statistically significant in absolute value ($2.76 > 1.66$). Because the dummy variable takes on a value of 1 when foreign investment is allowed, we can conclude that the volatility was lower with foreign investment.

    d.   Because the dependent variable is a measure of return volatility, we can conclude that average volatility before July 1993 was 0.0133 and after July 1993 was $0.0058 \ (0.0133 - 0.0075)$.

9. a.   In this case, the independent variable is qualitative: In today's age, the party that controls the White House is either Democratic or Republican. We can model this type of situation with the use of a zero-one dummy variable. Recall that to avoid multicollinearity problems, the number of dummy variables we need is one less than the number of possibilities of our qualitative variables. For this situation, we have two possibilities for our qualitative variable, Democratic or Republican, so we require only one dummy variable. The regression we would estimate would thus be

$$R_{mt} = b_0 + b_1 \text{Party}_t + \epsilon_{it}$$

    b.   The coefficient on the variable Party_t measures the average amount of differential annual return associated with a Republican controlling the White House (because $\text{Party}_t = 1$ when a Republican is president). To determine whether the political party affects the market's average returns, we need to test whether the coefficient on Party_t is significantly different from 0. We can test the null hypothesis using a *t*-test constructed as follows:

$$\frac{\hat{b}_2 - b_2}{s_{\hat{b}_2}} = \frac{-0.0435 - 0}{0.0446} = -0.9753$$

where

    $\hat{b}_2 = $ the regression estimate of b_2
    $b_2 = $ the hypothesized value of the coefficient (here, 0)
    $s_{\hat{b}_2} = $ the estimated standard error of $\hat{b}_2$

Because this regression has 73 observations and two coefficients, the *t*-test has $73 - 2 = 71$ degrees of freedom. At the 0.05 significance level, the critical value for the two-tailed test statistic is about 1.99. The absolute value of the test statistic is 0.9753; therefore, we cannot reject the null hypothesis that $b_2 = 0$. We can conclude that the political party in the White House does not, on average, affect the annual returns of the overall market as measured by the S&P 500.

10. a.   In a well-specified regression, the differences between the actual and predicted relationship should be random; the errors should not depend on the value of the independent variable. In this regression, the errors seem larger for smaller values of the book-to-market ratio. This finding indicates that we may have conditional heteroskedasticity in the errors and consequently, the standard errors will be incorrect. We cannot proceed with hypothesis testing until we test for and, if necessary, correct for the heteroskedasticity.

b. A simple test for heteroskedasticity is to regress the squared residuals from the estimated regression equation on the independent variables in the regression. As seen in Example 9-9, Breusch and Pagan showed that, under the null hypothesis of no conditional heteroskedasticity, $n \times R^2$ (from the regression of the squared residuals on the independent variables from the original regression) will be a χ^2 random variable, with the number of degrees of freedom equal to the number of independent variables in the regression.

c. The first method to correct for heteroskedasticity is to use robust standard errors. This method uses the parameter estimates from the linear regression model but corrects the standard errors of the estimated parameters to account for the heteroskedasticity. Many statistical software packages can easily compute robust standard errors, and we recommend using them.

11. a. $t = \dfrac{0.6360 - 1.0}{0.1156} = -3.1488$

We can reject the null hypothesis that $b_1 = 1$ and that long-term rates and short-term rates move together on a one-to-one basis.

b. With 60 observations and one slope parameter, the Durbin-Watson lower bound for the 5 percent level of significance is 1.55. The value of 1.23 indicates positive autocorrelation. The autocorrelation decreases the standard error and tends to make the t-statistic appear more significant than it actually is.

c. The coefficient estimates are the same, but the standard errors are different. The standard error on drs_t increased from 0.1156 to 0.1171. This change reduces the t-statistic from -3.1488 to $t = \dfrac{0.6360 - 1.0}{0.1171} = -3.108$. We can still reject the hypothesis that $b_1 = 1$ and reject the idea that long-term and short-term rates move together on a one-to-one basis.

12. a. This problem is known as multicollinearity. When some linear combinations of the independent variables in a regression model are highly correlated, the standard errors of the independent coefficient estimates become quite large even though the regression equation may fit rather well.

b. With only two independent variables (other than dummy variables) in a regression model, multicollinearity can exist only if the correlation between the two independent variables is high. If the correlation is low (say an absolute value of less than 0.5), then multicollinearity cannot exist.

c. Because the correlation of the two independent variables has a low absolute value (correlation $= -0.3509$), multicollinearity cannot exist. Given their t-statistics, the independent variables are not significant in explaining the variation in the dependent variable.

13. a. $R_{IBM,t} = b_0 + b_1 R_{S\&P500,t} + b_2 \Delta P_t + \epsilon_t$

b. We can test whether the coefficient on changes in the log of the price of oil are statistically significant in this regression. Our null hypothesis is that the coefficient is equal to 0 ($H_0: b_3 = 0$); our alternative hypothesis is that the coefficient is not equal to 0 ($H_a: b_3 \neq 0$). We can test the null hypothesis using a t-test constructed as follows:

$$\frac{\hat{b}_2 - b_2}{s_{\hat{b}_2}} = \frac{-1.1929 - 0}{14.0495} = -0.0849$$

where

$$\hat{b}_2 = \text{the regression estimate of } b_2$$
$$b_2 = \text{the hypothesized value of the coefficient (here, 0)}$$
$$s_{\hat{b}_2} = \text{the estimated standard error of } \hat{b}_2$$

This regression has 56 observations and three coefficients, so the t-test has $56 - 3 = 53$ degrees of freedom. At the 0.05 significance level, the critical value for the test statistic is between 2.01 and 2.0. The absolute value of the test statistic is 0.0849; therefore, we cannot reject the null hypothesis that $b_2 = 0$. We can conclude that the returns from IBM are not sensitive to changes in the log of the price of oil.

14. a. i. Sales forecast for 1999:

$$\text{SALES} = 8.530 + 8.078(\text{POP}) + 5.330(\text{INC}) + 7.380(\text{ADV})$$
$$= 8.530 + 8.078(34.7) + 5.330(27.4) + 7.380(8.2)$$
$$= 3.530 + 210.91 + 146.04 + 50.52$$
$$= \$426 \text{ million in U.S. dollars}$$

ii. Interpretation of R^2:

The R^2 is known as the "goodness of fit" or coefficient of determination. The R^2 indicates the percentage of the total variability of the dependent variable (SALES) that can be explained by the regression. The intercept and the independent variables (POP, INC, and ADV) together explain 80.4 percent of the variability of BoneMax sales. An R^2 of 80.4 percent is considered relatively high.

b. Significance of INC:

The critical t-value depends on the degrees of freedom, the level of significance, and whether the test is a one-tailed or two-tailed test. Degrees of freedom is the number of observations minus the number of parameters estimated—or number of observations minus number of independent variables minus 1; $\text{df} = n - (k + 1) = n - k - 1$:

$$\text{Degrees of freedom} = 20 - 3 - 1 = 20 - 4 = 16.$$

To evaluate whether the coefficient is different from 0 at the 5 percent significance level, use $5\%/2 = 2.5\%$ in the upper tail and 2.5% in the lower tail.

For 16 degrees of freedom and 2.5 percent in each tail, the critical t-value is 2.12.

The calculated t-value associated with the coefficient of the independent variable INC is 2.10, which is below the critical t-value of 2.12. Therefore, for the independent variable INC, we are not able to reject the null hypothesis that the coefficient is equal to 0. The coefficient of INC is not significantly different from 0 at a 5 percent significance level.

c. 95 percent Confidence Interval for POP:

To find the 95 percent confidence interval for the coefficient estimate of POP (the population of U.S. women over the age of 60), use the following relationship:

$$\text{Coefficient of POP} \pm (\text{Critical } t\text{-value} \times \text{Standard error of POP})$$
$$= 6.078 \pm (2.12 \times \text{Standard error of POP})$$

The critical t-value is the same as in 14(b), with 16 degrees of freedom and a two-tailed test with 2.5 percent in each tail.

To find the standard error, use the following formula:

Calculated t-value of POP = Coefficient of POP/Standard error of POP.

The standard error, then, is

Standard error of POP = Coefficient of POP/Calculated t-value of POP
= 6.078 / 2.23
= 2.7256

Using this standard error, the confidence interval is

6.078 $\pm$ (2.12 $\times$ 2.7256)
6.078 $\pm$ 5.778

A 95 percent confidence interval for the coefficient of POP in the regression model is from 0.300 to 11.856.

15. a.   An $R^2 = 0.9699$ is interpreted as 96.99 percent of the variation of the dependent variable being explained by the variation of the independent variables, or 96.99 percent of the variation of the dependent variable being explained by the regression. In this example, 96.99 percent of the variation of nominal toy sales ($SALES_t$) is explained by the variation of nominal per capita GDP (GDP_t) and the population of children age 3-14 ($CHILD_t$).

b. i.   The null hypothesis is H_0: $b_1 = b_2 = 0$.

The hypothesis is evaluated using the F-statistic. The first step is to determine the critical F-value that corresponds to the 95 percent significance level. To do this, we must compute the degrees of freedom (df) for both the numerator and denominator of the F-statistic, which is the ratio of the mean square regression (MSR) divided by the mean square error (MSE). The numerator df is the number of independent variables, $k = 2$, and the denominator df is 27, which is equal to the number of observations, $n = 30$, less $k + 1$, or df $= n - (k + 1) = 27$. The critical value (between 3.39 and 3.32) is then found from the F-tables in Appendix D.

If the F-statistic from the regression is larger than the critical value, then the null hypothesis is rejected at the 95 percent significance level. The F-statistic from the regression is 112.64, which is larger than the critical value, so the null is rejected at the 95 percent significance level.

We reject the hypothesis that the coefficients are simultaneously equal to 0. However, this still leaves open the possibility that a single coefficient could be equal to 0 (as we see in the case of $CHILD_t$, below).

ii.   To determine whether the individual estimates are not equal to 0, we use the t-statistic. The null hypotheses are

H_0: $b_i = 0, i = 1, 2$

We need to test two hypotheses, one each for the coefficient of each independent variable. The appropriate statistic is the two-tailed t-statistic. Similar to 15b(i) above, we first need to determine the df, which is the same as for the denominator of the F-statistic above, or df $= n - (k + 1) = 27$.

The critical t is found in Appendix B. The appropriate column is the 0.025 column, because we are using a two-tailed test. The critical value corresponding to the 95 percent significance level and df = 27 is 2.052. The t-values from the regression must be larger (in absolute value) than 2.052 for us to reject the null hypothesis at the 95 percent significance level. Using this critical t-value, $CHILD_t$ is not statistically different from 0 (although it is close); GDP_t is statistically different from 0 at this level of confidence.

c. i. Multicollinearity occurs when linear combinations of the independent variables themselves are highly correlated. We saw in the text that the only case in which correlation between variables may be a reasonable indicator of the absence of multicollinearity is when there are only two independent variables. In that case, multicollinearity will certainly not be a problem if the correlation between the two variables is low (say an absolute value of 0.5 or lower). Based on two indicators, it is likely that no multicollinearity exists in these regression results. First, the correlation between the two variables is 0.25, which is fairly low. Second, this correlation itself is not significantly different from 0 because the t-value of 0.75 is less than the critical t-value (2.048) for $n - 2 = 30 - 2 = 28$ df and $\alpha/2 = 0.025$.

ii. When the homoskedasticity assumption is violated, the standard errors of the regression coefficients may be incorrect (either too small or too large). If a standard error is understated (overstated), the t-value will be too large (too small). This may cause independent variables to appear significant when they are not, or it may cause independent variables to appear insignificant when they actually are significant. The remedy for this condition is to select other independent variables or to transform some of the variables.

d. The forecasted "industry nominal sales volume" is calculated (in US$ millions) as follows:

$$\text{SALES} = 62.10 + 87.5(100) + 0.1974(500) = \$8,910.80$$

e. When inflation can influence both dependent and independent variables, the results may be misleading. Yost suggests that both SALES and GDP should be inflation adjusted because, in the existing regression model, a spurious correlation may exist between nominal values that does not represent the underlying real economic relationship. Yost might argue that removing inflation from the variables will result in an analysis that may better represent the true economic relationships.

In the long run, consumer decisions are based more frequently on real values than on nominal values. Therefore, predictions based on real values may be more useful. Also, in this regression, current GDP is a nominal variable but CHILD is not. By inflation-adjusting SALES and GDP, all of the variables in the equation become comparable. After the analyst has estimated constant dollar (real) sales, current dollar (nominal) sales may be obtained by adjusting predicted constant dollar sales by the expected inflation rate. Therefore, Yost is justified in her comment.

10

TIME SERIES ANALYSIS

LEARNING OUTCOMES

After completing this chapter, you will be able to do the following:

- Compute the predicted trend value for a time series, given the estimated trend coefficients.
- Discuss the factors that determine whether a linear trend or a log-linear trend should be used with a particular time series.
- Discuss the limitations of trend models.
- List the requirements for a time series to be covariance stationary.
- Discuss the structure of an autoregressive model of order p.
- Explain how autocorrelations of the residuals from an autoregressive (AR) model can be used to test whether the AR model fits the time series.
- Compute the one-step-ahead forecast of a time series using an autoregressive model.
- Explain mean reversion.
- Compute the two-step-ahead forecast of a time series using an autoregressive model.
- Explain the difference between in-sample forecasts and out-of-sample forecasts.
- Discuss the instability of coefficients of time-series models.
- Define a random walk.
- Discuss the implications of unit roots for time-series analysis.
- Discuss when unit roots are likely to occur.
- Discuss how a time series with a unit root can be transformed so that it can be analyzed with an autoregressive model.
- Compute an n-period moving average of a time series.
- Discuss the structure of a moving-average model of order q.
- Determine the moving-average (MA) order of a time series from the autocorrelations of that series.
- Distinguish an autoregressive time series from a moving-average time series.
- Discuss how to test and correct for seasonality in a time-series model.
- Compute a forecast using an autoregressive model with a seasonal lag.
- Discuss the limitations of autoregressive moving-average (ARMA) models.

- Discuss how to test for autoregressive conditional heteroskedasticity.
- Discuss how to predict the variance of a time series using an autoregressive conditional heteroskedasticity (ARCH) model.

1 INTRODUCTION TO TIME SERIES ANALYSIS

As financial analysts, we often use time-series data to make investment decisions. A **time series** is a set of values of a particular variable in different time periods: the quarterly sales for a particular firm over the past five years, for example, or the daily returns on a traded security. In this chapter, we explore the two chief uses of time-series models: to explain the past and to predict the future of a time series. We also discuss how to estimate time-series models, and we examine how a model describing a particular time series can change over time. The following four examples illustrate the kinds of questions we might want to ask about time series.

Suppose we are deciding whether to invest in a fixed-income portfolio. Since an increase in inflation would lower the value of this portfolio, and vice-versa, our expectation of the future inflation may influence our decision. We may therefore want to model inflation, and see how an analysis of past inflation can help us in our decision making. Figure 10-1 shows monthly U.S. inflation (seasonally adjusted), as measured by the annualized percentage change in the U.S. Consumer Price Index (CPI) from January 1985 to December 1998.[1] Has inflation decreased on average during this period? Is inflation less volatile now than it was in previous years? How can we best use past inflation to predict future inflation?

FIGURE 10-1   Monthly CPI Inflation, Seasonally Adjusted

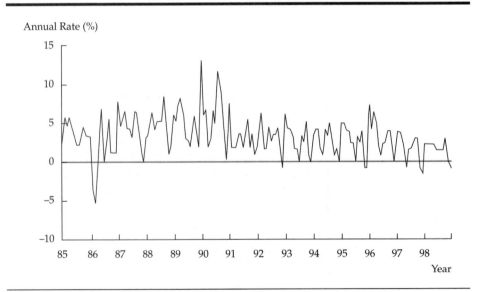

Source: U.S. Bureau of Labor Statistics

---

[1] Seasonally adjusted data correct for predictable seasonal patterns in variables. Seasonal adjustment will be discussed later in this chapter.

Suppose we are considering whether to invest in Intel Corporation's stock. For this purpose, we are interested in analyzing Intel's sales. Figure 10-2 shows Intel's quarterly sales from the first quarter of 1985 to the second quarter of 1999. Quarterly sales have increased more than twenty-fold during those 15 years. Does a simple linear trend model explain the increase in sales? Is sales growth more volatile now than it was in previous years? How can we best use Intel's past sales to predict its future sales?

FIGURE 10-2   Intel Quarterly Net Sales

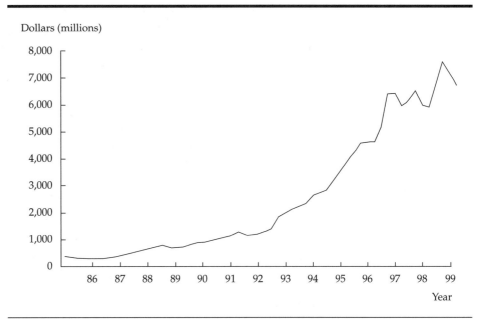

Source: Compustat®

Suppose we are managing a U.S.-based investment portfolio that includes some British stocks. Since the value of this portfolio would decrease if the pound sterling depreciates with respect to the dollar, and vice-versa, we are considering whether to hedge the exposure to the changes in the value of the pound sterling. To help us in making this decision, we want to model the dollar/pound sterling exchange rate. Figure 10-3 shows monthly data on the dollar/pound sterling exchange rate from January 1971 to December 1998. (The data are monthly averages of daily exchange rates.) Has the exchange rate been more stable since 1992 than it was in previous years? Has the exchange rate shown a long-term trend? How can we best use past exchange rates to predict future exchange rates?

Suppose we cover retail stores for a sell-side firm and we want to predict retail sales. Figure 10-4 shows monthly data on U.S. real retail sales from January 1971 to December 1998. The data are inflation-adjusted but not seasonally adjusted. Because the reported sales in the stores' financial statements are not seasonally adjusted, we model seasonally unadjusted retail sales. How can we model the trend in retail sales? How can we adjust for the extreme seasonality reflected in the peaks and troughs occurring at regular intervals? How can we best use past retail sales to predict future retail sales?

After examining the time series in Figures 10-1 through 10-4, five fundamental questions arise: How do we model trends? How do we predict the future value of a time series based on its past values? How do we model seasonality? How do we choose among time-series models? And how do we model changes in the variance of time series over time? We address each of these issues in this chapter.

FIGURE 10-3 UK/US Exchange Rate, Monthly Average of Daily Data

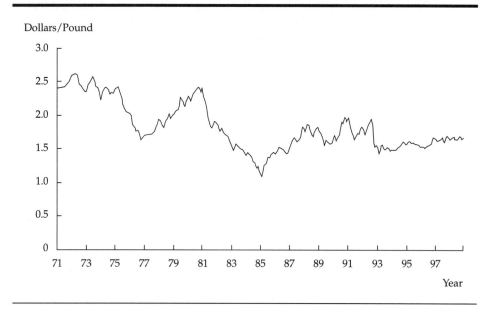

Source: Ibbotson Associates

FIGURE 10-4 Monthly U.S. Real Retail Sales (Not Seasonally Adjusted)

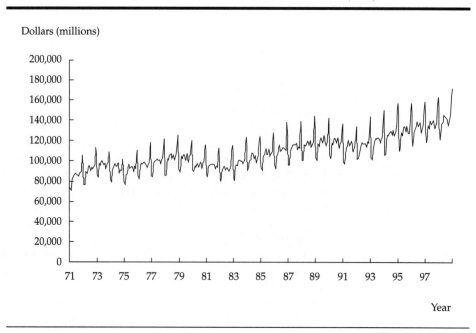

Source: Federal Reserve Bank of St. Louis

2 TRENDS

Estimating a trend in a time series and using that trend to predict future values of the time series is the simplest method of forecasting. For example, we saw clearly in Figure 10-2 that Intel's quarterly sales show a long-term pattern of upward movement—that is, a **trend.** In this section, we examine two types of trends, linear trends and log-linear trends, and discuss how to choose between them.

The simplest type of trend is a **linear trend.** If a time series, y_t, has a linear trend, then we can model the series using the following regression equation:

$$y_t = b_0 + b_1 t + \epsilon_t, t = 1, 2, \ldots, T \tag{10-1}$$

where

> y_t = the value of the time series at time t (this is the value of the dependent variable)
> b_0 = the y-intercept term
> b_1 = the slope coefficient
> t = time, the independent or explanatory variable
> ϵ_t = a random-error term

In Equation 10-1, the trend line, $b_0 + b_1 t$, predicts the value of the time series at time t (where t takes on a value of 1 in the first period of the sample and increases by 1 in each subsequent period). Because the coefficient b_1 is the slope of the trend line, we refer to b_1 as the trend coefficient. We can estimate the two coefficients, b_0 and b_1, using ordinary least squares (OLS), calling the values of the estimated coefficients $\hat{b}_0$ and $\hat{b}_1$.

Now we demonstrate how to use these estimates to predict the value of the time series in a particular period. Recall that t takes on a value of 1 in period 1. Therefore, the predicted or fitted value of y_t in period 1 is $\hat{y}_1 = \hat{b}_0 + \hat{b}_1(1)$. Similarly, in a subsequent period, say the sixth period, the fitted value is $\hat{y}_6 = \hat{b}_0 + \hat{b}_1(6)$. Now suppose that we want to predict the value of the time series for a period outside the sample, say period $T + 1$. The predicted value of y_t for period $T + 1$ is $\hat{y}_{T+1} = \hat{b}_0 + \hat{b}_1(T + 1)$.

EXAMPLE 10-1.   The Trend in the Consumer Price Index.

Suppose we are deciding whether to invest in a fixed-income portfolio. We are concerned about the future level of inflation because that would affect the value of this portfolio. Therefore, we want to predict future inflation rates. For this purpose, we first need to estimate the linear trend in inflation. To do so, we use the monthly CPI inflation data, expressed as an annual percentage rate,[2] shown previously in Figure 10-1. The data include 168 months from January 1985 to December 1998, and the model to be estimated is $y_t = b_0 + b_1 t + \epsilon_t, t = 1, 2, \ldots, 168$. Table 10-1 shows the results of estimating this equation. Both the intercept ($\hat{b}_0 = 4.3543$) and the trend coefficient ($\hat{b}_1 = -0.0132$) are highly statistically significant, as shown by the t-statistics for both coefficients, which are well above 3 in absolute value. Because the slope of the trend line is estimated to be -0.0132, we conclude that the linear trend model's best estimate is that the annualized rate of inflation declined at a rate

---

[2] In these data, 1 percent is represented as 1.0.

of about one one-hundredth of a percentage point per month during the sample time period.

TABLE 10-1   Estimating a Linear Trend in Inflation
                Monthly Data from January 1985 to December 1998

Regression Statistics		
R-squared	0.0636	
Standard error	2.4643	
Observations	168	
Durbin-Watson	1.29	

	Coefficient	Standard Error	t-Statistic
Intercept	4.3543	0.3820	11.4002
Trend	−0.0132	0.0039	−3.3589

Source for data: U.S. Bureau of Labor Statistics

FIGURE 10-5   Monthly CPI Inflation, With Trend

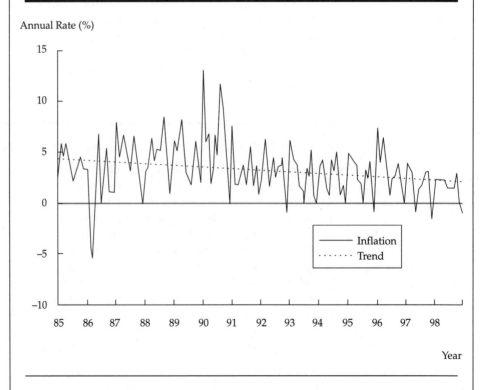

Source: U.S. Bureau of Labor Statistics

In January 1985, the first month of the sample, the predicted value of inflation is $\hat{y}_1 = 4.3543 - 0.0132(1) = 4.3411$ percent.[3] Similarly, in December 1998, the 168th or the last month of the sample, the predicted value of inflation is $\hat{y}_{168} = 4.3543 - 0.0132(168) = 2.1367$ percent. Note, though, that these predicted values are for the past. A comparison of these values with the actual values indicates how well our model fits the data; however, a main purpose of the estimated model is to predict the level of inflation for future periods. For example, for December 1999 (12 months after the end of the sample), $t = 168 + 12 = 180$, and the predicted level of inflation is $\hat{y}_{180} = 4.3543 - 0.0132(180) = 1.9783$ percent.

Figure 10-5 shows the inflation data along with the fitted trend. Note that inflation does not appear to be above or below the trend line for a long period of time. There are no persistent differences between the trend and actual inflation. Thus, it is reasonable to use a linear trend line to model changes in inflation since 1985. Furthermore, we can conclude that inflation has been steadily decreasing over time, a fact that can significantly affect investment decisions. Note also that the R^2 in this model is quite low, indicating great uncertainty in the inflation forecasts from this model. In fact, the trend explains only 6.36 percent of the variance in monthly inflation. Later in this chapter, we will examine whether we can build a better model of inflation than a model that uses only a trend line.

EXAMPLE 10-2.   Quarterly Sales at Intel.

Sometimes we cannot use trend lines to model time series because trend lines can lead to non-random errors. For example, suppose we want to use Equation 10-1 to fit the data on quarterly sales for Intel Corporation shown in Figure 10-2. We use 58 observations on Intel's sales from the first quarter of 1985 to the second quarter of 1999 to estimate the linear trend regression model $y_t = b_0 + b_1 t + \epsilon_t, t = 1, 2, \ldots, 58$. Table 10-2 shows the results of estimating this equation.

TABLE 10-2   Estimating a Linear Trend in Intel Sales

Regression Statistics	
R-squared	0.8680
Standard error	849.8342
Observations	58
Durbin-Watson	1.24

	Coefficient	Standard Error	t-Statistic
Intercept	−1227.9844	226.0949	−5.4313
Trend	127.9075	6.6657	19.1888

Source for data: Compustat®

---

[3] Some of the arithmetic results in this chapter are not exact because of rounding in the estimated coefficients.

At first glance, the results shown in Table 10-2 seem quite reasonable: both the intercept and the trend coefficient are highly statistically significant. When we plot the data on Intel's sales and the trend line, however, we see a different picture. As Figure 10-6 shows, before 1989 the trend line is persistently below sales. Between 1989 and 1995, the trend line is persistently above sales. After 1995, the trend line is once again persistently below sales.

FIGURE 10-6   Intel Quarterly Net Sales

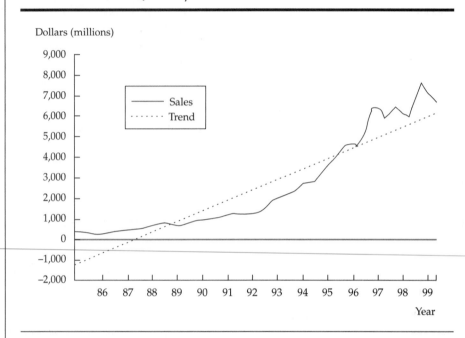

Source: Compustat®

Recall a key assumption underlying the regression model: that the regression errors are not correlated across observations. If a trend is persistently above or below the value of the time series, however, the residuals (that is, the difference between the time series and the trend) are serially correlated. Figure 10-7 shows the residuals (the difference between sales and the trend) from estimating a linear trend model with the raw sales data. The figure shows that the residuals are persistent. Because of this persistent serial correlation in the errors of the trend model, using a linear trend to fit sales at Intel would be inappropriate, even though the R^2 of the equation is high (0.87).

Thus, linear trend models don't work well if their residuals are persistent, and we then need to employ alternative models. For financial time series, an important alternative to a linear trend is a log-linear trend. Log-linear trends work well in fitting time series that have exponential growth.

How does exponential growth work? Suppose we describe a time series by the following equation:

$$y_t = e^{b_0 + b_1 t}, t = 1, 2, \ldots, T \tag{10-2}$$

In period 1, the time series would have the value $y_1 = e^{b_0 + b_1(1)}$ and in period 2, the series would have the value $y_2 = e^{b_0 + b_1(2)}$. The resulting ratio of the values of the time series in the first two periods is $y_2/y_1 = (e^{b_0 + b_1(2)})/(e^{b_0 + b_1(1)}) = e^{b_1(1)}$. Generally,

FIGURE 10-7   Residual from Predicting Intel Net Sales with a Trend

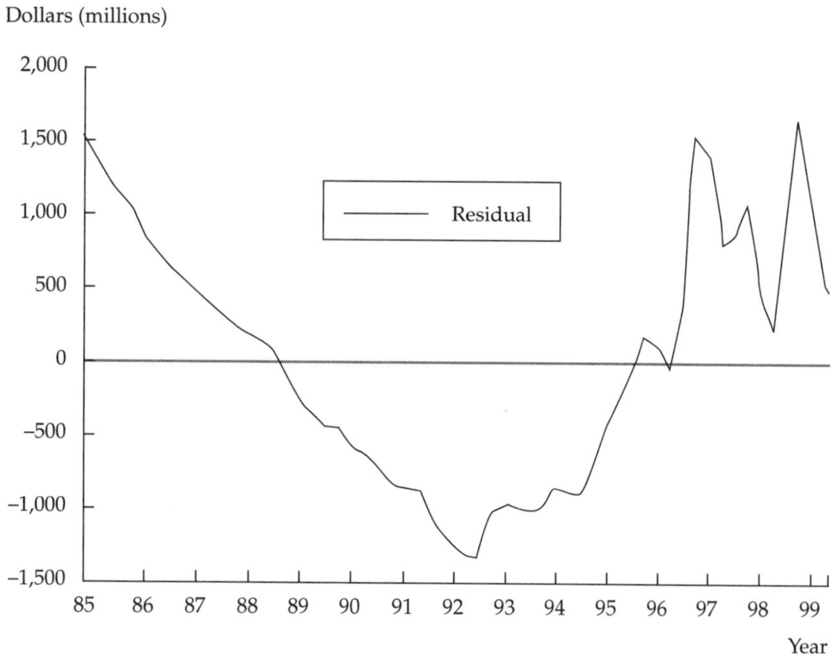

Source: Compustat®

in any period t, the time series has the value $y_t = e^{b_0 + b_1(t)}$. In period $t + 1$, the time series has the value $y_{t+1} = e^{b_0 + b_1(t+1)}$. The ratio of the values in the times series $(t + 1)$ and t is $y_{t+1}/y_t = e^{b_0 + b_1(t+1)}/e^{b_0 + b_1(t)} = e^{b_1(1)}$. Thus, the proportional rate of growth in the time series over two consecutive periods is always the same and the rate of growth is $(y_{t+1} - y_t)/y_t = y_{t+1}/y_t - 1 = e^{b_1} - 1$.[4] Exponential growth is growth at a constant rate with continuous compounding. Continuous compounding is just a mathematical convenience that allows us to restate the equation in a form that is easy to estimate.

If we take the natural log of both sides of Equation 10-2, the result is the following simpler equation:

$$\ln y_t = b_0 + b_1 t, \quad t = 1, 2, \dots, T$$

Note that this equation is linear in the coefficients b_0 and b_1. Therefore, if a time series grows at an exponential rate, we can model the natural log of that series using a linear trend.[5] Of course, no time series grows exactly at an exponential rate. Consequently, if we want to use a **log-linear model,** we must estimate the following equation:

$$\ln y_t = b_0 + b_1 t + \epsilon_t, \quad t = 1, 2, \dots, T \tag{10-3}$$

---

[4] For example, if we use annual periods and $e^{b_1} = 1.04$ for a particular series, then that series grows by $1.04 - 1 = 0.04$, that is, 4 percent per year.

[5] An exponential growth rate is a compound growth rate with continuous compounding. Continuous compounding is discussed in the chapter on the time value of money.

A log-linear model predicts that $\ln y_t$ will increase by b_1 from one time period to the next. The model predicts a constant growth rate in y_t of $e^{b_1} - 1$. For example, if $b_1 = 0.05$, then the predicted growth rate of y_t in each period is ($e^{0.05} - 1 = 0.051271$) or 5.13 percent. In contrast, the linear trend model (Equation 10-1) predicts that y_t grows by a constant amount from each period until the next.

EXAMPLE 10-3.   Quarterly Sales at Intel.

For this example, we return to the data we used in Example 10-2, quarterly sales for Intel Corporation from the first quarter of 1985 to the second quarter of 1999. Notice the curvature in the plot of the data in Figure 10-2. This shape is a hint that an exponential curve may fit the data. Consequently, we estimate the following linear equation:

$$\ln y_t = b_0 + b_1 t + \epsilon_t, \, t = 1, 2, \ldots, 58$$

This equation seems to fit the sales data much better than did Equation 10-1. As Table 10-3 shows, the R^2 for this equation is 0.98. (The R^2 with Equation 10-1 was 0.87.) An R^2 of 0.98 means that 98 percent of the variation in the natural log of Intel's sales is explained solely by a linear trend.

TABLE 10-3   Estimating a Linear Trend in Log-Normal Intel Sales

Regression Statistics		
R-squared	0.9835	
Standard error	0.1360	
Observations	58	
Durbin-Watson	1.49	

	Coefficient	Standard Error	t-Statistic
Intercept	5.5366	0.0362	153.0090
Trend	0.0617	0.0011	57.8359

Source for data: Compustat®

Figure 10-8 shows how well a linear trend fits the natural log of Intel's sales. The natural logs of the sales data lie very close to the linear trend during the sample period, and log sales are not above or below the trend for long periods of time. Thus, a log-linear trend model seems much better suited for modeling Intel's sales than a linear trend model.

How can we use the results of estimating Equation 10-3 to predict Intel's sales in the future? Suppose, for example, that we want to predict Intel's sales for the fourth quarter of 1999 ($t = 60$). The estimated value $\hat{b}_0$ is 5.5366, and the estimated

FIGURE 10-8   Ln Intel Quarterly Net Sales

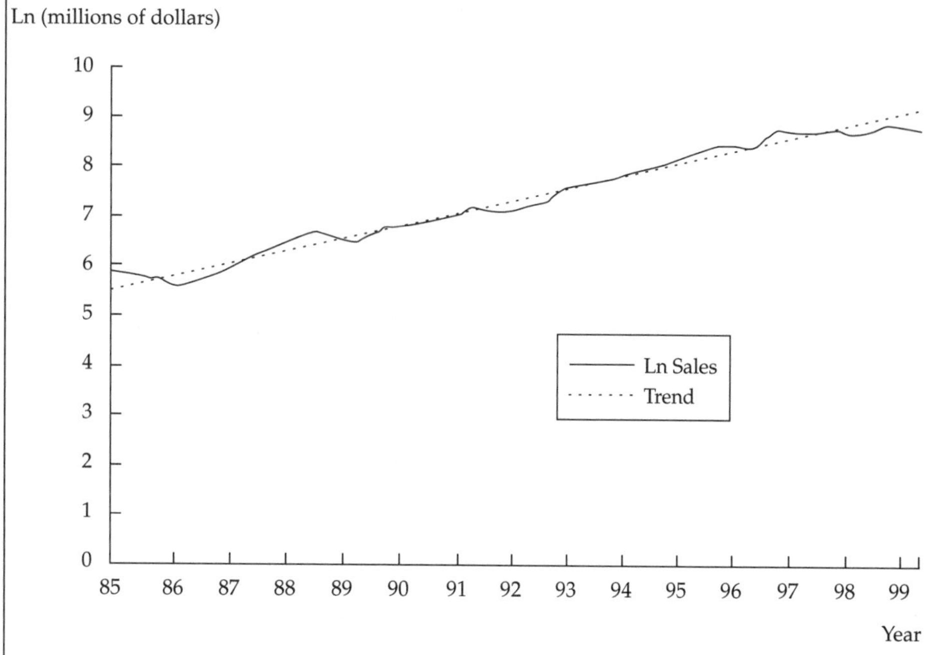

Ln (millions of dollars)

Source: Compustat®

value $\hat{b}_1$ is 0.0617. Thus, the estimated model predicts that $\text{l}\hat{\text{n}}\ y_{60} = 5.5366 + 0.0617(60) = 9.2386$ and sales will be $\hat{y}_{60} = e^{\text{l}\hat{\text{n}}\ y_{60}} = e^{9.2386} = \$10,286.63$ million.[6]

How much different is this forecast from the prediction of the linear trend model? Table 10-2 showed that for the linear trend model, the estimated value of $\hat{b}_0$ is -1227.9844 and the estimated value of $\hat{b}_1$ is 127.9075. Thus, if we predict Intel's sales for the fourth quarter of 1999 ($t = 60$) using this model, the forecast is $\hat{y}_{60} = -1227.9844 + 127.9075(60) = \$6,446.47$ million. This forecast is far below the prediction made by the log-linear regression model. Later in this chapter, we will examine whether we can build a better model of Intel's quarterly sales than a model that uses only a log-linear trend.

3   THE LIMITATIONS OF TREND MODELS

The trend in Examples 10-1 and 10-3 appears to fit the data well, but does it entirely capture the complex dynamics of the time series? In this section, we discuss how to test whether a trend by itself accurately predicts a time series.

Both the linear trend model and the log-linear trend model are single-variable regression models. If they are to be correctly specified, the regression-model assumptions

---

[6] Note that $\hat{b}_1 = 0.0617$ implies that the growth rate per quarter in Intel's sales will be 6.36 percent ($e^{0.0617} - 1 = 0.063643$).

must be satisfied. In particular, the regression error for one period must be uncorrelated with the regression error for all other periods.[7]

In the chapter on regression analysis, we showed that we could test whether regression errors are serially correlated using the Durbin-Watson statistic. If the trend models shown in Examples 10-1 and 10-3 really capture the time-series behavior of inflation and the log of Intel's sales, then the Durbin-Watson statistic for both of those models should not be significantly different from 2.0. Otherwise, the errors in the model are either positively or negatively serially correlated, and that correlation can be used to build a better forecasting model for those time series.

In Example 10-1, estimating a linear trend in the monthly CPI inflation yielded a Durbin-Watson statistic of 1.29. Is this result significantly different from 2.0? To find out, we need to test the null hypothesis of no serial correlation (H_0: $DW = 2$) against the alternative hypothesis (H_a: $DW \neq 2$). For a sample with 168 observations and one regressor, the critical value, d_l, for the Durbin-Watson test statistic at the 0.05 significance level is approximately 1.65. Because the value of the Durbin-Watson statistic (1.29) is below this critical value, we can reject the hypothesis of no significant serial correlation in the errors. We can conclude that a regression equation that uses a linear trend to model inflation has significant serial correlation in the errors.[8] We will need a different kind of regression model because this one violates the least-squares assumption of no serial correlation in the errors.

In Example 10-3, estimating a linear trend with the natural logarithm of sales for the Intel example yielded a Durbin-Watson statistic of 1.49. Suppose we wish to test the null hypothesis of no serial correlation (H_0: $DW = 2$) against the alternative hypothesis (H_a: $DW \neq 2$). The critical value, d_l, is 1.54 at the 0.05 significance level. The value of the Durbin-Watson statistic (1.49) is below this critical value, so we can reject the null hypothesis of no significant serial correlation in the errors. We can conclude that a regression equation that uses a trend to model the log of Intel's quarterly sales has significant serial correlation in the errors. So, for this series as well, we need to build a different kind of model.

Overall, we conclude that the trend models sometimes have the limitation that errors are serially correlated. Existence of serial correlation suggests that we can build better forecasting models for such time series than trend models.

4   FUNDAMENTAL ISSUES IN TIME SERIES

We have just seen that if we use a trend to model a time series, the residuals of the trend model may be serially correlated, thus violating a fundamental assumption of the linear regression model. If we find the residuals of the trend model to be serially correlated, how then should we model a time series?

One simple alternative to using a trend model might be to assume that the value of a time series in a particular period, say y_t, is related to its values in previous periods. For

---

[7] A key difference between cross-sectional data and time-series data is that time-series observations have a logical ordering. They must be processed in the order of the time periods involved. For example, we should not make a prediction of the inflation rate using a CPI series in which the order of the observations had been scrambled, because time patterns such as growth in the explanatory variables can negatively affect the statistical properties of the estimated regression coefficients.

[8] Significantly small values of the Durbin-Watson statistic indicate positive serial correlation; significantly large values point to negative serial correlation. Here the DW statistic of 1.29 indicates positive serial correlation. For more information, see the chapter on regression analysis.

example, if y_t depends only on its value from the previous period, we might want to estimate the equation

$$y_t = b_0 + b_1 y_{t-1} + \epsilon_t. \tag{10-4}$$

Note that the independent variable in Equation 10-4 is a random variable. This may seem like a mathematical subtlety, but it is not. If we use ordinary least squares to estimate Equation 10-4 when we have a randomly distributed independent variable that is a lagged value of the dependent variable, our statistical inference may be invalid. To conduct valid statistical inference, we must make a key assumption in time-series analysis: We must assume that the time series we are modeling is **covariance stationary.**[9]

What does it mean for a time series to be covariance stationary? The basic idea is that a time series is covariance stationary if its properties, such as mean and variance, do not change over time. A covariance stationary series must satisfy three principal requirements.[10] First, the expected value of the time series must be constant and finite in all periods; $E(y_t) = \mu$ and $|\mu| < \infty$, $t = 1, 2, \dots , T$. Second, the variance of the time series must be constant and finite in all periods. Third, the covariance of the time series with itself a fixed number of periods in the past or future must be constant and finite in all periods. The second and third requirements can be summarized as follows:[11]

$$\text{Cov}(y_t, y_{t-s}) = \lambda_s, \, |\lambda_s| < \infty, t = 1, 2, \dots , T; s = 0, \pm1, \pm2, \dots , \pm T$$

What are the consequences if a time series is not covariance stationary but we model it as in Equation 10-4? If we do, the estimation results will have no economic meaning. For a non-covariance stationary time series, estimating the regression in Equation 10-4 would yield spurious results. In particular, the estimate of b_1 will be biased and any hypothesis tests will not be valid. For example, as we discuss later in this section, Intel's quarterly sales are not covariance stationary. If we still model Intel's quarterly sales as in Equation 10-4, any forecast we make based on the estimated model and any hypothesis we test will not be valid. As we explain later, we will need to first adjust Intel's quarterly sales to make them covariance stationary before modeling them as in Equation 10-4.

How can we tell if a time series is covariance stationary? We can often answer this question by looking at a plot of the time series. If the plot shows roughly the same mean and variance over time without any significant seasonality, then we may want to assume that the time series is covariance stationary.

Some of the time series we looked at in Figures 10-1 to 10-4 appear to be covariance stationary. For example, the inflation data shown in Figure 10-1 appear to have roughly the same mean and variance over the sample period. Other time series, such as the data on Intel's quarterly sales in Figure 10-2, clearly show that the mean changes greatly over time. Thus, Intel's quarterly sales are not covariance stationary.

Figure 10-4 shows that monthly retail sales (not seasonally adjusted) are also not covariance stationary. Sales in December are always much higher than sales in other months (these are the regular large peaks), and sales in January are always much lower (these are the regular large drops after the December peaks). On average, sales also increase over time, so the mean of sales is not constant.

---

[9] *Weakly stationary* is a synonym for covariance stationary. You may also encounter the more restrictive concept of *strictly stationary,* which has little practical application. For details, see Diebold (1997).

[10] The absolute value is used to rule out the case where the mean is negative without limit (minus infinity).

[11] When s in this equation equals 0, then this equation imposes the condition that the variance of the time series is finite. This is so because the covariance of a random variable with itself is its variance: $\text{Cov}(y_t, y_t) = \text{Var}(y_t)$.

Later in this chapter, we will show how to adjust Intel's quarterly and monthly retail sales so that we can model a transformed version of those data as a covariance-stationary series. Once the data are adjusted, we can often use linear regression or other relatively simple statistical methods to successfully model the time series.

5 AUTOREGRESSIVE TIME-SERIES MODELS

Suppose we want to forecast a particular time series that we think is covariance stationary and has values related to its values in a previous period. In such an **autoregressive model** (AR), a time series is regressed on its own past values. When we use this model, we can drop the normal notation of y as the dependent variable and x as the independent variable because we no longer have that distinction to make. Here we simply use x_t. For example, a first-order autoregression, AR(1), for the variable x_t is shown by Equation 10-4 now using x_t rather than y_t:

$$x_t = b_0 + b_1 x_{t-1} + \epsilon_t$$

Thus, in an AR(1) model, we use only the most recent past value of x_t to predict the current value of x_t. In general, a pth-order autoregression, AR(p), for the variable x_t is shown by

$$x_t = b_0 + b_1 x_{t-1} + b_2 x_{t-2} + \cdots + b_p x_{t-p} + \epsilon_t. \tag{10-5}$$

In this equation, p past values of x_t are used to predict the current value of x_t.

If a time series is covariance stationary, then we can estimate an autoregressive model using ordinary least squares. But how do we know whether to use a first-order autoregression or a pth-order autoregression to model a particular time series? Before we can answer this question, we must examine a part of the regression equation that we have ignored so far in our discussion of autoregressive models: the error term, ϵ_t. In the linear regression model, we assumed that the error term was not correlated across observations. That assumption is even more critical in a time-series model than it is in a model in which the dependent and explanatory variables are different.

Suppose we use ordinary least squares to estimate the regression $y_t = b_0 + b_1 x_t + \epsilon_t$ where the explanatory and dependent variables are different, and for some reason the error term, ϵ_t, is correlated over time. As we discussed in the chapter on multiple regression, serial correlation of the errors in this model does not affect the accuracy of our estimates of b_0 and b_1.[12] Likewise, we can use ordinary least squares to estimate an autoregressive model (Equation 10-5) if the error term is uncorrelated across periods. In a time-series regression, however, serial correlation in the error term causes regression parameter estimates to be incorrect.[13] Suppose, for example, that the error terms in Equation 10-4 were serially correlated. Then we could not rely on the estimated values of b_0 and b_1 to make forecasts or to test hypotheses.[14]

This difference between time-series models and linear-regression models requires that we test for serial correlation in the errors of a time-series model before we conclude

---

[12] As we noted in the chapter on multiple regression, the use of the term *accuracy* here is helpful for a general understanding, but not entirely correct mathematically. The term *consistent* describes an estimator whose value converges to the true parameter estimate as the sample gets very large.

[13] That is, the parameters become inconsistent.

[14] See Diebold (1997) for this and other technical issues in this chapter.

that the model is valid for forecasting or testing hypotheses. Unfortunately, our previous test for serial correlation, the Durbin-Watson statistic, is not valid when the independent variables include past values of the dependent variable. Thus, for most time-series models, we cannot use the Durbin-Watson statistic.

Fortunately, we can use other tests to determine whether the errors in a time-series model are serially correlated. One such test reveals whether the autocorrelations of the error term are significantly different from 0. The autocorrelations of a time series are the correlations of that series with its own past values. For example, the first-order autocorrelation of a covariance-stationary series, x_t, which we denote as ρ_1, is as follows:

$$\rho_1 = \frac{E[(x_t - \mu)(x_{t-1} - \mu)]}{\sigma_x^2} = \frac{\text{Cov}(x_t, x_{t-1})}{\sigma_x^2}$$

In general, for a covariance-stationary series, x_t, the **kth order autocorrelation** (ρ_k) is

$$\rho_k = \frac{E[(x_t - \mu)(x_{t-k} - \mu)]}{\sigma_x^2} = \frac{\text{Cov}(x_t, x_{t-k})}{\sigma_x^2}$$

Note, for example, that the zeroth-order autocorrelation of x_t is $\dfrac{\text{Cov}(x_t, x_t)}{\sigma_x^2} = \dfrac{\text{Var}(x_t)}{\text{Var}(x_t)} = 1$.
Note also that we have the relationship $\text{Cov}(x_t, x_{t-k}) \leq \text{Var}(x_t)$ with equality holding when $k = 0$. This means that the absolute value of ρ_k is less than or equal to 1. The expected value of the error term in a time-series model is 0.[15] Therefore, the autocorrelations of the error term for a time-series model are

$$\rho_k = \frac{E[(\epsilon_t - 0)(\epsilon_{t-k} - 0)]}{\sigma_\epsilon^2} = \frac{\text{Cov}(\epsilon_t, \epsilon_{t-k})}{\sigma_\epsilon^2}$$

We can use autocorrelations to determine whether we are using the right time-series model by testing whether the autocorrelations of the error term are significantly different from 0. Of course, we can never directly observe the autocorrelations, ρ_k. Instead, we must estimate them. Thus, we replace the expected value of x_t, μ, by its estimated value, $\bar{x}$, to compute the estimated autocorrelations. The kth order estimated autocorrelation of time series, x_t, which we denote $\hat{\rho}_k$, is $\hat{\rho}_k = \dfrac{\displaystyle\sum_{t=k+1}^{T} [(x_t - \bar{x})(x_{t-k} - \bar{x})]}{\displaystyle\sum_{t=1}^{T} (x_t - \bar{x})^2}$

Even after we have estimated the autocorrelations, we still do not know whether they are significantly different from 0. To test the significance of the estimated autocorrelations, we must compute their standard error. Fortunately, the standard error of each estimated autocorrelation is easy to compute because it is $1/\sqrt{T}$.[16] Thus, if we have 100 observations on a time series, the standard error for each of the estimated autocorrelations is 0.1.

How can we use information about the autocorrelations to determine whether an autoregressive time-series model is correctly specified? We can use a simple three-step

---

[15] This is similar to the assumption made in the previous two chapters about the expected value of the error term.

[16] This is derived in Diebold (1997).

method. First, estimate a particular autoregressive model, say an AR(1) model. Second, compute the autocorrelations of the residuals from the model.[17] Third, test to see whether the autocorrelations are significantly different from 0. If significance tests show that the autocorrelations are significantly different from 0, the model is not correctly specified; we may need to modify the model in ways that we will discuss below.[18] We now present an example to demonstrate how this three-step method works.

EXAMPLE 10-4.   Predicting Gross Margins for Intel Corporation.

Suppose we want to predict Intel's gross margin [(Sales − Cost of goods sold)/Sales] with data from the first quarter of 1985 to the second quarter of 1999 using an autoregressive model. We do not really know the best model of gross margin, so we decide to start out with a first-order autoregressive model, AR(1): Gross margin$_t$ = $b_0 + b_1$ Gross margin$_{t-1}$ + ϵ_t. Table 10-4 shows the results of estimating this AR(1) model, along with the autocorrelations of the residuals from that model.

The first thing to note about Table 10-4 is that both the constant ($\hat{b}_0$ = 0.0748) and the first lag ($\hat{b}_1$ = 0.8785) of the gross margin are highly significant in the regression equation.[19] The t-statistic for the constant is about 2.2, whereas the t-statistic for the first lag of the gross margin is almost 16. With 57 observations and two parameters, this model has 55 degrees of freedom. At the 0.05 significance level, the critical value for a t-statistic is about 2.0. Therefore, we must reject the null hypotheses that the constant is equal to 0 ($b_0 = 0$) and the coefficient on the first lag is equal to 0 ($b_1 = 0$) in favor of the alternative hypothesis that the coefficients, individually, are not equal to 0. But are these statistics valid? We will know when we test whether the residuals from this model are serially correlated.

At the bottom of Table 10-4, the first four autocorrelations of the residual are displayed along with the standard error and the t-statistic for each of those autocorrelations.[20] The sample has 57 observations, so the standard error for each of the autocorrelations is $1/\sqrt{57}$ = 0.1325. Table 10-4 shows that none of the first four autocorrelations has a t-statistic larger than 1.25 in absolute value. Thus, we can conclude that none of these autocorrelations is significantly different from 0. Consequently, we can assume that the residuals are not serially correlated and that the model is correctly specified,[21] and we can use ordinary least squares to estimate the parameters and the parameters' standard errors in the autoregressive model.

Now that we have concluded that this model is correctly specified, how can we use it to predict Intel's gross margin in the next period? The estimated equation is Gross margin$_t$ = 0.0748 + 0.8785 × Gross margin$_{t-1}$ + ϵ_t. The expected value of

---

[17] We can compute these autocorrelations easily with most statistical packages. In Excel, for example, to compute the first-order autocorrelation, we compute the correlation of the residuals from observations 1 through $T - 1$ with the residuals from observations 2 through T.

[18] Often, econometricians use additional tests for the significance of autocorrelation coefficients. For example, the Box-Pierce Q statistic is frequently used to test the joint hypothesis that all autocorrelations of the residuals are equal to 0. For further discussion, see Diebold (1997).

[19] The first lag of a time series is the value of the time series in the previous period.

[20] For seasonally unadjusted data, analysts often compute the same number of autocorrelations as there are observations in a year (for example, four for quarterly data). The number of autocorrelations computed also often depends on sample size, as discussed in Diebold (1997).

[21] Statisticians have many other tests for serial correlation of the residuals in a time-series model. For details, see Diebold (1997).

TABLE 10-4 Autoregression: AR(1) Model
Gross Margin—Intel Corporation
Quarterly Data from February 1985 to February 1999

Regression Statistics

R-squared	0.8196
Standard error	0.0352
Observations	57
Durbin-Watson	1.8687

	Coefficient	Standard Error	t-Statistic
Constant	0.0748	0.0334	2.2421
Lag 1	0.8785	0.0556	15.8090

Autocorrelations of the Residual

Lag	Autocorrelation	Standard Error	t-Statistic
1	0.0020	0.1325	0.0154
2	−0.1652	0.1325	−1.2474
3	0.1135	0.1325	0.8569
4	−0.0462	0.1325	−0.3487

Source for data: Compustat®

the error term is 0 in any period. Thus, this model predicts that gross margin in period $t + 1$ will be Gross margin$_{t+1}$ = 0.0748 + 0.8785 × Gross margin$_t$. For example, if gross margin is 55 percent in this quarter (0.55), the model predicts that in the next quarter gross margin will be 0.5580 = 0.0748 + 0.8785(0.55). Gross margin is predicted to rise to 55.8 percent. On the other hand, if gross margin is currently 65 percent (0.65), the model predicts that in the next quarter, gross margin will be 0.6458 = 0.0748 + 0.8785(0.65). In this case, gross margin is predicted to fall to 64.58 percent. As we show in the following section, the model predicts gross margin to increase if it is below a certain level (61.56 percent) and to decrease if it is above that level.

5.1 MEAN REVERSION

We say that a time series shows **mean reversion** if it tends to fall when its level is above its mean and rise when its level is below its mean. Much like the temperature in a room controlled by a thermostat, a mean-reverting time series tends to return to its long-term mean. How can we determine the value that the time series tends toward? If a time series is currently at its mean-reverting level, then the model predicts that the value of the time series will be the same in the next period. At its mean-reverting level, we have the relationship $x_{t+1} = x_t$. For an AR(1) model ($x_{t+1} = b_0 + b_1 x_t$), the equality $x_{t+1} = x_t$ implies the level $x_t = b_0 + b_1 x_t$, or $x_t = b_0/(1 - b_1)$. So the AR(1) model predicts that the time series will stay the same if its current value is $b_0/(1 - b_1)$, increase if its current value is below $b_0/(1 - b_1)$, and decrease if its current value is above $b_0/(1 - b_1)$.

In the case of gross margins for Intel, the mean-reverting level for the model shown in Table 10-4 is $0.0748/(1 - 0.8785) = 0.6156$. If the current gross margin is above 0.6156, the model predicts that the gross margin will fall in the next period. If the current gross margin is below 0.6156, the model predicts that the gross margin will rise in the next period. As we will discuss later, all covariance-stationary time series have a finite mean-reverting level.

5.2   MULTIPERIOD FORECASTS AND THE CHAIN RULE OF FORECASTING

Often, financial analysts want to make forecasts for more than one period. For example, we might want to use a quarterly sales model to predict sales for a firm for each of the next four quarters. How can we use a time-series model to make forecasts for more than one period? We can answer this question by looking at how to make multiperiod forecasts from an AR(1) model. The one-period-ahead forecast of x_t from an AR(1) model is as follows:

$$\hat{x}_{t+1} = \hat{b}_0 + \hat{b}_1 x_t \tag{10-6}$$

If we want to forecast x_{t+2} using an AR(1) model, our forecast will have to be

$$\hat{x}_{t+2} = \hat{b}_0 + \hat{b}_1 x_{t+1} \tag{10-7}$$

Unfortunately, we do not know x_{t+1} in period t, so we cannot use Equation 10-7 directly to make a two-period-ahead forecast. We can, however, use our forecast of x_{t+1} and the AR(1) model to make a prediction of x_{t+2}. Using the **chain rule of forecasting,** we can substitute the predicted value of x_{t+1} into Equation 10-7 to get $\hat{x}_{t+2} = \hat{b}_0 + \hat{b}_1 \hat{x}_{t+1}$. We already know $\hat{x}_{t+1}$ from our one-period-ahead forecast in Equation 10-6. Now we have a simple way of predicting x_{t+2}.

Multiperiod forecasts are more uncertain than single-period forecasts because each forecast period has uncertainty. For example, in forecasting x_{t+2}, we first have the uncertainty associated with forecasting x_{t+1} using x_t, and then we have the uncertainty associated with forecasting x_{t+2} using the forecast of x_{t+1}. In general, the more periods a forecast has, the more uncertain it is.[22]

EXAMPLE 10-5.   Multiperiod Prediction of Intel's Gross Margin.

Suppose we want to predict Intel's gross margin in two periods using the model shown in Table 10-4. Assume that Intel's gross margin in the current period is 65 percent (0.65). The one-period-ahead forecast of Intel's gross margin from this model is $0.6458 = 0.0748 + 0.8785(0.65)$. By substituting the one-period-ahead forecast, 0.6458, back into the regression equation, we can derive the following two-period-ahead forecast: $0.6421 = 0.0748 + 0.8785(0.6458)$. Thus, if the current gross margin for Intel is 65 percent, the model predicts that Intel's gross margin in two quarters will be 64.21 percent.

---

[22] If a forecasting model is well specified, the prediction errors from the model will not be serially correlated. If the prediction errors for each period are not serially correlated, then the variance of a multiperiod forecast will be higher than the variance of a single-period forecast.

EXAMPLE 10-6. Modeling U.S. CPI Inflation.

As we discussed in the chapter on regression analysis, inflation and expectations about inflation have a significant effect on market returns to different assets. Suppose, for example, that we want to predict U.S. inflation using annualized monthly data on inflation as measured by the annualized percentage change in the consumer price index (CPI). Which model should we use? In this example, we first show how we decide which autoregressive model to use. This is similar to how we made the decision in Example 10-4 for Intel's gross margins. We then illustrate how two time-series models can make different forecasts of the same time series, reflecting the importance of using the appropriate model.

The first model that we estimate is an AR(1) model, using the previous month's inflation rate as the independent variable: $\text{Inflation}_t = b_0 + b_1 \text{Inflation}_{t-1} + \epsilon_t$, $t = 1, 2, \ldots, 335$. To estimate this model, we use monthly CPI inflation data from January 1971 to December 1998. Table 10-5 shows the results of estimating this model.

**TABLE 10-5 Monthly CPI Inflation at an Annual Rate: AR(1) Model
Monthly Data from February 1971 to December 1998**

Regression Statistics		
R-squared	0.3967	
Standard error	3.4143	
Observations	335	
Durbin-Watson	2.3351	

	Coefficient	Standard Error	t-Statistic
Constant	1.9545	0.2926	6.6804
Lag 1	0.6302	0.0426	14.7976

Autocorrelations of the Residual			
Lag	Autocorrelation	Standard Error	t-Statistic
1	−0.1679	0.0546	−3.0725
2	0.1334	0.0546	2.4417
3	0.0457	0.0546	0.8355
4	0.0944	0.0546	1.7272

Source for data: U.S. Bureau of Labor Statistics

As Table 10-5 shows, both the constant ($\hat{b}_0 = 1.9545$) and the first lagged value of inflation ($\hat{b}_1 = 0.6302$) are highly statistically significant, with large *t*-statistics. With 335 observations and two parameters, this model has 333 degrees of freedom. The critical value for a *t*-statistic at the 0.05 significance level is about 1.97. Therefore, we can reject the individual null hypotheses that the constant is equal to 0 ($b_0 = 0$) and the coefficient on the first lag is equal to 0 ($b_1 = 0$) in favor of the alternative hypothesis that the coefficients, individually, are not equal to 0.

Are these statistics valid? We will know when we test whether the residuals from this model are serially correlated. With 335 observations in this sample, the standard error for each of the estimated autocorrelations is $1/\sqrt{335} = 0.0546$. Both the first and the second estimated autocorrelation have *t*-statistics larger than 2.4 in absolute value. The critical value for the *t*-statistic is 1.97, so we can conclude that the autocorrelations are significantly different from 0. Thus, this model is misspecified because the residuals are serially correlated.

If the residuals in an autoregressive model are serially correlated, we can eliminate the correlation by estimating an autoregressive model with more lags of the dependent variable as explanatory variables. Table 10-6 shows the result of estimating a second time-series model, an AR(2) model using the same data as in the analysis shown in Table 10-5.[23] With 334 observations and three parameters, this model has 331 degrees of freedom. Because the degrees of freedom are almost the same as those for the estimates shown in Table 10-5, the critical value of the *t*-statistic at the 0.05 significance level is almost the same (1.97). If we estimate the equation Inflation$_t = b_0 + b_1$ Inflation$_{t-1} + b_2$ Inflation$_{t-2} + \epsilon_t$, we find that all three of the coefficients in the regression model (a constant and two lags of the dependent variable) are significantly different from 0. The bottom portion of Table 10-6 shows that none of the first four autocorrelations of the residual has a *t*-statistic greater than 1.61 in absolute value. The critical value is 1.97. Therefore, we fail to reject the hypothesis that the individual autocorrelations of the residual are significantly different from 0. We conclude that this model is correctly specified because we find no evidence of serial correlation in the residuals.

The choice between these two time-series models, AR(1) and AR(2), affects our prediction of future inflation. Suppose that in a given month, inflation had been 4 percent at an annual rate in the previous month and 3 percent in the month before that. The AR(1) model shown in Table 10-5 predicts that inflation in the next month will be $4.4755 = 1.9545 + 0.6302(4)$, whereas the AR(2) model shown in Table 10-6 predicts that inflation in the next month will be $4.0704 = 1.4142 + 0.4619(4) + 0.2695(3)$.

As we saw in Table 10-5, the residuals from the AR(1) model have significant serial correlation. We learn from Table 10-6, however, that residuals from the AR(2) model appear to have no significant serial correlation. This result suggests that we should use the AR(2) model, which predicts that inflation in the next month will be about 4.07 percent. If we had used the incorrect AR(1) model, we would have predicted inflation to be 31 basis points higher (4.48 percent vs. 4.07 percent) than we would have forecast using the AR(2) model. This incorrect forecast could have adversely affected our investment recommendations.

---

[23] Note that Table 10-6 shows only 334 observations in the regression because the extra lag of inflation requires the estimation sample to start one month later than the regression in Table 10-5. (With two lags, inflation for January and February 1973 must be known in order to estimate the equation starting in March 1973.)

TABLE 10-6 Monthly CPI Inflation at an Annual Rate: AR(2) Model
Monthly Data from March 1971 to December 1998

Regression Statistics			
Multiple R		0.6635	
R-squared		0.4402	
Standard error		3.2975	
Observations		334	
Durbin-Watson		2.0501	

	Coefficient	Standard Error	t-Statistic
Constant	1.4142	0.3023	4.6785
Lag 1	0.4619	0.0530	8.7191
Lag 2	0.2695	0.0530	5.0876

Autocorrelations of the Residual			
Lag	Autocorrelation	Standard Error	t-Statistic
1	−0.0282	0.0547	−0.5160
2	−0.0880	0.0547	−1.6074
3	−0.0304	0.0547	−0.5560
4	0.0287	0.0547	0.5244

Source for data: U.S. Bureau of Labor Statistics

5.3 COMPARING FORECAST MODEL PERFORMANCE

One way to compare the forecast performance of two models is to compare the variance of the forecast errors that the two models make. The model with the smaller forecast error variance will be the more accurate model, and it will also have the smaller standard error of the time-series regression. (This standard error will usually be directly reported in the output for the time-series regression.)

In comparing forecast accuracy among models, we must distinguish between **in-sample forecast errors** and **out-of-sample forecast errors.** In-sample forecast errors are the residuals from a fitted time-series model. For example, when we estimated a linear trend with raw inflation data from January 1971 to December 1998, the in-sample forecast errors were the residuals from January 1971 to December 1998. If we use this model to predict inflation outside this period, the differences between actual and predicted inflation are out-of-sample forecast errors.

EXAMPLE 10-7.   In-Sample Forecast Comparisons of U.S. CPI Inflation.

In Example 10-6, we compared an AR(1) forecasting model of monthly U.S. inflation with an AR(2) model of monthly U.S. inflation, and we decided that the AR(2) model was preferable. Table 10-5 showed that the standard error from the AR(1) model of inflation is 3.4143, and Table 10-6 showed that the standard error from the AR(2) model is 3.2975. Thus, the AR(2) model has a lower in-sample forecast variance than the AR(1) model, which is consistent with our belief that the AR(2) model is the preferable model. Its standard error is 3.2975/3.4143 = 96.58 percent of the forecast error of the AR(1) model.

Often, we want to compare the forecasting accuracy of different models after the sample period for which they were estimated. We wish to compare the out-of-sample forecast accuracy of the models. Out-of-sample forecast accuracy is important because the future is always out-of-sample. Though professional forecasters frequently distinguish between out-of-sample and in-sample forecasting performance, most articles that analysts will read contain only in-sample forecast evaluations. Analysts should be aware that out-of-sample performance is critical for evaluating the real-world contribution of a forecasting model.

Typically, we compare the out-of-sample forecasting performance of forecasting models by comparing their **root mean squared error** (RMSE). The root mean squared error is the square root of the average squared error. The model with the smallest root mean squared error is judged most accurate. The following example illustrates the computation and use of RMSE in comparing forecasting models.

EXAMPLE 10-8.   Out-of-Sample Forecast Comparisons of U.S. CPI Inflation.

Suppose we want to compare the forecasting accuracy of the AR(1) and AR(2) models of U.S. inflation estimated for Example 10-6 to predict U.S. inflation from January 1999 to June 2000.

For each month from January 1999 to June 2000, the first column of numbers in Table 10-7 shows the actual monthly inflation rate during the month. The second and third columns show the rate of inflation in the previous two months. The fourth column shows the out-of-sample error from the AR(1) model shown in Table 10-5. The fifth column shows the squared errors from the AR(1) model. The sixth column shows the out-of-sample errors from the AR(2) model shown in Table 10-6. The final column shows the squared errors from the AR(2) model. The bottom of the table displays the average squared error and the root-mean-squared error. According to these measures, the AR(1) model was slightly more accurate than the AR(2) model in its out-of-sample forecasts of inflation from January 1999 to June 2000. The root-mean-squared error from the AR(1) model was only 3.6738/3.8941 = 94.34 percent as large as the root-mean-squared error from the AR(2) model. Thus, even though the AR(2) model was more accurate in-sample, the AR(1) model was slightly more accurate out-of-sample. Of course, this was an extremely small sample to use in evaluating out-of-sample forecasting performance, so we should not view this difference as meaningful. Although we seem to have conflicting information on whether to choose an AR(1) or an AR(2) model here, regression coefficient stability is another factor to consider. The comparison between these two models will be continued in the following section.

TABLE 10-7   Out-of-Sample Forecast Error Comparisons
January 1999 to June 2000
U.S. CPI Inflation

	Infl(t)	Infl($t - 1$)	Infl($t - 2$)	AR(1) Err.	Sq. Err.	AR(2) Err.	Sq. Err.
January 1999	2.9682	−0.7293	0.0000	1.4733	2.1707	1.8909	3.5755
February 1999	1.4706	2.9682	−0.7293	−2.3545	5.5438	−1.1181	1.2502
March 1999	3.7090	1.4706	2.9682	0.8278	0.6852	0.8156	0.6652
April 1999	9.0850	3.7090	1.4706	4.7930	22.9733	5.5613	30.9276
May 1999	0.0000	9.0850	3.7090	−7.6798	58.9800	−6.6101	43.6938
June 1999	0.0000	0.0000	9.0850	−1.9545	3.8201	−3.8626	14.9197
July 1999	3.6704	0.0000	0.0000	1.7159	2.9445	2.2562	5.0906
August 1999	2.9177	3.6704	0.0000	−1.3499	1.8222	−0.1918	0.0368
September 1999	5.8988	2.9177	3.6704	2.1055	4.4332	2.1477	4.6126
October 1999	2.1653	5.8988	2.9177	−3.5066	12.2961	−2.7598	7.6167
November 1999	0.7158	2.1653	5.8988	−2.6033	6.7773	−3.2883	10.8130
December 1999	0.0000	0.7158	2.1653	−2.4056	5.7868	−2.3284	5.4213
January 2000	2.8896	0.0000	0.7158	0.9351	0.8745	1.2825	1.6449
February 2000	7.3498	2.8896	0.0000	3.5742	12.7751	4.6009	21.1678
March 2000	10.3616	7.3498	2.8896	3.7753	14.2527	4.7738	22.7891
April 2000	0.7036	10.3616	7.3498	−7.7808	60.5405	−7.4774	55.9113
May 2000	0.7032	0.7036	10.3616	−1.6947	2.8721	−3.8285	14.6571
June 2000	7.2346	0.7032	0.7036	4.8370	23.3962	5.3060	28.1535
				Average	13.4969	Average	15.1637
				RMSE	3.6738	RMSE	3.8941

Source for data: U.S. Bureau of Labor Statistics

5.4 INSTABILITY OF REGRESSION COEFFICIENTS

One of the important issues an analyst faces in modeling a time series is the sample period to use. The estimates of regression coefficients of the time-series model can change substantially across different sample periods used for estimating the model. Often, the regression coefficient estimates of a time series model estimated using an earlier sample period can be quite different from those of a model estimated using a later sample period. Similarly, the estimates can be different between models estimated using shorter and longer sample periods. Further, the choice of model for a particular time series can also depend on the sample period. For example, an AR(1) model may be appropriate for the sales of a company in one particular sample period, but an AR(2) model may be necessary for an earlier or later sample period (or for a longer or shorter sample period). Thus, the choice of a sample period is an important decision in modeling a financial time series.

Unfortunately, there is usually no clear-cut basis in economic or financial theory for determining whether data from a longer or shorter sample period should be used to estimate the time-series model. We can get some guidance, however, if we remember that our models are only valid for covariance-stationary time series. For example, we should not combine data from a period when exchange rates were fixed with data from a period when exchange rates were floating. The exchange rates in these two periods would not have the same variance because exchange rates are usually much more volatile under a floating-rate regime. Similarly, many U.S. analysts consider it inappropriate to model U.S. inflation or interest-rate behavior since the 1960s as a part of one sample period, because the Federal Reserve had distinct policy regimes during this period. The best way to determine appropriate samples for time-series estimation is to look at graphs of the data to see if the time series looks stationary before estimation begins. If we know that a government policy changed on a specific date, we might also test whether the time-series relation was the same before and after that date.

In the following example, we illustrate how the choice of a longer versus a shorter period can affect the order of the time-series model we choose. We then see how the choice of the time-series model (and the associated regression coefficients) affects our forecast. Finally, we discuss which sample period, and accordingly which model and corresponding forecast, is appropriate for the time series analyzed in the example.

EXAMPLE 10-9.   Instability in Time-Series Models of U.S. Inflation.

Suppose you want to model U.S. inflation. As in Example 10-6, you decide to use the monthly CPI data for the sample period 1971 to 1998. Based on the estimated models shown in Tables 10-5 and 10-6, you conclude that U.S. CPI inflation should be modeled as an AR(2) time series. Now suppose a colleague examines your results and questions estimating one time-series model for inflation in the United States since 1971, given that Federal Reserve policy changed dramatically in the late 1970s and early 1980s. She argues that the inflation time series from 1971 to 1998 has two **regimes** or underlying models generating the time series: one running from 1971 through 1984, and another starting in 1985. Therefore, she suggests that you estimate a new time-series model for U.S. inflation starting in 1985. Because of her suggestion, you first estimate an AR(1) model for inflation using data for a shorter sample period from 1985 to 1998. Your AR(1) estimates are shown in Table 10-8.

The bottom part of Table 10-8 shows that the first four autocorrelations of the residuals from the AR(1) model are quite small. In fact, none of these autocorrelations has a t-statistic larger than 0.7 in absolute value. Consequently, you cannot reject the null hypothesis that the residuals are serially uncorrelated. The AR(1) model is correctly specified for the sample period from 1985 to 1998, and there is no need to estimate the AR(2) model. This conclusion is very different from that reached in Example 10-6 using data from 1971 to 1998. In that example, we initially rejected the AR(1) model because its residuals exhibited serial correlation. When we used that larger sample, an AR(2) model initially appeared to fit the data much better than did an AR(1) model.

How deeply does our choice of sample period affect our forecast of future inflation? Suppose that in a given month inflation was 4 percent at an annual rate and 3 percent in the month before that. The AR(1) model shown in Table 10-8 predicts that inflation in the next month will be $3.5376 = 1.9569 + 0.3952(4)$. Therefore, the forecast of the next month's inflation using the 1985 to 1998 sample is 3.5376 percent. Remember from the analysis in Example 10-6 that the AR(2) model for the 1971 to 1998 sample predicts inflation of 4.0704 percent in the next month. Thus, using the correctly specified model for the shorter sample produces an inflation forecast almost 0.5 percentage points below the forecast made from the correctly specified model for the longer sample period. This difference might substantially affect a particular investment decision you plan to make.

Which model is correct? Figure 10-9 suggests an answer. Monthly U.S. inflation was, on average, so much higher and so much more volatile during the mid-

TABLE 10-8   Autoregression: AR(1) Model
             Monthly CPI Inflation at an Annual Rate
             Monthly Data from February 1985 to December 1998

Regression Statistics

R-squared	0.1540
Standard error	2.3485
Observations	167
Durbin-Watson	1.9367

	Coefficient	Standard Error	*t*-Statistic
Constant	1.9569	0.2974	6.5790
Lag 1	0.3952	0.0721	5.4800

Autocorrelations of the Residual

Lag	Autocorrelation	Standard Error	*t*-Statistic
1	0.0161	0.0774	0.2085
2	−0.0381	0.0774	−0.4920
3	−0.0513	0.0774	−0.6625
4	−0.0249	0.0774	−0.3220

Source for data: U.S. Bureau of Labor Statistics

FIGURE 10-9   Monthly CPI Inflation

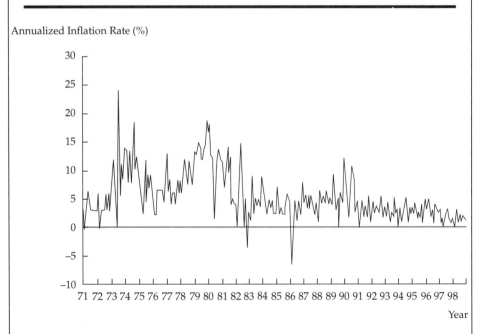

Annualized Inflation Rate (%)

Source: U.S. Bureau of Labor Statistics

511

1970s to early 1980s than it was after 1984 that inflation is probably not a covariance-stationary time series from 1971 to 1998. Therefore, we can reasonably believe that the data have more than one regime and we should estimate a separate model for inflation from 1985 to 1998, as we just did in this example. As the example shows, judgment and experience (such as knowledge of changes in government policy) play a vital role in determining how to model a time series. Simply relying on autocorrelations of the residuals from a time-series model cannot tell us the correct sample period for our analysis.

6   RANDOM WALKS AND UNIT ROOTS

So far, we have examined those time series in which the time series has a tendency to revert to its mean level as the change in variable from one period to the next follows a mean-reverting pattern. In contrast, there are many financial time series in which the changes follow a random pattern. Such time series are said to follow a random walk. We discuss random walks in the following section.

6.1   RANDOM WALKS

A random walk is one of the most widely studied time-series models for financial data. A **random walk** is a time series in which the value of the series in one period is the value of the series in the previous period plus an unpredictable random error. A random walk can be described by the following equation:

$$x_t = x_{t-1} + \epsilon_t, E(\epsilon_t) = 0, E(\epsilon_t^2) = \sigma^2, E(\epsilon_t \epsilon_s) = 0 \text{ if } t \neq s \tag{10-8}$$

Equation 10-8 means that the time series, x_t, is in every period equal to its value in the previous period plus an error term, ϵ_t, that has constant variance and is uncorrelated with the error term in previous periods. Note three important points. First, this equation is a special case of an AR(1) model with $b_0 = 0$ and $b_1 = 1$.[24] Second, the expected value of ϵ_t is zero. Therefore, the best forecast of x_t that can be made in period $t - 1$ is x_{t-1}. In fact, in this model x_{t-1} is the best forecast of x in every period after $t - 1$. Third, it is not the variable x that is random, but rather the change in variable, $x_t - x_{t-1}$, that equals ϵ_t and is thus random.

Random walks are quite common in financial time series. For example, many studies have tested and found that currency exchange rates follow a random walk. Consistent with the second point made above, some studies have found that sophisticated exchange rate forecasting models cannot outperform forecasts made on the basis of the random walk model, and that the best forecast of the future exchange rate is the current exchange rate.

Unfortunately, we cannot use the regression methods we have discussed so far to estimate an AR(1) model on a time series that is actually a random walk. To see why this is so, we must determine why a random walk has no finite mean-reverting level or finite variance. Recall that if x_t is at its mean-reverting level, then $x_t = b_0 + b_1 x_1$, or $x_t = b_0/(1 - b_1)$. In a random walk, however, $b_0 = 0$ and $b_1 = 1$, so $b_0/(1 - b_1) = 0/0$. Therefore, a random walk has an undefined mean-reverting level.

---

[24] Equation 10-8 with a non-zero intercept added is sometimes referred to as a random walk with drift. The focus of this chapter is on random walk without drift, Equation 10-8, and we refer to Equation 10-8 as a random walk without further qualification.

What is the variance of a random walk? Suppose that in period 1 the value of x_1 is 0. Then we know that $x_2 = 0 + \epsilon_2$. Therefore, the variance of $x_2 = \text{Var}(\epsilon_2) = \sigma^2$. Now $x_3 = x_2 + \epsilon_3 = \epsilon_2 + \epsilon_3$. Since the error term in each period is assumed to be uncorrelated with the error terms in all other periods, the variance of $x_3 = \text{Var}(\epsilon_2) + \text{Var}(\epsilon_3) = 2\sigma^2$. By a similar argument, we can show that for any period, t, the variance of $x_t = (t - 1)\sigma^2$. But this means that as t grows large, the variance of x_t grows without an upper bound: it approaches infinity. This, in turn, means that a random walk is not a covariance-stationary time series, because a covariance-stationary time series must have a finite variance.

What is the practical implication of these issues? We cannot use standard regression analysis on a time series that is a random walk. We can, however, convert the data to a covariance-stationary time series if we suspect that the time series is a random walk.[25] In statistical terms, we can difference it.

We difference a time series by creating a new time series, say y_t, that in each period is equal to the difference between x_t and x_{t-1}. This transformation is called **first-differencing** because it subtracts the value of the time series in the first prior period from the current value of the time series. Sometimes the first difference of x_t is written as $\Delta x_t = x_t - x_{t-1}$. Note that the first difference of the random walk in Equation 10-8 yields

$$y_t = x_t - x_{t-1} = \epsilon_t, E(\epsilon_t) = 0, E(\epsilon_t^2) = \sigma^2, E(\epsilon_t\epsilon_s) = 0 \text{ for } t \neq s$$

The expected value of ϵ_t is 0. Therefore, the best forecast of y_t that can be made in period $t - 1$ is 0. This implies that the best forecast is that there will be no change in the value of the current time series, x_{t-1}.

The first-differenced variable, y_t, is covariance stationary. How is this so? First, note that this model ($y_t = \epsilon_t$) is an AR(1) model with $b_0 = 0$ and $b_1 = 0$. We can compute the mean-reverting level of the first-differenced model as $b_0/(1 - b_1) = 0/1 = 0$. Therefore, a first-differenced random walk has a mean-reverting level of 0. Note also that the variance of y_t in each period is $\text{Var}(\epsilon_t) = \sigma^2$. Because the variance and the mean of y_t are constant and finite in each period, y_t is a covariance-stationary time series and we can model it using linear regression.[26] Of course, modeling the first-differenced series with an AR(1) model does not help us predict the future, as $b_0 = 0$ and $b_1 = 0$. We simply conclude that the time series is, in fact, a random walk.

If we had tried to estimate an AR(1) model for a time series that was a random walk, our statistical conclusions would have been incorrect because AR models cannot be used to estimate random walks or any time series that are not covariance stationary. The following example illustrates this issue with exchange rates.

EXAMPLE 10-10.   The Yen/Dollar Exchange Rate.

Financial analysts often assume that exchange rates are random walks. Suppose we want to test that hypothesis using month-end data on the yen/dollar exchange rate from January 1975 to December 1998. Table 10-9 shows the results of that regression.

---

[25] Statistical tests such as the Dickey-Fuller test determine whether a time series is a random walk using regression analysis. See Diebold (1997).

[26] All the covariances are finite, for two reasons: The variance is finite, and the covariance of a time series with its own past value can be no greater than the variance of the series.

TABLE 10-9   Yen/Dollar Exchange Rate: AR(1) Model
Month-End Data from January 1975 to December 1998

Regression Statistics	
R-squared	0.9908
Standard error	6.2118
Observations	288
Durbin-Watson	1.8610

	Coefficient	Standard Error	t-Statistic
Constant	0.9142	1.0918	0.8373
Lag 1	0.9914	0.0057	175.2497

Autocorrelations of the Residual			
Lag	Autocorrelation	Standard Error	t-Statistic
1	0.0653	0.0589	1.1079
2	0.0382	0.0589	0.6485
3	0.0954	0.0589	1.6182
4	0.0828	0.0589	1.4055

Source for data: Ibbotson Associates

The results in Table 10-9 suggest that the yen/dollar exchange rate is a random walk because the estimated constant does not appear to be significantly different from 0 and the estimated coefficient on the first lag of the exchange rate is very close to 1. Can we use the results in Table 10-9 to test whether the exchange rate is a random walk? Unfortunately, no, because the standard errors in an AR model are not valid if the model is estimated on a random walk (remember, a random walk is not covariance stationary). If the exchange rate is, in fact, a random walk, we might come to an incorrect conclusion based on faulty statistical tests and then invest incorrectly.

Fortunately, we have a way to resolve this dilemma. If the exchange rate is a random walk, then the first-differenced series, $y_t = x_t - x_{t-1}$, will be covariance stationary. We can then use the first-differenced series to test whether the exchange rate is a random walk using the following AR(1) regression: $y_t = b_0 + b_1 y_{t-1} + \epsilon_t$. If the exchange rate is a random walk, then $y_t = x_t - x_{t-1} = \epsilon_t$ and so $b_0 = 0$ and $b_1 = 0$. Additionally, the residuals from the regression will not be serially correlated. Table 10-10 shows the regression results for our AR(1) regression.

Table 10-10 shows that neither the constant nor the coefficient on the first lag of the first-differenced exchange rate is significantly different from 0. Further, the t-statistics on both of those coefficients are below 1.66 in absolute value, and we can-

TABLE 10-10   First Difference Yen/Dollar Exchange Rate: AR (1) Model
Month-End Data from January 1975 to December 1998

Regression Statistics			
R-squared	0.0042		
Standard error	6.2237		
Observations	288		
Durbin-Watson	1.9946		

	Coefficient	Standard Error	t-Statistic
Constant	−0.6110	0.3685	−1.6578
Lag 1	0.0652	0.0592	1.1014

Autocorrelations of the Residual			
Lag	Autocorrelation	Standard Error	t-Statistic
1	−0.0017	0.0589	−0.0282
2	0.0259	0.0589	0.4403
3	0.0898	0.0589	1.5231
4	0.0753	0.0589	1.2775

Source for data: Ibbotson Associates

not reject the null hypotheses that each coefficient is 0.[27] This result suggests that the yen/dollar exchange rate is a random walk.

We have concluded that the differenced regression is the model to choose. Now we can see that we would have been seriously misled if we had based our model choice on an R^2 comparison. In Table 10-9 the R^2 is 0.9908, whereas in Table 10-10 the R^2 is 0.0042. How can this be, if we just concluded that the model in Table 10-10 is the one that we should use? In Table 10-9, the R^2 measures how well the exchange rate in one period predicts the exchange rate in the next period. If the exchange rate is a random walk, its current value will be an extremely good predictor of its value in the next period, and thus the R^2 will be extremely high. At the same time, if the exchange rate is a random walk, then changes in the exchange rate should be completely unpredictable. Table 10-10 estimates whether changes in the exchange rate from one month to the next can be predicted by changes in the exchange rate over the previous month. If they cannot be predicted, the R^2 in Table 10-10 should be very low. In fact, it is low (0.0042). Furthermore, even though the R^2 in Table 10-9 is quite high, we cannot rely on the standard errors of the regression parameters because the undifferenced exchange-rate series appears to be a random

---

[27] See Greene (1999) for a test of the joint hypothesis that both coefficients are equal to 0.

walk and thus is not covariance stationary. This comparison provides a good example of the general rule that we cannot necessarily choose which model is correct based solely on a comparison of the R^2 from the two models.

So far, we have seen that we cannot reject the null hypothesis that $b_1 = 0$ or that $b_2 = 0$. This finding is evidence in favor of the possibility that x_t is a random walk. Before we can conclude that the exchange rate is a random walk, however, we also need to know whether the residuals from the first-differenced model are serially correlated. If they are serially correlated, then the exchange rate is not a random walk, because the residuals of a first-differenced random walk are not serially correlated. The bottom portion of Table 10-10 shows that each of the first four autocorrelations of the residuals in the first-differenced regression is quite small. In fact, none of the t-statistics for these autocorrelations is above 1.55 in absolute value. With 288 observations and two parameters, this model has 286 degrees of freedom. The critical value for a t-statistic in the model is about 1.97 at the 0.05 significance level. Thus, we cannot reject the null hypotheses that the autocorrelations, individually, are not significantly different from 0, because each of them has an absolute value smaller than the critical value of 1.97. Consequently, we can conclude that the residuals are not serially correlated and the exchange rate is a random walk.

The exchange rate is a random walk, and changes in a random walk are by definition unpredictable. Therefore, we cannot profit from an investment strategy that predicts changes in the exchange rate.

To this point, we have discussed only simple random walks; that is, random walks without drift. In a random walk without drift, the best predictor of the time series in the next period is its current value. A random walk with drift, however, is expected to increase or decrease by a constant amount in each period. The equation describing a random walk with drift is a special case of the AR(1) model:

$$x_t = b_0 + b_1 x_{t-1} + \epsilon_t$$

$$b_1 = 1, b_0 \neq 0, \text{ or}$$

$$x_t = b_0 + x_{t-1} + \epsilon_t, E(\epsilon_t) = 0 \tag{10-9}$$

A random walk with a drift has $b_0 \neq 0$ compared to a simple random walk which has $b_0 = 0$.

We have already seen that $b_1 = 1$ implies an undefined mean-reversion level and thus nonstationarity. Consequently, we cannot use an AR model to analyze a time series that is a random walk with drift until we transform the time series by taking first differences. If we first-difference Equation 10-9, the result is $y_t = x_t - x_{t-1}, y_t = b_0 + \epsilon_t, b_0 \neq 0$.

6.2   UNIT ROOTS

Random walks (with and without drift) are examples of time series that are not covariance stationary. If a time series comes from an AR(1) model, then to be covariance stationary, the absolute value of the lag coefficient, b_1, must be less than 1.0. So, we cannot rely on the statistical results of an AR(1) model if the absolute value of the lag coefficient is greater than or equal to 1.0 because the time series is not covariance stationary. If the lag coefficient is equal to 1.0, the time series is a random walk and is not covariance stationary. In that case, we say that the time series has a **unit root.**[28]

Unit roots are quite common in financial time series. What is the implication of the existence of a unit root in a time series? Since a time series with a unit root is not covari-

---

[28] When b_1 is greater than 1 in absolute value, we say that there is an explosive root. For details, see Diebold (1997).

ance stationary, modeling it without transforming it to make it covariance stationary is likely to lead to incorrect statistical conclusions, and any decisions made on the basis of these conclusions could be incorrect. So if a time series has a unit root, the analyst should first transform it to make it covariance stationary as illustrated later in this section.

When are unit roots likely to occur? They are most common in a time series that increases or decreases over time. For example, Intel's quarterly sales (Figure 10-2) and the level of the S&P 500 both increased significantly during the decade of the 1990s. Both these time series are likely to have a unit root.

EXAMPLE 10-11.   Intel's Quarterly Sales.

Earlier, we concluded that we could not model the log of Intel's quarterly sales using only a time-trend line (as shown in Example 10-3). Recall that the Durbin-Watson statistic from the log-linear regression caused us to reject the hypothesis that the errors in the regression were serially uncorrelated. Suppose, instead, that we decide to model the log of Intel's quarterly sales using an AR(1) model. We use ln Sales$_t$ = $b_0 + b_1$ ln Sales$_{t-1} + \epsilon_t$.

Table 10-11 shows the results of estimating that autoregression. We can see right away from the coefficient on the first lag of log sales that something seems

TABLE 10-11   Log Sales: AR(1) Model
Intel Corporation
Quarterly Data from January 1985 to February 1999

Regression Statistics		
R-squared	0.9942	
Standard error	0.0805	
Observations	58	
Durbin-Watson	1.3492	

	Coefficient	Standard Error	t-Statistic
Constant	0.0396	0.0752	0.5261
Lag 1	1.0012	0.0102	98.2545

Autocorrelations of the Residual			
Lag	Autocorrelation	Standard Error	t-Statistic
1	0.2803	0.1313	2.1346
2	0.0437	0.1313	0.3330
3	0.0193	0.1313	0.1471
4	0.1459	0.1313	1.1112

Source for data: Compustat®

wrong with this regression model. The estimated coefficient is above 1.0 ($\hat{b}_1 =$ 1.0012), suggesting that the time series we are modeling is not covariance stationary. Consequently, we can ignore the rest of the regression results because we cannot use an autoregressive model for a time series that is not covariance stationary. We might have saved ourselves some trouble by looking at a plot of the time series and seeing that it had a strong upward trend.

Though our discussion of unit roots has focused on AR(1) models, unit roots occur in time series that come from higher order autoregressive models as well. Again, these time series with unit roots are not covariance stationary. We briefly discuss unit roots in AR(2) models below, and provide an illustration in Example 10-12.

The regression equation for an AR(2) model is

$$x_t = b_0 + b_1 x_{t-1} + b_2 x_{t-2} + \epsilon_t,$$
$$E(\epsilon_t) = 0, E(\epsilon_t^2) = \sigma^2, E(\epsilon_t \epsilon_s) = 0 \text{ if } t \neq s \tag{10-10}$$

If an AR(2) model has a unit root, then the sum of b_1 and b_2 should be close to 1 and the estimated value of b_1 should be greater than 1. If an AR(2) regression shows these signs, it is safe to assume that the time series has a unit root and is not covariance stationary.[29]

EXAMPLE 10-12.   Intel's Quarterly Sales.

Suppose you model the log of Intel's quarterly sales as an AR(2) time series. You use $\ln \text{Sales}_t = b_0 + b_1 \ln \text{Sales}_{t-1} + b_2 \ln \text{Sales}_{t-2} + \epsilon_t$. Table 10-12 shows the results of that regression.

TABLE 10-12   Log Sales: AR(2) Model
Intel Corporation
Quarterly Data from February 1985 to February 1999

Regression Statistics		
Multiple R	0.9975	
R-squared	0.9949	
Standard error	0.0756	
Observations	57	
Durbin-Watson	2.0220	

	Coefficient	Standard Error	t-Statistic
Constant	0.0718	0.0719	0.99919
Lag 1	1.2916	0.1275	10.1323
Lag 2	−0.2965	0.1283	−2.31041

---

[29] See Diebold (1997).

Autocorrelations of the Residual			
Lag	Autocorrelation	Standard Error	t-Statistic
1	0.0048	0.1325	0.0361
2	−0.0280	0.1325	−0.2110
3	−0.0382	0.1325	−0.2881
4	0.1969	0.1325	1.4865

Source for data: Compustat®

Note that the sum of b_1 and b_2 (the two-lag coefficient) is very close to 1 and the estimated value of b_1 is greater than 1. These are clear signs that the log of Intel's quarterly sales probably contains a unit root and is not covariance stationary. Once again, this result should not be surprising, because the graph of the log of Intel's quarterly sales clearly showed a strong upward trend.

If a time series appears to have a unit root, how should we model it? One method that is often successful is to first-difference the time series (as discussed previously) and try to model the first-differenced series as an autoregressive time series. The following example demonstrates this method.

EXAMPLE 10-13.   Intel's Quarterly Sales.

Suppose you are convinced—from looking at the plot of the time series and from our analysis in Example 10-11 earlier—that the log of Intel's quarterly sales is not co-variance stationary (it has a unit root). So you create a new series, y_t, that is the first difference of the log of Intel's quarterly sales. Figure 10-10 shows that series.

If you compare Figure 10-10 to Figures 10-6 and 10-7, you will see that first-differencing the log of Intel's quarterly sales eliminates the strong upward trend that was present in both Intel's sale and the log of Intel's sales. Because the first-differenced series has no strong trend, you are better off assuming that the differenced series is covariance stationary rather than assuming that Intel's sales or the log of Intel's sales is a covariance-stationary time series.

Now suppose you decide to model the new series using an AR(1) model. You use $(\ln \text{Sales}_t - \ln \text{Sales}_{t-1}) = b_0 + b_1(\ln \text{Sales}_{t-1} - \ln \text{Sales}_{t-2}) + \epsilon_t$. Table 10-13 shows the results of that regression.

The lower part of Table 10-13 shows that the first four autocorrelations of residuals in this model are quite small. None of the t-statistics for these autocorrelations has an absolute value larger than 1.5. With 57 observations and two parameters, this model has 55 degrees of freedom. The critical value for a t-statistic in this model is about 2.0 at the 0.05 significance level. Therefore, we fail to reject the null hypotheses that each of these autocorrelations is equal to 0 and conclude instead that no significant autocorrelation is present in the residuals. This result suggests that the model is well specified and we could use the estimates. Both the constant ($\hat{b}_0 = 0.036$) and the coefficient ($\hat{b}_1 = 0.2884$) on the first lag of the new first-differenced series are statistically significant. How can we interpret the coefficients in the model? The value of the constant coefficient (0.0363) implies that if sales have not changed in the current quarter

FIGURE 10-10   Log Difference: Intel Quarterly Sales

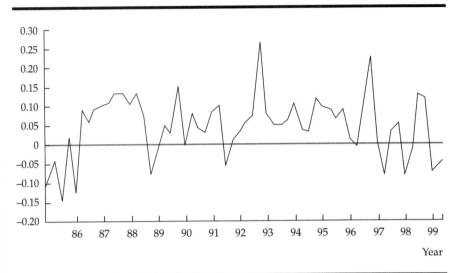

Source: Compustat®

TABLE 10-13   Log Difference Sales: AR(1) Model
Intel Corporation
Quarterly Data from February 1985 to February 1999

Regression Statistics

R-squared	0.0864
Standard error	0.0756
Observations	57
Durbin-Watson	2.0220

	Coefficient	Standard Error	*t*-Statistic
Constant	0.0363	0.0118	3.0860
Lag 1	0.2884	0.1264	2.2809

Autocorrelations of the Residual

Lag	Autocorrelation	Standard Error	*t*-Statistic
1	0.0077	0.1325	0.0581
2	−0.0349	0.1325	−0.2638
3	−0.0403	0.1325	−0.3044
4	0.1942	0.1325	1.4662

Source for data: Compustat®

($y_t = \ln \text{Sales}_t - \ln \text{Sales}_{t-1} = 0$), sales will grow by 3.63 percent next quarter.[30] If sales have changed during this quarter, however, the model predicts that sales will grow by 3.63 percent plus 0.2884 times the sales growth in this quarter.

Suppose we wanted to use this model at the end of the second quarter of 1999 to predict Intel's sales for the third quarter of 1999. Let us say that t is the second quarter of 1999, so $t - 1$ is the first quarter of 1999 and $t + 1$ is the third quarter of 1999. Then we would have to compute $\hat{y}_{t+1} = 0.0363 + 0.2884\, y_t$. To compute $\hat{y}_{t+1}$, we need to know $y_t = \ln \text{Sales}_t - \ln \text{Sales}_{t-1}$. In the first quarter of 1999, Intel's sales were \$7,103 million, so $\ln \text{Sales}_{t-1} = \ln(7,103) = 8.8683$. In the second quarter of 1999, Intel's sales were \$6,746 million, so $\ln(\text{Sales}_t) = \ln(6,746) = 8.8167$. Thus, $y_t = 8.8167 - 8.8683 = -0.0516$. Therefore, $\hat{y}_{t+1} = 0.0363 + 0.2884\,(-0.0516) = 0.0214$. If $\hat{y}_{t+1} = 0.0214$, then $0.0214 = \ln(\text{Sales}_{t+1}) - \ln(\text{Sales}_t) = \ln(\text{Sales}_{t+1}/\text{Sales}_t)$. If we exponentiate both sides of this equation, the result is

$$e^{0.0214} = (\text{Sales}_{t+1}/\text{Sales}_t)$$

$$\begin{aligned}
\text{Sales}_{t+1} &= \text{Sales}_t\, e^{0.0214} \\
&= \$6,746 \text{ million} \times 1.0216 \\
&= \$6,891 \text{ million}
\end{aligned}$$

Thus, in the second quarter of 1999, this model would have predicted that Intel's sales in the third quarter of 1999 would be \$6,891 million. This sales forecast might have affected our decision about whether to buy Intel's stock at the time.

7 MOVING-AVERAGE TIME-SERIES MODELS

So far, all of the forecasting models we have used have been autoregressive models. Since most financial time series have the qualities of an autoregressive process, autoregressive time-series models are the most frequently used time-series models in financial forecasting. Some financial time series, however, seem to better follow another kind of time series model called a moving-average model. For example, as we will see later, returns on the S&P 500 can be better modeled as a moving-average process than as an autoregressive process.

In this section, we present the fundamentals of moving-average models so that you can ask the right questions when presented with them. We first discuss how to smooth past values with a moving average and then how to forecast a time series using a moving-average model.

7.1 SMOOTHING PAST VALUES WITH AN N-PERIOD MOVING AVERAGE

Suppose you are analyzing the long-term trend in the past sales of a company. In order to focus on the trend, you may find it useful to remove short-term fluctuations or noise by smoothing out the time series of sales. One technique to smooth out period-to-period fluctuations in the value of a time series is an **n-period moving average.** An n-period moving average of the current and past $n - 1$ values of a time series, x_t, is calculated as

$$\frac{x_t + x_{t-1} + \cdots + x_{t-n+1}}{n} \tag{10-11}$$

---

[30] Note that 3.63 percent is the exponential growth rate, now [(Current quarter sales/Previous quarter sales) − 1]. The difference between these two methods of computing growth is usually small.

The following example demonstrates how to compute a moving average of Intel's quarterly sales.

EXAMPLE 10-14.   Intel's Quarterly Sales.

Suppose we want to compute the four-quarter moving average of Intel's sales at the end of the second quarter of 1999. Intel's sales in the previous four quarters were 1998:Q3, $6,731 million; 1998:Q4, $7,614 million; 1999:Q1 $7,103 million; and 1999:Q2, $6,746 million. The four-quarter moving average of sales in the second quarter of 1999 is thus $(6,731 + 7,614 + 7,103 + 6,746)/4 = \$7,048.5$ million.

We often plot the moving average of a series with large fluctuations to see whether the moving average provides a better sense of the data than the raw data provide. Figure 10-11 shows monthly real (inflation-adjusted) retail sales for the United States from January 1985 to September 1999, along with a 12-month moving average of the data.[31]

As Figure 10-11 shows, each year has a very strong peak in retail sales (December) followed by a sharp drop in sales (January). Because of the extreme seasonality in the data, a 12-month moving average can help us focus on the long-term movements in retail sales instead of seasonal fluctuations. Note that the moving average does not have the sharp sea-

FIGURE 10-11   Monthly Real Retail Sales and a 12-Month Moving Average of Retail Sales

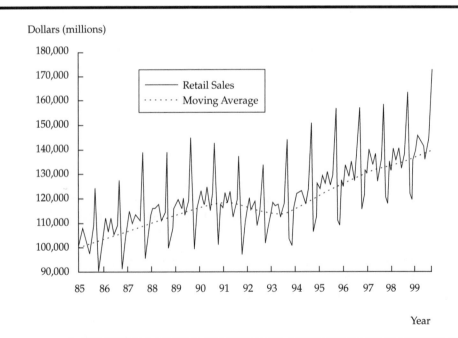

Source: Federal Reserve Bank of St. Louis

---

[31] A 12-month moving average is the average value of a time series over each of the last 12 months. Although the sample period starts in 1985, data from 1984 are used to compute the 12-month moving average for the months of 1985.

sonal fluctuations of the original retail sales data. Rather, the moving average of retail sales grows steadily from 1985 through 1990, then declines until 1993, and grows steadily thereafter. We can see that trend more easily by looking at a 12-month moving average than by looking at the time series itself.

Figure 10-12 shows monthly crude oil prices in the United States from January 1985 to September 1999, along with a 12-month moving average of oil prices. Although these data do not have the same sharp regular seasonality displayed in the retail sales data in Figure 10-11, the moving average smoothes out the monthly fluctuations in oil prices to show the longer-term movements.

FIGURE 10-12   Monthly Oil Price and a 12-Month Moving Average of Prices

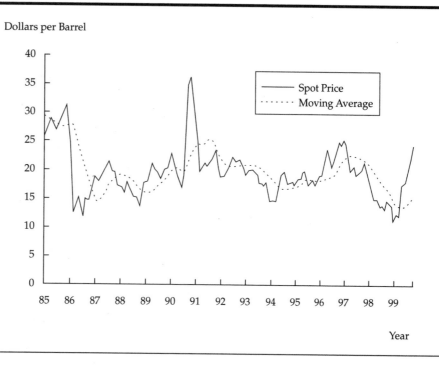

Source: Dow Jones Energy Service

Figure 10-12 also shows one weakness with a moving average: it always lags large movements in the actual data. For example, when oil prices fell sharply in 1985 and remained relatively low, the moving average fell only gradually. When oil prices rose quickly in 1999, the moving average also lagged. Consequently, a simple moving average of the recent past, though often useful in smoothing out a time series, may not be the best predictor of the future. A main reason for this is that a simple moving average gives equal weight to all the periods in the moving average. In order to forecast the future values of a time series, it is often better to use a more sophisticated moving-average time series model. We discuss such models below.

7.2   MOVING-AVERAGE TIME SERIES MODELS FOR FORECASTING

Suppose that a time series, x_t, is consistent with the following model:

$$x_t = \epsilon_t + \theta\epsilon_{t-1}, \ E(\epsilon_t) = 0, \ E(\epsilon_t^2) = \sigma^2, \ E(\epsilon_t\epsilon_s) = 0 \text{ for } t \neq s \tag{10-12}$$

This equation is called a moving-average model of order 1, or simply an MA(1) model. Theta (θ) is the parameter of the MA(1) model.

Equation 10-12 is a moving-average model because in each period, x_t is a moving average of ϵ_t and ϵ_{t-1}. Unlike the simple moving-average model of Equation 10-11, this moving-average model places different weights on the two terms in the moving average (1 on ϵ_t, and θ on ϵ_{t-1}).

We can see that a time series fits an MA(1) model by looking at its autocovariances and autocorrelations. First, we examine the variance of x_t in Equation 10-12 and its first two autocorrelations. Because the expected value of x_t is 0 in all periods and ϵ_t is uncorrelated with its own past values, the first autocovariance (and thus the first autocorrelation) is not equal to 0, but the second autocovariance and autocorrelation are equal to 0. Further analysis shows that all autocorrelations except for the first will be equal to 0 in an MA(1) model.

Of course, an MA(1) model is not the most complex moving-average model. A qth order moving-average model, denoted MA(q), can be written as

$$x_t = \epsilon_t + \theta_1\epsilon_{t-1} + \cdots + \theta_q\epsilon_{t-q}, E(\epsilon_t) = 0, E(\epsilon_t^2) = \sigma^2, \tag{10-13}$$

$$E(\epsilon_t\epsilon_s) = 0 \text{ for } t \neq s$$

How can we tell whether an MA(q) model fits a time series? We examine the autocorrelations. For an MA(q) model, the first q autocorrelations will be significantly different from 0, and all autocorrelations beyond that will be equal to 0. This result is critical for choosing the right value of q for an MA model. We discussed this result above for the specific case of $q = 1$ that all autocorrelations except for the first will be equal to 0 in an MA(1) model.

How can we distinguish an autoregressive time series from a moving-average time series? Once again, by examining the autocorrelations of the time series itself. The autocorrelations of most autoregressive time series start large and decline gradually, whereas the autocorrelations of an MA(q) time series suddenly drop to 0 after the first q autocorrelations. We are unlikely to know in advance whether a time series is autoregressive or moving average. Thus, the autocorrelations give us our best clue about how to model the time series. Most time series, however, are best modeled with an autoregressive model.

EXAMPLE 10-15.   Are Returns on the S&P 500 a Moving-Average Time Series?

Suppose we want to find out whether returns on the S&P 500 are a moving-average time series. The first thing we must do is compute the autocorrelations of the returns. Table 10-14 shows the first six autocorrelations of returns to the S&P 500 using monthly data from January 1975 to December 1998. Note that all of the autocorrelations are quite small. Do they reach significance? With 288 observations, the critical value for a t-statistic in this model is about 1.97 at the 0.05 significance level. In fact, none of the autocorrelations have a t-statistic larger in absolute value than 1.8, a value smaller than the critical value of 1.97. Consequently, we fail to reject the null hypothesis that those autocorrelations, individually, are not significantly different from 0.

If returns on the S&P 500 were an MA(q) time series, then the first q autocorrelations would be significantly different from 0. None of the autocorrelations are statistically significant, however, so returns to the S&P 500 appear to come from an

TABLE 10-14   Autocorrelations
Monthly Returns to the S&P 500 (Annualized)
Monthly Data from January 1975 to December 1998

	Autocorrelations		
Lag	Autocorrelation	Standard Error	t-Statistic
1	−0.0620	0.0589	−1.0526
2	0.0232	0.0589	0.3934
3	−0.0189	0.0589	−0.3201
4	−0.0433	0.0589	−0.7347
5	0.1041	0.0589	1.7664
6	−0.0530	0.0589	−0.8989
Observations	288		

Source for data: Ibbotson Associates

MA(0) time series. An MA(0) time series where we allow the mean to be non-zero has the following form:[32]

$$x_t = \mu + \epsilon_t, E(\epsilon_t) = 0, E(\epsilon_t^2) = \sigma^2, E(\epsilon_t\epsilon_s) = 0 \text{ for } t \neq s \qquad (10\text{-}14)$$

which means that the time series is not predictable. This result should not be too surprising, as most research suggests that short-term returns to stocks are difficult to predict.

We can see from this example how examining the autocorrelations allowed us to choose between the AR and MA models. If returns to the S&P 500 had come from an AR(1) time series, the first autocorrelation would have been significantly different from 0 and the autocorrelations would have declined gradually. Not even the first autocorrelation is significantly different from 0, however. Therefore, we can be sure that returns to the S&P 500 do not come from an AR(1) model—or from any higher order AR model, for that matter. This finding is consistent with our conclusion that the S&P 500 series is MA(0).

8 SEASONALITY IN TIME-SERIES MODELS

As we analyze the results of the time-series models in this chapter, we encounter complications. One complication frequently encountered is significant seasonality, a case in which the series shows regular patterns of movement within the year. At first glance,

---

[32] On the basis of investment theory and evidence, we expect that the mean monthly return on the S&P 500 is positive ($\mu > 0$). We can also generalize Equation 10-13 for an MA(q) time series by adding a constant term, μ. Including a constant term in a moving-average model does not change the expressions for the variance and autocovariances of the time series. A number of early studies of weak-form market efficiency used Equation 10-14 as the model for stock returns. See Garbade (1982).

seasonality might appear to rule out using autoregressive time-series models. After all, autocorrelations will differ by season. This problem can often be solved, however, by using seasonal lags in an autoregressive model.

What is a seasonal lag? A seasonal lag is usually the value of the time series one year before the current period. The seasonal lag is included as an extra term in an autoregressive model. Suppose, for example, that we model a particular quarterly time series using an AR(1) model, $x_t = b_0 + b_1 x_{t-1} + \epsilon_t$. If the time series had significant seasonality, this model would not be correctly specified. The seasonality would be easy to detect because the seasonal autocorrelation (in the case of quarterly data, the fourth autocorrelation) of the error term would be significantly different from 0. Suppose this quarterly model has significant seasonality. In this case, we might include a seasonal lag in the autoregressive model and estimate

$$x_t = b_0 + b_1 x_{t-1} + b_2 x_{t-4} + \epsilon_t \tag{10-15}$$

to test whether including the seasonal lag would eliminate statistically significant autocorrelation in the error term.

In Examples 10-16 and 10-17, we illustrate how to test and adjust for seasonality in a time-series model. We also illustrate how to compute a forecast using an autoregressive model with a seasonal lag.

EXAMPLE 10-16.   Seasonality in Sales at Proctor & Gamble.

Suppose we want to predict sales for Procter & Gamble. Based on the previous results in this chapter, we determine that the first difference of the log of sales is probably covariance stationary. Using quarterly data from the second quarter of 1985 to the second quarter of 1999, we estimate an AR(1) model using ordinary least squares on the first-differenced data. We estimate the following equation: $(\ln \text{Sales}_t - \ln \text{Sales}_{t-1}) = b_0 + b_1(\ln \text{Sales}_{t-1} - \ln \text{Sales}_{t-2}) + \epsilon_t$. Table 10-15 shows the results of the regression.

The first thing to note in Table 10-15 is the strong seasonal autocorrelation of the residuals. The bottom portion of the table shows that the fourth autocorrelation has a value of 0.5428 and a t-statistic of 4.10. With 57 observations and two parameters, this model has 55 degrees of freedom.[33] The critical value for a t-statistic is about 2.0 at the 0.05 significance level. Given this value of the t-statistic, we must reject the null hypothesis that the fourth autocorrelation is equal to 0 because 4.10 is larger than the critical value of 2.0.

In this model, the fourth autocorrelation is the seasonal autocorrelation because this AR(1) model is estimated with quarterly data. Table 10-15 shows the strong and statistically significant seasonal autocorrelation that occurs when a time series with strong seasonality is modeled without taking the seasonality into account. Therefore, the AR(1) model is misspecified and we cannot use it for forecasting.

Suppose we decide to use an autoregressive model with a seasonal lag because of the seasonal autocorrelation. We are modeling quarterly data, so we estimate Equation 10-15: $(\ln \text{Sales}_t - \ln \text{Sales}_t) = b_0 + b_1(\ln \text{Sales}_{t-1} - \ln \text{Sales}_{t-2}) +$

---

[33] Although the sample period begins in 1985, we use prior observations for the lags. Otherwise, the model would have fewer degrees of freedom because the sample size would be reduced with each increase in the number of lags.

TABLE 10-15 Log-Differenced Sales: AR(1) Model
Proctor & Gamble
Quarterly Data from February 1985 to February 1999

Regression Statistics		
R-squared	0.0186	
Standard error	0.0426	
Observations	57	
Durbin-Watson	2.0317	

	Coefficient	Standard Error	t-Statistic
Constant	0.0209	0.0062	3.3910
Lag 1	−0.1351	0.1323	−1.0208

Autocorrelations of the Residual			
Lag	Autocorrelation	Standard Error	t-Statistic
1	−0.0451	0.1325	−0.3406
2	−0.3876	0.1325	−2.9263
3	−0.0617	0.1325	−0.4655
4	0.5428	0.1325	4.0979

Source for data: Compustat®

$b_2(\ln \text{Sales}_{t-4} - \ln \text{Sales}_{t-5}) + \epsilon_t$. The estimates of this equation appear in Table 10-16.

Note the autocorrelations of the residual shown at the bottom of Table 10-16. When we include a seasonal lag in the regression, the absolute value of the seasonal autocorrelation (lag 4) drops by more than 50 percent. Although the fourth autocorrelation is still the largest one, the t-statistic on that autocorrelation now has an absolute value of less than 1.93.

Suppose we want to test whether we can reject the null hypothesis that the value of the fourth autocorrelation is 0 against the alternative hypothesis that it is not equal to 0. At the 0.05 significance level, with 57 observations and three parameters, this model has 54 degrees of freedom. The critical value of the t-statistic needed to reject the null hypothesis is thus about 2.0. The absolute value of the t-statistic (1.93) is less than 2.0, so we cannot reject the null hypothesis that the fourth autocorrelation is not significantly different from 0.

Now that we know that the residuals of this model do not have significant serial correlation, we can assume that the model is correctly specified. How can we interpret the coefficients in this model? To predict the current quarter's sales growth at Procter & Gamble, we need to know two things: sales growth in the previous quarter and sales growth four quarters ago. If sales remained constant in each of those two quarters, the model in Table 10-16 predicts that sales will grow by

TABLE 10-16   Log-Differenced Sales: AR(1) Model with Seasonal Lag
Proctor & Gamble
Quarterly Data from February 1985 to February 1999

Regression Statistics		
Multiple R		0.6109
R-squared		0.3732
Standard error		0.0344
Observations		57
Durbin-Watson		1.9734

	Coefficient	Standard Error	t-Statistic
Constant	0.0082	0.0055	1.5005
Lag 1	−0.0728	0.1073	−0.6784
Lag 4	0.6088	0.1101	5.5278

Autocorrelations of the Residual			
Lag	Autocorrelation	Standard Error	t-Statistic
1	0.0049	0.1325	0.0372
2	−0.0891	0.1325	−0.6727
3	−0.0379	0.1325	−0.2862
4	−0.2550	0.1325	−1.9250

Source for data: Compustat®

0.0082 (0.82 percent) in the current quarter. If sales grew by 1 percent last quarter and by 2 percent four quarters ago, then the model predicts that sales growth this quarter will be $0.0082 - 0.0728(0.01) + 0.6088(0.02) = 0.0196$ (1.96 percent).[34] Notice also that the R^2 in the model with the seasonal lag (0.3732 in Table 10-16) was almost 20 times higher than the R^2 in the model without the seasonal lag (0.0186 in Table 10-15). Again, the seasonal lag model does a much better job of explaining the data.

EXAMPLE 10-17.   Retail Sales Growth.

Suppose we want to predict the growth in U.S. monthly retail sales so that we can decide whether to recommend discount-store stocks. We decide to use non-seasonally adjusted data on retail sales, adjusted for inflation. To begin with, we estimate an AR(1) model with data on the annualized monthly growth in real retail sales from

---

[34] Note that all of these growth rates are exponential growth rates.

January 1971 to December 1998. We estimate the following equation: Sales growth$_t = b_0 + b_1$ Sales growth$_{t-1} + \epsilon_t$. Table 10-17 shows the results from this model.

TABLE 10-17 **Monthly Real Retail Sales Growth: AR(1) Model Not Seasonally Adjusted Monthly Data from February 1971 to December 1998**

Regression Statistics	
R-squared	0.1952
Standard error	235.1982
Observations	335
Durbin-Watson	2.0809

	Coefficient	Standard Error	t-Statistic
Constant	121.8693	13.8156	8.8211
Lag 1	-0.2605	0.0538	-4.8443

Autocorrelations of the Residual			
Lag	Autocorrelation	Standard Error	t-Statistic
1	-0.0552	0.0546	-1.0110
2	-0.1591	0.0546	-2.9125
3	0.1802	0.0546	3.2979
4	-0.0973	0.0546	-1.7812
5	-0.1310	0.0546	-2.3968
6	-0.2608	0.0546	-4.7726
7	-0.1351	0.0546	-2.4725
8	-0.0851	0.0546	-1.5574
9	0.1702	0.0546	3.1156
10	-0.1764	0.0546	-3.2295
11	-0.0678	0.0546	-1.2404
12	0.8611	0.0546	15.7614

Source for data: U.S. Federal Reserve Bank of St. Louis

The autocorrelations of the residuals from this model, shown at the bottom of Table 10-17, indicate that seasonality is extremely significant in this model. With 335 observations and two parameters, this model has 333 degrees of freedom. At the 0.05 significance level, the critical value for a t-statistic is about 1.97. The 12th-lag autocorrelation (this is the seasonal autocorrelation because we are using monthly data) has a value of 0.8611 and a t-statistic of 15.76. The t-statistic on this autocorrelation is so much larger than the critical value (1.97) that we can certainly reject the null hypothesis that the seasonal autocorrelation is 0. Consequently, the model shown in Table 10-17 is misspecified and we cannot rely on it to forecast sales growth. Note also that many of the other t-statistics for autocorrelations shown in the table are significantly different from 0.

Suppose we add the seasonal lag of sales growth (the 12th lag) to the AR(1) model to estimate the equation Sales growth$_t$ = b_0 + b_1 Sales growth$_{t-1}$ + b_2 Sales growth$_{t-12}$ + ϵ_t. Table 10-18 presents the results of estimating this equation. The estimated absolute value of the seasonal autocorrelation (the 12th autocorrelation) has fallen by more than 95 percent to -0.0232. None of the first 12 autocorrelations have a t-statistic with an absolute value greater than 1.66. The critical value at

TABLE 10-18   Monthly Real Retail Sales Growth: AR(1) Model with Seasonal Lag Not Seasonally Adjusted Monthly Data from February 1972 to December 1998

Regression Statistics	
Multiple R	0.9014
R-squared	0.8125
Standard error	105.9903
Observations	324
Durbin-Watson	2.1438

	Coefficient	Standard Error	t-Statistic
Constant	15.0085	7.0123	2.1403
Lag 1	−0.0472	0.0251	−1.8817
Lag 12	0.8954	0.0251	35.7132

Autocorrelations of the Residual			
Lag	Autocorrelation	Standard Error	t-Statistic
1	−0.0719	0.0556	−1.2936
2	−0.0211	0.0556	−0.3801
3	0.0921	0.0556	1.6576
4	−0.0722	0.0556	−1.2994
5	−0.0316	0.0556	−0.5682
6	0.0162	0.0556	0.2924
7	−0.0914	0.0556	−1.6451
8	0.0065	0.0556	0.1177
9	0.0115	0.0556	0.2067
10	−0.0568	0.0556	−1.0225
11	0.0083	0.0556	0.1486
12	−0.0232	0.0556	−0.4178

Source for data: U.S. Federal Reserve Bank of St. Louis

the 0.05 significance level is 1.97, so we cannot reject the individual null hypotheses that these autocorrelations are not significantly different from 0. We can conclude that there is no significant serial correlation in the residuals from this model. Because we can reasonably believe that the model is correctly specified, we can use it to predict retail sales growth. Note that the R^2 in Table 10-18 is 0.8125, more than four times as large as the R^2 in Table 10-17 (computed by the model without the seasonal lag).

How can we interpret the coefficients in the model? To predict growth in retail sales in this month, we need to know last month's retail sales growth and retail sales growth 12 months ago. If retail sales remained constant both last month and 12 months ago, the model in Table 10-18 predicts that retail sales will grow at an annual rate of approximately 15 percent this month.[35] If retail sales grew at an annual rate of 5 percent last month and at an annual rate of 10 percent 12 months ago, the model in Table 10-18 predicts that retail sales will grow in the current month at an annual rate of $15.0085 - 0.0472(5) + 0.8954(10) = 23.7265$, or 23.7 percent.

9 AUTOREGRESSIVE MOVING-AVERAGE MODELS

So far, we have presented autoregressive and moving-average models as alternatives for modeling a time series. The time series we have considered in examples have usually been explained quite well with a simple autoregressive model (with or without seasonal lags).[36] Some statisticians, however, have advocated using a more general model, the autoregressive moving-average (ARMA) model. The advocates of ARMA models argue that these models may fit the data better and provide better forecasts. However, as we discuss later in this section, there are severe limitations to estimating and using these models. Because you may encounter these models, we provide a brief overview below.

An ARMA model combines both autoregressive lags of the dependent variable and moving-average errors. The equation for such a model with p autoregressive terms and q moving-average terms, denoted ARMA(p, q), is

$$x_{t+1} = b_0 + b_1 x_t + \cdots + b_p x_{t-p} + \epsilon_t + \theta_1 \epsilon_{t-1} + \cdots + \theta_q \epsilon_{t-q} \qquad \text{(10-16)}$$

$$E(\epsilon_t) = 0, E(\epsilon_t^2) = \sigma^2, E(\epsilon_t \epsilon_s) = 0 \text{ for } t \neq s$$

where b_1, b_2, ... b_p are the autoregressive parameters and θ_1, θ_2, ... θ_q are the moving-average parameters.

There are severe limitations to estimating and using ARMA models. First, the parameters in ARMA models can be very unstable. In particular, slight changes in the data sample or the initial guesses for the values of the ARMA parameters can result in very different final estimates of the ARMA parameters. Second, choosing the right ARMA model is more of an art than a science. The criteria for deciding whether a particular time series is ARMA(p, q), ARMA($p + 1$, q), ARMA(p, $q + 1$), or ARMA($p + 1$, $q + 1$) are far from perfect. Moreover, even after a model is selected, that model may not forecast well.

---

[35] Unlike in Example 10-17, the models in Example 10-18 are estimated using data already expressed in percentage. Therefore, there is no need to multiply by 100 to get the growth rate in percentage.

[36] For the returns on the S&P 500 (see Example 10-15), we chose a moving-average model over an autoregressive model.

To reiterate, ARMA models can be very unstable, depending on the data sample used and the particular ARMA model estimated. Thus, you should be skeptical of claims that a particular ARMA model provides much better forecasts of a time series than any other ARMA model. In fact, in most cases, you can use an AR model to produce forecasts that are just as accurate as those from ARMA models without nearly as much complexity. Even some of the strongest advocates of ARMA models admit that these models should not be used with fewer than 80 observations, and they would not recommend using ARMA models for predicting quarterly sales or gross margins for a firm using even 15 years of quarterly data.

10   AUTOREGRESSIVE CONDITIONAL HETEROSKEDASTICITY

Up to now, we have ignored any issues of heteroskedasticity in time-series models and have assumed homoskedasticity. That is, we have assumed that the variance of the error term is constant, and does not depend on the value of the time series itself or on the size of previous errors. At times, however, this assumption is violated and the variance of the error term is not constant. In such a situation, the standard errors of the regression coefficients in AR, MA, or ARMA models will be incorrect, and our hypothesis tests would be invalid. Consequently, we can make poor investment decisions based on those tests.

For example, suppose you are building an autoregressive model of a company's sales. If there is heteroskedasticity, then the standard errors of the regression coefficients of your model are incorrect. It is likely that due to heteroskedasticity, one or more of the lagged sales terms may appear statistically significant whereas they actually are not. Thus, if you use this model for your decision making, you may make some sub-optimal decisions.

Engle (1982) first suggested a way of testing whether the variance of the error in a particular time-series model in one period depended on the variance of the error in previous periods. He called this type of heteroskedasticity autoregressive conditional heteroskedasticity (ARCH).

As an example, consider the ARCH(1) model

$$\epsilon_t \sim N(0, a_0 + a_1\epsilon_{t-1}^2) \qquad\qquad\qquad\qquad (10\text{-}17)$$

where the distribution of ϵ_t, conditional on its value the previous period, ϵ_{t-1}, is normal with mean 0 and variance $a_0 + a_1\epsilon_{t-1}^2$. If $a_1 = 0$, the variance of the error in every period is just a_0. The variance is constant over time and does not depend on past errors. Now suppose that $a_1 > 0$. Then the variance of the error in one period depends on how large the squared error was in the previous period. If a large error occurs in one period, the variance of the error in the next period will be even larger.

Engle shows that we can test whether a time series is ARCH(1) by regressing the squared residuals from a previously estimated time-series model (AR, MA, or ARMA) on a constant and one lag of the squared residuals. We can estimate the linear regression equation

$$\hat{\epsilon}_t^2 = a_0 + a_1\hat{\epsilon}_{t-1}^2 + u_t \qquad\qquad\qquad\qquad (10\text{-}18)$$

where u_t is an error term. If the coefficient a_1 is statistically significant, then the time series is ARCH(1). If a time-series model has ARCH(1) errors, then the variance of the errors in period $t + 1$ can be predicted in period t using the formula $\hat{\sigma}_{t+1}^2 = \hat{a}_0 + \hat{a}_1\hat{\epsilon}_t^2$.

EXAMPLE 10-18. Testing for ARCH(1) in Monthly Inflation.

Suppose you want to test whether monthly data on CPI inflation contain autoregressive conditional heteroskedasticity. You could estimate Equation 10-18 using the residuals from the time-series model. As discussed in Example 10-8, if you modeled monthly CPI inflation from 1971 to 1998, you would conclude that an AR(1) model was the best autoregressive model to use to forecast inflation out-of-sample. Table 10-19 shows the results of testing whether the errors in that model are ARCH(1).

TABLE 10-19 Test for ARCH(1)
Residuals from Monthly CPI Inflation at an Annual Rate
Monthly Data from February 1971 to December 1998:
AR(1) Model

Regression Statistics		
R-squared	0.0687	
Standard error	24.4584	
Observations	335	
Durbin-Watson	1.9420	

	Coefficient	Standard Error	t-Statistic
Constant	7.9068	1.4541	5.4375
Lag 1	0.2596	0.0524	4.9543

Source for data: U.S. Bureau of Labor Statistics

Because the t-statistic for the coefficient on the previous period's squared residuals is almost 5.0, we can easily reject the null hypothesis that the variance of the error does not depend on the variance of previous errors. Consequently, the test statistics we computed in Table 10-5 are not valid, and we should not use them in deciding our investment strategy.

It is possible our conclusion—that the AR(1) model for monthly inflation has ARCH in the errors—may have been due to the sample period employed (1971 to 1998). In Example 10-9, we used a shorter sample period of 1985 to 1998, and concluded that monthly CPI inflation follows an AR(1) process. (These results were shown in Table 10-8.) Table 10-19 shows that errors for a time-series model of inflation for the entire sample (1971 to 1988) have ARCH errors. Do the errors estimated with a shorter sample period (1985 to 1998) also display ARCH? For the shorter sample period, we estimated an AR(1) model using monthly inflation data. Now we test to see whether the errors display ARCH.[37] Table 10-20 shows the results.

---

[37] The AR(1) results are reported in Example 10-9.

TABLE 10-20   Test for ARCH(1)
Monthly CPI Inflation at an Annual Rate
Monthly Data from February 1985 to December 1998:
AR(1) Model

Regression Statistics	
R-squared	0.0024
Standard error	11.3893
Observations	167
Durbin-Watson	1.9997

	Coefficient	Standard Error	t-Statistic
Constant	5.1853	0.9773	5.3058
Lag 1	0.0487	0.0778	0.6257

Source for data: U.S. Bureau of Labor Statistics

In this sample, the coefficient on the previous period's squared residual is quite small and has a *t*-statistic of only 0.6257. Consequently, we fail to reject the null hypothesis that the errors in this regression have no autoregressive conditional heteroskedasticity. This is additional evidence that the AR(1) model for 1985–1998 is a good fit. The error variance appears to be homoskedastic and we can rely on the *t*-statistics. We again confirm that a single AR process for the entire period 1971–1998 is misspecified (that is, it does not describe the data well).

Suppose a model contains ARCH(1) errors. What are the consequences of that fact? First, if ARCH exists, the standard errors for the regression parameters will not be correct. As we discussed at the beginning of this section, this can have serious consequences for decision making. In case ARCH exists, we will need to use generalized least squares[38] or other methods that correct for heteroskedasticity to correctly estimate the standard error of the parameters in the time-series model. Second, if ARCH exists, we can predict the variance of the errors. Suppose, for instance, that we want to predict the variance of the error in inflation using the estimated parameters from Table 10-19: $\hat{\sigma}_t^2 = 7.9068 + 0.2596\,\hat{\epsilon}_{t-1}^2$. If the error in one period were 0 percent, the predicted variance of the error in the next period would be $7.9068 = 7.9068 + 0.2596(0)$. If the error in one period were 1 percent, the predicted variance of the error in the next period would be $8.1664 = 7.9068 + 0.2596(1^2)$.

Engle and other researchers have suggested many generalizations of the ARCH(1) model, including ARCH(*p*) and generalized autoregressive conditional heteroskedasticity (GARCH) models. In an ARCH(*p*) model, the variance of the error term in the current period depends linearly on the squared errors from the previous *p* periods: $\sigma_t^2 = a_0 + $

---

[38] See Greene (1999)

$a_1 \epsilon_{t-1}^2 + \cdots + a_p \epsilon_{t-p}^2$. GARCH models are similar to ARMA models of the error variance in a time series. Like ARMA models, they must be estimated with maximum likelihood, so they are outside the scope of this book. Just like ARMA models, GARCH models can be finicky and unstable: Their results can depend greatly on the sample period and the initial guesses of the parameters in the GARCH model. Financial analysts who use GARCH models should be well aware of how delicate they can be, and they should examine whether GARCH estimates are robust to changes in the sample and the initial guesses about the parameters.[39]

11   OTHER ISSUES IN TIME SERIES

Time series analysis is an extensive topic and includes many highly complex issues. Our objective in this chapter has been to present those issues in time series that are the most important for financial analysts and can also be handled with relative ease. In this section we briefly discuss some of the issues that we have not covered but could be useful for analysts.

In this chapter, we have shown how to use time-series models to make forecasts. We have also introduced the root-mean-squared error as a criterion for comparing forecasting models. However, we have not discussed measuring the uncertainty associated with forecasts made using time series models. The uncertainty of these forecasts can be very large, and should be taken into account when making investment decisions. Fortunately, the same techniques apply to evaluating the uncertainty of time-series forecasts as apply to evaluating the uncertainty about forecasts from linear regression models. To accurately evaluate forecast uncertainty, you need to consider both the uncertainty about the error term and the uncertainty about the estimated parameters in the time-series model. Evaluating this uncertainty is fairly complicated for regressions with more than one independent variable.

In this chapter, we used the U.S. CPI inflation series to illustrate some of the practical challenges you will face in using time-series models. We used information on Federal Reserve policy to explore the consequences of splitting the inflation series in two. In financial time-series work, we may suspect that a time series has more than one regime but not have the information to attempt to sort the data into different regimes. If you face such a problem, you may want to investigate other methods, especially switching regression models, to identify multiple regimes using only the time series itself.

You may be interested in modeling the joint behavior of two time series, such as inflation and interest rates. This important topic is known as multivariate time-series modeling. An important issue in analyzing multiple time series that has occupied the efforts of many researchers and financial analysts is the problem of cointegration. Cointegrated time series may each be a random walk, but they may be linked together through some financial or economic relationship. If one is analyzing cointegrated time series, ignoring cointegration could lead to incorrect statistical inference and sub-optimal forecasts.

To look at an example of cointegrated time series, consider the stock of British Airways that trades on the London Stock Exchange in pound sterling and trades on the New York Stock Exchange as an American Depository Receipt (ADR) in dollars. Now consider the three time series of US prices of the ADR in dollars, British prices in pound sterling, and the pound sterling/dollar exchange rates. Though each of these three series may

---

[39] For more on ARCH, GARCH, and other models of time-series variance, see Hamilton (1995).

individually be a random walk, they are likely to be cointegrated because there is a financial linkage between them.

If you are interested in these and other advanced time-series topics, you can learn more in Diebold (1997) and Hamilton (1995).

12 SUGGESTED STEPS IN TIME-SERIES FORECASTING

The following is a step-by-step guide to building a model to predict a time series.

1. Understand the investment problem you have, and make an initial choice of model. One alternative is a regression model that predicts the future behavior of a variable based on hypothesized causal relationships with other variables. Another is a time series model that attempts to predict the future behavior of a variable based on the past behavior of the same variable.

2. If you have decided to use a time series model, compile the time series and plot it to see whether it looks covariance stationary. The plot might show important deviations from covariance stationarity, including the following:

   • a linear trend,

   • an exponential trend,

   • seasonality, or

   • a significant shift in the time series during the sample period (for example, a change in mean or variance).

3. If you do not find significant seasonality or shift in the time series, then perhaps either a linear trend or an exponential trend will be sufficient to model the time series. In that case, take the following steps:

   • Determine whether a linear or exponential trend seems most reasonable (usually by plotting the series).

   • Estimate the trend.

   • Compute the residuals.

   • Use the Durbin-Watson statistic to determine whether the residuals have significant serial correlation. If you find no significant serial correlation in the residuals, then the trend model is sufficient to capture the dynamics of the time series and you can use that model for forecasting.

4. If you find significant serial correlation in the residuals from the trend model, use a more complex model, such as an autoregressive model. First, however, reexamine whether the time series is covariance stationary. Following is a list of violations of stationarity, along with potential methods to adjust the time series to make it covariance stationary:

   • If the time series has a linear trend, first-difference the time series.

   • If the time series has an exponential trend, take the natural log of the time series and then first-difference it.

   • If the time series shifts significantly during the sample period, estimate different time-series models before and after the shift.

   • If the time series has significant seasonality, include seasonal lags (discussed in Step 7 below).

5. After you have successfully transformed a raw time series into a covariance-stationary time-series, you can usually model the transformed series with a short autoregression.[40] To decide which autoregressive model to use, take the following steps:

   - Estimate an AR(1) model.

   - Test to see whether the residuals from this model have significant serial correlation.

   - If you find no significant serial correlation in the residuals, you can use the AR(1) model to forecast.

6. If you find significant serial correlation in the residuals, use an AR(2) model and test for significant serial correlation of the residuals of the AR(2) model.

   - If you find no significant serial correlation, use the AR(2) model.

   - If you find significant serial correlation of the residuals, keep increasing the order of the AR model until the residual serial correlation is no longer significant.

7. Your next move is to check for seasonality. There are two ways to detect seasonality in a time series:

   - Graph the data and check for regular seasonal patterns.

   - Examine the data to see whether the seasonal autocorrelations of the residuals from an AR model are significant (for example, the fourth autocorrelation for quarterly data) and the autocorrelations before and after the seasonal autocorrelations are not significant.

   To correct for seasonality, add seasonal lags to your AR model. For example, if you are using quarterly data, you might add the fourth lag of a time series as an additional variable in an AR(1) or an AR(2) model.

8. Next, test whether the residuals have autoregressive conditional heteroskedasticity. To test for ARCH(1), for example, do the following:

   - Regress the squared residual from your time-series model on a constant and a lagged value of the squared residual.

   - Test whether the coefficient on the squared lagged residual is significantly different from 0.

   - If the coefficient on the squared lagged residual is not significantly different from 0, the residuals do not display ARCH and you can rely on the standard errors from your time-series estimates.

   - If the coefficient on the squared lagged residual is significantly different from 0, use generalized least squares or other methods to correct for ARCH.

9. Finally, you may also want to perform tests of the model's out-of-sample forecasting performance to see how the model's out-of-sample performance compares to its in-sample performance.

After you have performed all of these steps, you can be reasonably sure that your model is correctly specified.

---

[40] Most financial time series can be modeled using an autoregressive process. For a few time series, a moving average model may fit better. To see if this is the case, examine the first 5 or 6 autocorrelations of the time series. If the autocorrelations suddenly drop to 0 after the first q autocorrelations, a moving average model (of order q) is appropriate. If the autocorrelations start large and decline gradually, an autoregressive model is more appropriate.

SUMMARY

- The prediction of a linear trend model for the value of a time series in period t is $\hat{b}_0 + \hat{b}_1 t$, where $\hat{b}_0$ and $\hat{b}_1$ are the estimated coefficients from the trend model.

- Time series that grow at a constant rate should be modeled using a log-linear trend model rather than a linear trend model.

- Trend models often do not capture the behavior of a time series, as indicated by serial correlation of the residuals. If the Durbin-Watson statistic from a trend model is significantly different from 2, then the next step is to try to model the time series with an autoregressive model.

- If a time series is not covariance stationary and we model it without transforming it to be covariance stationary, then the model estimated using least squares regression will not be valid. To be covariance stationary, a time series must have three properties: First, the expected value of the time series must be constant and finite in all periods. Second, the variance of the time series must be constant and finite in all periods. Third, the covariance of the time series with itself a fixed number of periods in the past or future must be constant and finite in all periods.

- An autoregressive model of order p uses p lags of a time series to predict its current value.

- An autoregressive model of order p adequately fits a time series if the residuals from the model show no significant serial correlation.

- The one-step-ahead forecast of a variable x_t from an AR(1) model made in period t for period $t + 1$ is $\hat{x}_{t+1} = \hat{b}_0 + \hat{b}_1 x_t$. This forecast can be used to create the two-period ahead forecast from the model made in period t, $\hat{x}_{t+2} = \hat{b}_0 + \hat{b}_1 \hat{x}_{t+1}$. Similar results hold for AR(p) models.

- A time series is mean-reverting if it tends to fall when its level is above its long-run mean and rise when its level is below its long-run mean. If a time series is covariance-stationary, then it will be mean-reverting.

- Out-of-sample forecasts are usually more valuable in evaluating the forecasting performance of a time series model than are in-sample forecasts. In-sample forecasts are the in-sample predicted values from the estimated time-series model. Out-of-sample forecasts are the forecasts made from the estimated time-series model for a time period different from the one for which the model was estimated.

- Just as in regression models, the coefficients in time-series models are often unstable across different sample periods.

- A random walk is a time series in which the value of the series in one period is the value of the series in the previous period plus an unpredictable random error. If the time series is a random walk, it is not covariance stationary. Random walks are quite common in financial time series.

- Unit roots occur if a time series is a random walk or a random walk with drift. Unit roots often occur in time series that increase or decrease steadily over time.

- If a time series has a unit root, then it will not be covariance stationary. As a consequence, we cannot model the series using AR, MA, or ARMA models estimated under the assumption of covariance stationarity.

- If a time series has a unit root, the unit root can often be successfully modeled by first-differencing the time series and estimating the first-differenced series as an autoregressive time series.

- An n-period moving average of the current and past $n - 1$ values of a time series, x_t, is calculated as $\dfrac{x_t + x_{t-1} + \cdots + x_{t-n+1}}{n}$.

- A moving-average model of order q uses q lags of the random error term to predict its current value.

- The order q of a moving average model can be determined using the fact that if a time series is a moving-average time series of order q, its autocorrelations suddenly drop to 0 after the first q autocorrelations.

- The autocorrelations of most autoregressive time series start large and decline gradually, whereas the autocorrelations of an MA(q) time series suddenly drop to 0 after the first q autocorrelations. This helps in distinguishing between autoregressive and moving-average time series.

- If the residuals of a time-series model (AR, MA, or ARMA) show significant serial correlation at seasonal lags, the time series has significant seasonality. This seasonality can often be modeled by including a seasonal lag in the model, such as adding the fourth lag in a quarterly model.

- The forecast made in time t for time $t + 1$ made by a quarterly AR(1) model with a seasonal lag is $x_{t+1} = \hat{b}_0 + \hat{b}_1 x_t + \hat{b}_2 x_{t-4}$.

- ARMA models have several limitations: the parameters in ARMA models can be very unstable; determining the AR and MA order of the model can be difficult; and even with their additional complexity, ARMA models may not forecast well.

- The variance of the error in a time-series model sometimes depends on the variance of previous errors. Analysts can test for first-order ARCH in a time series model by regressing the squared residual on a constant and the squared residual from the previous period. If the coefficient on the squared residual is statistically significant, the time-series model has ARCH(1) errors.

- If a time-series model has ARCH(1) errors, then the variance of the errors in period $t + 1$ can be predicted in period t using the formula $\hat{\sigma}^2_{t+1} = \hat{a}_0 + \hat{a}_1 \hat{\epsilon}^2_t$.

PROBLEMS

Note: In Chapter 10 Problems and Solutions, we use the hat (ˆ) to indicate an estimate if we are trying to differentiate between an estimated and an actual value. However, we suppress the hat when we are clearly showing regression output.

1. The civilian unemployment rate (UER) is an important component of many economic models. The following table gives regression statistics from estimating a linear trend model of the unemployment rate: $UER_t = b_0 + b_1 t + \epsilon_t$.

Estimating a Linear Trend in the Civilian Unemployment Rate
Monthly Data from January 1995 to December 1999

Regression Statistics			
R-squared		0.9314	
Standard error		0.1441	
Observations		60	
Durbin-Watson		0.9578	

Variable	Coefficient	Standard Error	t-Statistic
Intercept	5.8509	0.0377	155.1963
Trend	−0.0301	0.0011	−27.3636

a. Using the regression output in the above table, what is the model's prediction of the unemployment rate for July 1995, mid-way through the first year of the available data?

b. How should we interpret the Durbin-Watson (DW) statistic for this regression? What does the value of the DW statistic say about the validity of a t-test on the coefficient estimates?

2. The following figure compares the predicted civilian unemployment rate (PRED) with the actual civilian unemployment rate (UER). The predicted results come from estimating the linear time trend model $UER_t = b_0 + b_1 t + \epsilon_t$.

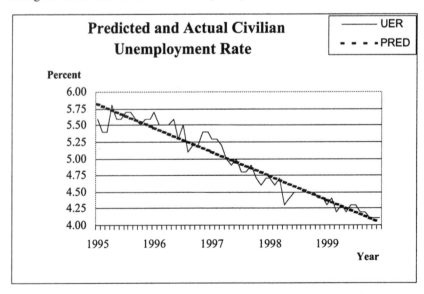

What can we conclude about the appropriateness of this model?

3. The figure below shows a plot of the first differences in the civilian unemployment rate, $\Delta UER_t = UER_t - UER_{t-1}$.

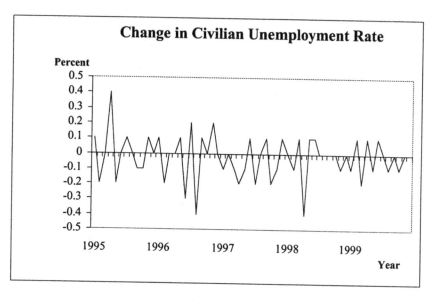

Change in Civilian Unemployment Rate

a. Has differencing the data made the new series, ΔUER_t, covariance stationary? Explain your answer.

b. Given the graph of the change in the unemployment rate shown in the figure, describe the steps we should take to determine the appropriate autoregressive time-series model specification for the series ΔUER_t.

4. The following table gives the regression output of an AR(1) model on first differences in the unemployment rate. Describe how to interpret the DW statistic for this regression.

Estimating an AR(1) Model in the Changes in the Civilian Unemployment Rate: Monthly Data from January 1995 to December 1999

Regression Statistics	
R-squared	0.1888
Standard error	0.1274
Observations	58
Durbin-Watson	2.1635

Variable	Coefficient	Standard Error	t-Statistic
Intercept	−0.0335	0.0170	−1.9706
ΔUER_{t-1}	−0.4288	0.1188	−3.6094

5. The autocorrelations of the errors from the estimated equation on first differences in the monthly civilian unemployment rate, $\Delta UER_t = b_0 + b_1 \Delta UER_{t-1} + \epsilon_t$, are given in the following table. What do these autocorrelations tell us about the appropriateness of the specification $\Delta UER_t = b_0 + b_1 \Delta UER_{t-1} + \epsilon_t$?

Different Order Autocorrelations of First Differences in the Civilian Unemployment Rate

Lag	Autocorrelation	Standard Error	t-Statistic
1	−0.0838	0.1313	−0.6382
2	−0.1147	0.1313	−0.8736
3	−0.0352	0.1313	−0.2681
4	−0.0257	0.1313	−0.1957
5	−0.1362	0.1313	−1.0373
6	0.0868	0.1313	0.6611
7	0.0138	0.1313	0.1051
8	−0.0288	0.1313	−0.2193
9	0.1305	0.1313	0.9939
10	−0.053	0.1313	−0.4037
11	0.0921	0.1313	0.7014
12	0.0167	0.1313	0.1272

6. Describe how to test for autoregressive conditional heteroskedasticity (ARCH) in the residuals from the AR(1) regression on first differences in the civilian unemployment rate, $\Delta UER_t = b_0 + b_1 \Delta UER_{t-1} + \epsilon_t$.

7. The following table shows the regression output for testing for ARCH(1) in the residuals from an AR(1) regression on first differences in the civilian unemployment rate: $\Delta UER_t = b_0 + b_1 \Delta UER_{t-1} + \epsilon_t$. Using the table, comment on whether we can reject the null hypothesis of no autoregressive conditional heteroskedasticity.

Testing for ARCH(1)
Squared Residuals from the Monthly Changes in Civilian Unemployment Rate

Regression Statistics			
R-squared	0.0114		
Standard error	0.0303		
Observations	57		
Durbin-Watson	1.3287		

Variable	Coefficient	Standard Error	t-Statistic
Intercept	0.0176	0.0045	3.9111
$\hat{\epsilon}_{t-1}^2$	−0.1068	0.1341	−0.7964

8. We conclude that changes in the civilian unemployment rate are covariance stationary and therefore mean-reverting. An AR(1) model adequately captures the behavior of changes in the unemployment rate. Specifically, we have $\Delta UER_t = -0.0335 - 0.4288\Delta UER_{t-1}$ (using the coefficient estimates given in problem 4). Given this equation, what is the mean-reverting level to which changes in the unemployment rate converge?

9. We are given the AR(1) model for changes in the civilian unemployment rate, $\Delta UER_t = -0.0335 - 0.4288\Delta UER_{t-1}$. If the current change (first difference) in the unemployment rate is 0.0300, what is the best prediction of the next change?

10. a. The AR(1) model for the civilian unemployment rate, $\Delta UER_t = -0.0335 - 0.4288\Delta UER_{t-1}$, was developed with five years of data. What would be the drawback to using the AR(1) model to predict changes in the civilian unemployment rate 12 months or more ahead, as compared with one month ahead?

   b. For purposes of estimating a predictive equation, what would be the drawback to using 30 years of civilian unemployment data rather than only five years?

11. You have been assigned to analyze whether the lightweight vehicle automobile industry would be a good sector in which to invest. As a first step in your analysis, you decide to model monthly sales in the lightweight vehicle sector to determine sales growth in the industry.

    a. The following figure gives lightweight vehicle monthly sales (annualized) from January 1991 to December 1999. Describe the salient features of the data shown in the figure.

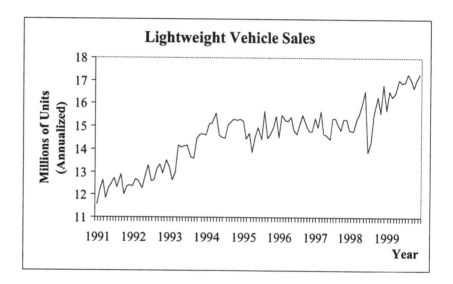

   b. Monthly sales in the lightweight vehicle sector have been increasing over time, but you suspect that the growth rate of monthly sales is relatively constant. Describe how to transform the $Sales_t$ data to model the growth rate of $Sales_t$.

   c. If $\ln(Sales_t)$ denotes the log of monthly annualized sales, write the regression equation for an AR(1) model for $\ln(Sales_t)$. Include a constant in the regression.

12. The following figure shows monthly observations on the natural log of lightweight vehicle sales, $\ln(Sales_t)$, for the period January 1991 to December 1999.

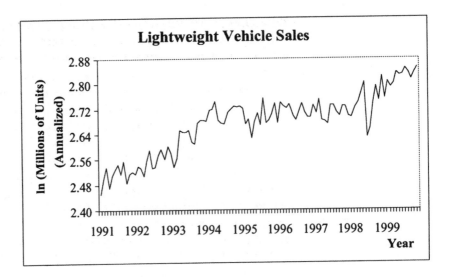

a. Using the figure, comment on whether the specification $\ln(\text{Sales}_t) = b_0 + b_1 \ln(\text{Sales}_{t-1}) + \epsilon_t$ is appropriate.

b. If $\ln(\text{Sales}_t)$ is not covariance stationary, discuss how to obtain a covariance-stationary time series.

13. The following figure shows a plot of first differences in the log of monthly lightweight vehicle sales. Has differencing the data made the resulting series, $\Delta\ln \text{Sales}_t = \ln \text{Sales}_t - \ln \text{Sales}_{t-1}$, covariance stationary?

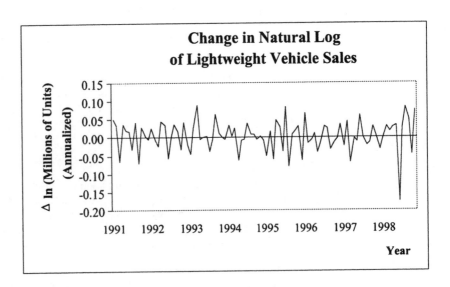

14. The table below shows regression statistics from estimating the following equation: $\Delta\ln(\text{Sales}_t) = b_0 + b_1\Delta \ln(\text{Sales}_{t-1}) + \epsilon_t$. In general, how can we use the residuals from estimating $\Delta\ln(\text{Sales}_t) = 0.0044 - 0.3012\Delta \ln(\text{Sales}_{t-1}) + \epsilon_t$ to determine whether the regression is correctly specified?

Estimating an AR(1) Model in the Changes in Lightweight Vehicle Sales Monthly Data from January 1991 to December 1998

Regression Statistics			
R-squared		0.0889	
Standard error		0.0395	
Observations		94	
Durbin-Watson		2.1607	

Variable	Coefficient	Standard Error	t-Statistic
Intercept	0.0044	0.0041	1.0754
$\Delta \ln(Sales_{t-1})$	−0.3012	0.1005	−2.9957

15. Using monthly data from January 1991 to December 1998, we estimate the following equation for lightweight vehicle sales: $\Delta \ln(Sales_t) = 0.0044 - 0.3012 \Delta \ln(Sales_{t-1}) + \epsilon_t$. The table below gives sample autocorrelations of the errors from this model.

Different Order Autocorrelations of Differences in the Logs of Vehicle Sales

Lag	Autocorrelation	Standard Error	t-Statistic
1	−0.0997	0.1031	−0.9667
2	−0.3013	0.1031	−2.9209
3	−0.1056	0.1031	−1.0242
4	0.0269	0.1031	0.2611
5	−0.1153	0.1031	−1.1180
6	0.2433	0.1031	2.3590
7	−0.0049	0.1031	−0.0478
8	−0.1701	0.1031	−1.6496
9	0.0965	0.1031	0.9358
10	0.1473	0.1031	1.4277
11	0.0346	0.1031	0.3352
12	−0.1990	0.1031	−1.9290

a. Use the information in the table to assess the appropriateness of this specification.
b. If the residuals from the AR(1) model above exhibit serial correlation, how would you modify the AR(1) specification for $\Delta \ln(Sales_t)$ to eliminate the serial correlation?

16. The following figure shows the quarterly sales of Avon Products, Inc., from 1989:Q1 to 1998:Q2. Describe the salient features of the data shown.

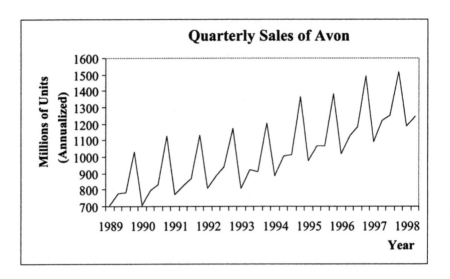

17. After sequentially estimating autoregressive models and testing the residuals for serial correlation, suppose we have arrived at an AR(4) model for the first differences of the natural logs of Avon sales data (given in the first table below). The second table below shows the regression statistics from the AR(4) specification.

Sales Data for Avon Products, Inc. (Million $)

Date Year:Quarter	Sales Sales$_t$	Natural Log of Sales ln(Sales$_t$)
1997:Q1	1087.6	6.99
1997:Q2	1225.0	7.11
1997:Q3	1249.4	7.13
1997:Q4	1517.4	7.32
1998:Q1	1183.4	7.08
1998:Q2	1247.2	7.13
1998:Q3	1233.2	7.12
1998:Q4	1548.9	7.35
1999:Q1	1213.8	7.10
1999:Q2	1258.1	7.14

Estimating an AR(4) Model in the Changes in Quarterly Sales for Avon Products from First Quarter 1989 to Second Quarter 1998

Regression Statistics	
R-squared	0.9807
Standard error	0.0323
Observations	33
Durbin-Watson	1.8438

Variable	Coefficient	Standard Error	t-Statistic
Intercept	0.0309	0.0105	2.9509
$\Delta \ln(\text{Sales}_{t-1})$	−0.5397	0.1621	−3.3300
$\Delta \ln(\text{Sales}_{t-2})$	0.5370	0.1627	−3.3014
$\Delta \ln(\text{Sales}_{t-3})$	−0.5339	0.1619	−3.2973
$\Delta \ln(\text{Sales}_{t-4})$	0.4222	0.1592	2.6524

Using the above information, answer the following questions.

a. The errors from a properly specified regression must be homoskedastic. Describe how to test for ARCH behavior in the errors from the AR(4) regression.

b. Use the regression estimates and the sales data to estimate sales in the second quarter of 1999 (an in-sample sales forecast).

18. The following figure shows the quarterly sales of Cisco Systems, Inc. from 1989:Q1 to 1998:Q2.

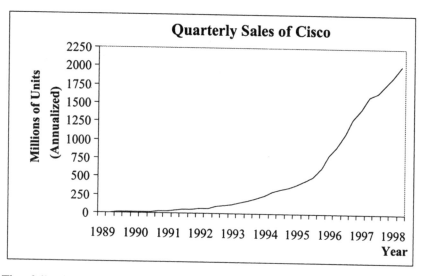

The following table gives the regression statistics from estimating the model $\Delta \ln(\text{Sales}_t) = b_0 + b_1 \Delta \ln(\text{Sales}_{t-1}) + \epsilon_t$.

Change in the Natural Log of Sales from Cisco Systems, Inc.
Quarterly Data from 1989:Q3 to 1998:Q2

Regression Statistics	
R-squared	0.3694
Standard error	0.0665
Observations	36
Durbin-Watson	1.7435

Variable	Coefficient	Standard Error	t-Statistic
Intercept	0.0624	0.0252	2.4755
$\Delta \ln(\text{Sales}_{t-1})$	0.5954	0.1334	4.4625

a. Describe the salient features of the quarterly sales series.
b. Describe the procedures we should use to determine whether the AR(1) specification is correct.
c. Assuming the model is correctly specified, what is the long-run change in the log of sales toward which the series will tend to converge?

19. For a regression model to be correctly specified, the errors from the regression must be serially uncorrelated and homoskedastic. One type of heteroskedasticity is ARCH behavior. The following table shows the regression output from the regression $\hat{\epsilon}_t^2 = a_0 + a_1\hat{\epsilon}_{t-1}^2 + u_t$ where $\hat{\epsilon}_t^2$ is the residual series from estimating the regression $\Delta \ln(Sales_t) = b_0 + b_1\Delta\ln(Sales_{t-1}) + \epsilon_t$.

Testing for ARCH(1)
Squared Residuals from Changes in the Log of Sales for Cisco Systems, Inc.

Regression Statistics	
R-squared	0.0016
Standard error	0.0091
Observations	35
Durbin-Watson	1.9792

Variable	Coefficient	Standard Error	t-Statistic
Intercept	0.0043	0.0017	2.5113
$\hat{\epsilon}_{t-1}^2$	−0.0395	0.1744	−0.2268

Interpret the output to determine whether ARCH is present in the errors from the regression model $\Delta\ln(Sales_t) = b_0 + b_1\Delta\ln(Sales_{t-1}) + \epsilon_t$.

20. The following table gives the actual change in the log of sales from 1998:Q3 to 1999:Q2, along with the forecasts from the regression model $\Delta\ln(Sales_t) = 0.0624 + 0.5954\Delta\ln(Sales_{t-1})$ estimated using data from 1989:Q3 to 1998:Q2. (Note that the observations after the second quarter of 1998 are out-of-sample.)

Date Year: Quarter	Actual Value of Changes in the Log of Sales $\Delta\ln(Sales_t)$	Forecast Value of Changes in the Log of Sales $\Delta\ln(Sales_t)$
1998:Q3	0.0798	0.1198
1998:Q4	0.0902	0.1338
1999:Q1	0.0796	0.1421
1999:Q2	0.0883	0.1470

Calculate the root mean squared error (RMSE) for the out-of-sample forecast errors.

21. The following table gives the actual sales, log of sales, and changes in the log of sales of Cisco Systems for the period 1998:Q3 to 1999:Q2.

Date Year:Quarter	Actual Sales	Log of Sales	Changes in Log of Sales $\Delta\ln(Sales_t)$
1998:Q3	2,183.7560	7.6888	0.0798
1998:Q4	2,389.9890	7.7790	0.0902
1999:Q1	2,588.0000	7.8586	0.0796
1999:Q2	2,827.0000	7.9470	0.0883
1999:Q3			
1999:Q4			

Forecast the third- and fourth-quarter sales of Cisco Systems for 1999 using the regression $\Delta\ln(Sales_t) = 0.0624 + 0.5954\Delta\ln(Sales_{t-1})$.

22. The first table below shows the autocorrelations of the residuals from an AR(1) model fit to the changes in the gross profit margin (GPM) of The Home Depot, Inc.

Autocorrelations of the Residuals from Estimating the Regression $\Delta GPM_t = 0.0007 - 0.2995_1 \Delta GPM_{t-1} + \epsilon_t$ Quarterly Data from 1989:Q3 to 1999:Q1 (39 observations)

Lag	Autocorrelation
1	−0.1591
2	−0.6352
3	−0.1243
4	0.8649
5	−0.1576

The next table shows the output from a regression on changes in the GPM for Home Depot, where we have changed the specification of the AR regression.

Change in Gross Profit Margin for The Home Depot, Inc. Quarterly Data 1990:Q2 to 1999:Q1

Regression Statistics			
R-squared	0.8919		
Standard error	0.0047		
Observations	36		
Durbin-Watson	2.310		

Variable	Coefficient	Standard Error	t-Statistic
Intercept	0.0003	0.0008	0.3548
ΔGPM_{t-1}	−0.0427	0.0600	−0.7112
ΔGPM_{t-4}	0.9621	0.0611	15.7584

a. Identify the change that was made to the regression model.
b. Discuss the rationale for changing the regression specification.

SOLUTIONS

1. a. The estimated forecasting equation is $\text{UER}_t = 5.8509 - 0.0301(t)$. The data begin in January 1995, and July 1995 is period 7. Thus, the linear trend model predicts the unemployment rate to be $\text{UER}_7 = 5.8509 - 0.0301(7) = 5.6402$ or approximately 5.64 percent.

b. The DW statistic is designed to detect first-order serial correlation of the errors of a regression equation. Under the null hypothesis of no first-order serial correlation, the DW statistic is 2.0. Positive serial correlation will lead to a DW statistic that is less than 2.0. From the table in Problem 1, we see that the DW statistic is 0.9578. To see whether this result is statistically different from 2.0, refer to the Durbin-Watson table at the end of the book, in the column marked $k = 1$ (one independent variable) and the row corresponding to 60 observations. We see that $d_l = 1.55$. Since our DW is clearly less than d_l, we reject the null hypothesis of no serial correlation at the 0.05 significance level.

The presence of serial correlation in the error terms violates one of the regression assumptions. The standard errors of the estimated coefficients will be biased downward and we cannot conduct hypothesis testing on the coefficients.

2. The difference between UER and its forecast value, $\hat{\text{UER}}$, is the forecast error. In an appropriately specified regression model, the forecast errors are randomly distributed around the regression line and have a constant variance. We can see that the errors from this model specification are persistent. The errors tend first to be above the regression line and then, starting in 1997, they tend to be below the regression line. This persistence suggests that the errors are positively serially correlated. Therefore, we conclude that the estimated model is not appropriate.

3. a. The plot of the series ΔUER_t seems to fluctuate around a constant mean; its volatility appears to be constant throughout the period. Our initial judgment is that the differenced series is covariance stationary.

b. The change in the unemployment rate seems covariance stationary, so we should first estimate an AR(1) model and test to see whether the residuals from this model have significant serial correlation. If the residuals do not display significant serial correlation, we should use the AR(1) model. If the residuals do display significant serial correlation, we should try an AR(2) model and test for serial correlation of the residuals of the AR(2) model. We should continue this procedure until the errors from the final AR(p) model are serially uncorrelated.

4. The DW statistic cannot be appropriately used for a regression that has a lagged value of the dependent variable as one of the explanatory variables. To test for serial correlation, we need to examine the autocorrelations.

5. None of the autocorrelations are significantly different from 0, as shown by the t-statistics. This finding indicates that the errors are serially uncorrelated; particularly note the absence of seasonality as evidenced by the insignificant autocorrelation at lag 12 (because of monthly data). An AR(1) model estimated on the first differences appears to fit this time series. However, we should still check to see that the errors are homoskedastic.

6. We should estimate the regression $\Delta\text{UER}_t = b_0 + b_1\Delta\text{UER}_{t-1} + \epsilon_t$ and save the residuals from the regression. Then we should create a new variable, $\hat{\epsilon}_t^2$, by squaring the residuals. Finally, we should estimate $\hat{\epsilon}_t^2 = a_0 + a_1\hat{\epsilon}_{t-1}^2 + u_t$ and test to see whether $\hat{a}_1$ is statistically different from 0.

7. The t-statistic for the coefficient on $\hat{\epsilon}_{t-1}^2$ is clearly not significant, indicating that we cannot reject the hypothesis that a_1 is 0 in the regression $\hat{\epsilon}_t^2 = a_0 + a_1\hat{\epsilon}_{t-1}^2 + u_t$. Therefore, we conclude that the regression $\Delta UER_t = b_0 + b_1\Delta UER_{t-1} + \epsilon_t$ for this time period is free from ARCH.

8. When a covariance-stationary series is at its mean-reverting level, the series will tend not to change until it receives a shock (ϵ_t) again. So, if the series ΔUER_t is at the mean reverting level, $\Delta UER_t = \Delta UER_{t-1}$. This implies that $\Delta UER_t = -0.0335 - 0.4288\Delta UER_t$, so that $(1 + 0.4288)\Delta UER_t = -0.0335$ and $\Delta UER_t = -0.0335/[1 - (-0.4288)] = -0.0234$. The mean-reverting level is -0.0234. The sample average of ΔUER_t over this period is -0.02333, close to the mean-reverting level.

    In an AR(1) model, the general expression for the mean-reverting level is $b_0/(1 - b_1)$.

9. The predicted change in the unemployment rate for next period is -4.64 percent, found by substituting 0.0300 into the forecasting model: $-0.0335 - 0.4288(0.03) = -0.0464$. An incorrect answer is the mean-reverting level of -0.0233, the answer to the previous question. The mean-reverting level is the average value over all possible paths, or long-run average value, for a stationary time series. If we did not know the current level of the series, -0.0233 would be our best forecast for next period's change. We do have relevant information, however—the current value of the time series (in first differences)—and we should use it. A stationary time series may need many periods to return to its equilibrium, mean-reverting level. In this case, however, if we substitute our one-period-ahead forecast of -0.0464 into the model (using the chain rule of forecasting), we get a two-period ahead forecast of -0.0136, quite close to the mean-reverting level.

10. a. Predictions too far ahead can be nonsensical. For example, the AR(1) model we have been examining, $\Delta UER_t = -0.0335 - 0.4288\Delta UER_t$, taken at face value, predicts declining civilian unemployment into the indefinite future. Because the civilian unemployment rate will probably not go below 3 percent frictional unemployment, and never below 0 percent unemployment, the long-range forecasts of this model are implausible. The model is designed for short-term forecasting, as are many time-series models.

    b. Using more years of data for estimation may lead to non-stationarity even in the series of first differences in the civilian unemployment rate. As we go further back, we increase the risk that the underlying civilian unemployment rate series has more than one regime (or true model). If the series has more than one regime, fitting one model to the entire period would not be correct.

11. a. The series shows an upward trend over time. The data plot suggests that the volatility of the time series may be larger in later time periods (as seen by the wider swings). If either the mean or variance is not constant, the time series is not covariance stationary.

    b. Take the natural log of $Sales_t$. If the growth rate of the time series is approximately constant, the time series probably has an exponential growth component. A log transformation of the time series is thus appropriate.

    c. With a constant included, the AR(1) regression equation in the log of Sales is $\ln(Sales_t) = b_0 + b_1 \ln(Sales_{t-1}) + \epsilon_t$.

12. a. The graph of $\ln Sales_t$ appears to trend upward over time. A series that trends upward or downward over time often has a unit root and is thus not covariance

stationary. Therefore, using an AR(1) regression on the undifferenced series is probably not correct. In practice, we need to examine regression statistics to confirm visual impressions such as this.

b.   The most common way to transform a time series with a unit root into a covariance stationary time series is to difference the data—that is, to create a new series $\Delta\ln(\text{Sales}_t) = \ln(\text{Sales}_t) - \ln(\text{Sales}_{t-1})$.

13.   The plot of the series $\Delta\ln(\text{Sales}_t)$ appears to fluctuate around a constant mean; its volatility seems constant throughout the period. Differencing the data appears to have made the time series covariance stationary.

14.   The errors from a correctly specified regression should be serially uncorrelated and homoskedastic. To see if the residuals satisfy these conditions, we should take the following steps:

  i. Graph the residuals to look for outliers and patterns.
  ii. Calculate the autocorrelations to be sure that the errors are serially uncorrelated and free of seasonality.
  iii. Test for homoskedasticity (absence of ARCH effects) in the data.

   We should remember that with an AR model, we cannot use the Durbin-Watson statistic (a standard output in regression software) to check for serial correlation.

15. a.   In a correctly specified regression, the residuals must be serially uncorrelated. The data contain 94 observations,[41] so the standard error of the autocorrelation is $\frac{1}{\sqrt{T}}$, or in this case $\frac{1}{\sqrt{94}} = 0.1031$. The t-statistic for the second lag is significant at the 0.01 level, and the sixth lag is significant at the 0.05 level. The 8th and 12th lags are both significant at the 0.10 level. We would have to modify the model specification before continuing with the analysis.

b.   Because the residuals from the AR(1) specification display significant serial correlation, we should estimate an AR(2) model and test for serial correlation of the residuals of the AR(2) model. If the residuals from the AR(2) model are serially uncorrelated, we should then test for seasonality and ARCH behavior. If any serial correlation remains in the residuals, we should estimate an AR(3) process and test the residuals from that specification for serial correlation. We should continue this procedure until the errors from the final AR(p) model are serially uncorrelated. When the serial correlation is eliminated, we should test for seasonality and ARCH behavior.

16.   The quarterly sales of Avon show an upward trend and a clear seasonal pattern, as indicated by the repeated regular cycle.

17. a.   We should save the residuals from the regression and create the squared residual series $\hat{\epsilon}_t^2$. We should then estimate, using OLS, the equation $\hat{\epsilon}_t^2 = a_0 + a_1\hat{\epsilon}_{t-1}^2 + u_t$ and test whether the coefficient $\hat{a}_1$ is significantly different from 0. If we cannot reject the hypothesis that $a_1 = 0$, we can conclude that the errors do not exhibit ARCH(1) behavior.

b.   As we compute below, the predicted value of sales for 1999:Q2 is $1,662.01 million. While modeling, we had transformed the original sales data by taking the natural log and differencing. We must reverse these transformations to get an estimate of the required sales.

---

[41] We lose two observations because we are looking at the first difference and because there is one lag.

With $\Delta\ln\text{Sales}_t = \ln\text{Sales}_t - \ln\text{Sales}_{t-1}$, the estimated equation is

$$\Delta\ln\text{Sales}_t = 0.0309 - 0.5397\Delta\ln\text{Sales}_{t-1} + 0.5370\Delta\ln\text{Sales}_{t-2}$$
$$- 0.5339\Delta\ln\text{Sales}_{t-3} + 0.4222\Delta\ln\text{Sales}_{t-4}$$

We need to substitute the appropriate observations from the last column of the second table in the statement of the problem. To keep track, let t stand for 1999:Q2, as follows:

$$\Delta\ln\text{Sales}_t = \ln\text{Sales}_t - \ln\text{Sales}_{t-1} = 0.0309 - 0.5397(7.10 - 7.35)$$
$$+ 0.5370(7.35 - 7.12) - 0.5339(7.12 - 7.13)$$
$$+ 0.4222(7.13 - 7.08) = 0.315784$$

Thus,

$$\ln\text{Sales}_t - \ln\text{Sales}_{t-1} = 0.315784.$$

So, $\ln\text{Sales}_t - 7.10 = 0.315784$, and $\ln\text{Sales}_t = 7.10 + 0.315784 = 7.415784$.

Therefore, $\ln\text{Sales}_t = 7.415784$ and $\text{Sales}_t = \exp(7.415784) = \$1{,}662.01$.

18. a. The series has a steady upward trend of growth, suggesting an exponential growth rate. This finding suggests transforming the series by taking the natural log and differencing the data.

b. First, we should determine whether the residuals from the AR(1) specification are serially uncorrelated. If the residuals are serially correlated, then we should try an AR(2) specification and then test the residuals from the AR(2) model for serial correlation. We should continue in this fashion until the residuals are serially uncorrelated. We should then look for seasonality in the residuals. If seasonality is present, we should add a seasonal lag. If no seasonality is present, we should test for ARCH. If ARCH is not present, we can conclude that the model is correctly specified.

c. If the model $\Delta\ln(\text{Sales}_t) = b_0 + b_1\Delta\ln(\text{Sales}_{t-1}) + \epsilon_t$ is correctly specified, then the series $\Delta\ln(\text{Sales}_t)$ is covariance-stationary. So, this series tends to its mean-reverting level, which is $b_0/(1 - b_1)$ or $0.0624/(1 - 0.5954) = 0.1542$.

19. A simple test for ARCH behavior is to regress the squared error terms from a regression on the lagged squared error terms. The coefficient on the $\hat{\epsilon}_{t-1}^2$ is not significantly different from 0, indicating that we cannot reject the hypothesis that the errors from the estimated equation $\Delta\ln(\text{Sales}_t) = b_0 + b_1\Delta\ln(\text{Sales}_{t-1}) + \epsilon_t$ do not exhibit ARCH behavior.

20. The root mean squared error of the out-of-sample forecast errors is 5.2 percent. Out-of-sample error refers to the difference between the forecasted value and the realized value of $\Delta\ln(\text{Sales}_t)$ for dates beyond the estimation period. In this case, the out-of-sample period is 1998:Q3 to 1999:Q2. These are the four quarters for which we have data that we did not use to obtain the estimated model $\Delta\ln(\text{Sales}_t) = 0.0624 + 0.5954\Delta\ln(\text{Sales}_{t-1})$.

The steps to calculate root mean squared error are as follows:

i. Take the difference between the forecast and the actual value. This is the error.
ii. Square the error.

iii. Sum the squared errors.
iv. Divide by the number of forecasts.
v. Take the square root of the average.

We show the calculations for RMSE in the table below.

Actual Value of Changes in the Log of Sales $\Delta\ln(\text{Sales}_t)$	Forecast Value of Changes in the Log of Sales $\Delta\ln(\text{Sales}_t)$	Error (Column 2 − Column 1)	Squared Error (Column 3 Squared)
0.0798	0.1198	0.0400	0.0016
0.0902	0.1338	0.0435	0.0019
0.0796	0.1421	0.0625	0.0039
0.0883	0.1470	0.0587	0.0034
		Sum	0.0108
		Mean (Average)	0.0027
		RMSE	0.0520
		(Square Root of Mean)	

21. The forecast of sales is $3,172 million for the third quarter of 1999 and $3,615 million for the fourth quarter of 1999, as the following table shows.

Date Year: Quarter	Sales	Log of Sales	Actual Value of Changes in the Log of Sales $\Delta\ln(\text{Sales}_t)$	Forecast Value of Changes in the Log of Sales $\Delta\ln(\text{Sales}_t)$
1998:Q3	2,183.7560	7.6888	0.0798	
1998:Q4	2,389.9890	7.7790	0.0902	
1999:Q1	2,588.0000	7.8586	0.0796	
1999:Q2	2,827.0000	7.9470	0.0883	
1999:Q3	3,171.6200	8.0620		0.1150
1999:Q4	3,615.1900	8.1929		0.1309

Using the estimated equation $\Delta\ln(\text{Sales}_t) = 0.0624 + 0.5954\Delta\ln(\text{Sales}_{t-1})$, we find the forecasted change in the log of sales for the third quarter of 1993 by inputting the value for the change in the log of sales from the previous quarter into the equation $\Delta\ln(\text{Sales}_t) = 0.0624 + 0.5954\Delta\ln(\text{Sales}_{t-1})$. Specifically, $\Delta\ln(\text{Sales}_t) = 0.0624 + 0.5954(0.0883) = 0.1150$, which means that we forecast the log of sales in the third quarter of 1999 to be $7.9470 + 0.1150 = 8.062$.

Next, we forecast the change in the log of sales for the fourth quarter of 1999 as $\Delta\ln(\text{Sales}_t) = 0.0624 + 0.5954(0.1150) = 0.1309$. (Note that we have to use our third quarter 1999 estimated value of the change in the log of sales as our input for $\Delta\ln(\text{Sales}_{t-1})$ because we are forecasting past the period for which we have actual data.)

With a forecasted change of 0.1309, we forecast the log of sales in the fourth quarter of 1999 to be $8.062 + 0.1309 = 8.1929$.

We have forecasted the log of sales in the third and fourth quarters of 1999 to be 8.062 and 8.1929, respectively. Finally, we take the antilog of our estimates of the log of sales in the third and fourth quarters of 1999 to get our estimates of the level of sales: $e^{8.062} = 3{,}171.62$ and $e^{8.1929} = 3{,}615.19$, respectively.

22. a. A second explanatory variable, the change in the gross profit margin lagged four quarters, ΔGPM_{t-4}, was added.

  b. The model was augmented to account for seasonality in the time series (with quarterly data, significant autocorrelation at the fourth lag indicates seasonality). The standard error of the autocorrelation coefficient equals 1 over the square root of the number of observations: $1\sqrt{39}$ or 0.160. The autocorrelation at the fourth lag (0.8649) is significant: $t = 0.8649/0.160 = 5.40$. This indicates seasonality, and accordingly we added ΔGPM_{t-4}. Note that in the augmented regression, the coefficient on ΔGPM_{t-4} is highly significant.

C H A P T E R

11

PORTFOLIO CONCEPTS

LEARNING OUTCOMES

After completing this chapter, you will be able to do the following:

- Define mean–variance analysis.
- List the assumptions of mean–variance analysis.
- Calculate the expected return and variance or standard deviation of return for a portfolio of two assets, given the expected returns, variances (or standard deviations), and correlation or covariance of the two assets.
- Calculate the expected return and variance or standard deviation of return for a portfolio of three assets, given the expected returns, variances (or standard deviations), and correlations or covariances of the three assets.
- Interpret the plot of the combinations of expected return and standard deviation of return attainable from two-asset portfolios.
- Define the minimum-variance frontier.
- Define the global minimum-variance portfolio.
- Define the efficient frontier.
- Explain the usefulness of the efficient frontier for portfolio management.
- Define diversification benefits.
- Explain how different correlations between two assets affect the diversification benefits achievable from a two-asset portfolio.
- Describe the minimum-variance frontiers for two-asset portfolios for correlations of $+1$, 0, and -1.
- Describe how to solve for the minimum-variance frontier for a set of assets, given expected returns, covariances, and constraints on portfolio weights.
- Describe the problem of instability of the minimum-variance frontier.
- Give two reasons that a minimum-variance frontier may be unstable when based on historical data for different sample time periods.
- Calculate the variance of an equally weighted portfolio of n stocks in terms of the average variance of returns, the average covariance between returns, and n.
- Calculate the ratio of the variance of an equally weighted portfolio with a small number of stocks to the variance of an equally weighted portfolio with a very large number of stocks, given the average variance and the average covariance between stocks, and holding average variance and average covariance constant.

- Characterize the relationship between diversification benefits and the number of stocks in a portfolio.
- Describe how the efficient frontier is used when a risk-free asset is available for investment.
- Calculate expected return and standard deviation of return for a portfolio of two assets when one of the assets is a risk-free asset.
- Define the capital allocation line.
- Calculate the value of one of the variables in the capital allocation line given the values of the remaining variables.
- Explain the slope coefficient in the capital allocation line.
- Define the capital market line.
- Explain the relationship between the capital allocation line and the capital market line.
- Define the market price of risk.
- Define the capital asset pricing model (CAPM).
- State the assumptions of the CAPM.
- Describe the relationship between the CAPM and the efficiency of the market portfolio.
- Explain the concept of a financial market equilibrium.
- Explain beta as defined in the capital asset pricing model.
- Discuss the difficulty with using historical variances and covariances of returns as inputs for tracing out the minimum-variance frontier.
- Define the market model.
- State the market model predictions about the expected asset returns, variances, and covariances.
- Calculate the correlation between two assets implied by the assets' betas, the assets' residual standard deviations from the market model, and the variance of return on the market.
- Discuss adjusted and unadjusted betas as predictors of future betas.
- Calculate an adjusted beta, given an adjustment model.
- Define a multifactor model.
- Describe three categories of multifactor models.
- Discuss the main features of a macroeconomic factor model.
- Define priced risk.
- Define systematic factors.
- Explain the use of systematic factors in multifactor models.
- Define factor sensitivity.
- Predict a stock return, given an estimated factor model.
- Describe the returns to a portfolio of two stocks, using a factor model.
- Define arbitrage pricing theory (APT).
- State and discuss the assumptions of APT.

- Explain the relationship between APT and multifactor models.
- Identify the factor risk premiums in an APT model.
- Calculate the expected return on an asset, given its factor sensitivities to a specified set of factors and the factor risk premiums.
- Define an arbitrage portfolio.
- Determine whether there is an arbitrage opportunity, given a set of portfolio expected returns and factor sensitivities.
- Define a factor portfolio.
- Calculate the weights of a factor portfolio for a specified factor, given three well-diversified portfolios and their estimated two-factor models.
- Define a tracking portfolio.
- Calculate the weights of a tracking portfolio, given three well-diversified portfolios, their estimated two-factor models, and a target configuration of factor sensitivities.
- Discuss the use of factor and tracking portfolios.
- Explain why an investor can possibly earn a substantial premium for holding dimensions of risk unrelated to market movements.
- Contrast the implications of the CAPM and a multifactor model for the investor's portfolio choice.

1 INTRODUCTION

No aspect of quantitative investment analysis is as widely studied or as vigorously debated as portfolio theory. Issues that portfolio managers have studied over the past 50 years include the following:

- Is there a trade-off between risk and return for portfolios?
- If a portfolio manager could know the distribution of asset returns, how would the manager select an optimal portfolio?
- What is the optimal way to combine risky and risk-free assets in a portfolio?
- What are the limitations to using historical return data to predict the future trade-off between risk and return?
- Must a portfolio manager believe all the assumptions of the capital asset pricing model to use mean–variance analysis?
- What quantitative methods do outstanding portfolio managers actually use in structuring their portfolios?
- What risk factors should a portfolio manager consider in addition to market risk?

In this chapter, we present key quantitative methods to support the management of portfolios. In Section 2, we focus on mean–variance analysis and related models and issues. Then in Section 3, we address some of the problems encountered using mean–variance analysis and how we can respond to them. We introduce the market model, which explains the return on assets in terms of a single variable: a market index. Because models that explain the returns on assets in terms of multiple factors are important in modern portfolio management, we end this chapter with a discussion of multifactor and related models and how we can use these tools to better measure and control risk.

2   MEAN–VARIANCE ANALYSIS AND DIVERSIFICATION

Is there a trade-off between risk and return? When does portfolio diversification reduce risk? Are there some asset portfolios that all risk-averse investors would avoid? These are some of the questions that Harry Markowitz addressed in the research for which he shared the 1990 Nobel Prize in economics.

Mean–variance analysis, the oldest and most accepted part of modern portfolio theory, provides the theoretical foundation for the trade-off between risk and return. In this section, we describe Markowitz's theory, illustrate the principles of portfolio diversification with several examples, and discuss the limitations of relying on mean–variance analysis to predict the actual trade-off between risk and return.

Mean–variance analysis is based on the following assumptions:

1. All investors are risk averse; they prefer less risk to more for the same level of expected return.[1]

2. Expected returns for all assets are known.

3. The variances and covariances of all asset returns are known.

4. Investors need only know the expected returns, variances, and covariances of returns to determine optimal portfolios. They can ignore skewness, kurtosis, and other attributes of a distribution.

5. There are no transaction costs or taxes.

Note that the first assumption does not mean that all investors have exactly the same tolerance for risk. Investors differ in the level of risk they are willing to tolerate for a given level of expected return. However, risk-averse investors prefer as little risk as possible for a given level of expected return.

The second, third, and fourth assumptions state that we need only know the expected returns, variances, and covariances of all asset returns to determine which combinations of assets make an optimal portfolio. With these assumptions in mind, consider the following examples, which illustrate the trade-off between risk and return.

EXAMPLE 11-1.   The Trade-Off between Risk and Return with Two Assets.

In this example, we explore how choosing the proportions of the two assets in a portfolio affects the risk and return to the portfolio. We make three points:

- The division of the portfolio's assets between bonds and stocks affects the expected return and risk of the portfolio.

---

[1] For more on risk aversion and its role in portfolio theory, see, for example, Sharpe, Alexander, and Bailey (1998) or Reilly and Brown (2000).

- The portfolio with the smallest variance (the **global minimum-variance portfolio**) in this example contains both stocks and bonds.
- All risk-averse investors would reject some portfolios of bonds and stocks because other portfolios offer greater expected return for the same level of risk.

Suppose we are managing a portfolio and we can choose between two asset classes: government bonds and large-cap stocks. What combination of assets should we purchase? Table 11-1 shows the assumptions we make about the expected returns of the two assets, along with the standard deviation of return for the two assets and the correlation between their returns.

TABLE 11-1   Assumed Returns, Variances, and Correlation: Two-Asset Case

	Asset 1 Large-Cap Stocks	Asset 2 Government Bonds
Expected return (%)	15	5
Variance	225	100
Standard deviation (%)	15	10
Correlation	0.5	

Mean–variance analysis assumes that investors are risk averse—for a given expected return, investors will always choose the portfolio with the least risk. Therefore, to determine the optimal asset combination for any given level of expected return, we must find the portfolio that has the minimum variance for that level of expected return.

We know from Table 11-1 that the standard deviation of the return to large-cap stocks (Asset 1) is 15 percent, the standard deviation of the return to government bonds (Asset 2) is 10 percent, and the correlation between the two asset returns is 0.5. Therefore, we can compute the variance of the portfolio's returns as a function of the fraction of the portfolio invested in large-cap stocks (w_1) and the fraction of the portfolio invested in government bonds (w_2). Because the portfolio is composed of only these two assets, we have the relationship $w_1 + w_2 = 1$. When the portfolio is 100 percent invested in Asset 1, w_1 is 1.0 and w_2 is 0; and when w_2 is 1.0, then w_1 is 0 and the portfolio is 100 percent invested in Asset 2. Also, when w_1 is 1.0, we know that our portfolio's expected return and variance of return are those of Asset 1. Conversely, when w_2 is 1.0, the portfolio's expected return and variance are those of Asset 2. Thus, in this case, the portfolio's maximum expected return is 15 percent if 100 percent of the portfolio is invested in large-cap stocks; its minimum expected return is 5 percent if 100 percent of the portfolio is invested in government bonds.

Before we can determine risk and return for all portfolios composed of large-cap stocks and government bonds, we must know how the expected return, variance, and standard deviation of the return for any two-asset portfolio depend on the expected returns of the two assets, their variances, and the correlation between the returns on the two assets.

For any portfolio composed of two assets, the expected return to the portfolio, $E(R_p)$, is

$$E(R_p) = w_1 E(R_1) + w_2 E(R_2)$$

where

$E(R_1) =$ the expected return to Asset 1
$E(R_2) =$ the expected return to Asset 2

The portfolio variance of return is

$$\sigma_p^2 = w_1^2\sigma_1^2 + w_2^2\sigma_2^2 + 2w_1w_2\rho_{1,2}\sigma_1\sigma_2$$

where

$\sigma_1 =$ the standard deviation of Asset 1
$\sigma_2 =$ the standard deviation of Asset 2
$\rho_{1,2} =$ the correlation between the two returns

and $\text{Cov}(R_1, R_2) = \rho_{1,2} \times \sigma_1 \times \sigma_2$ is the covariance between the two returns, recalling the definition of correlation as the covariance divided by the individual standard deviations. The portfolio standard deviation of return is

$$\sigma_p = [w_1^2\sigma_1^2 + w_2^2\sigma_2^2 + 2w_1w_2\rho_{1,2}\sigma_1\sigma_2]^{1/2}$$

In this case, the expected return to the portfolio is $E(R_p) = w_1(0.15) + w_2(0.05)$, and the portfolio variance is $\sigma_p^2 = w_1^2 \times 0.15^2 + w_2^2 \times 0.10^2 + 2w_1w_2(0.5)(0.15)(0.10)$.

Given our assumptions about the expected returns, variances, and return correlation for the two assets, we can determine both the variance and the expected return of the portfolio as a function of the proportion of assets invested in large-cap stocks and government bonds. Table 11-2 shows the portfolio expected return, variance, and standard deviation as the portion of the portfolio invested in large-cap stocks rises from 0 to 1.00.

TABLE 11-2　Relation between Expected Return and Risk for a Portfolio of Stocks and Bonds

Expected Return (%)	Portfolio Variance	Portfolio Standard Deviation (%)	Large-Cap Stocks, w_1	Government Bonds, w_2
5	100.00	10.00	0	1.00
6	96.75	9.84	0.10	0.90
7	97.00	9.85	0.20	0.80
8	100.75	10.04	0.30	0.70
9	108.00	10.39	0.40	0.60
10	118.75	10.90	0.50	0.50
11	133.00	11.53	0.60	0.40
12	150.75	12.28	0.70	0.30
13	172.00	13.11	0.80	0.20
14	196.75	14.03	0.90	0.10
15	225.00	15.00	1.00	0

As Table 11-2 shows, when 10 percent of the assets are in stocks, the expected portfolio return is 6 percent and the portfolio variance is 96.75.[2] That portfolio has a higher expected return and lower variance than a portfolio composed of only government bonds (which has an expected return of 5 percent and a variance of 100). This improved risk–return trade-off illustrates the power of diversification: Because the returns to large-cap stocks are not perfectly correlated with the returns to government bonds (they do not have a correlation of 1), by putting some of the portfolio into large-cap stocks, we increase the expected return and reduce the variance of return. Furthermore, there is no cost to improving the risk–return characteristics of the portfolio in this way.

Figure 11-1 graphs the possible combinations of risk and return for a portfolio composed of government bonds and large-cap stocks. Figure 11-1 plots the expected portfolio return on the y-axis and the portfolio variance on the x-axis.

FIGURE 11-1   Minimum-Variance Frontier: Large Cap Stocks and Government Bonds

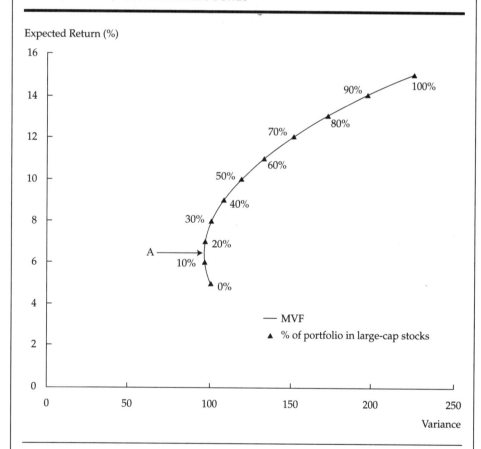

The two-asset case is special because all two-asset portfolios plot on the curve illustrated (there is a unique combination of two assets that provides a given level of expected return). We could call this curve a **portfolio possibilities curve.** We can

---

[2] Note that the 96.75 is actually percent squared. In decimals, the expected portfolio return is 0.06 and the portfolio variance is 0.009675. Often, percent squared is avoided by reporting the standard deviation, here 0.09836 or about 9.84 percent.

also call the curve in Figure 11-1 the **minimum-variance frontier** because it shows the minimum variance that can be achieved for a given level of expected return. The minimum-variance frontier is a more useful concept, because it also applies to portfolios with more than two assets. In the general case of more than two assets, any portfolio plotting on an imaginary horizontal line at any expected return level has the same expected return, and as we move left on that line, we have less variance of return. The point farthest to the left on a portfolio's minimum-variance frontier is the minimum variance for that level of expected return. With three or more assets, the minimum-variance frontier is a true frontier: It is the border of a region representing all combinations of expected return and risk that are possible (the border of the feasible region). We should note that with three or more assets, an unlimited number of portfolios can provide a given level of expected return.[3] In the three- or more asset case, if we move down and to the right on the minimum-variance frontier, we reach another portfolio but one with more risk and lower return.[4]

From Figure 11-1, note that the variance of the global minimum-variance portfolio (the one with the smallest variance) is approximately 96.43 (Point A) when the expected return of the portfolio is approximately 6.43. This global minimum-variance portfolio has 14.3 percent of assets in large-cap stocks and 85.7 percent of

FIGURE 11-2   Minimum-Variance Frontier: Large Cap Stocks
                       and Government Bonds

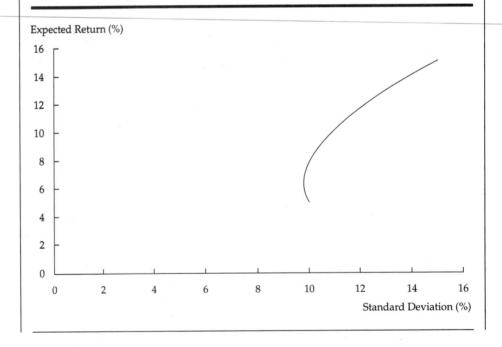

---

[3] For example, if we have three assets with expected returns of 5 percent, 12 percent, and 20 percent and we want an expected return of 11 percent on the portfolio, we would use the following equation to solve for the portfolio weights (using the fact that portfolio weights must sum to 1): $11\% = (5\% \times w_1) + (12\% \times w_2) + [14\% \times (1 - w_1 - w_2)]$. This single equation in two unknowns, w_1 and w_2, has an unlimited number of possible solutions, each solution representing a portfolio.

[4] The portfolios at the highest and lowest levels of expected return (the endpoints of the minimum-variance frontier), however, are unique.

assets in government bonds. Given these assumed returns and correlation, a portfolio manager should not choose a portfolio with less than 14.3 percent of assets in large-cap stocks because any such portfolio will have both a higher variance and a lower expected return than the global minimum-variance portfolio. All of the points on the minimum-variance frontier below Point A are inferior to the global minimum-variance portfolio, and they should be avoided.

Financial economists often say that portfolios located below the global minimum variance portfolio (Point A in Figure 11-1) are dominated by others that have the same variances but higher expected returns. Because these dominated portfolios use risk inefficiently, they are inefficient portfolios. The portion of the minimum-variance frontier beginning with the global minimum-variance portfolio and continuing above it is called the **efficient frontier.** Portfolios lying on the efficient frontier offer the maximum expected return for their level of variance of return. Efficient portfolios make efficient use of risk: Investors making portfolio choices in terms of mean return and variance of return can restrict their selection to portfolios lying on the efficient frontier. This reduction in the number of portfolios to be considered simplifies the task of portfolio selection. In practice, the efficient frontier is useful in focusing attention on one set of portfolios from the unlimited number of possible choices.

We can see the trade-off between risk and return by plotting the expected return of a portfolio against its standard deviation of return. Figure 11-2 plots the expected portfolio return for this example on the y-axis and the portfolio standard deviation of return on the x-axis.[5] Note that expected return and the standard deviation are measured in the same units (percent).

EXAMPLE 11-2. A Two-Asset Minimum-Variance Frontier Using Historical U.S. Return Data.

Portfolio managers need to understand the risk–return trade-off among various asset classes. Suppose, for example, that a portfolio manager wants to determine the risk–return trade-off between U.S. small-cap equities and U.S. long-term government bonds. The portfolio manager assumes that expected returns and variances can be estimated accurately using monthly historical returns from 1970 through 1999. She collects the data to compute the average returns, variances of returns, and correlation of returns for the two assets. Table 11-3 shows those historical statistics.

TABLE 11-3 Average Returns and Variances of Returns (Annualized, Based on Monthly Data, January 1970 to March 1999)

Asset Class	Average Return	Variance
U.S. small-cap stocks	15.12%	454.6
U.S. long-term government bonds	9.24%	113.2
Correlation	0.187	

Source: Ibbotson Associates

---

[5] For the remainder of this chapter, we will plot the expected return against standard deviation of return.

Given these statistics, the portfolio manager needs to determine how the allocation of the portfolio between the two assets affects the expected return and variance. To do so, she must calculate:

- the range of possible expected returns for the portfolio (minimum and maximum),
- the proportion of each of the two assets (asset weights) in the minimum-variance portfolio for each possible level of expected return, and
- the minimum variance[6] for each possible level of expected return.

Because U.S. government bonds have a lower expected return than U.S. small-cap stocks, the minimum expected return portfolio has 100 percent weight in U.S. long-term government bonds, 0 percent weight in U.S. small-cap stocks, and an expected return of 9.24 percent. In contrast, the maximum expected return portfolio has 100 percent weight in U.S. small-cap stocks, 0 percent weight in U.S. long-term government bonds, and an expected return of 15.12 percent. Therefore, the range of possible expected portfolio returns is 9.24 percent to 15.12 percent.

The next step in determining the minimum-variance frontier is to solve for the asset weights at different levels of expected return, starting at the minimum expected return of 9.24 percent and concluding at the maximum level of expected return of 15.12 percent. In this example, we assume the portfolio manager first solves for the portfolio weights for different levels in the expected return of the portfolio.[7] The weights at each level of expected return determine the variance for the portfolio consisting of these two asset classes. Table 11-4 shows several points on the minimum-variance frontier.

TABLE 11-4   Points on the Minimum-Variance Frontier for U.S. Small-Cap Stocks and U.S. Long-Term Government Bonds

Expected Return (%)	Variance	Standard Deviation (%)	Small-Cap Stocks, w_1	Government Bonds, w_2
9.24	113.2	10.6	0.000	1.000
9.34	110.9	10.5	0.017	0.983
9.44	108.9	10.4	0.034	0.966
10.10	102.9	10.1	0.147	0.853
10.76	108.9	10.4	0.259	0.741
10.86	110.9	10.5	0.276	0.724
15.12	454.6	21.3	1.000	0.000

Table 11-4 illustrates what happens to the weights in the individual asset classes as we move from the minimum expected return to the maximum expected return. When the expected return is 9.24 percent, the weight for the long-term government bonds is 100 percent. As we increase the expected return, the weight in long-term government bonds decreases; at the same time, the weight for U.S. small stocks increases. This result makes sense because we know that the maximum expected re-

---

[6] In the two-asset case, as previously stated, there is a unique combination of the two assets that provides a given level of expected return, so no minimization is needed.

[7] A basis point is 0.01 of 1 percent. Often these problems are solved for every 10 basis point increment.

turn of 15.12 percent must have a weight of 100 percent in U.S. small stocks. The weights in Table 11-4 reflect that property. Note that the global minimum-variance portfolio (which is also the global minimum-standard-deviation portfolio) contains some of both assets. A portfolio consisting only of bonds has more risk and a lower return than the global minimum-variance portfolio because diversification can reduce total portfolio risk in this case.

The portfolio manager must now choose her desired portfolio from those plotting on the efficient portion of the minimum-variance frontier. She knows the weights for the two asset classes at every point on the minimum-variance frontier for this two-asset portfolio. What asset allocations are appropriate given her risk tolerance and her expected return objective? This decision may seem rather straightforward. In fact, it is complicated because the portfolio manager does not—and cannot—really know the expected return or standard deviation over her future investment horizon. She is assuming that historical data on returns, variances, and correlations correctly estimate the future values of those statistics.

Figure 11-3 illustrates the minimum-variance frontier over the period 1970 to 1999 by graphing expected return as a function of standard deviation.

FIGURE 11-3 Minimum-Variance Frontier for U.S. Small-Cap Stocks and Long-Term Government Bonds, 1970–99

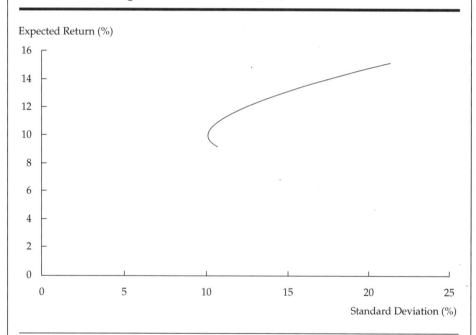

Although this figure clearly shows the historical trade-off between risk and return for small-cap stocks and government bonds, it does not actually show what the minimum-variance frontier will be over any future investment horizon. What the manager really needs to know are the expected *future* returns, variances, and correlations for the assets. The future may be very different from the past.[8]

---

[8] Also, this figure is based on monthly data corresponding to a monthly investment horizon. The figure could be quite different if we use data for a longer investment horizon.

The trade-off between risk and return for a portfolio depends not only on the expected asset returns and variances but also on the correlation of asset returns. In Example 11-1, we assumed that the correlation between returns to large-cap stocks and returns to government bonds was 0.5. The risk–return trade-off is quite different for other correlation values. Figure 11-4 shows the minimum-variance frontiers for portfolios containing large-cap stocks and government bonds for varying weights. The weights go from 100 percent in government bonds and 0 percent in large-cap stocks to 0 percent in government bonds and 100 percent in large-cap stocks, for four different values of the correlation coefficient. The correlations illustrated in Figure 11-4 are −1, 0, 0.5, and 1. In this figure, we use the following data from Table 11-1:

TABLE 11-1   (excerpted)

	Asset 1 Large-Cap Stocks	Asset 2 Government Bonds
Expected return (%)	15	5
Standard deviation (%)	15	10

FIGURE 11-4   Minimum-Variance Frontier: Large-Cap Stocks and Government Bonds for Varied Correlations

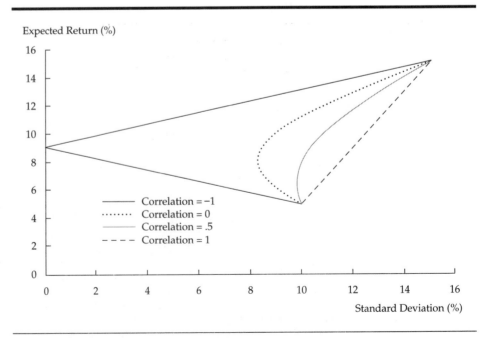

Figure 11-4 illustrates a number of interesting characteristics about minimum-variance frontiers and diversification:[9]

- The endpoints for all of the frontiers are the same. This fact should not be surprising, because at one endpoint all of the assets are in government bonds and at the other endpoint all of the assets are in large-cap stocks. At each endpoint, the expected return and standard deviation are simply the return and standard deviation for the relevant asset (stocks or bonds).

- When the correlation is +1, the minimum-variance frontier is an upward-sloping straight line. If we start at any point on the line, for each one percentage point increase in standard deviation we achieve the same constant increment in expected return. With a correlation of +1, the return (not just the expected return) on one asset is an exact positive linear function of the return on the other asset.[10] Because fluctuations in the returns on the two assets track each other in this way, the returns on one asset cannot dampen or smooth out the fluctuations in the returns on the other asset. For a correlation of +1, there are no potential benefits to diversification.

- When we move from a correlation of +1 to a correlation of 0.5, the minimum-variance frontier bows out to the left, in the direction of smaller standard deviation. With a correlation of 0.5, we can achieve any feasible level of expected return with a smaller standard deviation of return than for the +1 correlation case. As we move from a correlation of 0.5 to each smaller value of correlation, the minimum-variance frontier bows out further to the left.

- The frontiers for correlation of 0.5, 0, and −1 have a negatively sloped part.[11] This means that if we start at the lowest point (100 percent in government bonds) and shift money into stocks until we reach the global minimum-variance portfolio, we can get more expected return with less risk. Therefore, relative to an initial position fully invested in government bonds, there are benefits to diversification in each of these correlation cases. In general, diversification benefits occur when portfolio standard deviation of return can be reduced through diversification without decreasing expected return. Because the minimum-variance frontier bows out further to the left as we lower correlation, we can also conclude that as we lower correlation, holding all other values constant, there are increasingly larger potential benefits to diversification.

- When the correlation is −1, the minimum-variance frontier has two linear segments. The two segments join at the global minimum-variance portfolio, which has a stan-

---

[9] We are examining, and our observations generally pertain to, the practically interesting case in which neither of the two assets is dominated. In mean–variance analysis, an asset A is dominated by an asset B if (1) the mean return on B is equal to or larger than that on A, but B has a smaller standard deviation of return than A; or (2) the mean return on B is strictly larger than that on A, but A and B have the same standard deviation of return. The slope of a straight line connecting two assets, neither of which is dominated, is positive.

[10] If the correlation is +1, $R_1 = a + bR_2$, with $b > 0$.

[11] Frontiers of two assets for correlations of zero or below have a negatively sloped part. For positive correlations (between 0 and 1) a negatively sloped part is present when correlation is less than (standard deviation of the less risky asset) divided by (standard deviation of the more risky asset). Here this ratio is equal to 10/15 = 0.6667. Because 0.5 is less than 0.6667, the minimum-variance frontier for 0.5 has a negatively sloped part. We have not allowed short sales (negative asset weights). If we allow short sales, frontiers for any positive correlation will have a negatively sloped part, which may involve the short sale of the more risky asset, however. For details, see Elton and Gruber (1995).

dard deviation of zero. With a correlation of -1, portfolio risk can be reduced to zero, if desired.

- Between the two extreme correlations of $+1$ and -1, the minimum-variance frontier has a bullet-like shape. The minimum-variance frontier is sometimes therefore called the *bullet*.

- The efficient frontier is the positively sloped part of the minimum-variance frontier. Holding all other values constant, as we lower correlation, the efficient frontier improves in the sense of offering a higher expected return for a given feasible level of standard deviation of return.

In summary, when correlation is less than $+1$, there are potential benefits to diversification. As we lower the correlation coefficient toward -1, holding other values constant, the potential benefits to diversification increase.

2.1 OPTIMAL PORTFOLIOS WITH THREE ASSETS

In Example 11-1, we considered a portfolio composed of two assets: large-cap stocks and government bonds. For investors in our example who want to maximize expected return for a given level of risk (hold an efficient portfolio), the optimal portfolio combination of two assets contains some of each asset, unless the portfolio is placed entirely in the stock fund.

Now we can ask: Would adding a different asset to the possible choices for the portfolio improve the trade-off between risk and return? We can answer this question by contrasting the minimum-variance frontier for two assets with the minimum-variance frontier for three assets.

In our initial discussion of the risk–return trade-off, we assumed expected returns, variances, and correlations for large-cap stocks and government bonds. Table 11-1 showed these assumptions. Now suppose we assume that we can choose among three assets: large-cap stocks, government bonds, and small-cap stocks. Can choosing among these three assets provide a better trade-off between risk and return than choosing between only two assets, large-cap stocks and government bonds?

Table 11-5 shows our assumptions about the expected returns of all three assets, along with the standard deviations of the asset returns and their correlations.

TABLE 11-5   Assumed Returns, Variances, and Correlation: Three-Asset Case

	Asset 1 Large-Cap Stocks	Asset 2 Government Bonds	Asset 3 Small-Cap Stocks
Expected return (%)	15	5	15
Variance	225	100	225
Standard deviation (%)	15	10	15
Correlations			
Large-cap stocks and Bonds	0.5		
Large-cap stocks and Small-cap stocks	0.8		
Bonds and Small-cap stocks	0.5		

Now we can consider the relation between these statistics and the expected return and variance for the portfolio. For any portfolio composed of three assets, with portfolio weights w_1, w_2, and w_3, the expected return to the portfolio, $E(R_p)$, is

$$E(R_p) = w_1 E(R_1) + w_2 E(R_2) + w_3 E(R_3)$$

where

$E(R_1)$ = the expected return to Asset 1 (Large-cap stocks)
$E(R_2)$ = the expected return to Asset 2 (Government bonds)
$E(R_3)$ = the expected return to Asset 3 (Small-cap stocks)

The portfolio variance is

$$\sigma_p^2 = w_1^2\sigma_1^2 + w_2^2\sigma_2^2 + w_3^2\sigma_3^2 + 2w_1w_2\rho_{1,2}\sigma_1\sigma_2 + 2w_1w_3\rho_{1,3}\sigma_1\sigma_3 + 2w_2w_3\rho_{2,3}\sigma_2\sigma_3$$

where

σ_1 = the standard deviation for the return to Asset 1
σ_2 = the standard deviation for the return to Asset 2
σ_3 = the standard deviation for the return to Asset 3
$\rho_{1,2}$ = the correlation between Asset 1 and Asset 2
$\rho_{1,3}$ = the correlation between Asset 1 and Asset 3
$\rho_{2,3}$ = the correlation between Asset 2 and Asset 3

The portfolio standard deviation is

$$\sigma_p = [w_1^2\sigma_1^2 + w_2^2\sigma_2^2 + w_3^2\sigma_3^2 + 2w_1w_2\rho_{1,2}\sigma_1\sigma_2 + 2w_1w_3\rho_{1,3}\sigma_1\sigma_3 + 2w_2w_3\rho_{2,3}\sigma_2\sigma_3]^{1/2}$$

Given our assumptions, the expected return to the portfolio is

$$E(R_p) = w_1(0.15) + w_2(0.05) + w_3(0.15)$$

The portfolio variance is

$$\sigma_p^2 = w_1^2 0.15^2 + w_2^2 0.10^2 + w_3^2 0.15^2 + 2w_1w_2(0.5)(0.15)(0.10) + 2w_1w_3(0.8)(0.15)(0.15) + 2w_2w_3(0.5)(0.10)(0.15)$$

The portfolio standard deviation is

$$\sigma_p = [w_1^2 0.15^2 + w_2^2 0.10^2 + w_3^2 0.15^2 + 2w_1w_2(0.5)(0.15)(0.10) + 2w_1w_3(0.8)(0.15)(0.15) + 2w_2w_3(0.5)(0.10)(0.15)]^{1/2}$$

In this three-asset case, however, determining the optimal combinations of assets is much more difficult than it was in the two-asset example above. In the two-asset case, the percentage of assets in large-cap stocks was simply 100 percent minus the percentage of assets in government bonds. But with three assets, we need a method to determine what combination of assets will produce the lowest variance for any particular expected return. At least we know the minimum expected return (the return that would result from putting all assets in government bonds, 5 percent) and the maximum expected return (the return from putting all assets in either large-cap stocks or small-cap stocks, 15 percent). For any level of expected return between the minimum and maximum levels, we must solve for the portfolio weights that will result in the lowest risk for that level of expected return. We use an **optimizer** (a specialized computer program or a spreadsheet with this capability) to provide these weights.[12]

---

[12] These programs use a solution method called *quadratic programming*.

Notice that the new asset, small-cap stocks, has a correlation of less than $+1$ with both large-cap stocks and bonds, suggesting small-cap stocks may be useful in diversifying risk.

Table 11-6 shows the portfolio expected return, variance, standard deviation, and portfolio weights for the minimum-variance portfolio as the expected return rises from 5 percent to 15 percent.

TABLE 11-6   Points on the Minimum-Variance Frontier for the Three-Asset Case

Expected Return (%)	Portfolio Variance	Portfolio Standard Deviation (%)	Large-Cap (w_1)	Government Bonds (w_2)	Small Cap (w_3)
5	100.00	10.00	0	1.00	0
6	96.53	9.82	0.05	0.90	0.05
7	96.10	9.80	0.10	0.80	0.10
8	98.72	9.94	0.15	0.70	0.15
9	104.40	10.22	0.20	0.60	0.20
10	113.13	10.64	0.25	0.50	0.25
11	124.90	11.18	0.30	0.40	0.30
12	139.73	11.82	0.35	0.30	0.35
13	157.60	12.55	0.40	0.20	0.40
14	178.53	13.36	0.45	0.10	0.45
15	202.50	14.23	0.50	0	0.50

As Table 11-6 shows, the proportion of the portfolio in large-cap stocks and small-cap stocks is the same for every level of expected return in the three-asset case. This feature of the optimal portfolio stems from two facts: the expected returns for large-cap stocks are the same as the expected returns for small-cap stocks, and each of those returns has exactly the same standard deviation and correlation with the returns to government bonds. Without this highly unusual combination of returns, variances, and correlations, optimal portfolios in this example would contain different proportions of the large-cap stocks and small-cap stocks.

How does the minimum variance for each level of expected return in the three-asset case compare with the minimum variance for each level of expected return in the two-asset case? Figure 11-5 shows the comparison.

When 100 percent of the portfolio is invested in government bonds, the minimum-variance portfolio has the same expected return (5 percent) and standard deviation (10 percent) in both cases. For every other level of expected return, however, the minimum-variance portfolio in the three-asset case has a lower standard deviation than the minimum-variance portfolio in the two-asset case for the same expected return. Note also that the efficient frontier with three assets dominates the efficient frontier with two assets (we would choose our optimal portfolio from those on the efficient frontier). Adding an additional asset choice can never make things worse; the risk–return trade-off including the new asset will be at least as good as before the new asset was introduced.

From this three-asset example, we can draw two conclusions about the theory of portfolio diversification. First, we generally can improve the risk–return trade-off by considering more assets. Second, the composition of the minimum-variance portfolio for any particular level of expected return depends on the expected returns, the variances and correlations of those returns, and the number of assets.

FIGURE 11-5   Comparing Minimum-Variance Frontiers:
Three Assets versus Two Assets

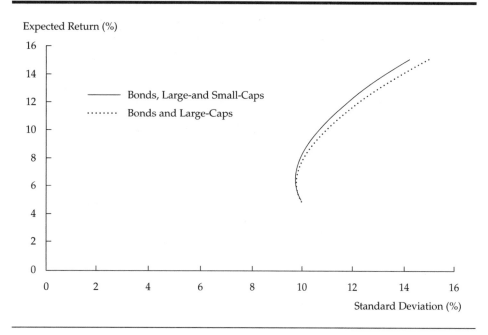

2.2 DETERMINING THE MINIMUM-VARIANCE FRONTIER FOR MANY ASSETS

We have shown examples of mean–variance analysis with two and three assets. Typically, however, portfolio managers form optimal portfolios using a large number of assets.[13] In this section, we show how to determine the minimum-variance frontier for a portfolio composed of many assets.

For a portfolio of n assets, the expected return on those assets is[14]

$$E(R_p) = \sum_{j=1}^{n} w_j E(R_j) \tag{11-1}$$

The variance of return on the portfolio is[15]

$$\sigma_p^2 = \sum_{i=1}^{n} \sum_{j=1}^{n} w_i w_j \mathrm{Cov}(R_i, R_j) \tag{11-2}$$

Before we determine the optimal portfolio weights, remember that the weights of the individual assets in the portfolio must sum to 1:

$$\sum_{j=1}^{n} w_j = 1$$

---

[13] Note that the mean–variance optimization can be based on either asset classes or individual assets. The most popular application of mean–variance analysis constructs portfolios from asset classes, not individual assets; this application greatly simplifies the problem. We can more easily determine the optimal portfolio allocation between stocks and bonds using classes rather than thousands of individual stocks.

[14] The summation notation says that we set j equal to 1 through n, then sum the resulting terms.

[15] The double summation notation says that we set i equal to 1 and let j run from 1 through n, then set i equal to two and let j run from 1 through n, and so forth until i equals n; then we sum all the terms.

To determine the minimum-variance frontier for a set of n assets, we must first determine the minimum and maximum expected returns possible with the set of assets (these are the minimum, $r_{\min}$, and the maximum, $r_{\max}$, expected returns for the individual assets). Then we must determine the portfolio weights that will create the minimum-variance portfolio for values of expected return between $r_{\min}$ and $r_{\max}$. In mathematical terms, we must solve the following problem: For specified values of z, $r_{\min} \le z \le r_{\max}$.

$$\text{Minimize}_{\text{by choice of } w\text{'s}} \ \sigma_p^2 = \sum_{i=1}^{n} \sum_{j=1}^{n} w_i w_j \, \text{Cov}(R_i, R_j) \tag{11-3}$$

$$\text{subject to } E(R_p) = \sum_{j=1}^{n} w_j E(R_j) = z \text{ and subject to } \sum_{j=1}^{n} w_j = 1$$

This optimization problem says that we solve for the portfolio weights (w_1, w_2, w_3, ... , w_n) that minimize the variance of return for a given level of expected return z, subject to the constraint that the weights sum to 1. The weights define a portfolio, and the portfolio is the minimum-variance portfolio for its level of expected return. We trace out the minimum-variance frontier by varying the value of expected return from the minimum to the maximum level.[16] We use an optimizer to actually solve the optimization problem. Example 11-3 shows a minimum-variance frontier that results from using historical data for three U.S. asset classes and non-U.S. stocks.

EXAMPLE 11-3.   A Minimum-Variance Frontier Using International Historical Return Data.

In this example, we examine a historical minimum-variance frontier with four asset classes. The three U.S. asset classes are the S&P 500 Index, U.S. small-cap stocks, and U.S. long-term government bonds. To these we add non-U.S. stocks (MSCI ex United States). We estimate the minimum-variance frontier based on historical monthly return data from January 1970 to August 1999. Table 11-7 presents the average returns, variances, and correlations of these four assets for the entire sample period.

Table 11-7 shows that the minimum average historical return from these four asset classes was 9.3 percent a year (bonds) and the maximum average historical return was 15.2 percent (U.S. small-cap stocks). To trace out the minimum-variance frontier, we use the optimization model. The optimization program solves for the mean-variance frontier using the following equations:

$$\text{Min } \sigma_p^2(R) = w_1^2 \sigma_1^2 + w_2^2 \sigma_2^2 + w_3^2 \sigma_3^2 + w_4^2 \sigma_4^2 + 2w_1 w_2 \rho_{1,2} \sigma_1 \sigma_2$$
$$+ 2w_1 w_3 \rho_{1,3} \sigma_1 \sigma_3 + 2w_1 w_4 \rho_{1,4} \sigma_1 \sigma_4 + 2w_2 w_3 \rho_{2,3} \sigma_2 \sigma_3$$
$$+ 2w_2 w_4 \rho_{2,4} \sigma_2 \sigma_4 + 2w_3 w_4 \rho_{3,4} \sigma_3 \sigma_4$$

---

[16] As a practical matter, we cannot solve for the optimal portfolio weights for every level of expected return, z, between $r_{\min}$ and $r_{\max}$, because z has an infinite number of possible values. Consequently, analysts often determine the optimal portfolio weights for a small set of z values by starting with $z = r_{\min}$, then increasing z by 10 basis points (0.10 percent) and solving for the optimal portfolio weights until $z = r_{\max}$.

TABLE 11-7   Average Annual Returns, Standard Deviations,
              and Correlation Matrix for Four Asset Classes:
              January 1970–August 1999

	S&P 500	U.S. Small-Cap Stocks	MSCI ex United States	U.S. Long-Term Government Bonds
Returns (%)	13.9	15.2	13.4	9.3
Standard deviation (%)	15.35	21.32	16.97	10.64
Correlation matrix				
S&P 500	1			
U.S. small-cap stocks	0.772	1		
MSCI ex United States	0.53	0.454	1	
U.S. long-term bonds	0.351	0.187	0.206	1

subject to $E(R_p) = w_1 E(R_1) + w_2 E(R_2) + w_3 E(R_3) + w_4 E(R_4) = z$
repeated for specified values of z, $0.093 \leq z \leq 0.152$

and $w_1 + w_2 + w_3 + w_4 = 1$

The weights w_1, w_2, w_3, and w_4 represent the four asset classes in the order listed in Table 11-7. The optimizer chooses the weights (allocations to the four asset classes) that result in the minimum-variance portfolio for each level of average return as we move from the minimum level (r_{min} = 9.3 percent) to the maximum level (r_{max} = 15.2 percent). Although we have not changed the notation in Equations 11-3, it is important to note that now $E(R_j)$ represents the sample mean return on asset class j, not a forward-looking expected return, and that the variances and covariances are also sample statistics. Unless we deliberately choose to use these historical data as our forward-looking estimates, we would not interpret the results of the optimization as a prediction about the future.

Figure 11-6 shows the minimum-variance frontier for the four assets classes based on the historical means, variances, and covariances from 1970 to 1999. The figure also shows the means and standard deviations of the four asset classes separately.

Although U.S. government bonds lie on the minimum-variance frontier, they are dominated by other assets that offer a better mean return for the same level of risk. Note also that the points representing large-cap stocks and the MSCI ex United States stocks plotted off and to the right of the minimum-variance frontier. If we move directly to the left from either, we reach a portfolio on the efficient frontier that has smaller risk with the same mean return. If we move directly up from either, we reach a portfolio that has greater mean return with the same level of risk. After the fact, at least, these two portfolios were not efficient for an investor who could invest in all four asset classes. Despite the fact that MSCI ex United States stocks is a very broad index itself, for example, there were benefits to further diversifying. Note that of the four asset classes, only U.S. small-cap stocks plotted on the efficient frontier.

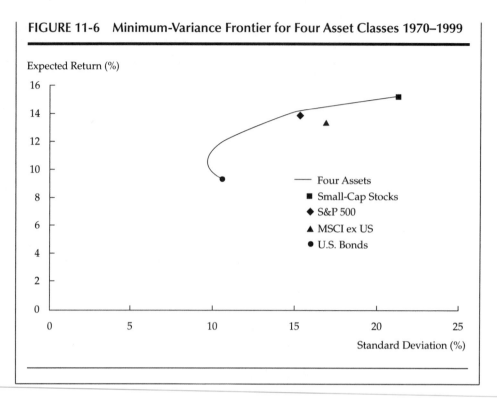

FIGURE 11-6   Minimum-Variance Frontier for Four Asset Classes 1970–1999

In this section, we have shown the process for tracing out a minimum-variance frontier. We also analyzed a frontier generated from actual data. In the next section, we address reasons to use care in analyzing and interpreting the results of mean–variance optimizations.

2.3 INSTABILITY IN THE MINIMUM-VARIANCE FRONTIER

Although standard mean–variance optimization, as represented by the model 11-3, is a convenient and objective procedure for portfolio formation, we need to use care in interpreting its results in practice. In this section, we discuss cautions regarding the use of mean–variance optimization. The problems that can arise have been widely studied, and remedies for them have been developed. With this knowledge, we can still find that mean–variance optimization is a useful tool.

The chief problem of mean–variance optimization is that small changes in input assumptions can lead to large changes in the minimum-variance (and efficient) frontier. This is the problem of **instability in the minimum-variance frontier.** It arises because, in practice, there is uncertainty about the expected returns, variances, and covariances used in tracing out the minimum-variance frontier.

Suppose, for example, that we use historical data to compute estimates to be used in an optimization. These means, variances, and covariances are sample quantities that are subject to random variation. In the chapter on sampling, for instance, we discussed how the sample mean has a probability distribution, called its sampling distribution. The sample mean is only a point estimate of the underlying or population mean.[17] The optimization process attempts to maximally exploit differences between assets. When these differences are statistically (and economically) insignificant (e.g., representing random variation), the

---

[17] The underlying means of asset returns are particularly difficult to estimate accurately. See Luenberger (1998, Chapter 8) for an introduction to this problem, and Black (1993).

resulting minimum-variance frontiers are misleading and not practically useful. Mean–variance optimization then overfits the data: It does too much with differences that are actually not meaningful. In an optimization with no limitation on short sales, assets can appear with very large negative weights, reflecting this overfitting. A negative weight for an asset means that the asset is sold short. Portfolios with very large short position are of little practical interest.[18] Because of sensitivity to small changes in inputs, mean–variance optimizations may suggest too frequent rebalancing of the portfolio, which is costly. Responses to instability include the following:

- Adding constraints against short sales (which is sometimes an institutional investment policy constraint as well). In model 11-3, we would add a no-short-sales constraint specifying that all asset weights must be positive: $w_j \geq 0, j = 1, 2, 3, \ldots, n$.[19]
- Improving the statistical quality of inputs to optimization.
- Using a statistical concept of the efficient frontier, reflecting the fact that the inputs to the optimization are random variables rather than constants.[20]

We stated above that mean–variance optimizations can recommend too-frequent portfolio rebalancing. Similarly, we find that the minimum-variance frontier is generally not stable when calculated using historical data for different time periods. One possible explanation is that the different frontiers reflect shifts in the parameters of the distribution of asset returns between sample time periods. Time instability of the minimum-variance frontier can also result from random variation in means, variances, and covariances, when the underlying parameters are actually unchanged. Small differences in sample periods used for mean–variance optimization may have a big effect even if the distribution of asset returns is stationary. Example 11-4 illustrates time instability with the data used for optimization.

EXAMPLE 11-4.   Time Instability of the Minimum-Variance Frontier.

In Example 11-3, we calculated a minimum-variance frontier for four asset classes for the period 1970 to 1999. What variation would we find among minimum-variance frontiers for subperiods of 1970 to 1999? To find out, we take the data for decades within the entire period, calculate the sample statistics, and then trace out the minimum-variance frontier for each decade. Table 11-8 shows the sample statistics of the monthly asset returns to these four asset classes for the 1970s, 1980s, 1990s, and the combined sample period.

As we might expect, variation occurs within subperiods in the sample means, variances, and covariances, for all asset classes. Initially, the correlations offer the impression of relative stability over time. For example, the correlation of the S&P 500 with the MSCI ex United States was 0.544, 0.512, and 0.551 for the 1970s, 1980s, and 1990s, respectively. In contrast to ranking by mean returns, the ranking of asset classes by standard deviation was the same in each decade, with U.S. small-cap

---

[18] In practice, few investors that engage in short sales would take a large short position as a result of an analysis restricted to means, variances, and correlations. Unlimited losses are possible in a short position.

[19] In practice, other, ad hoc constraints on the size of positions are sometimes used as well.

[20] For example, Michaud (1998) has suggested defining the efficient frontier as a *region* that defines, at a given confidence level, a set of statistically equivalent portfolios. He calls such portfolios "resampled efficient." A portfolio falling in the region is consistent with resampled efficiency and does not need to be rebalanced.

TABLE 11-8   Average Returns, Standard Deviations,
              and Correlation Matrixes

	S&P 500	U.S. Small-Cap Stocks	MSCI ex United States	U.S. Long-Term Government Bonds
Returns (%)				
1970s	7.0	14.4	11.8	5.0
1980s	17.6	16.7	21.1	12.9
1990s	17.2	14.3	7.1	9.2
Overall period	13.9	15.2	13.4	9.3
Standard Dev. (%)				
1970s	15.93	26.56	16.68	8.24
1980s	16.41	19.17	17.32	14.19
1990s	13.42	17.11	16.80	8.27
Overall period	15.35	21.32	16.97	10.64
Correlation matrixes				
1970s				
S&P 500	1			
U.S. small-cap	0.787	1		
MSCI ex U.S.	0.544	0.49	1	
U.S. L-T gov't	0.415	0.316	0.162	1
1980s				
S&P 500	1			
US small-cap	0.844	1		
MSCI ex U.S.	0.512	0.483	1	
U.S. L-T gov't	0.310	0.171	0.229	1
1990s				
S&P 500	1			
U.S. small-cap	0.695	1		
MSCI ex U.S.	0.551	0.399	1	
U.S. L-T gov't	0.385	0.075	0.162	1
Overall Period				
S&P 500	1			
U.S. small-cap	0.772	1		
MSCI ex U.S.	0.530	0.454	1	
U.S. L-T gov't	0.351	0.187	0.206	1

stocks the riskiest asset class and bonds the least risky. We could use statistical inference to explore interperiod differences. With these initial impressions in mind, however, let us view the decades' minimum-variance frontiers.

Figure 11-7 shows the minimum-variance frontiers computed using the historical return statistics shown in Table 11-8 for the 1970s, 1980s, 1990s, and the entire sample period. As this figure shows, the minimum-variance frontiers can differ dramatically in different periods. For example, note that the minimum-variance frontiers based on data from the 1970s and the 1980s do not overlap at all.

FIGURE 11-7   Historical Minimum-Variance Frontier Comparison

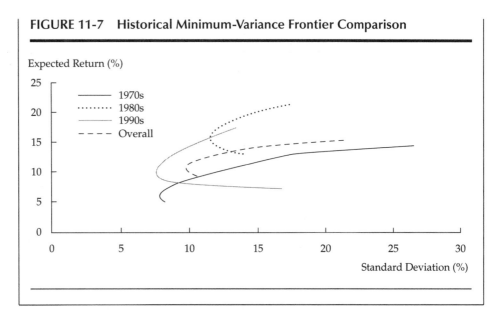

As mentioned, researchers have developed various methods to address portfolio managers' concerns about the issue of instability.

EXAMPLE 11-5.   How Yale University's Endowment Fund Uses Mean–Variance Analysis.

David Swensen, Yale University's chief investment officer (who also teaches portfolio management at Yale), wrote that "unconstrained mean–variance [optimization] usually provide[s] solutions unrecognizable as reasonable portfolios. ... Because the process involves material simplifying assumptions, adopting the unconstrained asset allocation point estimates produced by mean–variance optimization makes little sense."[21]

   Swensen's remarks highlight the concerns of practitioners about the usefulness of standard mean–variance optimization. Among the most important simplifying assumptions of mean–variance analysis is that the means, variances, and covariances are known. Because the optimization process tries to make much of small differences, and the true values of the means and other parameters are uncertain, this simplifying assumption has a large impact. As mentioned earlier, responses to instability include adding constraints on asset weights and modifying historical sample estimates of the inputs. Despite Swensen's criticism, Yale uses mean–variance analysis for allocating its portfolio; however, the Yale Investment Office adds constraints on weights and does not use raw historical inputs.

**2.4
DIVERSIFICATION
AND PORTFOLIO
SIZE**

Earlier, we illustrated the diversification benefits of adding a third asset to a two-asset portfolio. That discussion opened a question of practical interest that we further explore in this section: How many different stocks do we need to hold in order to have a well-diversified

---

[21] Swensen (2000).

portfolio? How does covariance or correlation interact with portfolio size in determining the portfolio's risk?

We address these questions using the example of an investor who holds an equally weighted portfolio. Suppose we purchase a portfolio of n stocks and put an equal fraction of the value of the portfolio into each of the stocks ($w_i = 1/n$, $i = 1, 2, \ldots, n$). The expected return on this portfolio is

$$E(R_p) = \sum_{i=1}^{n} w_i E(R_i)$$ (11-4)

The variance of return is

$$\sigma_p^2 = \sum_{i=1}^{n} \sum_{j=1}^{n} w_i w_j \text{Cov}(R_i, R_j)$$ (11-5)

Suppose we call the average variance of return across all stocks $\overline{\sigma}^2$ and the average covariance between all pairs of two stocks $\overline{\text{Cov}}$. It is possible to show[22] that Equation 11-5 simplifies to

$$\sigma_p^2 = \frac{1}{n}\overline{\sigma}^2 + \frac{n-1}{n}\overline{\text{Cov}}$$ (11-6)

Note that as the number of stocks, n, increases, the contribution of the variance of the individual stocks becomes very small because $\frac{1}{n}\overline{\sigma}^2$ has a limit of 0 as n becomes large. Note also that the contribution of the average covariance across stocks to the portfolio variance stays non-zero because $\frac{n-1}{n}\overline{\text{Cov}}$ has a limit of $\overline{\text{Cov}}$ as n becomes large. Thus, as the number of assets in the portfolio becomes large, portfolio variance approximately equals average covariance. In large portfolios, average covariance—capturing how assets move together—becomes more important than average individual risk or variance.

Besides this insight, Equation 11-6 allows us to gauge the reduction in portfolio variance from the completely undiversified position of holding only one stock. If the portfolio contained only one stock, then of course the variance of the portfolio would be the variance of the individual stock. This is the position of maximum variance.[23] If the portfolio contained a very large number of stocks, the variance of the portfolio would be close to the average covariance of any two stocks. This is the position of minimum variance. How large is the difference between these two levels of variance? How much of the maximum benefit can we obtain with a relatively small number of stocks?

The answers depend on the sizes of the average variance and the average covariance. Correlation is easier to interpret than covariance, so we will work with correlation rather than covariance. Suppose, for simplicity, that the correlation between the returns for any two stocks is the same and all stocks have the same standard deviation, σ. Assume that the common correlation is 0.25. This number has no special significance but is in a realistic range for the average correlation of U.S. equities for some time periods. The covariance of

---

[22] See Bodie, Kane, and Marcus (1999).

[23] For realistic values of correlation, average covariance is less than average variance.

two random variables is the correlation of those variables multiplied by the standard deviations of the two variables, so $\overline{\text{Cov}} = 0.25\sigma^2$.

Look back at Equation 11-6 and replace $\overline{\text{Cov}}$ with $0.25\sigma^2$:

$$\sigma_p^2 = \frac{1}{n}\sigma^2 + \frac{n-1}{n}(0.25\sigma^2)$$
$$= \frac{\sigma^2}{n} \times [1 + (n-1) \times 0.25]$$

or

$$\sigma_p^2 = \frac{\sigma^2}{n}[0.75 + 0.25 \times n]$$

and in general, under our assumptions

$$\sigma_p^2 = \sigma^2\left[\frac{1-\rho}{n} + \rho\right] \tag{11-7}$$

In this example, $\sigma_p^2 = \sigma^2\left[\frac{0.75}{n} + 0.25\right]$. If the portfolio contains one stock, the portfolio variance is σ^2. As n increases, portfolio variance drops rapidly. For example, if the portfolio contains 15 stocks, the portfolio variance is $0.3\sigma^2$, or only 30 percent of the variance of a portfolio with one stock. With 30 stocks, the portfolio variance is 27.5 percent of the variance of a single-stock portfolio. The smallest possible portfolio variance in this case is 25 percent of the variance of a single stock, because $\sigma_p^2 = 0.25\sigma^2$ when n is extremely large. With only 30 stocks, for example, the portfolio variance is only 110 percent of its minimum possible value and the variance is 72.5 percent smaller than the variance of a portfolio that contains only one stock.

For a reasonable assumed value of correlation, the previous example shows that a portfolio composed of many stocks has far less total risk than a portfolio composed of only one stock. In this example, we can diversify away 75 percent of the risk of an individual stock by holding many stocks. The practical implication for investors is that we may be able to obtain a large part of the risk reduction benefits of diversification with a surprisingly small number of securities.

What if the correlation among stocks is higher than 0.25? Suppose an investor wanted to be sure that his portfolio variance was 110 percent of the minimum possible portfolio variance of a diversified portfolio. How many stocks would the investor need? If the average correlation among stocks were 0.5, the investor would need only 10 stocks for the portfolio to have 110 percent of the minimum possible portfolio variance. With a higher correlation, fewer stocks are needed to obtain the same percentage of minimum possible portfolio variance. What if the correlation is lower than 0.25? If the correlation among stocks were 0.1, the investor would need 90 stocks in the portfolio to obtain 110 percent of the minimum possible portfolio variance.

EXAMPLE 11-6. How Many Stocks Are Needed Now for Diversification?

One common belief among investors is that almost all of the benefits of diversification can be achieved with a portfolio of only 30 stocks. In fact, Fisher and Lorie

(1970) showed that 95 percent of the benefits of diversification among NYSE-traded stocks from 1926 to 1965 were achieved with a portfolio of 32 stocks.

As we showed above, however, the number of stocks needed to achieve a particular diversification gain depends on the correlation among stock returns: The lower the correlation, the more stocks are needed. Campbell, Lettau, Malkiel, and Xu (2001) showed that although overall market volatility has not increased since 1963, individual stock returns have been more volatile recently (1986–97) and individual stock returns have been less correlated with each other. Consequently, more stocks are needed in a portfolio than in the period studied by Fisher and Lorie to achieve the same percentage of the risk-reducing benefits of diversification. They conclude that in 1963 through 1985 "a portfolio of 20 stocks reduced annualized excess standard deviation to about five percent, but in the 1986–1997 subsample, this level of excess standard deviation required almost 50 stocks."[24]

EXAMPLE 11-7.   Diversification at Berkshire Hathaway.

Berkshire Hathaway's highly successful CEO, Warren Buffett, is one of the harshest critics of modern portfolio theory and diversification. Buffett has said, for example, that "[I]f you are a know-something investor, able to understand business economics and find 5 to 10 sensibly priced companies that possess important long-term competitive advantages, conventional diversification makes no sense for you. It is apt simply to hurt your results and increase your risk."[25]

Does Buffett avoid diversification altogether? Certainly his investment record is phenomenal, but even Buffett engages in diversification to some extent. For example, consider the top three investment holdings of Berkshire Hathaway at the end of 1999.[26]

American Express Company	$ 8.4 billion (35%)
The Coca-Cola Company	$11.6 billion (49%)
The Gillette Company	<u>$ 3.9 billion</u> (16%)
Total	$23.9 billion

How much diversification do these three stocks provide? How much lower is the standard deviation of this portfolio than a portfolio consisting only of Gillette stock? To find answers to these questions, assume that the historical mean returns, return standard deviations, and return correlations of these stocks are the best estimates of the future expected returns, return standard deviations, and return correlations. Table 11-9 shows these historical statistics, based on monthly return data from 1990 through 2000.

---

[24] Campbell et al. defined "excess standard deviation" as the standard deviation of a randomly selected portfolio of a given size minus the standard deviation of an equally weighted market index.

[25] Buffett (1993).

[26] We consider only the top three holdings in order to simplify the computations in this example. Also for simplicity, we rounded the percentage allocations in the portfolio. The weights shown here are the relative weights among these three stocks, not their actual weights in the Berkshire Hathaway portfolio.

TABLE 11-9   Historical Returns, Variances, and Correlation:
Berkshire Hathaway's Largest Equity Holdings, 1999

	American Express	Coca-Cola	Gillette
Annual return	23.6%	23.8%	23.4%
Standard deviation	28.6%	25.7%	27.1%
Return correlations:	0.375	American Express and Coca-Cola	
	0.271	American Express and Gillette	
	0.486	Coca-Cola and Gillette	

Based on monthly return data, January 1990 to December 2000

Table 11-9 shows that for Gillette's stock, the mean annual return was 23.4 percent and the annualized standard deviation of the return was 27.1 percent. In contrast, a portfolio consisting of 35 percent American Express stock, 49 percent Coca-Cola stock, and 16 percent Gillette stock would have had an expected return of $0.35(0.236) + 0.49(0.238) + 0.16(0.234) = 0.236$, or 23.6 percent.

The expected standard deviation of the portfolio, based on these weights and the statistics in Table 11-9, would have been

$$\sigma_p = [w_1^2\sigma_1^2 + w_2^2\sigma_2^2 + w_3^2\sigma_3^2 + 2w_1w_2\rho_{1,2}\sigma_1\sigma_2 + 2w_1w_3\rho_{1,3}\sigma_1\sigma_3$$
$$+ 2w_2w_3\rho_{2,3}\sigma_2\sigma_3]^{1/2}$$

or

$$\sigma_p = [(0.35^2)(0.286^2) + (0.49^2)(0.257^2) + (0.16^2)(0.271^2)$$
$$+ 2(0.35)(0.49)(0.375)(0.286)(0.257)$$
$$+ 2(0.35)(0.16)(0.271)(0.286)(0.271)$$
$$+ 2(0.49)(0.16)(0.486)(0.257)(0.271)]^{1/2}$$
$$= 0.212 \text{ or } 21.2 \text{ percent}$$

The standard deviation of a portfolio with these three stocks is only $21.2/27.1 = 78.2$ percent of the standard deviation of a portfolio composed exclusively of Gillette stock. Therefore, Berkshire-Hathaway actually achieved substantial diversification, even considering only its top three holdings.

2.5   RISK-FREE ASSETS AND THE TRADE-OFF BETWEEN RISK AND RETURN

So far, we have considered only portfolios of risky securities, implicitly assuming that investors cannot also invest in a risk-free asset. But investors can hold their own government securities such as Treasury bills, which are virtually risk-free. What is the trade-off between risk and return when we can invest in a risk-free asset?

If an asset is risk-free, the standard deviation of its return is 0. The return is certain, and there is no risk of default. Suppose, for example, that the return to the risk-free asset is 4 percent a year. If we take the Treasury bill as risk-free, then 4 percent is the actual return, known in advance; it is not an expected return.[27] Because the standard deviation of the

---

[27] We assume here that the maturity of the T-bills is the same as the investment horizon so that there is no interest-rate risk.

risk-free asset return is 0, the covariance between the return of the risk-free asset and return of any other asset must also be 0. These observations help us understand how adding a risk-free asset to a portfolio can affect the mean–variance trade-off among assets.

Calculating and graphing the frontier reveals two important results that are true if investors can choose among risky assets and a risk-free asset. First, each investor has a unique optimal portfolio of risky assets, given the risk-free rate and the investor's beliefs about the expected returns and the variances and covariances of returns to the risky assets. We call that portfolio the tangent portfolio, for reasons we will discuss later.[28] The composition of this tangent portfolio does not depend on the investor's tolerance for risk. Second, for each investor, the efficient frontier combining risky assets and the risk-free asset is a straight line, called the **capital allocation line.** Recall that with risky assets only, the minimum-variance frontier typically looks like a bullet-shaped curve and the efficient frontier is the part of the curve above the global minimum-variance portfolio. The introduction of a risk-free asset dramatically changes the efficient frontier.

For each investor, the points on the capital allocation line represent the risk and return to various portfolios that combine the investor's risk-free asset with the investor's tangent portfolio. The investor's risk tolerance determines which point on the line he or she will choose. With these ideas in mind, we now expand on our original two-asset example, in which a portfolio manager must choose between investing in large-cap stocks and investing in government bonds.

EXAMPLE 11-8.   Trade-Off between Risk and Return with a Risk-Free Asset.

Assume that the portfolio manager wants to determine the effect of including risk-free Treasury bills in the portfolio. Table 11-10 shows hypothetical expected returns and correlations for the three asset classes.

TABLE 11-10   Expected Returns, Variances, and Correlations: Three-Asset Case with Risk-Free Asset

	Large-cap Stock	Government Bonds	T-Bills
Expected return (%)	15	5	4
Variance	225	100	0
Standard deviation (%)	15	10	0
Correlations:	0.5	Large-cap Stocks and Government Bonds	
	0	Large-cap Stocks and T-Bills	
	0	Government Bonds and T-Bills	

Suppose we decide to put the entire portfolio in risk-free Treasury bills with a return of 4 percent. In this case, then, the expected return to the portfolio is 4 percent and the expected variance in the portfolio is 0. Thus, if we limit the two assets available for investment to Treasury bills and the large-cap stocks, one endpoint on the efficient frontier (here, also a portfolio possibilities curve) is an expected return of 4 percent and a standard deviation of 0. Now assume that we put the entire portfolio

---

[28] Many tests assume that every investor has the same optimal portfolio. This assumption is not true if investors have differing expectations about asset returns, return standard deviations, and return correlations.

into large-cap stocks. The expected return is now 15 percent and the standard deviation of the portfolio is 15 percent; this return is the other endpoint on the efficient frontier for this two-asset case. What will happen if we divide the portfolio between Treasury bills and large-cap stocks? If the proportion of assets in large-cap stocks is w_1 and the proportion of assets in Treasury bills is $(1 - w_1)$, then the expected portfolio return is

$$E(R_p) = w_1(0.15) + (1 - w_1)(0.04)$$

and the portfolio standard deviation is

$$\sigma_p = [w_1(0.15)^2 + (1 - w_1)^2(0)^2]^{1/2} = w_1(0.15)$$

Note that both the expected return and the standard deviation of return are linearly related to w_1, the percentage of the portfolio in large-cap stocks. Figure 11-8 illustrates the trade-off between risk and return for Treasury bills and large-cap stocks in this example.

FIGURE 11-8   Portfolios of the Risk-Free Asset and Large-Cap Stocks

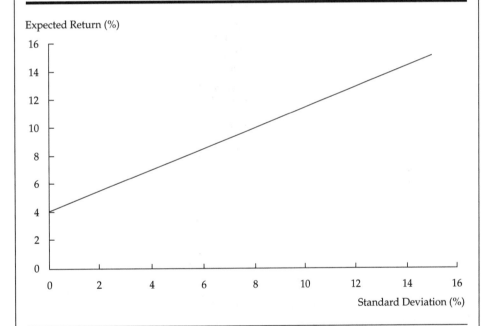

Now, let us consider the trade-off between risk and return for a portfolio containing Treasury bills and U.S. government bonds. Suppose we decide to put the entire portfolio in risk-free Treasury bills. In this case, the expected return to the portfolio is 4 percent and the expected variance in the portfolio is 0. Thus, one endpoint on the efficient frontier for the two-asset case of Treasury bills and U.S. government bonds is an expected return of 4 percent and a standard deviation of 0. (Again, this efficient frontier is a portfolio opportunities curve.) Now assume that we put the entire portfolio into U.S. government bonds. The expected return is now 5 percent and the standard deviation of the portfolio is 10 percent. What will happen if we divide the portfolio between Treasury bills and government bonds? If the proportion of assets in government bonds is w_1 and the proportion of assets in Treasury bills is $(1 - w_1)$, then the expected portfolio return is

$$E(R_p) = w_1(0.05) + (1 - w_1)(0.04)$$

and the portfolio standard deviation is

$$\sigma_p = [w_1(0.05)^2 + (1 - w_1)^2(0)^2]^{1/2} = w_1(0.05)$$

Note that both the expected return and the standard deviation of return are linearly related to w_1, the percentage of the portfolio in the government bonds. Figure 11-9 shows the trade-off between risk and return for Treasury bills and government bonds in this example.

FIGURE 11-9   Portfolios of the Risk-Free Asset and Government Bonds

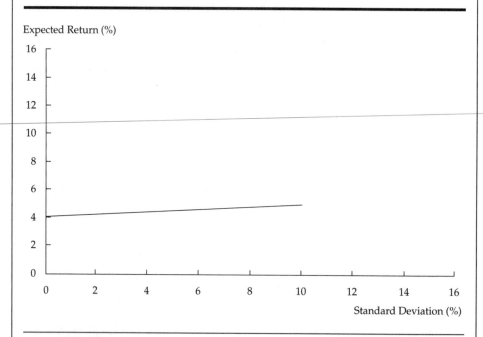

We have just seen the trade-off between risk and return for two different portfolios: one with Treasury bills and large-cap stocks, the other with Treasury bills and government bonds. How do these trade-offs between risk and return compare with the original risk–return trade-off between government bonds and large-cap stocks? Figure 11-10 illustrates the trade-off between risk and return for all three portfolios.

Notice that the frontier for Treasury bills and government bonds touches the minimum-variance frontier for bonds and stocks at the point of lowest return on the bond–stock minimum-variance frontier (the point where 100 percent of the portfolio is invested in bonds). Some points on the bill–bond frontier have lower risk and return than points on the bond–stock frontier; however, we can find no point on the bill–bond frontier where, for a given level of risk, the expected return is higher on the bill–bond frontier than on the bond–stock frontier. In fact, if we compute the efficient frontier for all three assets (bills, bonds, and stocks), the frontier is a straight line that shows the expected return and variance for portfolios formed only of

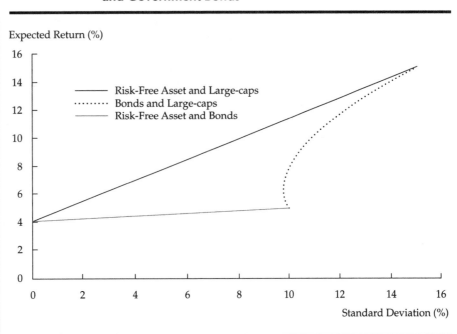

FIGURE 11-10   Portfolios of the Risk-Free Asset, Large-Cap Stocks and Government Bonds

Treasury bills and stocks.[29] (More typically, this line represents combinations of the risk-free asset and a broad combination of risky assets.) This line, the capital allocation line (CAL), is labeled Risk-Free Asset and Large-caps in Figure 11-10.

The capital allocation line shows the maximum expected return for a given level of risk for all portfolios containing both the risk-free asset and risky assets, given the portfolio manager's assumptions about expected returns, variances, and covariances. The CAL is the line from the risk-free rate of return that is tangent to the efficient frontier of risky assets; of all lines we could extend from the risk-free rate to the minimum-variance frontier, the CAL has maximum slope. Slope as rise (expected return) over run (standard deviation) measures the expected return to risk trade-off. The CAL is the line of maximum slope that touches the minimum-variance frontier; as a consequence, the capital allocation line offers the best risk–return trade-off achievable, given the manager's expectations.

The previous example showed three important general principles concerning the risk–return trade-off in a portfolio containing a risk-free asset:

- If a portfolio contains a risk-free asset, then the efficient frontier for all assets has a linear portion. That efficient frontier is called the capital allocation line.
- The CAL has a y-intercept equal to the risk-free rate.
- The CAL is tangent to the efficient frontier of all risky assets.

---

[29] In general, however, the point where the line from the risk-free asset touches the minimum-variance frontier of risky assets would not represent a portfolio composed of the highest expected return asset only.

EXAMPLE 11-9.   The CAL with Multiple Assets.

In Example 11-8, the CAL was tangent to the efficient frontier for all risky assets. We now illustrate how the efficient frontier changes depending on the **opportunity set** (the set of assets available for investment) and whether the investor wants to borrow to leverage his investments. We can illustrate this point by reconsidering our earlier example (Example 11-3) of optimal portfolio choice among the S&P 500, U.S. small-cap stocks, non-U.S. stocks (the MSCI ex United States), and U.S. government bonds, adding risk-free Treasury bills as an asset class.

We assume that the expected return to risk-free Treasury bills is now 5 percent. Because Treasury bills are risk-free, the standard deviation of bill returns is 0; the covariance between returns to bills and returns to the other assets is also 0. We demonstrate the following principles:

- The point of maximum expected return is not the point of tangency between the CAL and the efficient frontier for all assets (excluding the risk-free asset).

- The point of tangency between the CAL and the efficient frontier for risky assets represents a portfolio containing risky assets and none of the risk-free asset.

- If we rule out borrowing at the risk-free rate, then the efficient frontier for all the assets (including the risk-free asset) is not completely linear.

Figure 11-11 shows the mean–variance frontier for all five assets (the original four and the risk-free asset), assuming risk-free borrowing is not possible.

FIGURE 11-11   Efficient Frontier: The Effect of Adding a Risk-Free Asset to a Risky Portfolio

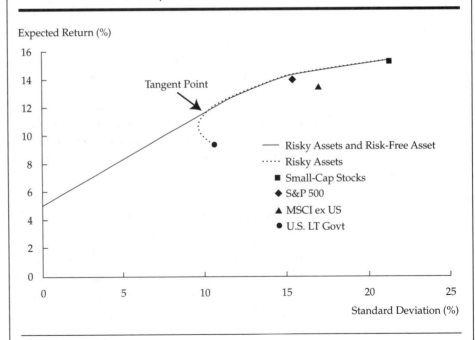

As the figure shows, the efficient frontier is linear from the y-intercept (the combination of risk and return for placing the entire portfolio in the risk-free asset) to the tangent point. If the investor wants additional return (and risk) beyond the tangent point without borrowing, however, the investor's efficient frontier is the portion of the efficient frontier for the four risky assets that lies to the right of the tangent point. The investor's efficient frontier has a linear and a curved portion.[30]

2.6 THE CAPITAL ALLOCATION LINE EQUATION

In the previous section, we discussed the graph of the capital allocation line, and how the efficient frontier can change depending on the set of assets available for investment as well as the portfolio manager's expectations. We now provide the equation of this line.

Suppose that an investor, given expectations about means, variances, and covariances for risky assets, plots the efficient frontier of risky assets. There is a risk-free asset. If w_T is the proportion of the portfolio the investor places in the tangent portfolio, then the expected return for the entire portfolio is

$$E(R_p) = (1 - w_T)R_F + w_T E(R_T)$$

and the standard deviation of the portfolio is

$$
\begin{aligned}
\sigma_p &= [(1 - w_T)^2 \sigma_{R_F} + w_T^2 \sigma_{R_T}^2 + 2\sigma_{R_F} \sigma_{R_T} \rho_{R_F,R_T}]^{1/2} \\
&= [(1 - w_T)^2 0 + w_T^2 \sigma_{R_T}^2 + 2 \times 0 \times \sigma_{R_T} \times 0]^{1/2} \\
&= (w_T^2 \sigma_{R_T}^2)^{1/2} \\
&= w_T \sigma_{R_T}
\end{aligned}
$$

where, for simplicity, we use R and σ_R to represent expected returns and standard deviation.

An investor can choose to invest any fraction of his assets in the risk-free asset or in the tangent portfolio; therefore, he can choose many combinations of risk and return. If he puts the entire portfolio in the risk-free asset, then

$$
\begin{aligned}
w_T &= 0 \\
E(R_p) &= (1 - 0)R_F + 0R_T = R_F, \text{ and} \\
\sigma_p &= 0\sigma_{R_T} \\
&= 0
\end{aligned}
$$

If he puts his entire portfolio in the tangent portfolio, $w_T = 1$

$$
\begin{aligned}
E(R_p) &= (1 - 1)R_F + 1E(R_T) = E(R_T), \text{ and} \\
\sigma_p &= 1 \times \sigma_{R_T} = \sigma_{R_T}
\end{aligned}
$$

In general, if he puts w_T percent of his portfolio in the tangent portfolio, his portfolio standard deviation will be $\sigma_p = w_T \times \sigma_{R_T}$.

To see how the portfolio weights, expected return, and risk are related, we use the relationship $w_T = \sigma_p/\sigma_{R_T}$. If we substitute this value of w_T back into the expression for expected return, $E(R_p) = (1 - w_T)R_F + w_T E(R_T)$, we get

$$E(R_p) = \left(1 - \frac{\sigma_p}{\sigma_{R_T}}\right)R_F + \frac{\sigma_p}{\sigma_{R_T}}E(R_T) \text{ or} \tag{11-8}$$

---

[30] If borrowing at the risk-free rate were possible (equivalent to buying on margin at the risk-free rate), the efficient frontier would be the straight line from the risk-free rate, now continued past the point of tangency.

$$E(R_p) = R_F + \frac{E(R_T) - R_F}{\sigma_{R_T}}\sigma_p \tag{11-9}$$

This equation shows the best possible trade-off between expected risk and return, given this investor's expectations. The term $\dfrac{E(R_T) - R_F}{\sigma_{R_T}}$ is the return that the investor demands to take on an extra unit of risk. Example 11-10 illustrates how we calculate the investor's price of risk and other aspects of his investment using the capital allocation line.

EXAMPLE 11-10.   CAL Calculations (1).

Suppose that the risk-free rate, R_F, is 5 percent, the expected return to the investor's tangent portfolio, R_T, is 15 percent, and the standard deviation of the tangent portfolio is 25 percent.

- What is the return that the investor demands to take on an extra unit of risk? In this case, $\dfrac{E(R_T) - R_F}{\sigma_{R_T}} = \dfrac{0.15 - 0.05}{0.25} = 0.4$. The investor demands an additional 40 basis points of expected return of the portfolio for every 1 percent increase in the standard deviation of portfolio returns.

- Suppose the investor is willing to have a portfolio standard deviation of 10 percent. What percentage of the assets is in the tangent portfolio and what is the expected return? Because $\sigma_p = w_T\sigma_{R_T}$, $w_T = 0.1/0.25 = 0.4$, or 40 percent. That is, 40 percent of the assets are in the tangent portfolio and 60 percent are in the risk-free asset. The expected return for the portfolio is $R_p = R_F + \dfrac{E(R_T) - R_F}{\sigma_{R_T}}\sigma_p = 0.05 + (0.4)(0.1) = 0.09$, or 9 percent.

- Suppose the investor wants to put 40 percent of the portfolio in the risk-free asset. What is the portfolio expected return? What is the standard deviation? In this case, $w_T = 1 - 0.4 = 0.6$. Therefore, the expected portfolio return is $R_p = (1 - w_T)R_F + w_TR_T = (1 - 0.6)(0.05) + (0.6)(0.15) = 0.11$ or 11 percent. The portfolio standard deviation is $\sigma_p = w_T\sigma_{R_T} = (0.6)(0.25) = 0.15$ or 15 percent.

EXAMPLE 11-11.   CAL Calculations (2).

Suppose that the risk-free rate, R_F, is 5 percent. The expected return on the tangent portfolio, $E(R_T)$, is 15 percent, and the standard deviation of the tangent portfolio is 25 percent (as perceived by the investor). Suppose also that the investor can both borrow and lend at the risk-free rate.

- What expected return should the investor demand for a portfolio with a standard deviation of 35 percent? As in Example 11-10, we know that the relation between risk and expected return for this portfolio is $E(R_p) = R_F + \dfrac{E(R_T) - R_F}{\sigma_{R_T}}\sigma_p = 0.05 + \dfrac{0.15 - 0.05}{0.25}\sigma_p = 0.05 + 0.4\sigma_p$. If the standard deviation for the portfolio's returns is 35 percent, then the investor can expect a return of $E(R_p) = 0.05 + 0.4\sigma_p = 0.05 + 0.4(0.35) = 0.19$, or 19 percent.

- What combination of the tangent portfolio and the risk-free asset does the investor need to hold in order to have a portfolio with this combination of risk and expected return? With an expected return of 19 percent, the asset allocation must be as follows:

$E(R_p) = (1 - w_T)R_F + w_T R_T$ or
$0.19 = (1 - w_T)(0.05) + w_T(0.15)$; $0.19 = 0.05 + 0.10w_T$; $w_T = 1.4$

How can the weight on the tangent portfolio be 140 percent? This weighting means that the investor has borrowed 40 percent of initial wealth at the risk-free rate. Therefore, the expected return is $(-0.4)(0.05) + (1.4)(0.15) = 0.19$ or 19 percent.

- If the investor has $10 million to invest, how much must she borrow at the risk-free rate? The investor would borrow $4 million dollars at the risk-free rate to increase the holdings of the tangent-asset portfolio to $14 million dollars. Therefore, the net value of the portfolio would be $14 million − $4 million = $10 million.

In this section, we have not assumed that investors have identical views about risky assets' mean returns, variances of returns, and correlations. Thus, each investor may perceive a different efficient frontier of risky assets and have a different tangent portfolio, the optimal portfolio of risky assets for each investor (which the investor may combine with risk-free borrowing or lending). In the next section, we review an influential model of capital market prices that attempts to describe expected returns that assets should offer, given a set of assumptions that includes identical views about risky assets.

2.7 THE CAPITAL ASSET PRICING MODEL

The capital asset pricing model (CAPM) has played a pivotal role in the development of quantitative investment management since its introduction in the early 1960s. In this section, we review some of its key aspects.

The CAPM makes the following assumptions:[31]

- Investors need only know the expected returns, the variances, and the covariances of returns to determine which portfolios are optimal for them. (This is an assumption of all of mean–variance theory.)

- Investors have identical views about risky assets' mean returns, variances of returns, and correlations.

- Investors can buy and sell assets in any quantity without affecting price, and all assets are marketable (can be traded).

- Investors can borrow and lend at the risk-free rate without limit, and can sell short any asset in any quantity.

- Investors pay no taxes on returns and pay no transaction costs on trades.

---

[31] For a complete list of assumptions, see Elton and Gruber (1995).

As a result of these assumptions, these conclusions follow:

- All investors face the same efficient frontier of risky assets. As a result, all investors combine the identical tangent portfolio with the risk-free asset to obtain their optimal portfolio.
- This tangent portfolio is the market portfolio of all risky assets (no risky asset is excluded). Every asset is represented in proportion to its capitalization, relative to the total market capitalization. So all investors combine two funds: the risk-free asset and the most diversified portfolio possible, the market portfolio.
- The CAL for all investors is the same. The tangency portfolio is the same portfolio, the market portfolio, for all investors. We define a new term, the capital market line (CML). The CML is the capital allocation line with the market portfolio as the tangency portfolio. The equation of the CML is

$$E(R_p) = R_F + \frac{E(R_M) - R_F}{\sigma_M}\sigma_p$$

where

$E(R_p)$ = the expected return of portfolio p lying on the capital market line
R_F = the risk-free rate
R_M = the market portfolio rate of return
σ_M = the standard deviation of return on the market portfolio
σ_p = the standard deviation of return on portfolio p

Note that the CML describes the expected return of only efficient portfolios. The slope of the CML, $[E(R_M) - R_F]/\sigma_M$, is called the market price of risk because it indicates the market risk premium for each unit of market risk.

The following equation describes the expected returns on all assets and portfolios, whether efficient or not:

$$E(R_i) = R_F + \beta_i[E(R_M) - R_F] \tag{11-10}$$

where

$E(R_i)$ = the expected return on asset i
R_F = the risk-free rate of return
$E(R_M)$ = the expected return on the market portfolio
β_i = $\text{Cov}(R_i, R_M)/\text{Var}(R_M)$

Equation 11-10 itself is referred to as the capital asset pricing model, and its graph is called the **security market line** (SML). The CAPM is an equation describing the expected return on any asset (or portfolio) as a linear function of its **beta,** β_i, which is a measure of the asset's sensitivity to movements in the market. The CAPM says that expected return has two components: first, the risk-free rate, R_F, and second, an extra return equal to $\beta_i[E(R_M) - R_F]$. The term $[E(R_M) - R_F]$ is the excess expected return on the market over the risk-free rate. This is the **market risk premium;** if we are 100 percent invested in the market, this is the extra return we expect to obtain, on average, compared with holding only the risk-free asset.

The market risk premium is multiplied by the asset's sensitivity to market movements, its beta. A beta of 1 represents average market sensitivity, and we expect an asset with that beta to earn the market risk premium exactly.[32] A beta greater than 1 indicates greater than average market risk and earns, according to the CAPM, a higher expected reward. Conversely, a beta less than 1 indicates less than average market risk and earns, according to the CAPM, a smaller expected reward. Rewards (expected returns) are related *only* to market risk, represented by beta. Sensitivity to the market return is the only source of difference in expected returns across assets.[33]

Like all theory-based models, the CAPM comes from a set of assumptions. The CAPM describes a financial market equilibrium in the sense that, if the model is correct and any asset's expected return differs from its expected return as given by the CAPM, market forces will come into play to restore the relationships specified by the model. For example, a stock that offers a higher expected return than justified by its beta will be bid up in price by investors expecting that any non-market risk the asset might carry will be offset by other assets in their extremely broad-based portfolio, lowering the stock's expected return.

Because it is all-inclusive, the market portfolio defined in CAPM is unobservable. In practice, we must use some broad index to represent it. Because the CAPM has been used primarily to value equities, a broad value-weighted stock index or market proxy is frequently used. The straight-line relationship between expected return and beta results from the efficiency of the market portfolio. As a result, the CAPM theory is equivalent to saying that an unobservable portfolio is efficient, but not that any particular proxy for the market is efficient.[34] Of more interest to practitioners than the strict truth of CAPM as a theory is whether beta computed using available market proxies is useful for evaluating the expected mean returns to various investment strategies. Here the evidence now favors the existence of multiple sources of systematic risk affecting the mean returns to investment strategies.

3 PRACTICAL ISSUES IN MEAN–VARIANCE ANALYSIS

Can we really use mean–variance analysis to estimate the mean–variance frontier for a large number of stocks? Unfortunately, even assuming that past variances and covariances are accurate estimates of the future distribution of returns for all assets, we will find it quite difficult to use mean–variance analysis to choose an optimal portfolio from a large number of stocks.

Our previous examples show that accurately predicting expected returns and the variances and correlations of those returns is essential for this task. Before we proceed, we need to ask two principal questions about how to predict expected returns and their variances and correlations. First, which methods are feasible? Second, which methods are most accurate?

---

[32] The market portfolio itself has a beta of 1, as $\beta_i = \mathrm{Cov}(R_m, R_m)/\mathrm{Var}(R_m) = \mathrm{Var}(R_m)/\mathrm{Var}(R_m) = 1$. Because the market portfolio includes all assets, the average asset must have a beta of 1. The same argument applies if we compute the betas of assets in an index, using the index to represent the market.

[33] One intuition for this idea is that the market is the perfectly diversified portfolio. We can cancel out any other risk by holding the market portfolio, and we can costlessly hold the market portfolio (by the no-transaction-costs assumption). Even risk with respect to personal assets such as human capital (representing earning power) can be diversified away (all assets are tradable). Investors should not require extra return for risks they can costlessly hedge.

[34] See Bodie, Kane, and Marcus (1999) for more on this topic. A proxy is something that represents something else.

In this section, we compare the feasibility and accuracy of several methods for computing the inputs needed for mean–variance optimization. These methods use the following:

- historical means, variances, and correlations,
- the market model, and
- an adjusted-beta market model.

3.1 ESTIMATES BASED ON HISTORICAL MEANS, VARIANCES, AND COVARIANCES

This method often requires estimating a very large number of parameters. As a result, it creates difficulties for using mean–variance analysis to choose among a large number of stocks, even assuming that past variances and covariances are accurate estimates for the future distribution of returns on all assets.

The number of parameters a portfolio manager needs to estimate for the minimum-variance frontier depends on the number of potential stocks in the portfolio. If a portfolio manager has n stocks in a portfolio and wants to use mean–variance analysis, she must estimate

- n parameters for the expected returns to the stocks,
- n parameters for the variances of the stock returns, and
- $n \times (n - 1)/2$ parameters for the covariances of all the stock returns with each other.

Together, the parameters total $n^2/2 + 3n/2$.

If the portfolio manager wanted to compute the minimum-variance frontier for a portfolio of 100 stocks, she would need to estimate $100^2/2 + 3(100)/2 = 5{,}150$ parameters. If she wanted to compute the minimum-variance frontier for 1,000 stocks, she would need to estimate 501,500 parameters. Not only is this task unappealing, it might be impossible. Consequently, portfolio managers who want to use the mean–variance model need an alternative method for computing the minimum-variance frontier for large numbers of assets.

3.2 THE MARKET MODEL

A simpler way to compute the variances and covariances of asset returns is to use the market model. The market model assumes that the returns to each asset are correlated with the returns to the market. For asset i, the return to the asset can be modeled as

$$R_i = \alpha_i + \beta_i R_m + \epsilon_i \tag{11-11}$$

where

R_i = the return to asset i
R_m = the return to the market portfolio
α_i = average return to asset i that is not related to the market return
β_i = the effect of the return on the market to asset i, or the sensitivity of asset i to the return on the market
ϵ_i = an error term

Consider first how to interpret β_i. If the market return increases by one percentage point, the market model predicts that the return to asset i will increase by β_i percentage points. (Recall that β_i is the slope in the market model.)

Now consider how to interpret α_i. If the market return is 0, the market model predicts that the return to asset i will be α_i, the intercept in the market model.

The market model makes several assumptions about Equation 11-11:

- The expected value of the error term is 0. That is, $E(\epsilon_i) = 0$.
- The market return (R_M) is uncorrelated with the error term, $\mathrm{Cov}(R_M, \epsilon_i) = 0$.
- The error terms, ϵ_i, are uncorrelated among different assets. For example, the error term for asset i is uncorrelated with the error term for asset j. Consequently, $E(\epsilon_i \epsilon_j) = 0$ for all i not equal to j.[35]

Note that some of these assumptions are very similar to those we made about the single-variable linear regression model in the chapter on correlation and regression. The market model, however, does not assume that the error term is normally distributed or that the variance of the error term is identical across assets.

Given these assumptions, the market model makes the following predictions about the expected returns of assets and the variances and covariances of asset returns:[36]

$$E(R_i) = \alpha_i + \beta_i E(R_M) \tag{11-12}$$

The expected return for asset i depends on the expected return to the market, $E(R_M)$, the effect of market returns on the return for asset i, β_i, and the portion of returns to asset i that are independent of market returns, α_i,

$$\mathrm{Var}(R_i) = \beta_i^2 \sigma_M^2 + \sigma_{\epsilon_i}^2 \tag{11-13}$$

The variance of the return to asset i depends on the variance of the return to the market, σ_M^2; the variance of the error for the return of asset i in the market model, $\sigma_{\epsilon_i}^2$; and the effect of market returns on the return for asset i, β_i.

$$\mathrm{Cov}(R_i, R_j) = \beta_i \beta_j \sigma_M^2 \tag{11-14}$$

The covariance of the return to asset i and the return to asset j depends on the variance of the return to the market, σ_M^2, and the effect of market returns on the return for asset i and asset j, β_i and β_j.

We can use the market model to greatly reduce the computational task of providing the inputs to a mean–variance optimization. For each of the n assets, we need to know α_i, β_i, $\sigma_{\epsilon_i}^2$, and σ_M^2 and and the expected return for the security. That is, we need to estimate $3n + 2$ parameters. Thus, if we use the market model, we need far fewer parameters to construct the minimum-variance frontier than we would if we estimated the historical means, variances, and covariances of asset returns. For example, if we estimated the minimum-variance frontier for 1,000 assets (say, 1,000 different stocks), the market model would use 3,002 parameters for computing the minimum-variance frontier, whereas the standard historical estimates would require 501,500 parameters, as discussed earlier.

---

[35] $\mathrm{Var}(\epsilon_i) = E[\epsilon_i - E(\epsilon_i)]^2 = E(\epsilon_i - 0)^2 = E(\epsilon_i)^2$. $\mathrm{Cov}(\epsilon_i, \epsilon_j) = E\{[\epsilon_i - E(\epsilon_i)][\epsilon_j - E(\epsilon_j)]\} = E[(\epsilon_i - 0)(\epsilon_j - 0)] = E(\epsilon_i \epsilon_j) = 0$. This assumption is not innocuous. If we have more than one factor that affects returns for assets, then this assumption will be incorrect and single-factor models will not produce accurate estimates of the covariance of asset returns. This error can be particularly severe when industry factors or macroeconomic factors affect asset returns (independent of the effect of the market return). We will discuss macroeconomic factor models later in this chapter.

[36] See Elton and Gruber (1995) for derivations of these results.

We do not know the parameters of the market model, so we must estimate them. But what method do we use? The most convenient way to estimate the model is to estimate a linear regression using time-series data on the returns to the market and the returns to each asset.

We can use the market model to estimate α_i and β_i (beta) by using a separate linear regression for each asset, using historical data on asset returns and market returns.[37] The regression output will give us an estimate, $\hat{\beta}_i$, of β_i; we call this estimate an unadjusted beta. Later in this section we will introduce an adjusted beta. We can use these estimates to compute the expected returns and the variances and covariances of those returns for mean–variance optimization.

EXAMPLE 11-12.   Computing Stock Correlations Using the Market Model.

We can compute this correlation from real data by estimating the market model for the returns to the two stocks. Suppose we regress the weekly change in the stock price on a constant and the weekly change in the S&P 500. The unadjusted beta for Cisco, β_{CSCO}, is 1.81, and the residual standard deviation from the market model, $\sigma_{\epsilon_{CSCO}}$, is 4.66. Therefore, $\sigma_{\epsilon_{CSCO}}^2 = 21.72$. The unadjusted beta for Exodus, β_{EXDS}, is 2.89, and the residual standard deviation from the market model, $\sigma_{\epsilon_{EXDS}}$, is 13.04. Therefore, $\sigma_{\epsilon_{EXDS}}^2 = 170.04$. If the value of σ_M^2 were given as 8.2, we could derive the correlation between the two asset returns.[38] Using the definition of correlation as covariance divided by the individual standard deviations, and using Equations 11-13 and 11-14, we have

$$\frac{\text{Cov}(R_{CSCO}, R_{EXDS})}{\text{Var}(R_{CSCO})^{1/2}\text{Var}(R_{EXDS})^{1/2}} =$$

$$\frac{\beta_{CSCO}\beta_{EXDS}(\sigma_M^2)}{[\beta_{CSCO}^2(\sigma_M^2) + \sigma_{\epsilon_{CSCO}}^2]^{1/2}[\beta_{EXDS}^2(\sigma_M^2) + \sigma_{\epsilon_{EXDS}}^2]^{1/2}} =$$

$$\frac{(1.81)\,(2.89)\,(8.2)}{[(1.81)^2(8.2) + 21.72]^{1/2}[(2.89)^2(8.2) + 170.04]^{1/2}} = 0.40$$

Thus, the market model predicts that the correlation between the two asset returns is 0.40. How does this result compare with the actual historical correlation between the two returns? The historical correlation is 0.5940.

One difficulty with using the market model is determining an appropriate return to use as the market return. Typically, analysts who use the market model to determine the risk of individual U.S. equities use returns on a market index, such as the S&P 500 or the

---

[37] One common practice is to use 60 months of monthly returns to estimate this model. The default setting on Bloomberg terminals uses two years of weekly data to estimate this model.

[38] Deriving the value of σ_M^2 is outside the scope of this text. Here we take it as given. The value of 8.2, however, is consistent with the other numeric values in this example. Note this is a value based on weekly data and corresponds to an annual standard deviation of about 20.6 percent.

Wilshire 5000 Index, as a proxy for returns on all U.S. equities. Using returns on an equity market index may create a reasonable market model for U.S. equities, but it may not be reasonable for modeling the risk of other asset classes.[39]

3.3 ADJUSTED BETA MARKET MODELS

Should we use historical betas from a market model for mean–variance optimization? Before we can answer this question, we need to restate our goal: We want to predict expected returns for a set of assets and the variances and covariances of those returns so we can estimate the minimum-variance frontier for those assets. We can use the historical betas from a market model to create an easy estimate of expected returns and their variances and covariances. This estimate, however, depends on the crucial assumption that the historical beta for a particular asset is the best predictor of the future beta for that asset. If beta changes over time, then this assumption is not true. Therefore, we may want to use some other measure instead of historical beta to estimate an asset's future beta. These other forecasts are known by the general term **adjusted beta.** Researchers have shown that adjusted beta is often a better forecast of future beta than is historical beta. As a consequence, practitioners often use adjusted beta.

Suppose, for example, we are in period t and we want to estimate the minimum-variance frontier for period $t + 1$ for a set of stocks. We need to use data available in period t to predict the expected stock returns and the variances and covariances of those returns in period $t + 1$. Note, however, that the historical estimate of beta in period t for a particular stock may not be the best estimate we can make in period t of beta in period $t + 1$ for that stock. And the minimum-variance frontier for period $t + 1$ must be based on the forecast of beta for period $t + 1$.

If beta for each stock were a random walk from one period to the next, then we could write the relation between the beta for stock i in period t and the beta for stock i in period $t + 1$ as

$$\beta_{i,t+1} = \beta_{i,t} + \epsilon_{i,t+1} \tag{11-15}$$

where $\epsilon_{i,t+1}$ is an error term. If beta follows a random walk, the best predictor of $\beta_{i,t+1}$ is $\beta_{i,t}$ because the error term has a mean value of 0. The historical beta is thus the best predictor of the future beta, and the historical beta need not be adjusted.

In reality, beta for each stock is not necessarily a random walk from one period to the next. Thus, the historical beta is not necessarily the best predictor of the future beta. For example, if beta can be represented as a first-order autoregression, then

$$\beta_{i,t+1} = \alpha_0 + \alpha_1 \beta_{i,t} + \epsilon_{i,t+1} \tag{11-16}$$

If we estimate this equation using time-series data on historical betas, the best predictor of $\beta_{i,t+1}$ is $\hat{\alpha}_0 + \hat{\alpha}_1 \beta_{i,t}$. In this case, the historical beta needs to be adjusted because the best prediction of beta in the next period is $\hat{\alpha}_0 + \hat{\alpha}_1 \beta_{i,t}$, not $\beta_{i,t}$.

Adjusted betas are better predictors of future betas than are historical betas because betas are, on average, mean reverting.[40] Therefore, we should use adjusted, rather than

---

[39] Using this model for estimating the risk of other asset classes may violate two assumptions of single-factor models discussed above: The market return, R_M, is independent of the error term, ϵ_i; and the error terms, ϵ_i, are independent across assets. If either of these assumptions is violated, the market model will not produce accurate predictions of expected returns or the variances and covariances of returns.

[40] See, for example, Klemkosky and Martin (1975).

historical, betas. One common method that practitioners use to adjust historical beta is to assume that $\alpha_0 = 0.333$ and $\alpha_1 = 0.667$. With this adjustment,

- if the historical beta is equal to 1.0, then the adjusted beta will be $0.333 + 0.667(1.0) = 1.0$;
- if the historical beta is equal to 1.5, then adjusted beta will be $0.333 + 0.667(1.5) = 1.333$;
- if the historical beta is equal to 0.5, then adjusted beta will be $0.333 + 0.667(0.5) = 0.667$.

Thus, the mean-reverting level of beta is 1.0. If the historical beta is above 1.0, then adjusted beta will be below historical beta; if historical beta is below 1.0, then adjusted beta will be above historical beta.[41]

4 MULTIFACTOR MODELS

The market model assumes that all explainable variation in asset returns is related to a single factor, the return to the market. Yet asset returns may be related to factors other than market return, such as interest-rate movements, inflation, or industry-specific returns. For many years, investment professionals have used multifactor models in portfolio management, risk analysis, and the evaluation of portfolio performance. Factor models have gained importance for the practical business of portfolio management because they explain asset returns better than the market model does.[42] For example, many stocks are affected not only by overall market risk but also by surprises in interest rates, inflation, and real economic growth. In this section, we explain the basic principles of factor models and discuss various types of these models. We also present arbitrage pricing theory, developed by Ross (1976), which relates the expected return of investments to their risk with respect to a set of factors.

A **factor** is a common or underlying element with which several variables are correlated. For example, the market factor is an underlying element with which individual company returns are correlated. Not all factors are useful for the purpose of explaining returns, however. We search for **systematic factors,** which affect the average return of a large number of different assets. These factors represent **priced risk,** for which investors require a return. Systematic factors should thus help explain returns.

Several types of multifactor models have been researched. We can categorize multifactor models into three groups, according to the type of factor used:

- In **macroeconomic factor models,** the factors are surprises in macroeconomic variables that significantly explain equity returns. The factors can be understood as af-

---

[41] Although practitioners regularly use this method for computing adjusted beta, we are not aware of any published research that suggests that $\alpha_0 = 0.333$ and $\alpha_1 = 0.667$ are the best coefficient values to use in computing adjusted beta. Some researchers suggest an additional adjustment to historical betas called fundamental betas. Fundamental betas predict beta based on fundamental data for a company (price–earnings ratio, earnings growth, market capitalization, volatility, and so forth). Consulting firms such as BARRA sell estimates of fundamental betas.

[42] See, for example, Burmeister and McElroy (1988). These authors show that at the 1 percent significance level, the CAPM can be rejected in favor of a factor model with several factors.

fecting either the expected future cash flows of companies or the interest rate used to discount these cash flows back to the present.

- In **fundamental factor models,** the factors are attributes of stocks or companies that are important in explaining cross-sectional differences in stock prices. Among the fundamental factors that have been used are book value to price, market capitalization, price–earnings ratio, and financial leverage.

- In **statistical factor models,** statistical methods are applied to a set of historical returns to determine portfolios that explain historical returns in one of two senses. In factor analysis models, the factors are the portfolios that best explain (reproduce) historical return covariances. In principal-components models, the factors are portfolios that best explain (reproduce) the historical return variances.

Our discussion will concentrate on macroeconomic factor models and fundamental factor models, because they are heavily used in portfolio management. Macroeconomic and fundamental factors are also much more readily understood and interpreted economically than statistical factors. We will focus in particular on a widely used structure of factor model that is also the basis of the arbitrage pricing theory. One principal difference between this factor model and the market model is how the independent variable is represented. The market model uses a return—the return on a market index—as the independent variable. The multifactor model we discuss uses unexpected components or surprises (for example, the surprise in inflation) as the independent variables, as we see in the next section.

4.1 THE STRUCTURE OF FACTOR MODELS

A widely used practical factor model assumes that the returns to each asset are correlated with only the surprises to some factors related to the aggregate economy, such as inflation or real output. This type of model is known as a macroeconomic factor model (or observable factor model).[43] If the return to asset i is explained by K factors, then the return for asset i is expressed by the following equation:

$$R_i = a_i + b_{i1}F_1 + b_{i2}F_2 + \ldots + b_{iK}F_K + \epsilon_i \qquad (11\text{-}17)$$

where

R_i = the return to asset i
a_i = the expected return to asset i
F_k = the surprise in the factor k, $k = 1, 2, \ldots, K$
b_{ik} = the sensitivity of the return on asset i to a surprise in factor k, $k = 1, 2, \ldots, K$
ϵ_i = an error term with a zero mean that represents the portion of the return to asset i not explained by the factor model

Before we go any further, we need to discuss what we mean by a surprise in a macroeconomic factor.[44] Suppose we are analyzing monthly returns for stocks. At the beginning of each month, we have a prediction of inflation for the month. The prediction may come from an econometric model or a professional economic forecaster, for example. Suppose our forecast at the beginning of the month is that inflation will be 0.4 percent during the

---

[43] See, for example, Burmeister, Roll, and Ross (1994).

[44] Note that we are not assuming that all factors (surprises) in the model are uncorrelated with each other. Later, we will discuss factor models that do assume all factors are uncorrelated with each other, although most factor models actually used in investment practice do not make that assumption.

month. At the end of the month, we find that inflation was actually 0.5 percent during the month. During any month,

Actual inflation = Predicted inflation + Surprise inflation

In this case, actual inflation was 0.5 percent and predicted inflation was 0.4 percent. Therefore, the surprise in inflation was $0.5 - 0.4 = 0.1$ percent. We can define **surprise** in general as the actual value minus predicted (or expected) value.

Why do we use surprises? Suppose we believe inflation and GNP growth are priced risk. We do not use the predicted values of these variables because the predicted values are already reflected in the stock prices and so are the expected returns of stocks. The intercept a_i, the expected return to asset i, reflects the effect of the predicted values of the macroeconomic variables on expected stock returns. The surprise in the macroeconomic variables during the month, on the other hand, contains new information about the variable. As a result, the surprise helps explain unexpected changes in stock returns during the month.

Consider a factor model in which the returns to each asset are correlated with two factors. For example, we might assume that the returns for a particular stock are correlated with surprises in interest rates and surprises in GDP growth. For stock i, the return to the stock can be modeled as

$$R_i = a_i + b_{i1}F_{INT} + b_{i2}F_{GDP} + \epsilon_i \tag{11-18}$$

where

R_i	= the return to stock i
a_i	= expected return to stock i
b_{i1}	= the effect of a surprise in interest rates on the return to stock i (sensitivity to interest rates)
F_{INT}	= the surprise in interest rates
b_{i2}	= the effect of a surprise in GDP growth on the return to stock i (sensitivity to GDP growth)
F_{GDP}	= the surprise in GDP growth
ϵ_i	= an error term with a zero mean that represents the portion of the return to asset i not explained by the factor model

Consider first how to interpret b_{i1}. If the surprise in interest rates during the period is 1 percentage point, the factor model predicts that a 1 percentage point surprise in interest rates will contribute b_{i1} percentage points to the return to stock i. Thus, b_{i1} is the slope coefficient for the interest rate surprise in the factor model.

Next, consider how to interpret b_{i2}. If the surprise in GDP growth during the period is 1 percentage point, the multi-factor model predicts that a 1 percentage point surprise in GDP will contribute b_{i2} percentage points to the return to stock i. Thus, b_{i2} is the slope coefficient for the GDP growth surprise in the multi-factor model.

Now consider how to interpret the intercept a_i. Recall that the error term has a mean or average value of 0. If the surprises in both interest rates and GDP growth are 0, the factor model predicts that the return to asset i will be a_i. Thus, a_i is the expected value of the return to stock i. We will discuss expected returns further when we present arbitrage pricing theory. Throughout our discussion, however, we assume that you do not estimate the parameters of the factor model yourself; instead you use parameter estimates from another source (for example, one of the many consulting companies that specialize in factor models).[45]

How can we use this example to account for the return to a particular stock, say Macrotech (MCTH)? First, assume that our investment horizon is one year. We want to know the contribution of expected return, surprises in interest rate changes and GDP growth, and company-specific factors to returns to Macrotech for the year. To use the two-factor model to account for Macrotech's returns, we need to know the following information:

- The coefficients of the model: expected return (a_{MCTH}), interest rate sensitivity ($b_{MCTH,1}$), and GDP growth sensitivity ($b_{MCTH,2}$)
- The surprise in the two factors, interest rate changes (F_{INT}) and GDP growth (F_{GDP})
- The company-specific surprise in returns (ϵ_{MCTH})

We assume that the expected return for Macrotech for the year (a_{MCTH}) was 12 percent. The sensitivity of Macrotech's stock to surprise changes in interest rates ($b_{MCTH,1}$) was −1.5. The sensitivity of Macrotech stock to surprise changes in GDP growth ($b_{MCTH,2}$) was 2.0. We will assume that these parameters are known. At the beginning of the year, interest rates were not predicted to change and GDP was predicted to grow by 4 percent (see Table 11-11). At the end of the year, we knew that interest rates increased by one percentage point. GDP grew at a rate of 2 percent during the year.

TABLE 11-11 Using a Two-Factor Model to Compute Returns for Macrotech

Macroeconomic Variable	Actual	Expected	Surprise	Factor Beta for Macrotech Stock	Contribution to Stock Return
Change in interest rate	1.0%	0.0%	1.0%	−1.5	−1.5%
Growth in GDP	2.0%	4.0%	−2.0%	2.0	−4.0%

As Table 11-11 shows, the surprise change in interest rates (Actual change − Predicted change) was $1 - 0 = 1\%$. The surprise in GDP growth (Actual change − Predicted change) was $2 - 4 = -2\%$.

If we knew only the expected return for Macrotech stock, the factor surprises, and the factor sensitivities of Macrotech stock, we would know what the return to Macrotech stock would have been if no company-specific surprises in returns occurred for the year. The return would have been

$$R_{MCTH} = 0.12 - 1.5R_{INT} + 2.0R_{GDP}$$
$$R_{MCTH} = 0.12 - 1.5(0.01) + 2.0(-0.02) = 0.065$$

---

[45] If you want to estimate your own macroeconomic factor model, follow these steps. First, estimate a time series for each macroeconomic surprise (for example, you could use the residuals from a time-series model for each different macroeconomic series). Then, use time-series data to regress the returns for a particular asset on the surprises to the different macroeconomic factors.

or 6.5 percent. If the company-specific surprise in returns for the year was 5 percent, then actual returns for the year would have been

$$R_{\text{MCTH}} = 0.12 - 1.5R_{\text{INT}} + 2.0R_{\text{GDP}} + \epsilon_{\text{MCTH}}$$
$$R_{\text{MCTH}} = 0.12 - 1.5(0.01) + 2.0(-0.02) + 0.05 = 0.115$$

or 11.5 percent.

EXAMPLE 11-13.   Factor Sensitivities for a Two-Stock Portfolio.

Suppose that stock returns are affected by two common factors: surprises in inflation and surprises in GDP growth. A portfolio manager plans to create a portfolio from two stocks, Manumatic (MANM) and Nextech (NXT). The following equations describe the returns for those stocks:

$$R_{\text{MANM}} = 0.09 - 1F_{\text{INFL}} + 1F_{\text{GDP}} + \epsilon_{\text{MANM}}$$
$$R_{\text{NXT}} = 0.12 + 2F_{\text{INFL}} + 4F_{\text{GDP}} + \epsilon_{\text{NXT}}$$

If one-third of the portfolio is invested in Manumatic stock and two-thirds is invested in Nextech stock, then the portfolio's returns are the following weighted-average of the returns to the two stocks:

$$R_P = (1/3)(0.09) + (2/3)(0.12) + [(1/3)(-1) + (2/3)(2)]F_{\text{INFL}} + [(1/3)(1)$$
$$+ (2/3)(4)]F_{\text{GDP}} + (1/3)\epsilon_{\text{MANM}} + (2/3)\epsilon_{\text{NXT}}$$

$$R_P = 0.11 + 1F_{\text{INFL}} + 3F_{\text{GDP}} + (1/3)\epsilon_{\text{MANM}} + (2/3)\epsilon_{\text{NXT}}$$

The expected return for the portfolio is 11 percent. The sensitivity of the portfolio to surprises in inflation is 1; if we have an inflation surprise of +1 percent, the portfolio return will be 1 percent higher than expected. The sensitivity of the portfolio to surprises in GDP growth is 3.

4.2 ARBITRAGE PRICING THEORY AND THE FACTOR MODEL

In the 1970s, Stephen Ross developed arbitrage pricing theory (APT) as an alternative to the CAPM. APT describes the expected return on an asset (or portfolio) as a linear function of the risk of the asset (or portfolio) with respect to a set of factors. Like the CAPM, the APT describes a financial market equilibrium. However, APT makes less-strong assumptions than the CAPM. The APT relies on three assumptions:

1. A factor model describes asset returns.

2. There are many assets, so investors can form well-diversified portfolios that eliminate asset-specific risk.

3. There are no arbitrage opportunities among well-diversified portfolios. **Arbitrage** is a riskless operation that requires no net investment of money.[46] An **arbitrage opportunity** is an opportunity to obtain an expected positive net cash flow using arbitrage.

---

[46] As we will see, arbitrage typically involves funding the investment in assets with proceeds from the short sale of other assets, so that net, no money is invested. A short sale is the sale of a borrowed asset. Note that the word *arbitrage* is also sometimes used for investment operations in which significant risk is present.

In the first assumption, the number of factors is not specified. The second assumption allows us to form portfolios with factor risk but without asset-specific risk. The third assumption is the condition of financial market equilibrium.

Empirical evidence indicates that Assumption 2 is reasonable. As the number of stocks in a portfolio gets large, we find that the asset-specific or nonsystematic risk of individual stocks makes almost no contribution to the variance of portfolio returns. Roll and Ross (2001) found that only 1 percent to 3 percent of the variance of a well-diversified portfolio comes from the nonsystematic variance of the individual stocks in the portfolio, as Figure 11-12 shows.

FIGURE 11-12   Sources of Volatility: The Case of a Well Diversified Portfolio

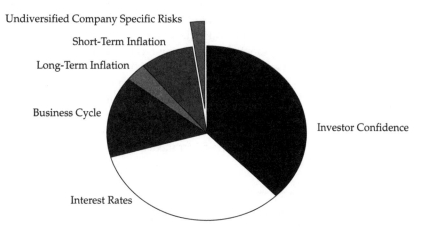

From *What Is the Arbitrage Pricing Theory*.
Retrieved May 25, 2001, from the World Wide Web: www.rollross.com/apt.html.
Reprinted with permission of Richard Roll.

According to APT, if the above three assumptions hold, the following equation holds:[47]

$$E(R_p) = R_F + \lambda_1\beta_{p,1} + \dots + \lambda_K\beta_{p,K} \tag{11-19}$$

where

$E(R_p)$ = the expected return to portfolio p
R_F = the risk-free rate
λ_j = the risk premium for factor j
$\beta_{p,j}$ = the sensitivity of the portfolio to factor j

The APT equation, Equation 11-19, says that the expected return on any well-diversified portfolio is linearly related to the **factor sensitivities** of that portfolio.[48]

---

[47] A risk-free asset is assumed. If a risk-free asset does not exist, in place of R_F we write λ_0 to represent the expected return on a risky portfolio with zero sensitivity to all the factors. The number of factors is not specified but needs to be much lower than the number of assets, a condition fulfilled in practice.

[48] The APT equation can also describe (at least approximately) the expected return on investments with asset-specific risk, under certain conditions. Factor sensitivities are sometimes called **factor betas** or **factor loadings.**

The **factor risk premium** (or **factor price**) λ_j represents the expected return in excess of the risk-free rate for a portfolio with a sensitivity of 1 to factor j and a sensitivity of 0 to all other factors. (Such a portfolio is called a **pure factor portfolio** for factor j; we will illustrate the process of constructing such portfolios shortly.)

For example, suppose we have a portfolio with a sensitivity of 1 with respect to Factor 1, and a sensitivity of 0 to all other factors. With E_1 being the expected return on this portfolio, Equation 11-19 shows that the expected return on this portfolio is $E_1 = R_F + \lambda_1 \times 1$, so $\lambda_1 = E_1 - R_F$. Suppose that $E_1 = 0.12$ and $R_F = 0.04$. Then the risk premium for factor 1 is $\lambda_1 = 0.12 - 0.04 = 0.08$ or 8 percent. We obtain an 8 percentage point increase in expected return per each unit of sensitivity to factor 1.

What is the relationship between the APT equation and the equation for a multifactor model, Equation 11-17? In discussing the multifactor model, we stated that the intercept term is the investment's expected return. The APT equation explains what an investment's expected return is in equilibrium. Thus if the APT holds, it places a restriction on the intercept term in the multifactor model in the sense that the APT model tells us what its value should be. We can in fact substitute the APT equation into the multifactor model to get an APT equation for return (as opposed to expected return).[49]

To use the APT equation, we need to estimate its parameters. The parameters of the APT equation are the risk-free rate and the factor risk premiums (the factor sensitivities are specific to individual investments). Example 11-14 shows how the expected returns and factor sensitivities of a set of portfolios can determine the parameters of the APT model in the case of a one-factor model.

EXAMPLE 11-14.   Determining the Parameters in a One-Factor Model.

Suppose we have three well-diversified portfolios with sensitivities to a single factor. Table 11-12 shows the expected returns and factor sensitivities of these portfolios. (We can assume that the expected returns reflect a one-year investment horizon.)

TABLE 11-12   Sample Portfolios for a One-Factor Model

Portfolio	Expected Return	Factor Sensitivity
A	0.075	0.5
B	0.150	2.0
C	0.070	0.4

We can use these data to determine the parameters of the APT equation. According to Equation 11-19, for any well-diversified portfolio and a single factor that explains returns, $E(R_p) = R_F + \lambda_1 \beta_{p,1}$. This is the equation of a straight line. The factor sensitivities and expected returns are known; thus there are two unknowns, the

---

[49] Another interesting question is the relationship between the APT and the CAPM. If the market is the factor in a single-factor model, APT (Equation 11-19) is consistent with the CAPM. The CAPM can also be consistent with multiple factors in an APT model, if the risk premiums in the APT model satisfy certain restrictions; these CAPM-related restrictions have been repeatedly rejected in statistical tests (see Burmeister and McElroy 1988, for example).

parameters R_F and λ_1. Because two points define a straight line, we need to set up only two equations. Selecting Portfolio A and B, we have

$$E(R_A) = 0.075 = R_F + 0.5\lambda_1$$

and

$$E(R_B) = 0.150 = R_F + 2\lambda_1$$

From the equation for Portfolio A, we have $R_F = 0.075 - 0.5\lambda_1$. Substituting this expression for the risk-free rate into the equation for Portfolio B gives

$$0.15 = 0.075 - 0.5\lambda_1 + 2\lambda_1$$
$$0.15 = 0.075 + 1.5\lambda_1$$

So we have $\lambda_1 = (0.15 - 0.075)/1.5 = 0.05$.

Substituting this value for λ_1 back into the equation for the expected return to Portfolio A yields

$$0.075 = R_F + 0.05 \times 0.5, \text{ or } R_F = 0.05$$

So the risk-free rate is 0.05 or 5 percent, and the factor premium for the common factor is also 0.05 or 5 percent. The APT equation is

$$E(R_p) = 0.05 + 0.05\beta_{p,1}$$

Portfolio C has a factor sensitivity of 0.4. Accordingly, $0.05 + (0.05 \times 0.4) = 0.07$ or 7 percent if no arbitrage opportunity exists. The expected return for Portfolio C given in Table 11-12 is 7 percent.

EXAMPLE 11-15. Checking Whether Portfolio Returns Are Consistent with No Arbitrage.

In this example, we demonstrate how to tell whether a set of expected returns for well-diversified portfolios is consistent with APT by testing whether an arbitrage opportunity exists. In Example 11-14, we had three portfolios with expected returns and factor sensitivities that were consistent with the one-factor APT model $E(R_p) = 0.05 + 0.05\beta_{p,1}$. Suppose we expand the set of portfolios to include a fourth well-diversified portfolio, Portfolio D. Table 11-13 repeats the data given in Table 11-12 for Portfolios A, B, and C, in addition to providing data on Portfolio D and a portfolio we form using A and C.

The expected return and factor sensitivity of a portfolio is the weighted average of the expected returns and factor sensitivities of the assets in the portfolio. Suppose we construct a portfolio consisting of 50 percent Portfolio A and 50 percent Portfolio C. Table 11-13 shows that the expected return of this portfolio is $(0.50)(0.0750) + (0.50)(0.07) = 0.0725$, or 7.25 percent. The factor sensitivity of this portfolio is $(0.50)(0.50) + (0.50)(0.40) = 0.45$.

Arbitrage pricing theory assumes that well-diversified portfolios present no arbitrage opportunities. If the initial investment is 0 and we do not bear risk, the final

TABLE 11-13   Sample Portfolios for a One-Factor Model

Portfolio	Expected Return	Factor Sensitivity
A	0.0750	0.50
B	0.1500	2.00
C	0.0700	0.40
D	0.0800	0.45
0.5A + 0.5C	0.0725	0.45

expected cash flow should be 0. In this case, the configuration of expected returns in relation to factor risk presents an arbitrage opportunity involving Portfolios A, C, and D. Portfolio D offers too high an expected rate of return given its factor sensitivity. According to the APT model estimated in Example 11-14, there is an arbitrage opportunity unless $E(R_D) = 0.05 + 0.05\beta_{D,1} = 0.05 + (0.05 \times 0.45) = 0.0725$, so that the expected return on D is 7.25 percent. In fact, the expected return on D is 8 percent. Portfolio D is undervalued relative to its factor risk. We will buy D (hold it long) in the arbitrage portfolio. We purchase D using the proceeds from selling short a portfolio consisting of A and C with exactly the same factor sensitivity as D, 0.45. As we showed above, an equally weighted portfolio of A and C has a factor sensitivity of 0.45.

The arbitrage thus involves the following strategy: Invest $10,000 in Portfolio D and fund that investment by selling short an equally weighted portfolio of Portfolios A and C; then close out the investment position at the end of one year (the investment horizon for expected returns). We calculate cash flows as follows. The expected return for Portfolio A, for example, is 0.0750. Thus, if we invest $10,000 in Portfolio A and plan to sell the portfolio after one year, we can expect to receive $10,750 = [$10,000 \times (1 + 0.075)] at the end of one year. Table 11-14 demonstrates the arbitrage profits to the arbitrage strategy. The final row of Table 11-14 shows the net cash flow to the arbitrage portfolio.

TABLE 11-14   Arbitrage Opportunity within Sample Portfolios

	Initial Cash Flow	Final Cash Flow	Factor Sensitivity
Portfolio D	−$10,000.00	$10,800.00	0.45
Portfolios A & C	$10,000.00	−$10,725.00	−0.45
Sum	$0.00	$75.00	0.00

As Table 11-14 shows, if we buy $10,000 of Portfolio D and sell $10,000 of an equally weighted portfolio of Portfolios A and C, we have an initial net cash flow of $0. The expected value of our investment in Portfolio D at the end of one year is $10,800 = [$10,000 \times (1 + 0.08)]. The expected value of our short position in Portfolios A and C at the end of one year is −$10,725 = [$10,000 \times (1.0725)]. So the combined expected cash flow from our investment position in one year is $75.

What about the risk? Table 11-14 shows that the factor risk has been eliminated: Purchasing D and selling short an equally weighted portfolio of A and C creates a portfolio with a factor sensitivity of $0.45 - 0.45 = 0$. The portfolios are well diversified, and we assume any asset-specific risk is negligible.

Because the arbitrage is possible, Portfolios A, C, and D cannot all be consistent with the same equilibrium. A unique set of parameters for the APT model does not describe the returns on these three portfolios. If Portfolio D actually had an expected return of 8 percent, investors would bid up its price until the expected return fell and the arbitrage opportunity vanished. Thus, arbitrage restores equilibrium relationships among expected returns.

In Example 11-14, we illustrated how the parameters of a single-factor APT model can be determined from data. Example 11-16 shows how we can also determine the model parameters in a model with more than one factor.

EXAMPLE 11-16. Determining the Parameters and Risk Premiums in a Two-Factor Model.

Suppose that two factors, surprise in inflation (Factor 1) and surprise in GDP growth (Factor 2), explain returns. According to APT, an arbitrage opportunity exists unless

$$E(R_p) = R_F + \lambda_1\beta_{p,1} + \lambda_2\beta_{p,2}$$

Our goal is to estimate the three parameters of the model R_F, λ_1, and λ_2. We also have hypothetical data on three well-diversified portfolios, J, K, and L, given in Table 11-15.

TABLE 11-15 Sample Portfolios for a Two-Factor Model

Portfolio	Expected Return	Sensitivity to Inflation Factor	Sensitivity to GDP Factor
J	0.12	1.0	1.5
K	0.12	0.5	1.0
L	0.11	1.5	2.5

If the market is in equilibrium (no arbitrage opportunities exist), the expected returns to three portfolios should be described by the two-factor APT with the same set of parameters. Using the expected returns and the return sensitivities shown in Table 11-15 yields

$$E(R_J) = 0.12 = R_F + 1.0\lambda_1 + 1.5\lambda_2$$
$$E(R_K) = 0.12 = R_F + 0.5\lambda_1 + 1.0\lambda_2$$
$$E(R_L) = 0.11 = R_F + 1.5\lambda_1 + 2.5\lambda_2$$

We have three equations with three unknowns. Thus, we can solve for the parameters using the method of substitution. We first want to get two equations with two unknowns. Solving the equation for $E(R_J)$ for the risk-free rate,

$$R_F = 0.12 - 1.0\lambda_1 - 1.5\lambda_2$$

Substituting this expression for the risk-free rate into the equation for $E(R_K)$, we find, after simplification, that $\lambda_1 = -\lambda_2$. Using $\lambda_1 = -\lambda_2$ to eliminate λ_1 in the equation for $E(R_J)$,

$$0.12 = R_F + 0.5\lambda_2$$

Using $\lambda_1 = -\lambda_2$ to eliminate λ_1 in the equation for $E(R_L)$,

$$0.11 = R_F + \lambda_2$$

Using the two equations in R_F and λ_2 immediately above we find that $\lambda_2 = -0.02$ (we solved for the risk-free rate in the first of these two equations and used the expression in the second equation). Because $\lambda_1 = -\lambda_2$, $\lambda_1 = 0.02$. Finally, $R_F = 0.12 - 1.0 \times 0.02 - 1.5 \times (-0.02) = 0.13$. To summarize

$R_F = 0.13$ (The risk-free rate is 13 percent.)
$\lambda_1 = 0.02$ (The inflation risk premium is 2 percent per unit of sensitivity.)
$\lambda_2 = -0.02$ (The GDP risk premium is -2 percent per unit of sensitivity.)

So, the APT equation for these three portfolios is

$$E(R_p) = 0.13 + 0.02\beta_{p,1} - 0.02\beta_{p,2}$$

This example illustrates the calculations for determining the parameters of an APT model. It also shows that the risk premium for a factor can actually be negative.

In explaining factor risk premiums, we introduced the concept of a factor portfolio. To review, a factor portfolio for any particular factor has a sensitivity of 1 for that factor and a sensitivity of 0 for all other factors. As a result, a factor portfolio exactly represents the risk of its factor. As a pure bet on a source of risk, factor portfolios are of interest to a portfolio manager who wants to hedge that risk or speculate on it. Example 11-17 shows how to create a factor portfolio.

**EXAMPLE 11-17.   Creating a Portfolio with Exposure to Only One
                                Risk Factor.**

A portfolio manager may want to bet that GDP will increase unexpectedly, inflation will drop unexpectedly, or that some other economic or financial factor affecting asset prices will change unexpectedly. To execute such a strategy, the manager may create a factor portfolio. In this example, we show how a manager constructs such a portfolio.

Suppose that only two factors affect asset returns: surprises in inflation, and surprises in GDP growth. We can take the same three well-diversified portfolios, J, K, and L, that we used in Example 11-16. Table 11-15 is repeated below.

TABLE 11-15   (repeated) Sample Portfolios for a Two-Factor Model

Portfolio	Expected Return	Sensitivity to Inflation Factor	Sensitivity to GDP Factor
J	0.12	1.0	1.5
K	0.12	0.5	1.0
L	0.11	1.5	2.5

The following two-factor model describes the returns on the three portfolios:

$$R_J = 0.12 + 1.0F_{\text{INFL}} + 1.5F_{\text{GDP}}$$
$$R_K = 0.12 + 0.5F_{\text{INFL}} + 1.0F_{\text{GDP}}$$
$$R_L = 0.11 + 1.5F_{\text{INFL}} + 2.5F_{\text{GDP}}$$

The portfolios' respective expected returns are the intercepts in the above three equations. Note that we have omitted the error term, ϵ_i, that appears in Equation 11-17. We have assumed that the three portfolios are so well diversified that asset-specific risk approaches 0.

How can we choose portfolio weights w_J, w_K, and w_L to create a factor portfolio for the inflation factor? We can determine the portfolio weights for this factor by solving three equations. First, the portfolio weights must sum to 1:

$$w_J + w_K + w_L = 1$$

A portfolio's factor sensitivity on a factor i is a weighted average of the factor sensitivities to i for the individual investments in the portfolio; a given weight is the proportion of the portfolio's market value that the investment represents. Therefore, this restriction implies that the weighted-average value of the inflation factor sensitivities of J, K, and L must equal 1. The second equation is

$$1.0w_J + 0.5w_K + 1.5w_L = 1$$

The factor weight on F_{GDP} must be 0. This restriction gives the third equation

$$1.5w_J + 1.0w_K + 2.5w_L = 0$$

How can we solve for the weights? If we solve the equation $w_J + w_K + w_L = 1$ for w_L and find that $w_L = (1 - w_J - w_K)$, we can substitute this result in the other two equations to find

$$1.0w_J + 0.5w_K + 1.5(1 - w_J - w_K) = 1, \text{ or } -0.5w_J - 1.0w_K = -0.5$$

and

$$1.5w_J + 1.0w_K + 2.5(1 - w_J - w_K) = 0, \text{ or } -1.0w_J - 1.5w_K = -2.5$$

If we multiply the equation $-0.5w_J - 1.0w_K = -0.5$ by -2 and add it to the equation $-1.0w_J - 1.5w_K = -2.5$, the result is

$$0.5w_K = -1.5 \text{ or } w_K = -3.0$$

Substituting $w_K = -3.0$ back into the equation $-1.0w_J - 1.5w_K = -2.5$ yields

$$-1.0w_J - 1.5(-3) = -2.5 \text{ or } w_J = 7.0$$

If we substitute $w_K = -3.0$ and $w_J = 7.0$ back into the equation $1.5w_J + 1.0w_K + 2.5w_L = 0$, we see that

$$1.5(7.0) + 1.0(-3.0) + 2.5w_L = 0$$

We can solve this equation to find that

$$w_L = -3.0$$

Therefore, the portfolio manager can construct a factor portfolio for the surprise in inflation by using portfolio weights $w_J = 7.0$, $w_K = -3.0$, and $w_L = -3.0$. If the inflation surprise is 1 percent, then the factor portfolio's return will be 1 percent higher than its expected level regardless of the level of the GDP surprise, because the factor portfolio has a sensitivity of 1 to surprises in inflation but no sensitivity to surprises in GDP. Thus the portfolio manager can create a portfolio that is a pure bet on inflation. Note that the expected return to the inflation factor portfolio is

$$w_J(0.12) + w_K(0.12) + w_L(0.11) =$$
$$(7.0)(0.12) + (-3.0)(0.12) + (-3.0)(0.11) = 0.15$$

or 15 percent.

A portfolio manager may want a specific set of factor risk exposures. To achieve his objective, the manager can create a **tracking portfolio.** A tracking portfolio is a portfolio that has a desired or target configuration of factor sensitivities. The configuration of factor sensitivities is often chosen to match that of a benchmark portfolio or other investment. For example, an investment manager may have the Russell 2000 Index (an index of U.S. small-cap stocks) as a benchmark. The portfolio manager may believe he can identify undervalued securities. One alternative for the portfolio manager is to pick small-cap stocks without otherwise quantitatively managing the risk of the portfolio. If the manager has definite stock-selection ability, this approach may have the highest long-run average return. Because the risk of the portfolio may be substantially different from the benchmark, however, the portfolio manager may underperform the benchmark substantially in some time periods. This risk arises because the portfolio may have very different sensitivities to one or more systematic factors than does the Russell 2000 (e.g., to surprises in inflation).

The portfolio manager might consider indexing a large part of the portfolio to the Russell 2000 while managing the balance actively (that is, picking stocks individually). This strategy has less variability with respect to the benchmark than the first strategy. The drawback of the second strategy is that the impact of the manager's stock selection ability is attenuated by indexing.

The portfolio manager has a third alternative of creating a tracking portfolio for the Russell 2000 from his individual stock picks (or a portfolio that matches certain risk exposures of the Russell 2000). This strategy is implemented by the selection of weights on the stocks. The manager hopes to thereby manage the tracking risk of his portfolio while continuing to pick stocks individually.[50] Besides application in investment management, tracking portfolios are useful in hedging risks to which a company may be exposed. The target factor sensitivities in the tracking portfolio are chosen to offset the risk exposures.

In Example 11-18 we illustrate how a tracking portfolio can be created.

EXAMPLE 11-18. Creating a Tracking Portfolio.

Suppose that a pension plan sponsor has placed money under the management of the portfolio manager that we met in Example 11-17. The money is to be fully invested in U.S. common stocks. The plan sponsor has specified an equity benchmark for the portfolio manager. The portfolio manager has decided to create a tracking portfolio for the benchmark. For the sake of illustrating the construction of a tracking portfolio with familiar data, let us continue with the three portfolios J, K, and L from Examples 11-16 and 11-17, and the same two-factor model.

The portfolio manager determines that the benchmark has a sensitivity of 1.5 to the surprise in inflation and a sensitivity of 2 to the surprise in GDP. A factor portfolio is just a special case of a tracking portfolio (a factor portfolio has a specified configuration of factor sensitivities). The steps in constructing a tracking portfolio for the benchmark from Portfolios J, K, and L are therefore quite similar. We repeat Table 11-15 below.

TABLE 11-15   (repeated) Sample Portfolios for a Two-Factor Model

Portfolio	Expected Return	Sensitivity to Inflation Factor	Sensitivity to GDP Factor
J	0.12	1.0	1.5
K	0.12	0.5	1.0
L	0.11	1.5	2.5

Recall the following two-factor model describes the returns on the three portfolios:

$$R_J = 0.12 + 1.0F_{INFL} + 1.5F_{GDP}$$
$$R_K = 0.12 + 0.5F_{INFL} + 1.0F_{GDP}$$
$$R_L = 0.11 + 1.5F_{INFL} + 2.5F_{GDP}$$

We need three equations to determine the portfolio weights w_J, w_K, and w_L in the tracking portfolio.

---

[50] Tracking risk is the standard deviation of the differences between the portfolio's and the benchmark's return. There is variation in usage: Some writers use *tracking error* instead of *tracking risk* for this concept.

- *Equation 1.* We have an equation that portfolio weights must sum to 1.

$$w_J + w_K + w_L = 1$$

- *Equation 2.* The second equation states that the weighted average of the sensitivities of J, K, and L to the surprise in inflation must equal the benchmark's sensitivity to the surprise in inflation, 1.5. This requirement ensures that the tracking portfolio has the same inflation risk as the benchmark.

$$1.0w_J + 0.5w_K + 1.5w_L = 1.5$$

- *Equation 3.* The third equation states that the weighted average of the sensitivities of J, K, and L to the surprise in GDP must equal the benchmark's sensitivity to the surprise in GDP, 2.0. This requirement ensures that the tracking portfolio has the same GDP risk as the benchmark.

$$1.5w_J + 1.0w_K + 2.5w_L = 2.0$$

We can solve for the weights as follows. From Equation 1, $w_L = (1 - w_J - w_K)$. We substitute this result in the other two equations to find

$$1.0w_J + 0.5w_K + 1.5(1 - w_J - w_K) = 1.5, \text{ simplifying to } w_K = -0.5w_J$$

and

$$1.5w_J + 1.0w_K + 2.5(1 - w_J - w_K) = 2,$$
$$\text{simplifying to } -w_J - 1.5w_K = -0.5$$

We next substitute $w_K = -0.5w_J$ into $-w_J - 1.5w_K = -0.5 - w_J - 1.5(-0.5w_J) = -0.5$ or $-w_J + 0.75w_J = -0.5$, so $w_J = 2$.
Using $w_K = -0.5w_J$ obtained earlier, $w_K = -0.5 \times 2 = -1.0$. Finally, from $w_L = (1 - w_J - w_K) = [1 - 2 - (-1.0)] = 0$. To summarize,

$$w_J = 2$$
$$w_K = -1.0$$
$$w_L = 0.$$

The tracking portfolio has an expected return of $(w_J \times 0.12) + (w_K \times 0.12) + (w_L \times 0.11) = (2 \times 0.12) + (-1.0 \times 0.12) + 0 = 0.24 - 0.12 = 0.12$. The tracking portfolio has the same expected return as Portfolio J or K, but with the benchmark's factor sensitivities.

Given a multifactor model, estimated factor sensitivities of the assets, and the target factor sensitivities, the procedure for determining the weights of assets in a tracking portfolio involves setting up two types of equations. First, we have an equation stating that the weights in the tracking portfolio sum to 1. Second, we have an equation for each target factor sensitivity. For each equation, on the left-hand side of the equal sign we have a weighted average of the factor sensitivities of the assets to the factor. On the right-hand side of the equal sign we have the targeted sensitivity of the tracking portfolio to the factor.

Having discussed the basics of multifactor models, APT, and the construction and uses of factor and tracking portfolios, we now review some specific factor models.

4.3 MULTIFACTOR MODELS IN CURRENT PRACTICE

In the previous section, we illustrated the concepts of multifactor models and APT with hypothetical one- and two-factor macroeconomic factor models. In this section, we introduce actual models. We illustrate one macroeconomic factor model in current use, as well as a practical application for it. Fundamental factor models are also popular in current investment practice. Earlier, we defined fundamental factor models as models that use attributes of a stock or the stock's issuer to explain equity returns. We end this section with more information on fundamental factor models.

Chen, Roll, and Ross (1986) pioneered the development of macroeconomic factor models. Following statistically based research suggesting that more than one factor was important in explaining the average returns on U.S. stocks, Chen et al. suggested that a relatively small set of macro factors were the primary influence on the U.S. stock market. The four factors in the Chen et al. study were the unanticipated changes in (1) inflation, (2) the slope of the term structure of interest rates (the yield curve), (3) the spread between low-rated and high-rated bonds (a risk premium), and (4) industrial production.[51]

The usefulness of any factor for explaining asset returns is generally evaluated using historical data. Our confidence that a factor will explain future returns increases if we can give an economic explanation of why a factor should be important in explaining average returns. We can give plausible explanations for Chen et al.'s four factors. For example, inflation affects the cash flows of businesses as well as the level of the discount rate applied to these cash flows by investors. Changes in industrial production affect the cash flows of businesses and the opportunities faced by investors. Example 11-19 presents a current macroeconomic factor model that expanded on the model of Chen et al.

EXAMPLE 11-19.   Expected Return in a Practical APT Model.

Burmeister, Roll, and Ross (1994) presented a macroeconomic factor model to explain the returns on U.S. equities. They included five factors:

1. Confidence risk: the unanticipated change in the return difference between risky corporate bonds and government bonds, both with maturities of 20 years. Risky corporate bonds bear much higher default risk than government debt. Investors' attitudes toward this risk should affect the average returns on equities. To explain the factor's name, when investors' confidence is high, they are willing to accept a smaller reward for bearing this risk.

2. Time horizon risk: the unanticipated change in the return difference between 20-year government bonds and 30-day Treasury bills. This factor reflects investors' willingness to invest for the long term.

3. Inflation risk: the unexpected change in the inflation rate. Nearly all stocks have negative exposure to this factor, as their returns decline with positive surprises in inflation.

4. Business-cycle risk: the unexpected change in the level of real business activity. A positive surprise or unanticipated change indicates that the expected growth rate of the economy, measured in constant dollars, has increased.

---

[51] "Unanticipated change in" a variable is the "surprise in the change of" the variable, using the terminology of this chapter.

5. Market-timing risk: the portion of the S&P 500's total return that is not explained by the first four risk factors.[52] Almost all stocks have positive sensitivity to this factor.

The first four factors are quite similar to the group of four factors in Chen et al. with
respect to the economic influences they seek to capture. The fifth factor acknowl-
edges the uncertainty we face about the correct set of underlying variables for asset
pricing; this fifth factor captures influences on the returns to the S&P 500 not explained by the first four factors.

The S&P 500 is a widely used index of 500 U.S. stocks of leading companies
in leading industries. Burmeister et al. used the S&P 500 to gauge the influence of
the five factors on the mean excess returns (above the Treasury bill rate) to a well-
diversified portfolio of U.S. equities. Table 11-16 shows their results.

TABLE 11-16   Explaining the Expected Excess Return for the S&P 500

Risk Factor	Factor Sensitivity	Risk Premium (%/Yr)	Effect of Factor on Expected Return (%/Yr)
Confidence risk	0.27	2.59	0.70
Time horizon risk	0.56	−0.66	−0.37
Inflation risk	−0.37	−4.32	1.60
Business-cycle risk	1.71	1.49	2.55
Market-timing risk	1.00	3.61	3.61
Expected excess return			8.09

The estimated APT model is $E(R_p)$ = T-bill rate + 2.59 × Confidence risk − 0.66 ×
Time horizon risk − 4.32 × Inflation risk + 1.49 × Business-cycle risk + 3.61 ×
Market-timing risk. The table shows that the S&P 500 had positive exposure to every
risk factor except inflation risk. The two largest contributions to excess return came
from market-timing risk and business-cycle risk. The table shows that this model
predicts that the S&P 500 has an expected excess return of 8.09 percent above the
T-bill rate. Thus, if the 30-day Treasury bill rate were 4 percent, for example, the
forecasted return for the S&P 500 would be 4 + 8.09 = 12.09 percent a year.

In Example 11-20, we illustrate how we might use the Burmeister et al. factor model
to assess the factor bets placed by a portfolio manager.

EXAMPLE 11-20.   Exposures to Economy-Wide Risks.

A core equity portfolio is an actively managed portfolio usually consisting of holdings in the stocks of leading companies. The S&P 500 is often used as a benchmark
for U.S. core equity portfolios. Because the portfolio manager's performance will be
evaluated relative to the S&P 500, it is useful to understand the active factor bets that

---

[52] Because of the way the factor is constructed, the S&P 500 itself has a sensitivity of 1 to market-timing risk.

the manager is placing relative to the S&P 500. With a focus on exposures to economy-wide risk, we use the Burmeister et al. model already presented. The data are given in Table 11-17.

TABLE 11-17   Excess Factor Sensitivities for a Core Equity Portfolio

Risk Factor	Core Portfolio's Factor Sensitivity	S&P 500 Factor Sensitivity	Core Portfolio's Excess Factor Sensitivity
Confidence risk	0.27	0.27	0.00
Time horizon risk	0.56	0.56	0.00
Inflation risk	−0.12	−0.37	0.25
Business-cycle risk	2.25	1.71	0.54
Market-timing risk	1.10	1.00	0.11

We see that the portfolio manager tracks the S&P 500 exactly on confidence and time horizon risk, but tilts toward greater business-cycle risk. The portfolio also has a small positive excess exposure to the market-timing factor.

We can use the excess exposure to business-cycle risk to illustrate the numerical interpretation of the excess sensitivities. Ignoring nonsystematic risk and holding the values of the other factors constant, if there is a +1 percent surprise in the business-cycle factor, we expect that the return on the portfolio would be $0.01 \times 0.54 = 0.0054$ or 0.54 percent higher than the return on the S&P 500. Conversely, we expect that the return on the portfolio would be lower than the S&P 500's return by an equal amount for a −1 percent surprise in business-cycle risk.

Because of the excess exposure of 0.54, the portfolio manager appears to be placing a bet on economic expansion, relative to the benchmark. Is the manager aware of this? If the factor bet is inadvertent, she is perhaps assuming an unwanted risk. If the manager is aware of the bet, what are the reasons for the bet?

Care must be taken in interpreting the portfolio manager's excess sensitivity of 0.25 to the inflation factor. The S&P 500 has a negative inflation factor exposure. The value of 0.25 represents a smaller negative exposure to inflation for the core portfolio; that is, less rather than more exposure to inflation risk. Note from Table 11-16 in Example 11-19 that, because the risk premium for inflation risk is negative, the manager is giving up expected return relative to the benchmark by his bet on inflation. Again, what are the portfolio's manager's reasons for the inflation factor bet?

The market-timing factor has an interpretation somewhat similar to that of the CAPM beta about how a stock tends to respond to changes in the broad market, with a higher value indicating higher sensitivity to market returns, all else equal. However, the market-timing factor reflects only the portion of the S&P 500's returns not explained by the other four factors, and the two concepts are distinct. We do not expect market-timing factor sensitivity to be proportional to CAPM beta, in general.

In addition to macroeconomic models, financial analysts often use fundamental factor models. A fundamental factor model explains the returns to individual stocks using observable fundamental factors that describe attributes of the securities themselves, or attributes of the securities' issuers. Industry membership, price-earnings ratios, book value-to-price, size, and financial leverage are examples of fundamental factors.

Fundamental factors differ from macroeconomic factors in several ways. In form, macroeconomic factors are changes, specifically the unanticipated part of the change in a variable. In contrast, dividend yield, for example, is not a change but the ratio of two different variables, dividend and price.[53] An investment's sensitivity to a macroeconomic factor is estimated using a statistical technique. In contrast, an investment's sensitivity to a fundamental factor such as dividend yield is the value of dividend yield itself, after scaling. Suppose, for example, that an investment has a dividend yield of 4.5 percent, and that the average dividend yield across all stocks being considered is 2.5 percent. Further, suppose that the standard deviation of dividend yields across all stocks is 2 percent. The investment sensitivity to the dividend factor would be calculated as the value of the attribute minus the average value of the attribute across all stocks, divided by the standard deviation of the attribute across all stocks. This scaling ensures that the average value of the factor sensitivity for an investment is 0 and that the standard deviation of factor sensitivities is 1. For our example, the investment's sensitivity to dividend yield is 1, computed as $(4.5\% - 2.5\%)/2\%$, which is above average. The time series of factor returns in a fundamental factor model are represented by the returns to pure factor portfolios constructed to have a sensitivity of 1 to a single factor and a sensitivity of 0 to other factors.

Example 11-21 reports a study that examined macroeconomic, fundamental, and statistical factor models.

EXAMPLE 11-21.   Alternative Factor Models.

Connor (1995) contrasted a macroeconomic factor model with a fundamental factor model to compare how well the models explain stock returns.[54]

Connor reported the results of applying a macroeconomic factor model to the returns for 779 large-cap U.S. stocks based on monthly data from January 1985 through December 1993. Using five macroeconomic factors, Connor was able to explain approximately 11 percent of the variance of return on these stocks.[55] Table 11-18 shows these results. Connor also reported a fundamental factor analysis of the same companies for which he conducted a macroeconomic factor analysis. Table 11-19 shows these results. In the table, "variability in markets" was the stock's volatility, "success" is a price momentum variable, "trade activity" distinguishes stocks by how often their shares trade, and "growth" distinguishes stocks by past and anticipated earnings growth.[56]

As Table 11-19 shows, the most important fundamental factor is the 55 industry dummies included in the model. The fundamental factor model explained approximately 43 percent of the variation in stock returns, compared with approximately 11 percent for the macroeconomic factor model. Connor's article does not

---

[53] Fundamental variables include other types of variables as well. For example, industry membership is measured on a nominal scale, because we can name the industry to which a company belongs but no more. A nominal variable can be represented in a regression by a dummy variable (a variable that takes on the value of 0 or 1). For more on dummy variables, see the chapter on multiple regression.

[54] We do not discuss results for statistical factor models also reported in Connor (1995).

[55] The explanatory power of a given model was computed as 1 − [(Average asset-specific variance of return across stocks)/(Average total variance of return across stocks)]. The variance estimates were corrected for degrees of freedom, so the marginal contribution of a factor to explanatory power can be 0 or negative. To summarize, explanatory power captures the proportion of the total variance of return that a given model explains for the average stock.

[56] The explanations of the variables are from Grinold and Kahn (1994); Connor (1995) does not supply definitions.

TABLE 11-18   The Explanatory Power of the Macroeconomic Factors

Factor	Explanatory Power from Using Each Factor Alone (%)	Increase in Explanatory Power from Adding Each Factor to All the Others (%)
Inflation	1.3	0.0
Term structure	1.1	7.7
Industrial production	0.5	0.3
Default premium	2.4	8.1
Unemployment	−0.3	0.1
All factors		10.9

Source: Connor (1995)

TABLE 11-19   The Explanatory Power of the Fundamental Factors

Factor	Explanatory Power from Using Each Factor Alone (%)	Increase in Explanatory Power from Adding Each Factor to All the Others (%)
Industries	16.3	18.0
Variability in markets	4.3	0.9
Success	2.8	0.8
Size	1.4	0.6
Trade activity	1.4	0.5
Growth	3.0	0.4
Earnings to price	2.2	0.6
Book to price	1.5	0.6
Earnings variability	2.5	0.4
Financial leverage	0.9	0.5
Foreign investment	0.7	0.4
Labor intensity	2.2	0.5
Dividend yield	2.9	0.4
All factors		42.6

Source: Connor (1995)

provide tests of the statistical significance of the various factors in the macroeconomic factor model or the fundamental factor model. Connor did find, however, strong evidence for the usefulness of fundamental factor models, and this evidence is mirrored by the wide use of those models in the investment community. Fundamental factor models are frequently used in portfolio performance attribution, for example.[57] Typically, fundamental factor models employ many more factors than

---

[57] Portfolio performance attribution analyzes the performance of portfolios in terms of the contributions from various sources of risk.

macroeconomic factor models, giving a more detailed picture of the sources of a portfolio manager's results.

We cannot conclude from this study that fundamental factor models are inherently superior to macroeconomic factors, however. Each of the major types of models has its uses. The factors in various macroeconomic factor models, including the model discussed in Example 11-19, are individually backed by statistical evidence that they represent systematic risk (i.e., risk that cannot be diversified away). In contrast, a portfolio manager can easily construct a portfolio that does not include a particular industry, so exposure to a particular industry is not systematic risk. The two types of factors, macroeconomic and fundamental, have different implication for managing risk, in general. The macroeconomic factor set is parsimonious (5 variables); the fundamental factors set is large (67 variables including the 55 industries dummies). Connor found that the macroeconomic factor model had no marginal explanatory power when added to the fundamental factor model, implying that the fundamental risk attributes capture all the risk characteristics represented by the macroeconomic factor betas. Because the fundamental factors supply such a detailed description of the characteristics of a stock and its issuer, however, this finding is not necessarily surprising.

4.4 CONCLUDING REMARKS

How can multifactor models help investors select portfolios? How does the portfolio advice for a multifactor world differ from the advice for a single-factor world? In earlier sections, we showed how models with multiple factors can help portfolio managers solve practical tasks in controlling risk, using techniques such as tracking portfolios. In this section, we provide additional insight into why some risks may be priced and how, as a result, the portfolio implications of a multifactor world differ from those of the world described by the CAPM. We show how an investor can make better portfolio decisions with a multifactor model than with a single-factor model.

The CAPM provides investors with useful and influential concepts for thinking about investments. Considerable evidence has accumulated, however, that shows that the CAPM provides an incomplete description of risk.[58] What is the portfolio advice of CAPM, and how can we improve on it when more than one source of systematic risk drives asset returns? An investor who believes that the CAPM explains asset returns would hold a portfolio consisting only of the risk-free asset and the market portfolio of risky assets. If the investor had a high tolerance for risk, she would put a greater proportion in the market portfolio. But to the extent the investor held risky assets, she would hold them in amounts proportional to their market-value weights, without consideration for any other dimension of risk. In reality, of course, everyone does not hold the same portfolio of risky assets. Practically speaking, this CAPM-oriented investor might hold a money market fund and a portfolio indexed on a broad market index.[59]

With more than one source of systematic risk, the *average* investor might still want to hold a broadly based portfolio and the risk-free asset. Other investors, however, may find it appropriate to tilt away from an index fund after considering dimensions of risk ignored by the CAPM. To make this argument, let us explore why, for example, the business cycle

---

[58] See Bodie, Kane, and Marcus (1999) for an introduction to the empirical evidence.

[59] Passive management is a distinct issue from holding a single portfolio. There are efficient-markets arguments for holding indexed investments that are separate from the CAPM. However, an index fund is reasonable for this investor.

is a source of systematic risk, as in the Burmeister et al. model discussed earlier. There is an economic intuition for why this risk is systematic:[60] Most investors hold jobs and are thus sensitive to recessions. Suppose, for example, that a working investor faces the risk of a recession. If this investor compared two stocks with the same CAPM beta, given his concern about recession risk, he would accept a lower return from the countercyclical stock and require a risk premium on the procyclical one. In contrast, an investor with inherited wealth and no job-loss concerns would be willing to accept the recession risk.

If the average investor holding a job bids up the price of the countercyclical stocks, then recession risk will be priced. In addition, procyclical stocks would have lower prices than if the recession factor were not priced. Investors can thus, as Cochrane (1999a) notes, "earn a substantial premium for holding dimensions of risk unrelated to market movements."

This view of risk has portfolio implications. The average investor is exposed to and negatively affected by cyclical risk, which is a priced factor. (Risks that do not affect the average investor should not be priced.) Investors with jobs (and thus with labor income) want lower cyclical risk and create a cyclical risk premium, whereas investors without labor income will accept more cyclical risk to capture a premium for a risk that they do not care about. As a result, an investor who faces lower-than-average recession risk optimally tilts towards greater-than-average exposure to the business-cycle factor, all else equal.

In summary, investors should know which priced risks they face and analyze the extent of their exposure. Compared with single-factor models, multifactor models offer a rich context for investors to search for ways to improve portfolio selection.

5 SUMMARY

In this chapter, we have presented a set of concepts, models, and tools that are key ingredients to quantitative portfolio management today.

- Mean–variance analysis is a part of modern portfolio theory that deals with the trade-offs between risk, as represented by variance or standard deviation of return, and expected return.
- Mean–variance analysis assumes:
  - Investors are risk averse.
  - Assets' expected returns, variances of returns, and covariances of returns are known.
  - Investors need to know only the expected returns, the variances of returns, and covariances between returns in order to determine which portfolios are optimal.
  - There are no transaction costs or taxes.
- For any portfolio composed of two assets, the expected return to the portfolio, $E(R_p)$, is $E(R_p) = w_1 E(R_1) + w_2 E(R_2)$, where $E(R_1)$ = the expected return to Asset 1 and $E(R_2)$ = the expected return to Asset 2.
- More generally, the expected return on a portfolio is a weighted average of the expected returns on the individual assets, where the weight applied to each asset's return is the fraction of the portfolio invested in that asset.

---

[60] This discussion follows Cochrane (1999a) and (1999b).

- The variance of return on a two-asset portfolio is

$$\sigma_p^2 = w_1^2\sigma_1^2 + w_2^2\sigma_2^2 + 2w_1w_2\rho_{1,2}\sigma_1\sigma_2$$

where

  σ_1 = the standard deviation of return on Asset 1
  σ_2 = the standard deviation of return on Asset 2
  $\rho_{1,2}$ = the correlation between the returns on Asset 1 and Asset 2

- In mean–variance analysis, the investment attributes of individual assets and portfolios are represented by points in a figure having standard deviation or variance of return as the x-axis and expected return as the y-axis.

- The minimum-variance frontier graphs the smallest variance of return attainable for each level of expected return.

- The global minimum-variance portfolio is the portfolio of risky assets having the minimum variance.

- An efficient portfolio is one providing the maximum expected return for its level of variance or standard deviation of return.

- The efficient frontier graphs all combinations of mean return and variance or standard deviation of return that can be attained by holding efficient portfolios.

- The efficient frontier is the upper portion of the minimum-variance frontier (the global minimum-variance portfolio and points above).

- According to mean–variance analysis, investors optimally select a portfolio from portfolios that lie on the efficient frontier.

- By restricting attention to the efficient portfolios, the investor's portfolio selection task is greatly simplified.

- Diversification benefits occur when portfolio standard deviation of return can be reduced through diversification without decreasing expected return.

- When the correlation between the returns on two assets is less than $+1$, there are potential benefits to diversification.

- For the two-asset case, the potential benefits from diversifying increase as we lower the correlation between the two portfolios towards -1, holding all else constant. For a correlation of -1, a portfolio of the two assets exists that eliminates risk. As we lower correlation, the efficient frontier improves in the sense of offering a higher expected return for a given feasible level of standard deviation of return, holding all other values constant.

- For the two-portfolio case, the risk–return trade-off improves as we lower the correlation between the two portfolios towards -1, holding all else constant. For a correlation of -1, a portfolio of the two assets exists that eliminates risk. The efficient frontier for a correlation of -1 dominates (is superior to) all efficient frontiers corresponding to larger values of the correlation coefficient.

- When we have three or more assets, the minimum-variance frontier is the curve that borders the set of all feasible portfolios (the feasible region) and defines portfolios having minimum variance for each specified return level.

- In general, to determine the minimum-variance frontier possible for a set of n assets, we first determine the minimum expected return and the maximum expected return among all the expected returns offered by the n assets. We then choose the individual asset weights that minimize portfolio variance of return for different levels of expected return, subject to the constraint that the individual asset weights sum to 1. This mean–variance optimization is a called a quadratic programming problem and is solved using a computer.

- Besides the constraints that individual asset weights sum to 1, other constraints on asset weights may be added that may change the shape of the minimum-variance frontier. One of the most common of such constraints specifies that the individual asset weights must be greater than or equal to 0; this is a constraint against short sales.

- A problem with standard mean–variance optimization is that small changes in inputs frequently lead to large changes in the weights of portfolios that appear on the minimum-variance frontier. This is the problem of instability. The problem of instability is practically important because the inputs to mean–variance optimization are often based on sample statistics, which are subject to random variation.

- Relatedly, the minimum-variance frontier is not stable over time. Besides the random variation in means, variances, and covariance, shifts in the distribution of asset returns between sample time periods can give rise to this time instability of the minimum-variance frontier.

- With $\overline{\sigma}^2$ the average variance of returns and $\overline{\text{Cov}}$ the average covariance between stocks, the variance of an equally weighted portfolio is

$$\sigma_p^2 = \frac{1}{n}\overline{\sigma}^2 + \frac{n-1}{n}\overline{\text{Cov}}$$

It follows from this expression that as the number of assets held in the portfolio increases, the variance of the portfolio approaches the average covariance, $\overline{\text{Cov}}$. For large portfolios, average covariance tends to be more important than average variance, which captures only the individual volatility of asset returns.

- If we now assume that all stocks have the same standard deviation of return, σ, and correlation, ρ, then we can express an equally weighted portfolio's variance of return as $\sigma_p^2 = \sigma^2\left[\dfrac{1-\rho}{n} + \rho\right]$, which highlights the impact of return correlation and number of assets held on portfolio variance of return.

- For realistic values for the assumed common correlation between stock returns, portfolio variance of return initially drops rapidly as we add securities to the portfolio, all else equal.

- The introduction of a risk-free asset into the portfolio selection problem results in the efficient frontier having a linear portion that is tangent to the efficient frontier defined only using risky assets. This line is called the capital allocation line (CAL).

- Portfolios on the CAL represent combinations of the risk-free asset and the tangency portfolio.

- The CAL relates the expected return on an efficient portfolio to its standard deviation of return (given the existence of a risk-free rate of return).

- The equation of the capital allocation line is

$$E(R_p) = R_F + \frac{E(R_T) - R_F}{\sigma_T}\sigma_p$$

where

$$E(R_p) = \text{the expected return of a portfolio lying on the CAL}$$
$$R_F = \text{the risk-free rate}$$
$$\sigma_T = \text{the standard deviation of return on the tangency portfolio}$$
$$\sigma_p = \text{the standard deviation of return on a portfolio}$$

- The market portfolio is the portfolio of all risky assets, in which the weight of each asset is its capitalization weight, equal to (Market value of asset)/ (Total market value of all assets).

- When the tangency portfolio is the market portfolio of risky assets, the capital allocation line is called the capital market line (CML).

- The equation of the CML is

$$E(R_p) = R_F + \frac{E(R_M) - R_F}{\sigma_M} \sigma_p$$

where

$$E(R_p) = \text{the expected return of a portfolio lying on the CAL}$$
$$R_F = \text{the risk-free rate}$$
$$\sigma_M = \text{the standard deviation of return on the tangency portfolio}$$
$$\sigma_p = \text{the standard deviation of return on a portfolio}$$

- Given the existence of a risk-free rate of return, the CML relates the expected return on an efficient portfolio to its standard deviation of return, assuming that the tangency portfolio is the market portfolio of risky assets.

- The slope of the CML, $\dfrac{E(R_M) - R_F}{\sigma_M}$, is called the market price of risk because it indicates the market risk premium per unit of market risk.

- The capital asset pricing model (CAPM) is an equation describing the expected return on an asset or portfolio (whether efficient or not), as a linear function of its beta.

- Beta is a measure of the sensitivity of an asset's returns to the return on the market portfolio.

- According to the CAPM,
    - The market portfolio of all risky assets is an efficient portfolio (the tangency portfolio in the CML).
    - All investors hold some combination of the market portfolio and the risk-free asset.
    - The CAPM describes the expected return on assets.

- If the market portfolio is efficient, the CAPM holds, and vice versa.

- The CAPM equation is

$$E(R_i) = R_F + \beta_i[E(R_M) - R_F]$$

where

$$E(R_i) = \text{the expected return on asset } i$$
$$R_F = \text{the risk-free rate of return}$$
$$E(R_M) = \text{the expected return on the market portfolio}$$
$$\beta_i = \text{Cov}(R_i, R_M)/\sigma_M^2, \text{ called beta.}$$

- The CAPM implies that the expected excess rate of return on an asset is directly proportional to its covariance with the market return. The implication is that investors are rewarded for bearing systematic risk (market-related risk) but not for bearing diversifiable risk.

- The CAPM describes a financial market equilibrium, in the sense that if the model is correct and any asset's expected return differs from its expected return as given by the CAPM, market forces will come into play to restore the relationships specified by the model.

- The graph of the CAPM is the security market line (SML).

- The beta on the market is 1. Assets with betas greater than 1 have greater-than-average market risk. Assets with betas less than 1 have lower-than-average market risk.

- The beta on a portfolio is a weighted average of the betas on the individual assets, where the weight on each asset is the fraction of the portfolio invested in that asset.

- To trace out the minimum-variance frontier with n assets, we need n expected returns, n variances, and $n(n - 1)/2$ covariances. For realistic values of n for individual assets, the number of parameters that need to be estimated is very large, owing largely to the number of covariances needed.

- The market model explains the return on a risky asset as a linear regression with the return on the market as the independent variable.

- The market model equation is

$$R_i = \alpha_i + \beta_i R_M + \epsilon_i$$

where

R_i = the return to asset i
R_M = the return to the market portfolio
α_i = average return to asset i that is not related to the market return
β_i = the effect of the return on the market to asset i
ϵ_i = an error term

We assume that the error term has a mean of zero, that the error term is uncorrelated with the market return, and that the error term is uncorrelated across assets.

- According to the market model,

$$\text{Var}(R_i) = \beta_i^2 \sigma_M^2 + \sigma_{\epsilon_i}^2 \text{ and } \text{Cov}(R_i, R_j) = \beta_i \beta_j \sigma_M^2$$

- We can use the expression for covariance from the market model to greatly simplify the calculational task of estimating the covariances needed to trace out the minimum-variance frontier.

- Using the parameters of the market model, we can express the correlation between the returns on two assets as

$$\text{Corr}(R_1, R_2) = \frac{\beta_1 \beta_2 \sigma_M^2}{(\beta_1^2 \sigma_M^2 + \sigma_{\epsilon_1}^2)^{1/2} (\beta_2^2 \sigma_M^2 + \sigma_{\epsilon_2}^2)^{1/2}}$$

- Historical beta is beta estimated from past returns on the asset and a market index.

- Historical betas tend, on average, to revert to the market average level of 1.

- Adjusted beta is a historical beta adjusted to reflect the tendency of beta to be mean reverting. For example, one common adjustment is

  Adjusted Beta = 0.33 + 0.67 Historical Beta.

- An adjusted beta tends to be a better predictor of future beta than does historical beta.
- Multifactor models describe the return on an asset in terms of the risk of the asset with respect to a set of factors.
- Multifactor models are categorized as macroeconomic factor models, fundamental factor models, and statistical factor models, according to the type of factor used.
- In macroeconomic factor models, the factors are surprises in macroeconomic variables that significantly explain equity returns. The factors can be understood as affecting either the expected future cash flows of companies or the interest rate used to discount these cash flows back to the present.
- In fundamental factor models, the factors are attributes of stocks or companies that are important in explaining cross-sectional differences in stock prices. Among the fundamental factors that have been used are book value to price, market capitalization, price–earnings ratio, and financial leverage.
- In statistical factor models, statistical methods are applied to a set of historical returns to determine portfolios that explain historical returns in one of two senses. In factor analysis models, the factors are the portfolios that best explain (reproduce) historical return covariances. In principal-components models, the factors are portfolios that best explain (reproduce) the historical return variances.
- The equation for a multifactor model with K factors is

$$R_i = a_i + b_{i1}F_1 + b_{i2}F_2 + \ldots + b_{iK}F_K + \epsilon_i$$

where

R_i = the return to asset i
F_k = the surprise in the factor k, $k = 1, 2, \ldots, K$
a_i = the expected return to asset i
b_{ik} = the sensitivity of the return on asset i to the surprise in factor k, $k = 1, 2, \ldots, K$
ϵ_i = a mean-zero error term that represents the portion of the return to asset i not explained by the factor model

- The K factors are generally selected to represent systematic factors. Systematic factors (also called common factors) affect the long-run average returns of a large number of different assets.
- Systematic factors represent priced risk. Priced risk is risk for which investors require an additional expected return.
- Surprise is defined as actual minus forecasted value, and has an expected value of zero.
- Surprise represents the new information about a factor that moves asset prices, in contrast to information already built into or reflected in asset prices.
- The terms b_{ik} ($k = 1, 2, \ldots, K$) in the equation of a multifactor model are known as factor sensitivities.

- A portfolio's factor sensitivity on a factor i is a weighted average of the factor sensitivities to i for the individual investments in the portfolio, where a given weight is the proportion of the portfolio's market value that each investment represents.
- A factor portfolio (or pure factor portfolio) is a portfolio of securities that has a factor sensitivity of 1 on a specified factor, factor sensitivities of 0 on all other factors, and no company-specific risk.
- A factor portfolio is formed from linear combinations of well-diversified portfolios.
- A factor portfolio is a special case of a tracking portfolio.
- A tracking portfolio is a portfolio that has a desired configuration of factor sensitivities. The configuration matches the factor sensitivities of the investment that is tracked.
- Factor portfolios and tracking portfolios illustrate the use of multifactor models in hedging and managing risks.
- Arbitrage pricing theory (APT) describes the expected return on an asset (or portfolio) as a linear function of the risk of the asset with respect to a set of factors.
- Like the CAPM, the APT describes a financial market equilibrium, but the APT makes less-strong assumptions.
- The major assumptions of the APT are:
  - Asset returns are described by a factor model.
  - There are many assets, so asset-specific risk can be diversified away.
  - Assets are priced so that there are no arbitrage possibilities.

$$E(R_P) = \lambda_0 + \lambda_1 \beta_{p,1} + \ldots + \lambda_K \beta_{p,K}$$

where

$E(R_p)$ = the expected return to portfolio p
λ_0 = the risk-free rate
λ_j = the factor risk premium for factor j
$\beta_{p,j}$ = the sensitivity of the portfolio to factor j

- APT explains the intercept term, a_i, in the equation of a multifactor model.
- The factor risk premium for a factor j can be interpreted as the expected return on a pure factor portfolio for factor j minus the risk-free rate.
- If expected returns do not conform to the APT, investors will form arbitrage portfolios to exploit the pricing discrepancy. Such actions should restore equilibrium relationships among expected returns.
- An arbitrage portfolio is a portfolio that has no factor risk (factor sensitivities are all 0) and that requires zero net investment (achieved by using the proceeds from short sales to establish the long positions in the arbitrage portfolio).
- If the expected return on an arbitrage portfolio is not 0, there is an opportunity to earn a profit without putting up any money or assuming any factor risk. The formation of arbitrage portfolios is the mechanism by which equilibrium relationships among expected returns are restored.
- Multifactor models permit a nuanced view of risk that may contrast with a single-factor perspective. From a CAPM perspective, investors should allocate their money between the risk-free asset and a broad-based index fund. With multiple sources of systematic risk, when an investor's factor risk exposures to other sources of income

and risk aversion differ from the average investor's, a tilt away from an indexed investment may be optimal.

- Multifactor models are widely used in portfolio performance attribution. In this role, a multifactor model can help identify the bets placed by a portfolio manager in achieving his or her results.

PROBLEMS

1. Given the large-cap stock index and the bond index data in the following table, calculate the expected mean return and standard deviation of return for a portfolio 75 percent invested in the stock index and 25 percent invested in the bond index.

Assumed Returns, Variances, and Correlation

	Large-Cap Stock Index	Government Bonds
Expected return (%)	15	5
Variance	225	100
Standard deviation (%)	15	10
Correlation	0.5	

For Problems 2 and 3, assume the following:

- Each stock has the same variance of return, denoted σ^2;
- The correlation between all pairs of stocks is the same, ρ; and
- Stocks are equally weighted.

2. Suppose 0.3 is the common correlation of returns between any two stocks in a portfolio containing 100 stocks. Also, suppose the average variance of stocks in the portfolio is 625 (corresponding to a standard deviation of return of 25 percent). Calculate the portfolio standard deviation of return.

3. Suppose the average variance of return of all stocks in a portfolio is 625 and the correlation between the returns of any two stocks is 0.3. Calculate the variance of return of an equally weighted portfolio of 24 stocks. Then state that variance as a percent of the variance achievable given an unlimited number of stocks, holding variance and correlation constant.

4. Suppose the risk-free rate is 5 percent and a second asset has an expected return of 13 percent with a standard deviation of 23 percent. Calculate the expected portfolio return and standard deviation of a portfolio consisting 10 percent of the risk-free asset and 90 percent of the second asset.

5. Suppose you have a $100,000 investment in an S&P 500 Index fund. You then replace 10 percent of your investment in the index fund with an investment in a stock having a beta of 2. Why is it not possible for your new portfolio, consisting of the index fund and the stock, to have a lower standard deviation of return than the original portfolio?

6. Suppose that the risk-free rate is 6 percent and the expected return on the investor's tangent portfolio is 14 percent, with a standard deviation of 24 percent.
   a. Calculate the investor's expected risk premium per extra unit of risk.
   b. Calculate the portfolio's expected return if the portfolio's standard deviation of return is 20 percent.

7. Suppose that the risk-free rate is 5 percent and the expected return on the market portfolio of risky assets is 13 percent. An investor with $1 million to invest wants to achieve a 17 percent rate of return on a portfolio combining the risk-free asset and the market portfolio of risky assets. Calculate how much this investor would need to borrow at the risk-free rate in order to establish this target expected return.

8. Two assets have betas of 1.5 and 1.2, respectively. The residual standard deviation from the market model is 2 for the first asset, and 4 for the second. The standard deviation of the market is given as 8. What is the correlation between the two assets?

9. Suppose that the best predictor for the future beta of a stock is determined to be Expected beta = 0.33 + 0.67(Historical beta). The historical beta is calculated as 1.2. The risk-free rate is 5 percent and the market risk premium is 8.5 percent. Calculate the expected return on the stock using expected (adjusted) beta in the capital asset pricing model.

10. Suppose that the expected return on the stock in the following table is 11 percent. Using a two-factor model, calculate the return on the stock if the company-specific surprise for the year is 3 percent.

Variable	Actual Value	Expected Value	Stock's Factor Beta
Change in interest rate	2.0%	0.0%	−1.5
Growth in GDP	1.0%	4.0%	2.0

11. A portfolio manager plans to create a portfolio from two stocks, Manumatic (MANM) and Nextech (NXT). The following equations describe the returns for those stocks:

$$R_{\text{MANM}} = 0.09 - 1F_{\text{INFL}} + 1F_{\text{GDP}} + \epsilon_{\text{MANM}}$$
$$R_{\text{NXT}} = 0.12 + 2F_{\text{INFL}} + 4F_{\text{GDP}} + \epsilon_{\text{NXT}}$$

You form a portfolio with market value weights of 50 percent Manumatic and 50 percent Nextech. Calculate the sensitivity of the portfolio to a 1 percent surprise in inflation.

12. Suppose we have the three portfolios with factor sensitivities given in the table below. Using the information in the following table, create an arbitrage portfolio using a short position in A and B and a long position in C. Calculate the expected cash flow on the arbitrage portfolio for a $10,000 investment in C.

Expected Returns and Factor Sensitivities (One-Factor Model)

Portfolio	Expected Return	Factor Sensitivity
A	0.1500	2.00
B	0.0700	0.40
C	0.0800	0.45

13. The expected returns and betas, as defined in the capital asset pricing model, are given in the table below. The question you want to address is whether the expected returns on Portfolios B, C, and D are consistent with the CAPM. Demonstrate that they are consistent by showing that a zero-beta, zero net investment portfolio long D and short B and C has an expected return of 0.

Portfolios and the CAPM

Portfolio	CAPM Beta	Expected Return
A	0.50	0.0750
B	1.5	0.1250
C	0.40	0.0700
D	0.60	0.0800

14. Suppose that an institution holds Portfolio K. The institution wants to use Portfolio L to hedge its exposure to inflation. Specifically, it wants to combine K and L to reduce exposure to the inflation factor to 0. Portfolios K and L are well-diversified, so the manager can ignore the risk of individual assets and assume that the only source of uncertainty in the portfolio is the surprises in the two factors. The returns to the two portfolios are

$$R_K = 0.12 + 0.5_{INFL} + 1.0F_{GDP}$$
$$R_L = 0.11 + 1.5F_{INFL} + 2.5F_{GDP}$$

Calculate the weights that a manager should have on K and L to achieve this goal.

15. Portfolio A has an expected return of 10.25 percent and a factor sensitivity of 0.5. Portfolio B has an expected return of 16.2 percent and a factor sensitivity of 1.2. The risk-free rate is 6 percent, and there is one factor. Determine the price of risk for the factor.

16. A portfolio manager uses the multifactor model shown in the following table:

Risk Factor	Portfolio A Factor Sensitivity	Portfolio B Factor Sensitivity	S&P 500 Factor Sensitivity	Portfolio A Excess Factor Sensitivity
Confidence risk	0.27	0.27	0.27	0.00
Time horizon risk	0.56	0.56	0.56	0.00
Inflation risk	−0.12	−0.45	−0.37	0.25
Business-cycle risk	2.25	1.0	1.71	0.54
Market-timing risk	1.00	1.00	1.00	0.00

The S&P 500 is the benchmark portfolio for Portfolios A and B. Calculate the weights the manager would put on Portfolios A and B in order to remove excess business-cycle factor sensitivity (relative to the business-cycle sensitivity of the S&P 500). Then calculate the inflation factor sensitivity of the resulting portfolio.

17. A wealthy investor has no other source of income beyond her investments. Her investment advisor recommends that she tilt her portfolio to cyclical stocks and high-yield bonds. Her advisor maintains that the average investor holds a job and is recession sensitive. Explain the advisor's advice.

SOLUTIONS

1. The expected return is $0.75 \times E(\text{return on stocks}) + 0.25 \times E(\text{return on bonds})$

$$= 0.75 \times 15 + 0.25 \times 5$$
$$= 12.5 \text{ percent}$$

The standard deviation is

$$\sigma = (w_{stocks}^2 \sigma_{stocks}^2 + w_{bonds}^2 \sigma_{bonds}^2 + 2w_{stocks}w_{bonds}\text{Corr}(R_{stocks},R_{bonds})\sigma_{stocks}\sigma_{bonds})^{1/2}$$
$$= (0.75^2 \times 225 + 0.25^2 \times 100 + 2 \times 0.75 \times 0.25 \times 0.5 \times 15 \times 10)^{1/2}$$
$$= (126.5625 + 6.25 + 28.125)^{1/2}$$
$$= (160.9375)^{1/2}$$
$$= 12.69 \text{ percent}$$

2. We use the expression

$$\sigma_p^2 = \sigma^2\left[\frac{1-\rho}{n} + \rho\right]$$

The square root of this expression is standard deviation.
With variance equal to 625 and correlation equal to 0.3,

$$\sigma_p = \sqrt{625 \times \left[\frac{(1-0.3)}{100} + 0.3\right]}$$
$$= 13.85 \text{ percent}$$

3. We find portfolio variance using the following expression

$$\sigma_p^2 = \sigma^2\left[\frac{1-\rho}{n} + \rho\right]$$

$$\sigma_p^2 = 625[(1-0.3)/24 + 0.3] = 205.73$$

With 24 stocks, variance of return is 205.73 (equivalent to a standard deviation of 14.34 percent). With an unlimited number of securities, the first term in square brackets is 0 and the smallest variance is achieved:

$$\sigma_{min}^2 = \sigma^2 \times \rho = 625 \times 0.30 = 187.5$$

This result is equivalent to a standard deviation of 13.69 percent. The ratio of the variance of the 24-stock portfolio to the portfolio with an unlimited number of securities is

$$\frac{\sigma_p^2}{\sigma_{min}^2} = \frac{205.73}{187.5} = 1.097, \text{ or approximately } 110\%$$

The variance of the 24-stock portfolio is approximately 110 percent of the variance of the portfolio with an unlimited number of securities.

4. Define

R_p = return on the portfolio
R_1 = return on the risk-free asset
R_2 = return on the risky asset
w_1 = fraction of the portfolio invested in the risk-free asset
w_2 = fraction of the portfolio invested in the risky asset

Then the expected return on the portfolio is

$$E(R_p) = w_1 E(R_1) + w_2 E(R_2) = 0.10 \times 5\% + 0.9 \times 13\%$$
$$= 0.5 + 11.7 = 12.2\%$$

To calculate standard deviation of return, we calculate variance of return and take the square root of variance:

$$\sigma^2(R_P) = w_1^2 \, \sigma^2(R_1) + w_2^2 \, \sigma^2(R_2) + 2w_1 w_2 \text{Cov}(R_1, R_2)$$
$$= 0.1^2 \times 0^2 + 0.9^2 \times 23^2 + 2 \times 0.1 \times 0.9 \times 0$$
$$= 0.9^2 \times 23^2$$
$$= 428.49$$

Thus, portfolio standard deviation of return is $\sigma(R_P) = (428.49)^{1/2} = 20.7$ percent.

5. The total risk of a portfolio (variance of return) is the sum of systematic risk and diversifiable risk. Because an S&P 500 index fund is very well diversified, the initial portfolio has almost no diversifiable risk: The risk of the index fund is almost exclusively systematic risk. By replacing 10 percent of the initial portfolio with a single stock, we are adding both systematic and diversifiable risk. The systematic risk of the new stock (and hence the new portfolio) is higher than the systematic risk of the original portfolio. By itself, the additional systematic risk would increase total risk and so standard deviation of return. In addition, we are adding to the diversifiable risk of the portfolio by liquidating part of the original portfolio and investing it in a single stock.

6. a. With R_T the return on the tangency portfolio and R_F the risk-free rate

$$\text{Expected risk premium per unit of risk} = \frac{E(R_T) - R_F}{\sigma(R_T)} = \frac{14 - 6}{24} = 0.33$$

b. First, we find the weight w of the tangency portfolio in the investor's portfolio using the expression $\sigma^2(R_P) = w^2 \, \sigma^2(R_T)$, which reflects the fact the return risk-free asset is nonrandom and so has zero variance of return and zero correlation with the return on the tangency portfolio. Because $\sigma^2(R_P) = 20^2 = 400$,

$$400 = w^2 \times 24^2 = w^2 \times 24^2$$
$$\text{so } w = (400/576)^{1/2} = 0.833333$$

Then,

$$E(R_p) = wE(R_T) + (1 - w)R_F$$
$$= 0.833333 \times 14\% + 0.166667 \times 6\% = 12.67\%$$

7.   With R_m the return on the market portfolio, and all the other terms as defined in previous answers, we have

$$E(R_p) = wE(R_m) + (1 - w)R_F$$
$$17\% = w \times 13 + (1 - w) \times 5 = (8 \times w) - 5\%$$
$$12\% = (8 \times w)$$
$$w = 1.5$$

Thus $1 - 1.5 = -0.5$ of initial wealth goes into the risk-free asset. The negative sign indicates borrowing. We have $-0.5 \times \$1$ million $= -\$500,000$. The investor borrows \$500,000.

8.   We start from the definition of correlation (first line below). In the numerator, we substitute for covariance using Equation 11-13; in the denominator we use Equation 11-12 to substitute the standard deviations of return.

$$\text{Corr } (R_1, R_2) = \frac{\text{Cov}(R_1, R_2)}{\sigma_1 \times \sigma_2}$$

$$= \frac{\beta_1 \beta_2 \sigma_m^2}{\sqrt{\beta_1^2 \sigma_m^2 + \sigma_\epsilon^2} \sqrt{\beta_2^2 \sigma_m^2 + \sigma_\epsilon^2}}$$

$$= \frac{1.5 \times 1.2 \times 8^2}{\sqrt{1.5^2 \times 8^2 + 2^2} \sqrt{1.2^2 \times 8^2 + 4^2}}$$

$$= 0.91$$

9. $\beta_{adj} = 0.33 + (0.67 \times 1.2)$
      $= 0.33 + 0.80$
      $= 1.13$

$$E(R_p) = E(R_i) = R_F + \beta_i[E(R_M) - R_F]$$
$$= 5\% + 1.13 \times 8.5\%$$
$$= 14.6\%$$

10.   The surprise in a factor is actual value minus expected value. For the interest rate factor, the surprise was 2 percent; for the GDP factor, the surprise was -3 percent.

$$R = \text{expected return} - 1.5 \times (\text{interest rate surprise}) + 2 \times (\text{GDP surprise})$$
$$+ \text{company-specific surprise}$$
$$R = 11\% - 1.5 \times 2\% + 2 \times (-3\%) + 3\%$$
$$= 5\%$$

11.   Factor sensitivity is the portfolio weight on Manumatic stock multiplied by its inflation sensitivity, plus the portfolio weight on Nextech stock multiplied by its inflation sensitivity: $0.5 \times (-1) + 0.5 \times 2 = 0.5$. So a 1 percent interest rate surprise increase in inflation is expected to produce a 50 basis point increase in the portfolio's return.

12.   The arbitrage portfolio must have a zero sensitivity to the factor. We first need to find the proportions of A and B in the short position that combine to produce a factor sensitivity equal to 0.45, the factor sensitivity of C, which we will hold long. Using w as the weight on A in the short position,

$$w \times 2 + (1 - w)\,0.4 = 0.45$$
$$2w + 0.4 - 0.4w = 0.45$$
$$1.6w = 0.05$$
$$w = 0.05/1.6 = 0.03125$$

Hence, the weights on A and B are -0.03125 and -0.96875, respectively. These sum to -1. The arbitrage portfolio has zero net investment. The weight on C in the arbitrage portfolio must be 1, so that combined with the short position, the net investment is 0. The expected return on the arbitrage portfolio is $1 \times 0.08 - 0.03125 \times 0.15 - 0.96875 \times 0.07 = 0.08 - 0.0725 = 0.0075$ or 0.75%. For $\$10,000$ invested in C, this represents a $\$10,000 \times 0.0075 = \$75$ arbitrage profit.

13.   Because the beta of the arbitrage portfolio is 0, using w as the weight of portfolio B in the arbitrage portfolio

$$0 = 1.0 \times \beta_D - w \times \beta_B - (1 - w) \times \beta_C$$
$$= 0.6 - w \times 1.5 - (1 - w) \times 0.4$$

or

$$1.5w + 0.4 - 0.4w = 0.6$$
$$1.1w = 0.2$$
$$w = 0.2/1.1 = 0.181818$$
$$1 - w = 0.818182$$

Now we show that the expected return on this zero-beta portfolio is 0:

$$E(R_p) = E(R_D) - wE(R_B) - (1 - w)E(R_C)$$
$$E(R_p) = 0.08 - 0.181818 \times 0.125 - 0.818182 \times 0.07$$
$$E(R_p) = 0$$

Hence, eliminating beta risk leads to a 0 percent expected return. The CAPM beta correctly prices the assets.

14.   We need to combine Portfolios K and L in such a way that sensitivity to the inflation factor is zero. The inflation sensitivity of Portfolios K and L is 0.5 and 1.5, respectively. With w the weight on Portfolio L, we have

$$0 = 0.5(1 - w) \times 0.5 + w \times 1.5$$
$$0 = 0.5 - (w \times 0.5) + (w \times 1.5)$$
$$0 = 0.5 + (w \times 1)$$
$$w = -0.5$$

The weight on Portfolio L in the new portfolio is -0.5, and the weight on Portfolio K is 1.5 $(-0.5 + 1.5 = 1)$. For every $\$1.50$ invested in Portfolio K, the institution shorts $\$0.50$ of Portfolio L. The new portfolio's return is

$$R = 0.125 + 0.25F_{GDP}$$

The intercept is computed as $(1.50 \times 0.12) + (-0.5 \times 0.11) = 0.125$, and the sensitivity to the GDP factor is computed as $(1.50 \times 1.0) + (-0.5 \times 2.5) = 0.25$.

15. $E(R_A) = 6 + 0.5 \times \lambda = 10.25$
$E(R_B) = 6 + 1.2\lambda = 16.2$
Using either equation, we can calculate the price of factor risk as

$$\lambda = \frac{10.25 - 6}{0.5} = \frac{16.2 - 6}{1.2} = 8.5$$

The risk premium for each unit of factor risk, or price of risk, is 8.5 percent.

16. With w the weight on Portfolio A, $(1 - w)$ the weight on Portfolio B, and 1.71 the sensitivity of the S&P 500 to the business-cycle factor, we have

$$2.25 \times w + 1.00(1 - w) = 1.71$$
$$2.25 \times w + 1 - w = 1.71$$
$$1.25 \times w = 0.71$$

Thus,

$w = 0.568$, weight on Portfolio A
$1 - w = 0.432$, weight on Portfolio B

With a weight of 0.568 on A and 0.432 on B, the resulting inflation factor sensitivity would be $0.568(-0.12) + 0.432(-0.45) = -0.263$.

17. If the average investor has income from employment, then this income makes this investor recession-sensitive. Hence, the average investor requires a risk premium to hold securities that are sensitive to recessions. This need for a risk premium for these stocks by the average investor influences the price of these securities. Cyclical stocks and high-yield bonds are both very sensitive to economic conditions. For example, the debt-paying ability of high-yield bond issuers is strongly affected by recessions. The wealthy investor with no labor income can take the recession risk for which she would receive a premium (pays a lower price than would be the case if the average investor were not recession-sensitive). The high-wealth investor can afford to take the risk, because she does not face recession risk from labor income.

APPENDICES

Appendix A   Cumulative Probabilities for a Standard Normal Distribution
$P(Z \leq x) = N(x)$ for $x \geq 0$ or $P(Z \leq z) = N(z)$ for $z \geq 0$

x or z	0	0.01	0.02	0.03	0.04	0.05	0.06	0.07	0.08	0.09
0.00	0.5000	0.5040	0.5080	0.5120	0.5160	0.5199	0.5239	0.5279	0.5319	0.5359
0.10	0.5398	0.5438	0.5478	0.5517	0.5557	0.5596	0.5636	0.5675	0.5714	0.5753
0.20	0.5793	0.5832	0.5871	0.5910	0.5948	0.5987	0.6026	0.6064	0.6103	0.6141
0.30	0.6179	0.6217	0.6255	0.6293	0.6331	0.6368	0.6406	0.6443	0.6480	0.6517
0.40	0.6554	0.6591	0.6628	0.6664	0.6700	0.6736	0.6772	0.6808	0.6844	0.6879
0.50	0.6915	0.6950	0.6985	0.7019	0.7054	0.7088	0.7123	0.7157	0.7190	0.7224
0.60	0.7257	0.7291	0.7324	0.7357	0.7389	0.7422	0.7454	0.7486	0.7517	0.7549
0.70	0.7580	0.7611	0.7642	0.7673	0.7704	0.7734	0.7764	0.7794	0.7823	0.7852
0.80	0.7881	0.7910	0.7939	0.7967	0.7995	0.8023	0.8051	0.8078	0.8106	0.8133
0.90	0.8159	0.8186	0.8212	0.8238	0.8264	0.8289	0.8315	0.8340	0.8365	0.8389
1.00	0.8413	0.8438	0.8461	0.8485	0.8508	0.8531	0.8554	0.8577	0.8599	0.8621
1.10	0.8643	0.8665	0.8686	0.8708	0.8729	0.8749	0.8770	0.8790	0.8810	0.8830
1.20	0.8849	0.8869	0.8888	0.8907	0.8925	0.8944	0.8962	0.8980	0.8997	0.9015
1.30	0.9032	0.9049	0.9066	0.9082	0.9099	0.9115	0.9131	0.9147	0.9162	0.9177
1.40	0.9192	0.9207	0.9222	0.9236	0.9251	0.9265	0.9279	0.9292	0.9306	0.9319
1.50	0.9332	0.9345	0.9357	0.9370	0.9382	0.9394	0.9406	0.9418	0.9429	0.9441
1.60	0.9452	0.9463	0.9474	0.9484	0.9495	0.9505	0.9515	0.9525	0.9535	0.9545
1.70	0.9554	0.9564	0.9573	0.9582	0.9591	0.9599	0.9608	0.9616	0.9625	0.9633
1.80	0.9641	0.9649	0.9656	0.9664	0.9671	0.9678	0.9686	0.9693	0.9699	0.9706
1.90	0.9713	0.9719	0.9726	0.9732	0.9738	0.9744	0.9750	0.9756	0.9761	0.9767
2.00	0.9772	0.9778	0.9783	0.9788	0.9793	0.9798	0.9803	0.9808	0.9812	0.9817
2.10	0.9821	0.9826	0.9830	0.9834	0.9838	0.9842	0.9846	0.9850	0.9854	0.9857
2.20	0.9861	0.9864	0.9868	0.9871	0.9875	0.9878	0.9881	0.9884	0.9887	0.9890
2.30	0.9893	0.9896	0.9898	0.9901	0.9904	0.9906	0.9909	0.9911	0.9913	0.9916
2.40	0.9918	0.9920	0.9922	0.9925	0.9927	0.9929	0.9931	0.9932	0.9934	0.9936
2.50	0.9938	0.9940	0.9941	0.9943	0.9945	0.9946	0.9948	0.9949	0.9951	0.9952
2.60	0.9953	0.9955	0.9956	0.9957	0.9959	0.9960	0.9961	0.9962	0.9963	0.9964
2.70	0.9965	0.9966	0.9967	0.9968	0.9969	0.9970	0.9971	0.9972	0.9973	0.9974
2.80	0.9974	0.9975	0.9976	0.9977	0.9977	0.9978	0.9979	0.9979	0.9980	0.9981
2.90	0.9981	0.9982	0.9982	0.9983	0.9984	0.9984	0.9985	0.9985	0.9986	0.9986
3.00	0.9987	0.9987	0.9987	0.9988	0.9988	0.9989	0.9989	0.9989	0.9990	0.9990
3.10	0.9990	0.9991	0.9991	0.9991	0.9992	0.9992	0.9992	0.9992	0.9993	0.9993
3.20	0.9993	0.9993	0.9994	0.9994	0.9994	0.9994	0.9994	0.9995	0.9995	0.9995
3.30	0.9995	0.9995	0.9995	0.9996	0.9996	0.9996	0.9996	0.9996	0.9996	0.9997
3.40	0.9997	0.9997	0.9997	0.9997	0.9997	0.9997	0.9997	0.9997	0.9997	0.9998
3.50	0.9998	0.9998	0.9998	0.9998	0.9998	0.9998	0.9998	0.9998	0.9998	0.9998
3.60	0.9998	0.9998	0.9999	0.9999	0.9999	0.9999	0.9999	0.9999	0.9999	0.9999
3.70	0.9999	0.9999	0.9999	0.9999	0.9999	0.9999	0.9999	0.9999	0.9999	0.9999
3.80	0.9999	0.9999	0.9999	0.9999	0.9999	0.9999	0.9999	0.9999	0.9999	0.9999
3.90	1.0000	1.0000	1.0000	1.0000	1.0000	1.0000	1.0000	1.0000	1.0000	1.0000
4.00	1.0000	1.0000	1.0000	1.0000	1.0000	1.0000	1.0000	1.0000	1.0000	1.0000

For example, to find the z-value leaving 2.5 percent of the area/probability in the upper tail, find the element 0.9750 in the body of the table. Read 1.90 at the left end of the element's row and 0.06 at the top of the element's column, to give $1.90 + 0.06 = 1.96$. *Table generated with Excel.*

Appendix A (continued)	Cumulative Probabilities for a Standard Normal Distribution $P(Z \le x) = N(x)$ for $x \le 0$ or $P(Z \le z) = N(z)$ for $z \le 0$								
x or z	0	0.01	0.02	0.03	0.04	0.05	0.06	0.07	0.08	0.09
0.00	0.5000	0.4960	0.4920	0.4880	0.4840	0.4801	0.4761	0.4721	0.4681	0.4641
−0.10	0.4602	0.4562	0.4522	0.4483	0.4443	0.4404	0.4364	0.4325	0.4286	0.4247
−0.20	0.4207	0.4168	0.4129	0.4090	0.4052	0.4013	0.3974	0.3936	0.3897	0.3859
−0.30	0.3821	0.3783	0.3745	0.3707	0.3669	0.3632	0.3594	0.3557	0.3520	0.3483
−0.40	0.3446	0.3409	0.3372	0.3336	0.3300	0.3264	0.3228	0.3192	0.3156	0.3121
−0.50	0.3085	0.3050	0.3015	0.2981	0.2946	0.2912	0.2877	0.2843	0.2810	0.2776
−0.60	0.2743	0.2709	0.2676	0.2643	0.2611	0.2578	0.2546	0.2514	0.2483	0.2451
−0.70	0.2420	0.2389	0.2358	0.2327	0.2296	0.2266	0.2236	0.2206	0.2177	0.2148
−0.80	0.2119	0.2090	0.2061	0.2033	0.2005	0.1977	0.1949	0.1922	0.1894	0.1867
−0.90	0.1841	0.1814	0.1788	0.1762	0.1736	0.1711	0.1685	0.1660	0.1635	0.1611
−1.00	0.1587	0.1562	0.1539	0.1515	0.1492	0.1469	0.1446	0.1423	0.1401	0.1379
−1.10	0.1357	0.1335	0.1314	0.1292	0.1271	0.1251	0.1230	0.1210	0.1190	0.1170
−1.20	0.1151	0.1131	0.1112	0.1093	0.1075	0.1056	0.1038	0.1020	0.1003	0.0985
−1.30	0.0968	0.0951	0.0934	0.0918	0.0901	0.0885	0.0869	0.0853	0.0838	0.0823
−1.40	0.0808	0.0793	0.0778	0.0764	0.0749	0.0735	0.0721	0.0708	0.0694	0.0681
−1.50	0.0668	0.0655	0.0643	0.0630	0.0618	0.0606	0.0594	0.0582	0.0571	0.0559
−1.60	0.0548	0.0537	0.0526	0.0516	0.0505	0.0495	0.0485	0.0475	0.0465	0.0455
−1.70	0.0446	0.0436	0.0427	0.0418	0.0409	0.0401	0.0392	0.0384	0.0375	0.0367
−1.80	0.0359	0.0351	0.0344	0.0336	0.0329	0.0322	0.0314	0.0307	0.0301	0.0294
−1.90	0.0287	0.0281	0.0274	0.0268	0.0262	0.0256	0.0250	0.0244	0.0239	0.0233
−2.00	0.0228	0.0222	0.0217	0.0212	0.0207	0.0202	0.0197	0.0192	0.0188	0.0183
−2.10	0.0179	0.0174	0.0170	0.0166	0.0162	0.0158	0.0154	0.0150	0.0146	0.0143
−2.20	0.0139	0.0136	0.0132	0.0129	0.0125	0.0122	0.0119	0.0116	0.0113	0.0110
−2.30	0.0107	0.0104	0.0102	0.0099	0.0096	0.0094	0.0091	0.0089	0.0087	0.0084
−2.40	0.0082	0.0080	0.0078	0.0075	0.0073	0.0071	0.0069	0.0068	0.0066	0.0064
−2.50	0.0062	0.0060	0.0059	0.0057	0.0055	0.0054	0.0052	0.0051	0.0049	0.0048
−2.60	0.0047	0.0045	0.0044	0.0043	0.0041	0.0040	0.0039	0.0038	0.0037	0.0036
−2.70	0.0035	0.0034	0.0033	0.0032	0.0031	0.0030	0.0029	0.0028	0.0027	0.0026
−2.80	0.0026	0.0025	0.0024	0.0023	0.0023	0.0022	0.0021	0.0021	0.0020	0.0019
−2.90	0.0019	0.0018	0.0018	0.0017	0.0016	0.0016	0.0015	0.0015	0.0014	0.0014
−3.00	0.0013	0.0013	0.0013	0.0012	0.0012	0.0011	0.0011	0.0011	0.0010	0.0010
−3.10	0.0010	0.0009	0.0009	0.0009	0.0008	0.0008	0.0008	0.0008	0.0007	0.0007
−3.20	0.0007	0.0007	0.0006	0.0006	0.0006	0.0006	0.0006	0.0005	0.0005	0.0005
−3.30	0.0005	0.0005	0.0005	0.0004	0.0004	0.0004	0.0004	0.0004	0.0004	0.0003
−3.40	0.0003	0.0003	0.0003	0.0003	0.0003	0.0003	0.0003	0.0003	0.0003	0.0002
−3.50	0.0002	0.0002	0.0002	0.0002	0.0002	0.0002	0.0002	0.0002	0.0002	0.0002
−3.60	0.0002	0.0002	0.0001	0.0001	0.0001	0.0001	0.0001	0.0001	0.0001	0.0001
−3.70	0.0001	0.0001	0.0001	0.0001	0.0001	0.0001	0.0001	0.0001	0.0001	0.0001
−3.80	0.0001	0.0001	0.0001	0.0001	0.0001	0.0001	0.0001	0.0001	0.0001	0.0001
−3.90	0.0000	0.0000	0.0000	0.0000	0.0000	0.0000	0.0000	0.0000	0.0000	0.0000
−4.00	0.0000	0.0000	0.0000	0.0000	0.0000	0.0000	0.0000	0.0000	0.0000	0.0000

For example, to find the z-value leaving 2.5 percent of the area/probability in the lower tail, find the element 0.0250 in the body of the table. Read −1.90 at the left end of the element's row and 0.06 at the top of the element's column, to give −1.90 − 0.06 = −1.96. *Table generated with Excel.*

Appendix B   Table of the Student's *t*-Distribution (One-Tailed Probabilities)

df	p = 0.10	p = 0.05	p = 0.025	p = 0.01	p = 0.005	df	p = 0.10	p = 0.05	p = 0.025	p = 0.01	p = 0.005
1	3.078	6.314	12.706	31.821	63.657	31	1.309	1.696	2.040	2.453	2.744
2	1.886	2.920	4.303	6.965	9.925	32	1.309	1.694	2.037	2.449	2.738
3	1.638	2.353	3.182	4.541	5.841	33	1.308	1.692	2.035	2.445	2.733
4	1.533	2.132	2.776	3.747	4.604	34	1.307	1.691	2.032	2.441	2.728
5	1.476	2.015	2.571	3.365	4.032	35	1.306	1.690	2.030	2.438	2.724
6	1.440	1.943	2.447	3.143	3.707	36	1.306	1.688	2.028	2.434	2.719
7	1.415	1.895	2.365	2.998	3.499	37	1.305	1.687	2.026	2.431	2.715
8	1.397	1.860	2.306	2.896	3.355	38	1.304	1.686	2.024	2.429	2.712
9	1.383	1.833	2.262	2.821	3.250	39	1.304	1.685	2.023	2.426	2.708
10	1.372	1.812	2.228	2.764	3.169	40	1.303	1.684	2.021	2.423	2.704
11	1.363	1.796	2.201	2.718	3.106	41	1.303	1.683	2.020	2.421	2.701
12	1.356	1.782	2.179	2.681	3.055	42	1.302	1.682	2.018	2.418	2.698
13	1.350	1.771	2.160	2.650	3.012	43	1.302	1.681	2.017	2.416	2.695
14	1.345	1.761	2.145	2.624	2.977	44	1.301	1.680	2.015	2.414	2.692
15	1.341	1.753	2.131	2.602	2.947	45	1.301	1.679	2.014	2.412	2.690
16	1.337	1.746	2.120	2.583	2.921	46	1.300	1.679	2.013	2.410	2.687
17	1.333	1.740	2.110	2.567	2.898	47	1.300	1.678	2.012	2.408	2.685
18	1.330	1.734	2.101	2.552	2.878	48	1.299	1.677	2.011	2.407	2.682
19	1.328	1.729	2.093	2.539	2.861	49	1.299	1.677	2.010	2.405	2.680
20	1.325	1.725	2.086	2.528	2.845	50	1.299	1.676	2.009	2.403	2.678
21	1.323	1.721	2.080	2.518	2.831	60	1.296	1.671	2.000	2.390	2.660
22	1.321	1.717	2.074	2.508	2.819	70	1.294	1.667	1.994	2.381	2.648
23	1.319	1.714	2.069	2.500	2.807	80	1.292	1.664	1.990	2.374	2.639
24	1.318	1.711	2.064	2.492	2.797	90	1.291	1.662	1.987	2.368	2.632
25	1.316	1.708	2.060	2.485	2.787	100	1.290	1.660	1.984	2.364	2.626
26	1.315	1.706	2.056	2.479	2.779	110	1.289	1.659	1.982	2.361	2.621
27	1.314	1.703	2.052	2.473	2.771	120	1.289	1.658	1.980	2.358	2.617
28	1.313	1.701	2.048	2.467	2.763	200	1.286	1.653	1.972	2.345	2.601
29	1.311	1.699	2.045	2.462	2.756	∞	1.282	1.645	1.960	2.326	2.576
30	1.310	1.697	2.042	2.457	2.750						

To find a critical *t*-value, enter the table with df and a specified value for α, the significance level. For example, with 5 df, $\alpha = 0.05$ and a one-tailed test, the desired probability in the tail would be $p = 0.05$ and the critical *t*-value would be $t(5, 0.05) = 2.015$. With $\alpha = 0.05$ and a two-tailed test, the desired probability in each tail would be $p = 0.025 = \alpha/2$, giving $t(0.025) = 2.571$. *Table generated using Excel.*

Appendix C   Values of χ^2 (Degrees of Freedom, Level of Significance)

Degrees of Freedom	Probability in Right Tail								
	0.99	0.975	0.95	0.9	0.1	0.05	0.025	0.01	0.005
1	0.000157	0.000982	0.003932	0.0158	2.706	3.841	5.024	6.635	7.879
2	0.020100	0.050636	0.102586	0.2107	4.605	5.991	7.378	9.210	10.597
3	0.1148	0.2158	0.3518	0.5844	6.251	7.815	9.348	11.345	12.838
4	0.297	0.484	0.711	1.064	7.779	9.488	11.143	13.277	14.860
5	0.554	0.831	1.145	1.610	9.236	11.070	12.832	15.086	16.750
6	0.872	1.237	1.635	2.204	10.645	12.592	14.449	16.812	18.548
7	1.239	1.690	2.167	2.833	12.017	14.067	16.013	18.475	20.278
8	1.647	2.180	2.733	3.490	13.362	15.507	17.535	20.090	21.955
9	2.088	2.700	3.325	4.168	14.684	16.919	19.023	21.666	23.589
10	2.558	3.247	3.940	4.865	15.987	18.307	20.483	23.209	25.188
11	3.053	3.816	4.575	5.578	17.275	19.675	21.920	24.725	26.757
12	3.571	4.404	5.226	6.304	18.549	21.026	23.337	26.217	28.300
13	4.107	5.009	5.892	7.041	19.812	22.362	24.736	27.688	29.819
14	4.660	5.629	6.571	7.790	21.064	23.685	26.119	29.141	31.319
15	5.229	6.262	7.261	8.547	22.307	24.996	27.488	30.578	32.801
16	5.812	6.908	7.962	9.312	23.542	26.296	28.845	32.000	34.267
17	6.408	7.564	8.672	10.085	24.769	27.587	30.191	33.409	35.718
18	7.015	8.231	9.390	10.865	25.989	28.869	31.526	34.805	37.156
19	7.633	8.907	10.117	11.651	27.204	30.144	32.852	36.191	38.582
20	8.260	9.591	10.851	12.443	28.412	31.410	34.170	37.566	39.997
21	8.897	10.283	11.591	13.240	29.615	32.671	35.479	38.932	41.401
22	9.542	10.982	12.338	14.041	30.813	33.924	36.781	40.289	42.796
23	10.196	11.689	13.091	14.848	32.007	35.172	38.076	41.638	44.181
24	10.856	12.401	13.848	15.659	33.196	36.415	39.364	42.980	45.558
25	11.524	13.120	14.611	16.473	34.382	37.652	40.646	44.314	46.928
26	12.198	13.844	15.379	17.292	35.563	38.885	41.923	45.642	48.290
27	12.878	14.573	16.151	18.114	36.741	40.113	43.195	46.963	49.645
28	13.565	15.308	16.928	18.939	37.916	41.337	44.461	48.278	50.994
29	14.256	16.047	17.708	19.768	39.087	42.557	45.722	49.588	52.335
30	14.953	16.791	18.493	20.599	40.256	43.773	46.979	50.892	53.672
50	29.707	32.357	34.764	37.689	63.167	67.505	71.420	76.154	79.490
60	37.485	40.482	43.188	46.459	74.397	79.082	83.298	88.379	91.952
80	53.540	57.153	60.391	64.278	96.578	101.879	106.629	112.329	116.321
100	70.065	74.222	77.929	82.358	118.498	124.342	129.561	135.807	140.170

To have a probability of 0.05 in the right tail when df = 5, the tabled value is $\chi^2(5, 0.05) = 11.070$.

Appendix D   Table of the F-Distribution

Panel A. Critical values for right-hand tail area equal to 0.05

Numerator: df_1 and Denominator: df_2

df1:	1	2	3	4	5	6	7	8	9	10	11	12	15	20	21	22	23	24	25	30	40	60	120	∞
df2: 1	161	200	216	225	230	234	237	239	241	242	243	244	246	248	248	249	249	249	249	250	251	252	253	254
2	18.5	19.0	19.2	19.2	19.3	19.3	19.4	19.4	19.4	19.4	19.4	19.4	19.4	19.4	19.4	19.5	19.5	19.5	19.5	19.5	19.5	19.5	19.5	19.5
3	10.1	9.55	9.28	9.12	9.01	8.94	8.89	8.85	8.81	8.79	8.76	8.74	8.70	8.66	8.65	8.65	8.64	8.64	8.63	8.62	8.59	8.57	8.55	8.53
4	7.71	6.94	6.59	6.39	6.26	6.16	6.09	6.04	6.00	5.96	5.94	5.91	5.86	5.80	5.79	5.79	5.78	5.77	5.77	5.75	5.72	5.69	5.66	5.63
5	6.61	5.79	5.41	5.19	5.05	4.95	4.88	4.82	4.77	4.74	4.70	4.68	4.62	4.56	4.55	4.54	4.53	4.53	4.52	4.50	4.46	4.43	4.40	4.37
6	5.99	5.14	4.76	4.53	4.39	4.28	4.21	4.15	4.10	4.06	4.03	4.00	3.94	3.87	3.86	3.86	3.85	3.84	3.83	3.81	3.77	3.74	3.70	3.67
7	5.59	4.74	4.35	4.12	3.97	3.87	3.79	3.73	3.68	3.64	3.60	3.57	3.51	3.44	3.43	3.43	3.42	3.41	3.40	3.38	3.34	3.30	3.27	3.23
8	5.32	4.46	4.07	3.84	3.69	3.58	3.50	3.44	3.39	3.35	3.31	3.28	3.22	3.15	3.14	3.13	3.12	3.12	3.11	3.08	3.04	3.01	2.97	2.93
9	5.12	4.26	3.86	3.63	3.48	3.37	3.29	3.23	3.18	3.14	3.10	3.07	3.01	2.94	2.93	2.92	2.91	2.90	2.89	2.86	2.83	2.79	2.75	2.71
10	4.96	4.10	3.71	3.48	3.33	3.22	3.14	3.07	3.02	2.98	2.94	2.91	2.85	2.77	2.76	2.75	2.75	2.74	2.73	2.70	2.66	2.62	2.58	2.54
11	4.84	3.98	3.59	3.36	3.20	3.09	3.01	2.95	2.90	2.85	2.82	2.79	2.72	2.65	2.64	2.63	2.62	2.61	2.60	2.57	2.53	2.49	2.45	2.40
12	4.75	3.89	3.49	3.26	3.11	3.00	2.91	2.85	2.80	2.75	2.72	2.69	2.62	2.54	2.53	2.52	2.51	2.51	2.50	2.47	2.43	2.38	2.34	2.30
13	4.67	3.81	3.41	3.18	3.03	2.92	2.83	2.77	2.71	2.67	2.63	2.60	2.53	2.46	2.45	2.44	2.43	2.42	2.41	2.38	2.34	2.30	2.25	2.21
14	4.60	3.74	3.34	3.11	2.96	2.85	2.76	2.70	2.65	2.60	2.57	2.53	2.46	2.39	2.38	2.37	2.36	2.35	2.34	2.31	2.27	2.22	2.18	2.13
15	4.54	3.68	3.29	3.06	2.90	2.79	2.71	2.64	2.59	2.54	2.51	2.48	2.40	2.33	2.32	2.31	2.30	2.29	2.28	2.25	2.20	2.16	2.11	2.07
16	4.49	3.63	3.24	3.01	2.85	2.74	2.66	2.59	2.54	2.49	2.46	2.42	2.35	2.28	2.26	2.25	2.24	2.24	2.23	2.19	2.15	2.11	2.06	2.01
17	4.45	3.59	3.20	2.96	2.81	2.70	2.61	2.55	2.49	2.45	2.41	2.38	2.31	2.23	2.22	2.21	2.20	2.19	2.18	2.15	2.10	2.06	2.01	1.96
18	4.41	3.55	3.16	2.93	2.77	2.66	2.58	2.51	2.46	2.41	2.37	2.34	2.27	2.19	2.18	2.17	2.16	2.15	2.14	2.11	2.06	2.02	1.97	1.92
19	4.38	3.52	3.13	2.90	2.74	2.63	2.54	2.48	2.42	2.38	2.34	2.31	2.23	2.16	2.14	2.13	2.12	2.11	2.11	2.07	2.03	1.98	1.93	1.88
20	4.35	3.49	3.10	2.87	2.71	2.60	2.51	2.45	2.39	2.35	2.31	2.28	2.20	2.12	2.11	2.10	2.09	2.08	2.07	2.04	1.99	1.95	1.90	1.84
21	4.32	3.47	3.07	2.84	2.68	2.57	2.49	2.42	2.37	2.32	2.28	2.25	2.18	2.10	2.08	2.07	2.06	2.05	2.05	2.01	1.96	1.92	1.87	1.81
22	4.30	3.44	3.05	2.82	2.66	2.55	2.46	2.40	2.34	2.30	2.26	2.23	2.15	2.07	2.06	2.05	2.04	2.03	2.02	1.98	1.94	1.89	1.84	1.78
23	4.28	3.42	3.03	2.80	2.64	2.53	2.44	2.37	2.32	2.27	2.24	2.20	2.13	2.05	2.04	2.02	2.01	2.01	2.00	1.96	1.91	1.86	1.81	1.76
24	4.26	3.40	3.01	2.78	2.62	2.51	2.42	2.36	2.30	2.25	2.22	2.18	2.11	2.03	2.01	2.00	1.99	1.98	1.97	1.94	1.89	1.84	1.79	1.73
25	4.24	3.39	2.99	2.76	2.60	2.49	2.40	2.34	2.28	2.24	2.20	2.16	2.09	2.01	2.00	1.98	1.97	1.96	1.96	1.92	1.87	1.82	1.77	1.71
30	4.17	3.32	2.92	2.69	2.53	2.42	2.33	2.27	2.21	2.16	2.13	2.09	2.01	1.93	1.92	1.91	1.90	1.89	1.88	1.84	1.79	1.74	1.68	1.62
40	4.08	3.23	2.84	2.61	2.45	2.34	2.25	2.18	2.12	2.08	2.04	2.00	1.92	1.84	1.83	1.81	1.80	1.79	1.78	1.74	1.69	1.64	1.58	1.51
60	4.00	3.15	2.76	2.53	2.37	2.25	2.17	2.10	2.04	1.99	1.95	1.92	1.84	1.75	1.73	1.72	1.71	1.70	1.69	1.65	1.59	1.53	1.47	1.39
120	3.92	3.07	2.68	2.45	2.29	2.18	2.09	2.02	1.96	1.91	1.87	1.83	1.75	1.66	1.64	1.63	1.62	1.61	1.60	1.55	1.50	1.43	1.35	1.25
Infinity	3.84	3.00	2.60	2.37	2.21	2.10	2.01	1.94	1.88	1.83	1.79	1.75	1.67	1.57	1.56	1.54	1.53	1.52	1.51	1.46	1.39	1.32	1.22	1.00

With 1 degree of freedom (df) in the numerator and 3 df in the denominator, the critical F-value is 10.1 for a right-hand tail area equal to 0.05.

Appendix D Table of the F-Distribution

Panel B. Critical values for right-hand tail area equal to 0.025

Numerator: df$_1$ and Denominator: df$_2$

df2: \ df1:	1	2	3	4	5	6	7	8	9	10	11	12	15	20	21	22	23	24	25	30	40	60	120	∞
1	648	799	864	900	922	937	948	957	963	969	973	977	985	993	994	995	996	997	998	1001	1006	1010	1014	1018
2	38.51	39.00	39.17	39.25	39.30	39.33	39.36	39.37	39.39	39.40	39.41	39.41	39.43	39.45	39.45	39.45	39.45	39.46	39.46	39.46	39.47	39.48	39.49	39.50
3	17.44	16.04	15.44	15.10	14.88	14.73	14.62	14.54	14.47	14.42	14.37	14.34	14.25	14.17	14.16	14.14	14.13	14.12	14.12	14.08	14.04	13.99	13.95	13.90
4	12.22	10.65	9.98	9.60	9.36	9.20	9.07	8.98	8.90	8.84	8.79	8.75	8.66	8.56	8.55	8.53	8.52	8.51	8.50	8.46	8.41	8.36	8.31	8.26
5	10.01	8.43	7.76	7.39	7.15	6.98	6.85	6.76	6.68	6.62	6.57	6.52	6.43	6.33	6.31	6.30	6.29	6.28	6.27	6.23	6.18	6.12	6.07	6.02
6	8.81	7.26	6.60	6.23	5.99	5.82	5.70	5.60	5.52	5.46	5.41	5.37	5.27	5.17	5.15	5.14	5.13	5.12	5.11	5.07	5.01	4.96	4.90	4.85
7	8.07	6.54	5.89	5.52	5.29	5.12	4.99	4.90	4.82	4.76	4.71	4.67	4.57	4.47	4.45	4.44	4.43	4.41	4.40	4.36	4.31	4.25	4.20	4.14
8	7.57	6.06	5.42	5.05	4.82	4.65	4.53	4.43	4.36	4.30	4.24	4.20	4.10	4.00	3.98	3.97	3.96	3.95	3.94	3.89	3.84	3.78	3.73	3.67
9	7.21	5.71	5.08	4.72	4.48	4.32	4.20	4.10	4.03	3.96	3.91	3.87	3.77	3.67	3.65	3.64	3.63	3.61	3.60	3.56	3.51	3.45	3.39	3.33
10	6.94	5.46	4.83	4.47	4.24	4.07	3.95	3.85	3.78	3.72	3.66	3.62	3.52	3.42	3.40	3.39	3.38	3.37	3.35	3.31	3.26	3.20	3.14	3.08
11	6.72	5.26	4.63	4.28	4.04	3.88	3.76	3.66	3.59	3.53	3.47	3.43	3.33	3.23	3.21	3.20	3.18	3.17	3.16	3.12	3.06	3.00	2.94	2.88
12	6.55	5.10	4.47	4.12	3.89	3.73	3.61	3.51	3.44	3.37	3.32	3.28	3.18	3.07	3.06	3.04	3.03	3.02	3.01	2.96	2.91	2.85	2.79	2.72
13	6.41	4.97	4.35	4.00	3.77	3.60	3.48	3.39	3.31	3.25	3.20	3.15	3.05	2.95	2.93	2.92	2.91	2.89	2.88	2.84	2.78	2.72	2.66	2.60
14	6.30	4.86	4.24	3.89	3.66	3.50	3.38	3.29	3.21	3.15	3.09	3.05	2.95	2.84	2.83	2.81	2.80	2.79	2.78	2.73	2.67	2.61	2.55	2.49
15	6.20	4.77	4.15	3.80	3.58	3.41	3.29	3.20	3.12	3.06	3.01	2.96	2.86	2.76	2.74	2.73	2.71	2.70	2.69	2.64	2.59	2.52	2.46	2.40
16	6.12	4.69	4.08	3.73	3.50	3.34	3.22	3.12	3.05	2.99	2.93	2.89	2.79	2.68	2.67	2.65	2.64	2.63	2.61	2.57	2.51	2.45	2.38	2.32
17	6.04	4.62	4.01	3.66	3.44	3.28	3.16	3.06	2.98	2.92	2.87	2.82	2.72	2.62	2.60	2.59	2.57	2.56	2.55	2.50	2.44	2.38	2.32	2.25
18	5.98	4.56	3.95	3.61	3.38	3.22	3.10	3.01	2.93	2.87	2.81	2.77	2.67	2.56	2.54	2.53	2.52	2.50	2.49	2.44	2.38	2.32	2.26	2.19
19	5.92	4.51	3.90	3.56	3.33	3.17	3.05	2.96	2.88	2.82	2.76	2.72	2.62	2.51	2.49	2.48	2.46	2.45	2.44	2.39	2.33	2.27	2.20	2.13
20	5.87	4.46	3.86	3.51	3.29	3.13	3.01	2.91	2.84	2.77	2.72	2.68	2.57	2.46	2.45	2.43	2.42	2.41	2.40	2.35	2.29	2.22	2.16	2.09
21	5.83	4.42	3.82	3.48	3.25	3.09	2.97	2.87	2.80	2.73	2.68	2.64	2.53	2.42	2.41	2.39	2.38	2.37	2.36	2.31	2.25	2.18	2.11	2.04
22	5.79	4.38	3.78	3.44	3.22	3.05	2.93	2.84	2.76	2.70	2.65	2.60	2.50	2.39	2.37	2.36	2.34	2.33	2.32	2.27	2.21	2.14	2.08	2.00
23	5.75	4.35	3.75	3.41	3.18	3.02	2.90	2.81	2.73	2.67	2.62	2.57	2.47	2.36	2.34	2.33	2.31	2.30	2.29	2.24	2.18	2.11	2.04	1.97
24	5.72	4.32	3.72	3.38	3.15	2.99	2.87	2.78	2.70	2.64	2.59	2.54	2.44	2.33	2.31	2.30	2.28	2.27	2.26	2.21	2.15	2.08	2.01	1.94
25	5.69	4.29	3.69	3.35	3.13	2.97	2.85	2.75	2.68	2.61	2.56	2.51	2.41	2.30	2.28	2.27	2.26	2.24	2.23	2.18	2.12	2.05	1.98	1.91
30	5.57	4.18	3.59	3.25	3.03	2.87	2.75	2.65	2.57	2.51	2.46	2.41	2.31	2.20	2.18	2.16	2.15	2.14	2.12	2.07	2.01	1.94	1.87	1.79
40	5.42	4.05	3.46	3.13	2.90	2.74	2.62	2.53	2.45	2.39	2.33	2.29	2.18	2.07	2.05	2.03	2.02	2.01	1.99	1.94	1.88	1.80	1.72	1.64
60	5.29	3.93	3.34	3.01	2.79	2.63	2.51	2.41	2.33	2.27	2.22	2.17	2.06	1.94	1.93	1.91	1.90	1.88	1.87	1.82	1.74	1.67	1.58	1.48
120	5.15	3.80	3.23	2.89	2.67	2.52	2.39	2.30	2.22	2.16	2.10	2.05	1.94	1.82	1.81	1.79	1.77	1.76	1.75	1.69	1.61	1.53	1.43	1.31
Infinity	5.02	3.69	3.12	2.79	2.57	2.41	2.29	2.19	2.11	2.05	1.99	1.94	1.83	1.71	1.69	1.67	1.66	1.64	1.63	1.57	1.48	1.39	1.27	1.00

Appendix D — Table of the F-Distribution

Panel C. Critical values for right-hand tail area equal to 0.01

Numerator: df_1 and Denominator: df_2

df_2 : df_1	1	2	3	4	5	6	7	8	9	10	11	12	15	20	21	22	23	24	25	30	40	60	120	∞
1	4052	5000	5403	5625	5764	5859	5928	5982	6023	6056	6083	6106	6157	6209	6216	6223	6229	6235	6240	6261	6287	6313	6339	6366
2	98.5	99.0	99.2	99.2	99.3	99.3	99.4	99.4	99.4	99.4	99.4	99.4	99.4	99.4	99.5	99.5	99.5	99.5	99.5	99.5	99.5	99.5	99.5	99.5
3	34.1	30.8	29.5	28.7	28.2	27.9	27.7	27.5	27.3	27.2	27.1	27.1	26.9	26.7	26.7	26.6	26.6	26.6	26.6	26.5	26.4	26.3	26.2	26.1
4	21.2	18.0	16.7	16.0	15.5	15.2	15.0	14.8	14.7	14.5	14.5	14.4	14.2	14.0	14.0	14.0	13.9	13.9	13.9	13.8	13.7	13.7	13.6	13.5
5	16.3	13.3	12.1	11.4	11.0	10.7	10.5	10.3	10.2	10.1	10.0	9.89	9.72	9.55	9.53	9.51	9.49	9.47	9.45	9.38	9.29	9.20	9.11	9.02
6	13.7	10.9	9.78	9.15	8.75	8.47	8.26	8.10	7.98	7.87	7.79	7.72	7.56	7.40	7.37	7.35	7.33	7.31	7.30	7.23	7.14	7.06	6.97	6.88
7	12.2	9.55	8.45	7.85	7.46	7.19	6.99	6.84	6.72	6.62	6.54	6.47	6.31	6.16	6.13	6.11	6.09	6.07	6.06	5.99	5.91	5.82	5.74	5.65
8	11.3	8.65	7.59	7.01	6.63	6.37	6.18	6.03	5.91	5.81	5.73	5.67	5.52	5.36	5.34	5.32	5.30	5.28	5.26	5.20	5.12	5.03	4.95	4.86
9	10.6	8.02	6.99	6.42	6.06	5.80	5.61	5.47	5.35	5.26	5.18	5.11	4.96	4.81	4.79	4.77	4.75	4.73	4.71	4.65	4.57	4.48	4.40	4.31
10	10.0	7.56	6.55	5.99	5.64	5.39	5.20	5.06	4.94	4.85	4.77	4.71	4.56	4.41	4.38	4.36	4.34	4.33	4.31	4.25	4.17	4.08	4.00	3.91
11	9.65	7.21	6.22	5.67	5.32	5.07	4.89	4.74	4.63	4.54	4.46	4.40	4.25	4.10	4.08	4.06	4.04	4.02	4.01	3.94	3.86	3.78	3.69	3.60
12	9.33	6.93	5.95	5.41	5.06	4.82	4.64	4.50	4.39	4.30	4.22	4.16	4.01	3.86	3.84	3.82	3.80	3.78	3.76	3.70	3.62	3.54	3.45	3.36
13	9.07	6.70	5.74	5.21	4.86	4.62	4.44	4.30	4.19	4.10	4.02	3.96	3.82	3.66	3.64	3.62	3.60	3.59	3.57	3.51	3.43	3.34	3.25	3.17
14	8.86	6.51	5.56	5.04	4.70	4.46	4.28	4.14	4.03	3.94	3.86	3.80	3.66	3.51	3.48	3.46	3.44	3.43	3.41	3.35	3.27	3.18	3.09	3.00
15	8.68	6.36	5.42	4.89	4.56	4.32	4.14	4.00	3.89	3.80	3.73	3.67	3.52	3.37	3.35	3.33	3.31	3.29	3.28	3.21	3.13	3.05	2.96	2.87
16	8.53	6.23	5.29	4.77	4.44	4.20	4.03	3.89	3.78	3.69	3.62	3.55	3.41	3.26	3.24	3.22	3.20	3.18	3.16	3.10	3.02	2.93	2.84	2.75
17	8.40	6.11	5.19	4.67	4.34	4.10	3.93	3.79	3.68	3.59	3.52	3.46	3.31	3.16	3.14	3.12	3.10	3.08	3.07	3.00	2.92	2.83	2.75	2.65
18	8.29	6.01	5.09	4.58	4.25	4.01	3.84	3.71	3.60	3.51	3.43	3.37	3.23	3.08	3.05	3.03	3.02	3.00	2.98	2.92	2.84	2.75	2.66	2.57
19	8.19	5.93	5.01	4.50	4.17	3.94	3.77	3.63	3.52	3.43	3.36	3.30	3.15	3.00	2.98	2.96	2.94	2.92	2.91	2.84	2.76	2.67	2.58	2.49
20	8.10	5.85	4.94	4.43	4.10	3.87	3.70	3.56	3.46	3.37	3.29	3.23	3.09	2.94	2.92	2.90	2.88	2.86	2.84	2.78	2.69	2.61	2.52	2.42
21	8.02	5.78	4.87	4.37	4.04	3.81	3.64	3.51	3.40	3.31	3.24	3.17	3.03	2.88	2.86	2.84	2.82	2.80	2.79	2.72	2.64	2.55	2.46	2.36
22	7.95	5.72	4.82	4.31	3.99	3.76	3.59	3.45	3.35	3.26	3.18	3.12	2.98	2.83	2.81	2.78	2.77	2.75	2.73	2.67	2.58	2.50	2.40	2.31
23	7.88	5.66	4.76	4.26	3.94	3.71	3.54	3.41	3.30	3.21	3.14	3.07	2.93	2.78	2.76	2.74	2.72	2.70	2.69	2.62	2.54	2.45	2.35	2.26
24	7.82	5.61	4.72	4.22	3.90	3.67	3.50	3.36	3.26	3.17	3.09	3.03	2.89	2.74	2.72	2.70	2.68	2.66	2.64	2.58	2.49	2.40	2.31	2.21
25	7.77	5.57	4.68	4.18	3.86	3.63	3.46	3.32	3.22	3.13	3.06	2.99	2.85	2.70	2.68	2.66	2.64	2.62	2.60	2.53	2.45	2.36	2.27	2.17
30	7.56	5.39	4.51	4.02	3.70	3.47	3.30	3.17	3.07	2.98	2.91	2.84	2.70	2.55	2.53	2.51	2.49	2.47	2.45	2.39	2.30	2.21	2.11	2.01
40	7.31	5.18	4.31	3.83	3.51	3.29	3.12	2.99	2.89	2.80	2.73	2.66	2.52	2.37	2.35	2.33	2.31	2.29	2.27	2.20	2.11	2.02	1.92	1.80
60	7.08	4.98	4.13	3.65	3.34	3.12	2.95	2.82	2.72	2.63	2.56	2.50	2.35	2.20	2.17	2.15	2.13	2.12	2.10	2.03	1.94	1.84	1.73	1.60
120	6.85	4.79	3.95	3.48	3.17	2.96	2.79	2.66	2.56	2.47	2.40	2.34	2.19	2.03	2.01	1.99	1.97	1.95	1.93	1.86	1.76	1.66	1.53	1.38
Infinity	6.63	4.61	3.78	3.32	3.02	2.80	2.64	2.51	2.41	2.32	2.25	2.18	2.04	1.88	1.85	1.83	1.81	1.79	1.77	1.70	1.59	1.47	1.32	1.00

Appendix D Table of the F-Distribution

Panel D. Critical values for right-hand tail area equal to **0.005**

Numerator: df_1 and Denominator: df_2

df1:	1	2	3	4	5	6	7	8	9	10	11	12	15	20	21	22	23	24	25	30	40	60	120	∞
df2: 1	16211	20000	21615	22500	23056	23437	23715	23925	24091	24222	24334	24426	24630	24836	24863	24892	24915	24940	24959	25044	25146	25253	25359	25464
2	198.5	199.0	199.2	199.2	199.3	199.3	199.4	199.4	199.4	199.4	199.4	199.4	199.4	199.4	199.4	199.4	199.4	199.4	199.4	199.5	199.5	199.5	199.5	200
3	55.55	49.80	47.47	46.20	45.39	44.84	44.43	44.13	43.88	43.68	43.52	43.39	43.08	42.78	42.73	42.69	42.66	42.62	42.59	42.47	42.31	42.15	41.99	41.83
4	31.33	26.28	24.26	23.15	22.46	21.98	21.62	21.35	21.14	20.97	20.82	20.70	20.44	20.17	20.13	20.09	20.06	20.03	20.00	19.89	19.75	19.61	19.47	19.32
5	22.78	18.31	16.53	15.56	14.94	14.51	14.20	13.96	13.77	13.62	13.49	13.38	13.15	12.90	12.87	12.84	12.81	12.78	12.76	12.66	12.53	12.40	12.27	12.14
6	18.63	14.54	12.92	12.03	11.46	11.07	10.79	10.57	10.39	10.25	10.13	10.03	9.81	9.59	9.56	9.53	9.50	9.47	9.45	9.36	9.24	9.12	9.00	8.88
7	16.24	12.40	10.88	10.05	9.52	9.16	8.89	8.68	8.51	8.38	8.27	8.18	7.97	7.75	7.72	7.69	7.67	7.64	7.62	7.53	7.42	7.31	7.19	7.08
8	14.69	11.04	9.60	8.81	8.30	7.95	7.69	7.50	7.34	7.21	7.10	7.01	6.81	6.61	6.58	6.55	6.53	6.50	6.48	6.40	6.29	6.18	6.06	5.95
9	13.61	10.11	8.72	7.96	7.47	7.13	6.88	6.69	6.54	6.42	6.31	6.23	6.03	5.83	5.80	5.78	5.75	5.73	5.71	5.62	5.52	5.41	5.30	5.19
10	12.83	9.43	8.08	7.34	6.87	6.54	6.30	6.12	5.97	5.85	5.75	5.66	5.47	5.27	5.25	5.22	5.20	5.17	5.15	5.07	4.97	4.86	4.75	4.64
11	12.23	8.91	7.60	6.88	6.42	6.10	5.86	5.68	5.54	5.42	5.32	5.24	5.05	4.86	4.83	4.80	4.78	4.76	4.74	4.65	4.55	4.45	4.34	4.23
12	11.75	8.51	7.23	6.52	6.07	5.76	5.52	5.35	5.20	5.09	4.99	4.91	4.72	4.53	4.50	4.48	4.45	4.43	4.41	4.33	4.23	4.12	4.01	3.90
13	11.37	8.19	6.93	6.23	5.79	5.48	5.25	5.08	4.94	4.82	4.72	4.64	4.46	4.27	4.24	4.22	4.19	4.17	4.15	4.07	3.97	3.87	3.76	3.65
14	11.06	7.92	6.68	6.00	5.56	5.26	5.03	4.86	4.72	4.60	4.51	4.43	4.25	4.06	4.03	4.01	3.98	3.96	3.94	3.86	3.76	3.66	3.55	3.44
15	10.80	7.70	6.48	5.80	5.37	5.07	4.85	4.67	4.54	4.42	4.33	4.25	4.07	3.88	3.86	3.83	3.81	3.79	3.77	3.69	3.59	3.48	3.37	3.26
16	10.58	7.51	6.30	5.64	5.21	4.91	4.69	4.52	4.38	4.27	4.18	4.10	3.92	3.73	3.71	3.68	3.66	3.64	3.62	3.54	3.44	3.33	3.22	3.11
17	10.38	7.35	6.16	5.50	5.07	4.78	4.56	4.39	4.25	4.14	4.05	3.97	3.79	3.61	3.58	3.56	3.53	3.51	3.49	3.41	3.31	3.21	3.10	2.98
18	10.22	7.21	6.03	5.37	4.96	4.66	4.44	4.28	4.14	4.03	3.94	3.86	3.68	3.50	3.47	3.45	3.42	3.40	3.38	3.30	3.20	3.10	2.99	2.87
19	10.07	7.09	5.92	5.27	4.85	4.56	4.34	4.18	4.04	3.93	3.84	3.76	3.59	3.40	3.37	3.35	3.33	3.31	3.29	3.21	3.11	3.00	2.89	2.78
20	9.94	6.99	5.82	5.17	4.76	4.47	4.26	4.09	3.96	3.85	3.76	3.68	3.50	3.32	3.29	3.27	3.24	3.22	3.20	3.12	3.02	2.92	2.81	2.69
21	9.83	6.89	5.73	5.09	4.68	4.39	4.18	4.01	3.88	3.77	3.68	3.60	3.43	3.24	3.22	3.19	3.17	3.15	3.13	3.05	2.95	2.84	2.73	2.61
22	9.73	6.81	5.65	5.02	4.61	4.32	4.11	3.94	3.81	3.70	3.61	3.54	3.36	3.18	3.15	3.12	3.10	3.08	3.06	2.98	2.88	2.77	2.66	2.55
23	9.63	6.73	5.58	4.95	4.54	4.26	4.05	3.88	3.75	3.64	3.55	3.47	3.30	3.12	3.09	3.06	3.04	3.02	3.00	2.92	2.82	2.71	2.60	2.48
24	9.55	6.66	5.52	4.89	4.49	4.20	3.99	3.83	3.69	3.59	3.50	3.42	3.25	3.06	3.04	3.01	2.99	2.97	2.95	2.87	2.77	2.66	2.55	2.43
25	9.48	6.60	5.46	4.84	4.43	4.15	3.94	3.78	3.64	3.54	3.45	3.37	3.20	3.01	2.99	2.96	2.94	2.92	2.90	2.82	2.72	2.61	2.50	2.38
30	9.18	6.35	5.24	4.62	4.23	3.95	3.74	3.58	3.45	3.34	3.25	3.18	3.01	2.82	2.80	2.77	2.75	2.73	2.71	2.63	2.52	2.42	2.30	2.18
40	8.83	6.07	4.98	4.37	3.99	3.71	3.51	3.35	3.22	3.12	3.03	2.95	2.78	2.60	2.57	2.55	2.52	2.50	2.48	2.40	2.30	2.18	2.06	1.93
60	8.49	5.79	4.73	4.14	3.76	3.49	3.29	3.13	3.01	2.90	2.82	2.74	2.57	2.39	2.36	2.33	2.31	2.29	2.27	2.19	2.08	1.96	1.83	1.69
120	8.18	5.54	4.50	3.92	3.55	3.28	3.09	2.93	2.81	2.71	2.62	2.54	2.37	2.19	2.16	2.13	2.11	2.09	2.07	1.98	1.87	1.75	1.61	1.43
Infinity	7.88	5.30	4.28	3.72	3.35	3.09	2.90	2.74	2.62	2.52	2.43	2.36	2.19	2.00	1.97	1.95	1.92	1.90	1.88	1.79	1.67	1.53	1.36	1.00

Appendix E   Critical Values for the Durbin-Watson Statistic (α = .05)

n	K = 1		K = 2		K = 3		K = 4		K = 5	
	d_l	d_u	d_l	d_u	d_l	d_u	d_l	d_u	d_l	d_u
15	1.08	1.36	0.95	1.54	0.82	1.75	0.69	1.97	0.56	2.21
16	1.10	1.37	0.98	1.54	0.86	1.73	0.74	1.93	0.62	2.15
17	1.13	1.38	1.02	1.54	0.90	1.71	0.78	1.90	0.67	2.10
18	1.16	1.39	1.05	1.53	0.93	1.69	0.82	1.87	0.71	2.06
19	1.18	1.40	1.08	1.53	0.97	1.68	0.86	1.85	0.75	2.02
20	1.20	1.41	1.10	1.54	1.00	1.68	0.90	1.83	0.79	1.99
21	1.22	1.42	1.13	1.54	1.03	1.67	0.93	1.81	0.83	1.96
22	1.24	1.43	1.15	1.54	1.05	1.66	0.96	1.80	0.86	1.94
23	1.26	1.44	1.17	1.54	1.08	1.66	0.99	1.79	0.90	1.92
24	1.27	1.45	1.19	1.55	1.10	1.66	1.01	1.78	0.93	1.90
25	1.29	1.45	1.21	1.55	1.12	1.66	1.04	1.77	0.95	1.89
26	1.30	1.46	1.22	1.55	1.14	1.65	1.06	1.76	0.98	1.88
27	1.32	1.47	1.24	1.56	1.16	1.65	1.08	1.76	1.01	1.86
28	1.33	1.48	1.26	1.56	1.18	1.65	1.10	1.75	1.03	1.85
29	1.34	1.48	1.27	1.56	1.20	1.65	1.12	1.74	1.05	1.84
30	1.35	1.49	1.28	1.57	1.21	1.65	1.14	1.74	1.07	1.83
31	1.36	1.50	1.30	1.57	1.23	1.65	1.16	1.74	1.09	1.83
32	1.37	1.50	1.31	1.57	1.24	1.65	1.18	1.73	1.11	1.82
33	1.38	1.51	1.32	1.58	1.26	1.65	1.19	1.73	1.13	1.81
34	1.39	1.51	1.33	1.58	1.27	1.65	1.21	1.73	1.15	1.81
35	1.40	1.52	1.34	1.58	1.28	1.65	1.22	1.73	1.16	1.80
36	1.41	1.52	1.35	1.59	1.29	1.65	1.24	1.73	1.18	1.80
37	1.42	1.53	1.36	1.59	1.31	1.66	1.25	1.72	1.19	1.80
38	1.43	1.54	1.37	1.59	1.32	1.66	1.26	1.72	1.21	1.79
39	1.43	1.54	1.38	1.60	1.33	1.66	1.27	1.72	1.22	1.79
40	1.44	1.54	1.39	1.60	1.34	1.66	1.29	1.72	1.23	1.79
45	1.48	1.57	1.43	1.62	1.38	1.67	1.34	1.72	1.29	1.78
50	1.50	1.59	1.46	1.63	1.42	1.67	1.38	1.72	1.34	1.77
55	1.53	1.60	1.49	1.64	1.45	1.68	1.41	1.72	1.38	1.77
60	1.55	1.62	1.51	1.65	1.48	1.69	1.44	1.73	1.41	1.77
65	1.57	1.63	1.54	1.66	1.50	1.70	1.47	1.73	1.44	1.77
70	1.58	1.64	1.55	1.67	1.52	1.70	1.49	1.74	1.46	1.77
75	1.60	1.65	1.57	1.68	1.54	1.71	1.51	1.74	1.49	1.77
80	1.61	1.66	1.59	1.69	1.56	1.72	1.53	1.74	1.51	1.77
85	1.62	1.67	1.60	1.70	1.57	1.72	1.55	1.75	1.52	1.77
90	1.63	1.68	1.61	1.70	1.59	1.73	1.57	1.75	1.54	1.78
95	1.64	1.69	1.62	1.71	1.60	1.73	1.58	1.75	1.56	1.78
100	1.65	1.69	1.63	1.72	1.61	1.74	1.59	1.76	1.57	1.78

Source: From J. Durbin and G. S. Watson, "Testing for Serial Correlation in Least Squares Regression, II." *Biometrika* 38 (1951): 159–178. Reproduced by permission of the *Biometrika* trustees.

Note: K = the number of slope parameters in the model.

REFERENCES

Altman, Edward I. 1968. "Financial Ratios, Discriminant Analysis and the Prediction of Corporate Bankruptcy." *Journal of Finance.* Vol. 23: 589–699.

Altman, Edward I. and Vellore M. Kishore. 1996. "Almost Everything You Wanted to Know about Recoveries on Defaulted Bonds." *Financial Analysts Journal.* Vol. 52, No. 6: 57–64.

Altman, Edward, R. Haldeman, and P. Narayanan. 1977. "Zeta Analysis: A New Model to Identify Bankruptcy Risk of Corporations." *Journal of Banking and Finance.* Vol. 1.

Ambachtsheer, Keith, Ronald Capelle, and Tom Scheibelhut. 1998. "Improving Pension Fund Performance." *Financial Analysts Journal.* Vol. 54, No. 6: 15–21.

Baks, Klaas P., Andres Metrick, and Jessica Wachter. 2001. "Should Investors Avoid All Actively Managed Mutual Funds?" *Journal of Finance.* Vol. 56: 45–85.

Bauman, W. Scott, C. Mitchell Conover, and Robert E. Miller. 1998. "Growth versus Value and Large-Cap versus Small-Cap Stocks in International Markets." *Financial Analysts Journal.* Vol. 54, No. 2: 75–89.

Black, Fischer. 1993. "Estimating Expected Return." *Financial Analysts Journal.* Vol. 49, No. 5: 36–38.

Block, Stanley B. 1999. "A Study of Financial Analysts: Practice and Theory." *Financial Analysts Journal,* Vol. 55, No. 4: 86–95.

Blume, Marshall. 1984. "The Use of "Alphas" to Improve Performance," *Journal of Portfolio Management.* Vol. 11: 86–92.

Bodie, Zvi, Alex Kane, and Alan J. Marcus. 1999. *Investments,* 4th edition. Irwin/McGraw-Hill.

Bowerman, Bruce L. and Richard T. O'Connell. 1997. *Applied Statistics.* Chicago: Irwin.

Brealey, Richard A. and Stewart C. Myers. 1999. *Principles of Corporate Finance,* 6th edition. New York: McGraw-Hill.

Breusch, T. and A. Pagan 1979. "A Simple Test for Heteroskedasticity and Random Coefficient Variation." *Econometrica.* Vol. 47: 1287–1294.

Brown, Stephen, William Goetzmann, and Stephen Ross. 1995. "Survival." *Journal of Finance.* Vol. 50: 853–873.

Buetow, Gerald W., Jr., Robert R. Johnson, and David E. Runkle. 2000. "The Inconsistency of Return-Based Style Analysis." *Journal of Portfolio Management.* Vol. 26, No. 3: 61–77.

Buffett, Warren. 1993. *Berkshire Hathaway Chairman's Letter.* Retrieved May 25, 2001, from the World Wide Web: www.berkshirehathaway.com/letters/1983.html.

Burmeister, Edwin and Marjorie B. McElroy. 1988. "Joint Estimation of Factor Sensitivities and Risk Premia for the Arbitrage Pricing Theory." *Journal of Finance.* Vol. 43: 721–733.

Burmeister, Edwin, Richard Roll, and Stephen A. Ross. 1994. "A Practitioner's Guide to Arbitrage Pricing Theory." *A Practitioner's Guide to Factor Models.* Charlottesville, VA: The Research Foundation of the Institute of Chartered Financial Analysts.

Campbell, John Y., Andrew W. Lo, and A. Craig MacKinlay. 1997. *The Econometrics of Financial Markets.* Princeton, NJ: Princeton University Press.

Campbell, John Y., Andrew W. Lo, and A. Craig MacKinlay. 1990. "Data Snooping Biases in Tests of Financial Asset Pricing Models." *Review of Financial Studies.* Vol. 3: 175–208.

Campbell, John Y., Martin Lettau, Burton G. Malkiel, and Yexiao Xu. 2001. "Have Individual Stocks Become More Volatile? An Empirical Exploration of Idiosyncratic Risk." *Journal of Finance.* Vol. 56, No. 1: 1–43.

Campbell, Stephen K. 1974. *Flaws and Fallacies in Statistical Thinking.* Englewood Cliffs, NJ: Prentice-Hall.

Chen, Nai-fu, Richard Roll, and Stephen Ross. 1986. "Economic Forces and the Stock Market." *Journal of Business.* Vol. 59, July: 386–403.

Chua, Jess H., Richard S. Woodward, and Eric C. To. 1987. "Potential Gains From Stock Market Timing in Canada." *Financial Analysts Journal.* Sept-Oct: 50–56.

Clarke, Roger G. and Mark P. Kritzman. 1996. *Currency Management: Concepts and Practices.* Charlottesville, VA: Research Foundation of the Institute of Chartered Financial Analysts.

Cochrane, John H. 1999a. "New Facts in Finance." *Economic Perspectives.* Federal Reserve Bank of Chicago. Vol. 23, No. 3: 36–58. (Revision of NBER Working Paper 7169).

Cochrane, John H. 1999b. "Portfolio Advice for a Multifactor World." *Economic Perspectives.* Federal Reserve Bank of Chicago. Vol. 23, No. 3: 59–78. (Revision of NBER Working Paper 7170).

Connor, Gregory. 1995. "The Three Types of Factor Models: A Comparison of their Explanatory Power." *Financial Analysts Journal.* Vol. 51, No. 3: 42–46.

Cox, Jonathan, Stephen Ross, and Mark Rubinstein. 1979. "Options Pricing: A Simplified Approach." *Journal of Financial Economics.* Vol. 7: 229–263.

Damodoran, Aswath. 1996. *Investment Valuation: Tools and techniques for determining the value of any asset.* New York: John Wiley & Sons.

Daniel, Wayne W. and James C. Terrell. 1979. *Business Statistics, Basic Concepts and Methodology.* Boston: Houghton Mifflin.

Daniel, Wayne W. and James C. Terrell. 1995. *Business Statistics for Management & Economics*, 7th edition. Boston: Houghton-Mifflin.

Davidson, Russell and James G. MacKinnon. 1993. *Estimation and Inference in Econometrics.* New York: Oxford University Press.

Diebold, Francis X. 1997. *Elements of Forecasting.* Cincinnati, OH: South-Western College Publishing.

Dimson, Elroy, Paul Marsh, and Mike Staunton. 2000. *The Millennium Book: A Century of Investment Returns.* London: ABN-AMRO and London Business School.

Durbin, J. and G.S. Watson. 1951. "Testing for Serial Correlation in Least Squares Regression, II." *Biometrika* 38: 159–178.

Dybvig, Philip H. and Stephen A. Ross. 1985a. "Differential Information and Performance Measurement Using a Security Market Line." *Journal of Finance.* Vol. 40: 383–399.

Dybvig, Philip H. and Stephen A. Ross. 1985b. "The Analytics of Performance Measurement Using a Security Market Line." *Journal of Finance.* Vol. 40: 401–416.

Elton, Edward J., Martin J. Gruber, and Joel Rentzler. 1987. "Professionally Managed Publicly Traded commodity Funds." *Journal of Business.* Vol. 60, No. 2: 175–199.

Elton, Edward J., Martin J. Gruber, and Joel Rentzler. 1990. "The Performance of Publicly Offered Commodity Funds." *Financial Analysts Journal.* Vol. 46, No. 4: 23–30.

Elton, Edwin J. and Martin J. Gruber. 1995. *Modern Portfolio Theory and Investment Analysis*, 5th edition. New York: Wiley.

Engle, R.F. 1982. "Autoregressive Conditional Heteroskedasticity with Estimates of the Variance of United Kingdom Inflations." *Econometrica.* Vol. 50: 987–1008.

Fabozzi, Frank J. 1999. *Investment Management,* 2nd edition. 593–598. Englewood Cliffs, NJ: Prentice Hall.

Fabozzi, Frank J. 2000. *Fixed Income Analysis for the Chartered Financial Analyst® Program.* New Hope, PA: Frank J. Fabozzi Associates.

Fabozzi, Frank J. 2000b. *Fixed Income Readings for the Chartered Financial Analyst® Program.* New Hope, PA: Frank J. Fabozzi Associates. p. 87.

Fama, Eugene F. and Kenneth R. French. 1992. "The Cross-Section of Expected Stock Returns." *Journal of Finance.* Vol. 47, No. 2: 427–466.

Fama, Eugene F. and Kenneth R. French. 1993. "Common Risk Factors in the Returns on Stocks and Bonds." *Journal of Financial Economics.* Vol. 33, No. 1: 3–56.

Fama, Eugene. 1976. *Foundations of Finance.* New York: Basic Books.

Feller, William. 1957. *An Introduction to Probability Theory and its Applications*, Vol. I, 2nd edition. New York: Wiley.

Ferguson, Robert. 1993. "Some Formulas for Evaluating Two Popular Option Strategies." *Financial Analysts Journal.* Vol. 49, No. 5: 71–78.

Fisher, Lawrence and James H. Lorie. 1970. "Some Studies Of Variability Of Returns On Investments In Common Stocks." *Journal of Business.* Vol. 43, No. 2: 99–134.

French, Kenneth R. and James M. Poterba. 1991. "Investor Diversification and International Equity Markets." *American Economic Review.* Vol. 81, No. 2: 222–226.

Freund, John E., and Frank J. Williams. 1977. *Elementary Business Statistics*, 3rd edition. Englewood Cliffs, NJ: Prentice-Hall.

Fridson, Martin S. and M. Christopher Garman. 1998. "Determinants of Spreads on New High-Yield Bonds." *Financial Analysts Journal.* Vol. 54, No. 2: 28–39.

Garbade, Kenneth. 1982. *Securities Markets.* New York: McGraw-Hill.

Goldberger, Arthur S. 1998. *Introductory Econometrics.* Cambridge, MA: Harvard University Press.

Greene, William H. 1999. *Econometric Analysis*, 4th edition. Upper Saddle River, NJ: Prentice Hall.

Grinold, Richard and Ronald N. Kahn. 1994. "Multi-Factor Models for Portfolio Risk." *A Practitioner's Guide to Factor Models.* Charlottesville, VA: The Research Foundation of the Institute of Chartered Financial Analysts.

Hamilton, James D. 1995. *Time Series Analysis.* Princeton, NJ: Princeton University Press.

Hansen, Lars Peter. 1982. "Large Sample Properties of Generalized Method of Moments Estimators." *Econometrica.* Vol. 50: 1029–1054.

Henriksson, Roy D. and Robert C. Merton. 1981. "On Market Timing and Investment Performance. II. Statistical Procedures for Evaluating Forecasting Skills." *Journal of Business.* Vol. 54: 513–33.

Hettmansperger, T. P. and J. W. McKean. 1998. *Robust Nonparametric Statistical Methods.* London: Arnold.

Hillier, Frederick S. and Gerald J. Lieberman. 2000. *Introduction to Operations Research*, 7th edition. New York: McGraw-Hill.

Hull, John. 1999. *Options, Futures, and Other Derivatives*, 4th edition. Upper Saddle River, NJ: Prentice Hall.

Kahn, Ronald N. and Andrew Rudd. 1995. "Does Historical Performance Predict Future Performance? *Financial Analysts Journal.* Vol. 51, No. 6: 43–52.

Keane, Michael P. and David E. Runkle. 1990. "Testing the Rationality of Price Forecasts: New Evidence from Panel Data." *American Economic Review.* Vol. 80, No. 4: 714–735.

Keane, Michael P. and David E. Runkle. 1998. "Are Financial Analysts' Forecasts of Corporate Profits Rational?" *Journal of Political Economy.* Vol. 106, No. 4: 768–805.

Kemeny, John G., Arthur Schleifer, Jr., J. Laurie Snell, and Gerald L. Thompson. 1972. *Finite Mathematics with Business Applications*, 2nd edition. Englewood Cliffs, NJ: Prentice Hall.

Klemkosky, Robert C. and John D. Martin. 1975. "The Adjustment of Beta Forecasts." *Journal of Finance*. Vol. 30, No. 4: 1123.

Kolb, Robert W., Gerald D. Gay, and William C. Hunter. 1985. "Liquidity Requirements for Financial Futures Investments." *Financial Analysts Journal*. Vol. 41, No. 3: 60–68.

Kon, Stanley J. 1984. "Models of Stock Returns-A Comparison." *Journal of Finance*. Vol. 34: 147–165.

Kool, Clemens J. M. 2000. "International Bond Markets and the Introduction of the Euro." *Review* of the Federal Reserve Bank of St. Louis. Vol. 82, No. 5: 41–56.

Kothari, S.P., Jay Shanken, and Richard G. Sloan. 1995. "Another Look at the Cross-section of Expected Returns." *Journal of Finance*. Vol. 50, No. 1: 185–224.

Leibowitz, Martin L. and Roy D. Henriksson. 1989. "Portfolio Optimization with Shortfall Constraints: A Confidence-Limit Approach to Managing Downside Risk." *Financial Analysts Journal*. Vol. 45, No. 2: 34–41.

Liang, Bing. 1999. "On the Performance of Hedge Funds." *Financial Analysts Journal*. Vol. 55, No. 4: 72–85.

Linsmeier, Thomas J. and Neil D. Pearson. 2000. "Value at Risk." *Financial Analysts Journal*. Vol. 56, No. 2: 47–67.

Lo, Andrew W. 1999. "The Three P's of Total Risk Management." *Financial Analysts Journal*. Vol. 55, No. 1:13–26.

Luenberger, David G. 1998. *Investment Science*. New York: Oxford University Press.

MacKinlay, A. Craig and Matthew P. Richardson. 1991. "Using Generalized Methods of Moments to Test Mean–Variance Efficiency." *Journal of Finance*. Vol. 46, No. 2: 511–527.

McQueen, Grant, and Steven Thorley. 1999. "Mining Fools Gold." *Financial Analysts Journal*. Vol. 55, No. 2: 61–72.

McQueen, Grant, Kay Shields, and Steven R. Thorley. 1997. "Does the "Dow-10 Investment Strategy" Beat the Dow Statistically and Economically?" *Financial Analysts Journal*. Vol. 53, No. 4: 67–72.

Michaud, Richard O. 1998. *Efficient Asset Allocation*. Boston: Harvard Business School Press.

Moore, David S. and George P. McCabe. 1998. *Introduction to the Practice of Statistics*, 3rd edition. New York: W. H. Freeman.

Nayar, Nandkumar and Michael S. Rozeff. 1994. "Ratings, Commercial Paper, and Equity Returns." *Journal of Finance*. Vol. 49, No. 4: 1431–1449.

Pindyck, Robert S. and Daniel L. Rubinfeld. 1998. *Econometric Models and Economic Forecasts*, 4th edition. Boston, MA: Irwin/McGraw-Hill.

Ramsey, Frank P. 1931. "Truth and Probability." *The Foundations of Mathematics and Other Logical Essays*. R.B. Braithwaite, ed. London: Routledge and Kegan Paul.

Reilly, Frank K. and Keith C. Brown. 2000. *Investment Analysis and Portfolio Management*, 6th edition. Fort Worth, TX: Dryden.

Roll, Richard and Stephen A. Ross. 2001. *What Is the Arbitrage Pricing Theory*. Retrieved May 25, 2001, from the World Wide Web: www.rollross.com/apt.html.

Ross, Sheldon M. 1997. *A First Course in Probability*, 5th edition. Englewood, NJ: Prentice-Hall.

Ross, Stephen A. 1976. "The Arbitrage Theory of Capital Asset Pricing." *Journal of Economic Theory*. December: 341–360.

Roy, A.D. 1952. "Safety-First and the Holding of Assets." *Econometrica*, Vol. 20: 431–439.

Sharpe, William F. 1992. "Asset Allocation: Management Style and Performance Measurement." *Journal of Portfolio Management*. Vol. 18, No. 2: 7–19.

Sharpe, William F., Gordon J. Alexander, and Jeffery V. Bailey. 1998. *Investments*. Upper Saddle River, NJ: Prentice Hall.

Shumay, Tyler and Vincent A. Warther. 1999. "The Delisting Bias in CRSP's Nasdaq Data and Its Implications for the Size Effect." *Journal of Finance*. Vol. 54, No. 6: 2361–2379.

Siegel, Jeremy J. 1998. *Stocks for the Long Run*, 2nd edition. New York: McGraw-Hill.

Siegel, Sidney. 1956. *Nonparametric Statistics for the Behavioral Sciences*. New York: McGraw-Hill.

Swensen, David F. 2000. *Pioneering Portfolio Management: An Unconventional Approach to Institutional Investment*. New York: Free Press.

White, Halbert. 1980. "A Heteroskedasticity-Consistent Covariance Matrix Estimator and a Direct Test for Heteroskedasticity." *Econometrica*. Vol. 48: 817–838.

GLOSSARY

A priori probability One based on logical analysis rather than on observation or personal judgment.

Absolute dispersion The amount of variability present without comparison to any reference point or benchmark.

Absolute frequency The number of observations in a given interval (for grouped data).

Accrued interest Interest earned, but not yet paid.

Addition rule for probabilities Given events A and B, the probability that A or B occurs, or both occur, is equal to the probability that A occurs, plus the probability that B occurs, minus the probability that both A and B occur.

Additivity principle The principle that dollar amounts indexed at the same point in time are additive.

Adjusted beta Beta, adjusted for autoregression.

Adjusted R^2 An adjusted multiple R^2, the square of the correlation of the actual values of y with the forecast value s, adjusted for the degrees of freedom. Adjusted R^2 does not automatically increase when another variable is added to a regression model.

Alternative hypothesis The hypothesis accepted when the null hypothesis is rejected.

Analysis of variance (ANOVA) The technique for conducting a test which provides the inputs for an F-test on the hypothesis that all of the coefficients in the regression model are simultaneously equal to 0.

Annual percentage rate (APR) A measure of the cost of credit, expressed as a yearly rate.

Annuity A finite stream of periodic, level cash flows.

Annuity due An annuity that has the first cash flow paid or received immediately.

Arbitrage A riskless operation which requires no net investment.

Arbitrage opportunity An opportunity to obtain an expected positive net cash flow using arbitrage.

Arbitrage-free valuation approach An approach to valuing a fixed-income instrument as a portfolio of zero-coupon bonds.

Asian call option A call option exercisable only at maturity and having a strike price equal to the average value of the underlying stock price during the life of the option.

Autoregressive model (AR) A model in which a variable in one period depends linearly on its value in previous period(s).

Bank discount basis Discount divided by face value, and annualized on the basis of a 360-day year.

Bayes' formula Rule for updating your probability of an event, given a set of prior probabilities for an event and receipt of new information.

Bernoulli random variable A random variable having the outcomes 0 and 1.

Bernoulli trial An experiment with two outcomes, which can represent success or failure, up move or down move, or another binary outcome.

Beta A measure of an asset's sensitivity to movements in the market.

Binomial random variable The number of successes in n Bernoulli trials.

Binomial tree The graphical representation of a model of asset price dynamics in which, at each period, the asset moves up with probability p or down with probability $(1 - p)$.

Bond-equivalent basis Annualizing a semiannual yield by doubling it.

Bond-equivalent yield The yield to maturity which ignores compounding within a year.

Breusch–Pagan test A test for conditional heteroskedasticity using the $n \times R^2$ statistic based on a regression of the squared residuals from the original regression and the same set of independent variables.

Capital allocation line A line showing the maximum expected return for a given level of risk for all portfolios containing both the risk-free asset and risky assets, given the portfolio manager's assumptions about expected returns and the variances and covariances of expected returns.

Capital budgeting The allocation of funds to relatively long-range projects or investments.

Capital market line The capital market line is the capital allocation line with the market portfolio as the tangency portfolio.

Capital structure The specific mixture of long-term financing a firm uses to finance its operations.

CD equivalent yield A yield equal to the annualized holding period yield, assuming a 360-day year, r_{MM} = HPY $\times$ (360/t), where t = days in holding period and HPY is the holding period yield.

Certain world A world in which the exact amount and timing of the future cash flows on all investments are known today.

Chain rule of forecasting The principle of chaining forward forecasts period-by-period to obtain a forecast for a distant period.

Chebyshev's inequality A result due to P. L. Chebyshev (1821–1894) stating that, for any distribution, at least 75 (89) percent of the values will fall within 2 (3) standard deviations of the mean.

Coefficient of variation A relative measure of dispersion equal to the standard deviation divided by the mean.

Combination A listing in which order does not matter.

Combination formula (binomial formula) The number of ways we can choose r objects from a total of n objects, where the order in which the r objects are chosen does not matter.

Complement The complement of the set S is the set of elements not included in S. If we have an event or scenario S, the event not-S, called the complement of S, is written S^C

Compounding The process of accumulating interest on interest on an investment over time.

Conditional expected values Expectations or forecasts based on a set of information or events.

Conditional heteroskedasticity Heteroskedasticity in the error variance that is correlated with (conditional on) the values of the independent variables in the regression.

Conditional probability The probability of a stated event, given that another event has occurred.

Conditional variances The variance of one variable, given the outcome of another.

Confidence interval An interval that has a given probability of including the population parameter it is intended to estimate.

Consistent probability The same probability of a particular event is used in different asset valuations that depend on that probability.

Consistent estimator An estimator for which the probability of accurate estimates (estimates close to the value to the population parameter) increases as sample size increases.

Constant growth dividend discount model An equity valuation model giving the value P_0 of a share of stock as $P_0 = D_1/(k - g)$, where D_1 is the dividend to be received at $t = 1$, k is the required rate of return or discount rate on equity for the equity's level of risk, and g is the assumed constant growth rate in dividends.

Continuous random variable A continuous random variable is one which we cannot describe with a complete list of outcomes such as z_1, z_2, ..., because the outcome $(z_1 + z_2)/2$, not on the list, would always be possible.

Continuously compounded return The natural logarithm of 1 plus the holding period return, or, equivalently, the natural logarithm of the ending price over the beginning price.

Correlation analysis A technique that expresses the strength of the linear relation between two series with a single number.

Coupon The periodic interest payment to the owners of a coupon bond.

Coupon bond Bonds on which interest is paid periodically.

Coupon bond interest The coupon paid periodically through to the maturity date of the bond.

Covariance matrix A matrix or square array whose entries are covariances, noting that variance is a special case of covariance.

Covariance stationary Said of a time-series for which the expected value and variance are constant and finite in all periods, and for which the covariance with itself a fixed number of periods in the past or future is also constant and finite.

Critical value A value against which the computed test statistic is compared to decide whether or not to reject the null hypothesis.

Cross-sectional data Observations over individual units at a point in time, as opposed to time-series data.

Cumulative absolute frequency The number of observations less than or equal to a given value.

Cumulative distribution function Gives the probability that a random variable X is less than or equal to a specified value.

Cumulative frequency distribution A display of data showing how many observations lie at or below a given value.

Cumulative relative frequency The proportion of observations less than or equal to a given value.

Data mining The practice of finding forecasting models by extensive searching through databases for patterns or trading rules; repeatedly "drilling" in the same data until statistical significance is "discovered."

Data-snooping bias   The bias in the inference drawn as a result of prying into the empirical results of others to guide your own analysis.

Deciles   Quantiles that divide the data into 10 equal parts.

Default risk   The risk of failing to make a contractually promised payment.

Degree of confidence   The probability that the confidence interval includes the unknown population parameter.

Degrees of freedom   The number of independent observations used; called "degrees of freedom" because in a random sample, observations are to be selected independently of each other.

Dependent events   Events such that the occurrence of one event affects the probability of occurrence of the other event.

Dependent variable   The variable whose variance is to be explained by a regression.

Descriptive statistics   The study of how data can be summarized effectively to describe the important aspects of large data sets.

Diffuse prior   The assumption of equal prior probabilities.

Discount   To calculate the present value of some future amount; or the amount by which an instrument is priced below its face value.

Discount bond   A bond that sells for less than its par value.

Discrete random variable   A random variable that can take on at most a countable number of possible values.

Discriminant analysis   A multivariate technique that yields a linear function which can then be used to compute an overall score which is then used to categorize an observation.

Dispersion   The variability around the central tendency.

Diversification benefits   Benefits occurring when portfolio standard deviation of return can be reduced without decreasing expected return.

Down transition probability   The probability that an asset's value moves down.

Dummy variable   A variable which takes on the value of 1 if a particular condition is true and 0 if that condition is false.

Dutch Book Theorem   A result in probability theory stating that inconsistent probabilities create profit opportunities.

Earnings yield   Earnings per share divided by stock price.

Effective annual rate (EAR)   The total interest paid or earned in a year expressed as a percentage of the principal amount at the beginning of the year, taking full account of compounding within the year.

Effective annual yield (EAY)   Takes the quantity 1 plus the holding period yield and compounds it forward to one year, then subtracts 1 to compute an annualized return that accounts for the effect of interest-on-interest.

Efficient frontier   The set of portfolios on the minimum variance frontier, but with maximum expected return for each given level of standard deviation.

Empirical probability   A probability based on relative frequency of occurrence.

Error term   The portion of the dependent variable that cannot be explained by the independent variable(s) in a regression.

Estimate   The particular value calculated from sample observations using an estimator.

Estimated or fitted parameters   The intercept and slope coefficients in a regression; they serve as population parameter estimates.

Estimation   A procedure addressing the question, "What is this parameter's (e.g., the population mean's) value?"

Estimator   The formulas used to compute the sample mean and all the other sample statistics.

Event   Any outcome or specified set of outcomes of a random variable.

Excess kurtosis   Degree of peakedness (fatness of tails) in excess of the peakedness of the normal distribution.

Excess return   The extra return that investors receive or require for the risk taken.

Exhaustive events   Events that cover all the distinct possible outcomes.

Expected value   The probability-weighted average of the possible outcomes of a random variable.

Face value   The promised payment at maturity separate from any coupon payment.

Factor   A common or underlying element with which several variables are correlated.

Factor betas or factor loadings   The sensitivity of a portfolio to a factor.

Factor risk premium (or factor price)   The expected return in excess of the risk-free rate for a portfolio with a sensitivity of one to factor i and a sensitivity of zero to all other factors.

Factor sensitivities   Measures of factor risk associated with a portfolio.

Financial risk The uncertainty of future income due to the company's financing. Also, the uncertainty due to possible losses in the financial markets.

Financial risk management Managing future income variability due to the company's financing. Also, managing the uncertainty due to possible losses in the financial markets.

First-differencing The procedure of subtracting the value of the time series in the first prior period from the current value of the time series.

Fractile A synonym for quantile.

Frequency distribution A tabular display of data summarized into a relatively small number of intervals.

Frequency polygon A graph of a frequency distribution obtained by drawing straight lines joining successive points representing the class frequencies.

Full price The price of a security with accrued interest.

Fundamental factor models Factor models in which the factors are attributes of stocks or companies that are important in explaining cross-sectional differences in stock prices.

Future value The amount to which a payment or series of payments will grow by a stated future date.

Geometric mean A measure of central tendency computed by taking the nth root of the product of n values.

Global minimum-variance portfolio The portfolio with the smallest variance.

Gordon model An equity valuation model giving the value P_0 of a share of stock as $P_0 = D_1/(k - g)$, where D_1 is the dividend to be received at $t = 1$, k is the discount rate, and g is the assumed constant growth rate in dividends.

Growing perpetuity A stream of cash flows that grow at a constant rate forever.

Heteroskedastic An error term descriptor when the variance of the errors differs across observations.

Histogram A bar chart of continuous data that have been grouped into a frequency distribution.

Historic simulation (also called back simulation) Samples from a historical record of returns (or other underlying variables) to simulate a process.

Holding period return A synonym for total return.

Holding period yield (HPY) The total return from income and capital appreciation over a stated holding period; the holding period return on a bond.

Hurdle rate A rate of return that has to be met.

Hypothesis A statement about one or more populations.

Hypothesis testing Using rules to decide whether to accept or reject a hypothesis.

IID Independently and identically distributed.

Incremental cash flows Changes in cash flows, usually resulting from a decision.

Independent events Two events are independent if the occurrence of one event does not affect the probability of occurrence of the other event.

Independent variable A variable used to explain the reliability of a dependent variable in a regression.

Inferential statistics The branch of statistics that deals with making forecasts, estimates, or judgments about a larger group from the smaller group actually observed.

Inflation premium An extra return required as compensation for expected inflation.

In-sample forecast error An error in forecasting within the sample period on which a model is estimated.

Instability in the minimum-variance frontier Changes in the minimum-variance frontier caused by the phenomenon that small changes in input assumptions frequently lead to large changes in the weights of portfolios that appear on the minimum-variance (and efficient) frontiers.

Internal rate of return (IRR) That discount rate which causes net present value to equal 0.

Interpolation formula A formula for determining the value of a quantity of interest as a function of two known values bracketing the quantity.

Interval A set of values within which an observation falls.

Interval scale A measurement scale in which values can be added or subtracted meaningfully, but ratios cannot be formed meaningfully.

IRR rule An investment decision rule that accepts an investment for which the IRR is greater than the opportunity cost of capital.

Joint probability The probability of both events happening.

Joint probability function The joint probability function of two random variables X and Y gives the probability of joint occurrences of values of X and Y.

kth order correlation The correlation of a time series with itself k periods in the past.

Kurtosis A statistical measure that indicates when a distribution is more or less peaked than a normal distribution.

Leptokurtic A distribution that is more peaked than normal.

Level of significance The probability of a Type I error in testing a hypothesis, denoted by the Greek letter alpha, α.

Likelihood The probability of an observation, given a state of the world.

Linear association An association between variables that can be expressed as $y = b_0 + b_1 x_1 + b_2 x_2 \ldots$

Linear regression A technique to estimate a hypothesized linear relationship between the dependent and the independent variables.

Linear trend The underlying linear movement of a time series.

Log-linear model A regression model in which the natural logarithm of the dependent variable is a linear function of the independent variable(s).

Look-ahead bias A bias caused by using information that was not available on the test date.

Lookback call option An option which has a value at maturity equal to (Value of the stock at maturity − Minimum value of stock during the life of the option) or $0, whichever is greater.

Macroeconomic factor models Factor models in which the factors are surprises (differences from expectations) in macroeconomic variables that significantly explain equity returns.

Marginal probability The unconditional probability, or simply the probability of an event occurring.

Market risk premium The excess expected return on the market (over the risk-free rate).

Markowitz decision rule A decision rule for choosing between two investments based on their means and variances.

Mean reversion The characteristic of a time series that tends to revert to a long-run mean value; a property of covariance stationary time-series. A time series has mean reversion if it tends to fall when its level is above its mean and rise when its level is below its mean.

Mean–variance analysis Analysis of investment opportunities based on their means, variances, and covariances.

Measurement scales A scheme of measuring differences. The four types of measurement scales are nominal, ordinal, interval, and ratio.

Measures of central tendency Statistics that attempt to define the middle point of the distribution.

Median The middle item of a data set sorted in ascending or descending order; the 50th percentile.

Minimum variance frontier The set of portfolios with minimum variance (standard deviation) for each given level of expected return.

Modal interval The most frequently occurring interval.

Mode The most frequently occurring value in a set of observations.

Money market The market for low-risk, highly liquid, short-term debt instruments (with maturity of one year or less).

Money market yield A yield equal to the annualized holding period yield, assuming a 360-day year, r_{MM} = HPY $\times$ (360/t).

Monte Carlo simulation A methodology which involves the use of a computer to find approximate solutions to complex problems.

Multicollinearity A regression assumption violation in which linear combinations of the independent variables are correlated with each other, resulting in standard errors that are quite large even though the regression equation seems to fit rather well.

Multiple linear regression model A linear regression model with more than one independent variable.

Multiple R The correlation of the actual values of Y with the forecast values of Y in a regression.

Multiplication rule for probabilities The probability of the first event times the probability of the second, given the first.

Multivariate distribution A probability distribution that specifies the probabilities for a group of related random variables.

Multivariate normal A probability distribution which is normal for each remaining variable when all others are held constant, and which is completely defined by the means and variance of the original variables plus their pairwise correlations.

Mutually exclusive events Events such that only one can occur at a time.

N factorial $n! = n \times (n - 1) \times (n - 2) \ldots \times 1$ and where $0! = 1$

Negative serial correlation Serial correlation in which a positive error in one period increases the probability of a negative error in the next period, and a negative error in one period increases the probability of a positive error in the next period.

Net present value (NPV) The present value of an investment's cash inflows minus the present value of its cash outflows.

Node A boxed value from which successive moves or outcomes branch in a tree.

Nominal cost of money The stated cost of funds, as opposed to the cost adjusted for inflation.

Nominal scale A measurement scale that names but does not meaningfully order.

Nonlinear relation An association between variables that cannot be expressed as $y = b_0 + b_1x_1 + b_2x_2 \ldots$

Nonparametric A test that is not concerned with a parameter, or that makes minimal assumptions about the population from which the sample comes.

Not statistically significant A result indicating that the null hypothesis cannot be rejected, or that a population parameter cannot be said to be different from zero, for example.

n-period moving average A technique to smooth out period-to-period fluctuations in the value of a time series.

NPV rule An investment decision rule that accepts an investment if the investment's NPV is positive.

Null hypothesis The hypothesis to be tested against an alternative.

Objective probabilities Probabilities that generally do not vary from person to person.

One-sided (or one-tailed) hypothesis test A test where the null is rejected only if the evidence indicates that the population parameter is greater than (smaller than) θ_0. The alternative hypothesis has one side.

Opportunity cost The value that investors forgo by making a given choice; the value in the best alternative use.

Opportunity set The set of assets available for investment.

Optimizer A specialized computer program or a spreadsheet with the capability to solve for the portfolio weights that will result in the lowest risk for that level of expected return.

Ordinal scale A measurement scale that orders data, but does not allow meaningful addition and subtraction.

Ordinary annuity An annuity that has the first cash flow occurring one period from the starting date.

Outcome A value taken by a random variable.

Outliers Small numbers of observations at either extreme (small or large) of a sample.

Out-of-sample forecast error An error in forecasting outside the sample period on which a model is estimated.

Paired comparisons test A test of the difference in means between two populations where the observations from the two populations are paired.

Paired observations Two observations treated as a matched unit, although they come from different populations.

Pairs arbitrage trade A trade in two closely related stocks involving the short sale of one and the purchase of the other.

Parameter A descriptive measure computed from or used to describe a population, by convention represented by Greek letters.

Parametric test Any test or procedure with either of these two characteristics: First, they are concerned with parameters; and second, their validity depends on a definite set of assumptions.

Percentiles Quantiles that divide the data into 100 equal parts.

Perfect collinearity A condition obtained when one of the independent variables is an exact linear combination of other independent variables.

Performance evaluation Judging the quality of investment decision outcomes.

Performance measurement The calculation of returns in a logical and consistent manner.

Permutation An ordered listing.

Permutation formula The number of ways that r objects can be chosen from a total of n objects, where the order in which the r objects is listed matters.

Perpetuity A perpetual annuity or infinite series of level, sequential cash flows, with the first cash flow occurring one period from now.

Platykurtic A distribution that is less peaked than normal.

Point estimate The single estimate of an unknown population parameter calculated as a sample mean.

Pooled Combined from two samples.

Population All members of a specified group.

Population mean The average, μ, calculated for all the members of a finite population.

Portfolio possibilities curve The set of all portfolios that may possibly be created by assigning differing weights to assets.

Positive serial correlation Serial correlation in which a positive error in one period increases the probability of a positive error for the next period; also that a negative error in one period is likely to be followed by a negative error in the next period.

Posterior probability A probability that reflects or is calculated after new information is available.

Power of a test The probability of correctly rejecting the null (rejecting the null hypothesis when it is false).

Premium bond A bond selling at a price above its face value.

Present value The current (discounted) value of future cash flows.

Price relative A ratio of end-of-period price to beginning price.

Priced risk A risk for which investors require a return as compensation for bearing.

Principal   The capital sum as opposed to interest; the face value to be paid at maturity.

Prior probabilities   Probabilities determined before new information is available.

Probability   Defined by the following two properties: (1) the probability of any event is a number between 0 and 1, and (2) the sum of the probabilities of any list of mutually exclusive and exhaustive events equals 1.

Probability density function   A function with non-negative values such that probability can be described by areas under the curve graphing the function.

Probability distribution   A distribution that specifies the probabilities of a variable's possible outcomes.

Probability function   A function that specifies the probability that the random variable takes on a specific value.

Probit and logit models   Models which estimate the probability of a zero-one discrete outcome given the values of the independent variables used to explain that outcome.

Pseudo-random numbers   Numbers produced by random number generators.

Pure discount instrument   A fixed-income security with a single cash flow.

Pure factor portfolio   A portfolio with non-zero factor sensitivity to only the factor in question.

P-value   The smallest level of significance at which the null hypothesis can be rejected.

Qualitative dependent variables   Dummy variables that are used as dependent variables.

Quantile   In a frequency distribution, the value at or below which a stated fraction of the data lies.

Quartiles   Quantiles that divide the data into 4 equal parts.

Quintiles   Quantiles that divided the data into 5 equal parts.

Quoted interest rate   The stated annual interest rate.

Random number   An observation drawn from a uniform distribution.

Random number generator   An algorithm that produces uniformly distributed random numbers between 0 and 1.

Random variable   A quantity whose future outcomes are uncertain.

Random walk   A time series in which the value of the series in one period is the value of the series in the previous period plus an unpredictable random error.

Range   The difference between the maximum value and minimum value in a data set.

Ratio scale   A measurement scale that permits ratios to be formed meaningfully; the strongest measurement scale.

Real rate   The cost of funds adjusted for expected inflation; the cost of funds in units of constant purchasing power.

Regimes   States of the world yielding different underlying models that generate time series.

Rejection point   A value against which the computed test statistic is compared to decide whether or not to reject the null hypothesis.

Relative dispersion   The amount of variability present in comparison to a reference point or benchmark.

Relative frequency   The absolute frequency of each return interval divided by the total number of observations.

Risk premium   The expected return on an investment minus the risk-free rate.

Robust   A descriptor of a statistic if the required probability calculations are insensitive to violations from assumptions.

Root mean squared error   The square root of the average squared error.

Safety-first rules   Rules to minimize the probability of falling below a specified level.

Sample   A subset of a population.

Sample mean   The sum of the sample observations, divided by the sample size.

Sample selection bias   When data availability leads to certain observations being excluded from the analysis.

Sample statistic   A measure calculated on the basis of a sample.

Sampling   The process of obtaining a sample.

Sampling distribution   The distribution of all the distinct possible values that the statistic can assume when computed from samples of the same size randomly drawn from the same population.

Sampling error   The difference between the observed value of a statistic and the parameter it is intended to estimate.

Sampling plan   The set of rules used to select a sample.

Scatter plot   A graph that shows the relationship between the observations for two data series in two dimensions.

Security market line   An equilibrium relationship giving $E(r) = \text{RFR} + [E(R_m) - \text{RFR}] \times \beta$ where β is the market factor sensitivity and $E(R_m) - \text{RFR}$ is the market risk premium.

Semi-logarithmic A scale constructed so that equal intervals on the vertical scale represent equal rates of change, and equal intervals on the horizontal scale represent equal amounts of change.

Serially correlated A description of errors when they are not independent across observations.

Sharpe ratio (or Sharpe measure) The average return in excess of the risk-free rate divided by the standard deviation of returns; measures the excess return earned per unit of standard deviation of return.

Shortfall risk The risk that portfolio value will fall below some minimum acceptable level over some time horizon.

Simple interest Interest calculated on the principal only. Simple interest is contrasted with compound interest, which is interest earned on both the principal and interest reinvested from prior periods.

Simple random sample A sample obtained in such a way that each element of the population has an equal probability of being selected.

Simple random sampling The procedure of drawing a sample to satisfy the definition of a simple random sample.

Simulation trial A complete pass through the steps of a simulation.

Skewed A distribution that is not symmetrical.

Skewness A measure of the lack of symmetry.

Spot interest rate The yield to maturity on a zero-coupon bond; used as an interest rate appropriate for discounting a cash flow of some given maturity.

Spot yield curve The graph of spot rates versus term to maturity.

Spurious correlation A correlation between two variables that is not based on any theoretical relationship, but rather a relation that arises in the data solely because each of those variables is related to some third variable.

Standard deviation The positive square root of the variance; a measure of dispersion in the same units as the original data, as opposed to the variance, which is in squared units.

Standard error of estimate The standard error of the residual in a multiple regression model, the same as in a linear regression with only one independent variable.

Standard error of the sample mean The standard deviation of the sample mean.

Standard normal distribution The normal density with $\mu = 0$ and $\sigma = 1$.

Standardizing A transformation achieved by subtracting the mean and dividing the result by the standard deviation.

Stated annual interest rate An interest rate that does not account for compounding within the year.

Statistic A measure calculated on the basis of a sample.

Statistical factor models Factor models in which statistical methods are applied to a set of historical returns to determine portfolios that explain historical return variances or covariances.

Statistical inference Using a sample statistic to infer the value of an unknown population parameter.

Statistically significant A result indicating that the null hypothesis can be rejected, or that a population parameter can be said to be different from zero.

Statistics (1) The science of describing, analyzing, and drawing conclusions from data; (2) a collection of numerical data.

Stratified random sampling A procedure by which the population is subdivided into subpopulations (strata) based on one or more classification criteria. Simple random samples are then drawn from each stratum in sizes proportional to the relative size of each stratum in the population. These samples are then pooled.

Stress testing/scenario analysis A set of techniques for estimating losses in extremely unfavorable combinations of events or scenarios.

Subjective probability A probability drawing on personal judgment.

Supernormal growth Unusually high growth that is expected to last for a finite amount of time.

Surprise The actual value minus predicted (or expected) value.

Survivorship bias A test design that fails to account for companies that have gone bankrupt, merged, or are otherwise no longer reported in the database.

Systematic factors Factors which affect the average return of a large number of different assets.

Systematic sampling A procedure of selecting every kth member until we have a sample of the desired size that should be approximately random.

Term to maturity The time difference between today's date and the date on which the issuer will redeem the issue by paying the face or par value.

Test statistic A quantity, calculated on the basis of a sample, whose value is the basis for deciding whether or not to reject the null hypothesis.

Time series A set of values of a particular variable in sequential time periods.

Time-period bias A bias from a test design based on a time period that may make the results time-period specific.

Time-series data Observations of a variable over time.

Time-weighted Averaged over time.

Total probability rule Explains the unconditional probability of the event in terms of probabilities conditional on the scenarios.

Total probability rule for expected value The probability of an event is the sum of the conditional probabilities of that event, given each of the mutually exclusive scenarios in which the event can occur.

Total return A measure of the return over a stated period that incorporates both the return from price appreciation and the return from investment income.

Tracking error The total return on a portfolio (gross of fees) minus the total return on a benchmark.

Tracking portfolio A portfolio that has a desired or target configuration of factor sensitivities.

Tree diagram A diagram with branches emanating from nodes representing mutually exclusive chance events or else mutually exclusive decisions. Probabilities and payoffs are shown on the tree.

Trend A long-term pattern of movement in one direction.

t-**test** A hypothesis test using a statistic (*t*-statistic) that follows the Student's *t*-distribution.

Two-sided (or two-tailed) hypothesis test A test in which the null is rejected in favor of the alternative if the evidence indicates that the population parameter is either smaller or larger than θ_0.

Two-stage dividend discount model A variation of the constant growth dividend discount model in which a short-term supernormal growth period is followed by a long-term constant growth period.

Type I error The error of rejecting a true null hypothesis.

Type II error The error of not rejecting a false null hypothesis.

Unbiased estimator An estimator whose expected value (the mean of its sampling distribution) equals the parameter it is intended to estimate.

Unconditional heteroskedasticity Heteroskedasticity in the error variance that is not correlated with the independent variables in the multiple regression.

Unconditional probability The marginal probability, or simply the probability of an event occurring.

Unit normal distribution The normal density with $\mu = 0$ and $\sigma = 1$.

Unit root A characteristic of a time series model that indicates that remedial steps need to be taken to deal with nonstationarity.

Univariate distribution A distribution which specifies the probabilities for a single random variable.

Up transition probability The probability that an asset moves up.

Value at Risk The worst loss that can happen over a specified horizon under normal market conditions, at a specified confidence level (such as 95% or 99%).

Variance The expected value (the probability-weighted average) of squared deviations from a random variable's expected value.

Volatility A measure of the standard deviation of very short-term returns on the underlying asset.

Weighted average cost of capital (WACC) A weighted average of the after-tax required rates of return on the firm's common stock, preferred stock, and long-term debt where the weights are the fraction of each source of financing in the firm's target capital structure.

Weighted mean An average in which each observation is weighted by an index of its relative importance.

Working capital management The management of the firm's short-term assets (such as inventory) and short-term liabilities (such as money owed to suppliers).

Yield to maturity Double the semi-annual internal rate of return on a semi-annual bond, or simply the internal rate of return for an annual pay bond.

Zero-coupon bonds or pure discount bonds Bonds that do not pay any periodic coupon interest over their term to maturity.